VAMPIRE
CHEERLEADERS
IN SPACE...AND TIME?!

ART
MICHAEL
SHELFER

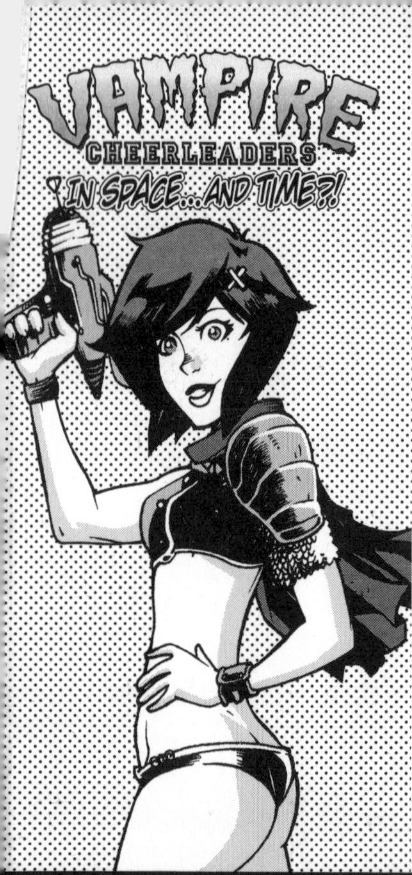
VAMPIRE
CHEERLEADERS
IN SPACE...AND TIME?!

STAFF CREDITS

lettering & design **Nicky Lim**
toning **Ludwig Sacramento**
proofreader **Shanti Whitesides**
editor **Alexis Roberts**

publisher **Jason DeAngelis**
Seven Seas Entertainment

Special Thanks to Shiei, Gisèle Lagacé, Kisai Yuki, Shouri, David Lumsdon, Clay Gardner, Devon Collins, Matthew Pollock, Amy Shelfer, Adrienne Shelfer, Lucy Shelfer, and all the readers who supported us over the years!

ISBN: 978-1-626920-98-9
Printed in Canada
First Printing: March 2015
10 9 8 7 6 5 4 3 2 1

Seven Seas

READING DIRECTIONS

This book reads from ***right to left***, Japanese style. If this is your first time reading manga, you start reading from the top right panel on each page and take it from there. If you get lost, just follow the numbered diagram here. It may seem backwards at first, but you'll get the hang of it! Have fun!!

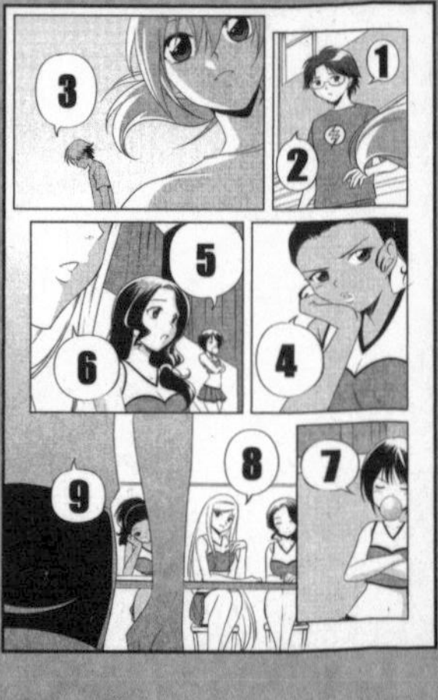
1
2
3
4
5
6
7
8
9

ALL RIGHT, KATIE, MY DEAR, DEAR LYCANTHROPE SISTER... DECISION TIME.

WHAT FLAVOR DO *YOU*, KATIE ELIZABETH KANE, CHOOSE FOR *YOUR* ULTRA-SPECIAL, *STEPHANIE KANE VICTORY PANCAKES™*?!

FO GOOF!

PARANORMAL MYSTERY SQUAD'S SORCERESS SUPREME, CHARLOTTE ROTH, PICKED BLUEBERRY-BANANA.

STEPHANIE KANE OF EARTH, YOU HAVE PROVEN YOURSELF.

CHOCOLATE IT IS!

HMMMM. I'LL HAVE... SNOZBERRY.

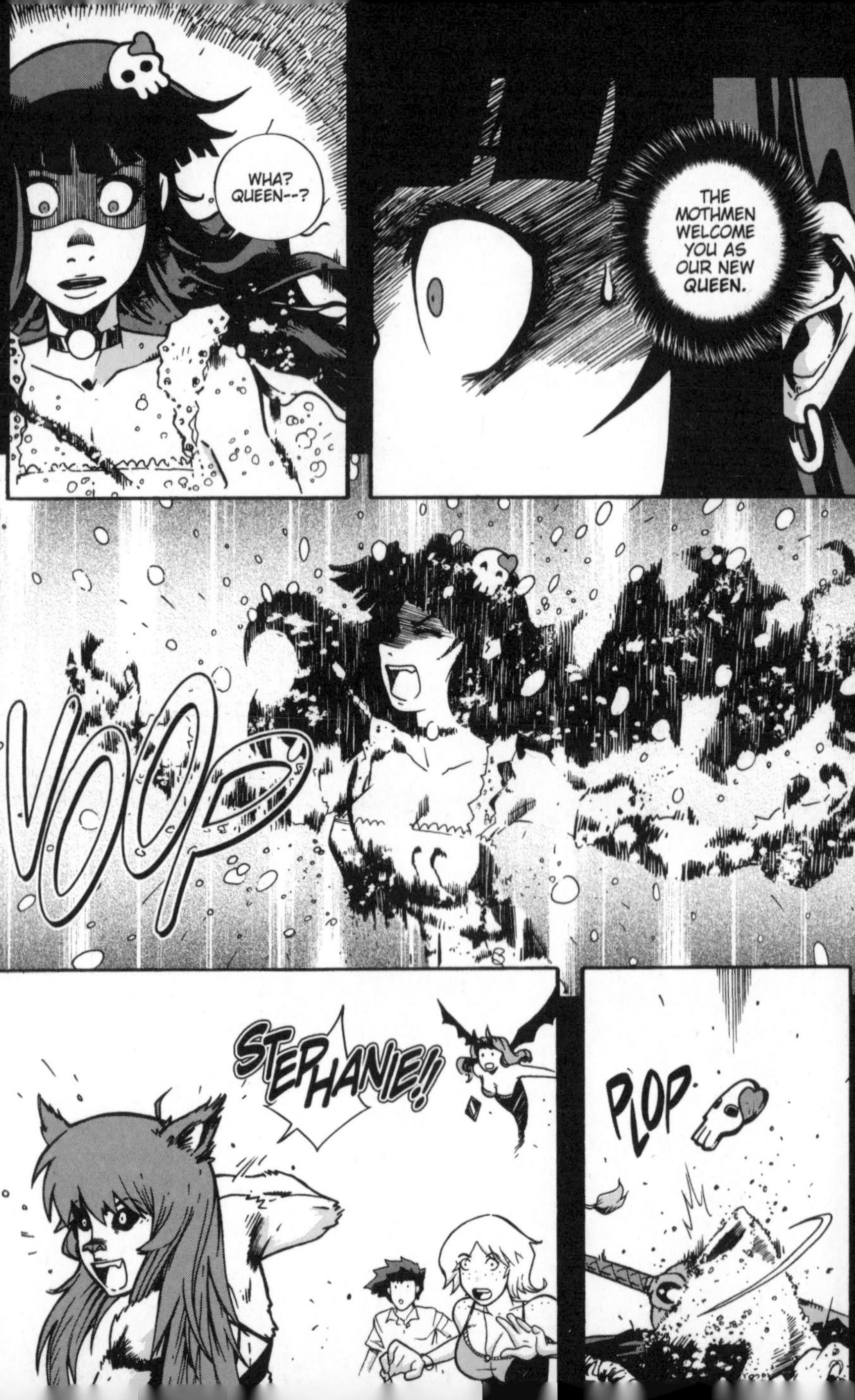
THE MOTHMEN WELCOME YOU AS OUR NEW QUEEN.
WHA? QUEEN--?
VOOP
PLOP
STEPHANIE!!

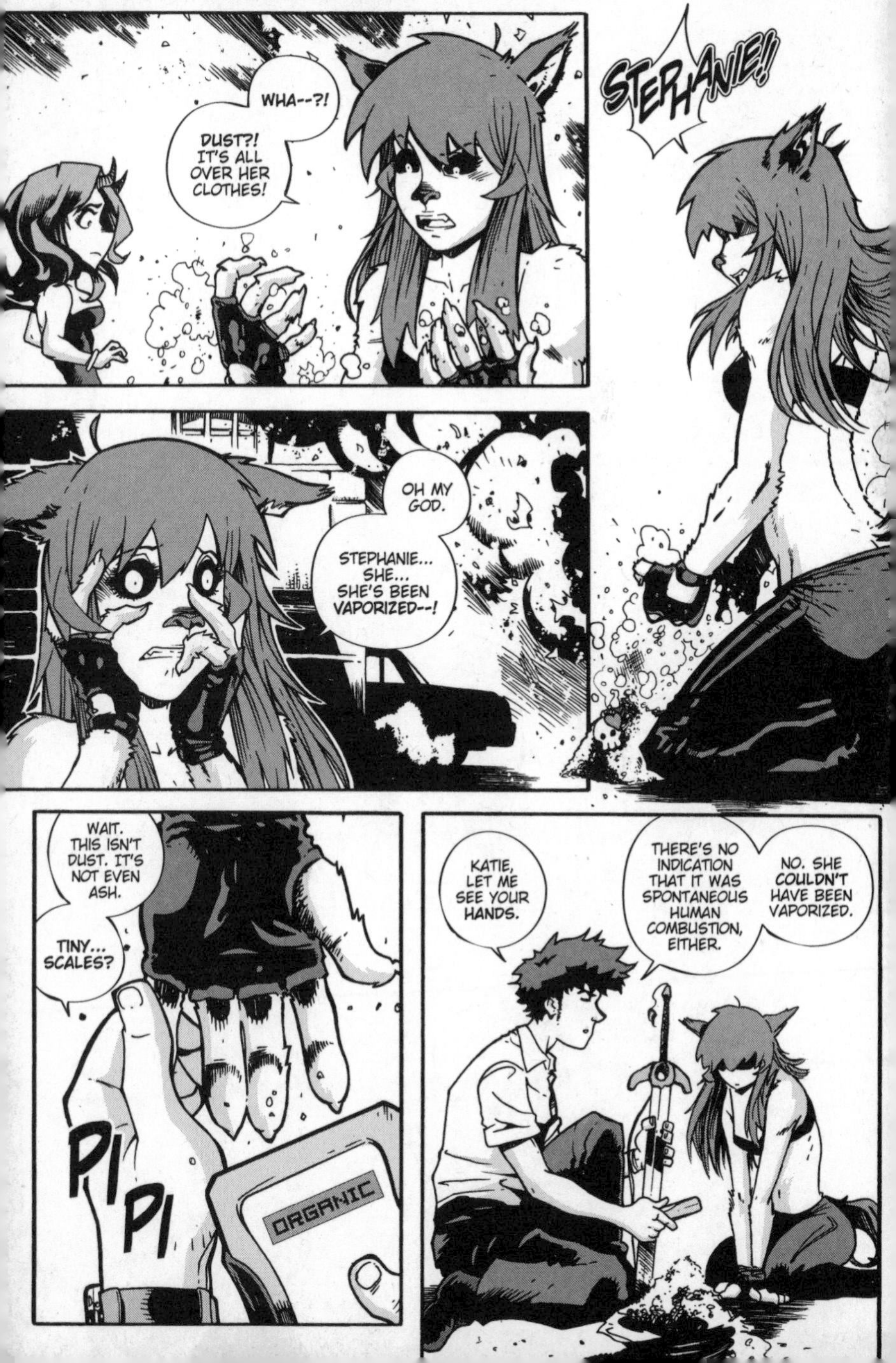
STEPHANIE!!
WHA--?!
DUST?! IT'S ALL OVER HER CLOTHES!
OH MY GOD.
STEPHANIE... SHE... SHE'S BEEN VAPORIZED--!
NO. SHE COULDN'T HAVE BEEN VAPORIZED.
THERE'S NO INDICATION THAT IT WAS SPONTANEOUS HUMAN COMBUSTION, EITHER.
KATIE, LET ME SEE YOUR HANDS.
WAIT. THIS ISN'T DUST. IT'S NOT EVEN ASH.
TINY... SCALES?
PI PI
ORGANIC

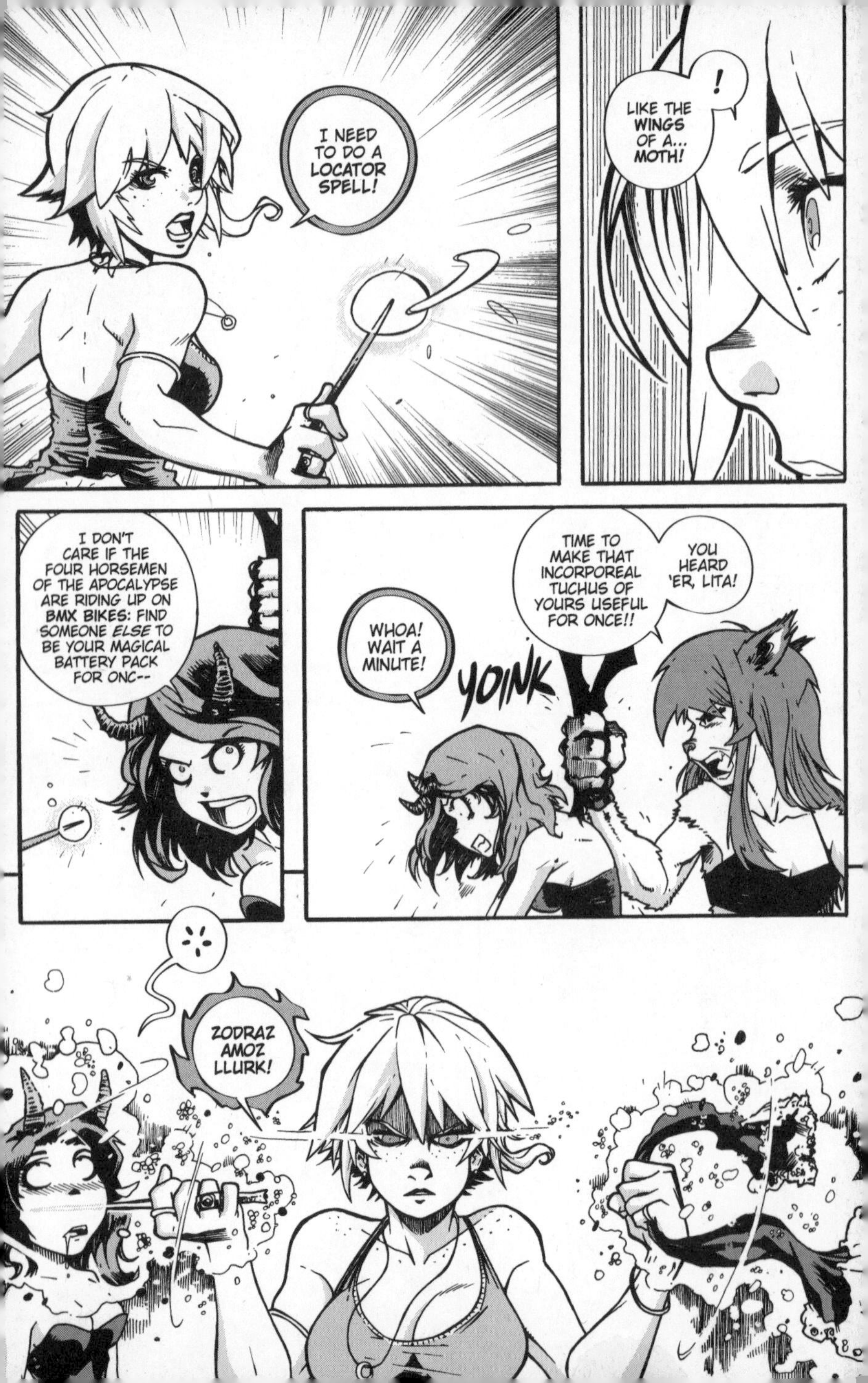
!
LIKE THE WINGS OF A... MOTH!
I NEED TO DO A LOCATOR SPELL!
YOU HEARD 'ER, LITA!
TIME TO MAKE THAT INCORPOREAL TUCHUS OF YOURS USEFUL FOR ONCE!!
WHOA! WAIT A MINUTE!
YOINK
I DON'T CARE IF THE FOUR HORSEMEN OF THE APOCALYPSE ARE RIDING UP ON BMX BIKES: FIND SOMEONE ELSE TO BE YOUR MAGICAL BATTERY PACK FOR ONC--
ZODRAZ AMOZ LLURK!

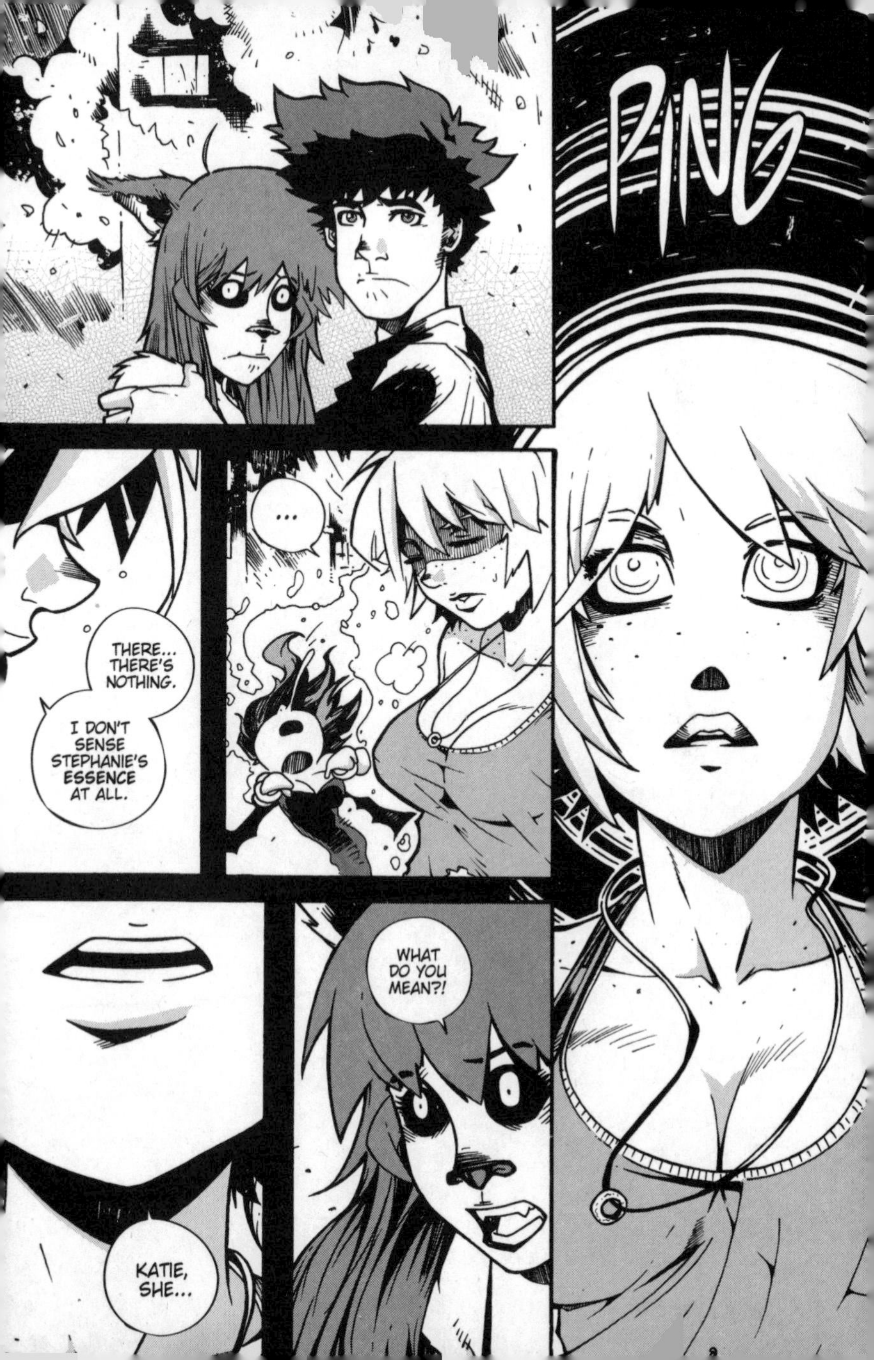
PING
...
THERE... THERE'S NOTHING.
I DON'T SENSE STEPHANIE'S ESSENCE AT ALL.
WHAT DO YOU MEAN?!
KATIE, SHE...

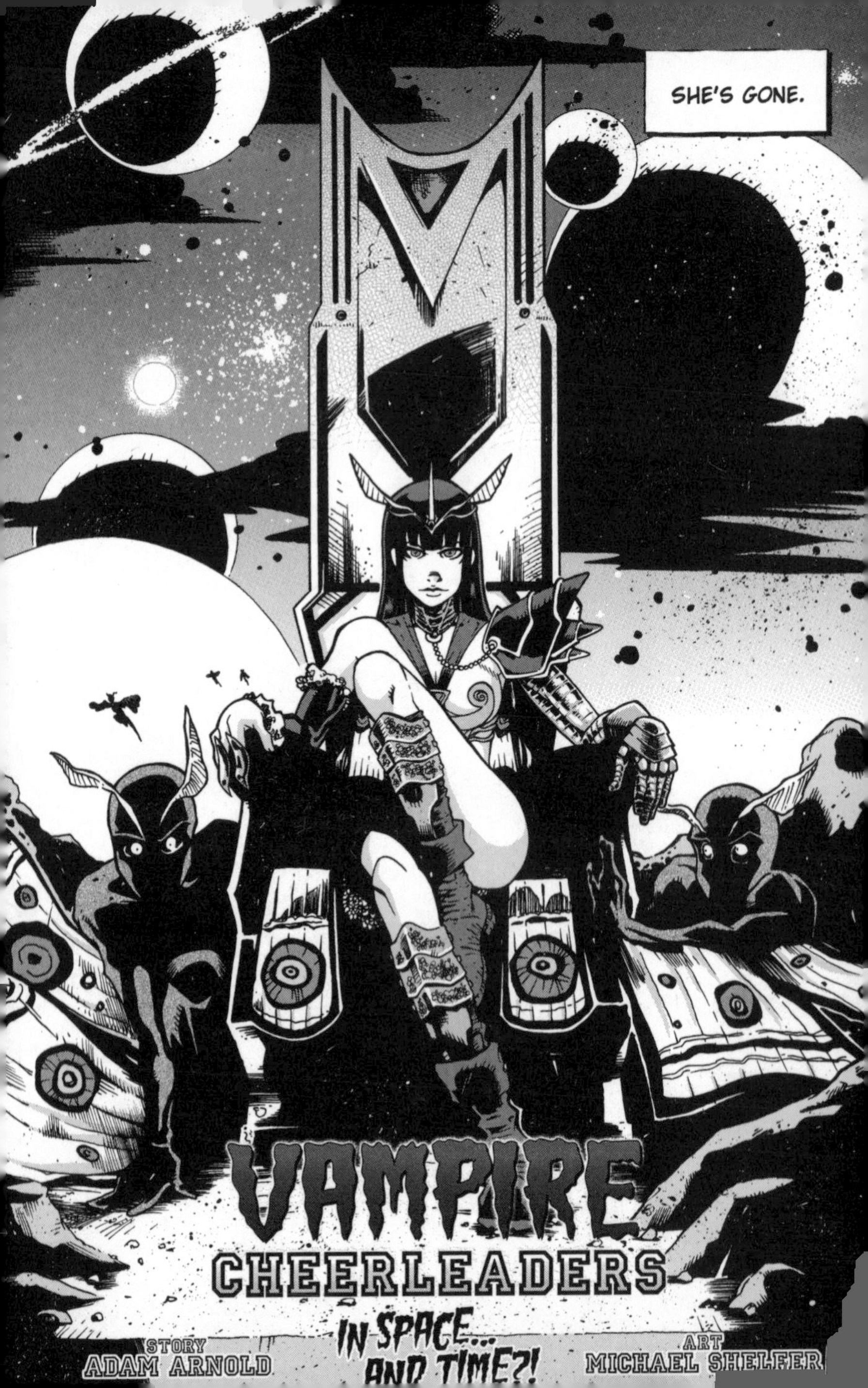
SHE'S GONE.
VAMPIRE
CHEERLEADERS
IN SPACE... AND TIME?!
STORY
ADAM ARNOLD
ART
MICHAEL SHELFER

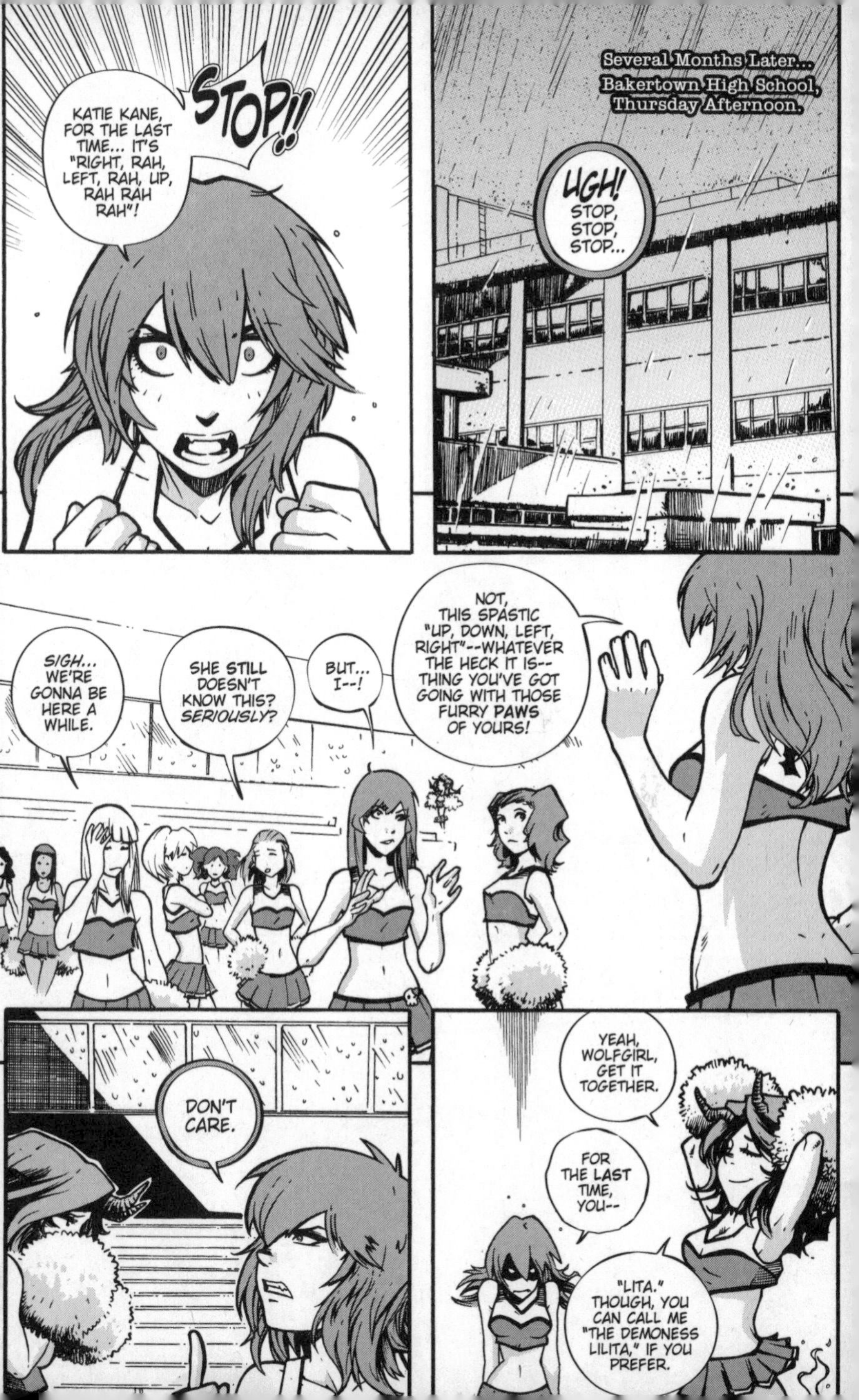
Several Months Later... Bakertown High School, Thursday Afternoon.
UGH! STOP, STOP, STOP...
STOP!!
KATIE KANE, FOR THE LAST TIME... IT'S "RIGHT, RAH, LEFT, RAH, UP, RAH RAH RAH"!
NOT, THIS SPASTIC "UP, DOWN, LEFT, RIGHT"--WHATEVER THE HECK IT IS--THING YOU'VE GOT GOING WITH THOSE FURRY PAWS OF YOURS!
BUT... I--!
SHE STILL DOESN'T KNOW THIS? SERIOUSLY?
SIGH... WE'RE GONNA BE HERE A WHILE.
YEAH, WOLFGIRL, GET IT TOGETHER.
FOR THE LAST TIME, YOU--
"LITA." THOUGH, YOU CAN CALL ME "THE DEMONESS LILITA," IF YOU PREFER.
DON'T CARE.

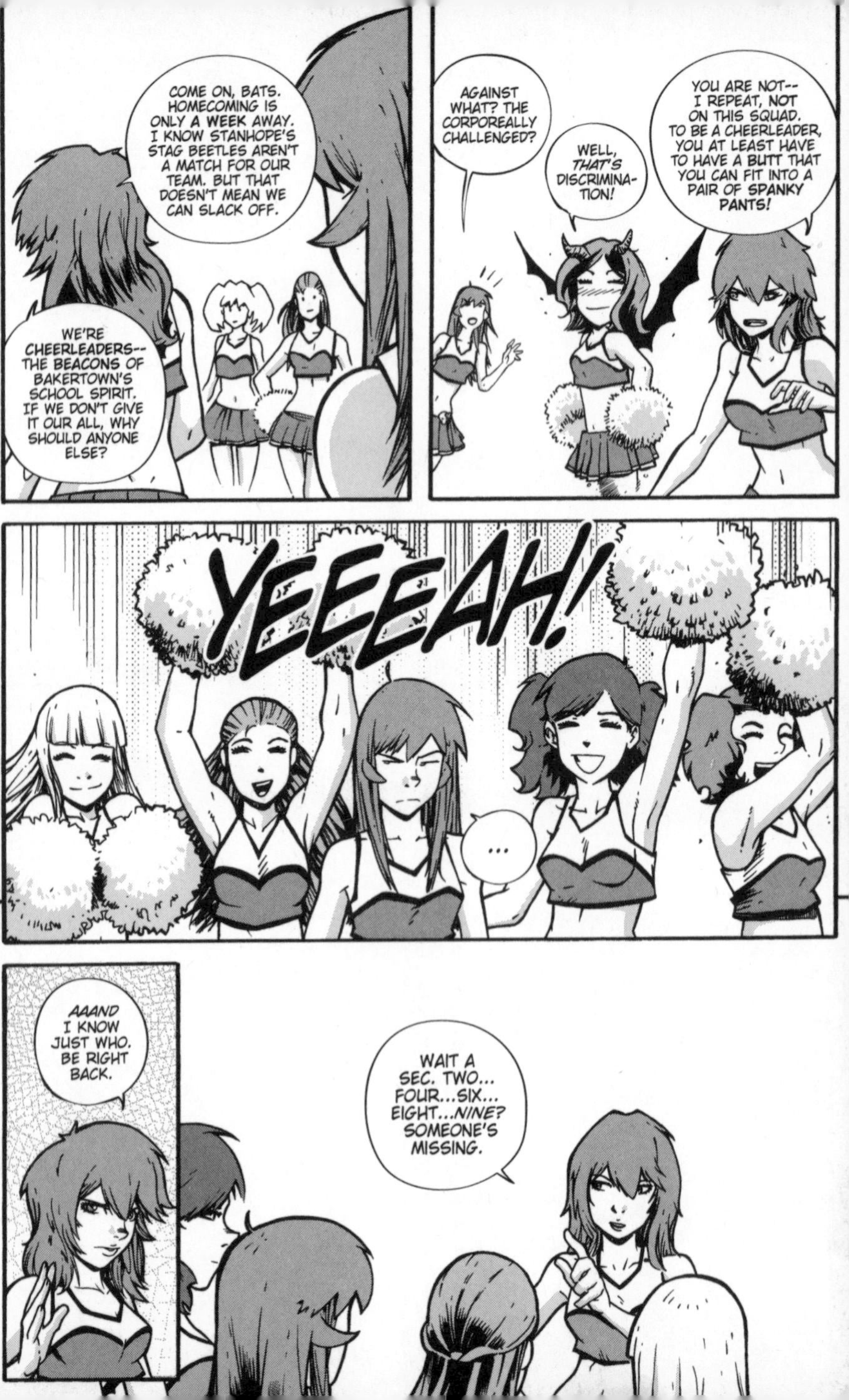
YOU ARE NOT-- I REPEAT, NOT ON THIS SQUAD. TO BE A CHEERLEADER, YOU AT LEAST HAVE TO HAVE A BUTT THAT YOU CAN FIT INTO A PAIR OF SPANKY PANTS!
AGAINST WHAT? THE CORPOREALLY CHALLENGED?
WELL, *THAT'S* DISCRIMINATION!
COME ON, BATS. HOMECOMING IS ONLY A **WEEK** AWAY. I KNOW STANHOPE'S STAG BEETLES AREN'T A MATCH FOR OUR TEAM. BUT THAT DOESN'T MEAN WE CAN SLACK OFF.
WE'RE CHEERLEADERS-- THE BEACONS OF BAKERTOWN'S SCHOOL SPIRIT. IF WE DON'T GIVE IT OUR ALL, WHY SHOULD ANYONE ELSE?
YEEEAH!
...
WAIT A SEC. TWO... FOUR...SIX... EIGHT...*NINE*? SOMEONE'S MISSING.
AAAND I KNOW JUST WHO. BE RIGHT BACK.

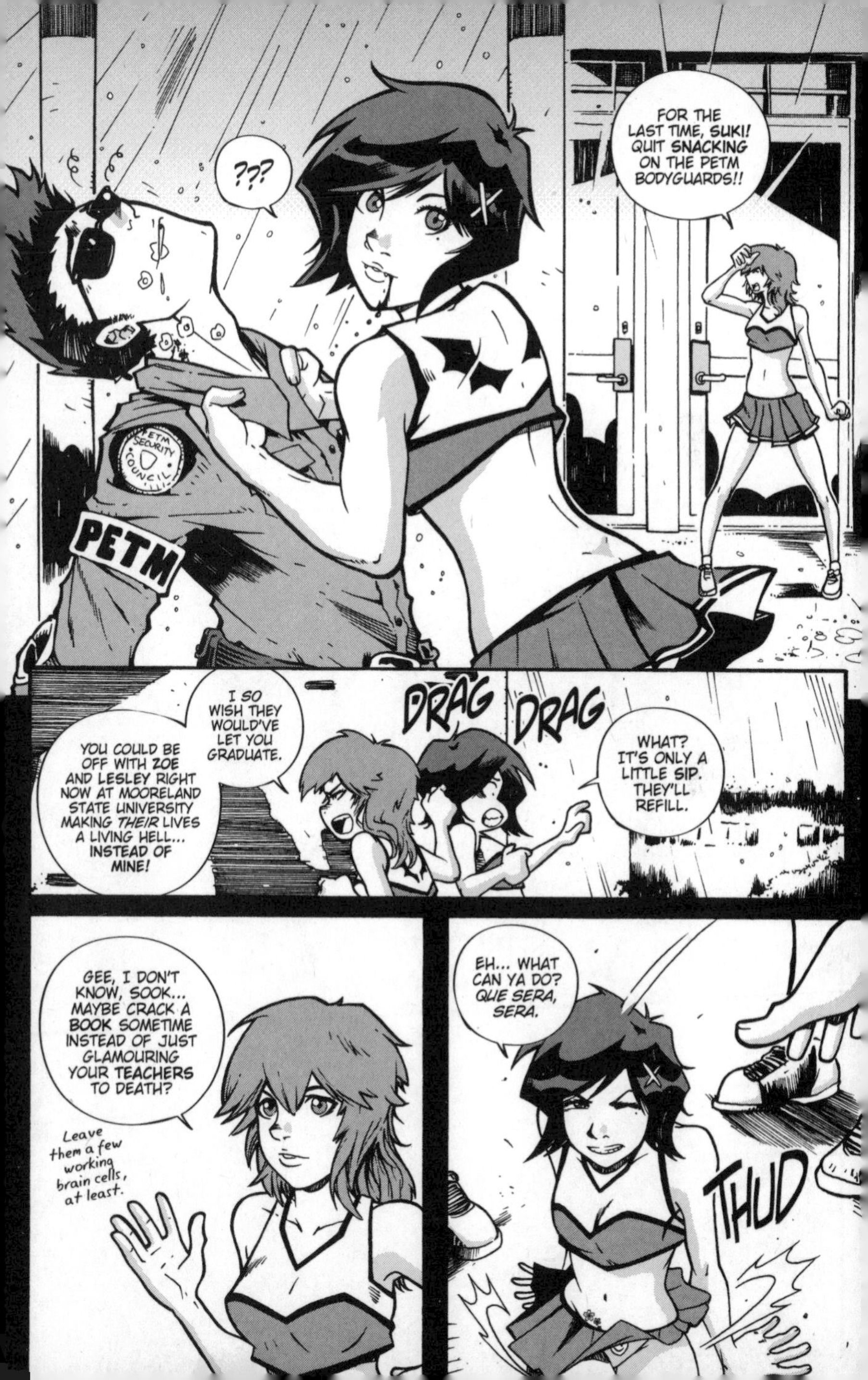
FOR THE LAST TIME, SUKI! QUIT SNACKING ON THE PETM BODYGUARDS!!
???
PETM SECURITY COUNCIL
PETM
DRAG
DRAG
WHAT? IT'S ONLY A LITTLE SIP. THEY'LL REFILL.
I SO WISH THEY WOULD'VE LET YOU GRADUATE.
YOU COULD BE OFF WITH ZOE AND LESLEY RIGHT NOW AT MOORELAND STATE UNIVERSITY MAKING THEIR LIVES A LIVING HELL... INSTEAD OF MINE!
EH... WHAT CAN YA DO? QUE SERA, SERA.
THUD
GEE, I DON'T KNOW, SOOK... MAYBE CRACK A BOOK SOMETIME INSTEAD OF JUST GLAMOURING YOUR TEACHERS TO DEATH?
Leave them a few working brain cells, at least.

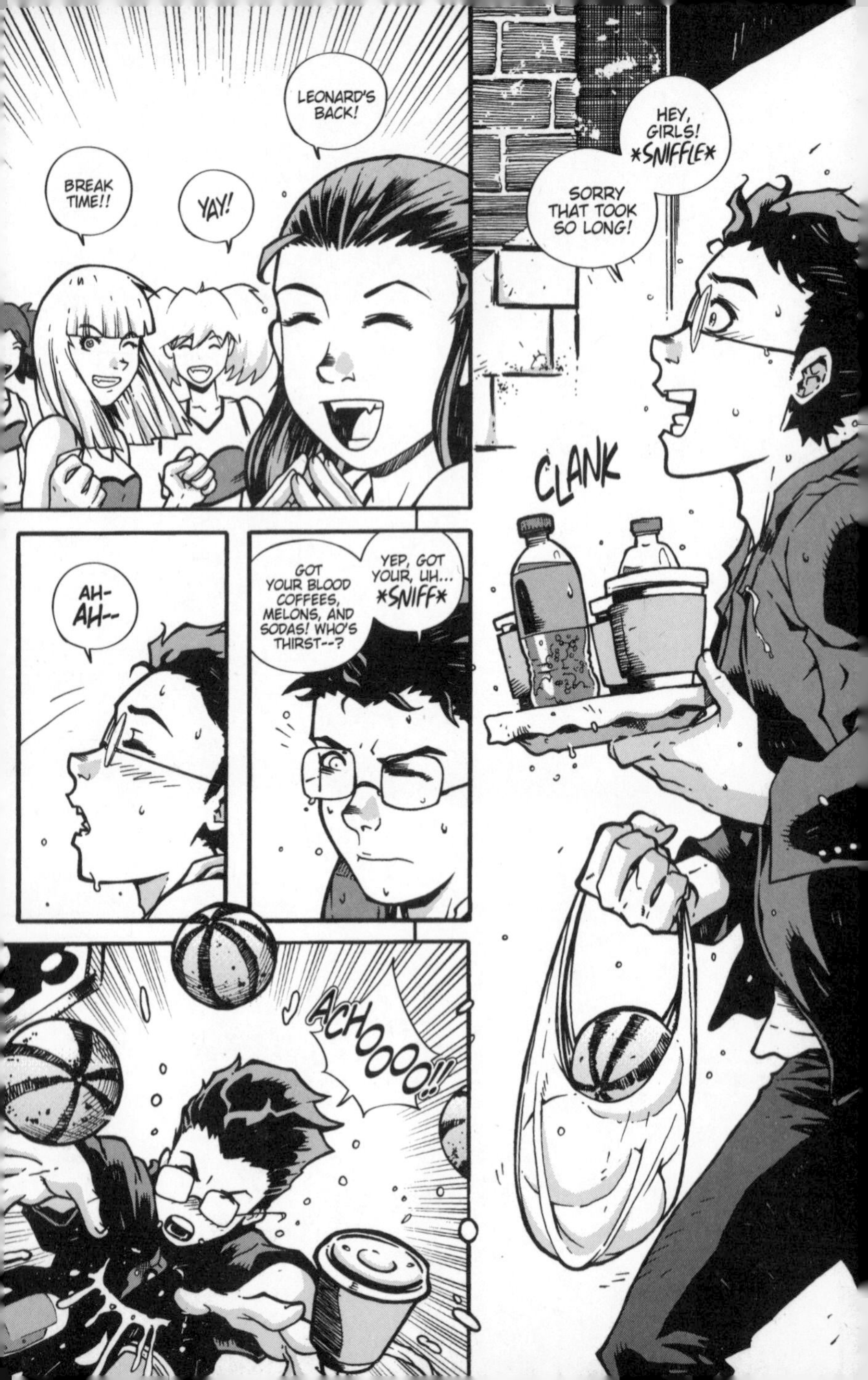
HEY, GIRLS! *SNIFFLE*
SORRY THAT TOOK SO LONG!
CLANK
LEONARD'S BACK!
YAY!
BREAK TIME!!
YEP, GOT YOUR, UH... *SNIFF*
GOT YOUR BLOOD COFFEES, MELONS, AND SODAS! WHO'S THIRST--?
AH-AH--
ACHOOOO!!

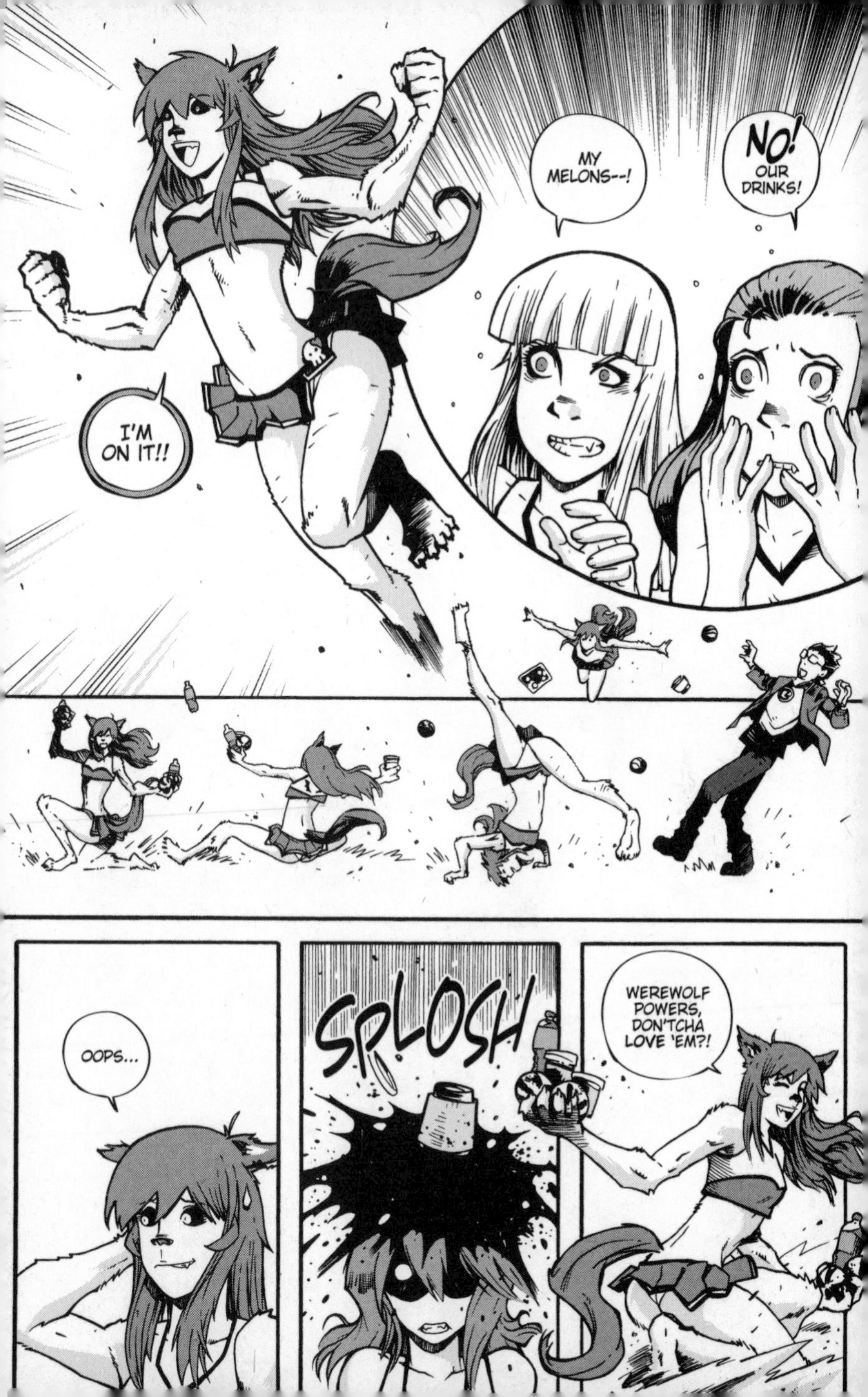
NO! OUR DRINKS!
MY MELONS--!
I'M ON IT!!
WEREWOLF POWERS, DON'TCHA LOVE 'EM?!
SPLOSH
OOPS...

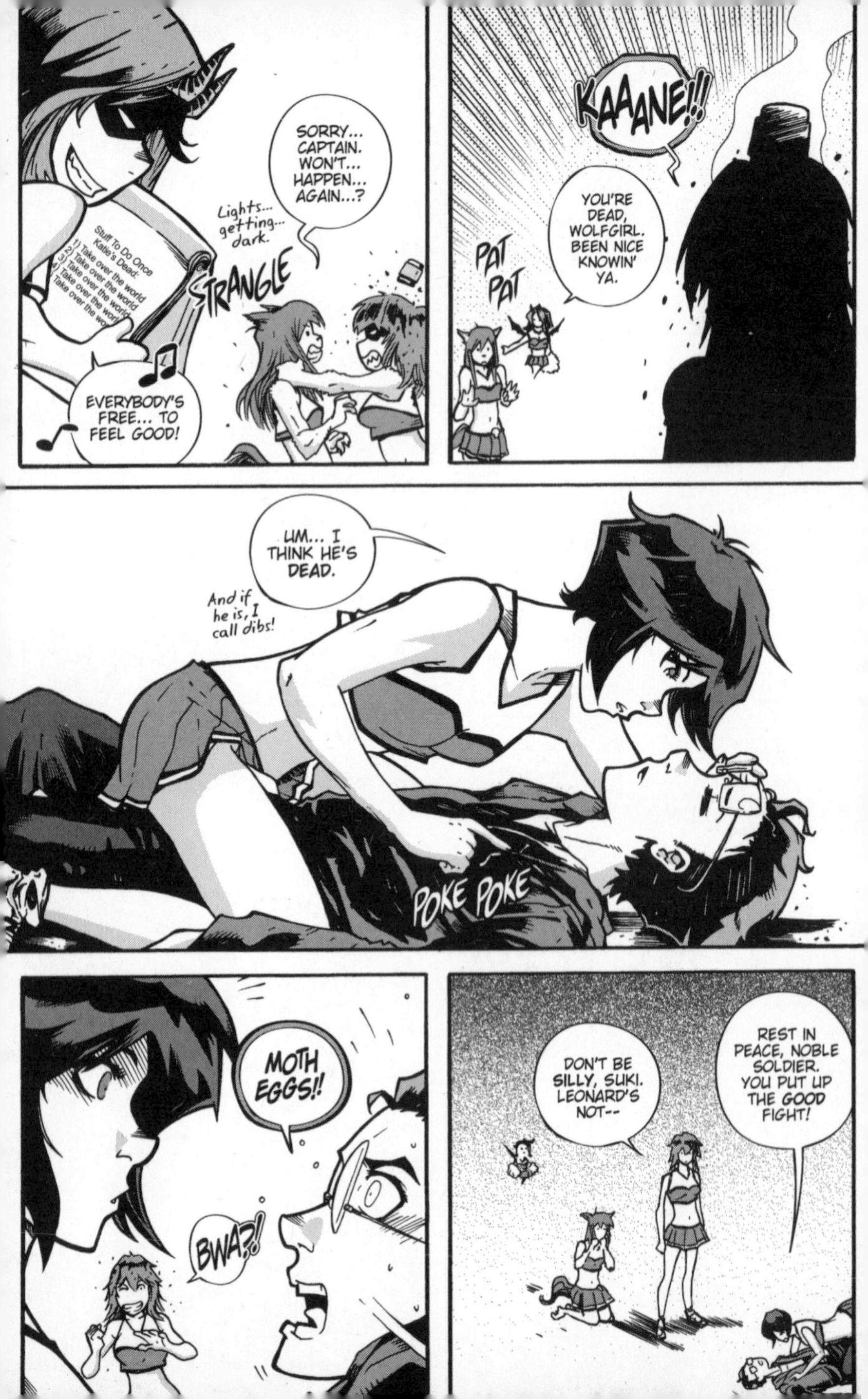
KAAANE!!!
YOU'RE DEAD, WOLFGIRL. BEEN NICE KNOWIN' YA.
PAT PAT
SORRY... CAPTAIN. WON'T... HAPPEN... AGAIN...?
Lights... getting... dark.
Stuff To Do Once Katie's Dead:
1) Take over the world
2) Take over the world
3) Take over the world
4) Take over the world
STRANGLE
EVERYBODY'S FREE... TO FEEL GOOD!
UM... I THINK HE'S DEAD.
And if he is, I call dibs!
POKE POKE
REST IN PEACE, NOBLE SOLDIER. YOU PUT UP THE GOOD FIGHT!
DON'T BE SILLY, SUKI. LEONARD'S NOT--
MOTH EGGS!!
BWA?!

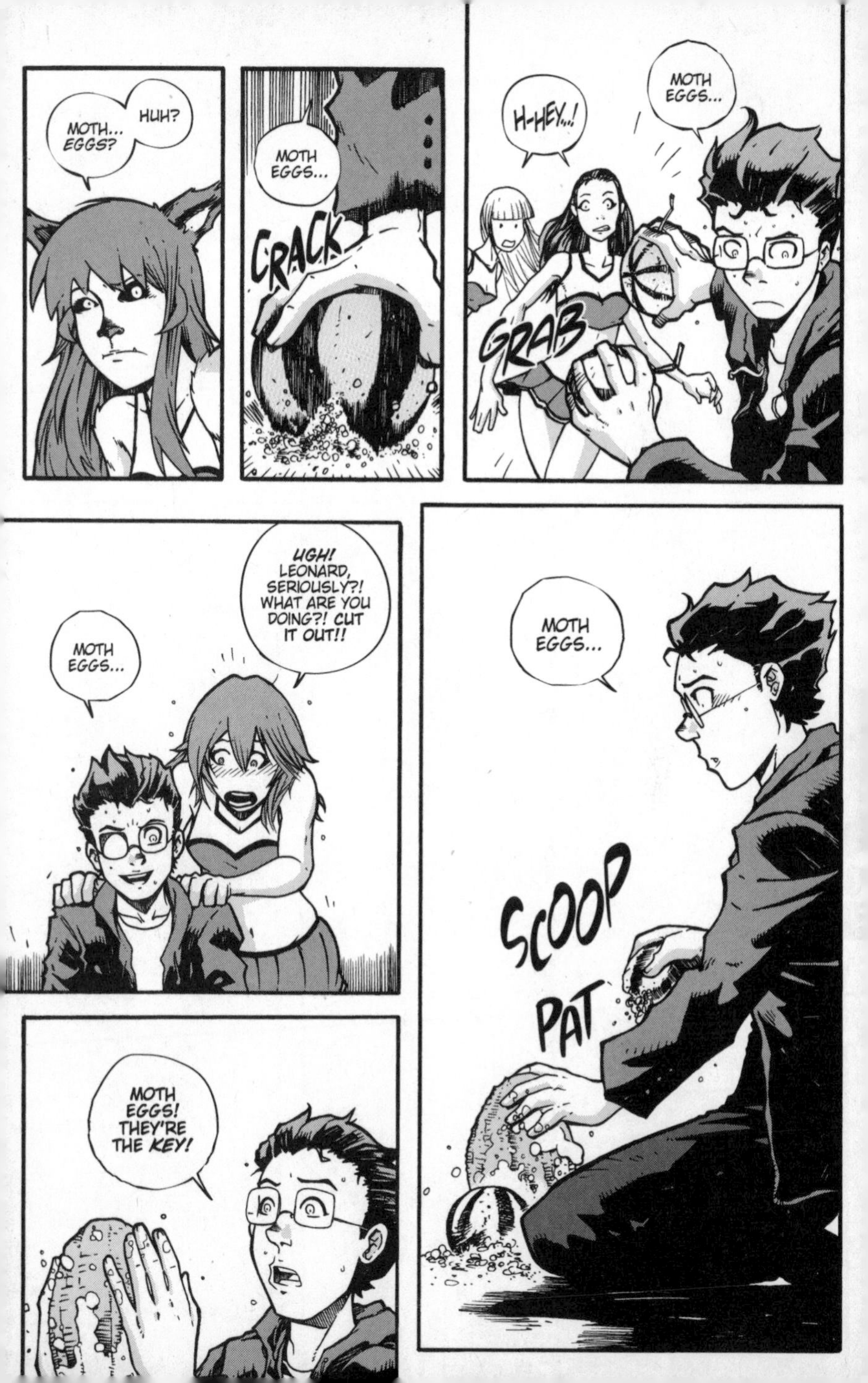
MOTH EGGS...
H-HEY...!
GRAB
MOTH EGGS...
CRACK
HUH?
MOTH... EGGS?
MOTH EGGS...
SCOOP
PAT
UGH! LEONARD, SERIOUSLY?! WHAT ARE YOU DOING?! CUT IT OUT!!
MOTH EGGS...
MOTH EGGS! THEY'RE THE KEY!

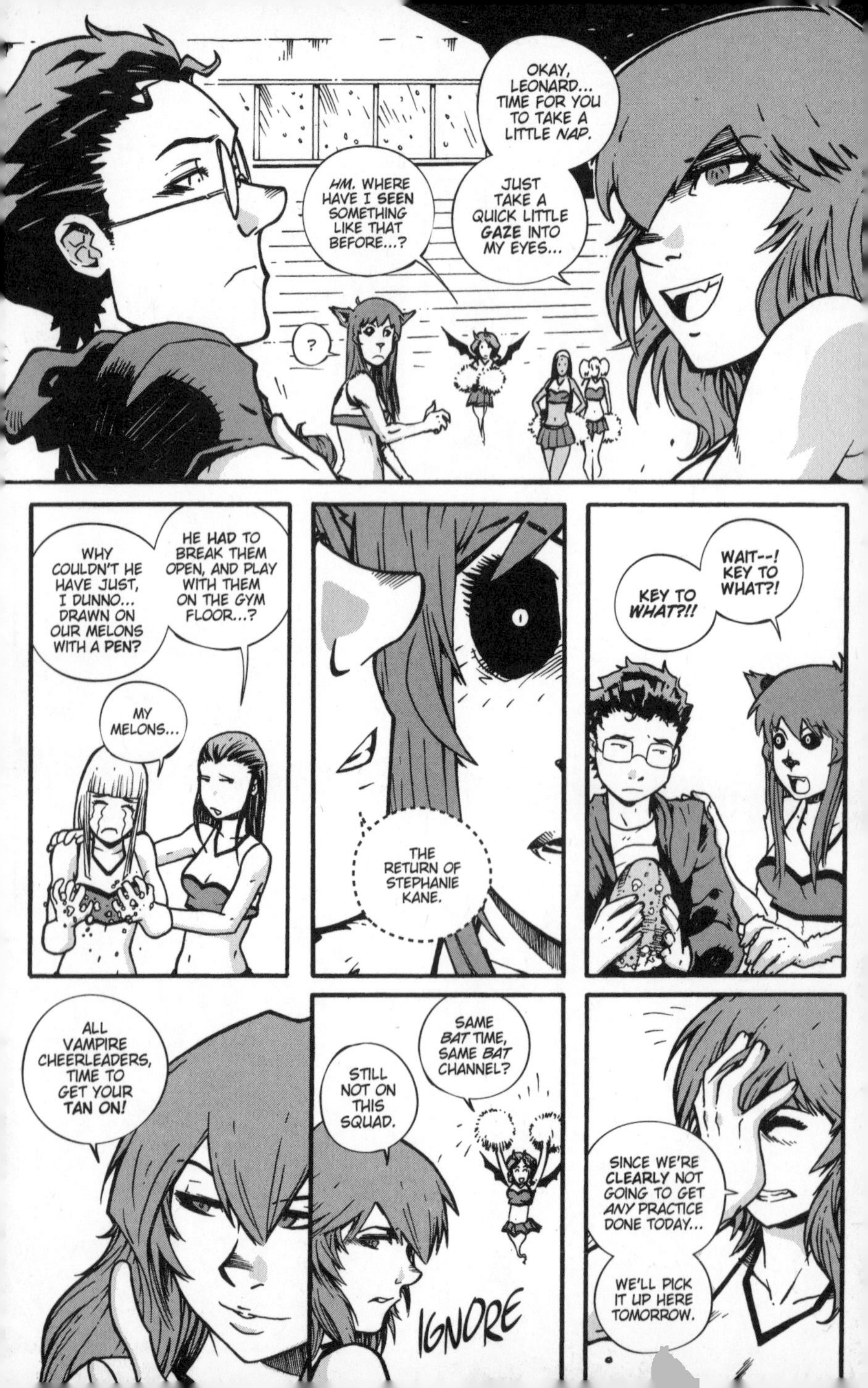
OKAY, LEONARD... TIME FOR YOU TO TAKE A LITTLE NAP.
JUST TAKE A QUICK LITTLE GAZE INTO MY EYES...
HM. WHERE HAVE I SEEN SOMETHING LIKE THAT BEFORE...?
?
WAIT--! KEY TO WHAT?!
KEY TO WHAT?!!
THE RETURN OF STEPHANIE KANE.
HE HAD TO BREAK THEM OPEN, AND PLAY WITH THEM ON THE GYM FLOOR...?
WHY COULDN'T HE HAVE JUST, I DUNNO... DRAWN ON OUR MELONS WITH A PEN?
MY MELONS...
SINCE WE'RE CLEARLY NOT GOING TO GET ANY PRACTICE DONE TODAY...
WE'LL PICK IT UP HERE TOMORROW.
SAME BAT TIME, SAME BAT CHANNEL?
STILL NOT ON THIS SQUAD.
IGNORE
ALL VAMPIRE CHEERLEADERS, TIME TO GET YOUR TAN ON!

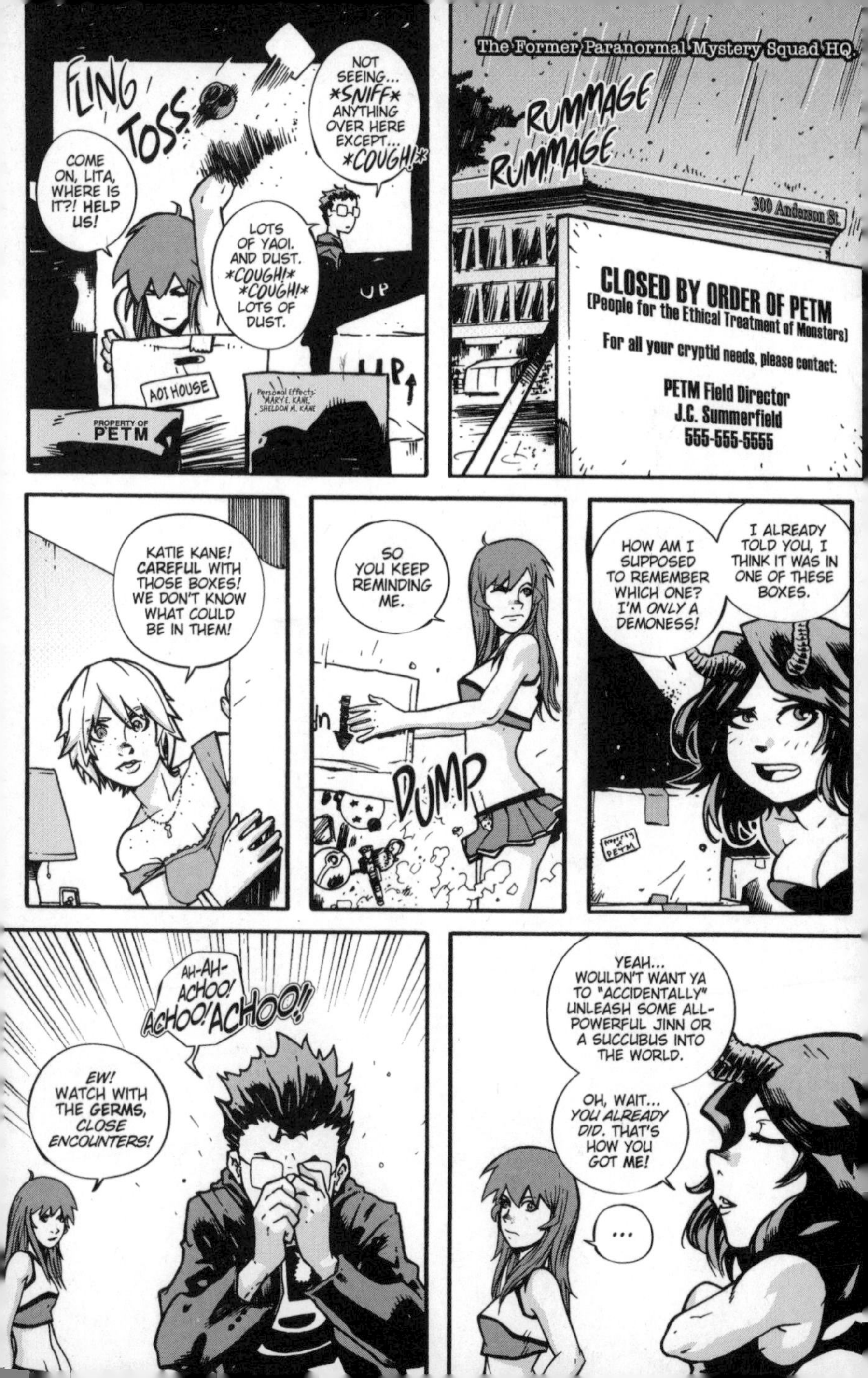
The Former Paranormal Mystery Squad HQ.
RUMMAGE RUMMAGE
300 Anderson St.
CLOSED BY ORDER OF PETM
(People for the Ethical Treatment of Monsters)
For all your cryptid needs, please contact:
PETM Field Director
J.C. Summerfield
555-555-5555
FLING
TOSS
NOT SEEING... *SNIFF* ANYTHING OVER HERE EXCEPT... *COUGH!*
COME ON, LITA, WHERE IS IT?! HELP US!
LOTS OF YAOI. AND DUST. *COUGH!* *COUGH!* LOTS OF DUST.
UP
UP
AOI HOUSE
Personal Effects: MARY E. KANE, SHELDON M. KANE
PROPERTY OF PETM
I ALREADY TOLD YOU, I THINK IT WAS IN ONE OF THESE BOXES.
HOW AM I SUPPOSED TO REMEMBER WHICH ONE? I'M *ONLY* A DEMONESS!
Property of PETM
SO YOU KEEP REMINDING ME.
DUMP
KATIE KANE! CAREFUL WITH THOSE BOXES! WE DON'T KNOW WHAT COULD BE IN THEM!
YEAH... WOULDN'T WANT YA TO "ACCIDENTALLY" UNLEASH SOME ALL-POWERFUL JINN OR A SUCCUBUS INTO THE WORLD.
OH, WAIT... *YOU ALREADY DID*. THAT'S HOW YOU GOT ME!
...
AH-AH-ACHOO! ACHOO! ACHOO!
EW! WATCH WITH THE GERMS, *CLOSE ENCOUNTERS!*

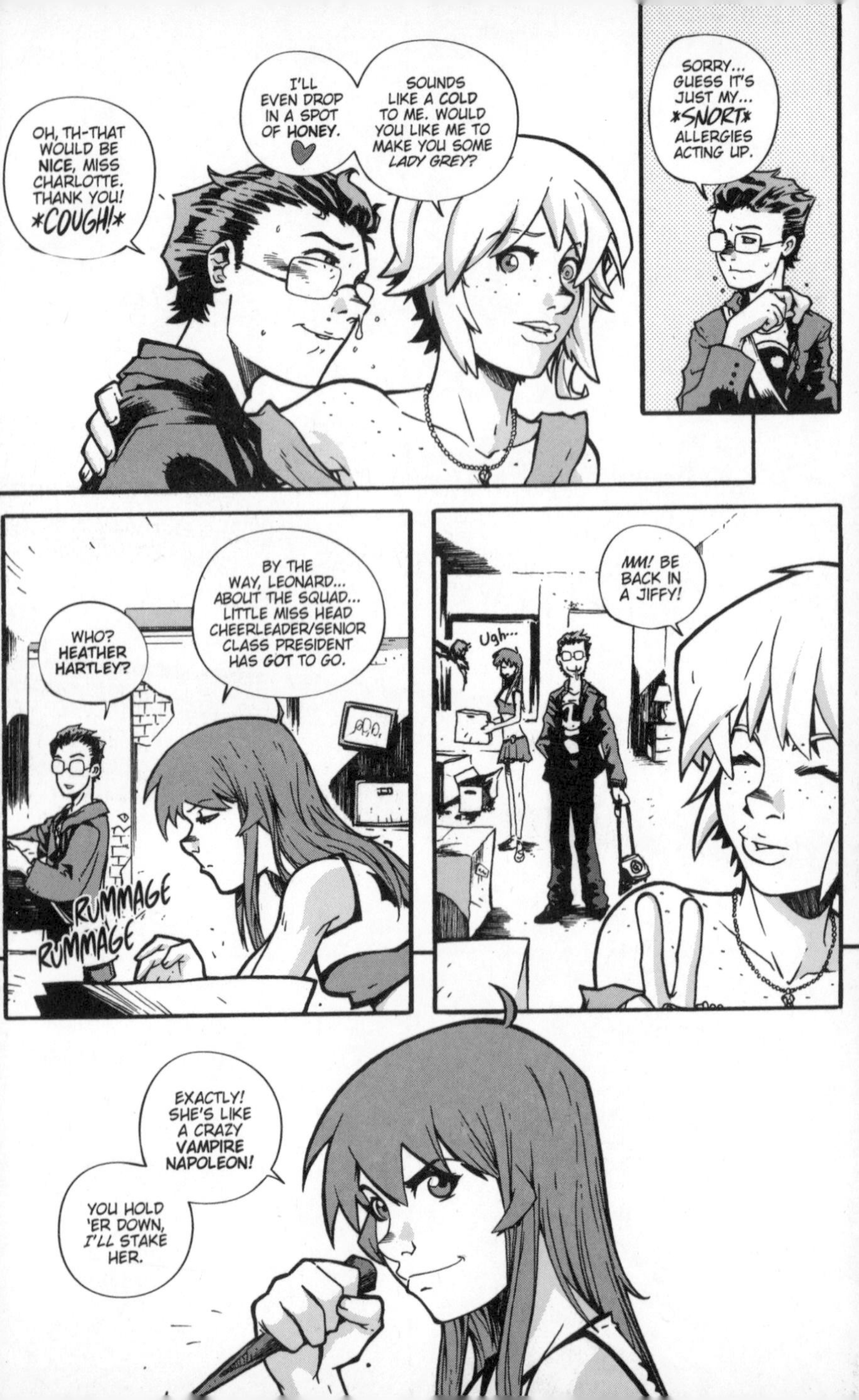
SORRY... GUESS IT'S JUST MY... *SNORT* ALLERGIES ACTING UP.
SOUNDS LIKE A COLD TO ME. WOULD YOU LIKE ME TO MAKE YOU SOME LADY GREY?
I'LL EVEN DROP IN A SPOT OF HONEY.
OH, TH-THAT WOULD BE NICE, MISS CHARLOTTE. THANK YOU! *COUGH!*
MM! BE BACK IN A JIFFY!
Ugh...
BY THE WAY, LEONARD... ABOUT THE SQUAD... LITTLE MISS HEAD CHEERLEADER/SENIOR CLASS PRESIDENT HAS GOT TO GO.
WHO? HEATHER HARTLEY?
RUMMAGE
RUMMAGE
EXACTLY! SHE'S LIKE A CRAZY VAMPIRE NAPOLEON!
YOU HOLD 'ER DOWN, I'LL STAKE HER.

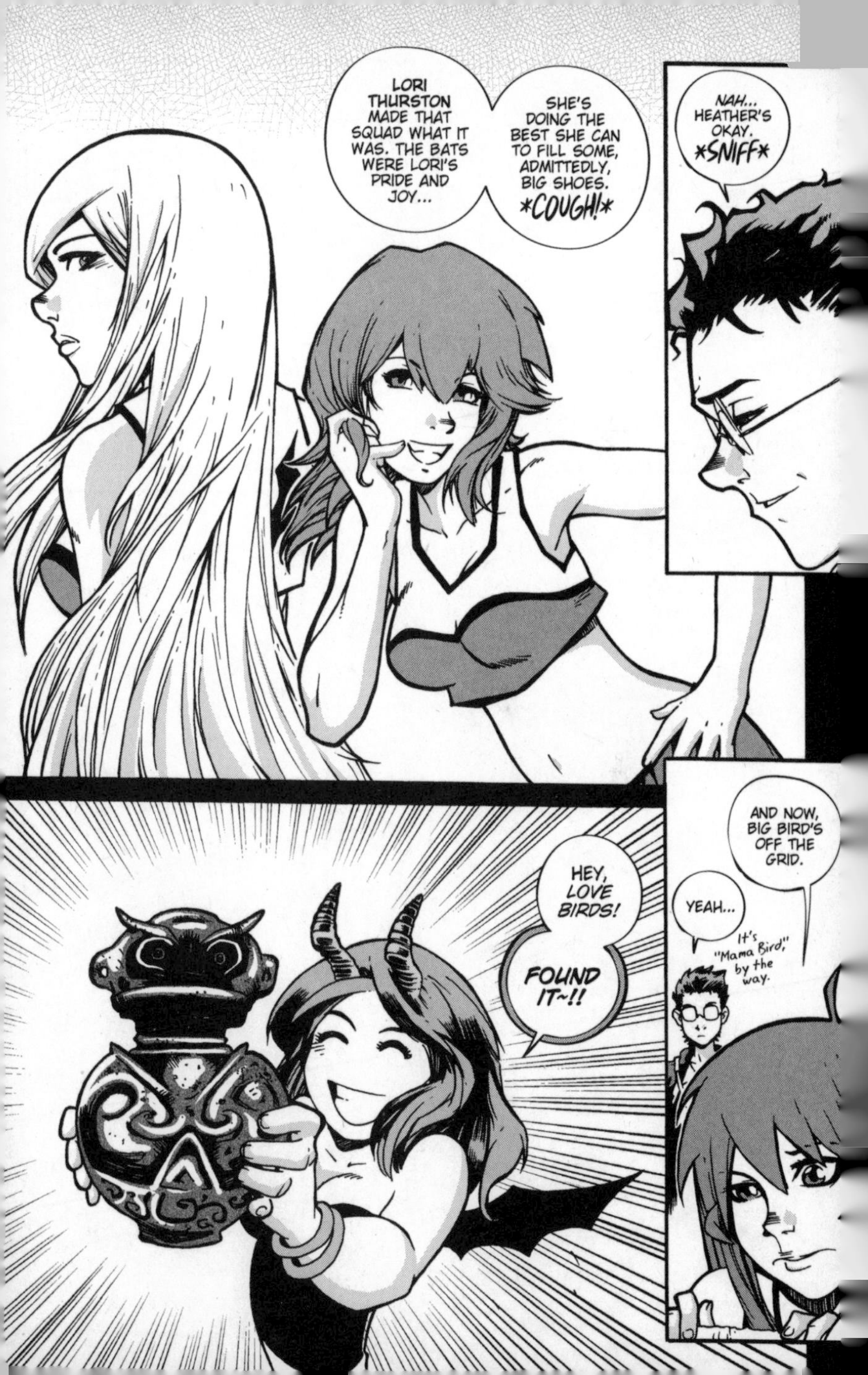
NAH... HEATHER'S OKAY. *SNIFF*
SHE'S DOING THE BEST SHE CAN TO FILL SOME, ADMITTEDLY, BIG SHOES. *COUGH!*
LORI THURSTON MADE THAT SQUAD WHAT IT WAS. THE BATS WERE LORI'S PRIDE AND JOY...
AND NOW, BIG BIRD'S OFF THE GRID.
YEAH...
It's "Mama Bird," by the way.
HEY, LOVE BIRDS!
FOUND IT~!!

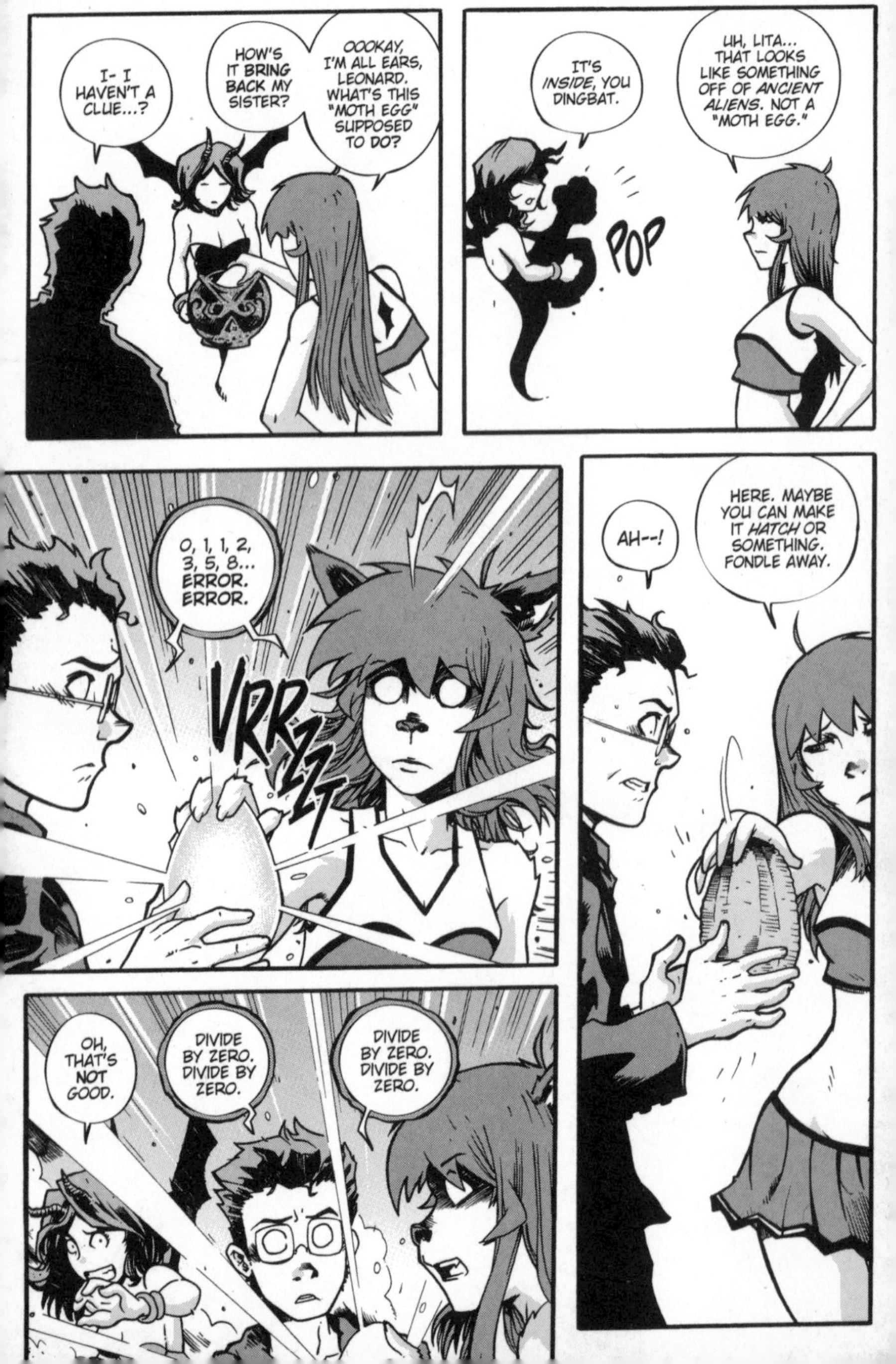
UH, LITA... THAT LOOKS LIKE SOMETHING OFF OF *ANCIENT ALIENS*. NOT A "MOTH EGG."
IT'S *INSIDE*, YOU DINGBAT.
POP
OOOKAY, I'M ALL EARS, LEONARD. WHAT'S THIS "MOTH EGG" SUPPOSED TO DO?
HOW'S IT BRING BACK MY SISTER?
I- I HAVEN'T A CLUE...?
HERE. MAYBE YOU CAN MAKE IT *HATCH* OR SOMETHING. FONDLE AWAY.
AH--!
0, 1, 1, 2, 3, 5, 8... ERROR. ERROR.
VRRZZZT
DIVIDE BY ZERO. DIVIDE BY ZERO.
DIVIDE BY ZERO. DIVIDE BY ZERO.
OH, THAT'S NOT GOOD.

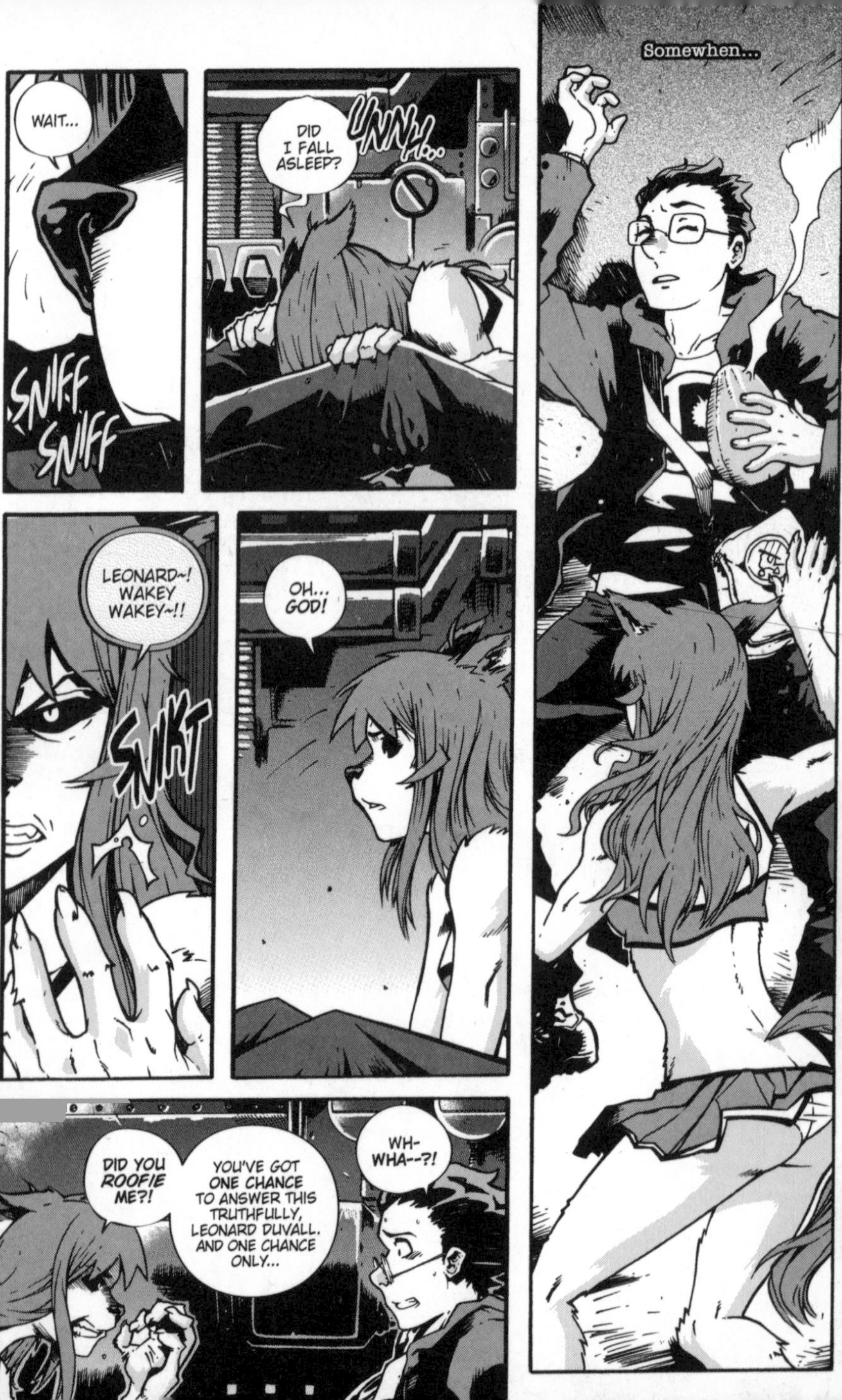
Somewhen...
UNNH...
DID I FALL ASLEEP?
WAIT...
SNIFF SNIFF
OH... GOD!
LEONARD~! WAKEY WAKEY~!!
SNIKT
WH- WHA--?!
YOU'VE GOT ONE CHANCE TO ANSWER THIS TRUTHFULLY, LEONARD DUVALL. AND ONE CHANCE ONLY...
DID YOU ROOFIE ME?!

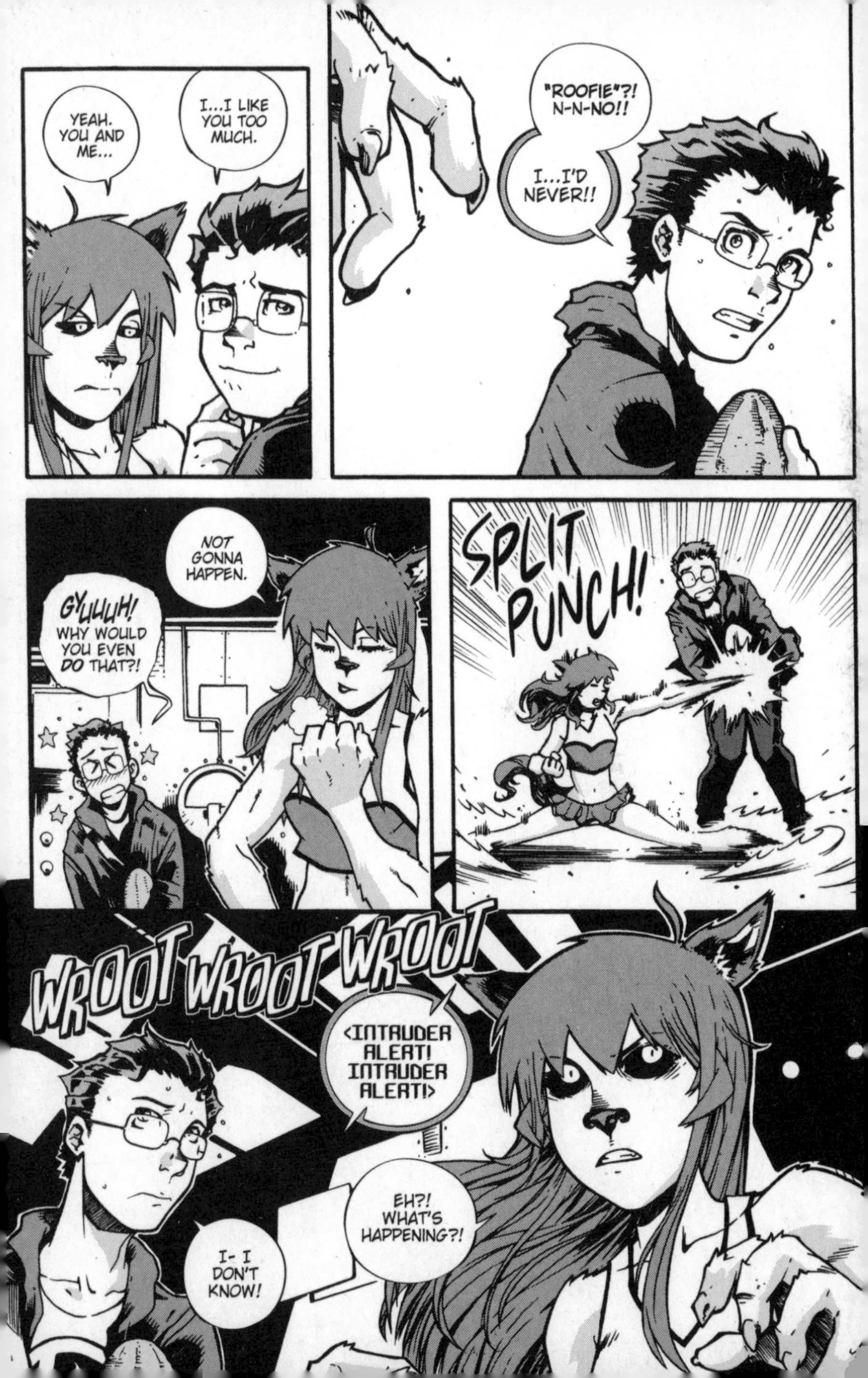
"ROOFIE"?! N-N-NO!!
I...I'D NEVER!!
I...I LIKE YOU TOO MUCH.
YEAH. YOU AND ME...
SPLIT PUNCH!
NOT GONNA HAPPEN.
GYUUUH! WHY WOULD YOU EVEN DO THAT?!
WROOT WROOT WROOT
<INTRUDER ALERT! INTRUDER ALERT!>
EH?! WHAT'S HAPPENING?!
I- I DON'T KNOW!

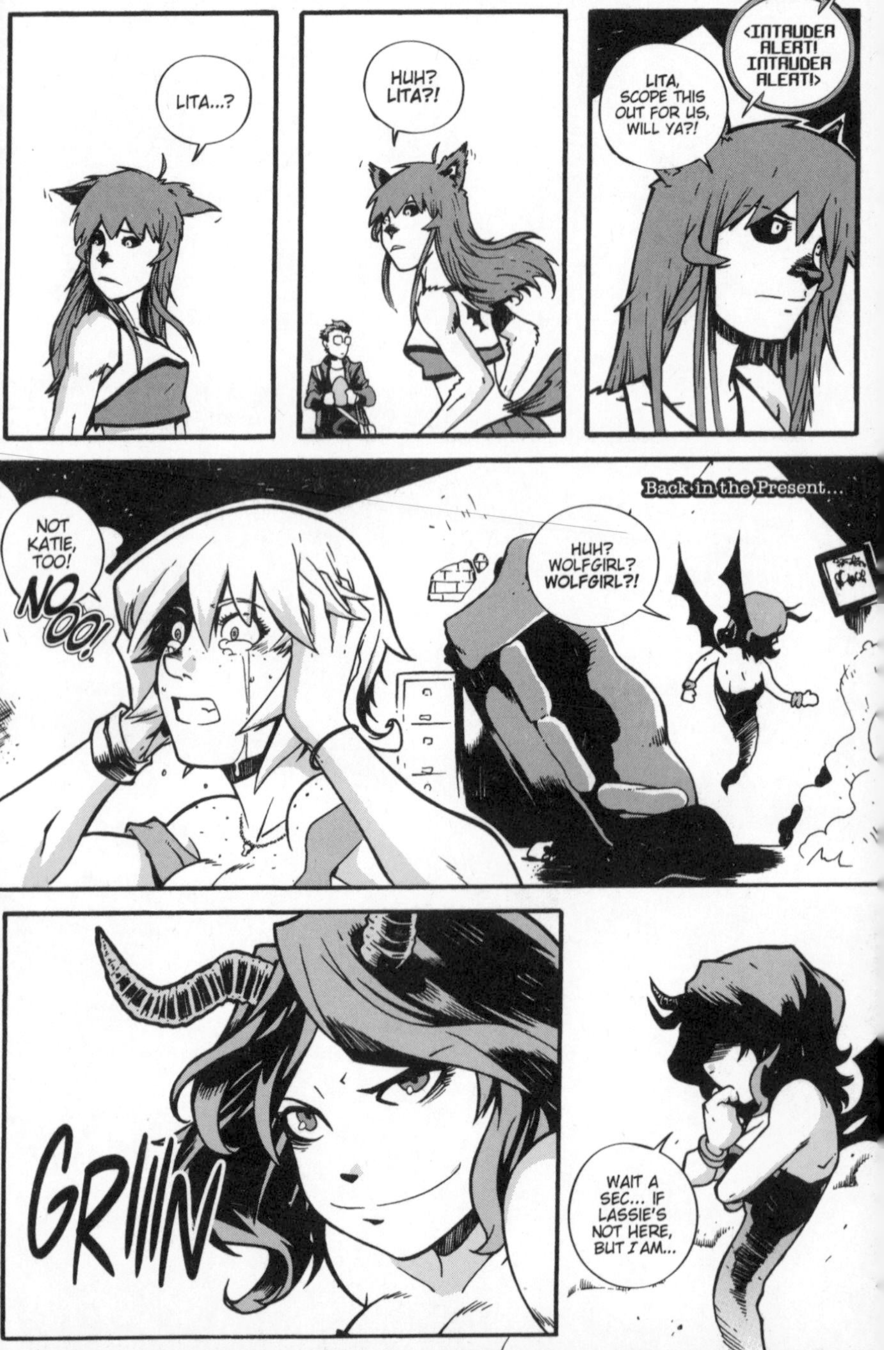
<INTRUDER ALERT! INTRUDER ALERT!>
LITA, SCOPE THIS OUT FOR US, WILL YA?!
HUH? LITA?!
LITA...?
Back in the Present...
HUH? WOLFGIRL? WOLFGIRL?!
NOT KATIE, TOO!
NOOO!
WAIT A SEC... IF LASSIE'S NOT HERE, BUT *I* AM...
GRIIIN

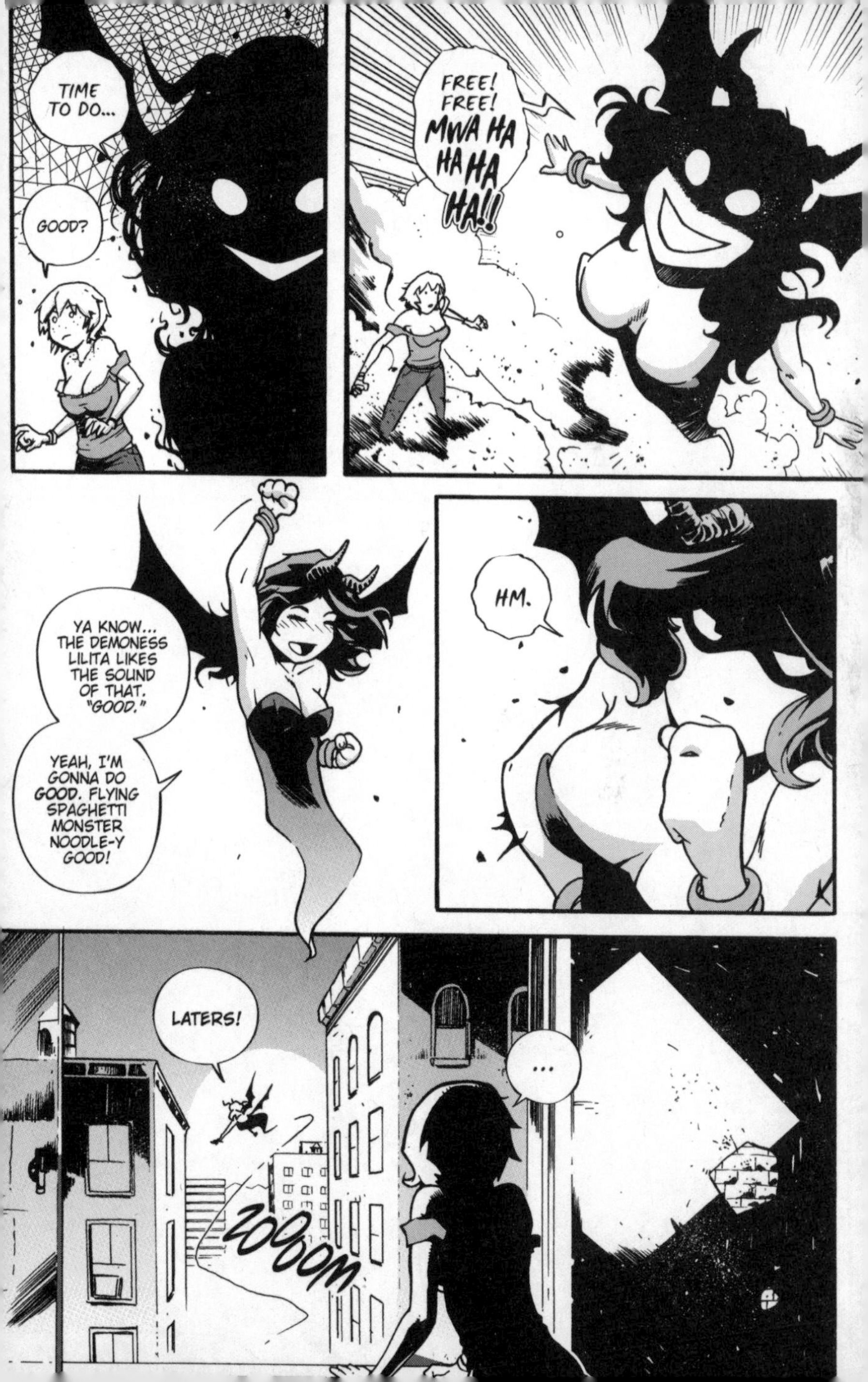
FREE! FREE! MWA HA HA HA HA!!
TIME TO DO...
GOOD?
HM.
YA KNOW... THE DEMONESS LILITA LIKES THE SOUND OF THAT. "GOOD."
YEAH, I'M GONNA DO GOOD. FLYING SPAGHETTI MONSTER NOODLE-Y GOOD!
...
LATERS!
ZOOOOOM

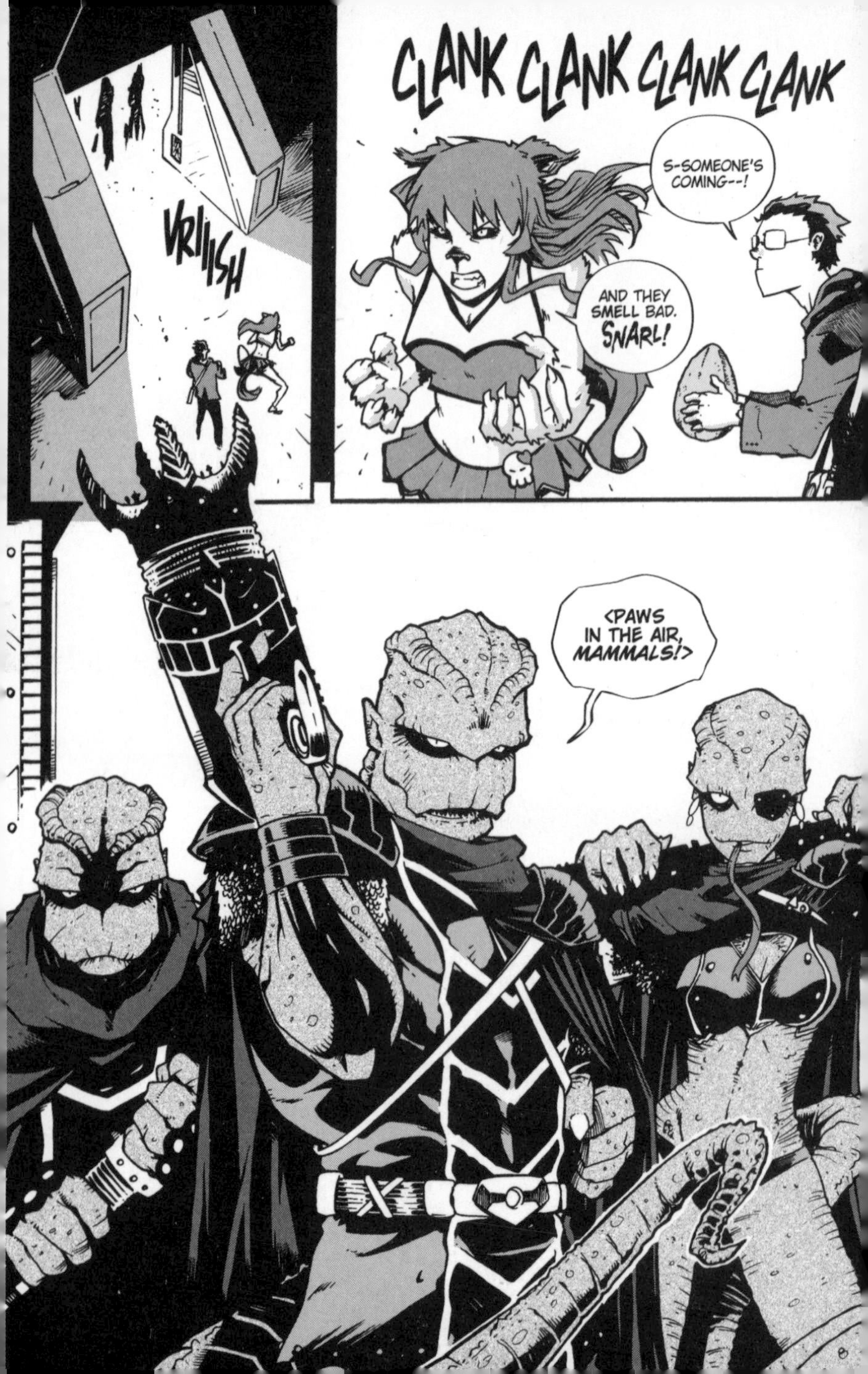
CLANK CLANK CLANK CLANK
S-SOMEONE'S COMING--!
AND THEY SMELL BAD. SNARL!
VRIIISH
<PAWS IN THE AIR, MAMMALS!>

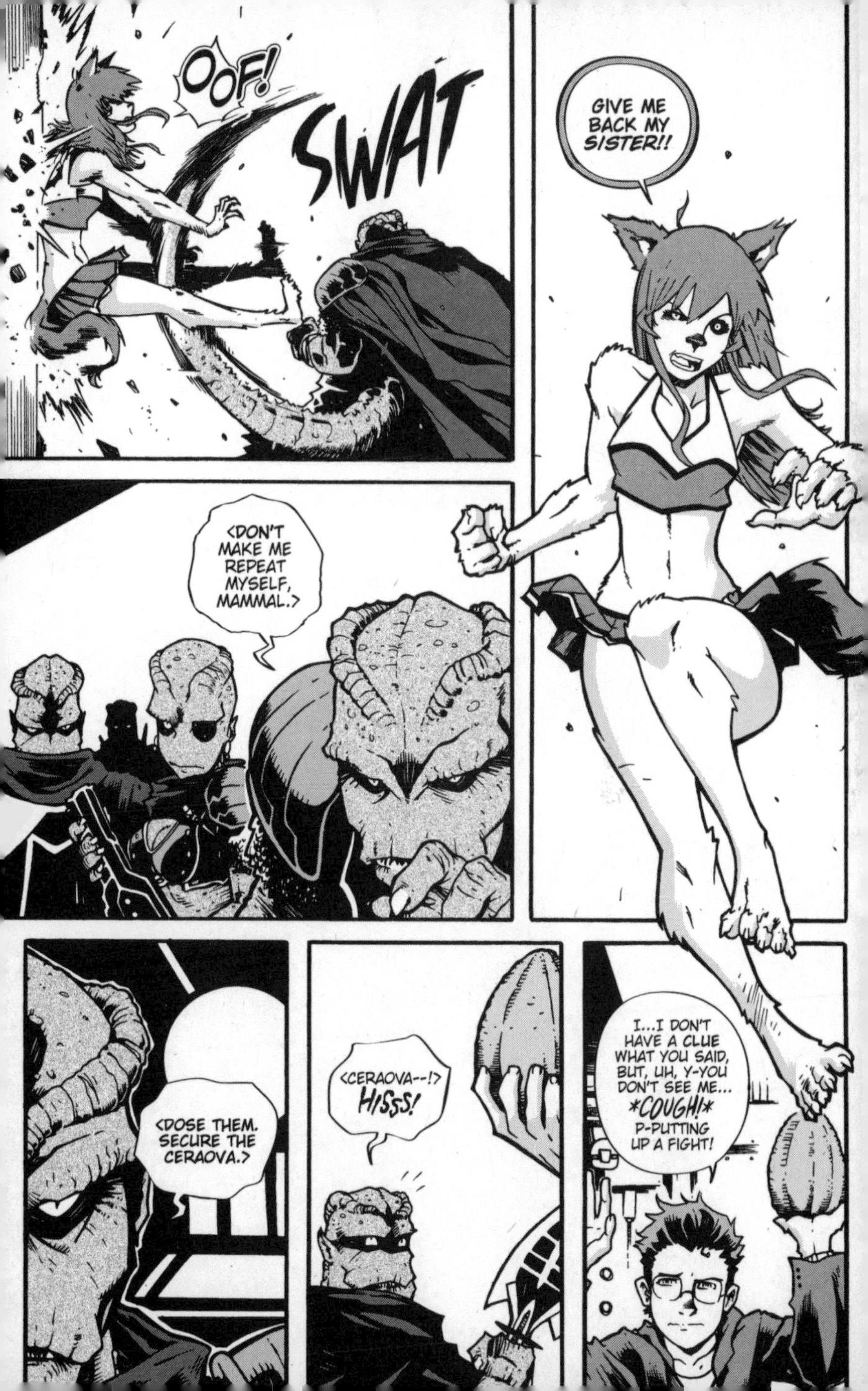
GIVE ME BACK MY SISTER!!
OOF!
SWAT
<DON'T MAKE ME REPEAT MYSELF, MAMMAL.>
I...I DON'T HAVE A CLUE WHAT YOU SAID, BUT, UH, Y-YOU DON'T SEE ME... *COUGH!* P-PUTTING UP A FIGHT!
<CERAOVA--!>
HISSS!
<DOSE THEM. SECURE THE CERAOVA.>

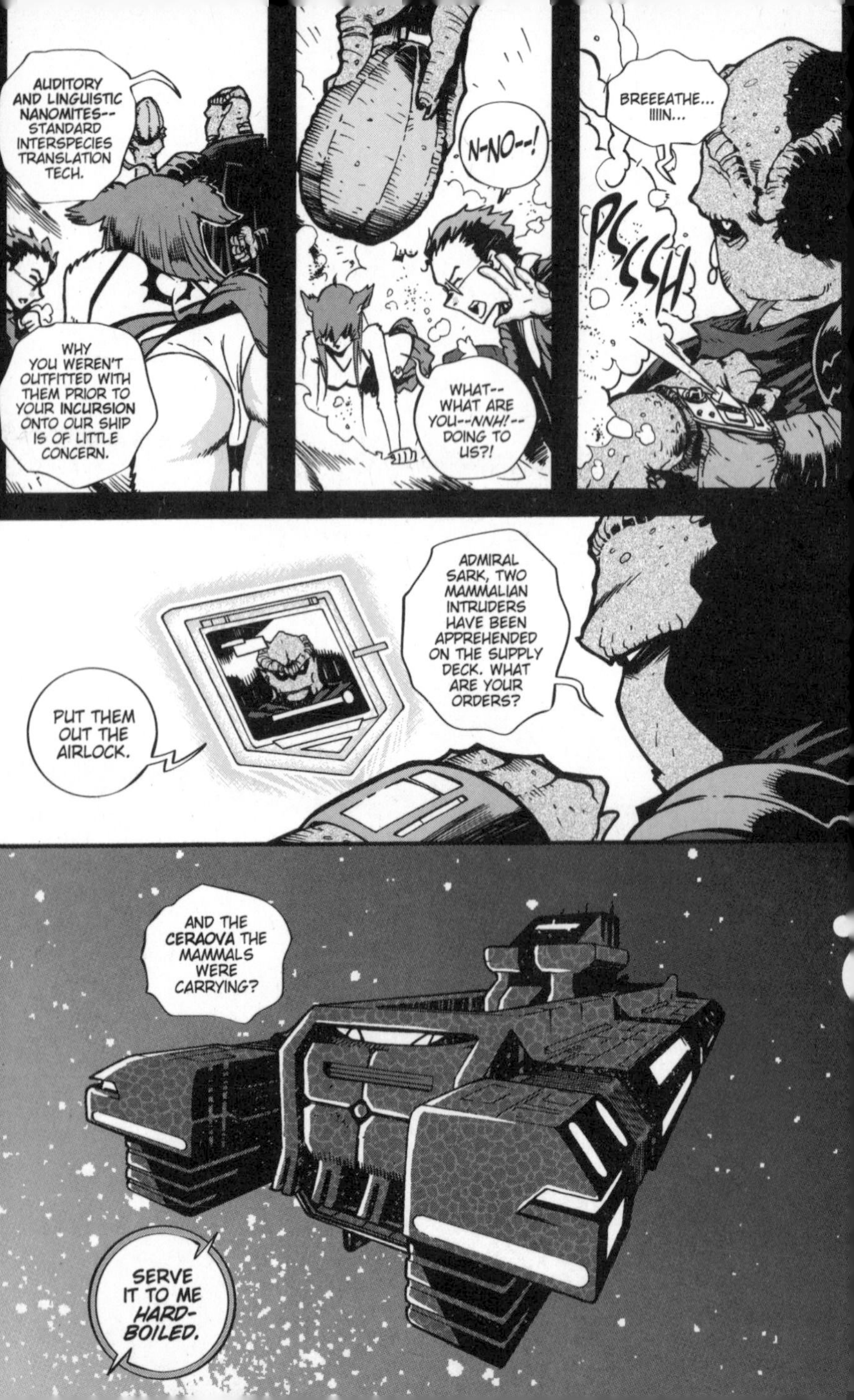
BREEEATHE... IIIIN...
PSSSH
N-NO--!
WHAT-- WHAT ARE YOU--NNH!-- DOING TO US?!
AUDITORY AND LINGUISTIC NANOMITES-- STANDARD INTERSPECIES TRANSLATION TECH.
WHY YOU WEREN'T OUTFITTED WITH THEM PRIOR TO YOUR INCURSION ONTO OUR SHIP IS OF LITTLE CONCERN.
ADMIRAL SARK, TWO MAMMALIAN INTRUDERS HAVE BEEN APPREHENDED ON THE SUPPLY DECK. WHAT ARE YOUR ORDERS?
PUT THEM OUT THE AIRLOCK.
AND THE CERAOVA THE MAMMALS WERE CARRYING?
SERVE IT TO ME HARD-BOILED.

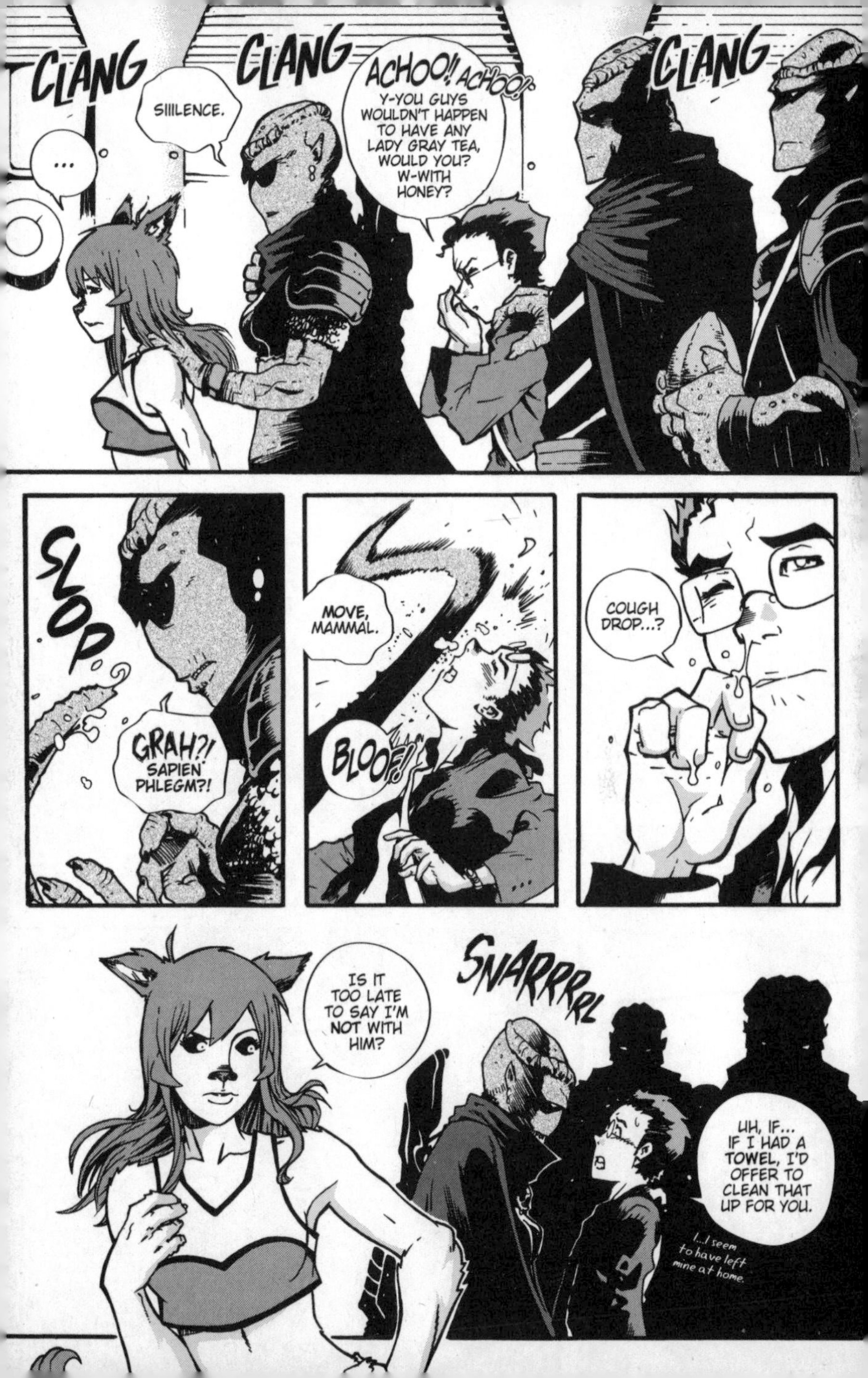
CLANG
ACHOO!! ACHOO!! Y-YOU GUYS WOULDN'T HAPPEN TO HAVE ANY LADY GRAY TEA, WOULD YOU? W-WITH HONEY?
CLANG
SIIILENCE.
CLANG
...
COUGH DROP...?
MOVE, MAMMAL.
BLOOF!
SLOP
GRAH?! SAPIEN PHLEGM?!
SNARRRRL
UH, IF... IF I HAD A TOWEL, I'D OFFER TO CLEAN THAT UP FOR YOU.
I...I seem to have left mine at home.
IS IT TOO LATE TO SAY I'M NOT WITH HIM?

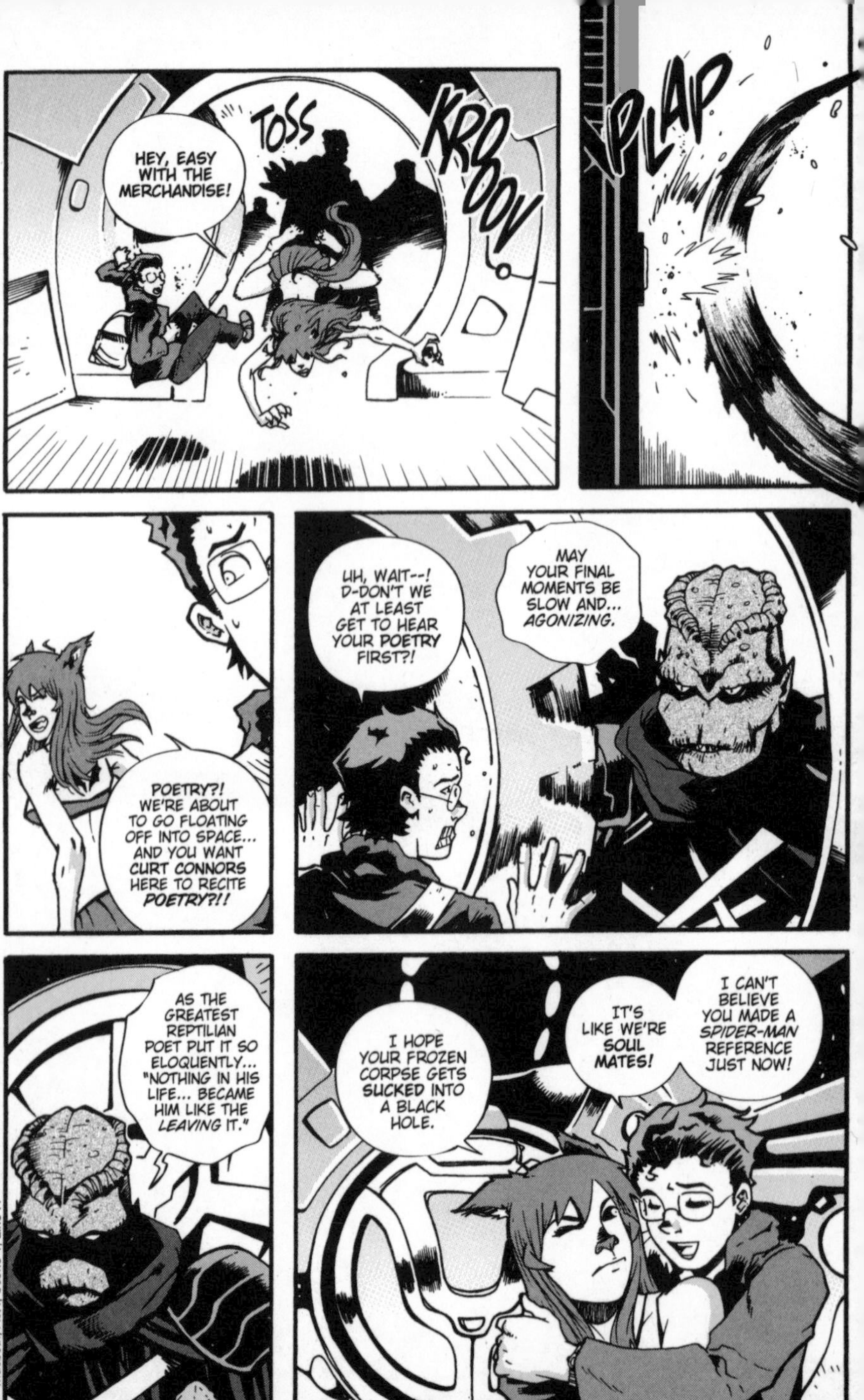
PLAP
KROOOV!
TOSS
HEY, EASY WITH THE MERCHANDISE!
MAY YOUR FINAL MOMENTS BE SLOW AND... *AGONIZING.*
UH, WAIT--! D-DON'T WE AT LEAST GET TO HEAR YOUR **POETRY** FIRST?!
POETRY?! WE'RE ABOUT TO GO FLOATING OFF INTO SPACE... AND YOU WANT **CURT CONNORS** HERE TO RECITE ***POETRY?!!***
I CAN'T BELIEVE YOU MADE A *SPIDER-MAN* REFERENCE JUST NOW!
IT'S LIKE WE'RE **SOUL MATES!**
I HOPE YOUR FROZEN CORPSE GETS **SUCKED** INTO A BLACK HOLE.
AS THE GREATEST REPTILIAN POET PUT IT SO ELOQUENTLY... "NOTHING IN HIS LIFE... BECAME HIM LIKE THE *LEAVING* IT."

Macbeth, Act I, Scene 4, Line 7.

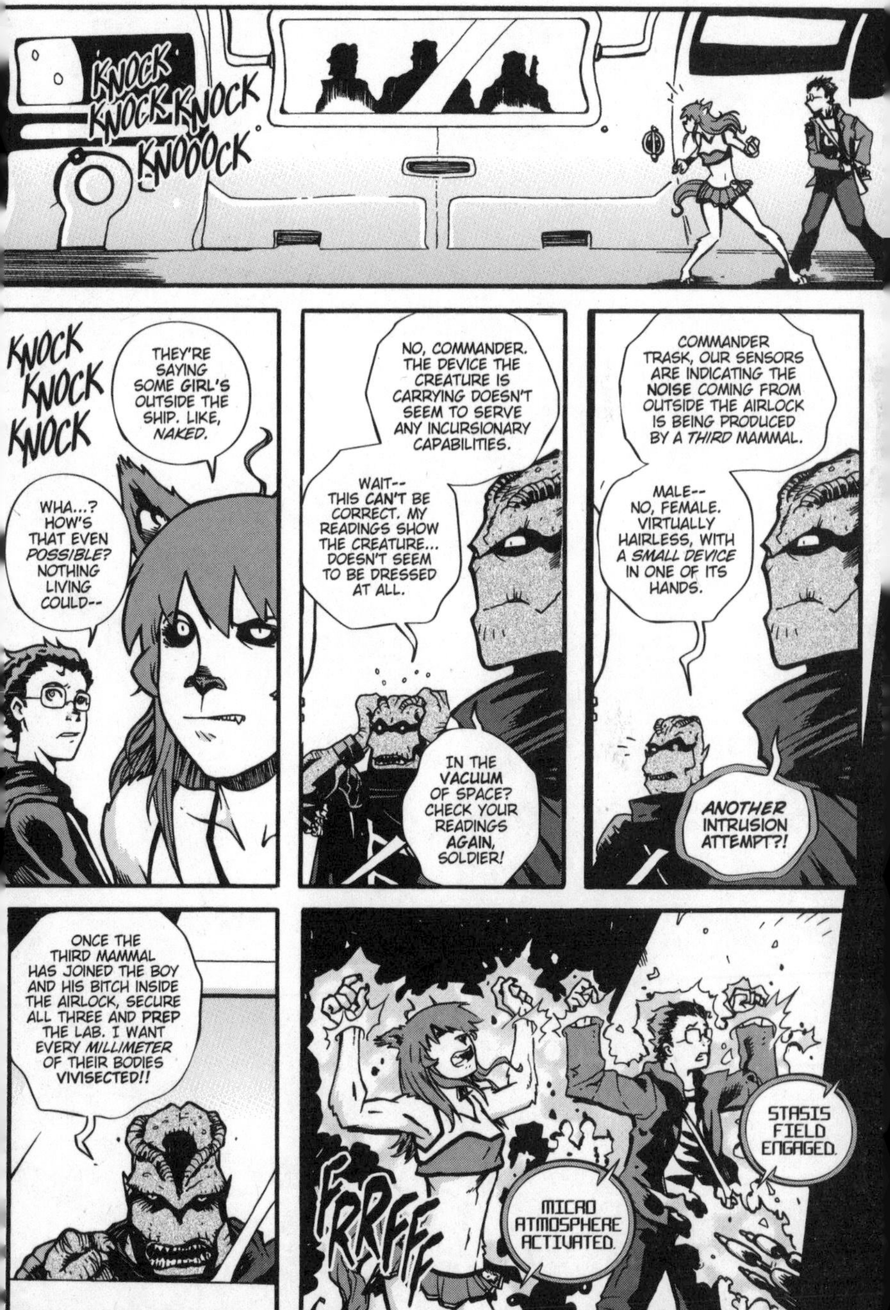
KNOCK KNOCK KNOCK KNOOOCK
COMMANDER TRASK, OUR SENSORS ARE INDICATING THE NOISE COMING FROM OUTSIDE THE AIRLOCK IS BEING PRODUCED BY A *THIRD* MAMMAL.
MALE-- NO, FEMALE. VIRTUALLY HAIRLESS, WITH A *SMALL DEVICE* IN ONE OF ITS HANDS.
ANOTHER INTRUSION ATTEMPT?!
NO, COMMANDER. THE DEVICE THE CREATURE IS CARRYING DOESN'T SEEM TO SERVE ANY INCURSIONARY CAPABILITIES.
WAIT-- THIS **CAN'T** BE CORRECT. MY READINGS SHOW THE CREATURE... DOESN'T SEEM TO BE DRESSED AT ALL.
IN THE **VACUUM** OF SPACE? CHECK YOUR READINGS **AGAIN**, SOLDIER!
THEY'RE SAYING SOME **GIRL'S** OUTSIDE THE SHIP. LIKE, *NAKED*.
KNOCK KNOCK KNOCK
WHA...? HOW'S THAT EVEN *POSSIBLE?* NOTHING LIVING COULD--
STASIS FIELD ENGAGED.
MICRO ATMOSPHERE ACTIVATED.
FRRFFF
ONCE THE THIRD MAMMAL HAS JOINED THE BOY AND HIS BITCH INSIDE THE AIRLOCK, SECURE ALL THREE AND PREP THE LAB. I WANT EVERY *MILLIMETER* OF THEIR BODIES **VIVISECTED!!**

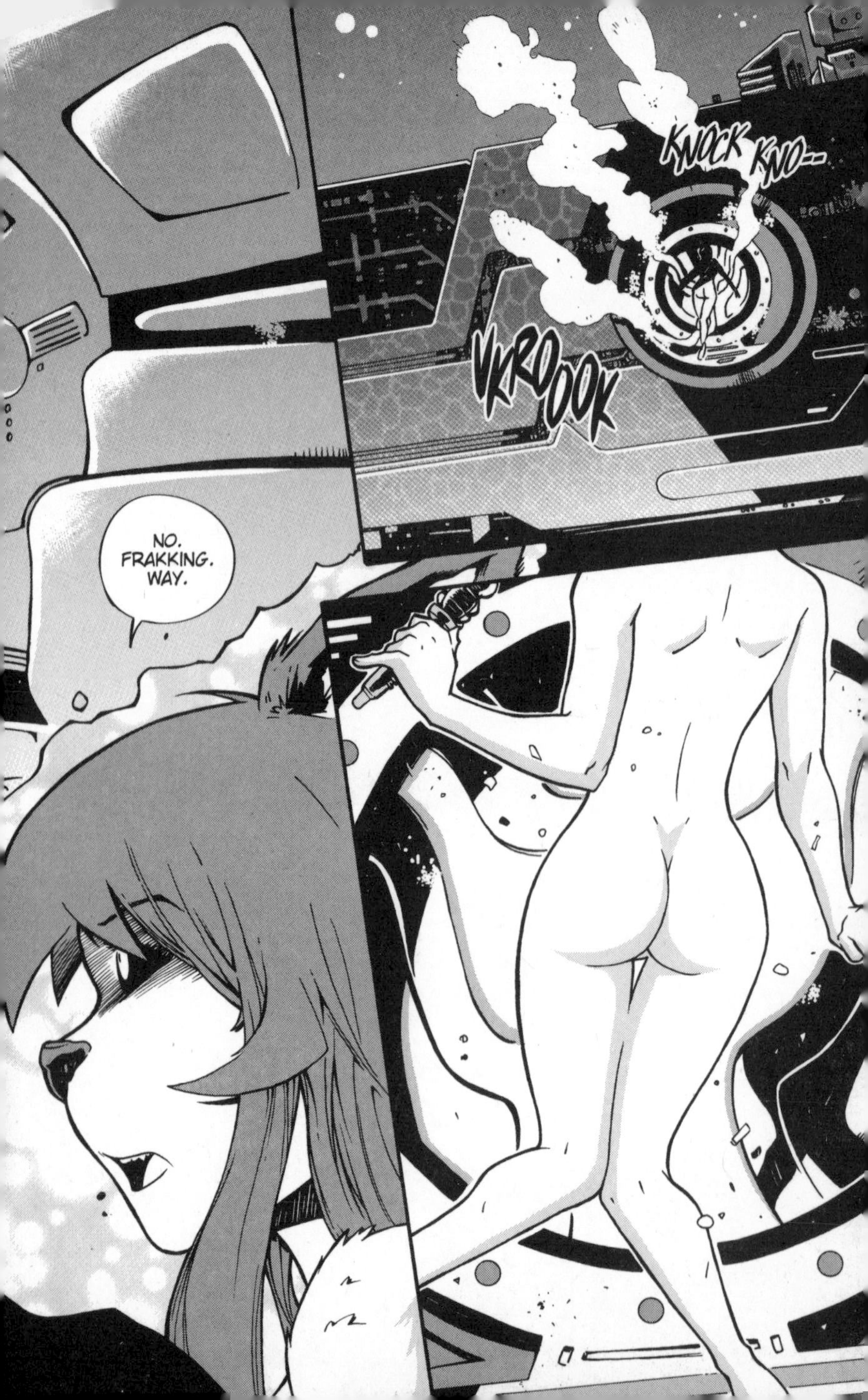
KNOCK KNO--
VKROOOK
NO. FRAKKING. WAY.

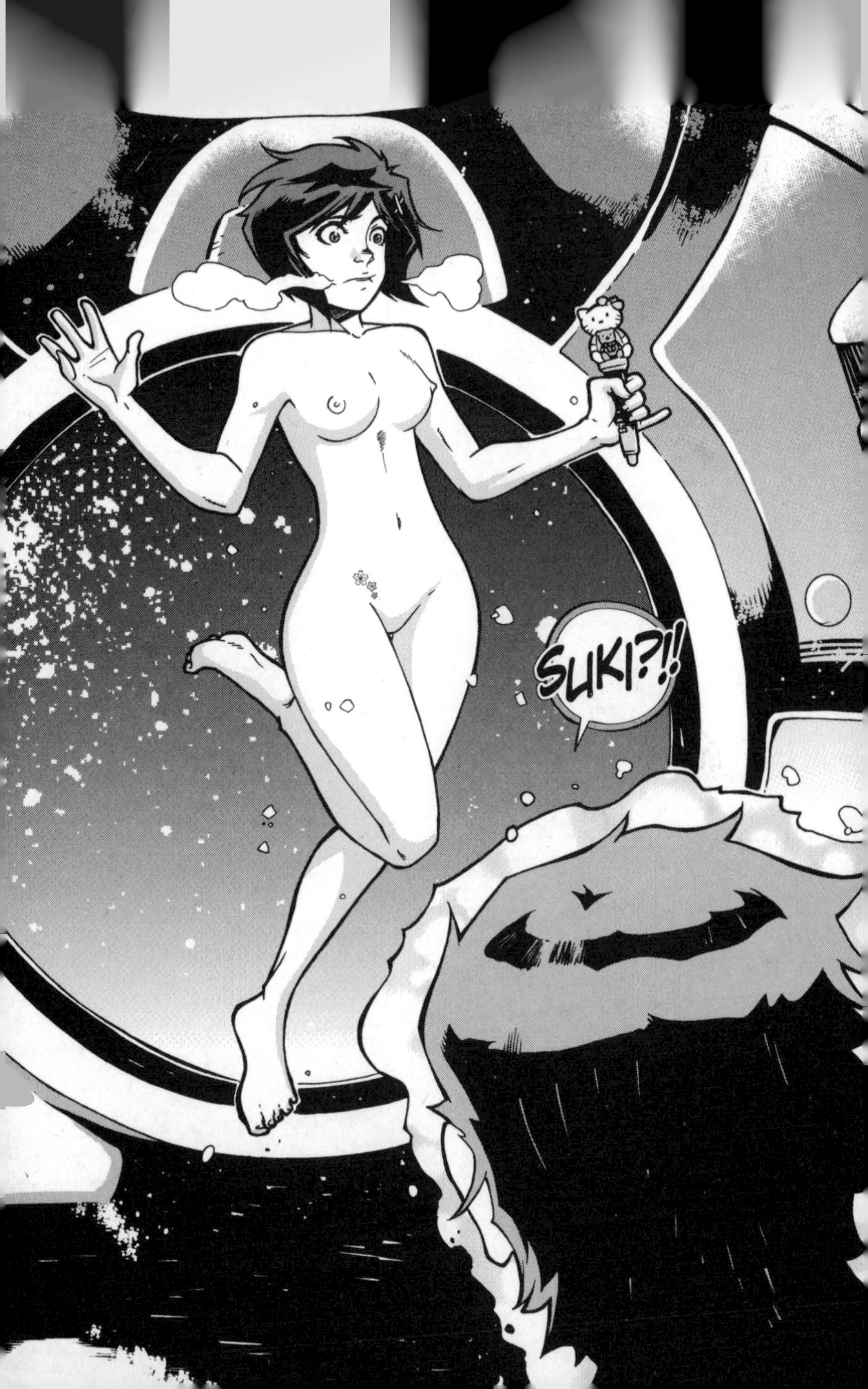
SUKI?!!

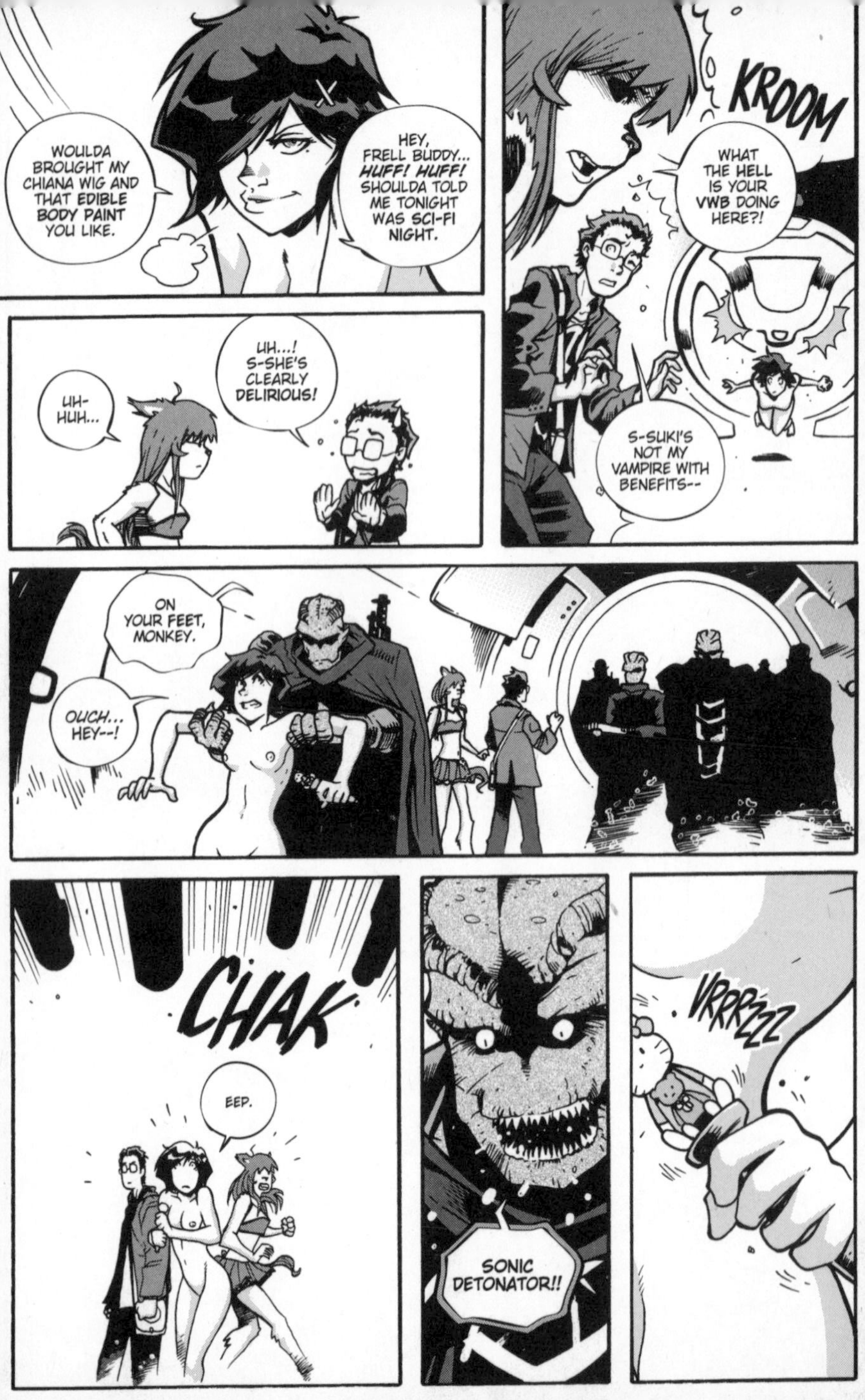
KROOM
WHAT THE HELL IS YOUR VWB DOING HERE?!
S-SUKI'S NOT MY VAMPIRE WITH BENEFITS--
HEY, FRELL BUDDY... *HUFF! HUFF!* SHOULDA TOLD ME TONIGHT WAS SCI-FI NIGHT.
WOULDA BROUGHT MY CHIANA WIG AND THAT EDIBLE BODY PAINT YOU LIKE.
UH...! S-SHE'S CLEARLY DELIRIOUS!
UH-HUH...
ON YOUR FEET, MONKEY.
OUCH... HEY--!
VRRRZZZ
SONIC DETONATOR!!
CHAK
EEP.

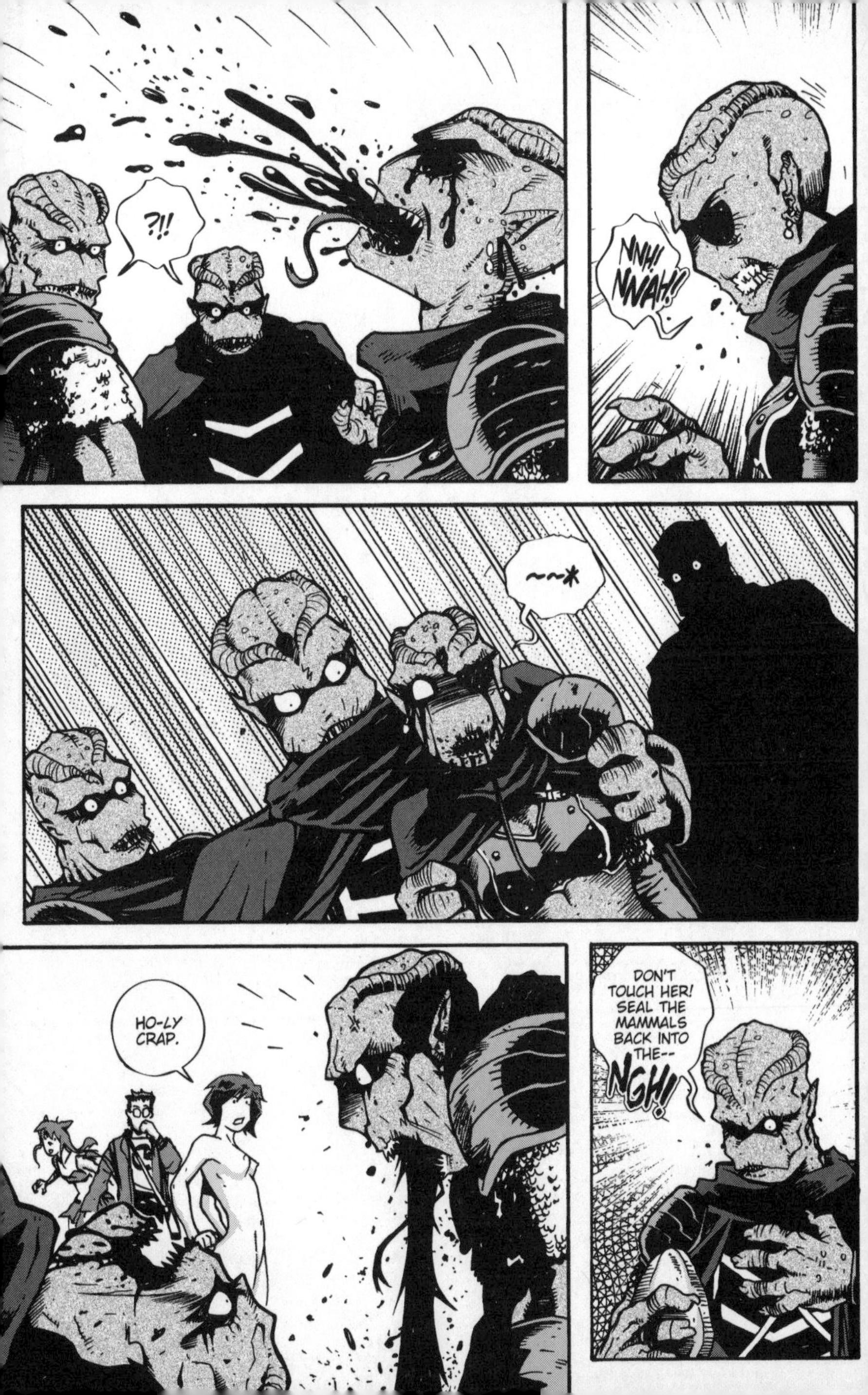
NNH! NNAH!!
?!!
~~*
DON'T TOUCH HER! SEAL THE MAMMALS BACK INTO THE--
NGH!
HO-LY CRAP.

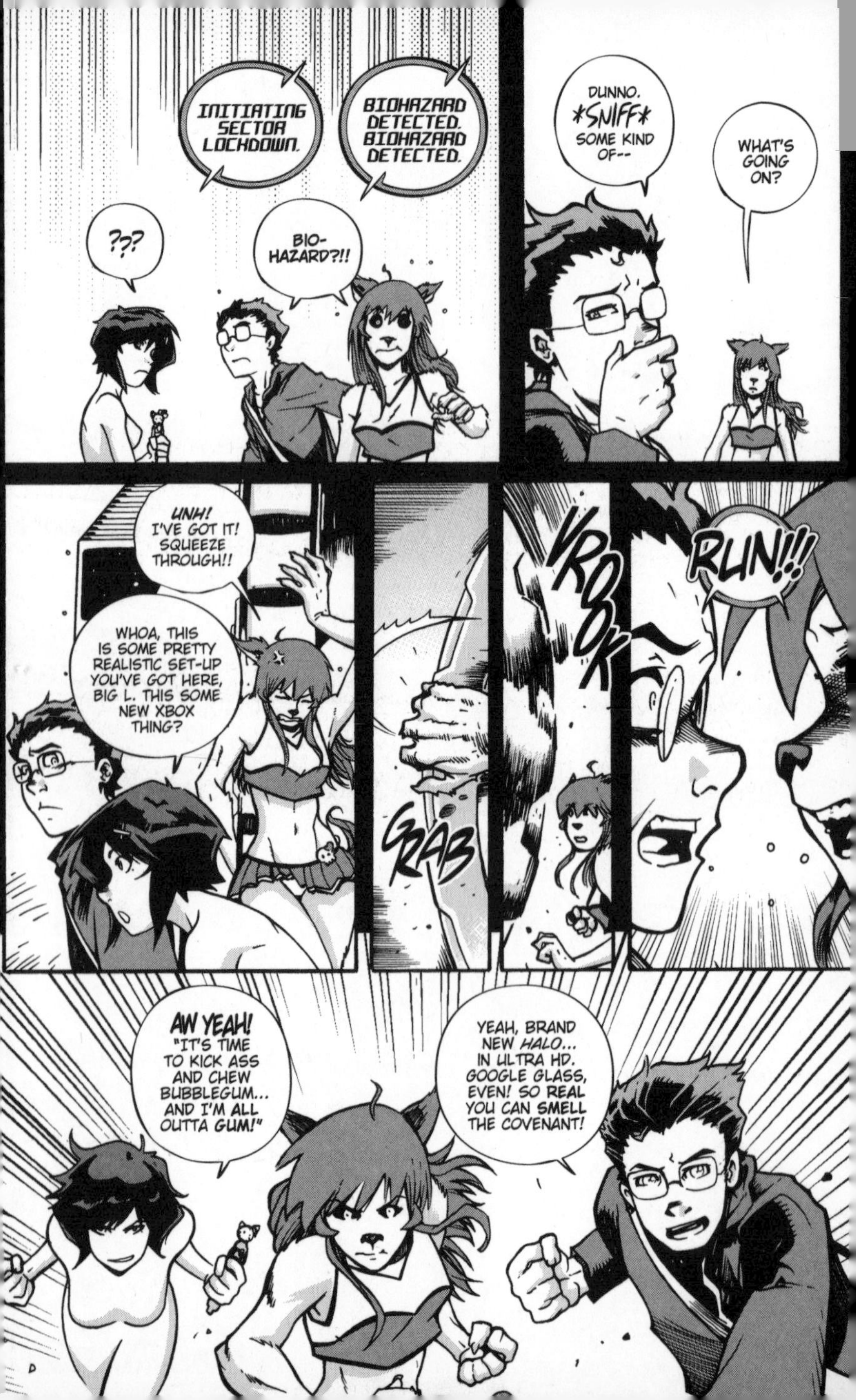
WHAT'S GOING ON?
DUNNO. *SNIFF* SOME KIND OF--
BIOHAZARD DETECTED. BIOHAZARD DETECTED.
INITIATING SECTOR LOCKDOWN.
BIO-HAZARD?!!
???
RUN!!!
VROOOK
GRAB
UNH! I'VE GOT IT! SQUEEZE THROUGH!!
WHOA, THIS IS SOME PRETTY REALISTIC SET-UP YOU'VE GOT HERE, BIG L. THIS SOME NEW XBOX THING?
YEAH, BRAND NEW HALO... IN ULTRA HD. GOOGLE GLASS, EVEN! SO REAL YOU CAN SMELL THE COVENANT!
AW YEAH! "IT'S TIME TO KICK ASS AND CHEW BUBBLEGUM... AND I'M ALL OUTTA GUM!"

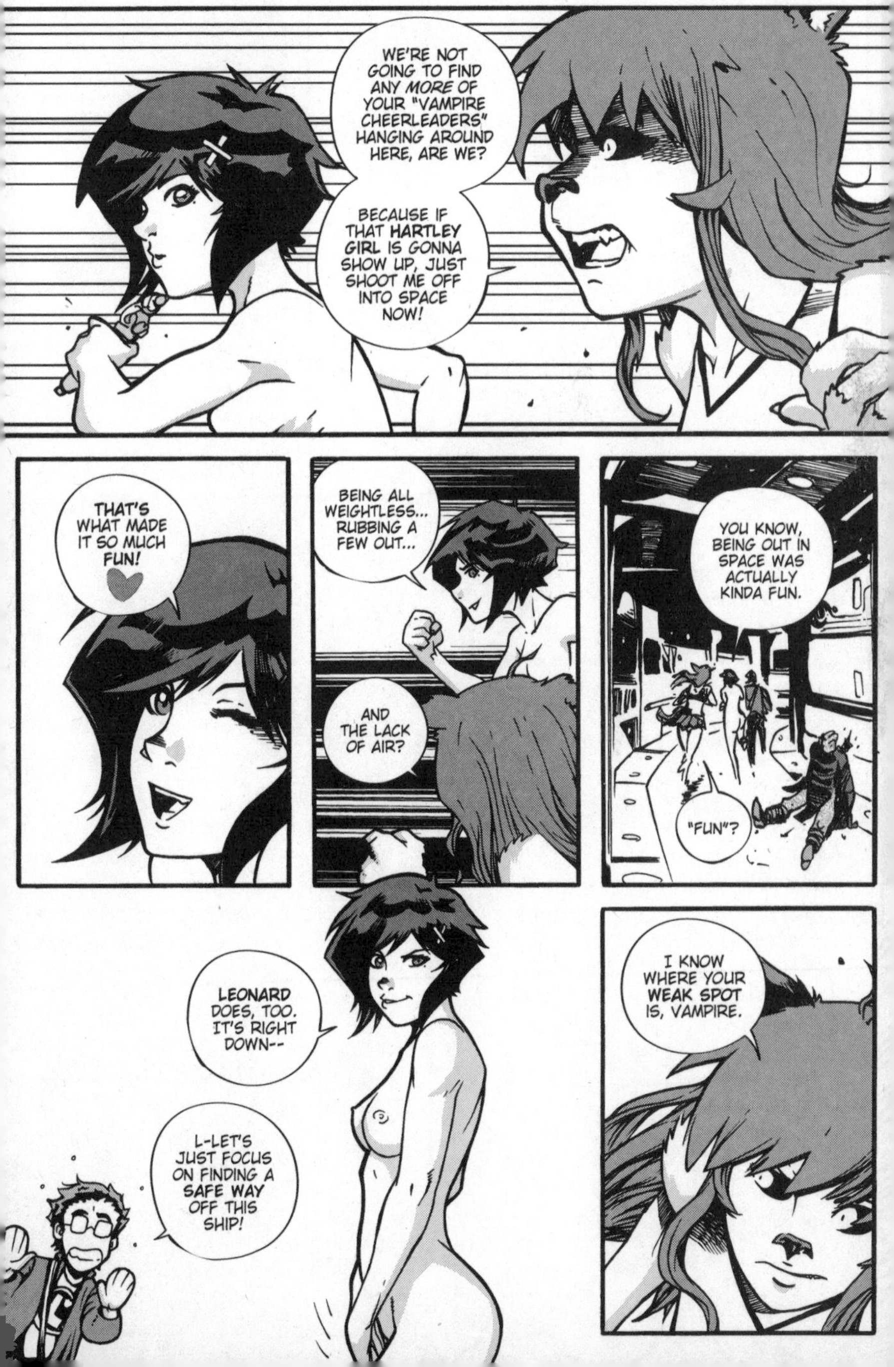
WE'RE NOT GOING TO FIND ANY *MORE* OF YOUR "VAMPIRE CHEERLEADERS" HANGING AROUND HERE, ARE WE?
BECAUSE IF THAT **HARTLEY GIRL** IS GONNA SHOW UP, JUST SHOOT ME OFF INTO SPACE NOW!
YOU KNOW, BEING OUT IN SPACE WAS ACTUALLY KINDA FUN.
"FUN"?
BEING ALL WEIGHTLESS... RUBBING A FEW OUT...
AND THE LACK OF AIR?
THAT'S WHAT MADE IT SO MUCH **FUN!**
I KNOW WHERE YOUR **WEAK SPOT** IS, VAMPIRE.
LEONARD DOES, TOO. IT'S RIGHT DOWN--
L-LET'S JUST FOCUS ON FINDING A **SAFE WAY** OFF THIS SHIP!

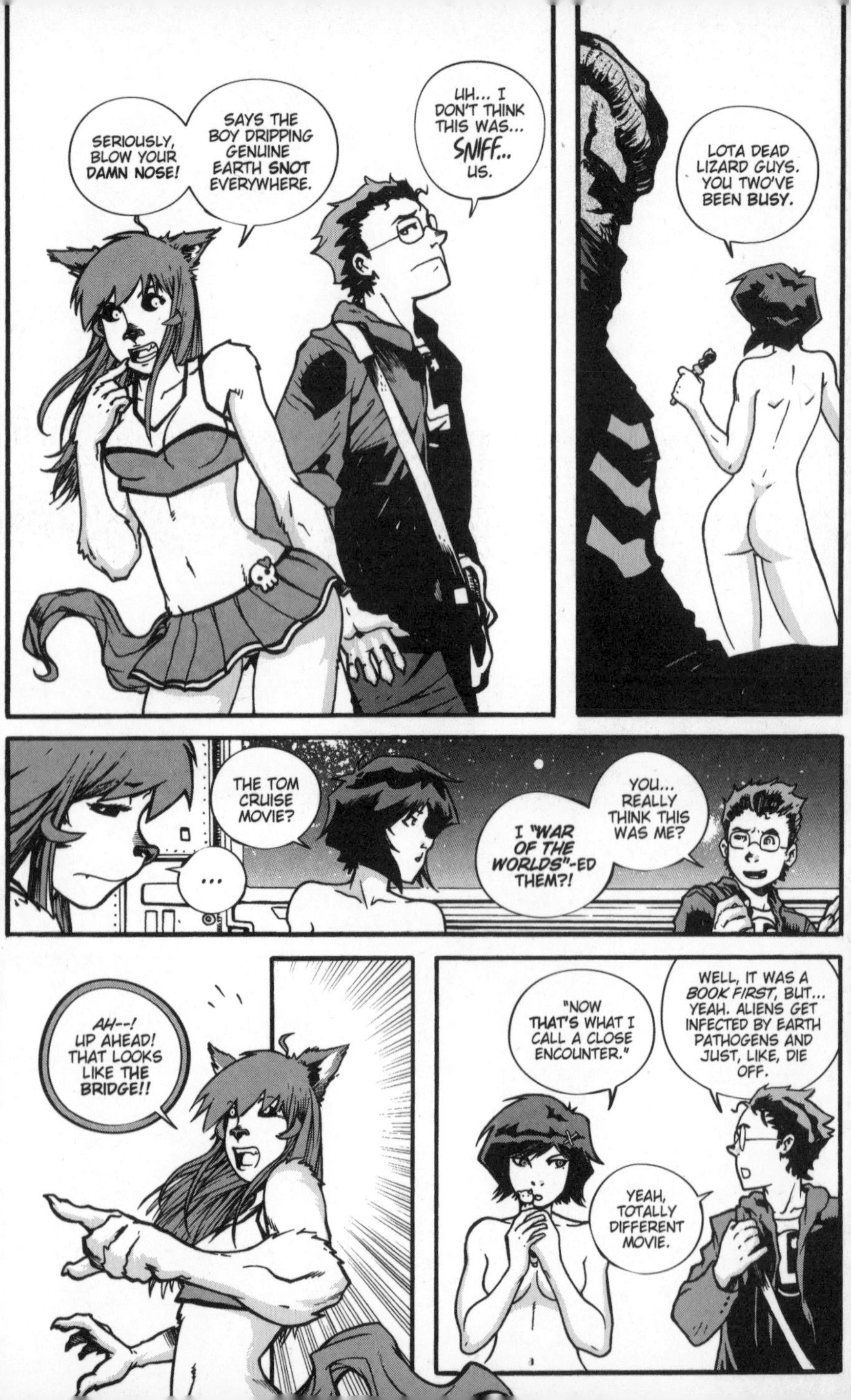
LOTA DEAD LIZARD GUYS. YOU TWO'VE BEEN **BUSY.**
UH... I DON'T THINK THIS WAS... SNIFF... US.
SAYS THE BOY DRIPPING GENUINE EARTH **SNOT** EVERYWHERE.
SERIOUSLY, BLOW YOUR **DAMN NOSE!**
YOU... REALLY THINK THIS WAS ME?
I ***"WAR OF THE WORLDS"***-ED THEM?!
THE TOM CRUISE MOVIE?
...
WELL, IT WAS A *BOOK FIRST*, BUT... YEAH. ALIENS GET INFECTED BY EARTH PATHOGENS AND JUST, LIKE, DIE OFF.
"NOW THAT'S WHAT I CALL A CLOSE ENCOUNTER."
YEAH, TOTALLY DIFFERENT MOVIE.
AH--! UP AHEAD! THAT LOOKS LIKE THE **BRIDGE!!**

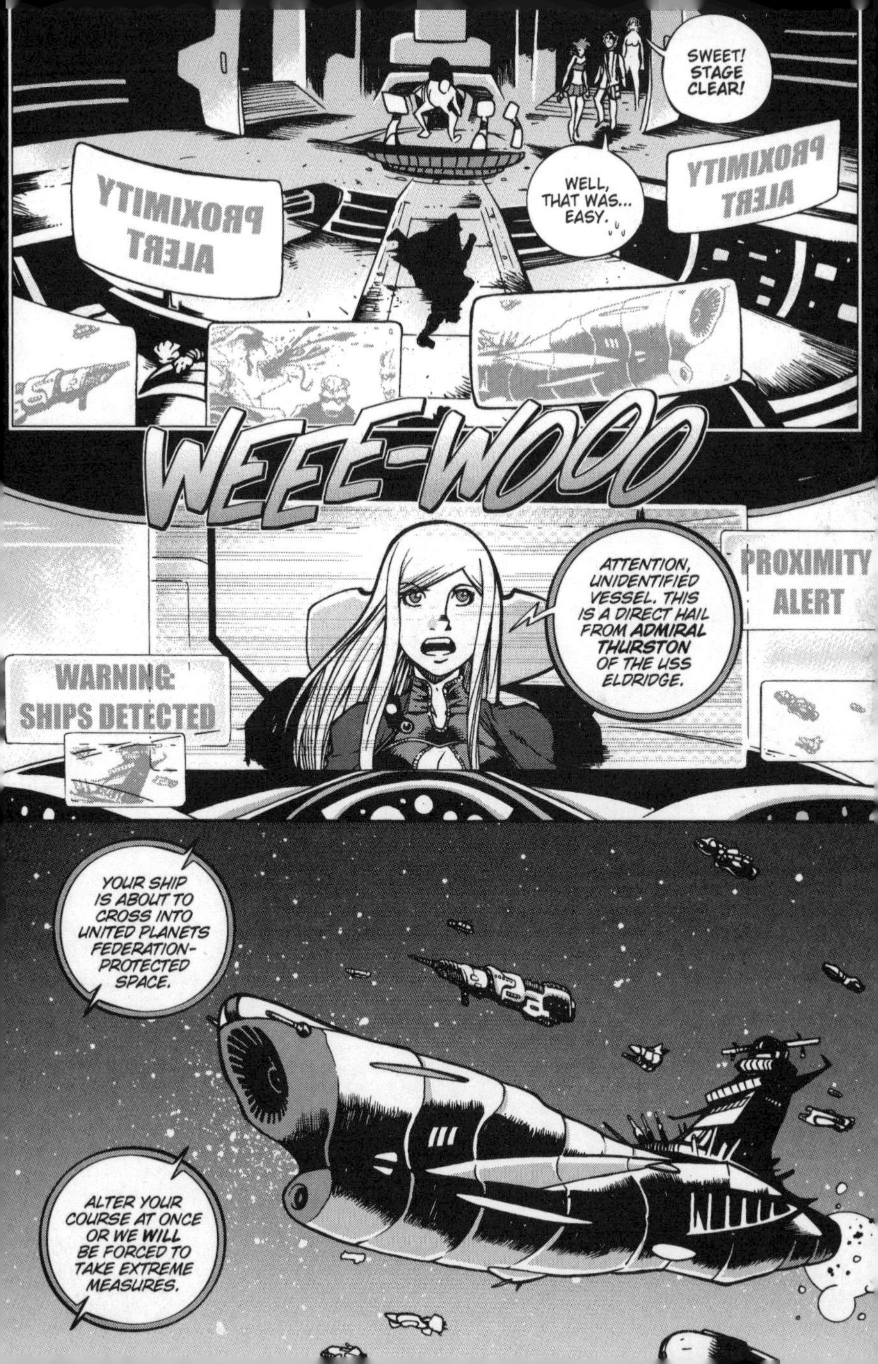
SWEET! STAGE CLEAR!
PROXIMITY ALERT
WELL, THAT WAS... EASY.
PROXIMITY ALERT
WEEE-WOOO
PROXIMITY ALERT
ATTENTION, UNIDENTIFIED VESSEL. THIS IS A DIRECT HAIL FROM ADMIRAL THURSTON OF THE USS ELDRIDGE.
WARNING: SHIPS DETECTED
YOUR SHIP IS ABOUT TO CROSS INTO UNITED PLANETS FEDERATION-PROTECTED SPACE.
ALTER YOUR COURSE AT ONCE OR WE WILL BE FORCED TO TAKE EXTREME MEASURES.

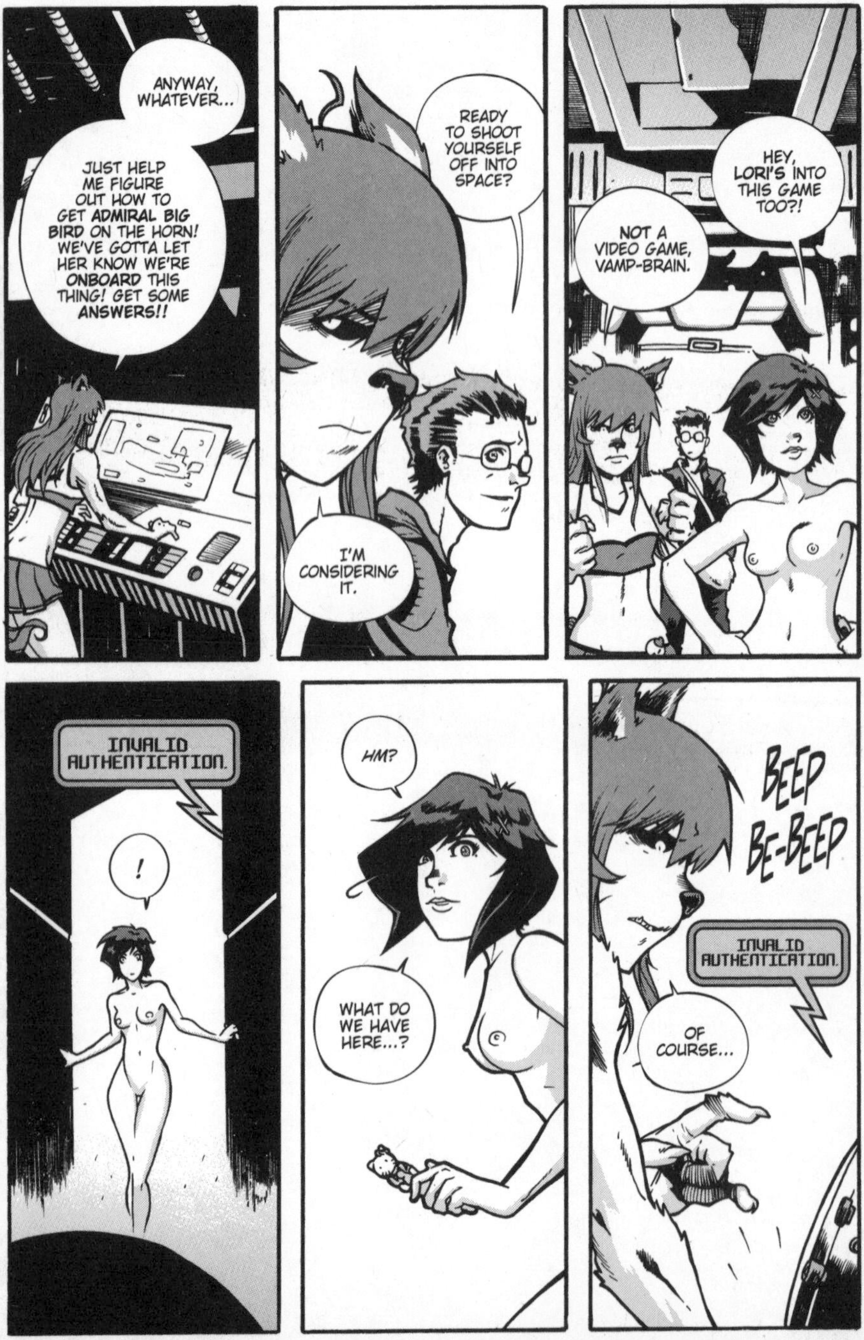
HEY, LORI'S INTO THIS GAME TOO?!
NOT A VIDEO GAME, VAMP-BRAIN.
READY TO SHOOT YOURSELF OFF INTO SPACE?
I'M CONSIDERING IT.
ANYWAY, WHATEVER...
JUST HELP ME FIGURE OUT HOW TO GET **ADMIRAL BIG BIRD** ON THE HORN! WE'VE GOTTA LET HER KNOW WE'RE **ONBOARD** THIS THING! GET SOME **ANSWERS!!**
BEEP BE-BEEP
INVALID AUTHENTICATION.
OF COURSE...
HM?
WHAT DO WE HAVE HERE...?
INVALID AUTHENTICATION.
!

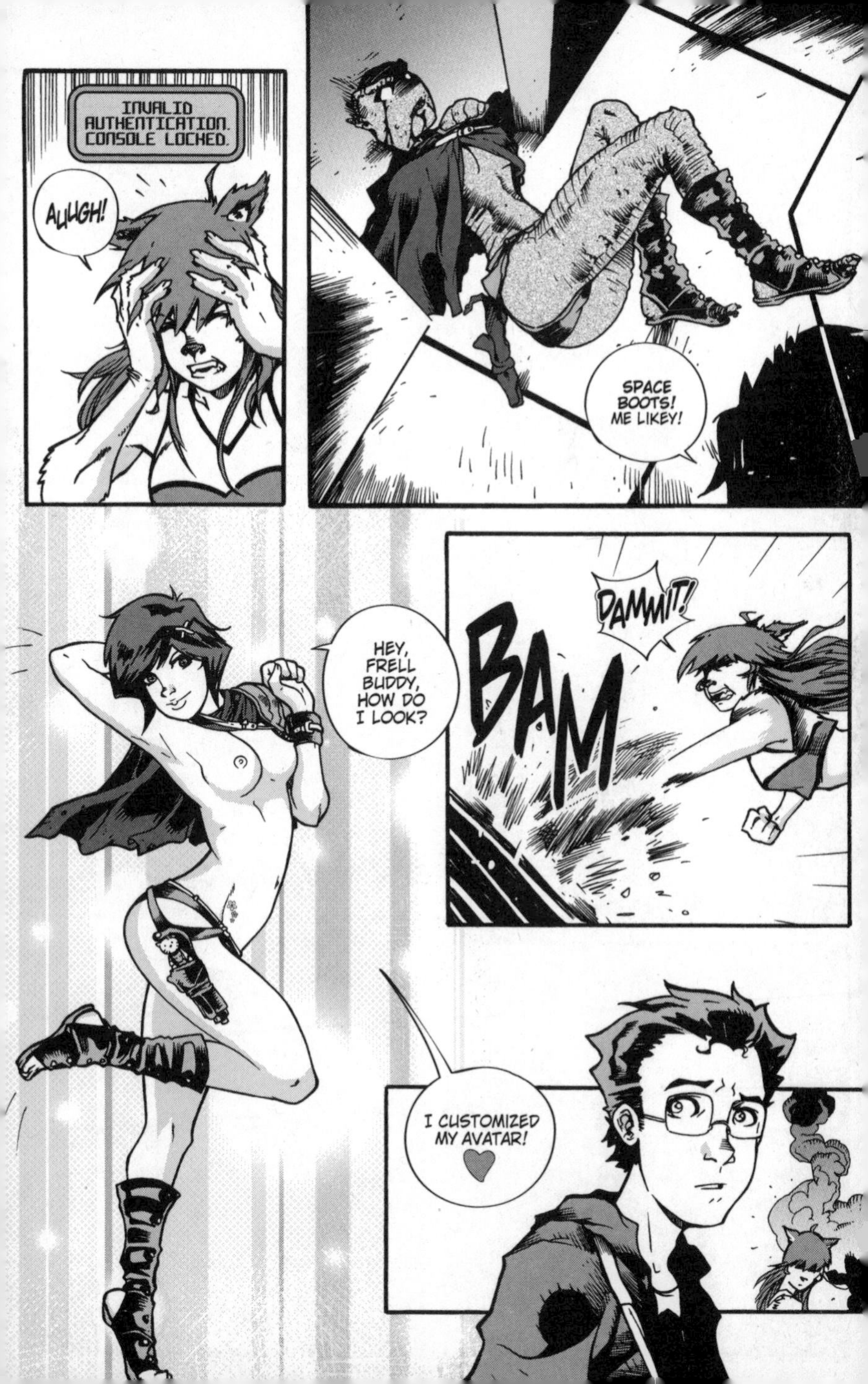
SPACE BOOTS! ME LIKEY!
INVALID AUTHENTICATION. CONSOLE LOCKED.
AUUGH!
DAMMIT!
BAM
I CUSTOMIZED MY AVATAR!
HEY, FRELL BUDDY, HOW DO I LOOK?

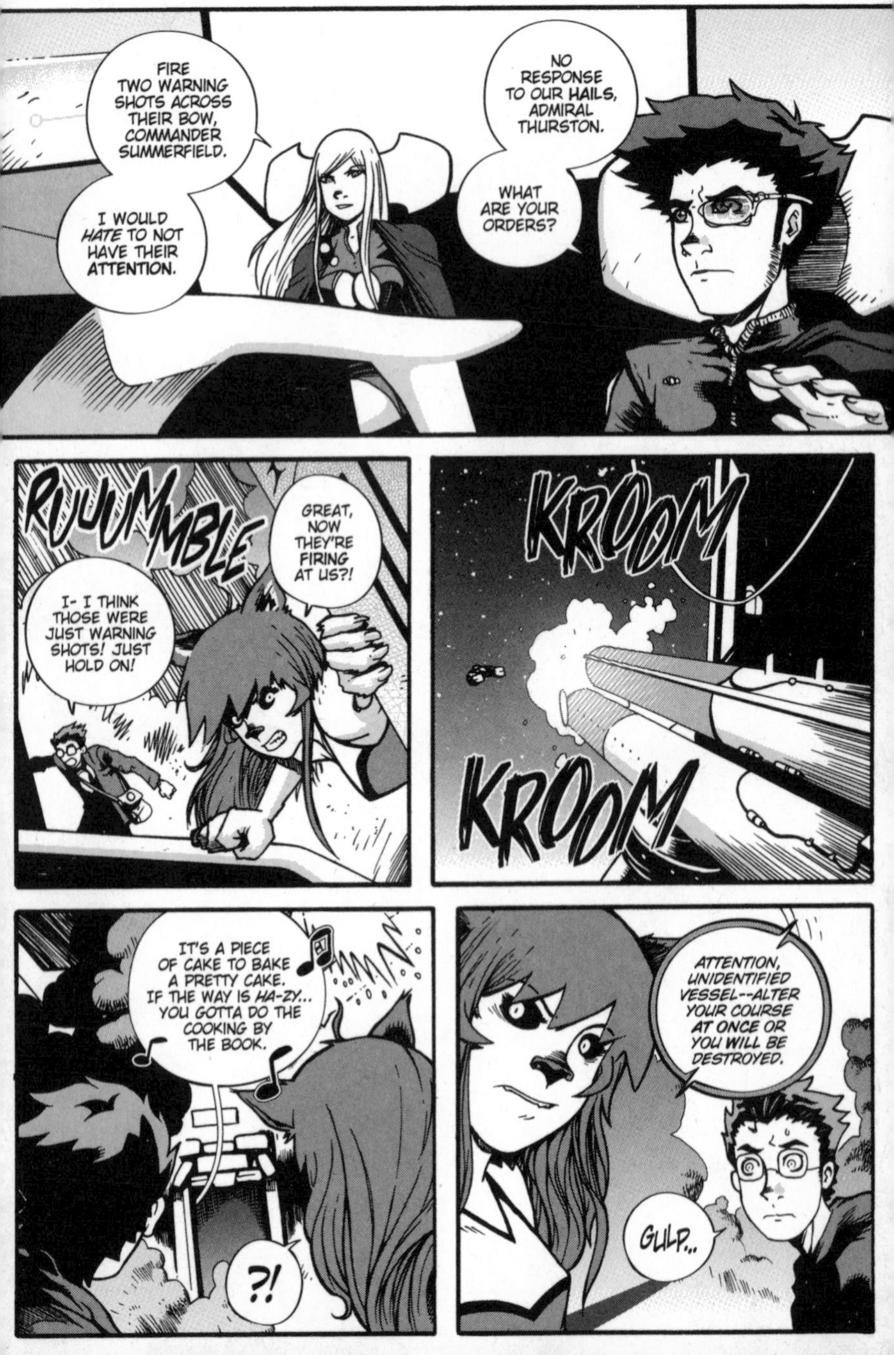
NO RESPONSE TO OUR HAILS, ADMIRAL THURSTON.
WHAT ARE YOUR ORDERS?
FIRE TWO WARNING SHOTS ACROSS THEIR BOW, COMMANDER SUMMERFIELD.
I WOULD *HATE* TO NOT HAVE THEIR ATTENTION.
KROOM
KROOM
RUUUMMBLE
GREAT, NOW THEY'RE FIRING AT US?!
I- I THINK THOSE WERE JUST WARNING SHOTS! JUST HOLD ON!
ATTENTION, UNIDENTIFIED VESSEL--ALTER YOUR COURSE AT ONCE OR YOU WILL BE DESTROYED.
GULP...
IT'S A PIECE OF CAKE TO BAKE A PRETTY CAKE. IF THE WAY IS *HA-ZY*... YOU GOTTA DO THE COOKING BY THE BOOK.
?!

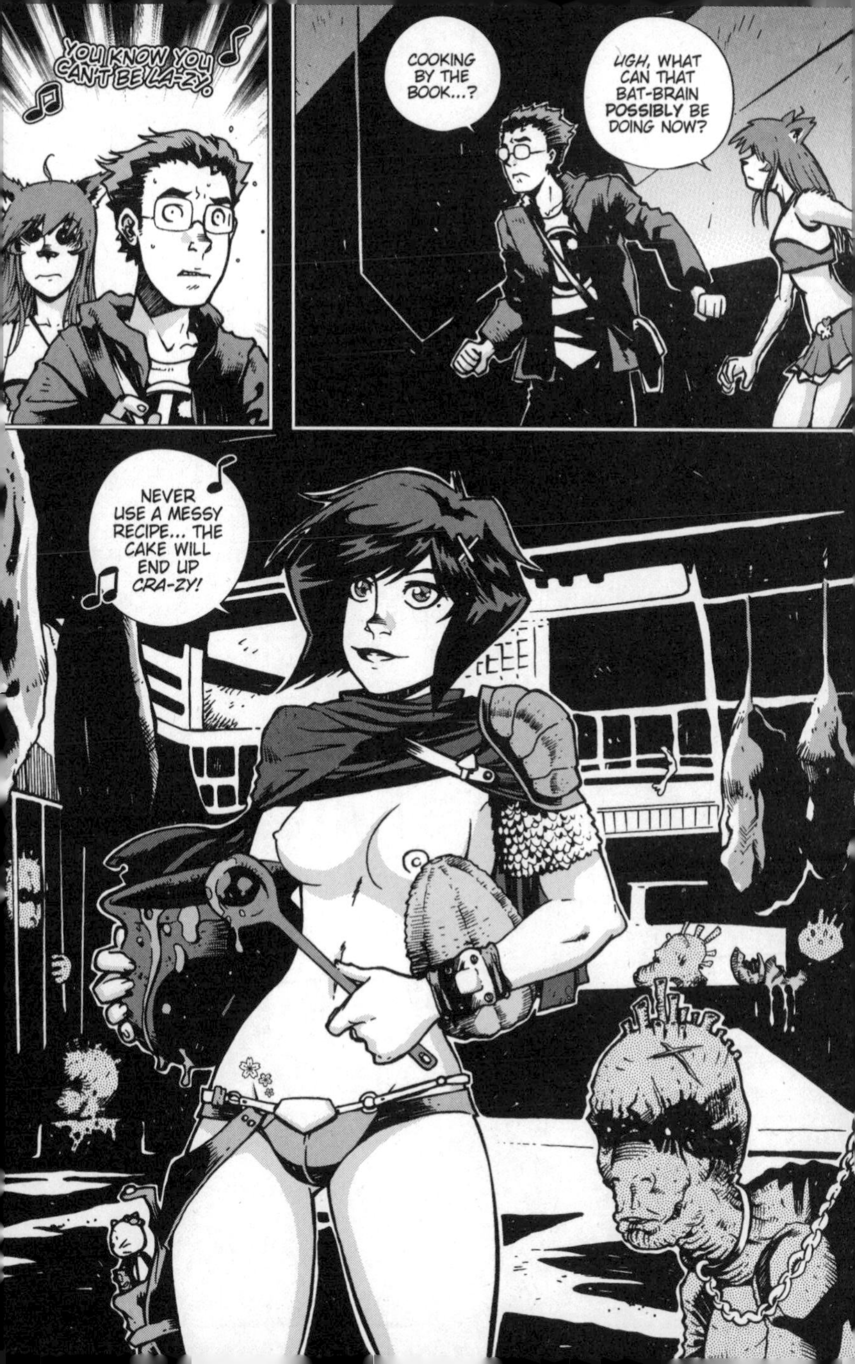
UGH, WHAT CAN THAT BAT-BRAIN POSSIBLY BE DOING NOW?
COOKING BY THE BOOK...?
YOU KNOW YOU CAN'T BE LA-ZY.
NEVER USE A MESSY RECIPE... THE CAKE WILL END UP CRA-ZY!

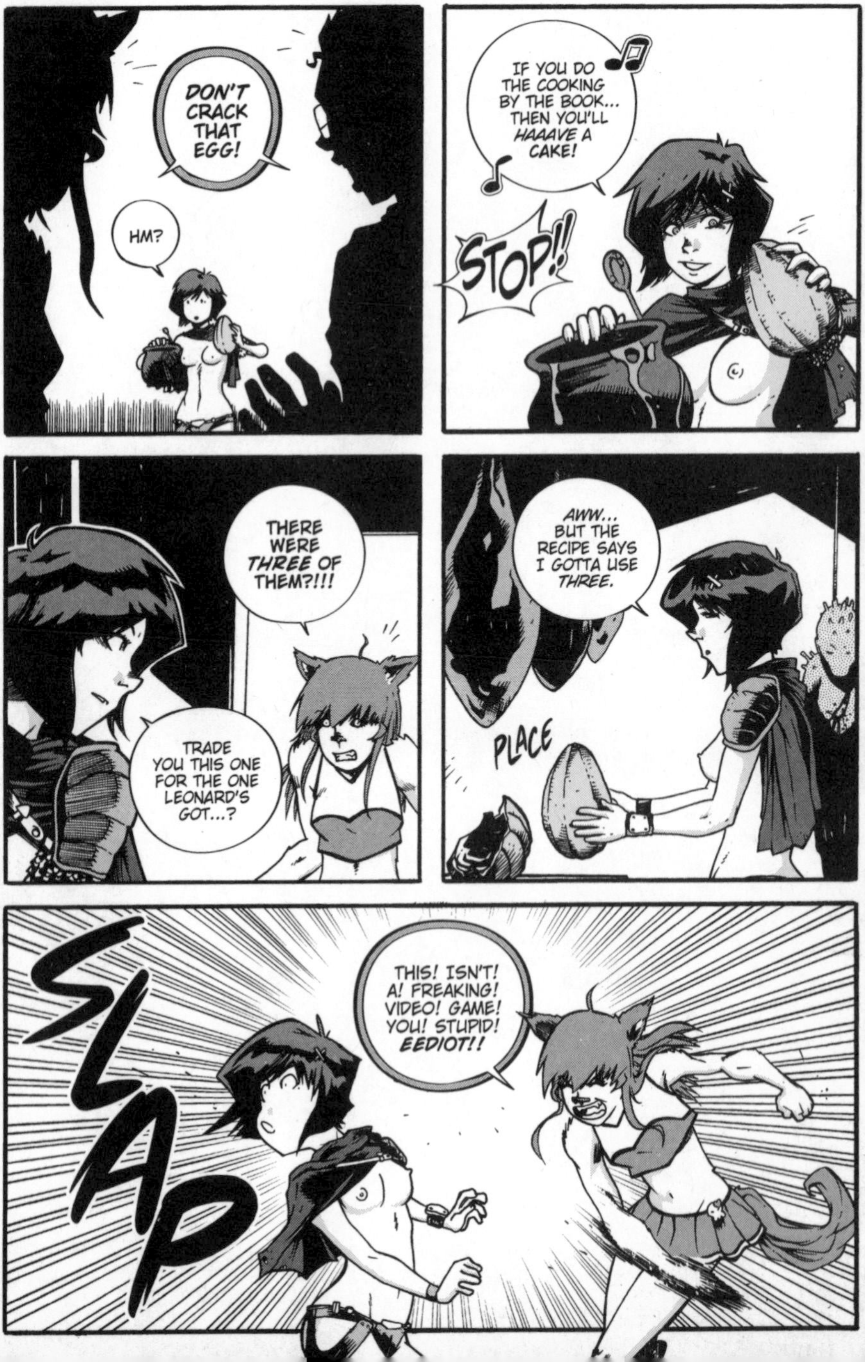
IF YOU DO THE COOKING BY THE BOOK... THEN YOU'LL *HAAAVE* A CAKE!
STOP!!
DON'T CRACK THAT EGG!
HM?
AWW... BUT THE RECIPE SAYS I GOTTA USE *THREE.*
PLACE
THERE WERE *THREE* OF THEM?!!!
TRADE YOU THIS ONE FOR THE ONE LEONARD'S GOT...?
THIS! ISN'T! A! FREAKING! VIDEO! GAME! YOU! STUPID! ***EEDIOT!!***
SLAP

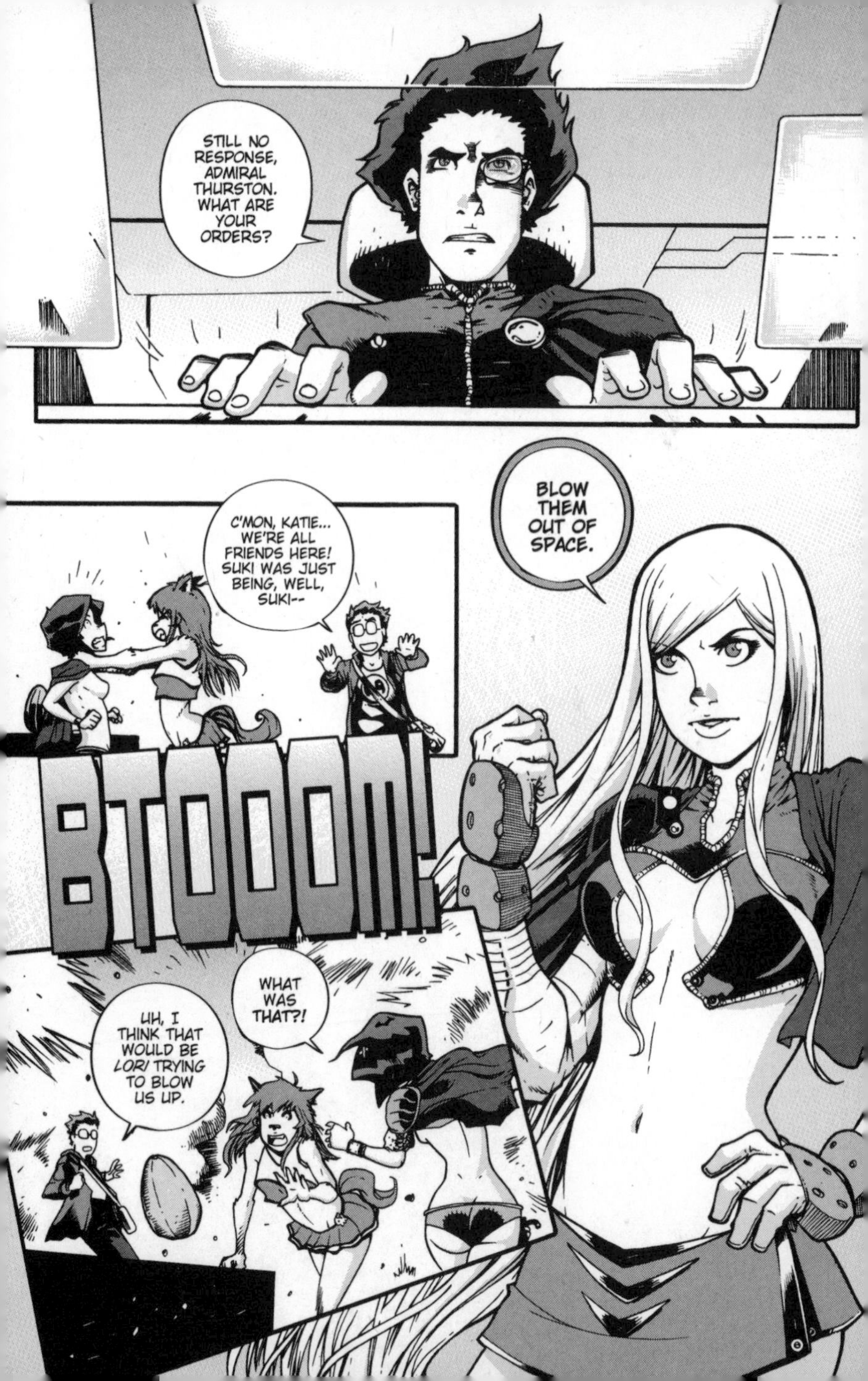
STILL NO RESPONSE, ADMIRAL THURSTON. WHAT ARE YOUR ORDERS?
BLOW THEM OUT OF SPACE.
C'MON, KATIE... WE'RE ALL FRIENDS HERE! SUKI WAS JUST BEING, WELL, SUKI--
BTOOOM!
WHAT WAS THAT?!
UH, I THINK THAT WOULD BE *LORI* TRYING TO BLOW US UP.

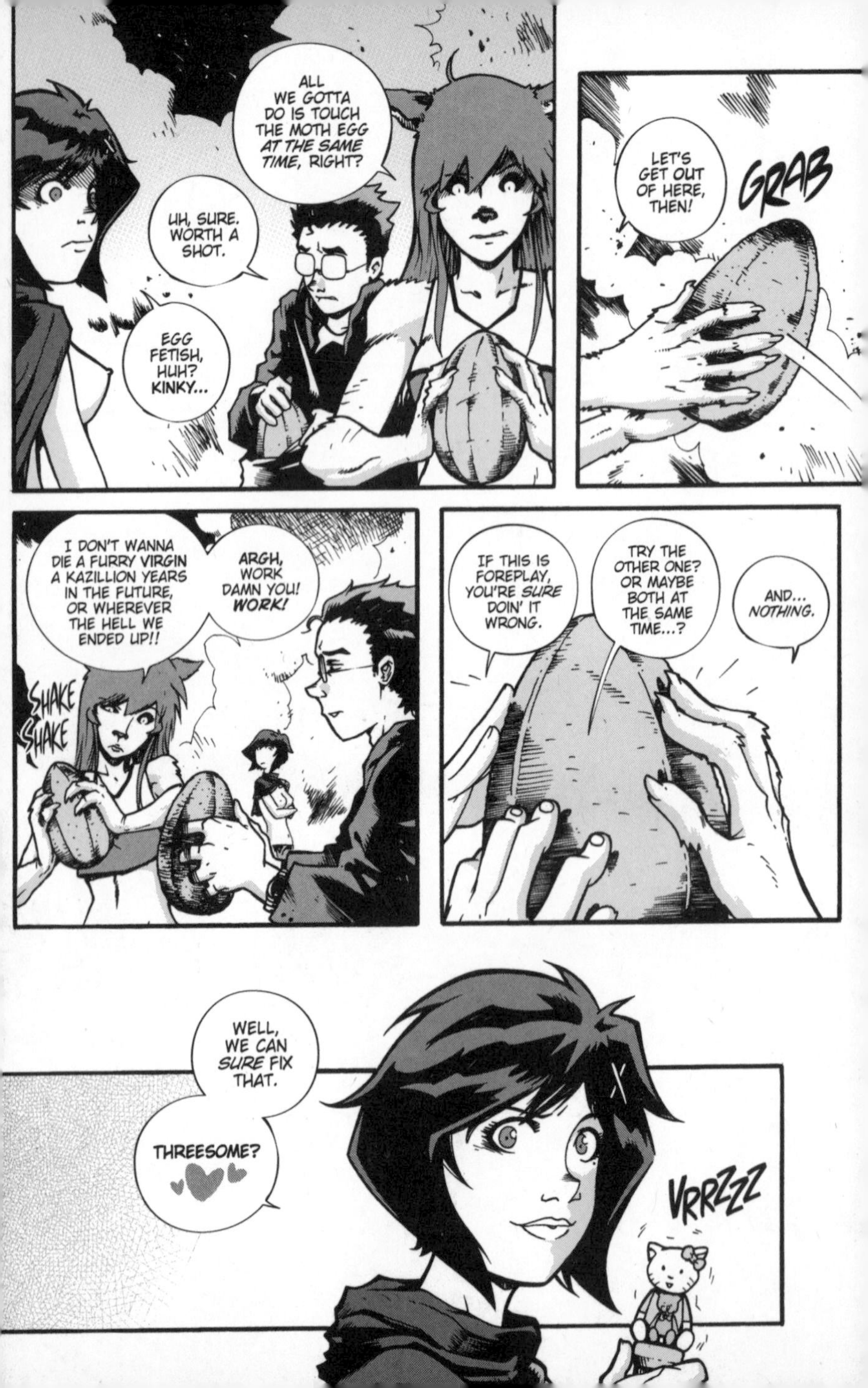
LET'S GET OUT OF HERE, THEN!
GRAB
ALL WE GOTTA DO IS TOUCH THE MOTH EGG *AT THE SAME TIME*, RIGHT?
UH, SURE. WORTH A SHOT.
EGG FETISH, HUH? **KINKY...**
AND... *NOTHING.*
TRY THE OTHER ONE? OR MAYBE BOTH AT THE SAME TIME...?
IF THIS IS FOREPLAY, YOU'RE *SURE* DOIN' IT WRONG.
ARGH, WORK DAMN YOU! ***WORK!***
I DON'T WANNA DIE A FURRY *VIRGIN* A KAZILLION YEARS IN THE FUTURE, OR WHEREVER THE HELL WE ENDED UP!!
SHAKE SHAKE
WELL, WE CAN *SURE* FIX THAT.
THREESOME?
VRRZZZ

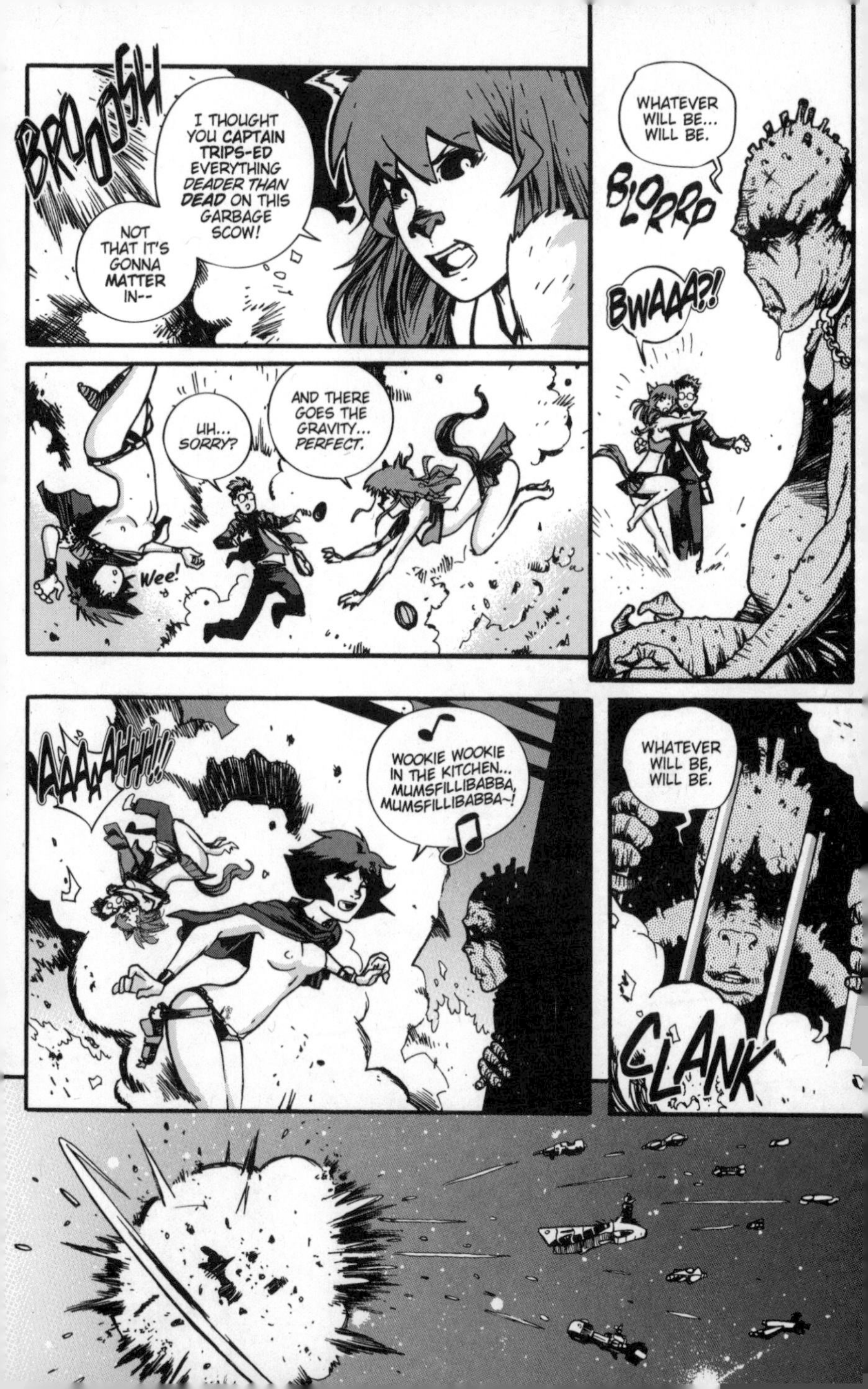
WHATEVER WILL BE... WILL BE.
BLORRRP
BWAAA?!
BROOOSH
I THOUGHT YOU CAPTAIN TRIPS-ED EVERYTHING DEADER THAN DEAD ON THIS GARBAGE SCOW!
NOT THAT IT'S GONNA MATTER IN--
AND THERE GOES THE GRAVITY... PERFECT.
UH... SORRY?
Wee!
WHATEVER WILL BE, WILL BE.
CLANK
WOOKIE WOOKIE IN THE KITCHEN... MUMSFILLIBABBA, MUMSFILLIBABBA~!
AAAAAHHH!!

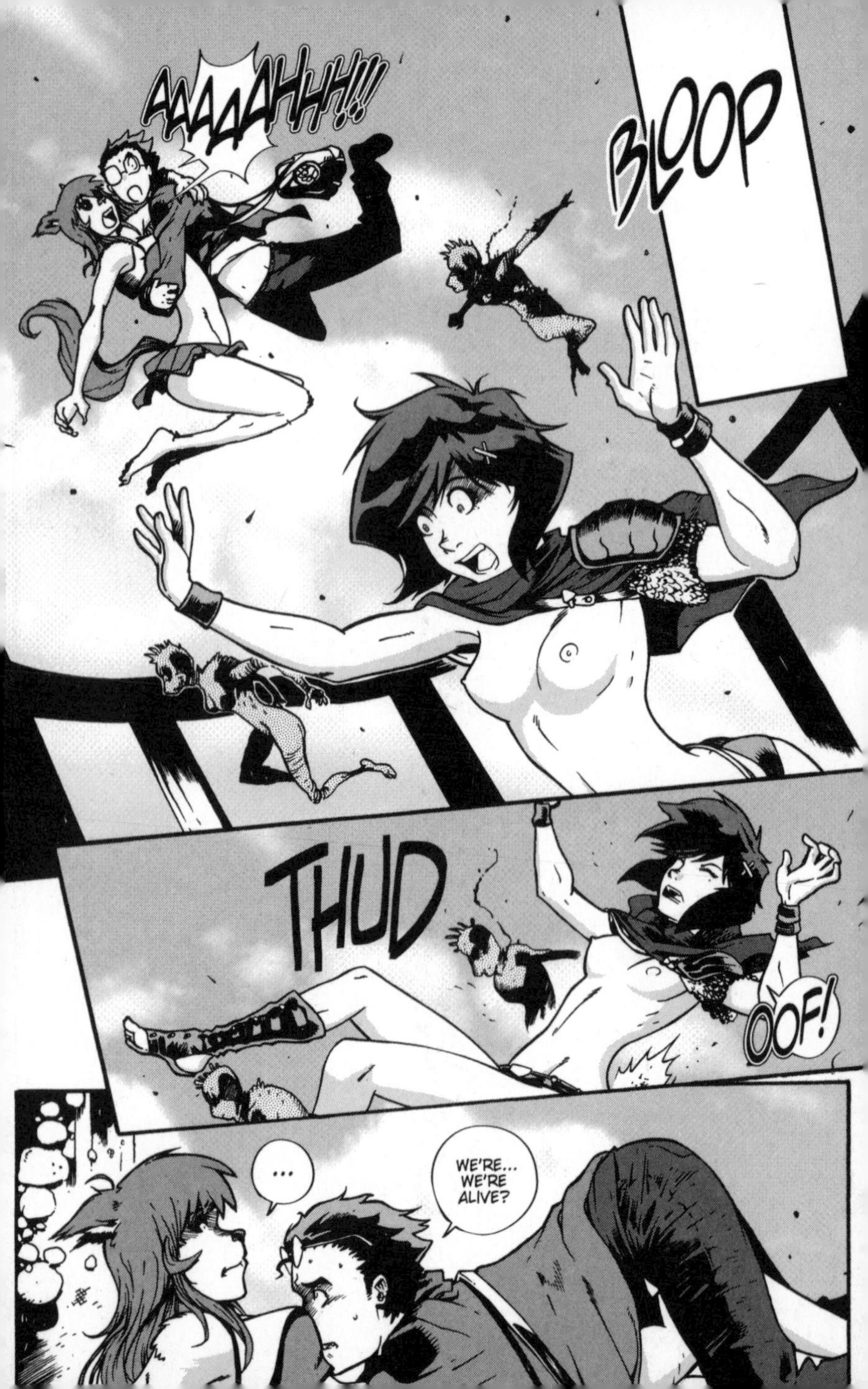
BLOOP
AAAAAHHH!!!
OOF!
THUD
WE'RE... WE'RE ALIVE?
...

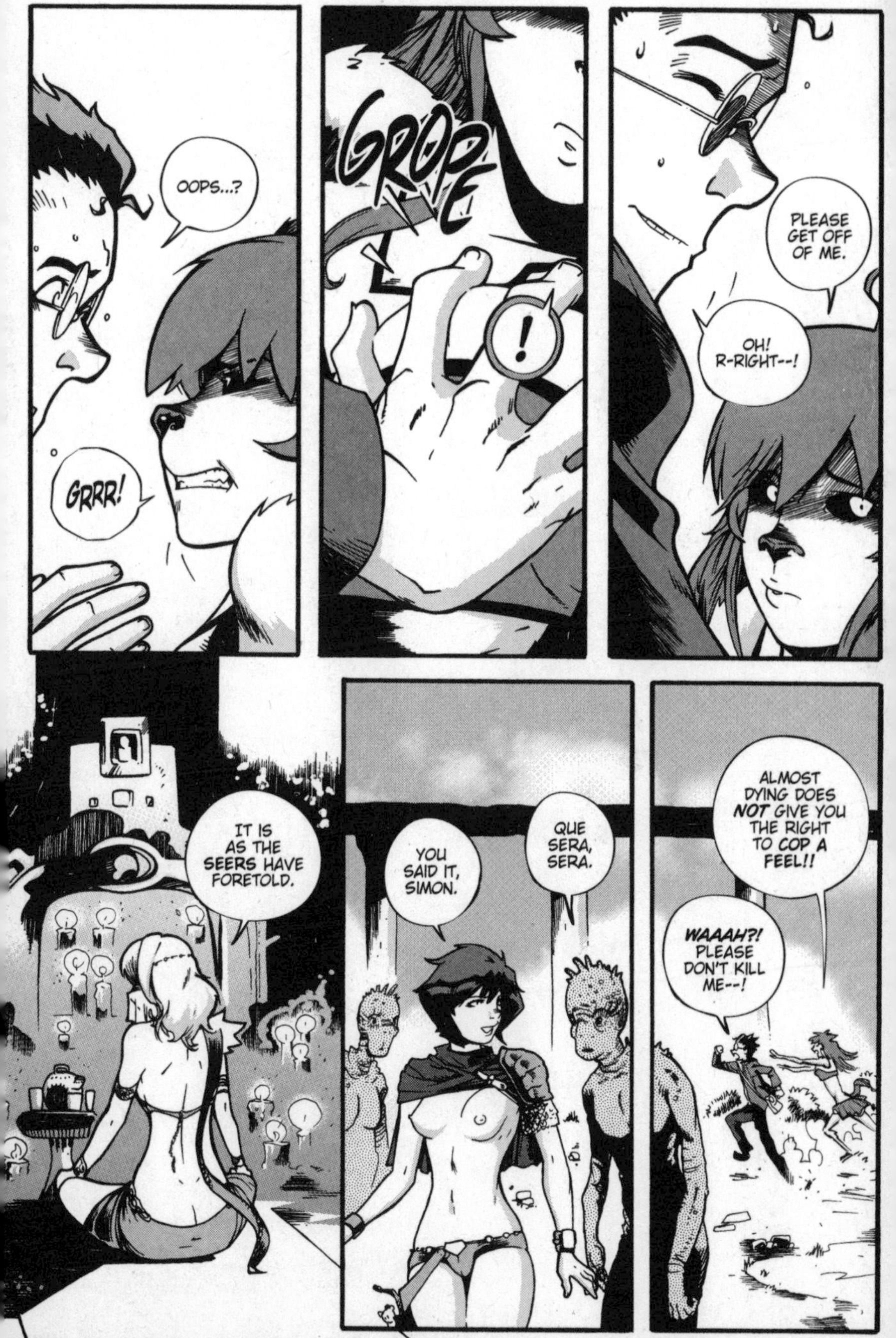
PLEASE GET OFF OF ME.
OH! R-RIGHT--!
GROPE
!
OOPS...?
GRRR!
ALMOST DYING DOES **NOT** GIVE YOU THE RIGHT TO COP A FEEL!!
WAAAH?! PLEASE DON'T KILL ME--!
QUE SERA, SERA.
YOU SAID IT, SIMON.
IT IS AS THE SEERS HAVE FORETOLD.

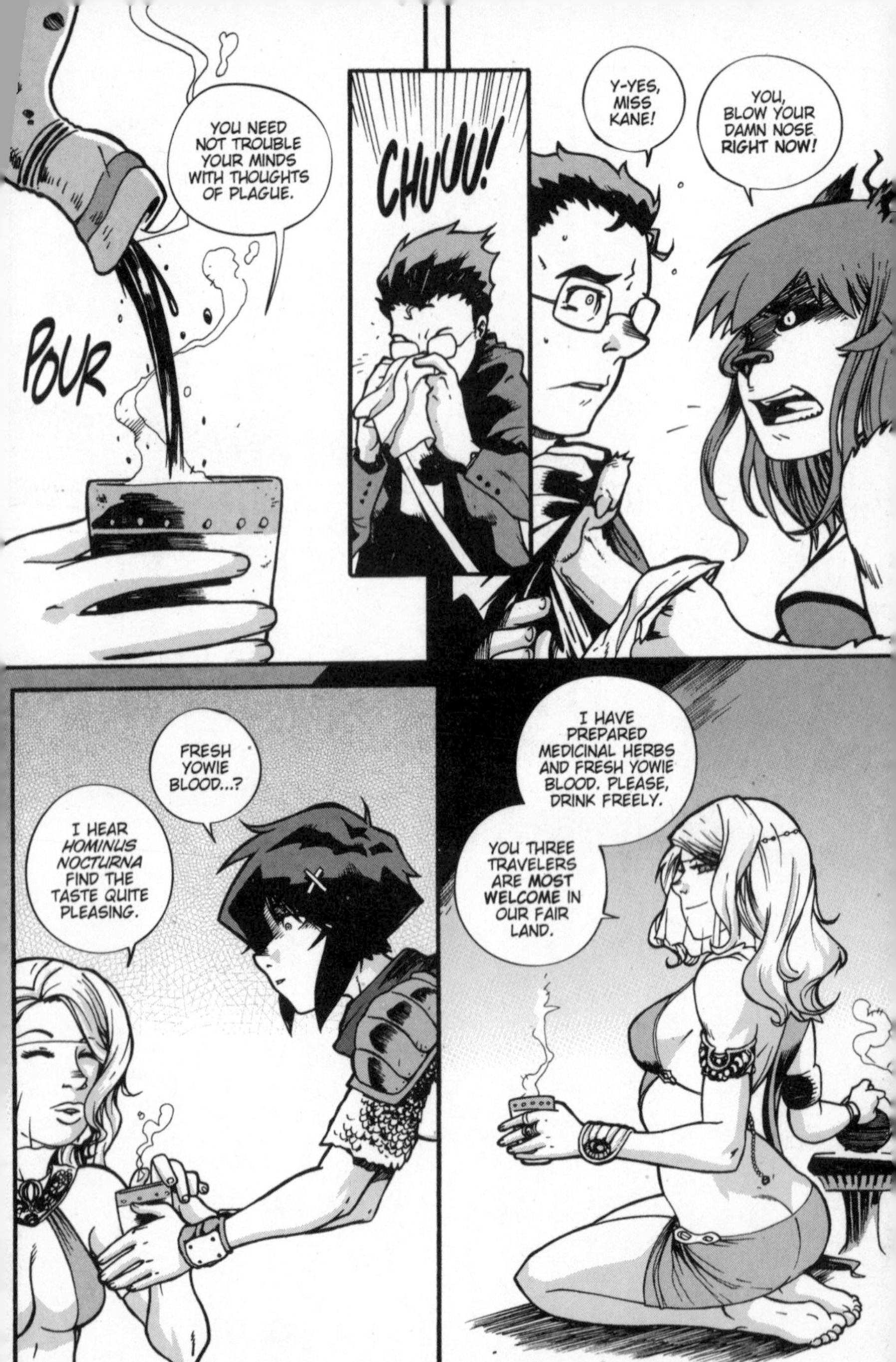
YOU, BLOW YOUR DAMN NOSE RIGHT NOW!
Y-YES, MISS KANE!
CHUUU!
YOU NEED NOT TROUBLE YOUR MINDS WITH THOUGHTS OF PLAGUE.
POUR
I HAVE PREPARED MEDICINAL HERBS AND FRESH YOWIE BLOOD. PLEASE, DRINK FREELY.
YOU THREE TRAVELERS ARE **MOST WELCOME** IN OUR FAIR LAND.
FRESH YOWIE BLOOD...?
I HEAR *HOMINUS NOCTURNA* FIND THE TASTE QUITE PLEASING.

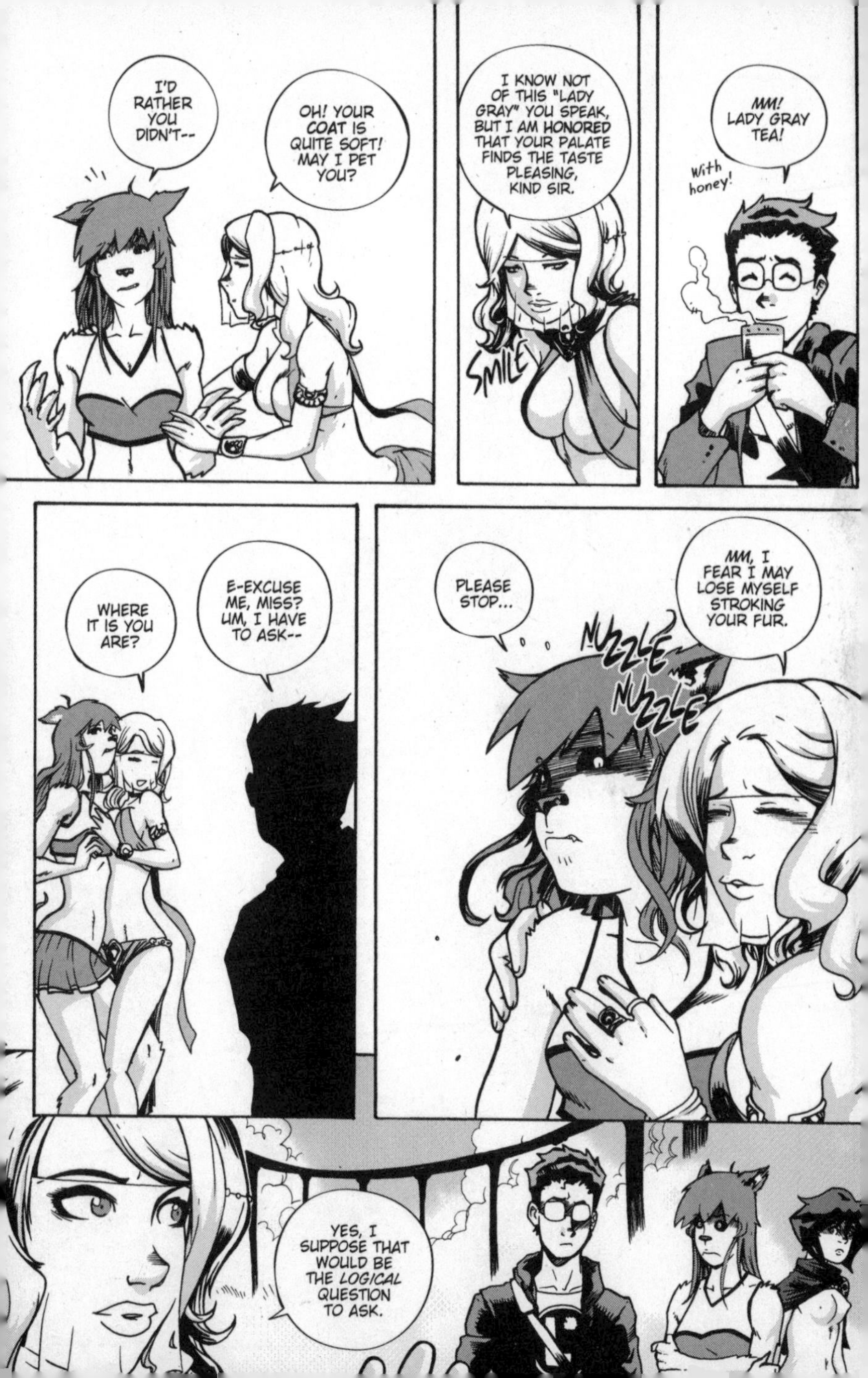
MM! LADY GRAY TEA!
With honey!
I KNOW NOT OF THIS "LADY GRAY" YOU SPEAK, BUT I AM HONORED THAT YOUR PALATE FINDS THE TASTE PLEASING, KIND SIR.
SMILE
OH! YOUR COAT IS QUITE SOFT! MAY I PET YOU?
I'D RATHER YOU DIDN'T--
MM, I FEAR I MAY LOSE MYSELF STROKING YOUR FUR.
NUZZLE
NUZZLE
PLEASE STOP...
E-EXCUSE ME, MISS? UM, I HAVE TO ASK--
WHERE IT IS YOU ARE?
YES, I SUPPOSE THAT WOULD BE THE LOGICAL QUESTION TO ASK.

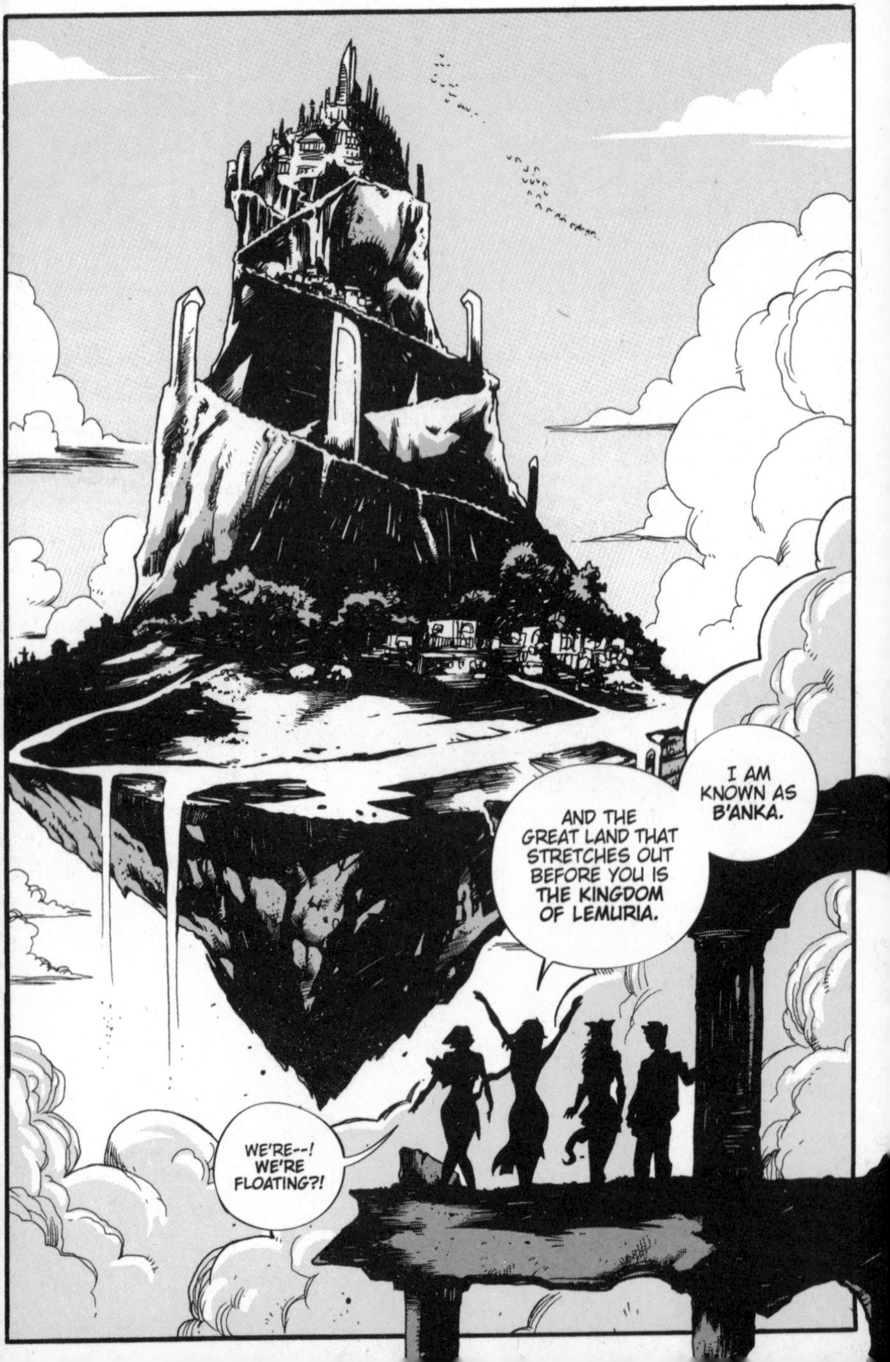
I AM KNOWN AS B'ANKA.
AND THE GREAT LAND THAT STRETCHES OUT BEFORE YOU IS THE KINGDOM OF LEMURIA.
WE'RE--! WE'RE FLOATING?!

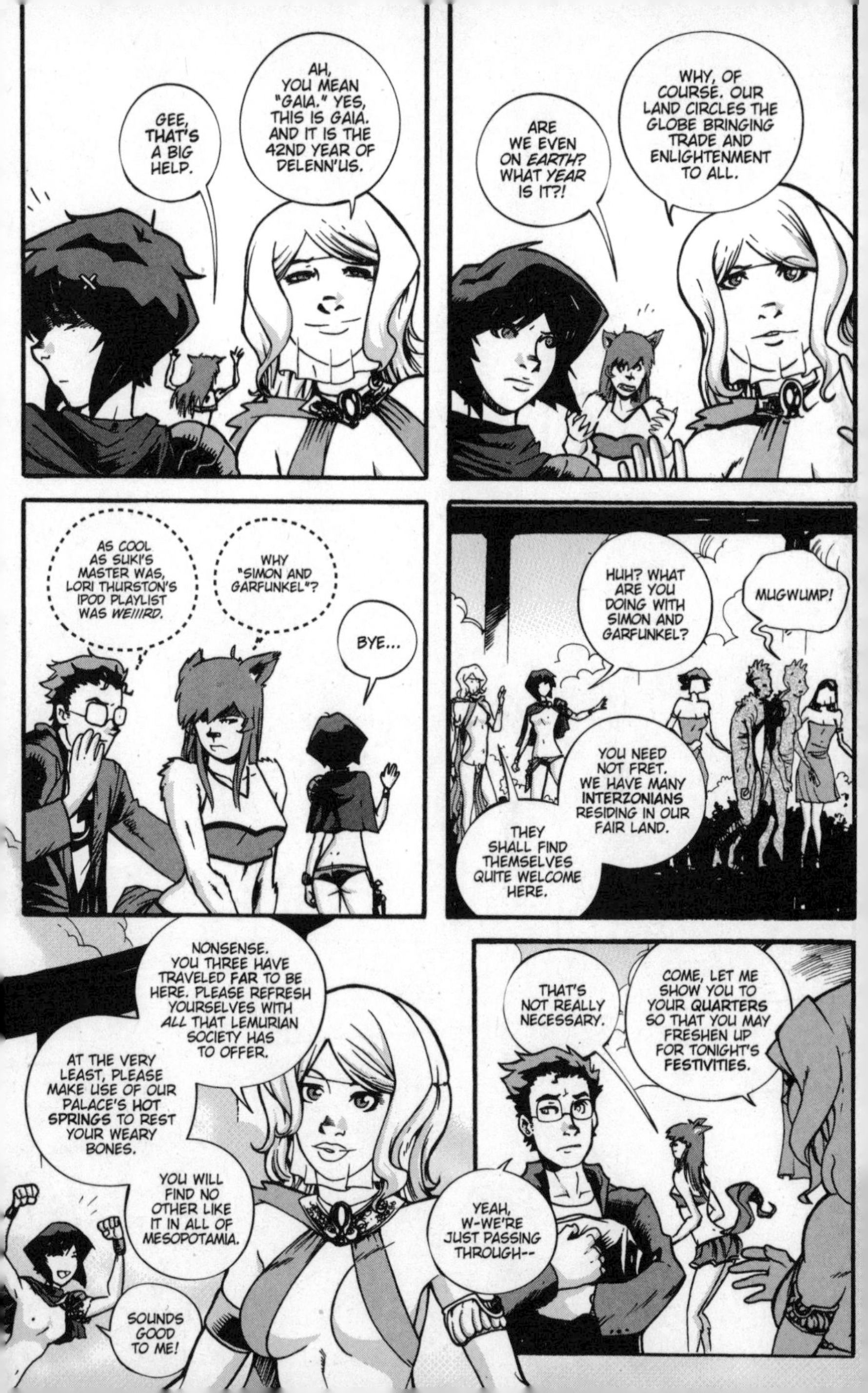
ARE WE EVEN ON *EARTH?* WHAT *YEAR* IS IT?!
WHY, OF COURSE. OUR LAND CIRCLES THE GLOBE BRINGING TRADE AND ENLIGHTENMENT TO ALL.
AH, YOU MEAN "GAIA." YES, THIS IS GAIA. AND IT IS THE 42ND YEAR OF DELENN'US.
GEE, **THAT'S** A BIG HELP.
HUH? WHAT ARE YOU DOING WITH SIMON AND GARFUNKEL?
MUGWUMP!
YOU NEED NOT FRET. WE HAVE MANY **INTERZONIANS** RESIDING IN OUR FAIR LAND.
THEY SHALL FIND THEMSELVES QUITE WELCOME HERE.
WHY "SIMON AND GARFUNKEL"?
AS COOL AS SUKI'S MASTER WAS, LORI THURSTON'S IPOD PLAYLIST WAS *WEIIIRD.*
BYE...
COME, LET ME SHOW YOU TO YOUR **QUARTERS** SO THAT YOU MAY FRESHEN UP FOR TONIGHT'S **FESTIVITIES.**
THAT'S NOT REALLY NECESSARY.
YEAH, W-WE'RE JUST PASSING THROUGH--
NONSENSE. YOU THREE HAVE TRAVELED **FAR** TO BE HERE. PLEASE REFRESH YOURSELVES WITH *ALL* THAT LEMURIAN SOCIETY HAS TO OFFER.
AT THE VERY LEAST, PLEASE MAKE USE OF OUR PALACE'S **HOT SPRINGS** TO REST YOUR WEARY BONES.
YOU WILL FIND NO OTHER LIKE IT IN ALL OF MESOPOTAMIA.
SOUNDS GOOD TO ME!

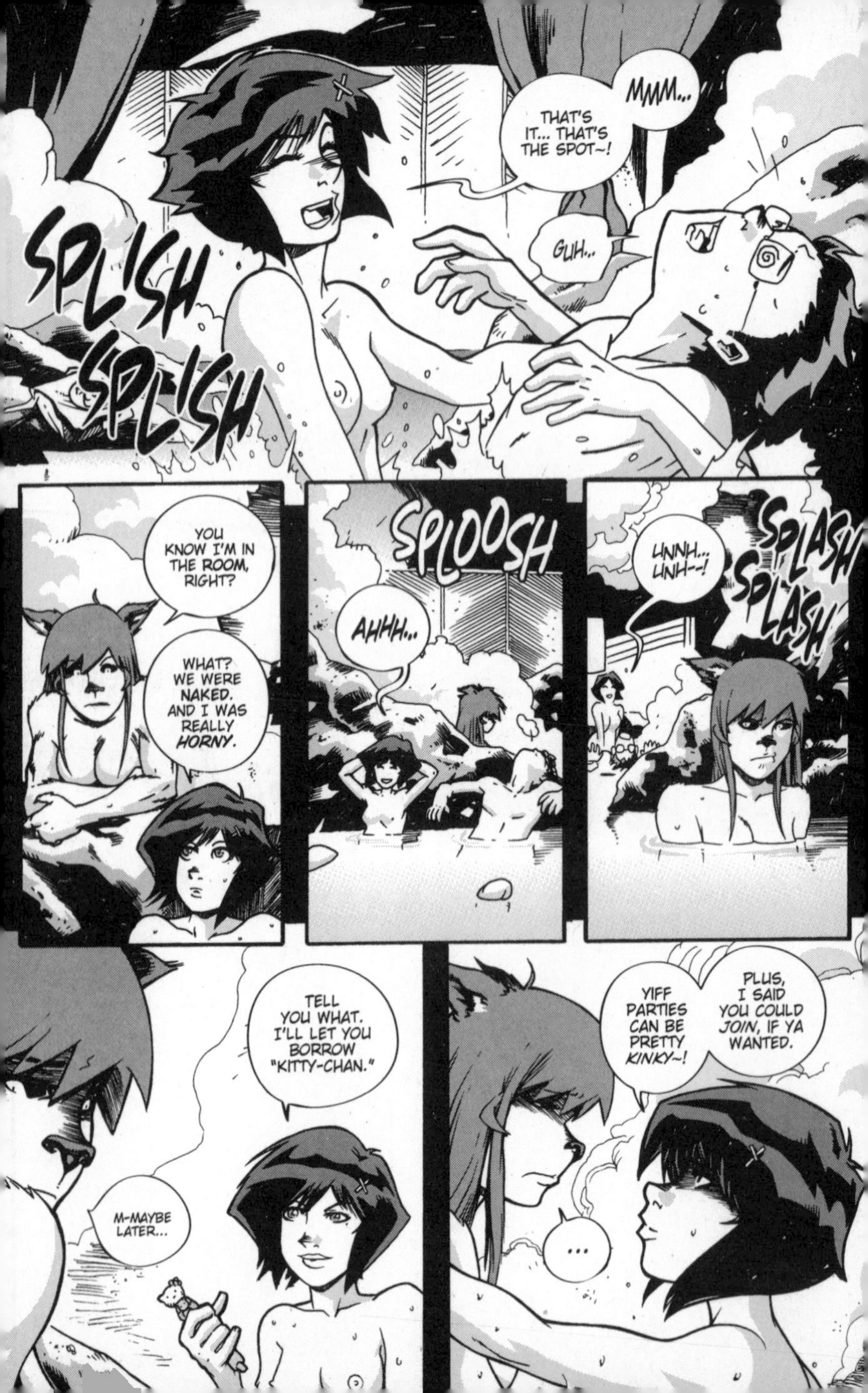
MMM...
THAT'S IT... THAT'S THE SPOT~!
GUH..
SPLISH SPLISH
SPLASH SPLASH
UNNH... UNH--!
SPLOOSH
AHHH...
YOU KNOW I'M IN THE ROOM, RIGHT?
WHAT? WE WERE NAKED. AND I WAS REALLY *HORNY*.
PLUS, I SAID YOU COULD *JOIN*, IF YA WANTED.
YIFF PARTIES CAN BE PRETTY *KINKY*~!
...
TELL YOU WHAT. I'LL LET YOU BORROW "KITTY-CHAN."
M-MAYBE LATER...

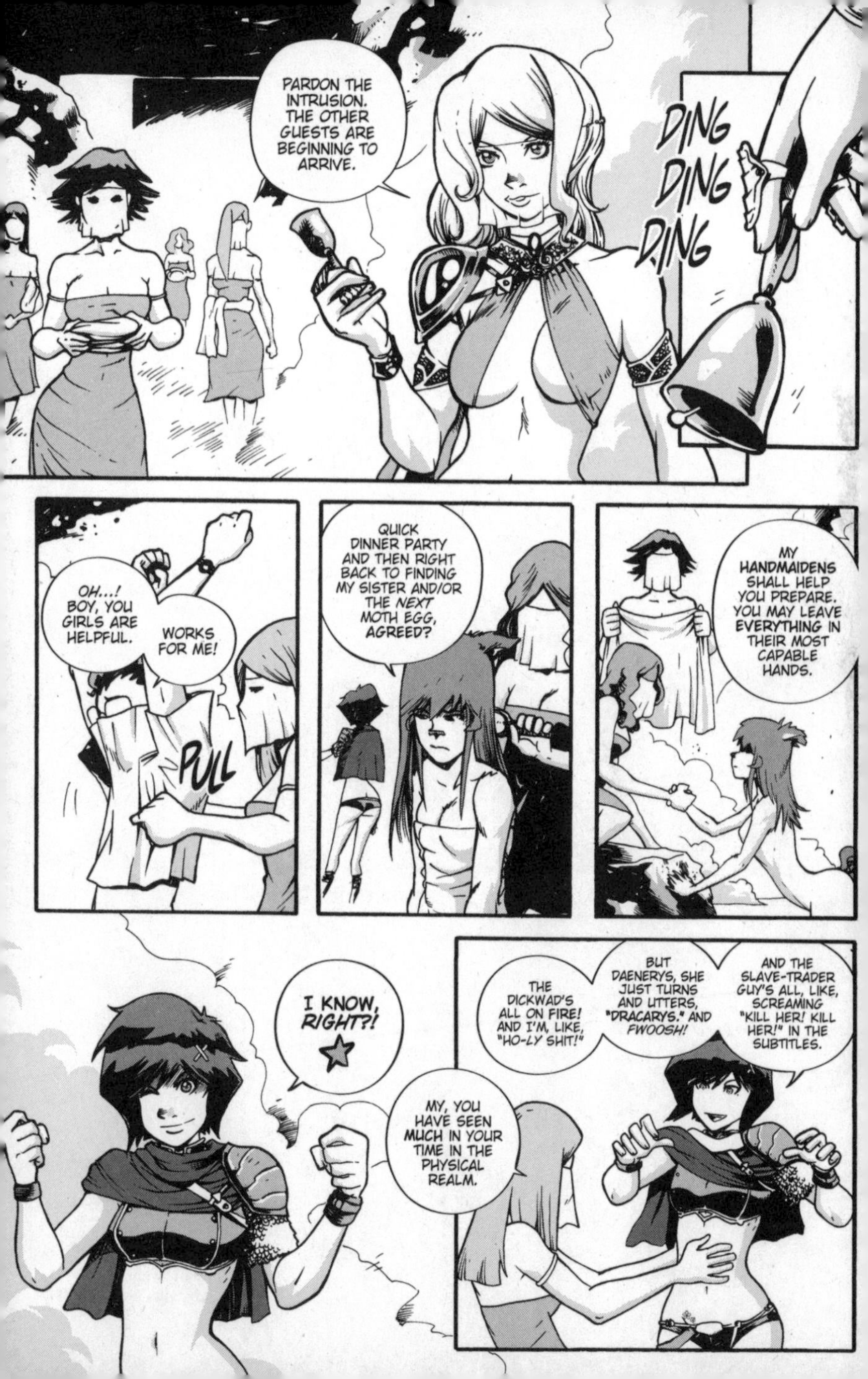
DING DING DING
PARDON THE INTRUSION. THE OTHER GUESTS ARE BEGINNING TO ARRIVE.
MY HANDMAIDENS SHALL HELP YOU PREPARE. YOU MAY LEAVE EVERYTHING IN THEIR MOST CAPABLE HANDS.
QUICK DINNER PARTY AND THEN RIGHT BACK TO FINDING MY SISTER AND/OR THE NEXT MOTH EGG, AGREED?
WORKS FOR ME!
OH...! BOY, YOU GIRLS ARE HELPFUL.
PULL
AND THE SLAVE-TRADER GUY'S ALL, LIKE, SCREAMING "KILL HER! KILL HER!" IN THE SUBTITLES.
BUT DAENERYS, SHE JUST TURNS AND UTTERS, "DRACARYS." AND FWOOSH!
THE DICKWAD'S ALL ON FIRE! AND I'M, LIKE, "HO-LY SHIT!"
MY, YOU HAVE SEEN MUCH IN YOUR TIME IN THE PHYSICAL REALM.
I KNOW, RIGHT?!

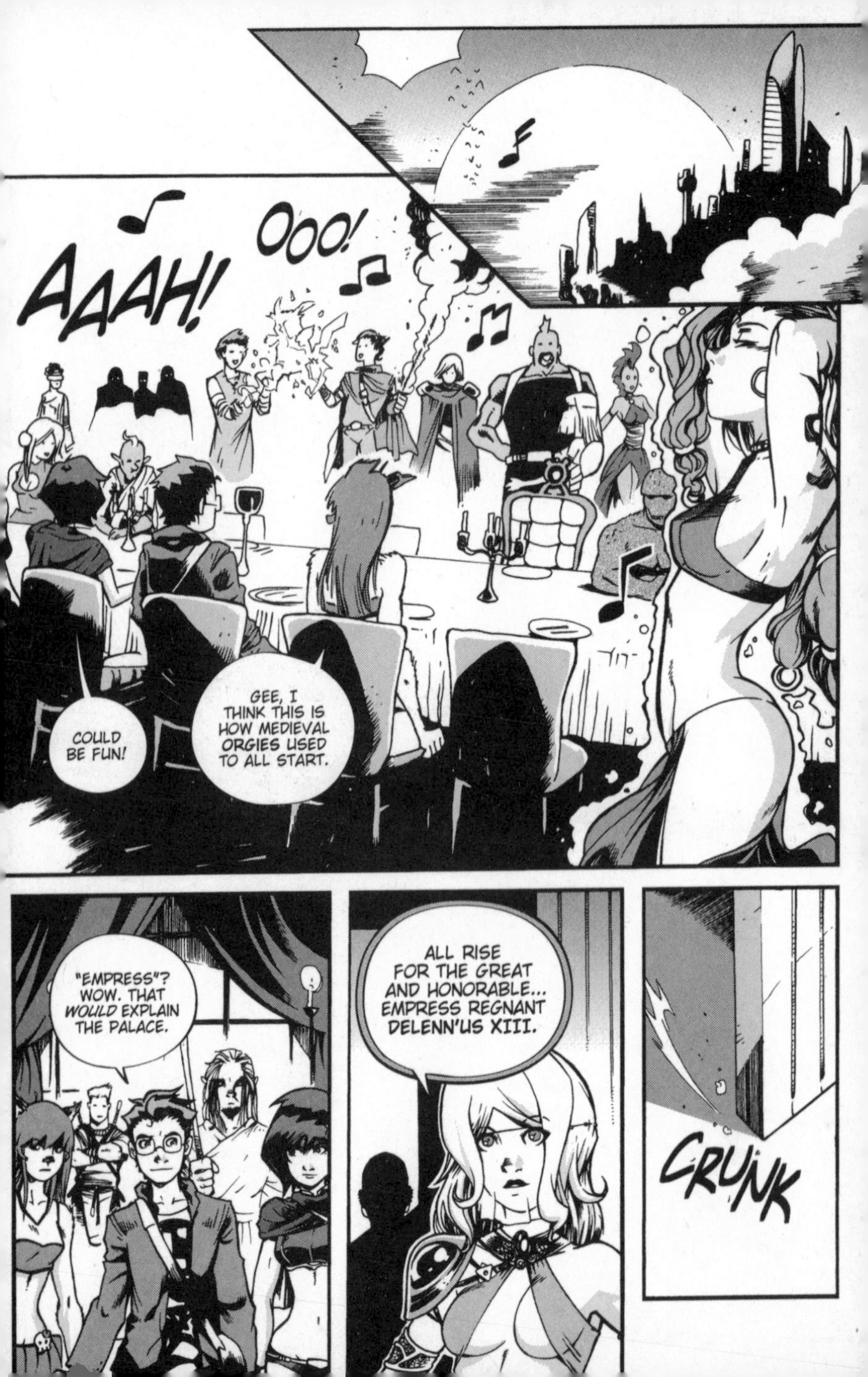
AAAH!
OOO!
COULD BE FUN!
GEE, I THINK THIS IS HOW MEDIEVAL ORGIES USED TO ALL START.
"EMPRESS"? WOW. THAT *WOULD* EXPLAIN THE PALACE.
ALL RISE FOR THE GREAT AND HONORABLE... EMPRESS REGNANT DELENN'US XIII.
CRUNK

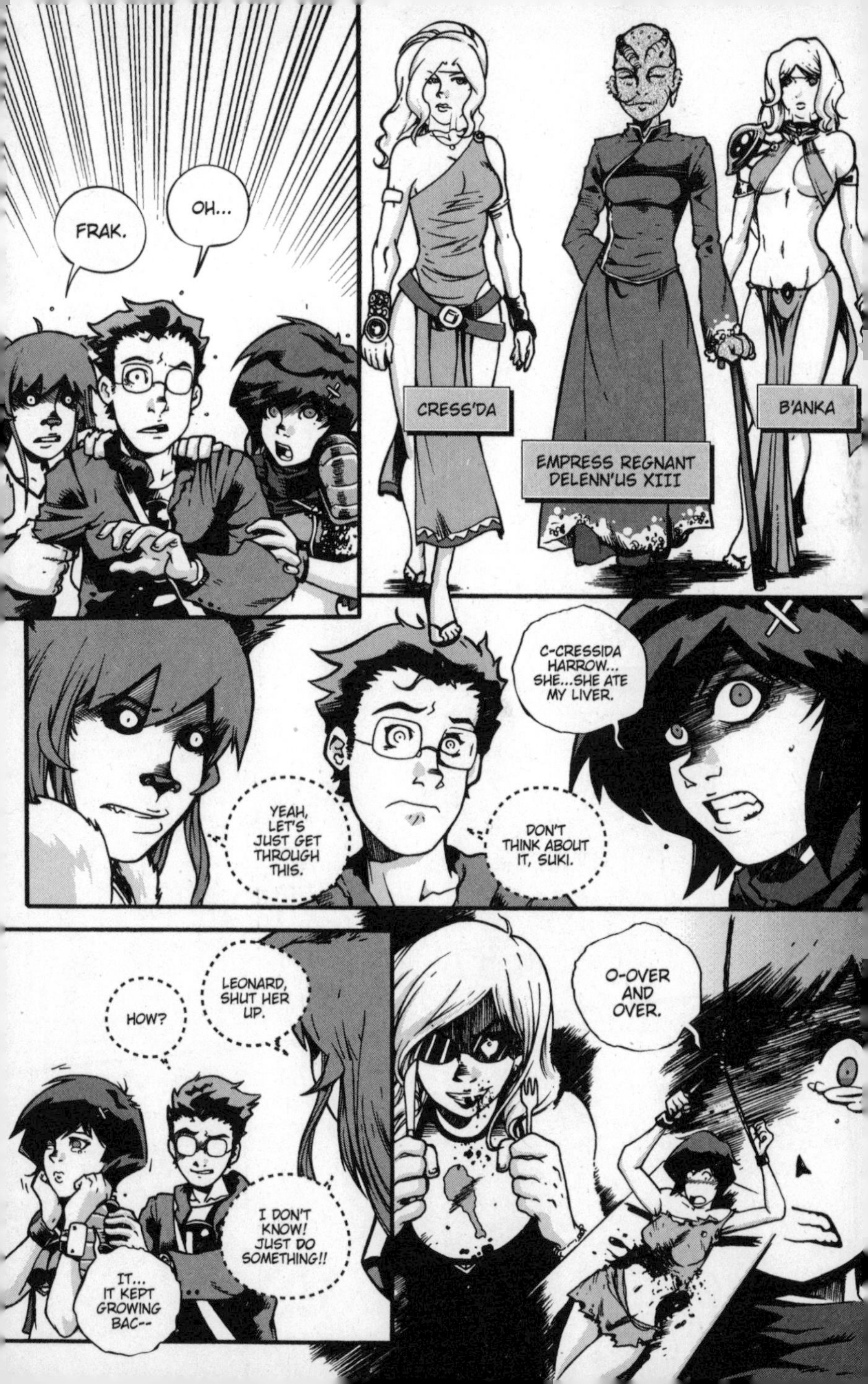
B'ANKA
CRESS'DA
EMPRESS REGNANT DELENN'US XIII
OH...
FRAK.
C-CRESSIDA HARROW... SHE...SHE ATE MY LIVER.
DON'T THINK ABOUT IT, SUKI.
YEAH, LET'S JUST GET THROUGH THIS.
O-OVER AND OVER.
LEONARD, SHUT HER UP.
HOW?
I DON'T KNOW! JUST DO SOMETHING!!
IT... IT KEPT GROWING BAC--

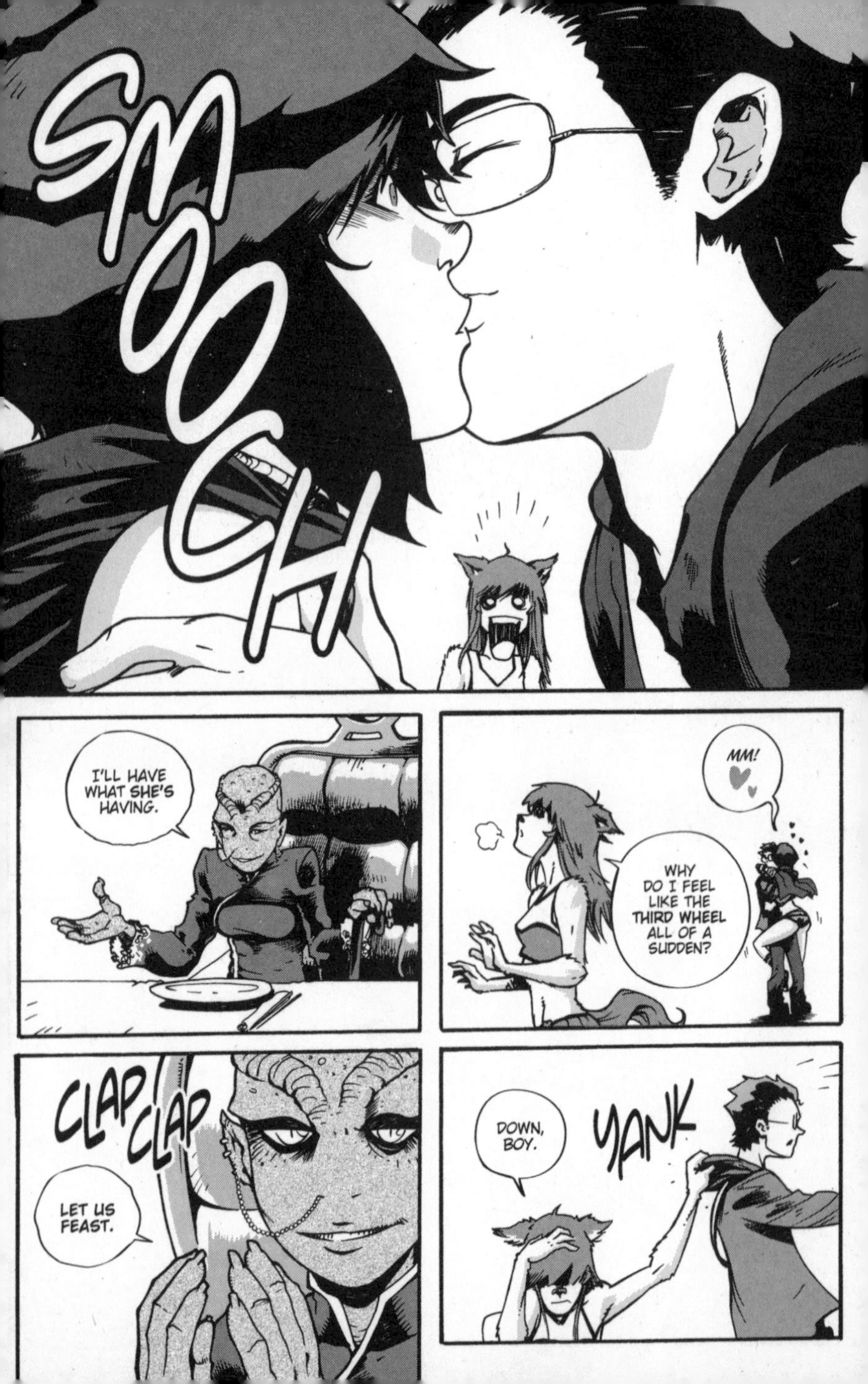
SMOOCH
MM!
WHY DO I FEEL LIKE THE THIRD WHEEL ALL OF A SUDDEN?
I'LL HAVE WHAT SHE'S HAVING.
YANK
DOWN, BOY.
CLAP CLAP
LET US FEAST.

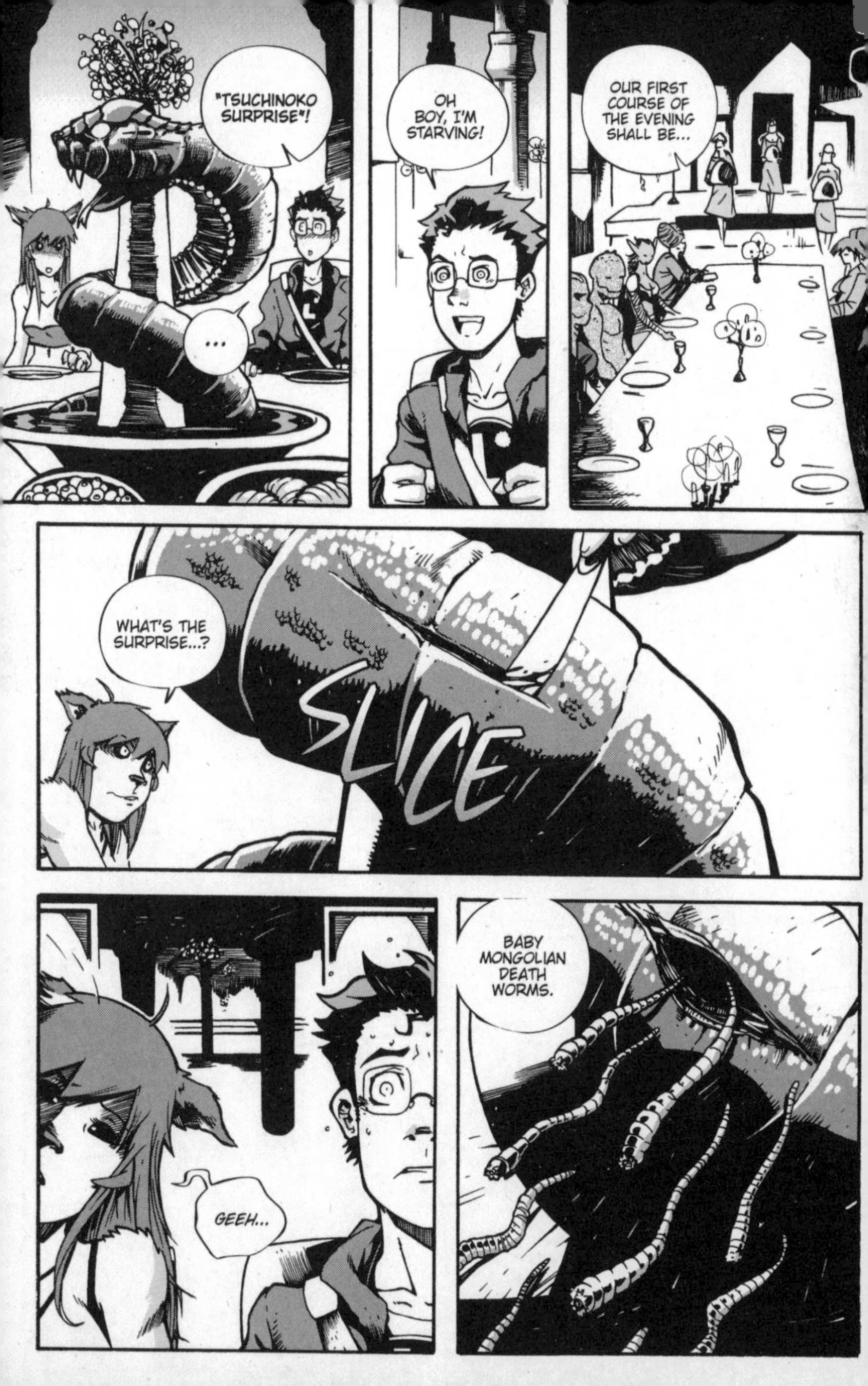

OUR FIRST COURSE OF THE EVENING SHALL BE...
OH BOY, I'M STARVING!
"TSUCHINOKO SURPRISE"!
...
WHAT'S THE SURPRISE...?
SLICE
BABY MONGOLIAN DEATH WORMS.
GEEH...

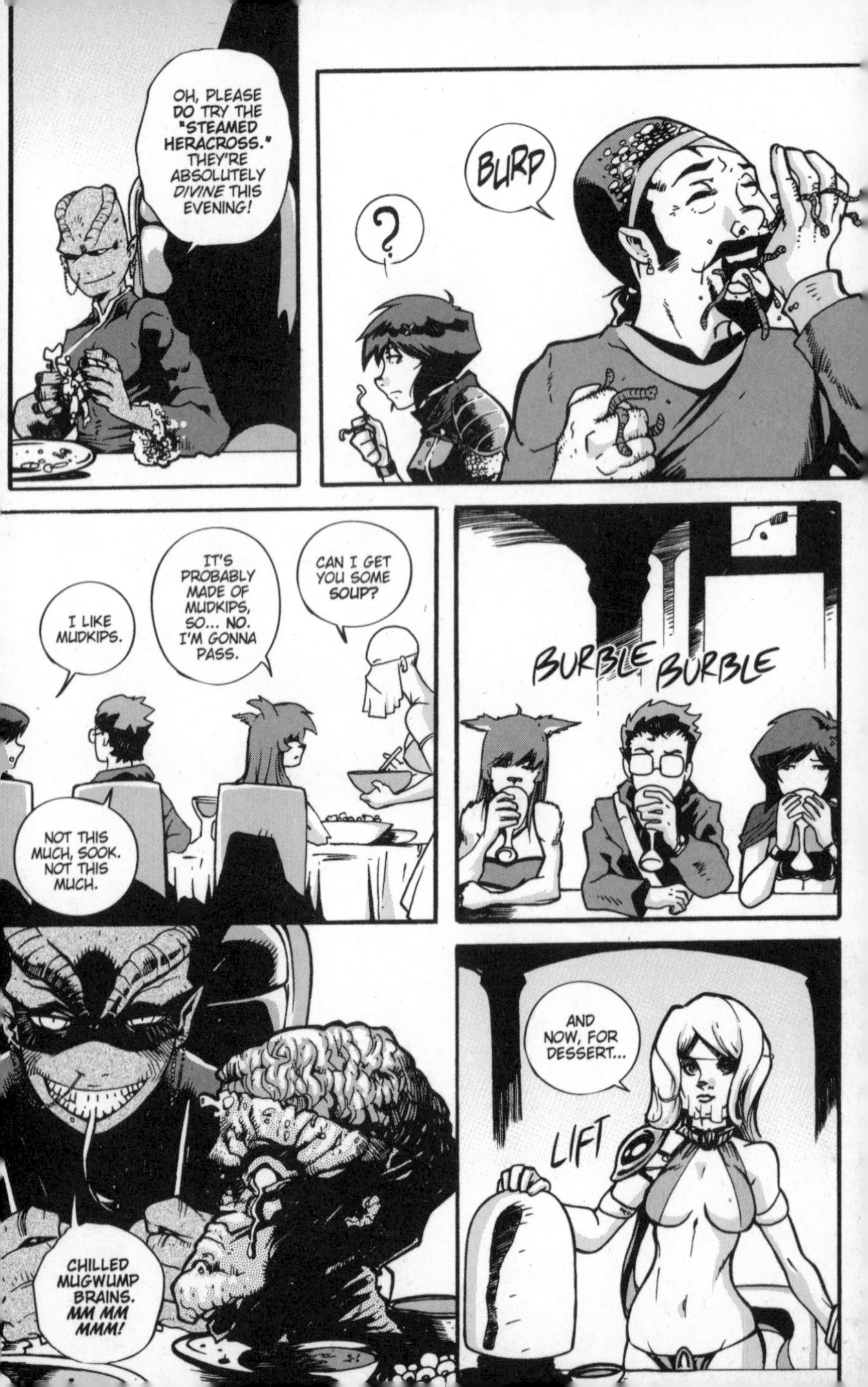
BURP
?
OH, PLEASE DO TRY THE "STEAMED HERACROSS." THEY'RE ABSOLUTELY *DIVINE* THIS EVENING!
BURBLE BURBLE
CAN I GET YOU SOME SOUP?
IT'S PROBABLY MADE OF MUDKIPS, SO... NO. I'M GONNA PASS.
I LIKE MUDKIPS.
NOT THIS MUCH, SOOK. NOT THIS MUCH.
AND NOW, FOR DESSERT...
LIFT
CHILLED MUGWUMP BRAINS. **MM MM MMM!**

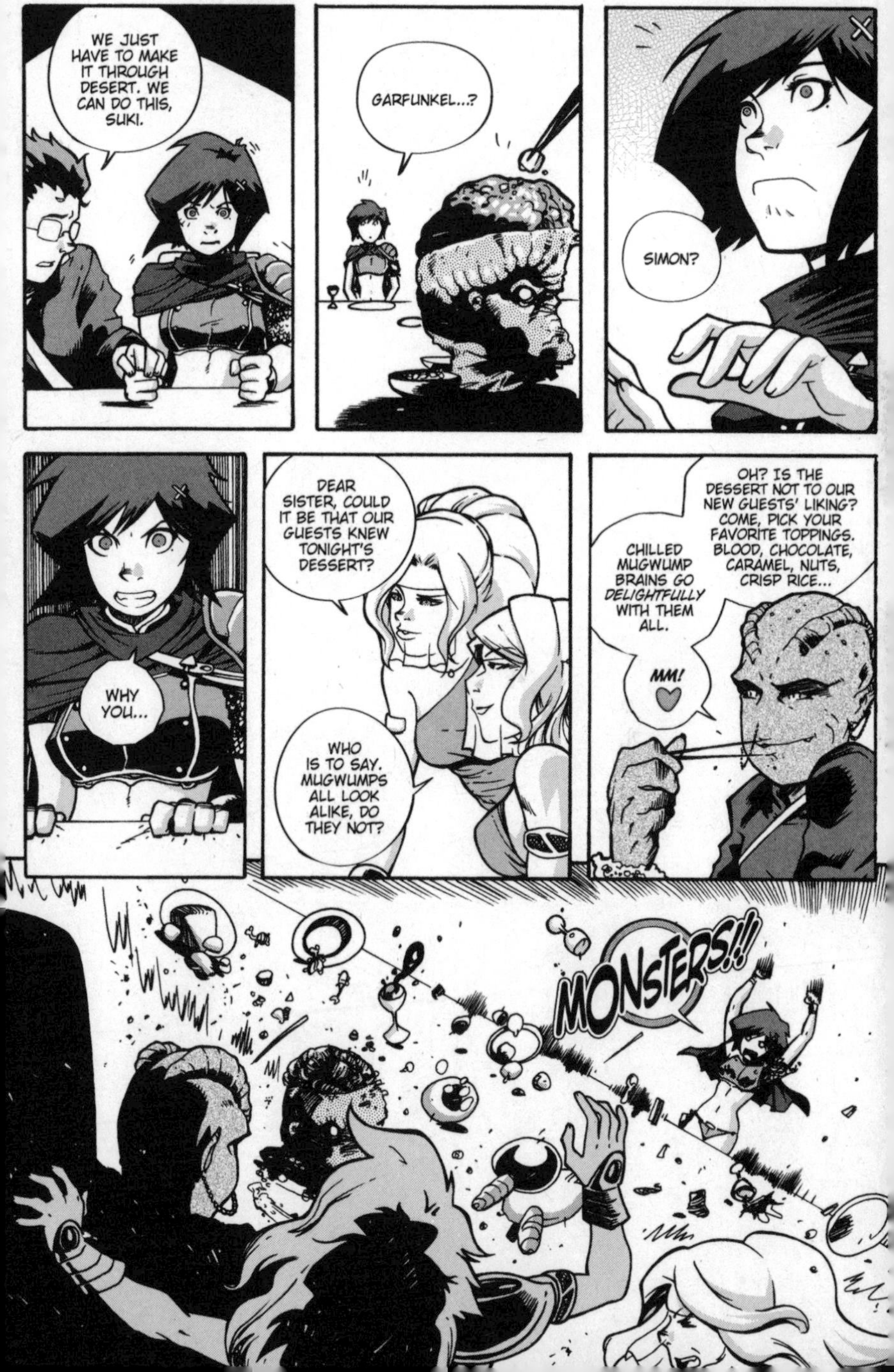
SIMON?
GARFUNKEL...?
WE JUST HAVE TO MAKE IT THROUGH DESERT. WE CAN DO THIS, SUKI.
OH? IS THE DESSERT NOT TO OUR NEW GUESTS' LIKING? COME, PICK YOUR FAVORITE TOPPINGS. BLOOD, CHOCOLATE, CARAMEL, NUTS, CRISP RICE...
CHILLED MUGWUMP BRAINS GO *DELIGHTFULLY* WITH THEM ALL.
MM! ♥
DEAR SISTER, COULD IT BE THAT OUR GUESTS KNEW TONIGHT'S DESSERT?
WHO IS TO SAY. MUGWUMPS ALL LOOK ALIKE, DO THEY NOT?
WHY YOU...
MONSTERS!!!

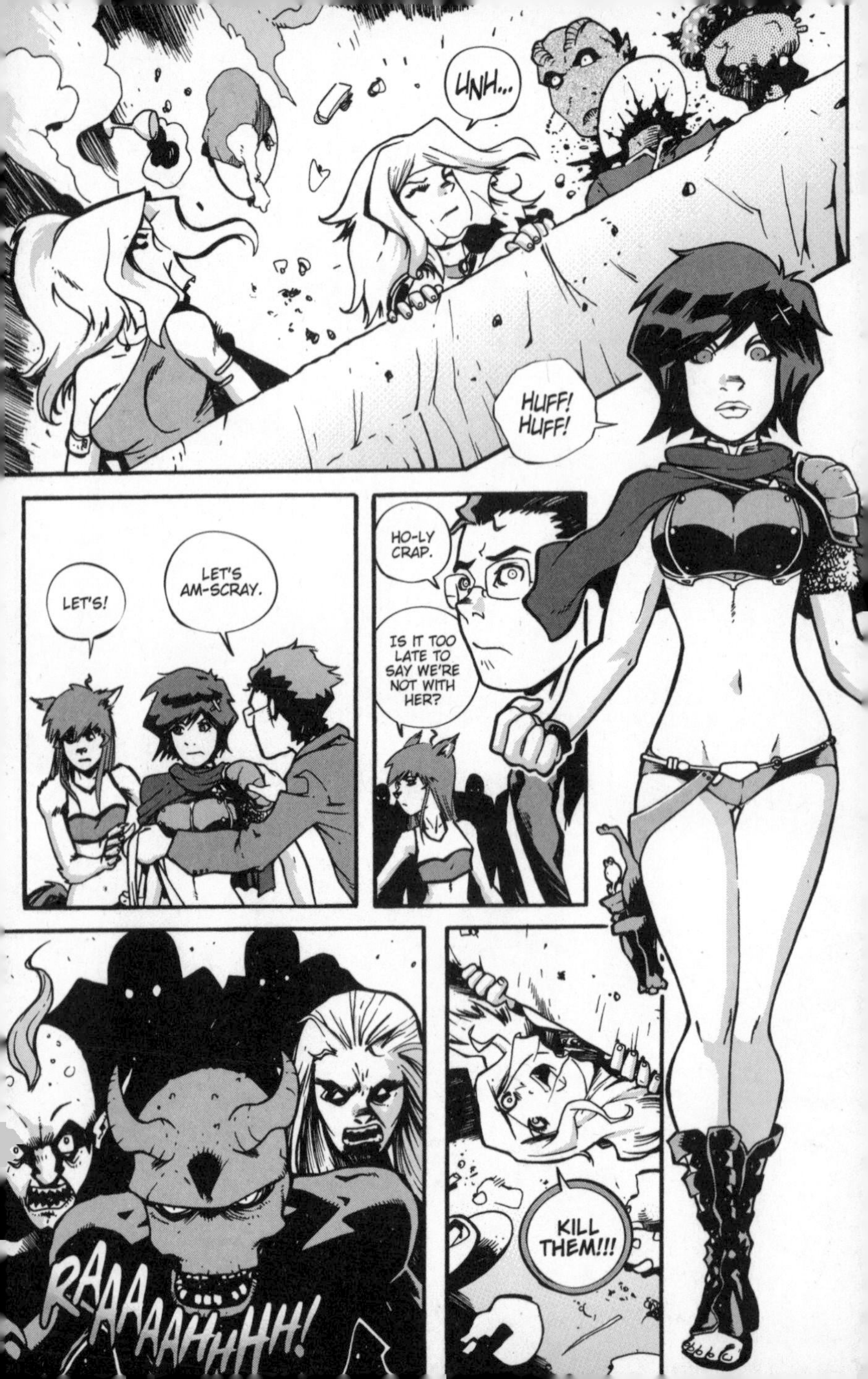
UNH...
HUFF! HUFF!
HO-LY CRAP.
IS IT TOO LATE TO SAY WE'RE NOT WITH HER?
LET'S AM-SCRAY.
LET'S!
KILL THEM!!!
RAAAAAHHHHHH!

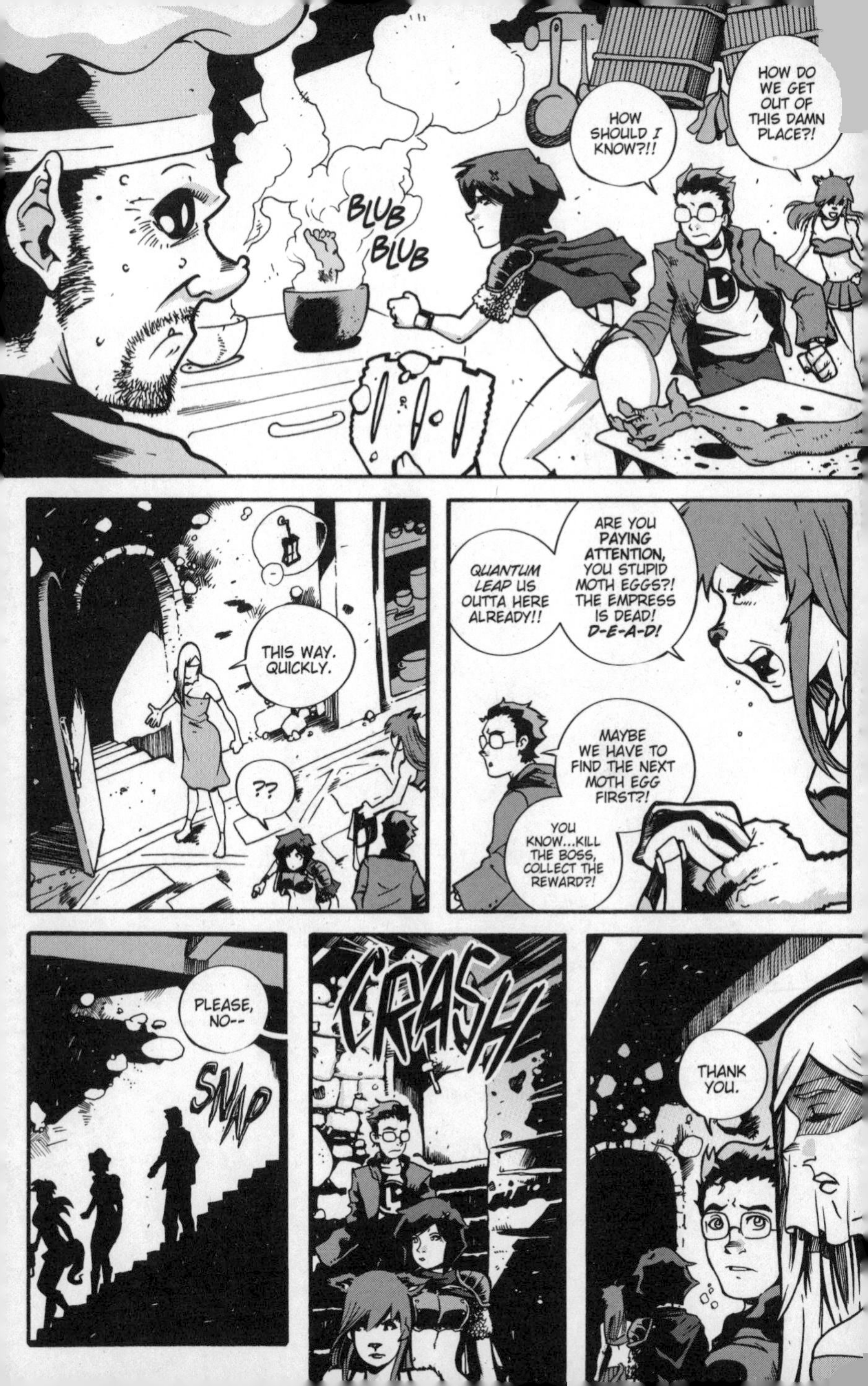
HOW DO WE GET OUT OF THIS DAMN PLACE?!
HOW SHOULD I KNOW?!!
BLUB BLUB
ARE YOU PAYING ATTENTION, YOU STUPID MOTH EGGS?! THE EMPRESS IS DEAD! D-E-A-D!
QUANTUM LEAP US OUTTA HERE ALREADY!!
MAYBE WE HAVE TO FIND THE NEXT MOTH EGG FIRST?!
YOU KNOW...KILL THE BOSS, COLLECT THE REWARD?!
THIS WAY. QUICKLY.
??
THANK YOU.
CRASH
PLEASE, NO--
SNAP

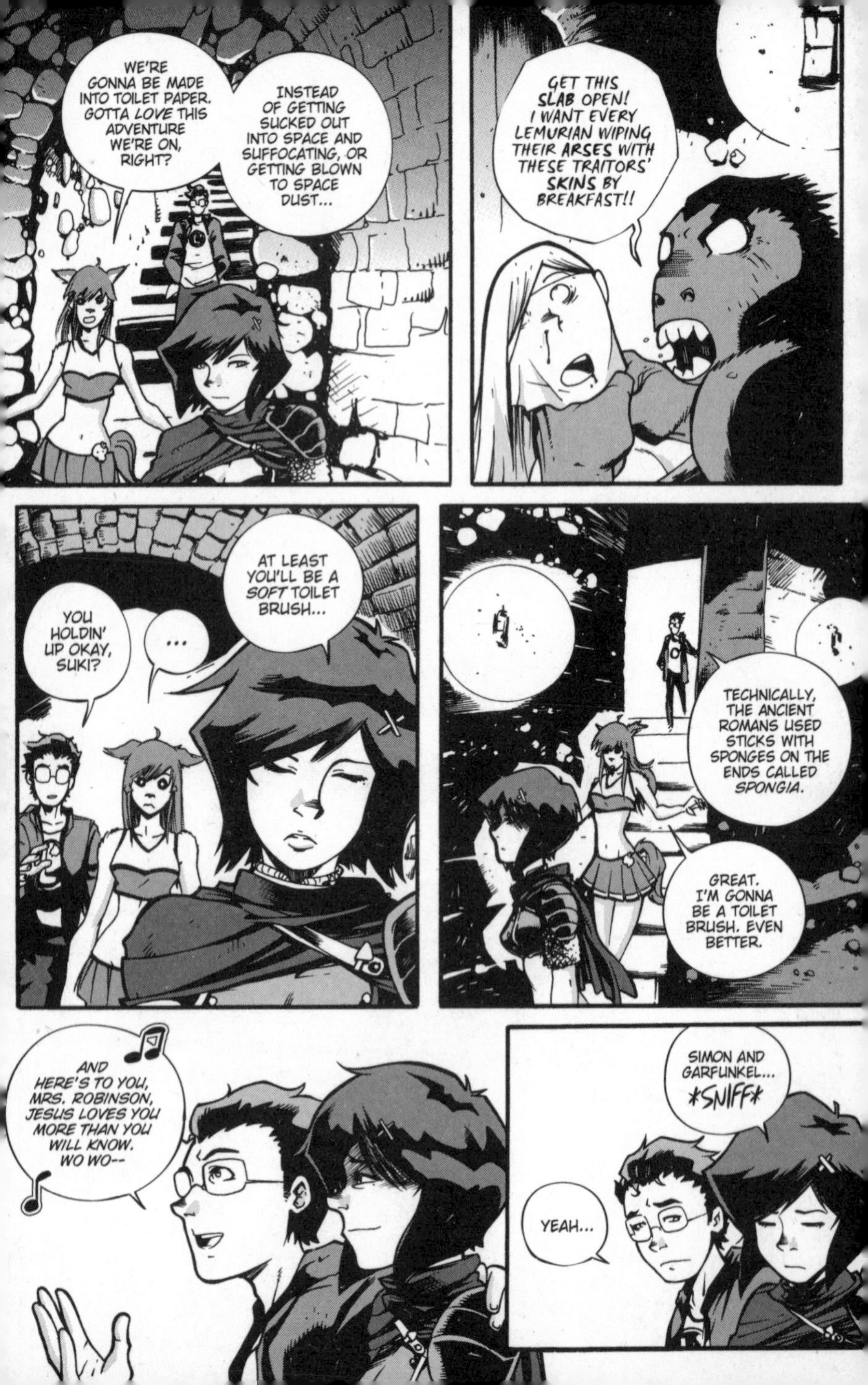
WE'RE GONNA BE MADE INTO TOILET PAPER. GOTTA *LOVE* THIS ADVENTURE WE'RE ON, RIGHT?
INSTEAD OF GETTING SUCKED OUT INTO SPACE AND SUFFOCATING, OR GETTING BLOWN TO SPACE DUST...
GET THIS **SLAB** OPEN! I WANT EVERY LEMURIAN WIPING THEIR **ARSES** WITH THESE TRAITORS' **SKINS** BY BREAKFAST!!
YOU HOLDIN' UP OKAY, SUKI?
...
AT LEAST YOU'LL BE A *SOFT* TOILET BRUSH...
TECHNICALLY, THE ANCIENT ROMANS USED STICKS WITH SPONGES ON THE ENDS CALLED *SPONGIA*.
GREAT. I'M GONNA BE A TOILET BRUSH. EVEN BETTER.
AND HERE'S TO YOU, MRS. ROBINSON, JESUS LOVES YOU MORE THAN YOU WILL KNOW. WO WO--
SIMON AND GARFUNKEL... *SNIFF*
YEAH...

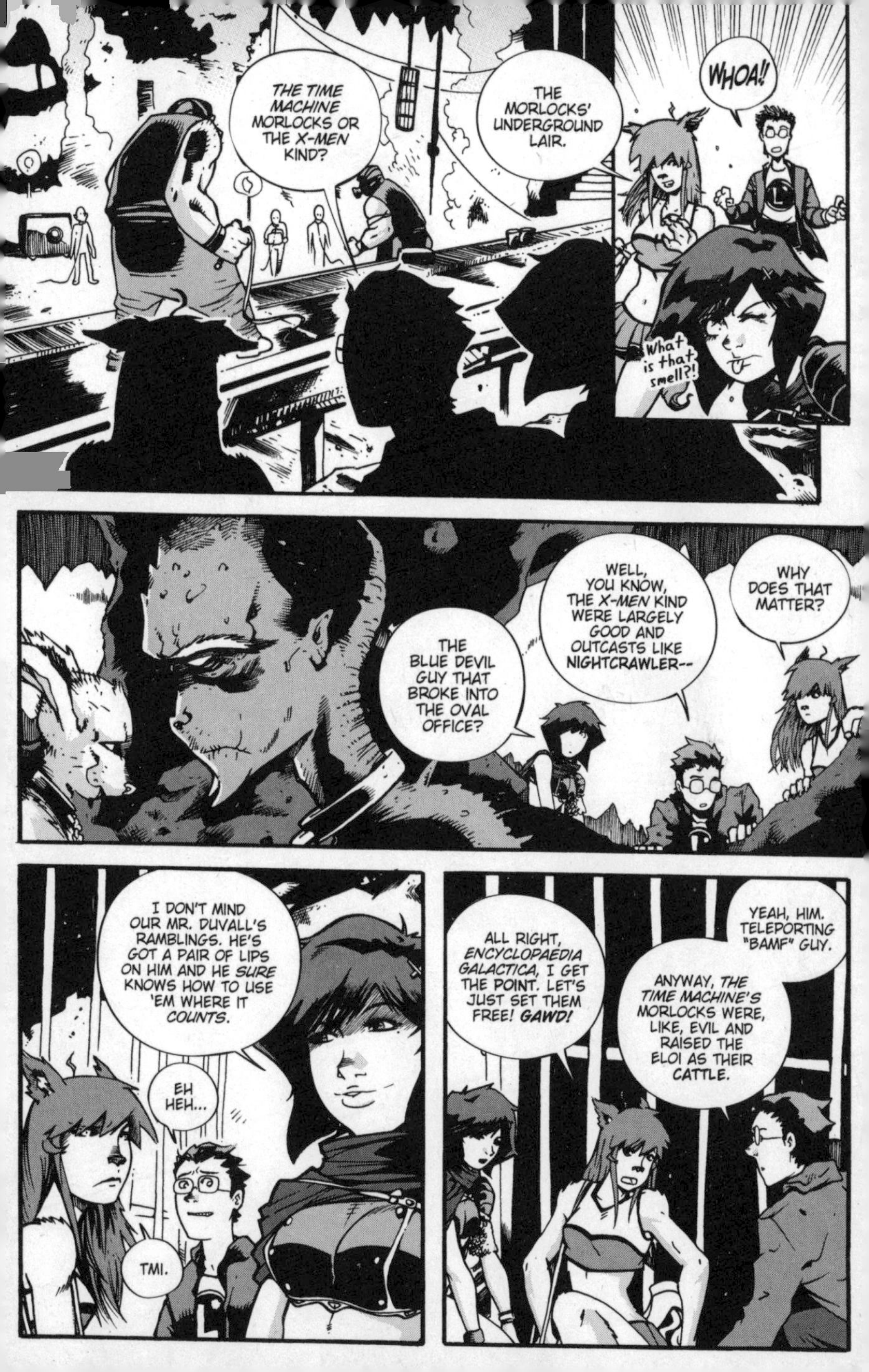
WHOA!!
What is that smell?!
THE MORLOCKS' UNDERGROUND LAIR.
THE TIME MACHINE MORLOCKS OR THE *X-MEN* KIND?
WHY DOES THAT MATTER?
WELL, YOU KNOW, THE *X-MEN* KIND WERE LARGELY GOOD AND OUTCASTS LIKE **NIGHTCRAWLER**--
THE BLUE DEVIL GUY THAT BROKE INTO THE OVAL OFFICE?
YEAH, HIM. TELEPORTING "BAMF" GUY.
ANYWAY, *THE TIME MACHINE'S* MORLOCKS WERE, LIKE, EVIL AND RAISED THE ELOI AS THEIR CATTLE.
ALL RIGHT, *ENCYCLOPAEDIA GALACTICA*, I GET THE POINT. LET'S JUST SET THEM FREE! ***GAWD!***
I DON'T MIND OUR MR. DUVALL'S RAMBLINGS. HE'S GOT A PAIR OF LIPS ON HIM AND HE *SURE* KNOWS HOW TO USE 'EM WHERE IT *COUNTS*.
EH HEH...
TMI.

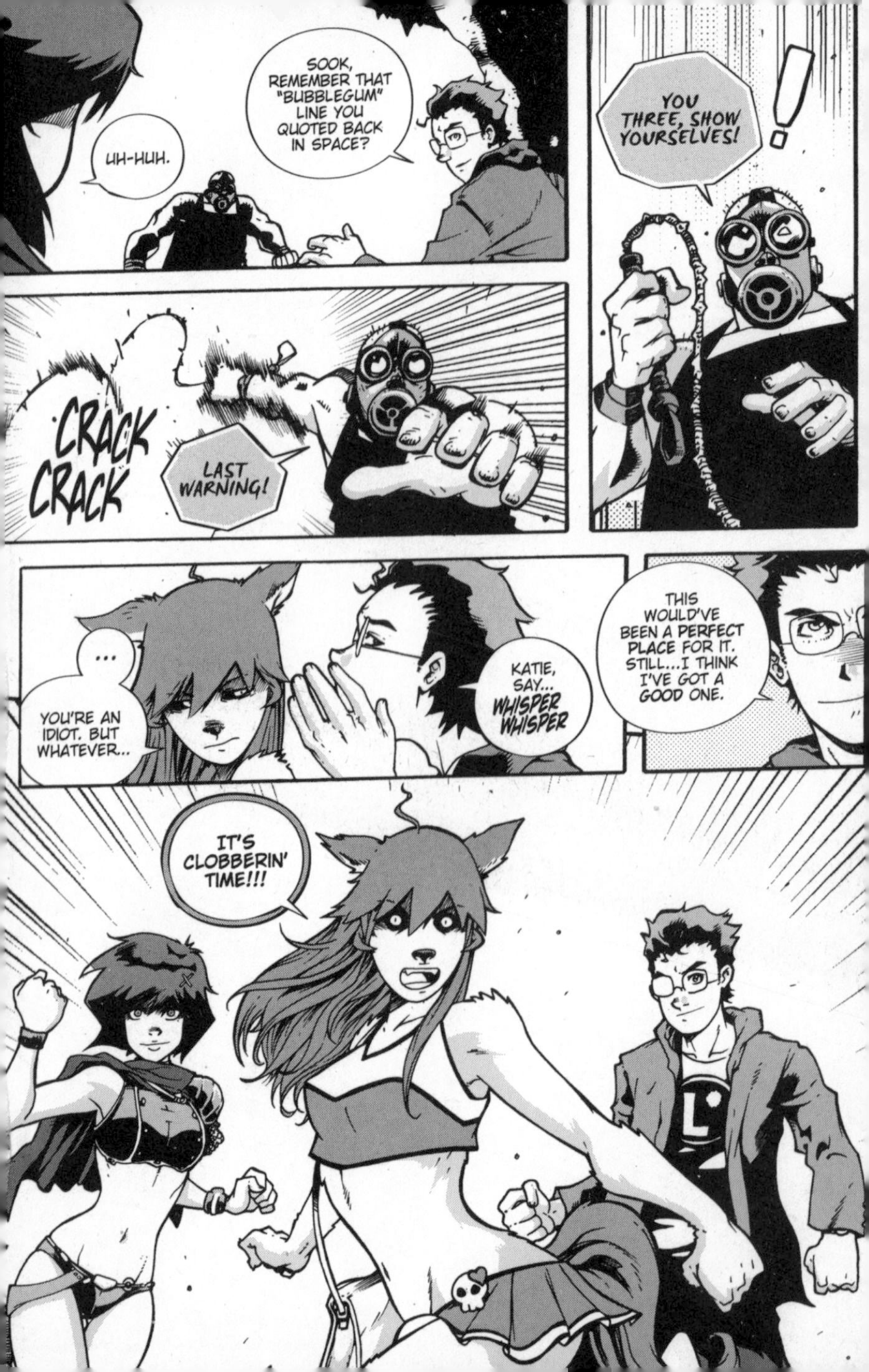

YOU THREE, SHOW YOURSELVES!
!
SOOK, REMEMBER THAT "BUBBLEGUM" LINE YOU QUOTED BACK IN SPACE?
UH-HUH.
LAST WARNING!
CRACK CRACK
THIS WOULD'VE BEEN A PERFECT PLACE FOR IT. STILL...I THINK I'VE GOT A GOOD ONE.
KATIE, SAY... WHISPER WHISPER
...
YOU'RE AN IDIOT. BUT WHATEVER...
IT'S CLOBBERIN' TIME!!!

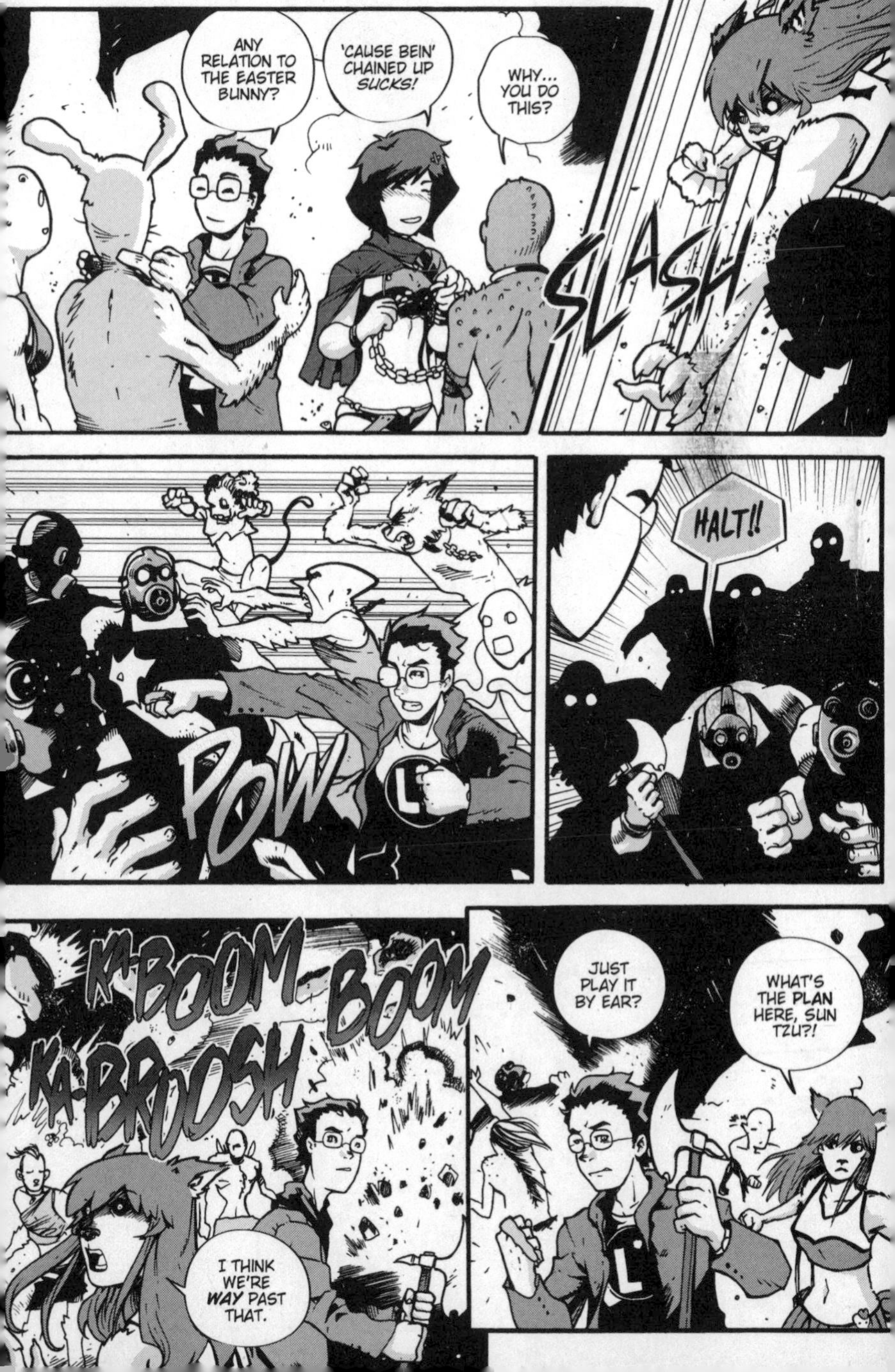
SLASH
WHY... YOU DO THIS?
'CAUSE BEIN' CHAINED UP SUCKS!
ANY RELATION TO THE EASTER BUNNY?
HALT!!
POW
WHAT'S THE PLAN HERE, SUN TZU?!
JUST PLAY IT BY EAR?
K-BOOM-BOOM
KA-BROOSH
I THINK WE'RE WAY PAST THAT.

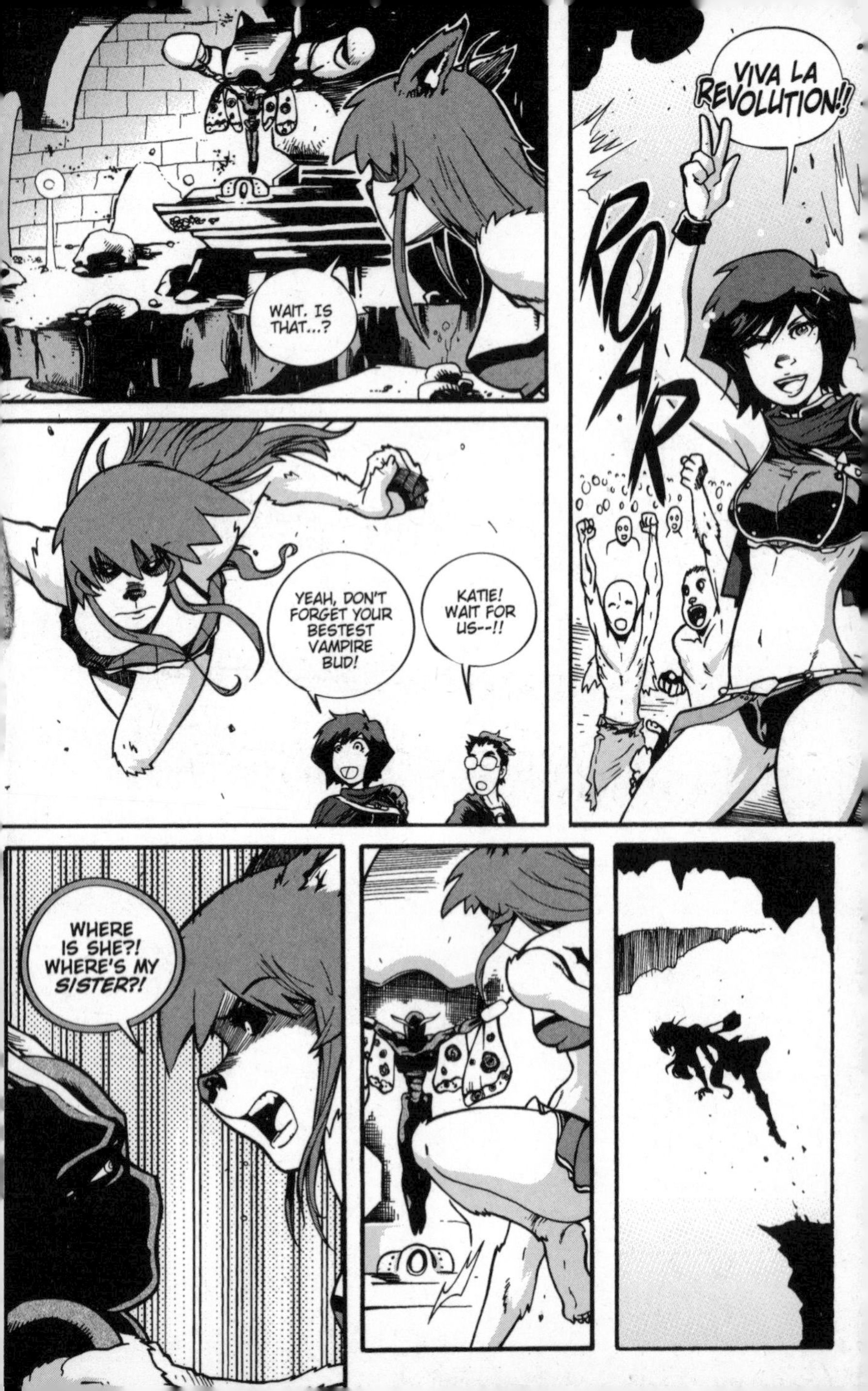
VIVA LA REVOLUTION!!
ROAR
WAIT. IS THAT...?
KATIE! WAIT FOR US--!!
YEAH, DON'T FORGET YOUR BESTEST VAMPIRE BUD!
WHERE IS SHE?! WHERE'S MY SISTER?!

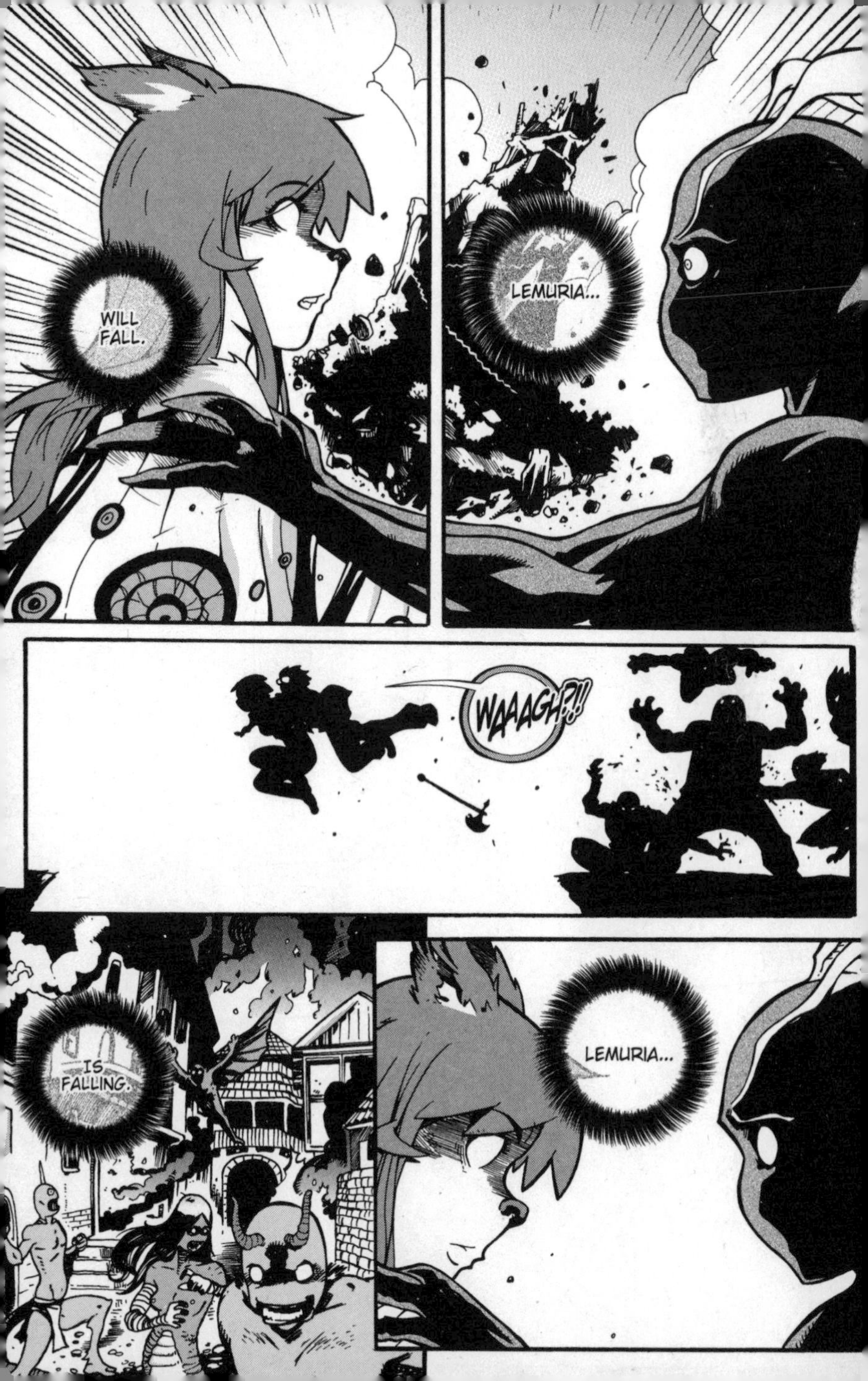
LEMURIA...
WILL FALL.
WAAAGH?!!
LEMURIA...
IS FALLING.

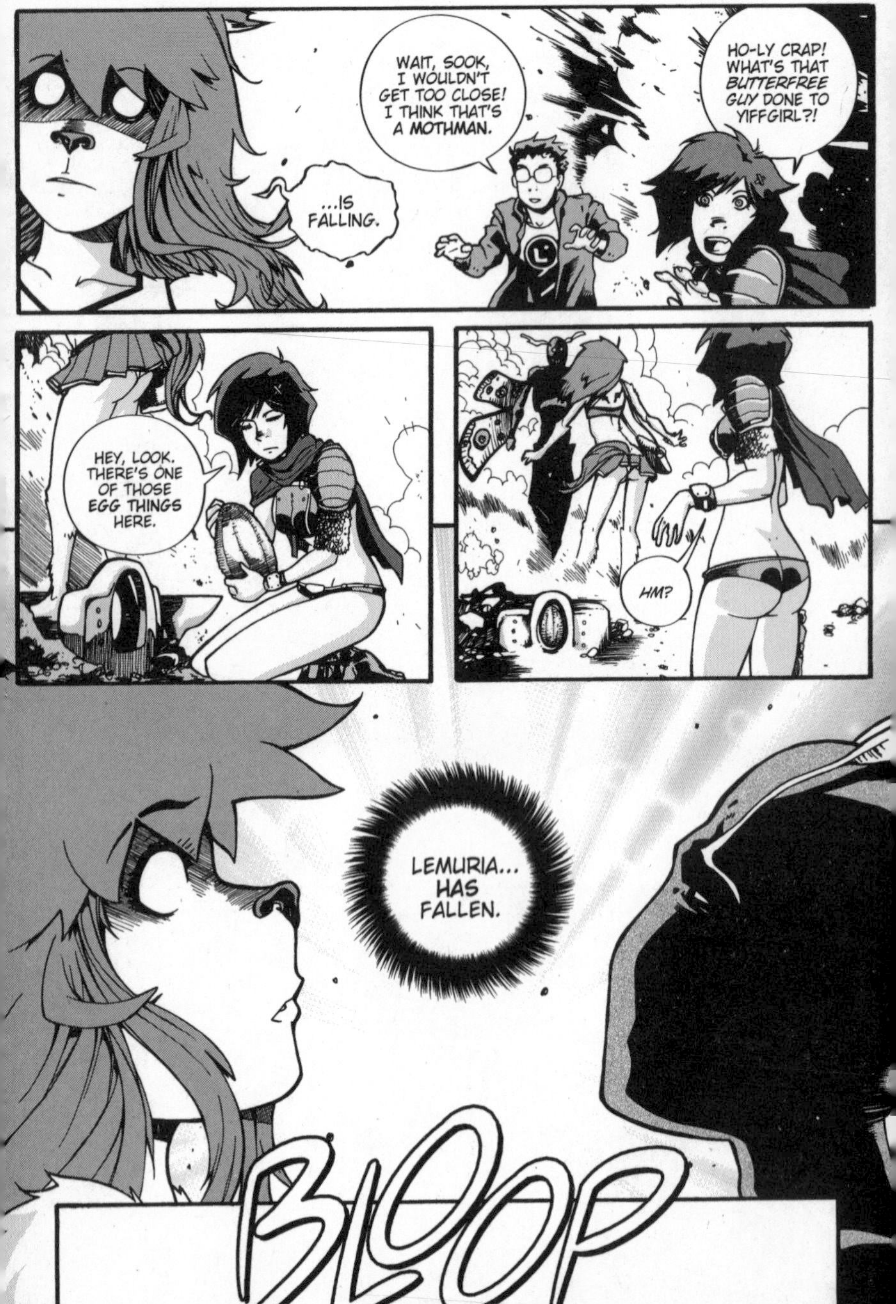
HO-LY CRAP! WHAT'S THAT *BUTTERFREE GUY* DONE TO YIFFGIRL?!
WAIT, SOOK, I WOULDN'T GET TOO CLOSE! I THINK THAT'S A **MOTHMAN**.
...IS FALLING.
HM?
HEY, LOOK. THERE'S ONE OF THOSE **EGG THINGS** HERE.
LEMURIA... HAS FALLEN.
BLOOP

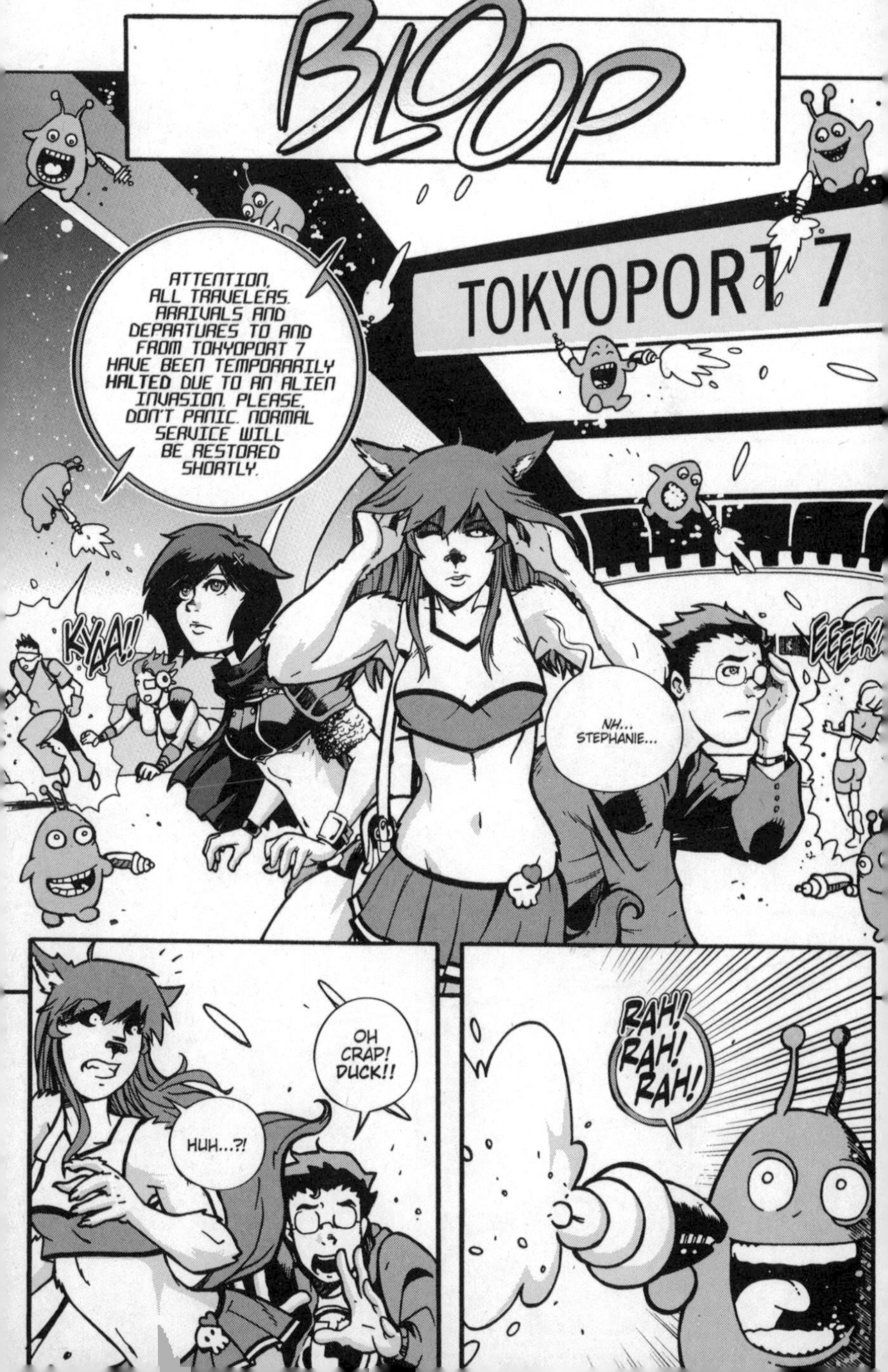
BLOOP
TOKYOPORT 7
ATTENTION, ALL TRAVELERS. ARRIVALS AND DEPARTURES TO AND FROM TOKYOPORT 7 HAVE BEEN TEMPORARILY HALTED DUE TO AN ALIEN INVASION. PLEASE, DON'T PANIC. NORMAL SERVICE WILL BE RESTORED SHORTLY.
EEEEK!
NH... STEPHANIE...
KYAA!!
RAH! RAH! RAH!
OH CRAP! DUCK!!
HUH...?!

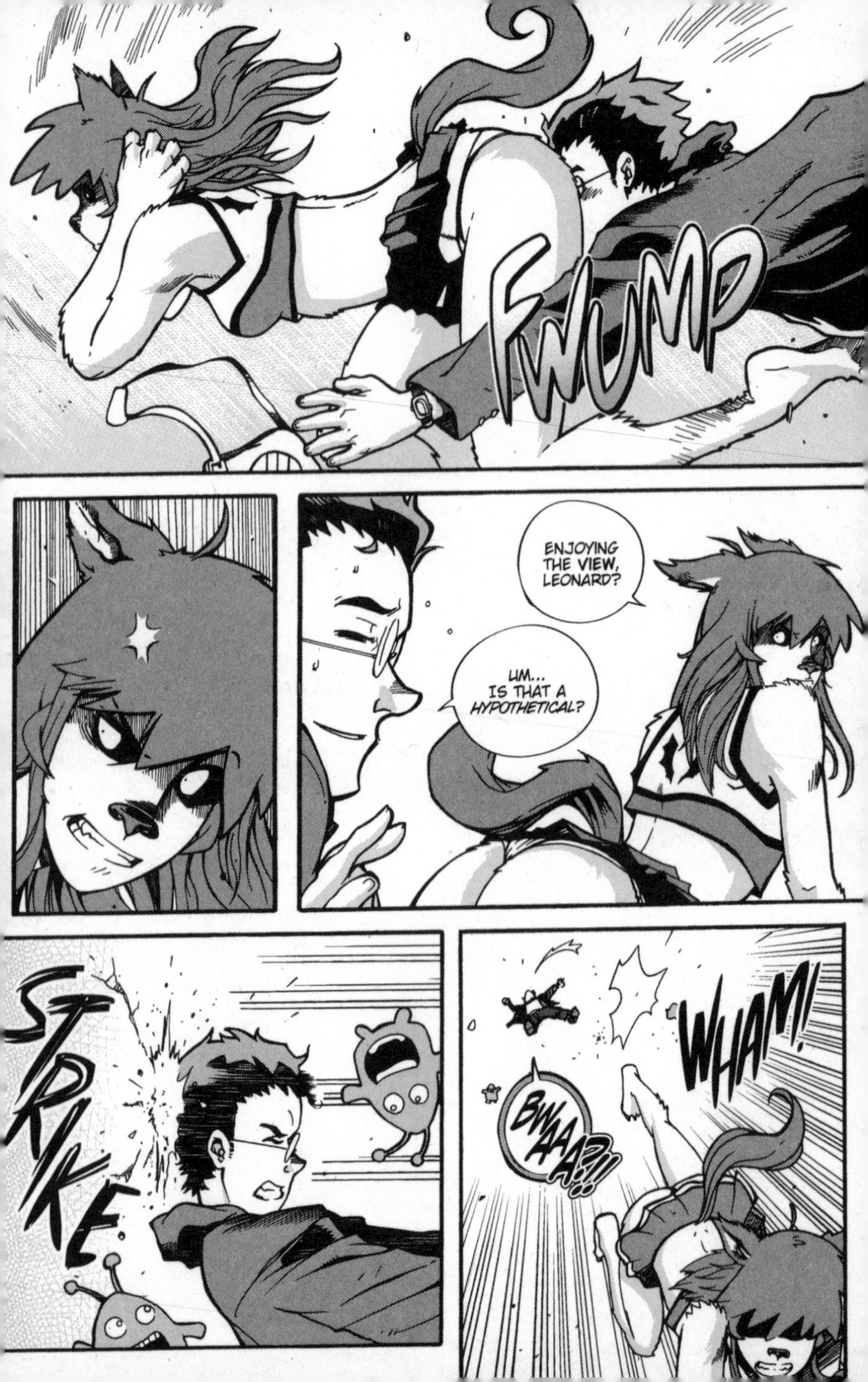
FWUMP
ENJOYING THE VIEW, LEONARD?
UM... IS THAT A *HYPOTHETICAL?*
WHAM!
BWAAAA?!!
STRIKE

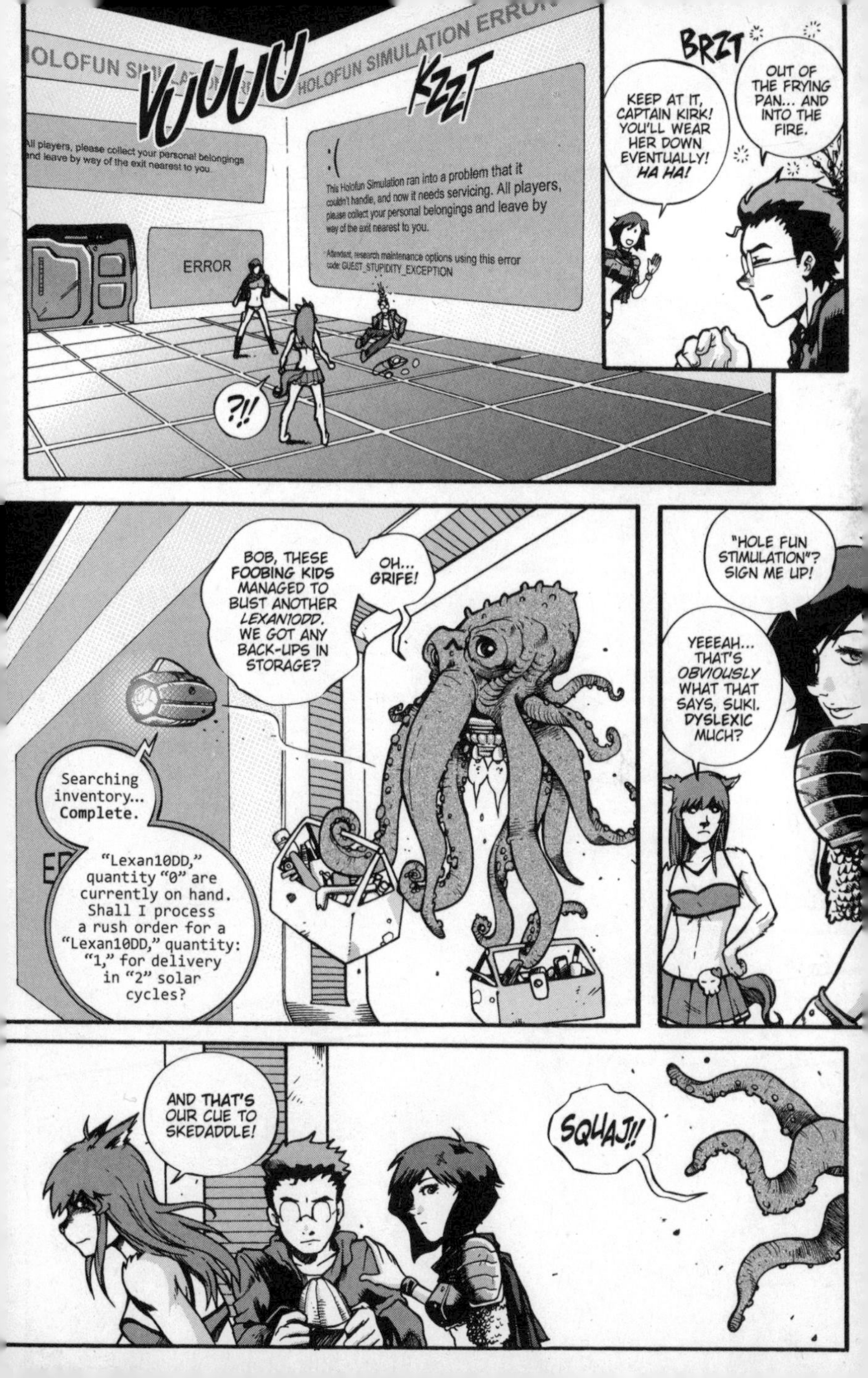
BRZT
OUT OF THE FRYING PAN... AND INTO THE FIRE.
KEEP AT IT, CAPTAIN KIRK! YOU'LL WEAR HER DOWN EVENTUALLY! HA HA!
HOLOFUN SIMULATION ERROR
KZZT
:(
This Holofun Simulation ran into a problem that it couldn't handle, and now it needs servicing. All players, please collect your personal belongings and leave by way of the exit nearest to you.
Attendant, research maintenance options using this error code: GUEST_STUPIDITY_EXCEPTION
VUUUU
All players, please collect your personal belongings and leave by way of the exit nearest to you.
ERROR
?!!
"HOLE FUN STIMULATION"? SIGN ME UP!
YEEEAH... THAT'S OBVIOUSLY WHAT THAT SAYS, SUKI. DYSLEXIC MUCH?
OH... GRIFE!
BOB, THESE FOOBING KIDS MANAGED TO BUST ANOTHER LEXAN10DD. WE GOT ANY BACK-UPS IN STORAGE?
Searching inventory... Complete.
"Lexan10DD," quantity "0" are currently on hand. Shall I process a rush order for a "Lexan10DD," quantity: "1," for delivery in "2" solar cycles?
SQUAJ!!
AND THAT'S OUR CUE TO SKEDADDLE!

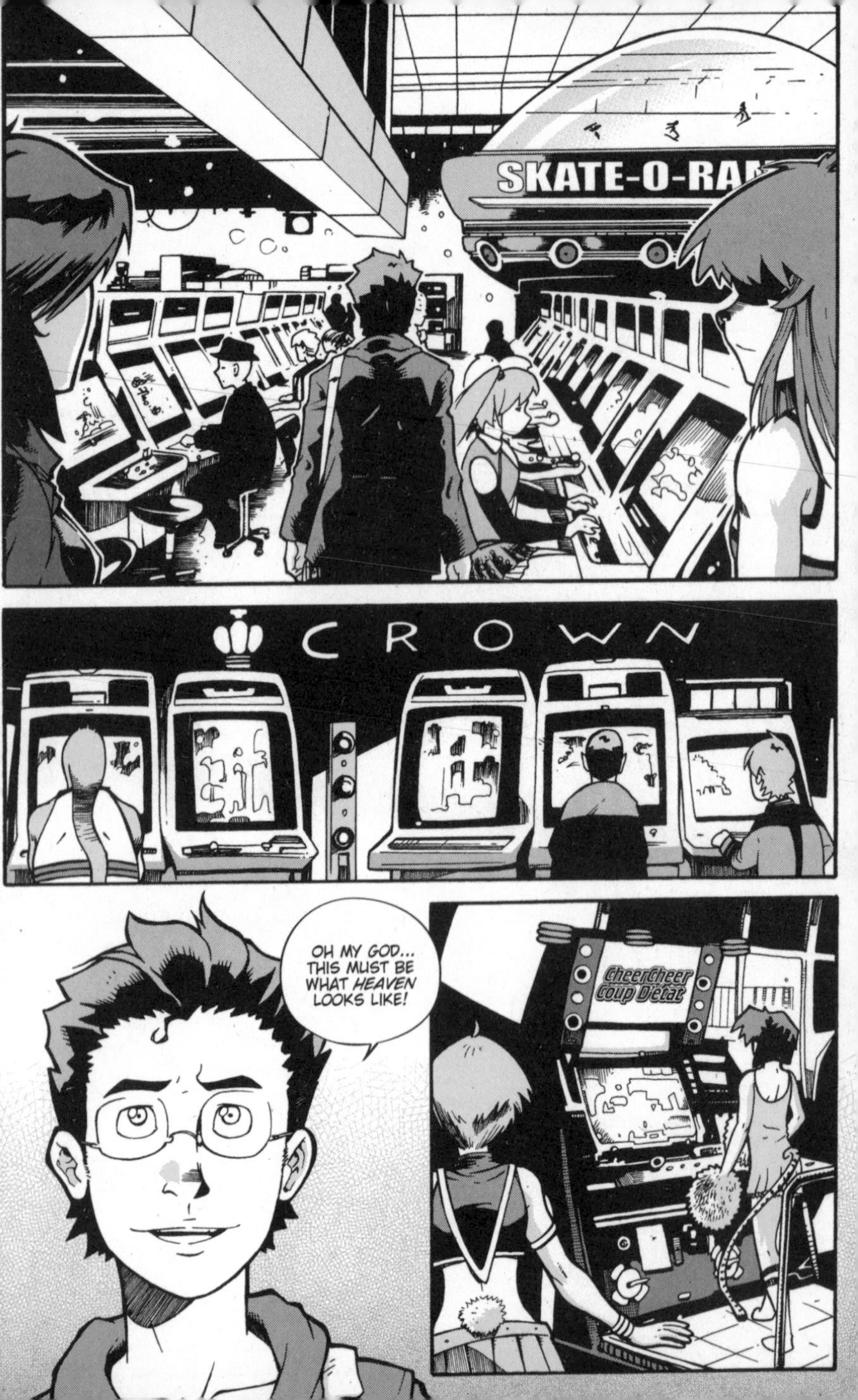
SKATE-O-RA
CROWN
CheerCheer Coup D'etat
OH MY GOD... THIS MUST BE WHAT *HEAVEN* LOOKS LIKE!

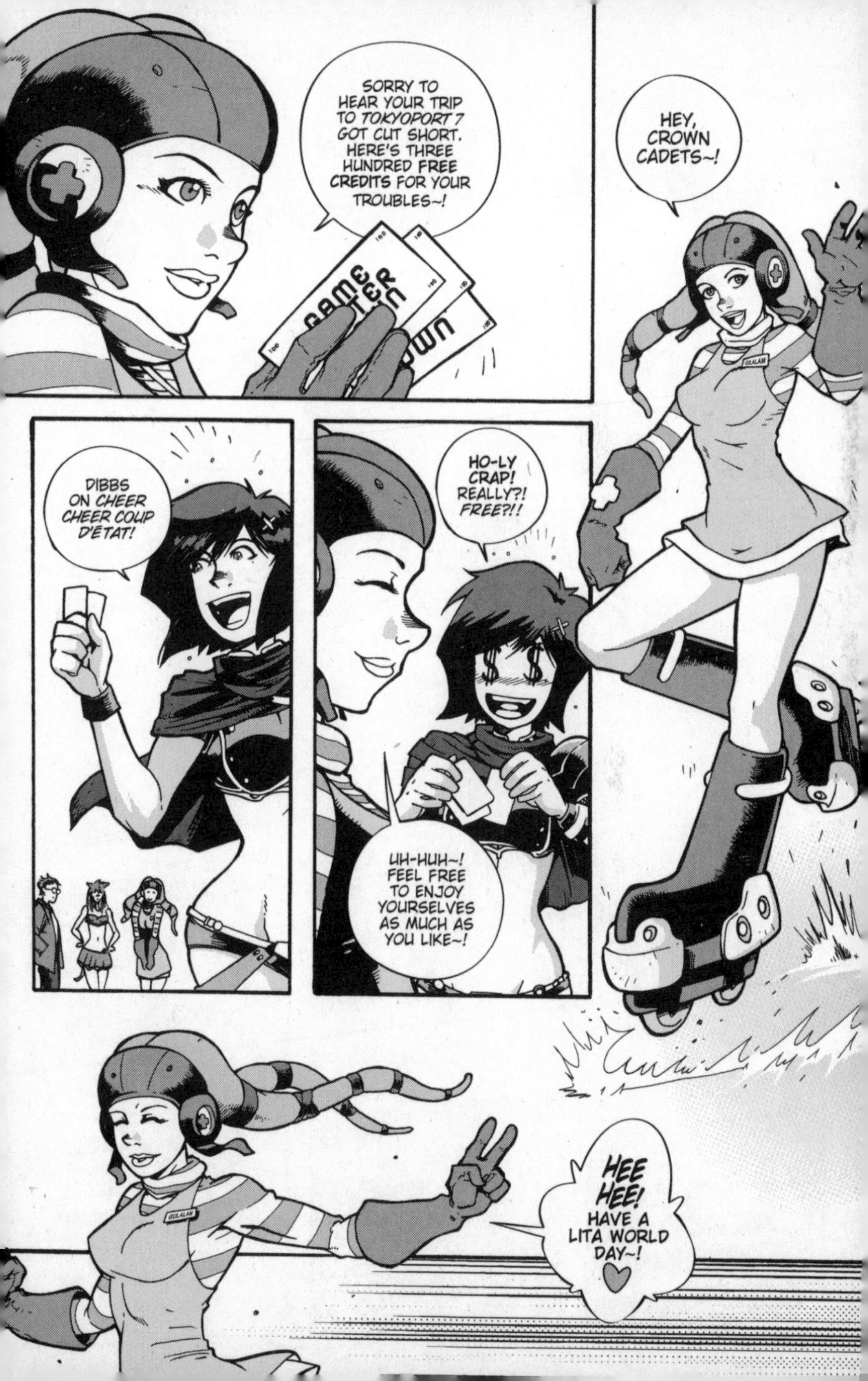
HEY, CROWN CADETS~!
SORRY TO HEAR YOUR TRIP TO *TOKYOPORT 7* GOT CUT SHORT. HERE'S THREE HUNDRED FREE CREDITS FOR YOUR TROUBLES~!
HO-LY CRAP! REALLY?! *FREE?!!*
UH-HUH~! FEEL FREE TO ENJOY YOURSELVES AS MUCH AS YOU LIKE~!
DIBBS ON *CHEER CHEER COUP D'ÉTAT!*
HEE HEE! HAVE A LITA WORLD DAY~!

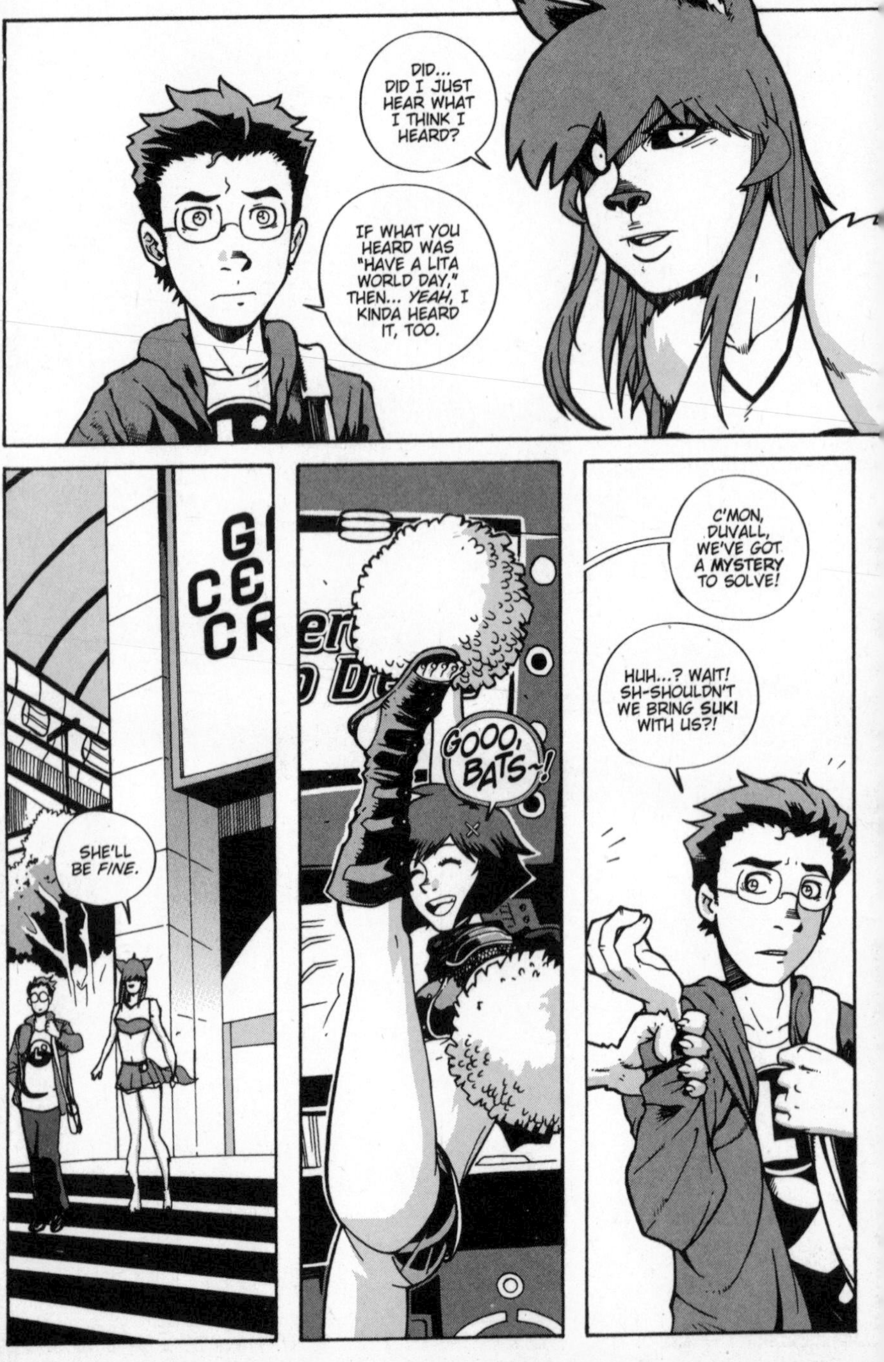
DID... DID I JUST HEAR WHAT I THINK I HEARD?
IF WHAT YOU HEARD WAS "HAVE A LITA WORLD DAY," THEN... *YEAH*, I KINDA HEARD IT, TOO.
C'MON, DUVALL, WE'VE GOT A MYSTERY TO SOLVE!
HUH...? WAIT! SH-SHOULDN'T WE BRING SUKI WITH US?!
GOOO, BATS~!
SHE'LL BE *FINE*.

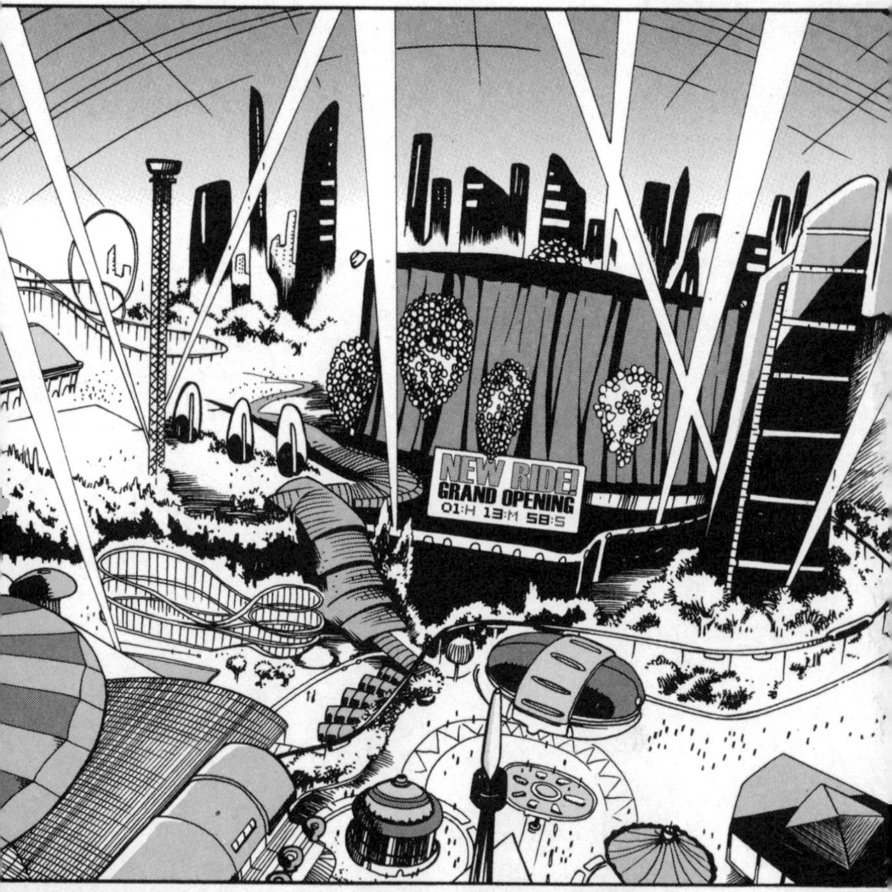
NEW RIDE!
GRAND OPENING
01:H 13:M 58:S

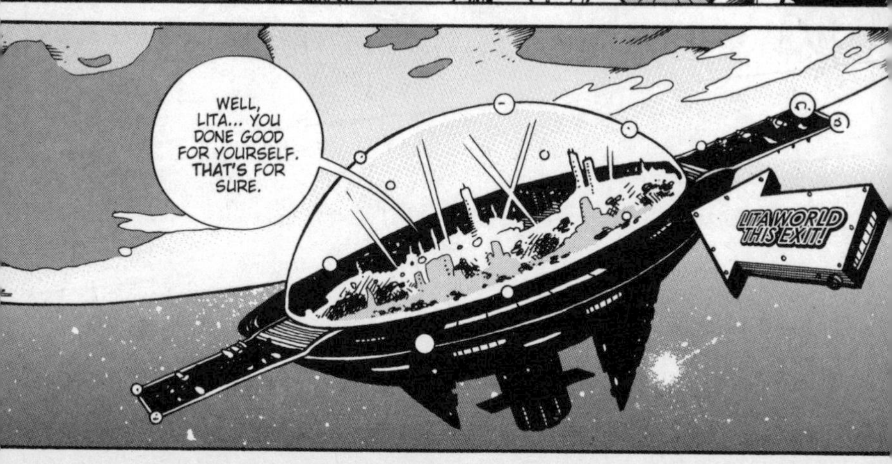
WELL, LITA... YOU DONE GOOD FOR YOURSELF. THAT'S FOR SURE.
LITA WORLD THIS EXIT!

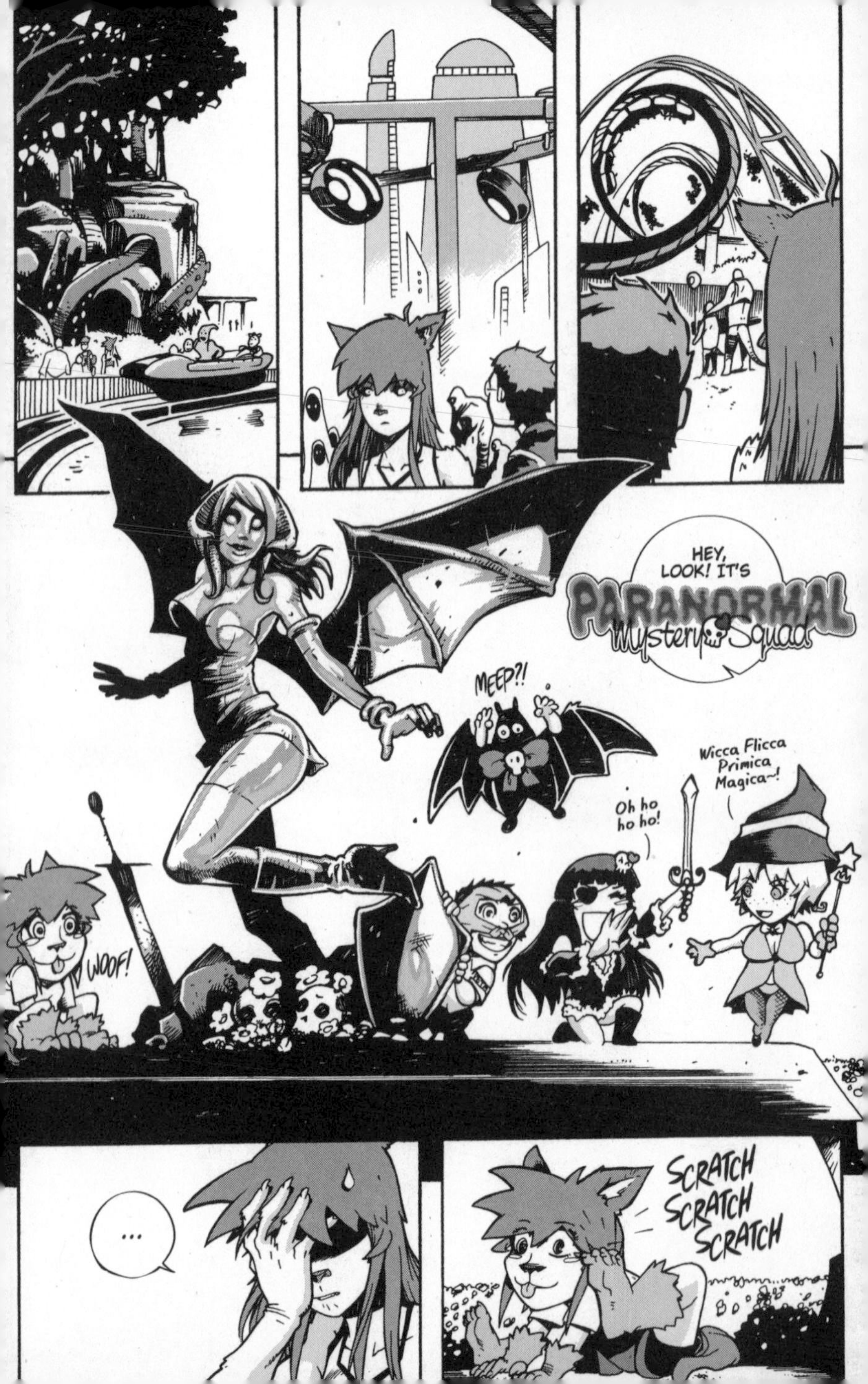
HEY, LOOK! IT'S
PARANORMAL Mystery Squad
Wicca Flicca Primica Magica~!
Oh ho ho ho!
MEEP?!
WOOF!
SCRATCH SCRATCH SCRATCH
...

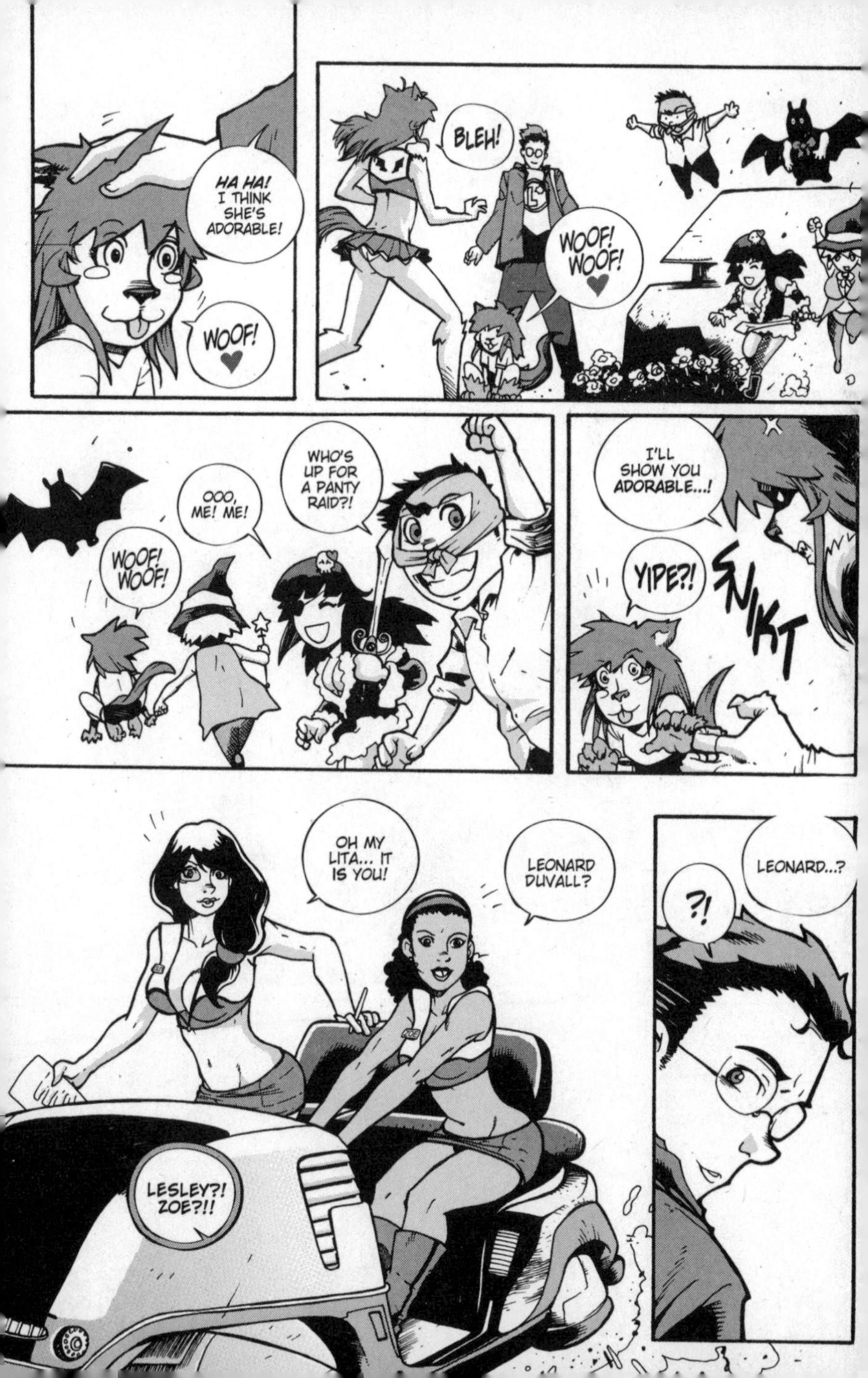
BLEH!
WOOF! WOOF!
HA HA! I THINK SHE'S ADORABLE!
WOOF!
I'LL SHOW YOU ADORABLE...!
YIPE?!
SNIKT
WHO'S UP FOR A PANTY RAID?!
OOO, ME! ME!
WOOF! WOOF!
LEONARD...?
?!
LEONARD DUVALL?
OH MY LITA... IT IS YOU!
LESLEY?! ZOE?!!

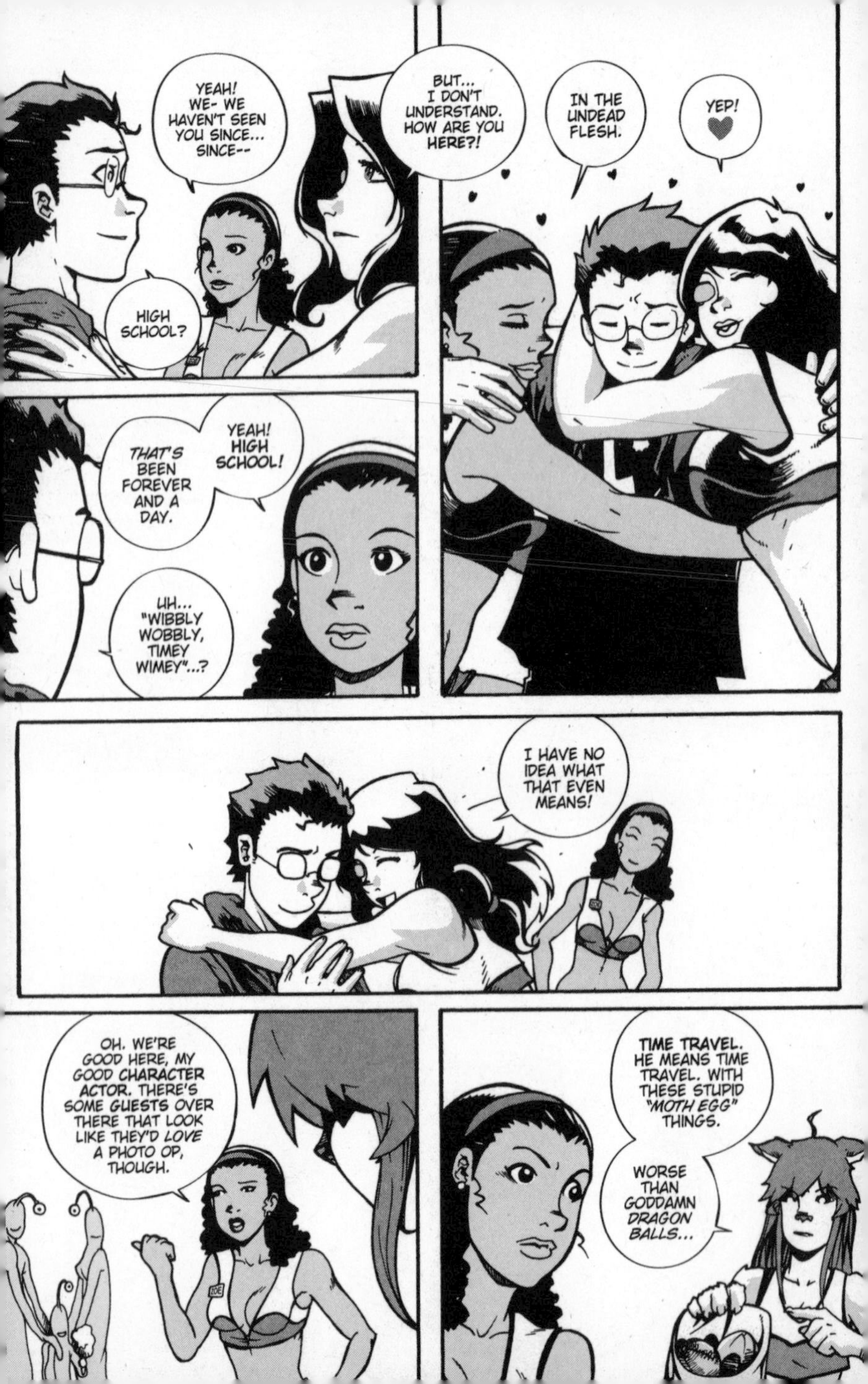
YEP! ♥
IN THE UNDEAD FLESH.
BUT... I DON'T UNDERSTAND. HOW ARE YOU HERE?!
YEAH! WE- WE HAVEN'T SEEN YOU SINCE... SINCE--
HIGH SCHOOL?
YEAH! HIGH SCHOOL!
THAT'S BEEN FOREVER AND A DAY.
UH... "WIBBLY WOBBLY, TIMEY WIMEY"...?
I HAVE NO IDEA WHAT THAT EVEN MEANS!
TIME TRAVEL. HE MEANS TIME TRAVEL. WITH THESE STUPID *"MOTH EGG"* THINGS.
WORSE THAN GODDAMN *DRAGON BALLS*...
OH. WE'RE GOOD HERE, MY GOOD **CHARACTER ACTOR**. THERE'S SOME **GUESTS** OVER THERE THAT LOOK LIKE THEY'D *LOVE* A PHOTO OP, THOUGH.

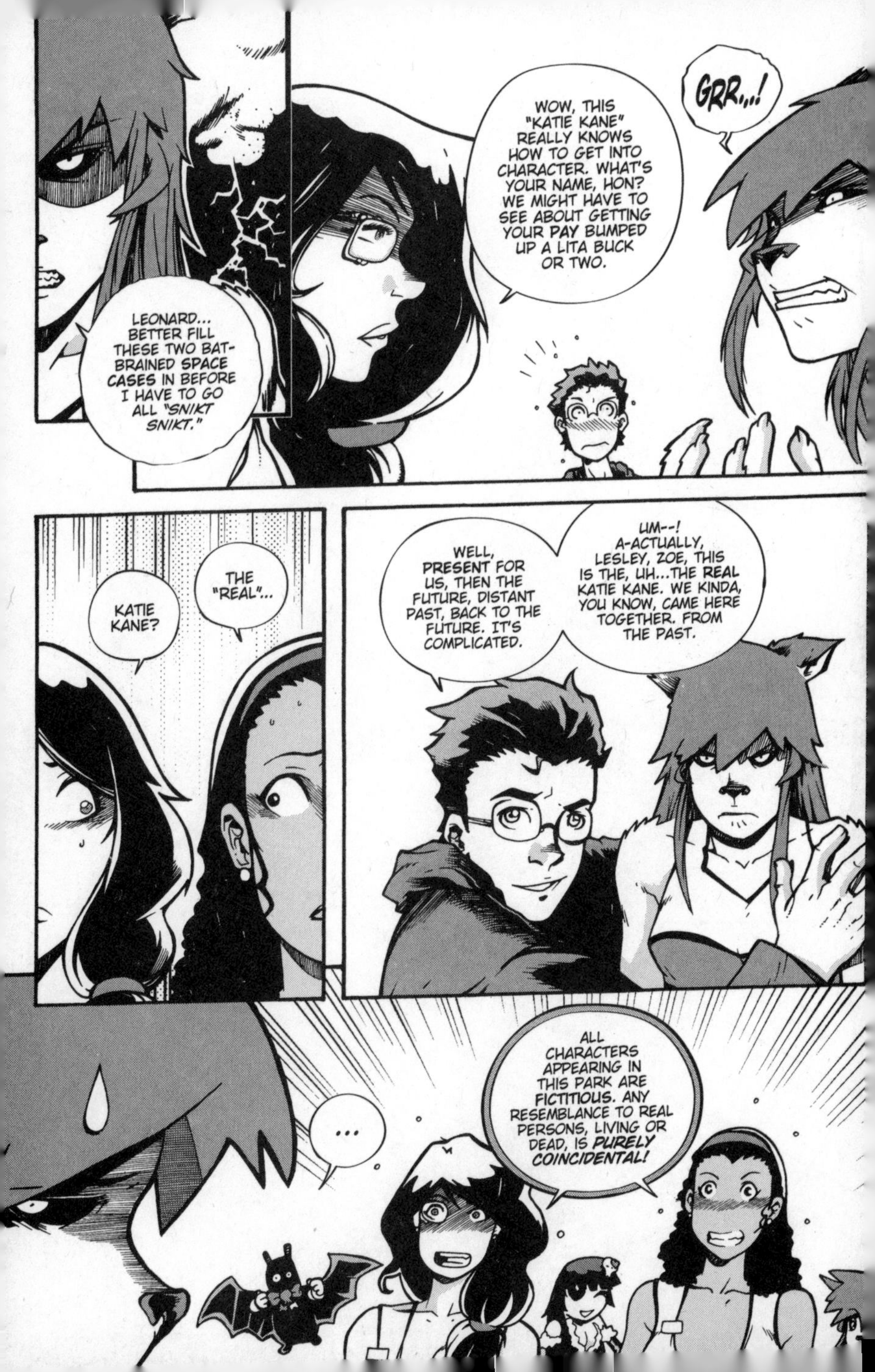
WOW, THIS "KATIE KANE" REALLY KNOWS HOW TO GET INTO CHARACTER. WHAT'S YOUR NAME, HON? WE MIGHT HAVE TO SEE ABOUT GETTING YOUR PAY BUMPED UP A LITA BUCK OR TWO.
GRR...!
LEONARD... BETTER FILL THESE TWO BAT-BRAINED SPACE CASES IN BEFORE I HAVE TO GO ALL "SNIKT SNIKT."
THE "REAL"...
KATIE KANE?
UM--! A-ACTUALLY, LESLEY, ZOE, THIS IS THE, UH...THE REAL KATIE KANE. WE KINDA, YOU KNOW, CAME HERE TOGETHER. FROM THE PAST.
WELL, PRESENT FOR US, THEN THE FUTURE, DISTANT PAST, BACK TO THE FUTURE. IT'S COMPLICATED.
...
ALL CHARACTERS APPEARING IN THIS PARK ARE FICTITIOUS. ANY RESEMBLANCE TO REAL PERSONS, LIVING OR DEAD, IS PURELY COINCIDENTAL!

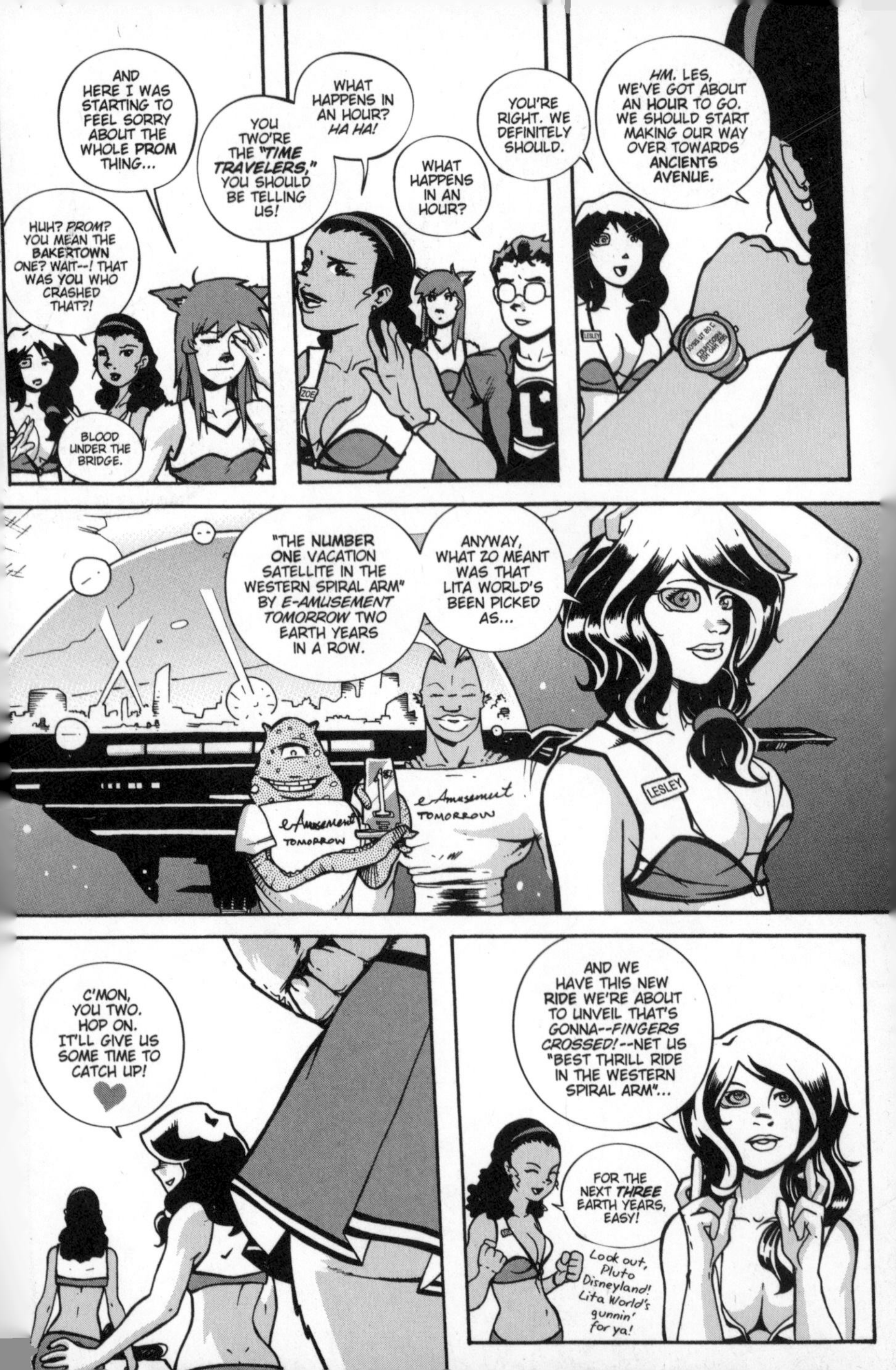

HM. LES, WE'VE GOT ABOUT AN HOUR TO GO. WE SHOULD START MAKING OUR WAY OVER TOWARDS ANCIENTS AVENUE.
LESLEY
YOU'RE RIGHT. WE DEFINITELY SHOULD.
WHAT HAPPENS IN AN HOUR?
WHAT HAPPENS IN AN HOUR? HA HA!
YOU TWO'RE THE "TIME TRAVELERS," YOU SHOULD BE TELLING US!
ZOE
AND HERE I WAS STARTING TO FEEL SORRY ABOUT THE WHOLE PROM THING...
HUH? PROM? YOU MEAN THE BAKERTOWN ONE? WAIT--! THAT WAS YOU WHO CRASHED THAT?!
BLOOD UNDER THE BRIDGE.
ANYWAY, WHAT ZO MEANT WAS THAT LITA WORLD'S BEEN PICKED AS...
"THE NUMBER ONE VACATION SATELLITE IN THE WESTERN SPIRAL ARM" BY E-AMUSEMENT TOMORROW TWO EARTH YEARS IN A ROW.
LESLEY
e-Amusement TOMORROW
e-Amusement TOMORROW
AND WE HAVE THIS NEW RIDE WE'RE ABOUT TO UNVEIL THAT'S GONNA--FINGERS CROSSED!--NET US "BEST THRILL RIDE IN THE WESTERN SPIRAL ARM"...
FOR THE NEXT THREE EARTH YEARS, EASY!
Look out, Pluto Disneyland! Lita World's gunnin' for ya!
C'MON, YOU TWO. HOP ON. IT'LL GIVE US SOME TIME TO CATCH UP!

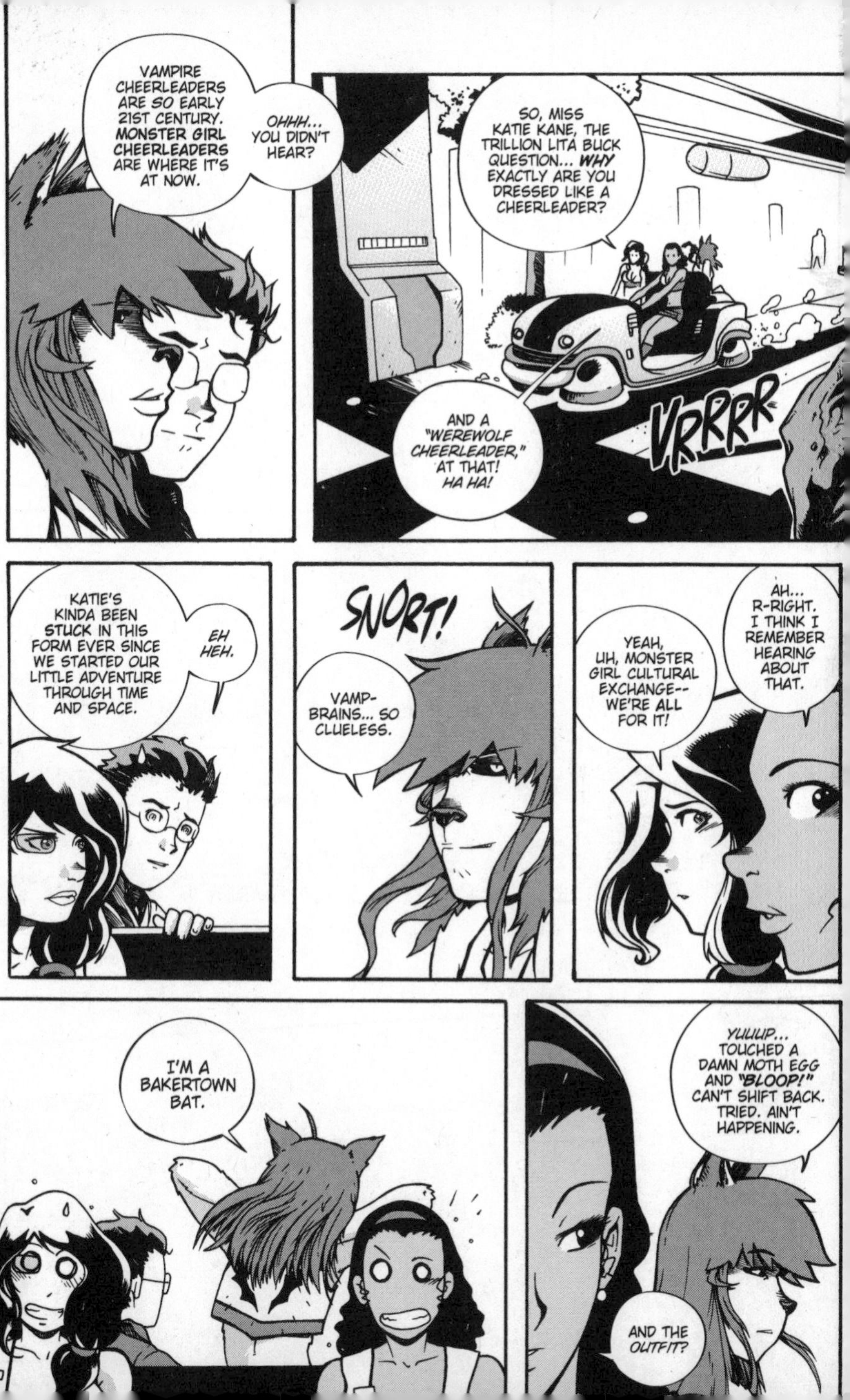
SO, MISS KATIE KANE, THE TRILLION LITA BUCK QUESTION... *WHY* EXACTLY ARE YOU DRESSED LIKE A CHEERLEADER?
AND A *"WEREWOLF CHEERLEADER,"* AT THAT! *HA HA!*
VRRRR
OHHH... YOU DIDN'T HEAR?
VAMPIRE CHEERLEADERS ARE *SO* EARLY 21ST CENTURY. **MONSTER GIRL CHEERLEADERS** ARE WHERE IT'S AT NOW.
AH... R-RIGHT. I THINK I REMEMBER HEARING ABOUT THAT.
YEAH, UH, MONSTER GIRL CULTURAL EXCHANGE-- WE'RE **ALL** FOR IT!
SNORT!
VAMP-BRAINS... SO CLUELESS.
EH HEH.
KATIE'S KINDA BEEN **STUCK** IN THIS FORM EVER SINCE WE STARTED OUR LITTLE ADVENTURE THROUGH TIME AND SPACE.
YUUUP... TOUCHED A DAMN MOTH EGG AND ***"BLOOP!"*** CAN'T SHIFT BACK. TRIED. AIN'T HAPPENING.
AND THE *OUTFIT?*
I'M A BAKERTOWN BAT.

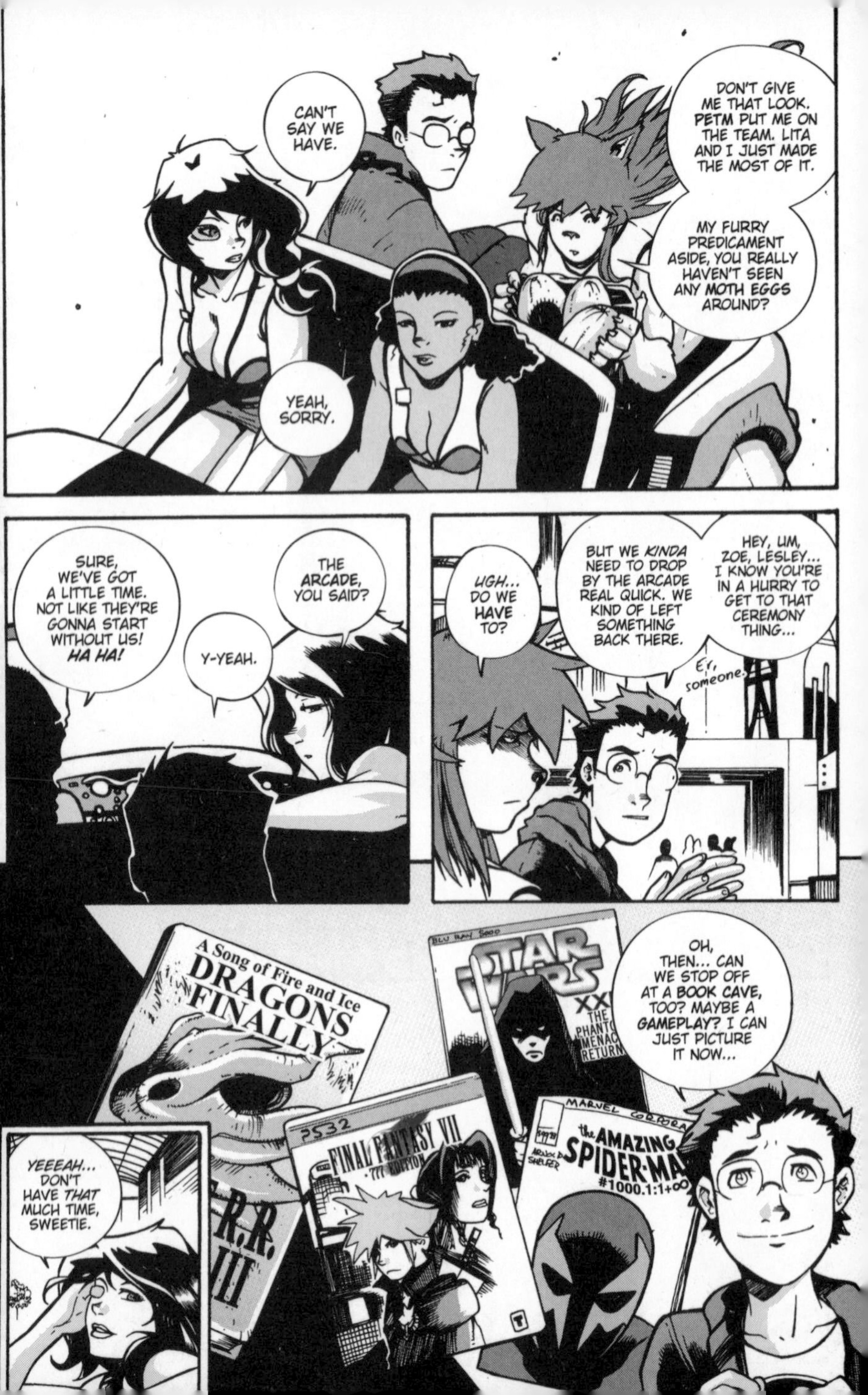
DON'T GIVE ME THAT LOOK. PETM PUT ME ON THE TEAM. LITA AND I JUST MADE THE MOST OF IT.
MY FURRY PREDICAMENT ASIDE, YOU REALLY HAVEN'T SEEN ANY MOTH EGGS AROUND?
CAN'T SAY WE HAVE.
YEAH, SORRY.
HEY, UM, ZOE, LESLEY... I KNOW YOU'RE IN A HURRY TO GET TO THAT CEREMONY THING...
BUT WE *KINDA* NEED TO DROP BY THE ARCADE REAL QUICK. WE KIND OF LEFT SOMETHING BACK THERE.
Er, someone.
UGH... DO WE HAVE TO?
THE ARCADE, YOU SAID?
SURE, WE'VE GOT A LITTLE TIME. NOT LIKE THEY'RE GONNA START WITHOUT US! ***HA HA!***
Y-YEAH.
OH, THEN... CAN WE STOP OFF AT A BOOK CAVE, TOO? MAYBE A GAMEPLAY? I CAN JUST PICTURE IT NOW...
BLU RAY 5000
A Song of Fire and Ice
DRAGONS FINALLY
PS32
FINAL FANTASY VII
the AMAZING SPIDER-MA
#1000.1:1+∞
YEEEAH... DON'T HAVE *THAT* MUCH TIME, SWEETIE.

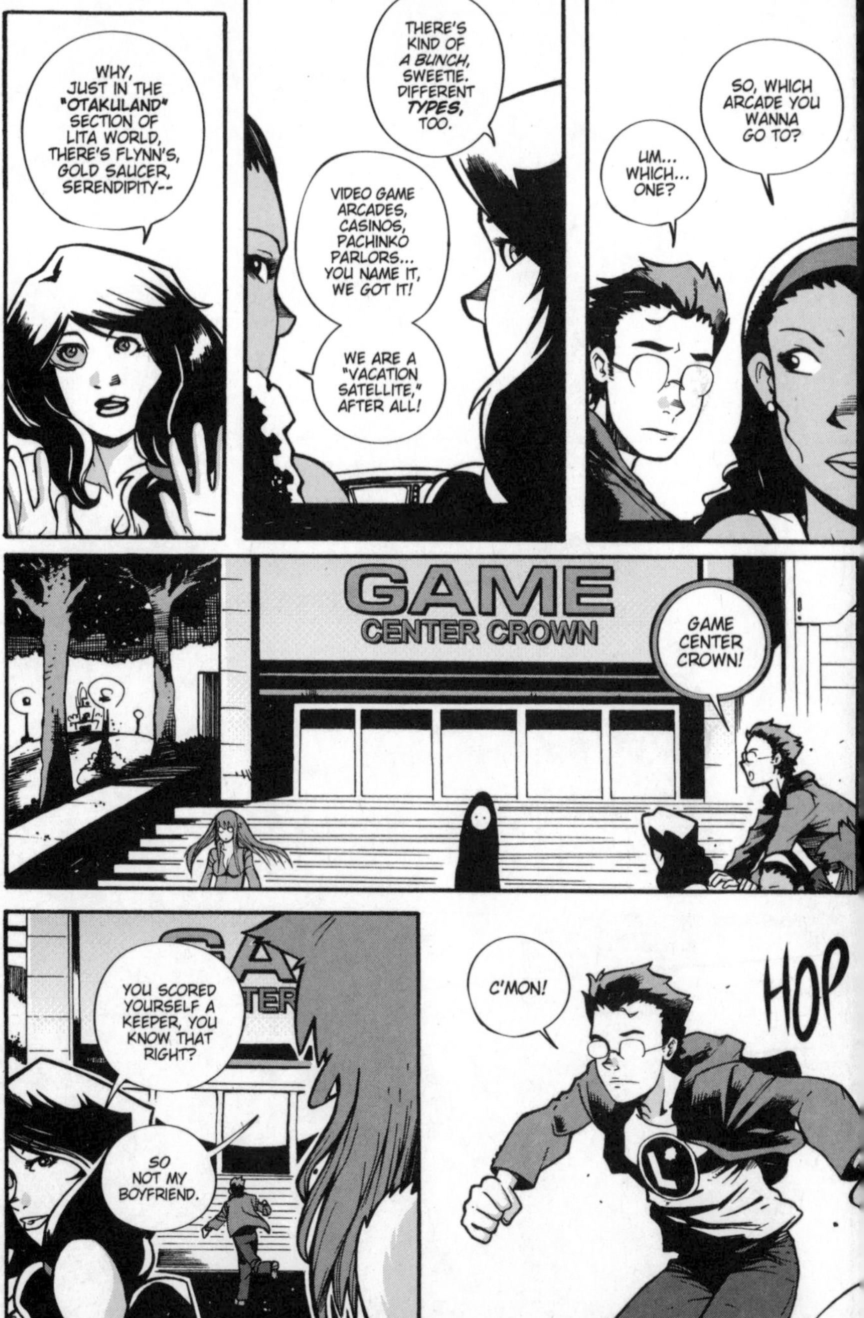
SO, WHICH ARCADE YOU WANNA GO TO?
UM... WHICH... ONE?
THERE'S KIND OF *A BUNCH,* SWEETIE. DIFFERENT *TYPES,* TOO.
VIDEO GAME ARCADES, CASINOS, PACHINKO PARLORS... YOU NAME IT, WE GOT IT!
WE ARE A "VACATION SATELLITE," AFTER ALL!
WHY, JUST IN THE **"OTAKULAND"** SECTION OF LITA WORLD, THERE'S FLYNN'S, GOLD SAUCER, SERENDIPITY--
GAME
CENTER CROWN
GAME CENTER CROWN!
HOP
C'MON!
YOU SCORED YOURSELF A KEEPER, YOU KNOW THAT RIGHT?
SO NOT MY BOYFRIEND.

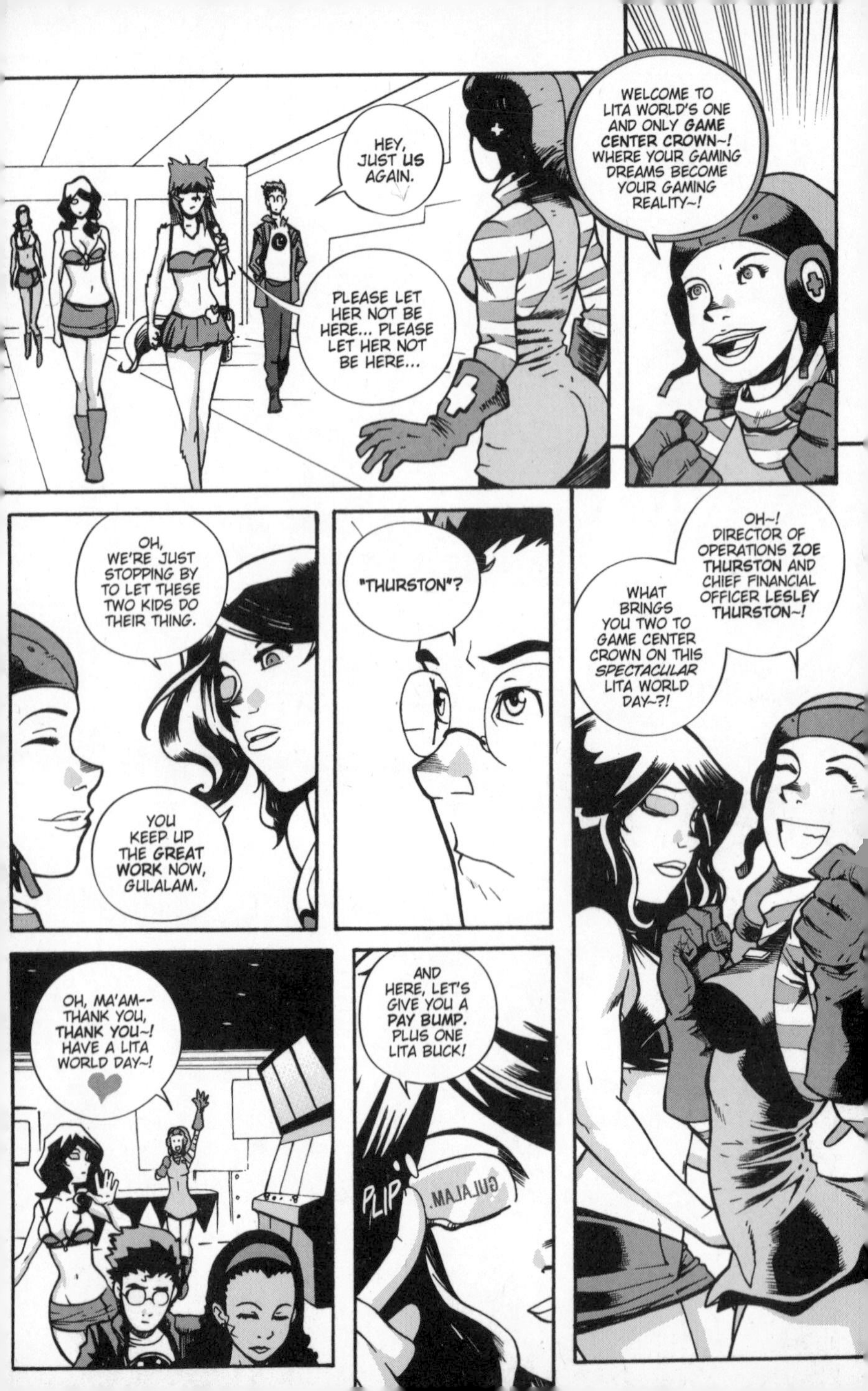
WELCOME TO LITA WORLD'S ONE AND ONLY **GAME CENTER CROWN**~! WHERE YOUR GAMING DREAMS BECOME YOUR GAMING REALITY~!
HEY, JUST **US** AGAIN.
PLEASE LET HER NOT BE HERE... PLEASE LET HER NOT BE HERE...
OH~! DIRECTOR OF OPERATIONS **ZOE THURSTON** AND CHIEF FINANCIAL OFFICER **LESLEY THURSTON**~!
WHAT BRINGS YOU TWO TO GAME CENTER CROWN ON THIS *SPECTACULAR* LITA WORLD DAY~?!
"THURSTON"?
OH, WE'RE JUST STOPPING BY TO LET THESE TWO KIDS DO THEIR THING.
YOU KEEP UP THE **GREAT WORK** NOW, GULALAM.
AND HERE, LET'S GIVE YOU A **PAY BUMP**. PLUS ONE LITA BUCK!
PLIP
OH, MA'AM-- THANK YOU, **THANK YOU**~! HAVE A LITA WORLD DAY~!

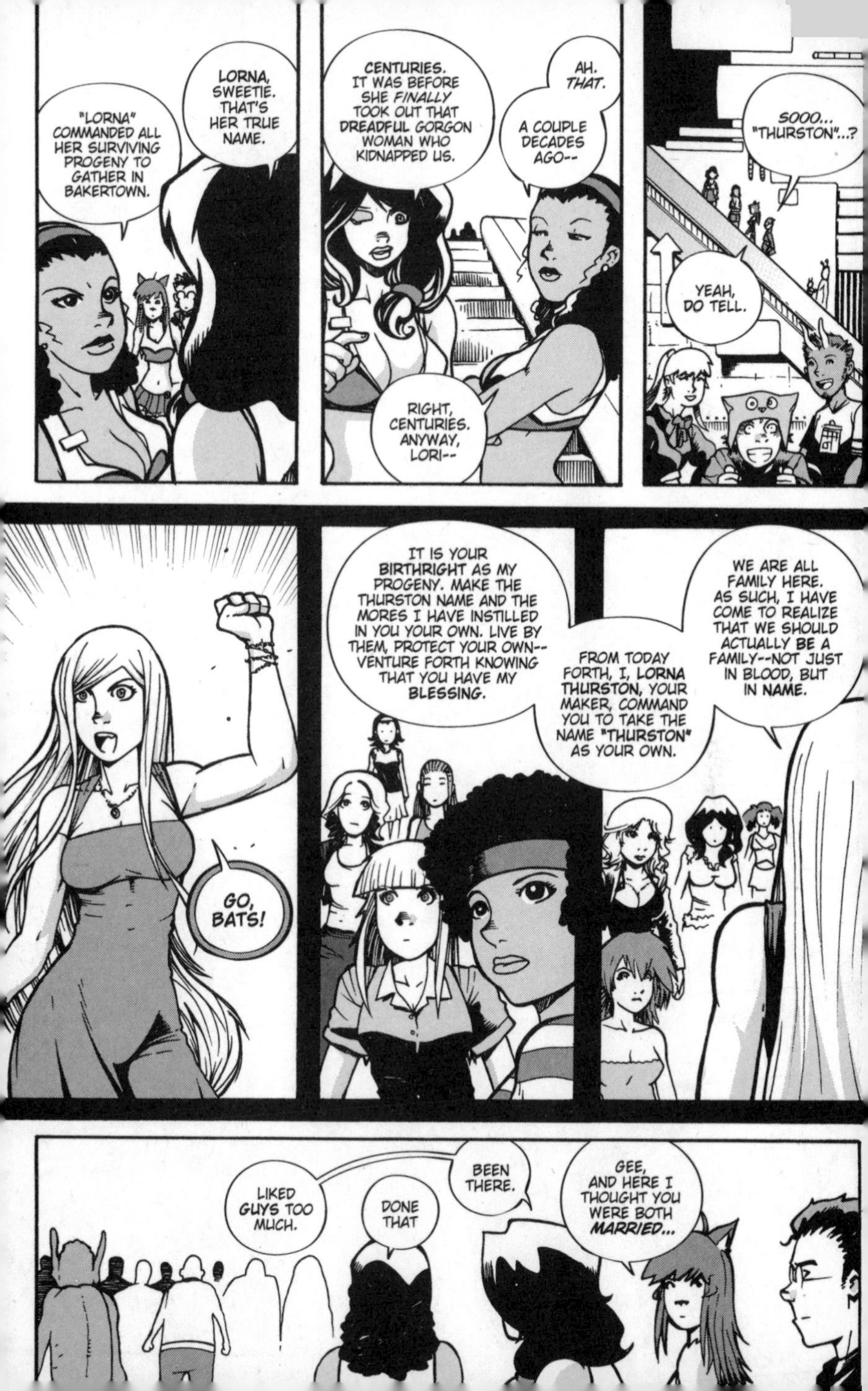

SOOO... "THURSTON"...?
YEAH, DO TELL.
AH. *THAT.*
A COUPLE DECADES AGO--
CENTURIES. IT WAS BEFORE SHE *FINALLY* TOOK OUT THAT DREADFUL GORGON WOMAN WHO KIDNAPPED US.
RIGHT, CENTURIES. ANYWAY, LORI--
LORNA, SWEETIE. THAT'S HER TRUE NAME.
"LORNA" COMMANDED ALL HER SURVIVING PROGENY TO GATHER IN BAKERTOWN.
WE ARE ALL FAMILY HERE. AS SUCH, I HAVE COME TO REALIZE THAT WE SHOULD ACTUALLY **BE** A FAMILY--NOT JUST IN BLOOD, BUT IN **NAME.**
FROM TODAY FORTH, I, **LORNA THURSTON,** YOUR MAKER, COMMAND YOU TO TAKE THE NAME **"THURSTON"** AS YOUR OWN.
IT IS YOUR **BIRTHRIGHT** AS MY PROGENY. MAKE THE THURSTON NAME AND THE MORES I HAVE INSTILLED IN YOU YOUR OWN. LIVE BY THEM, PROTECT YOUR OWN--VENTURE FORTH KNOWING THAT YOU HAVE MY **BLESSING.**
GO, BATS!
GEE, AND HERE I THOUGHT YOU WERE BOTH ***MARRIED...***
BEEN THERE.
DONE THAT
LIKED **GUYS** TOO MUCH.

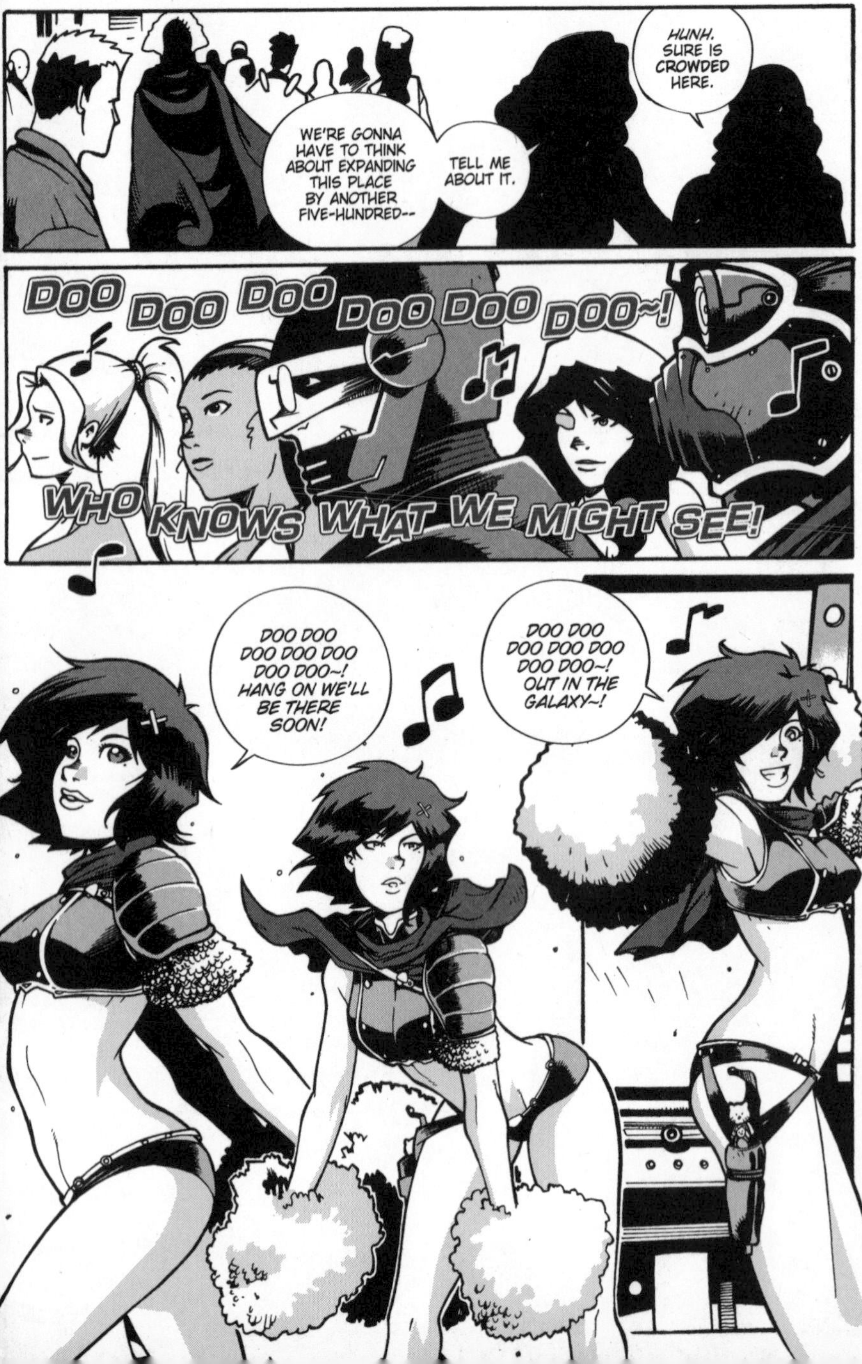
HUNH. SURE IS CROWDED HERE.
TELL ME ABOUT IT.
WE'RE GONNA HAVE TO THINK ABOUT EXPANDING THIS PLACE BY ANOTHER FIVE-HUNDRED--
DOO DOO DOO DOO DOO DOO~!
WHO KNOWS WHAT WE MIGHT SEE!
DOO DOO DOO DOO DOO DOO DOO~! OUT IN THE GALAXY~!
DOO DOO DOO DOO DOO DOO DOO~! HANG ON WE'LL BE THERE SOON!

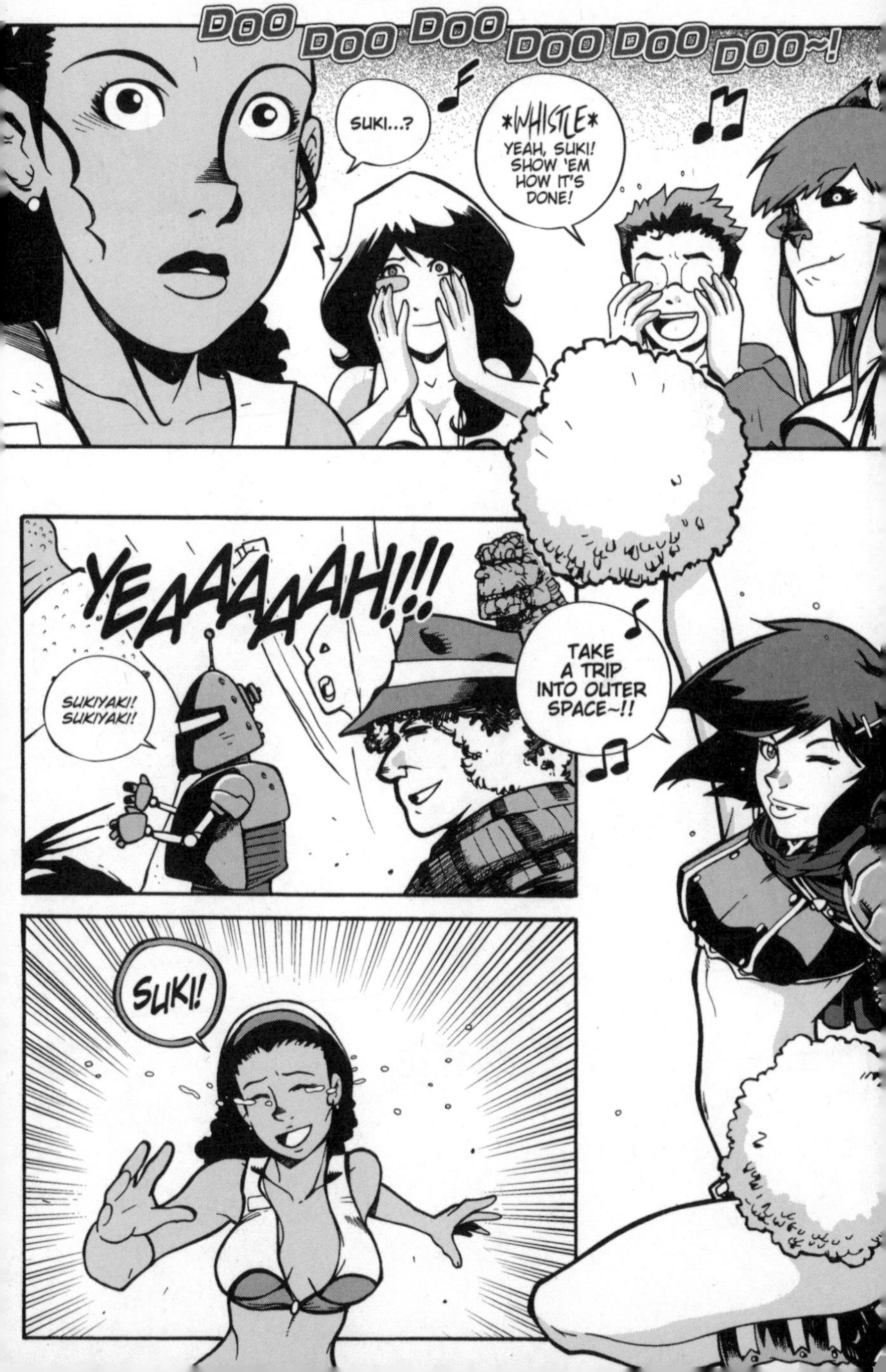
DOO DOO DOO DOO DOO DOO~!
WHISTLE YEAH, SUKI! SHOW 'EM HOW IT'S DONE!
SUKI...?
TAKE A TRIP INTO OUTER SPACE~!!
YEAAAAAH!!!
SUKIYAKI! SUKIYAKI!
SUKI!

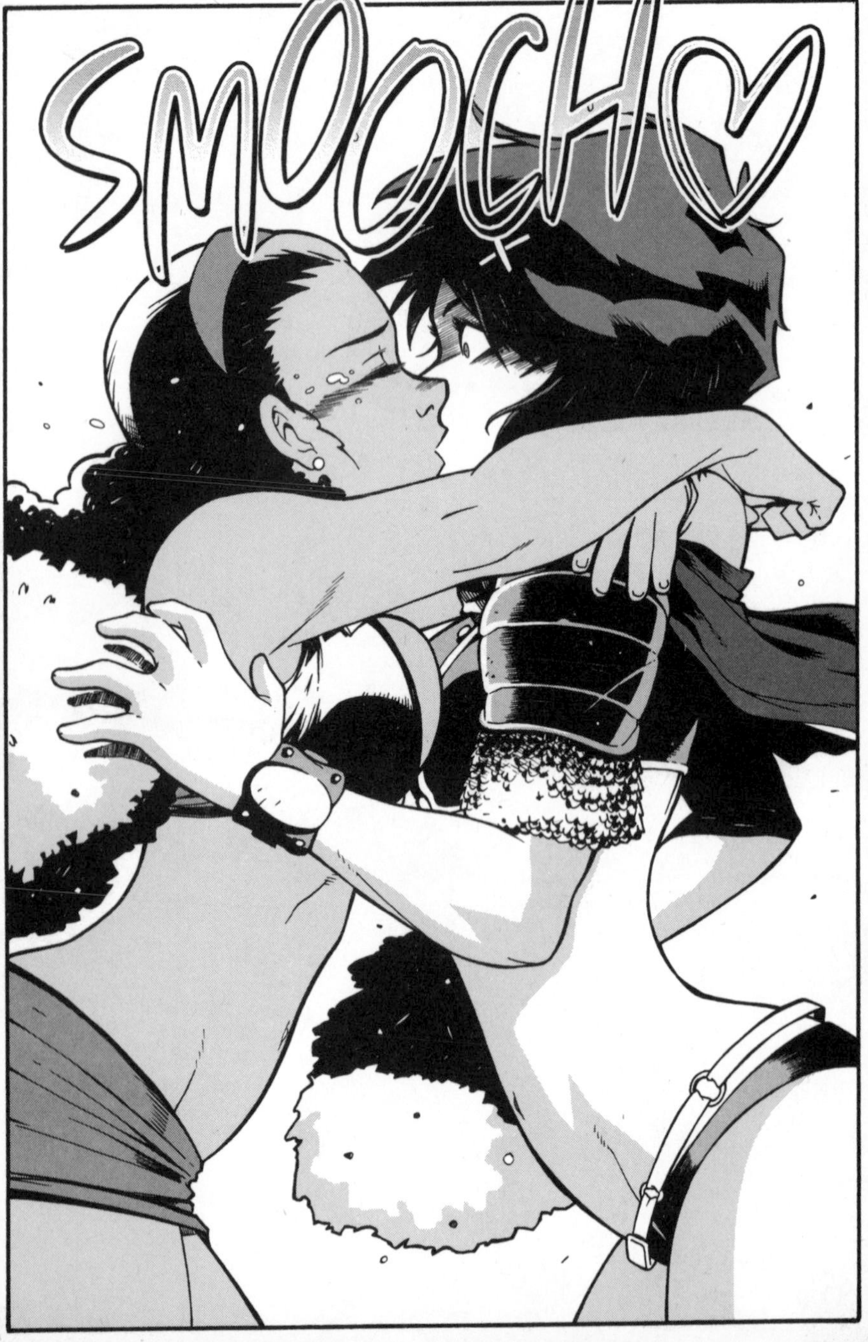
SMOOCH♡

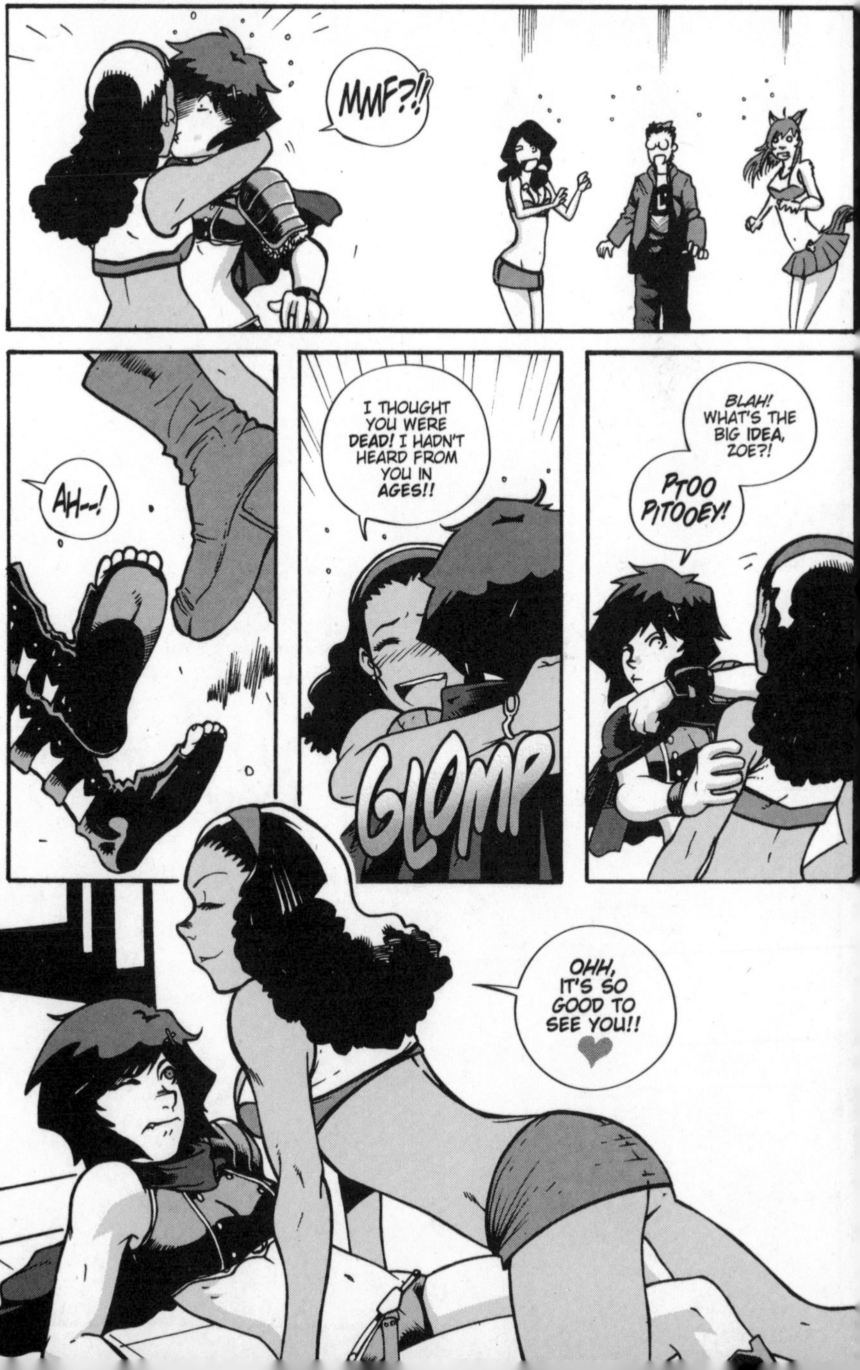
MMF?!!
BLAH! WHAT'S THE BIG IDEA, ZOE?!
PTOO PITOOEY!
I THOUGHT YOU WERE DEAD! I HADN'T HEARD FROM YOU IN AGES!!
GLOMP
AH--!
OHH, IT'S SO GOOD TO SEE YOU!! ♥

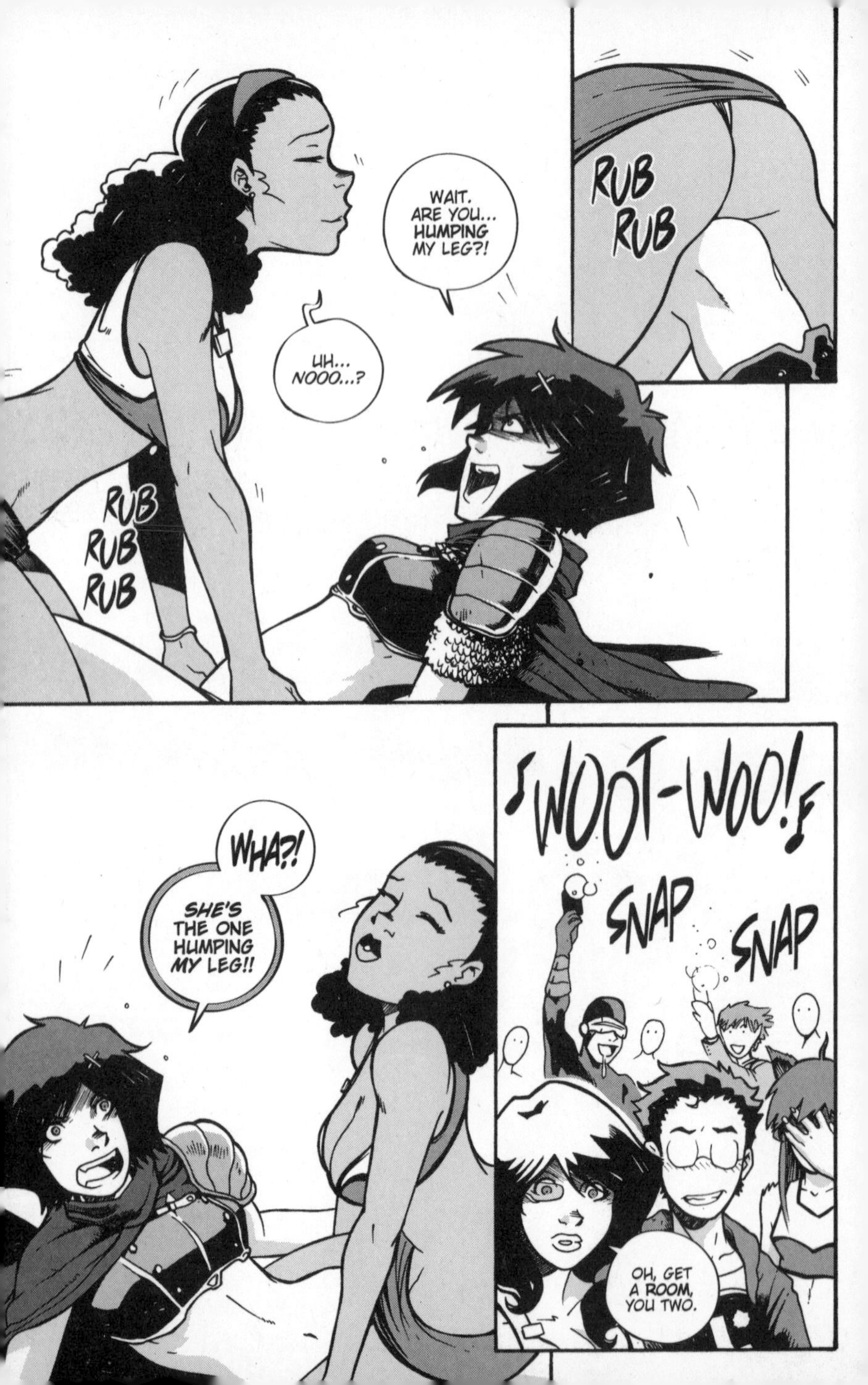
RUB RUB
WAIT. ARE YOU... HUMPING MY LEG?!
UH... NOOO...?
RUB RUB RUB
WOOT-WOO!
SNAP
SNAP
OH, GET A ROOM, YOU TWO.
WHA?!
SHE'S THE ONE HUMPING MY LEG!!

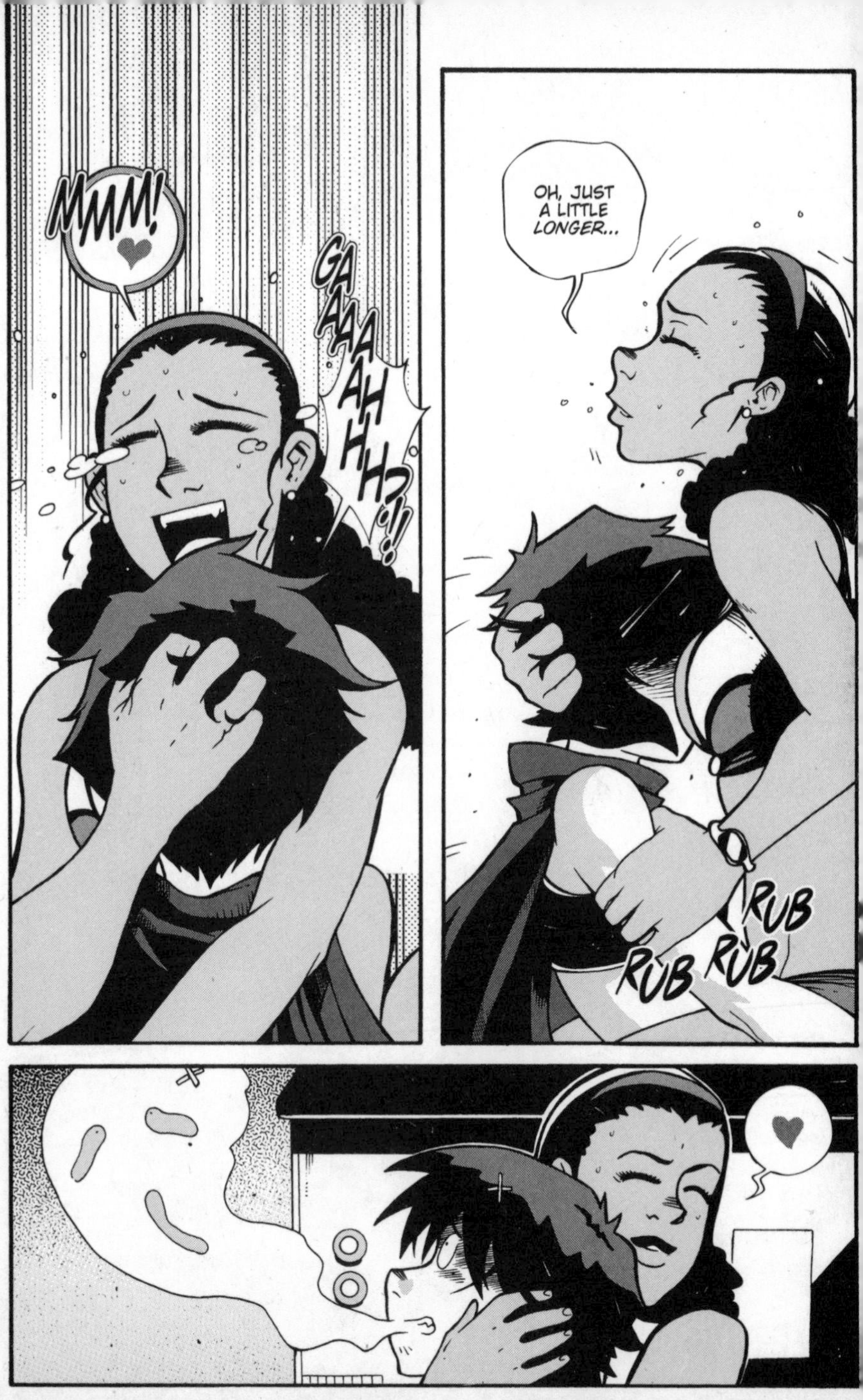
OH, JUST A LITTLE LONGER...
RUB RUB
RUB
MMM!
GAAAAAHHH?!!

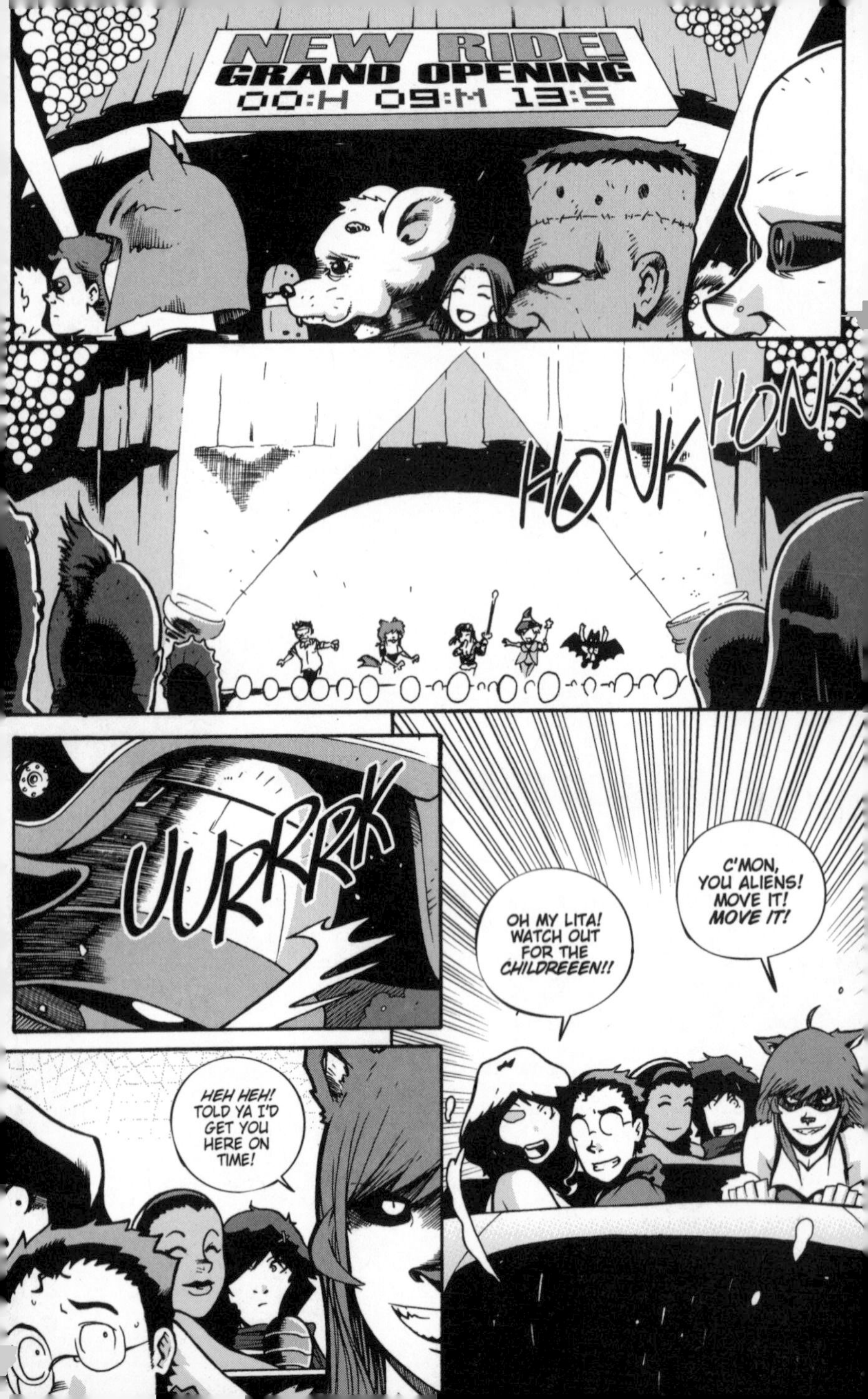
NEW RIDE!
GRAND OPENING
00:H 09:M 13:S
HONK HONK
C'MON, YOU ALIENS! MOVE IT! *MOVE IT!*
OH MY LITA! WATCH OUT FOR THE *CHILDREEEN!!*
UURRRRK
HEH HEH! TOLD YA I'D GET YOU HERE ON TIME!

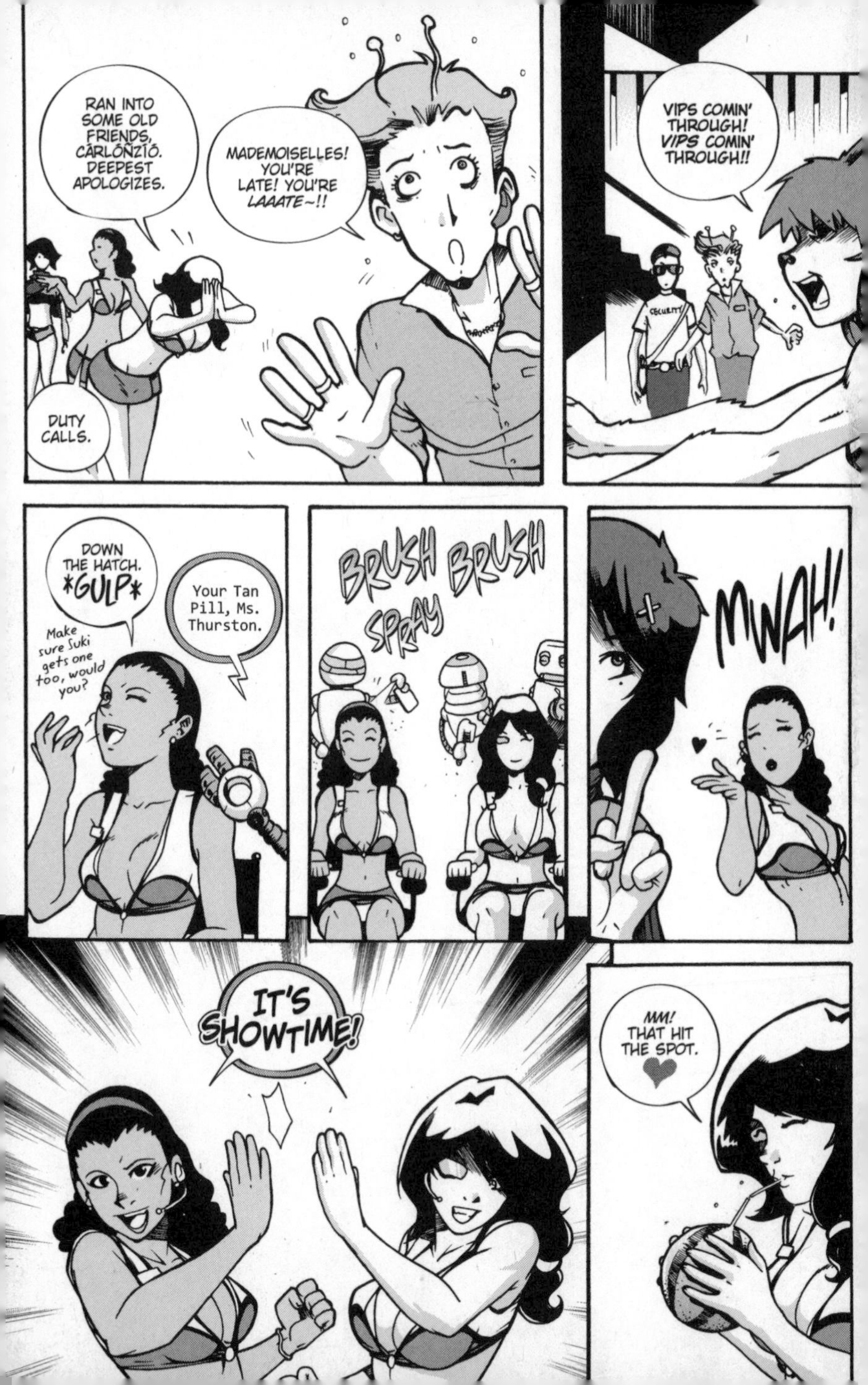
VIPS COMIN' THROUGH! VIPS COMIN' THROUGH!!
MADEMOISELLES! YOU'RE LATE! YOU'RE LAAATE~!!
RAN INTO SOME OLD FRIENDS, CĀRLŌÑZĪŌ. DEEPEST APOLOGIZES.
DUTY CALLS.
MWAH!
BRUSH BRUSH
SPRAY
Your Tan Pill, Ms. Thurston.
DOWN THE HATCH. *GULP*
Make sure Suki gets one too, would you?
MM! THAT HIT THE SPOT.
IT'S SHOWTIME!

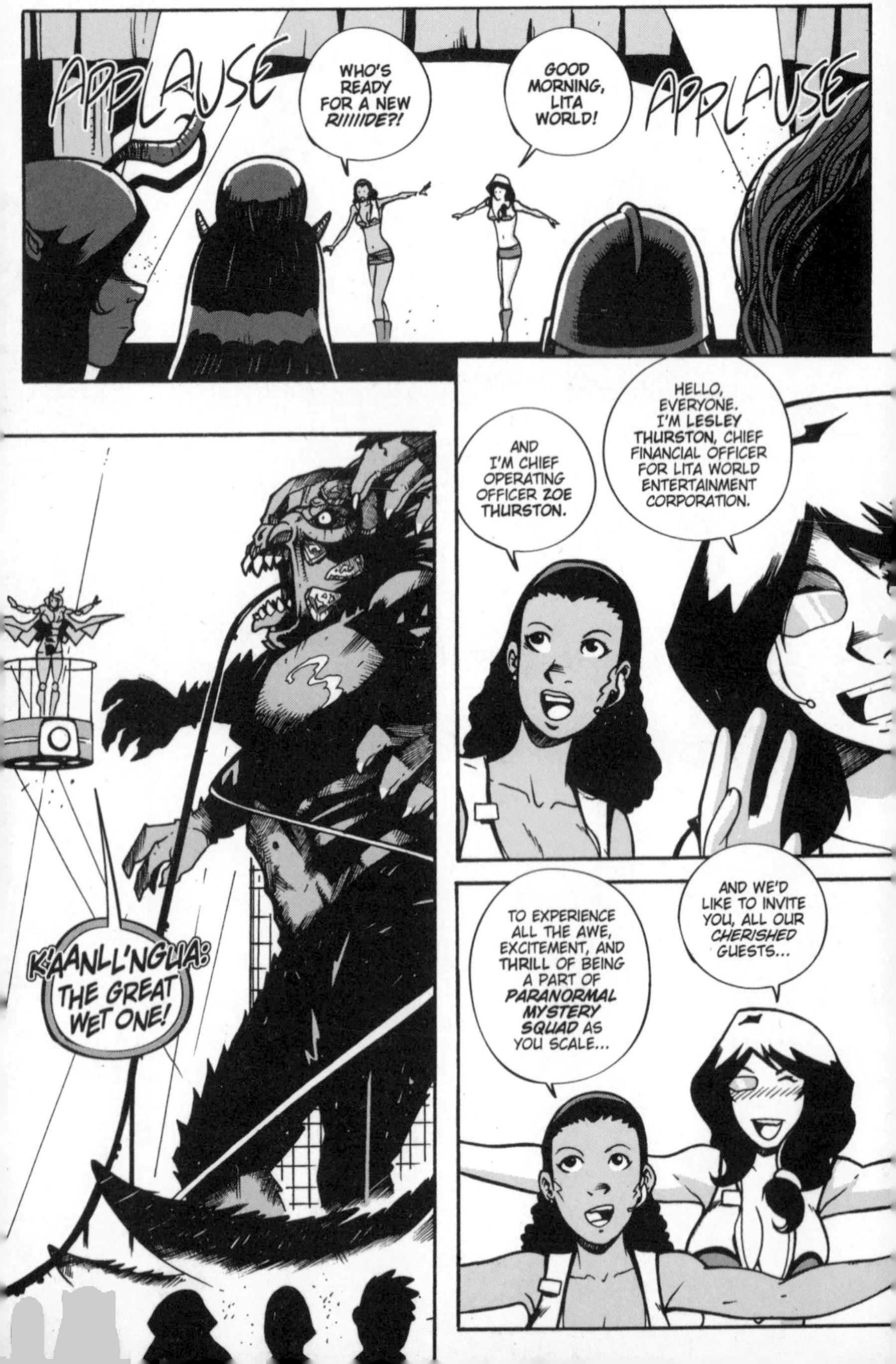
APPLAUSE
GOOD MORNING, LITA WORLD!
WHO'S READY FOR A NEW *RIIIIIDE?!*
APPLAUSE
HELLO, EVERYONE. I'M **LESLEY THURSTON**, CHIEF FINANCIAL OFFICER FOR LITA WORLD ENTERTAINMENT CORPORATION.
AND I'M CHIEF OPERATING OFFICER **ZOE THURSTON.**
AND WE'D LIKE TO INVITE YOU, ALL OUR *CHERISHED* GUESTS...
TO EXPERIENCE ALL THE AWE, EXCITEMENT, AND THRILL OF BEING A PART OF ***PARANORMAL MYSTERY SQUAD*** AS YOU SCALE...
K'AANLL'NGLIA: THE GREAT WET ONE!

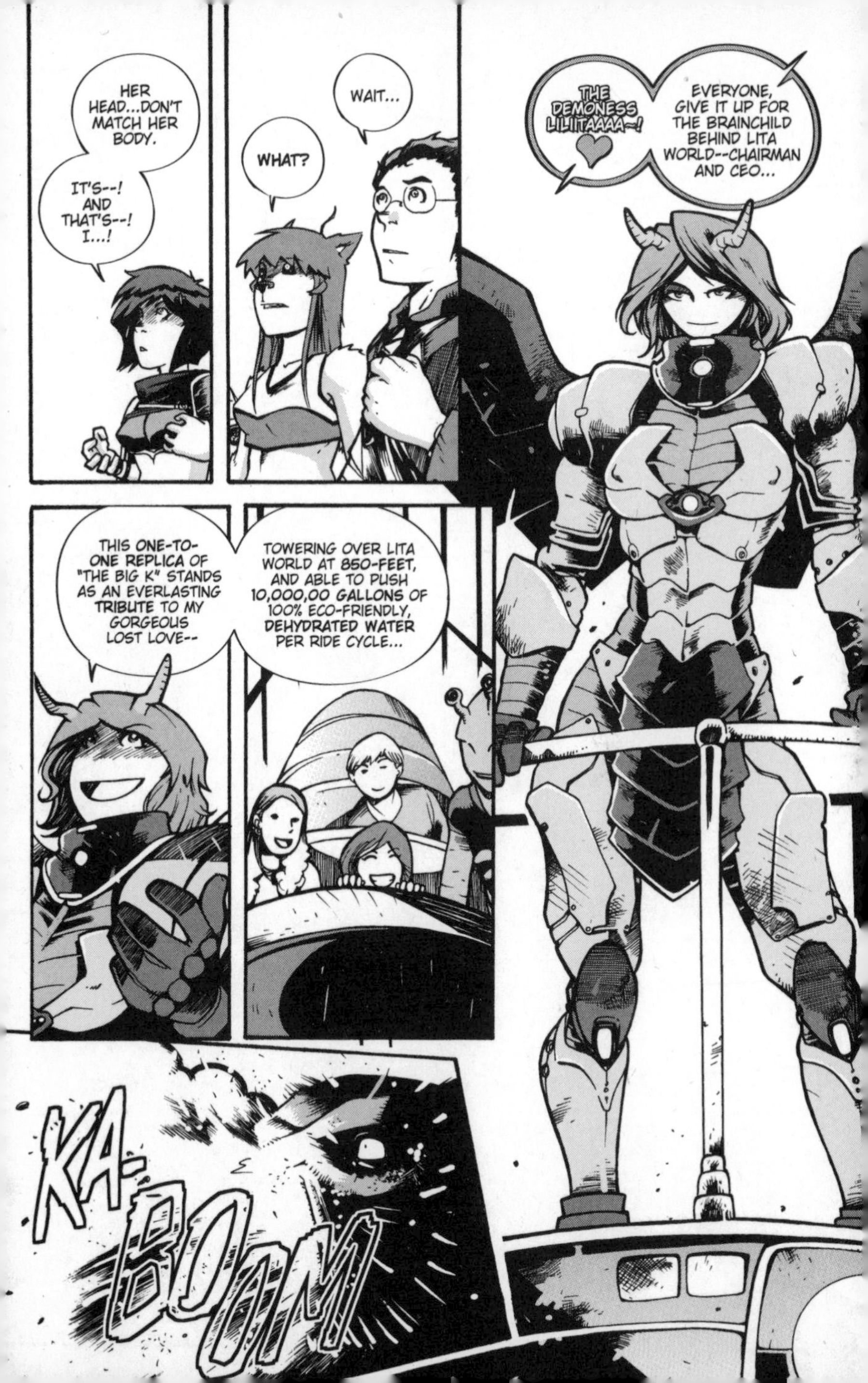
EVERYONE, GIVE IT UP FOR THE BRAINCHILD BEHIND LITA WORLD--CHAIRMAN AND CEO...
THE DEMONESS LILIITAAAA~!
WAIT...
WHAT?
HER HEAD...DON'T MATCH HER BODY.
IT'S--! AND THAT'S--! I...!
TOWERING OVER LITA WORLD AT 850-FEET, AND ABLE TO PUSH 10,000,00 GALLONS OF 100% ECO-FRIENDLY, DEHYDRATED WATER PER RIDE CYCLE...
THIS ONE-TO-ONE REPLICA OF "THE BIG K" STANDS AS AN EVERLASTING TRIBUTE TO MY GORGEOUS LOST LOVE--
KA-BOOM

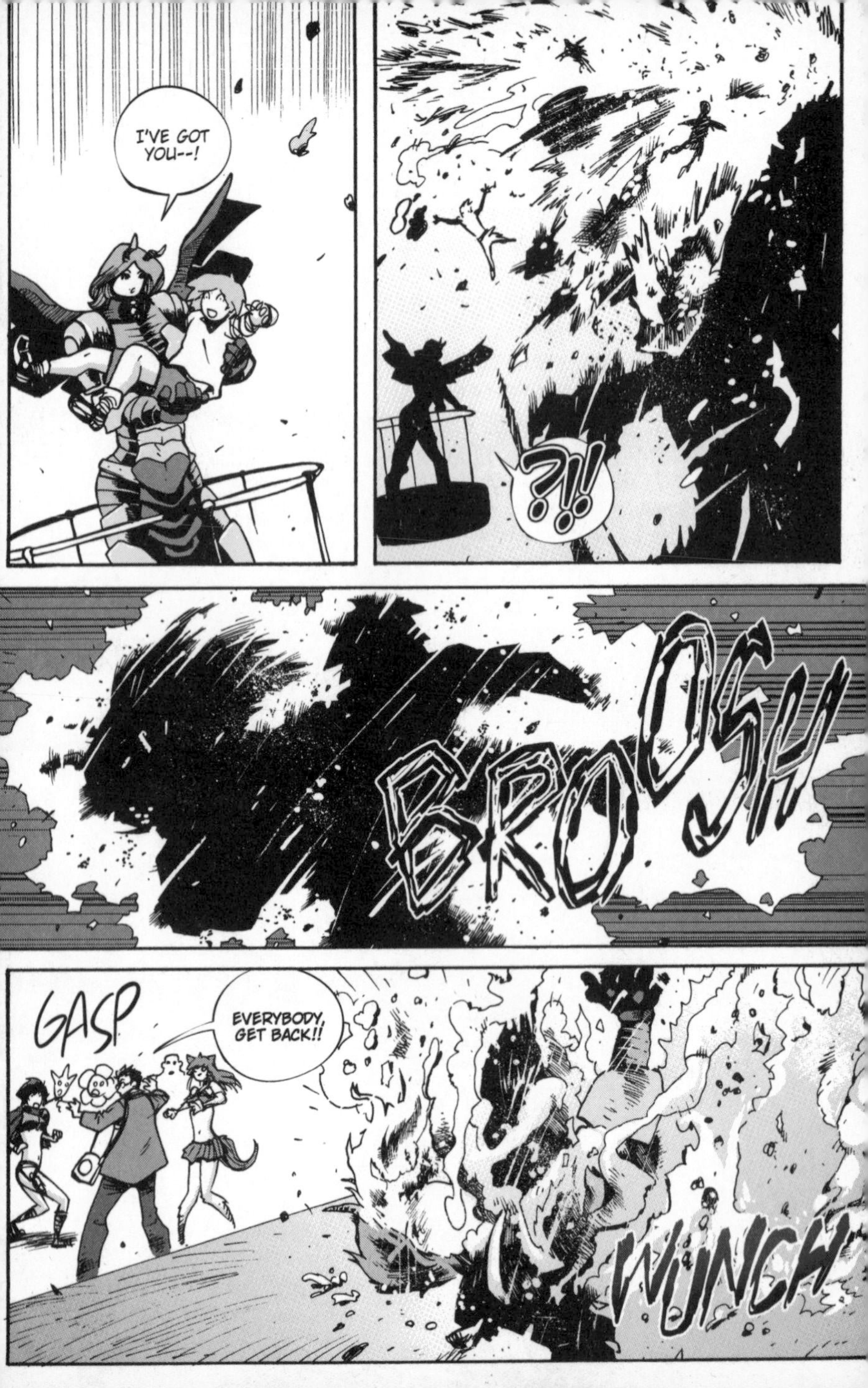
?!!
I'VE GOT YOU--!
BROOSH
EVERYBODY, GET BACK!!
GASP
WUNCH

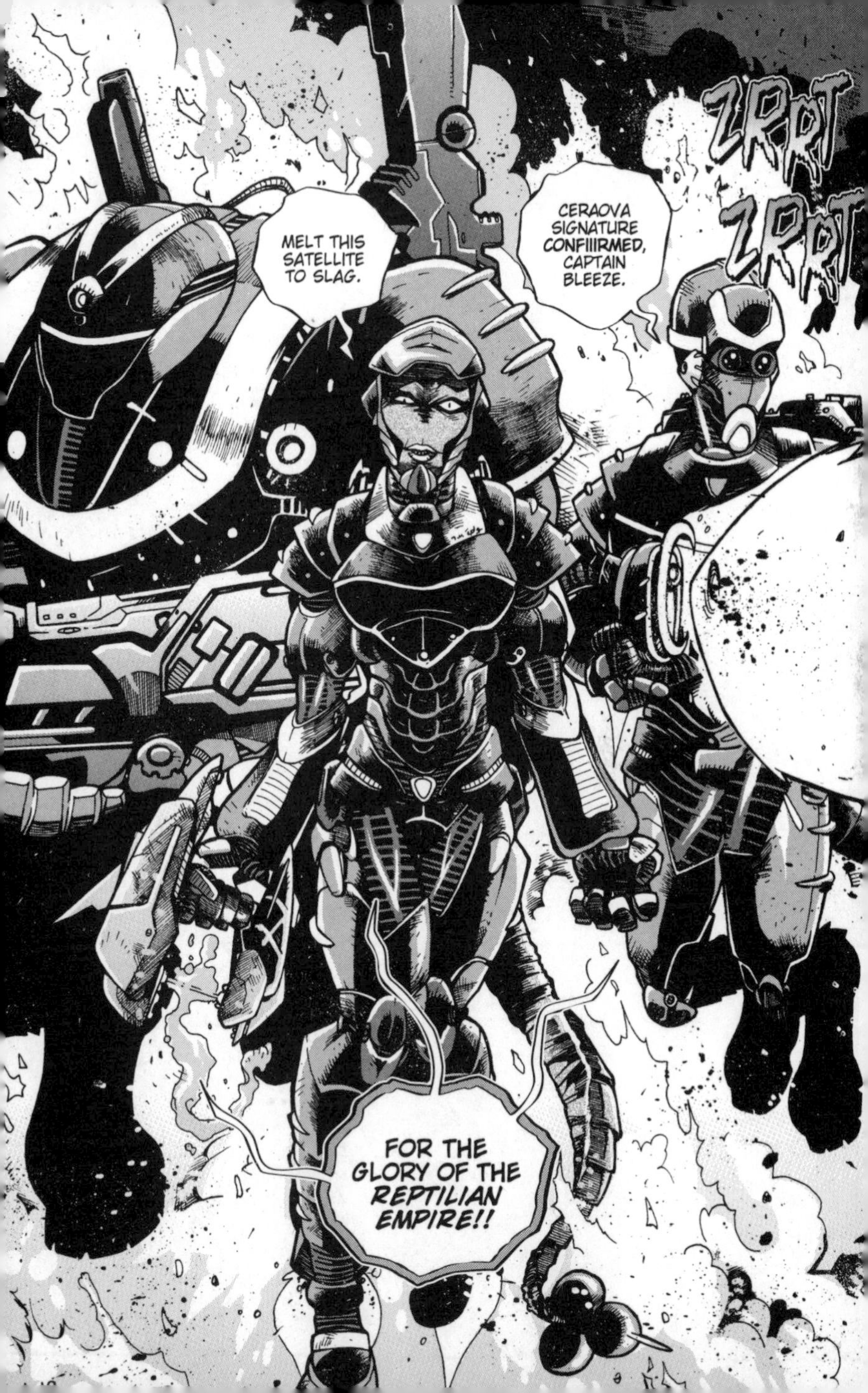
ZRRT
ZRRT
CERAOVA SIGNATURE CONFIIIRMED, CAPTAIN BLEEZE.
MELT THIS SATELLITE TO SLAG.
FOR THE GLORY OF THE *REPTILIAN EMPIRE!!*

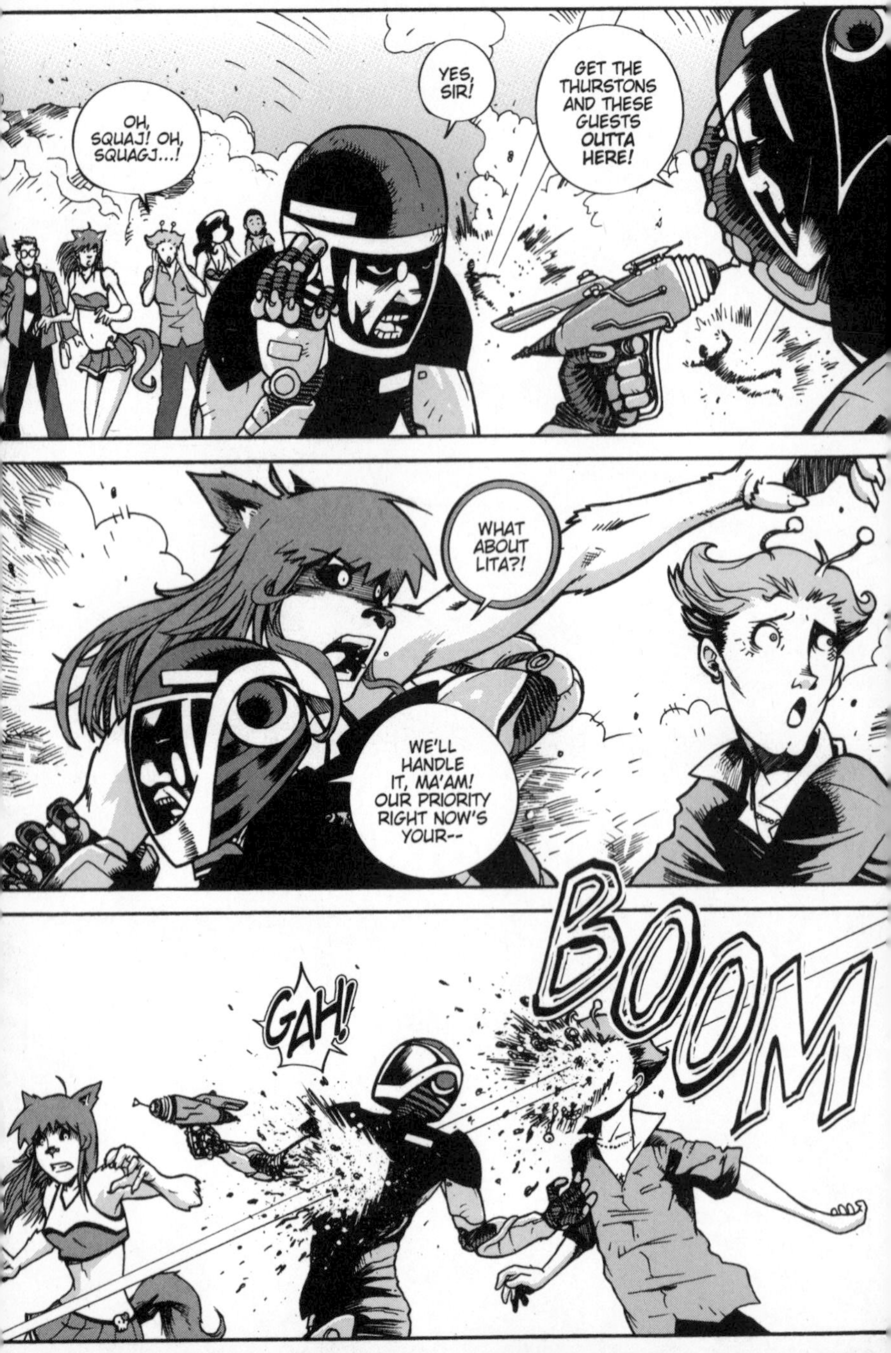
GET THE THURSTONS AND THESE GUESTS OUTTA HERE!
YES, SIR!
OH, SQUAJ! OH, SQUAGJ...!
WHAT ABOUT LITA?!
WE'LL HANDLE IT, MA'AM! OUR PRIORITY RIGHT NOW'S YOUR--
BOOM
GAH!

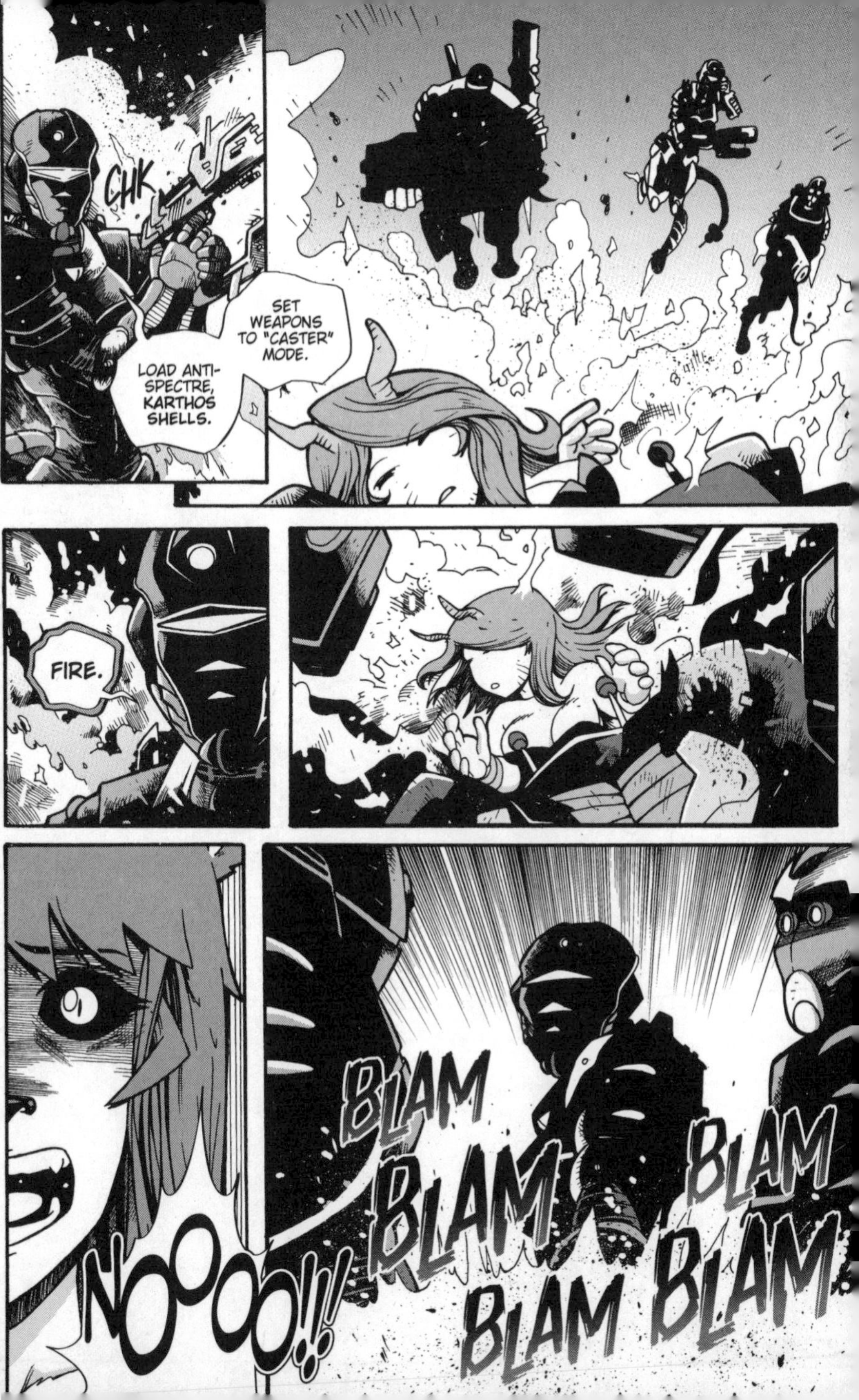
CHK
SET WEAPONS TO "CASTER" MODE.
LOAD ANTI-SPECTRE, KARTHOS SHELLS.
FIRE.
BLAM
BLAM
BLAM
BLAM
BLAM
BLAM
NOOOO!!

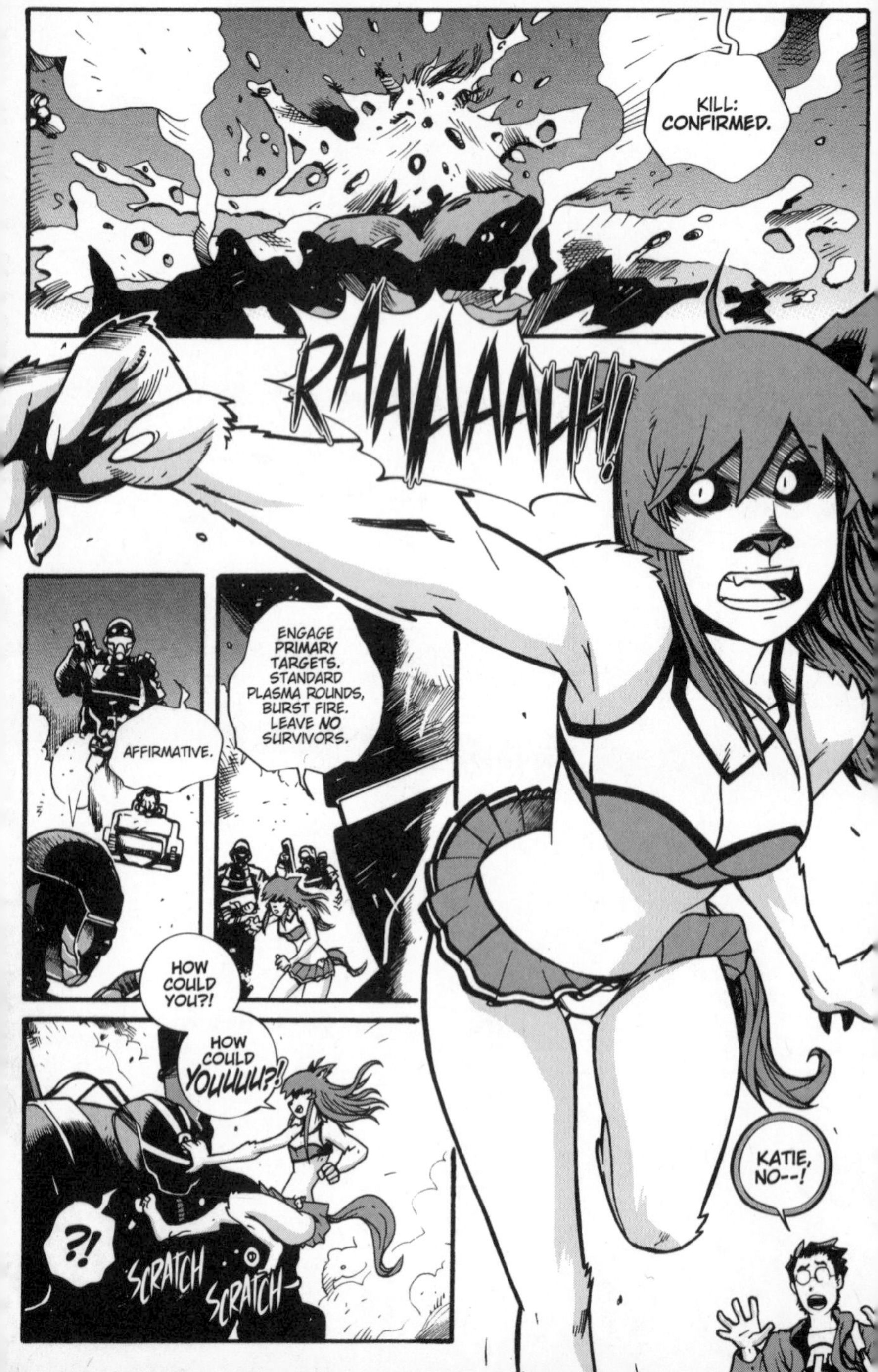
KILL: CONFIRMED.
RAAAAAHH!!
KATIE, NO--!
ENGAGE PRIMARY TARGETS. STANDARD PLASMA ROUNDS, BURST FIRE. LEAVE NO SURVIVORS.
AFFIRMATIVE.
HOW COULD YOU?!
HOW COULD YOUUUU?!
?!
SCRATCH
SCRATCH

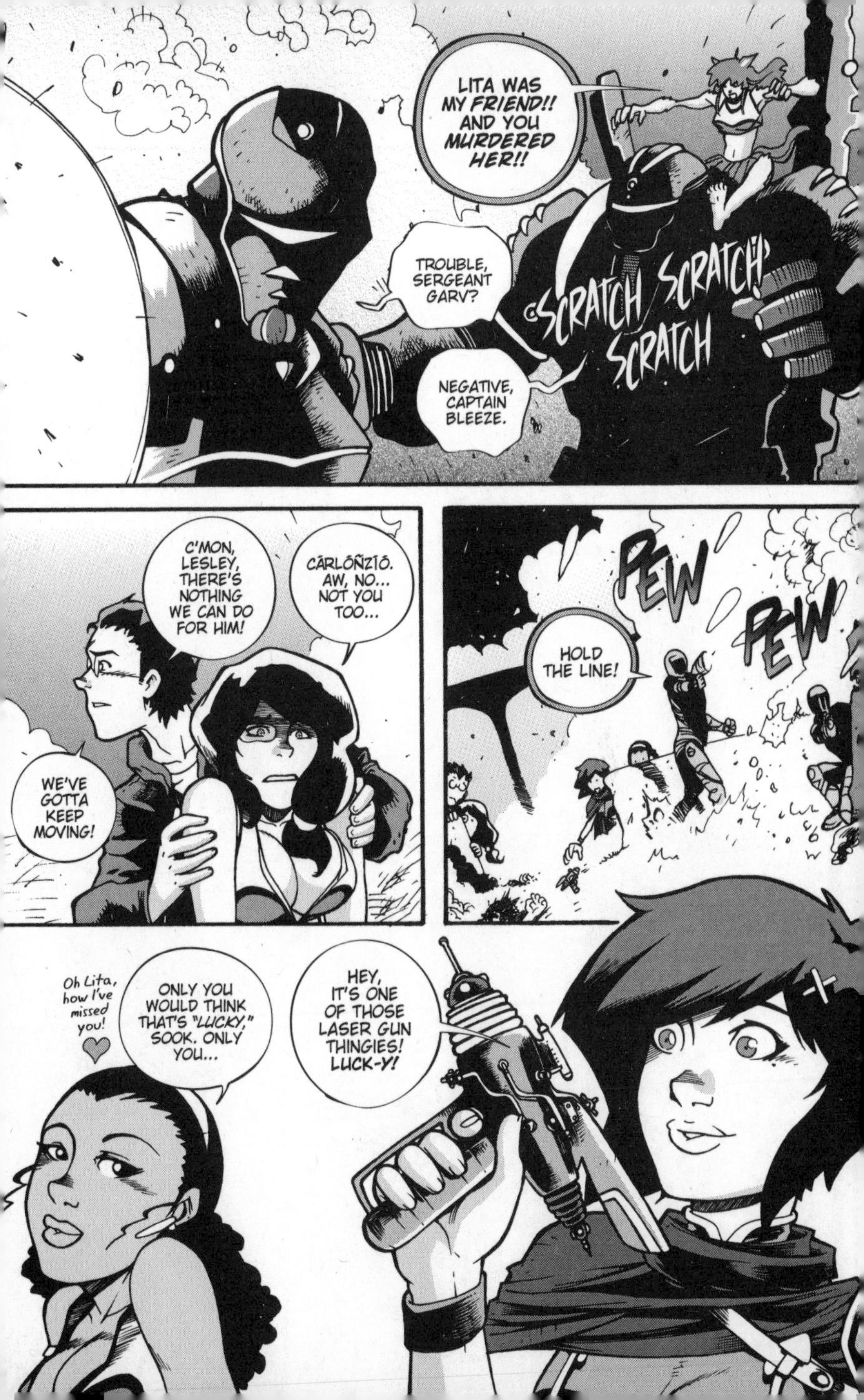

LITA WAS MY FRIEND!! AND YOU MURDERED HER!!
SCRATCH SCRATCH SCRATCH SCRATCH
TROUBLE, SERGEANT GARV?
NEGATIVE, CAPTAIN BLEEZE.
PEW PEW
HOLD THE LINE!
CĀRLŌÑZĪŌ. AW, NO... NOT YOU TOO...
C'MON, LESLEY, THERE'S NOTHING WE CAN DO FOR HIM!
WE'VE GOTTA KEEP MOVING!
HEY, IT'S ONE OF THOSE LASER GUN THINGIES! LUCK-Y!
ONLY YOU WOULD THINK THAT'S "LUCKY," SOOK. ONLY YOU...
Oh Lita, how I've missed you! ♥

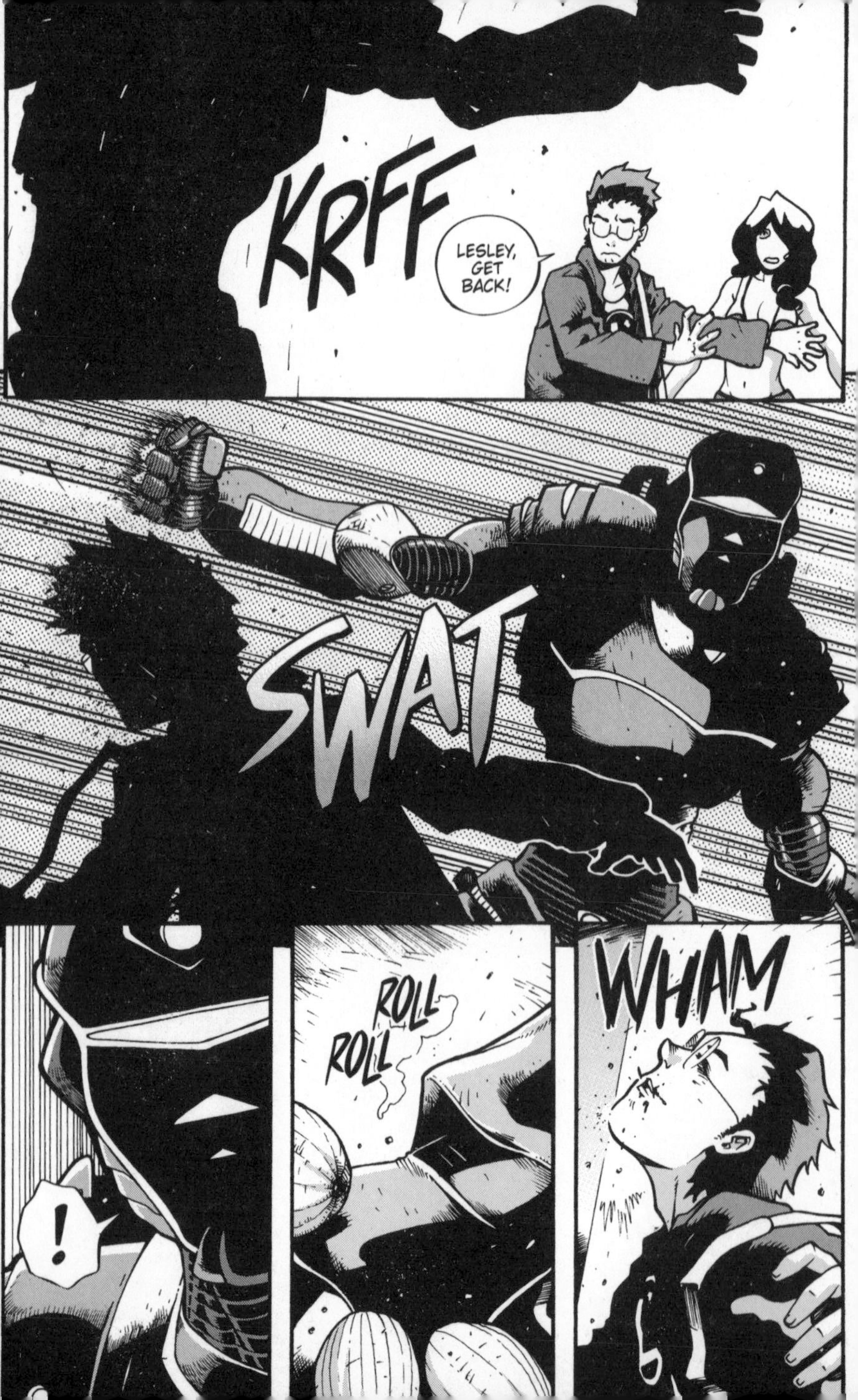
KRFF
LESLEY, GET BACK!
SWAT
WHAM
ROLL
ROLL
!

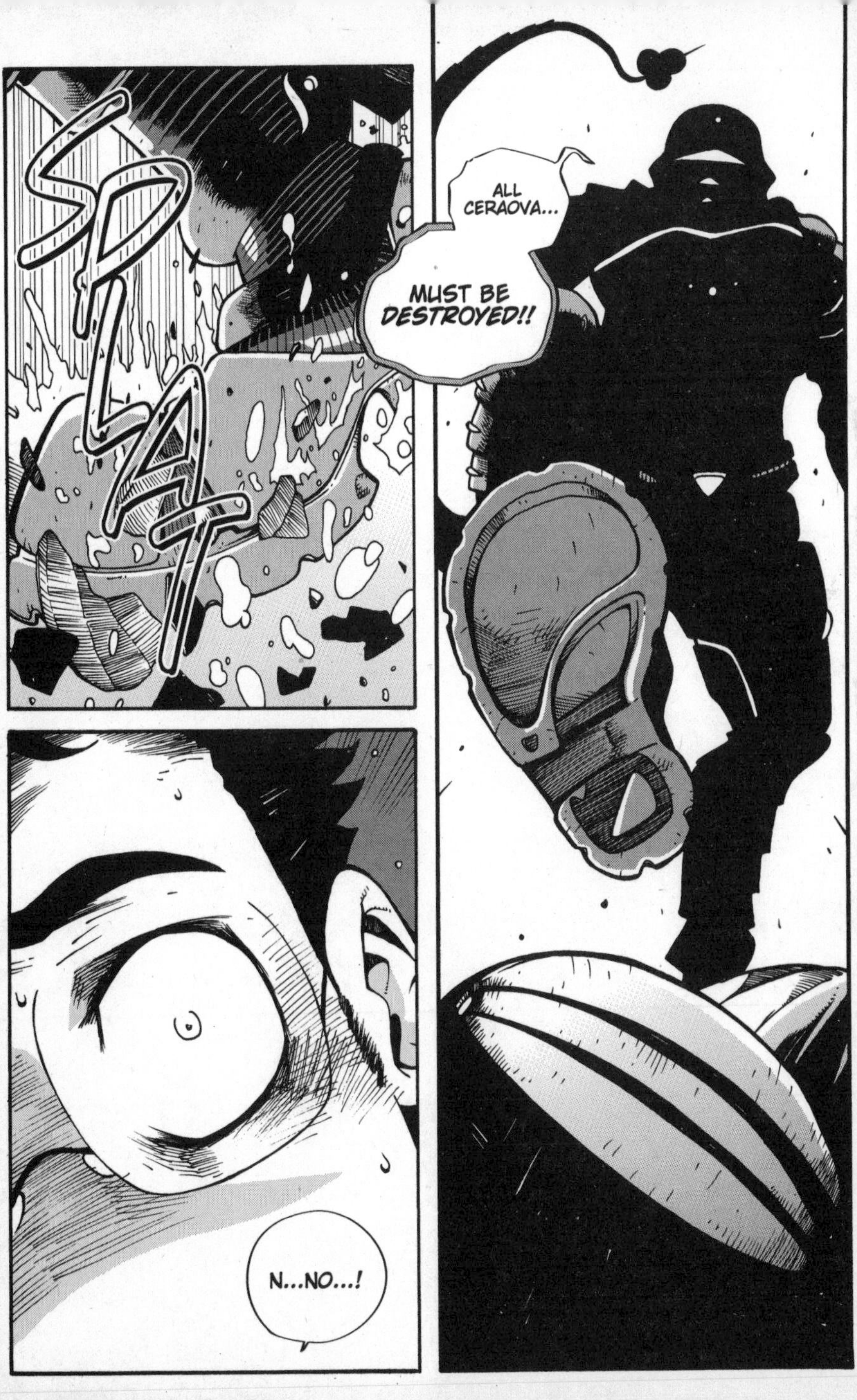
ALL CERAOVA...
MUST BE DESTROYED!!
SPLAT
N...NO...!

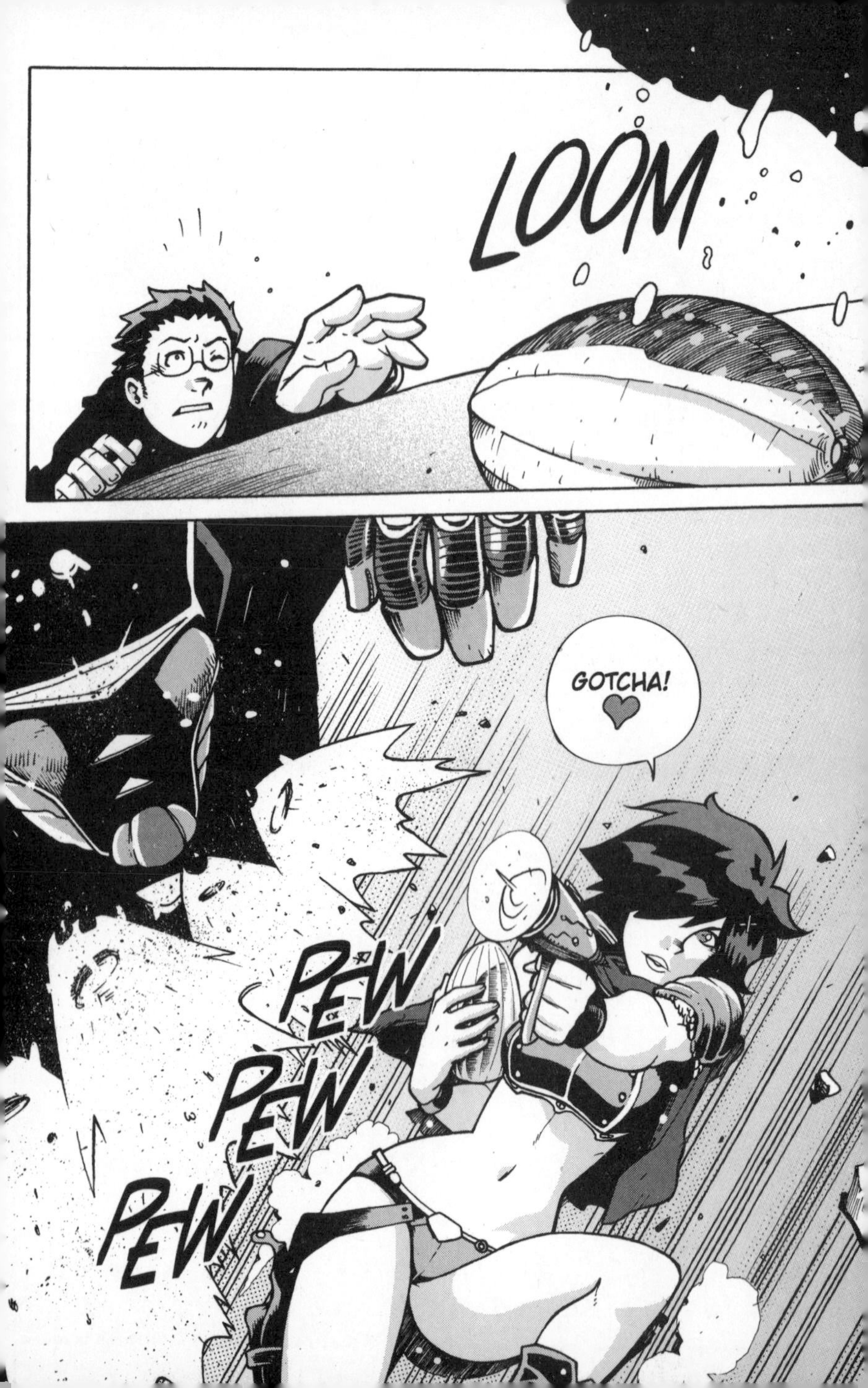
LOOM
GOTCHA! ♥
PEW
PEW
PEW

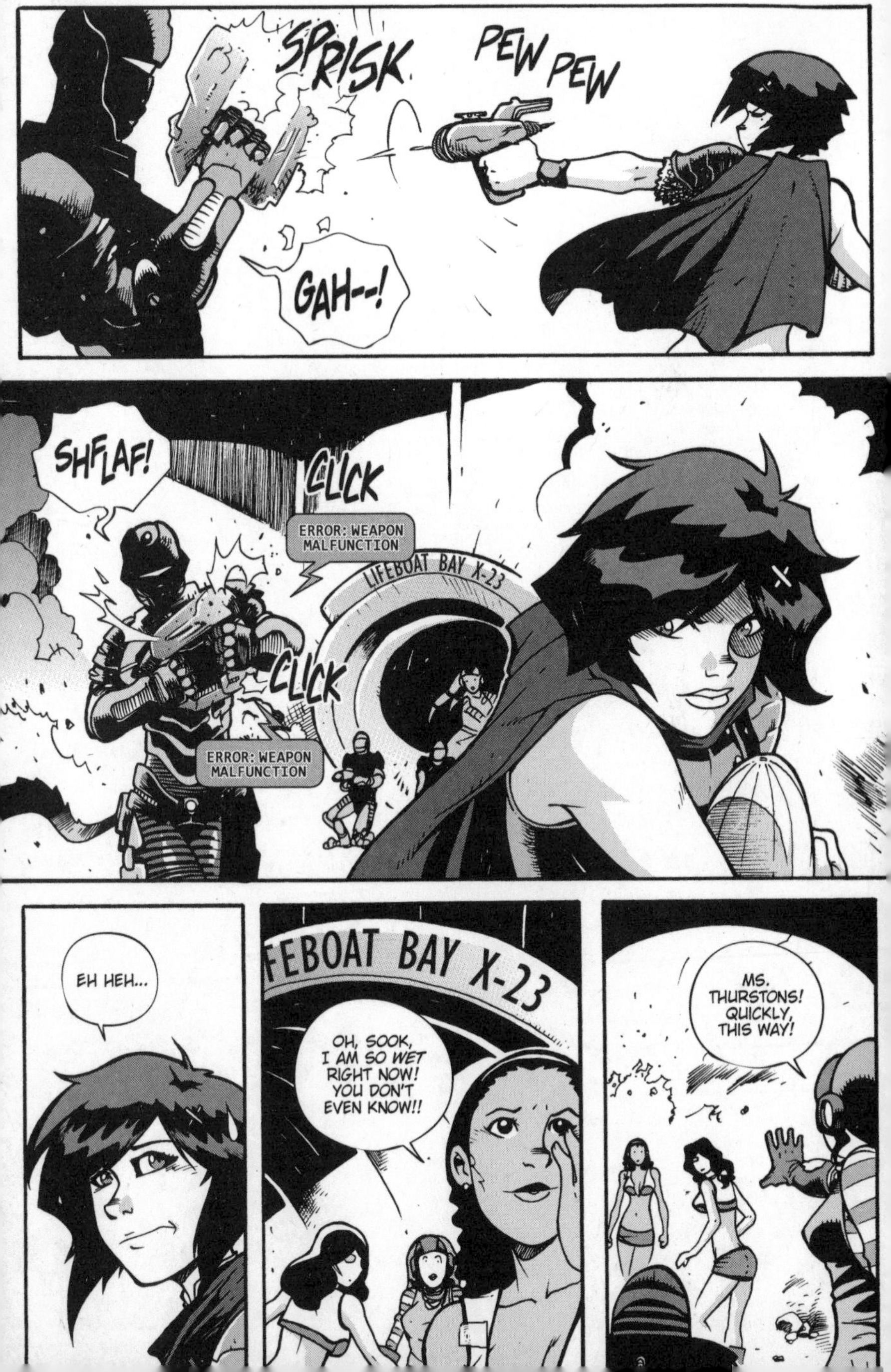
PEW PEW
SPRISK
GAH--!
CLICK
SHFLAF!
ERROR: WEAPON MALFUNCTION
LIFEBOAT BAY X-23
CLICK
ERROR: WEAPON MALFUNCTION
MS. THURSTONS! QUICKLY, THIS WAY!
FEBOAT BAY X-23
OH, SOOK, I AM SO *WET* RIGHT NOW! YOU DON'T EVEN KNOW!!
EH HEH...

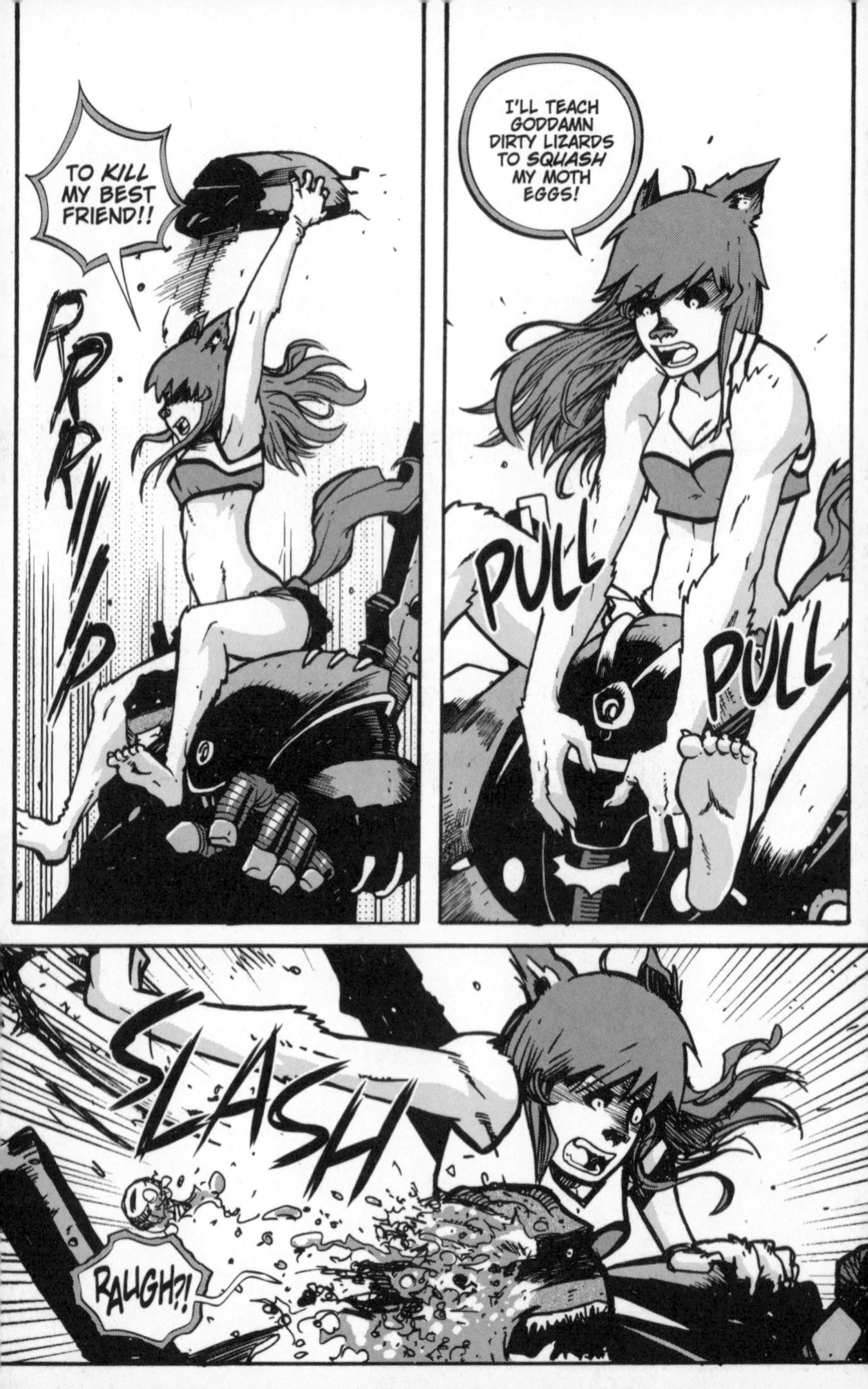
I'LL TEACH GODDAMN DIRTY LIZARDS TO SQUASH MY MOTH EGGS!
PULL
PULL
TO KILL MY BEST FRIEND!!
RRRIIIP
SLASH
RAUGH?!

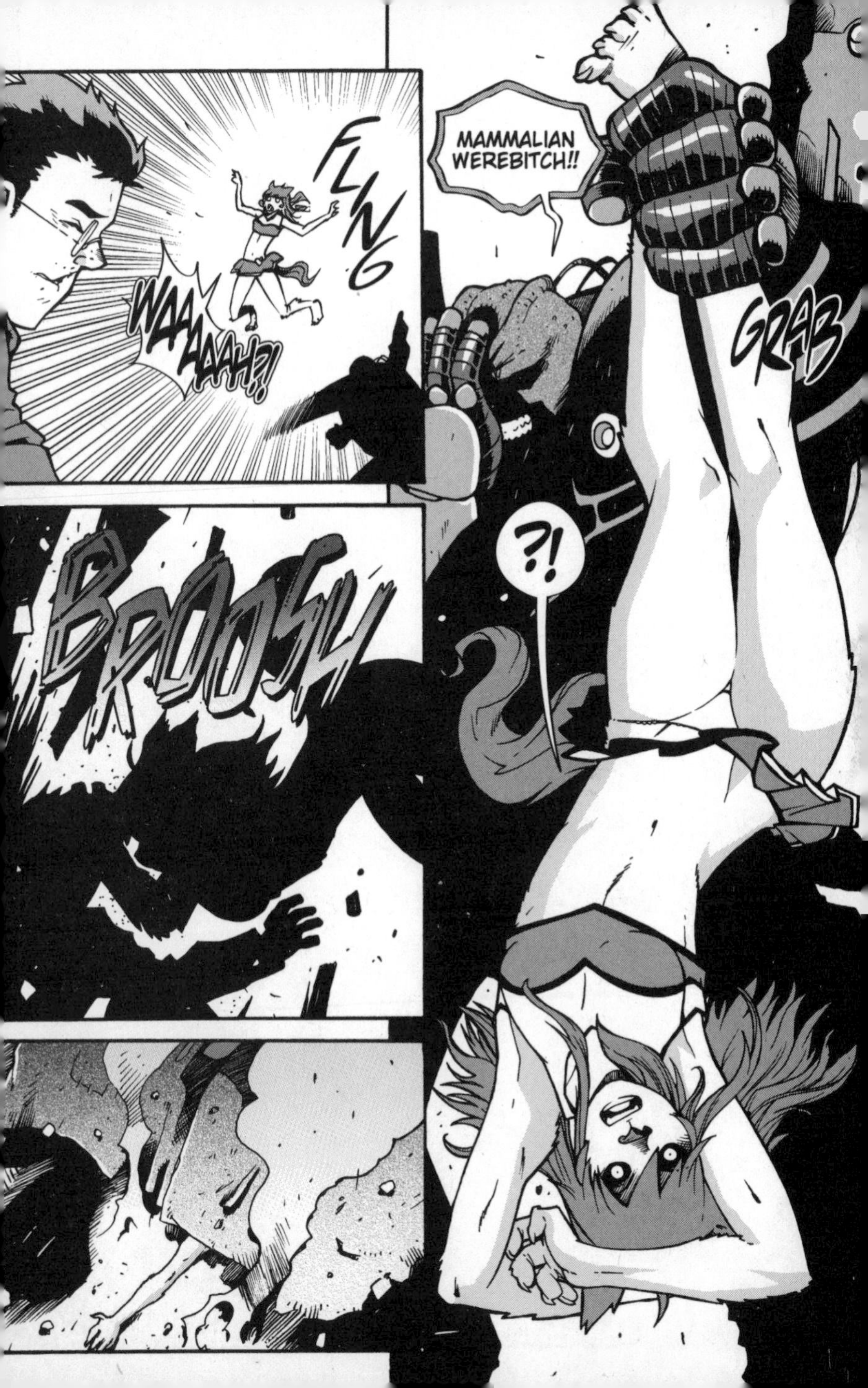
MAMMALIAN WEREBITCH!!
GRAB
?!
FLING
WAAAAAAH?!
BROOSH

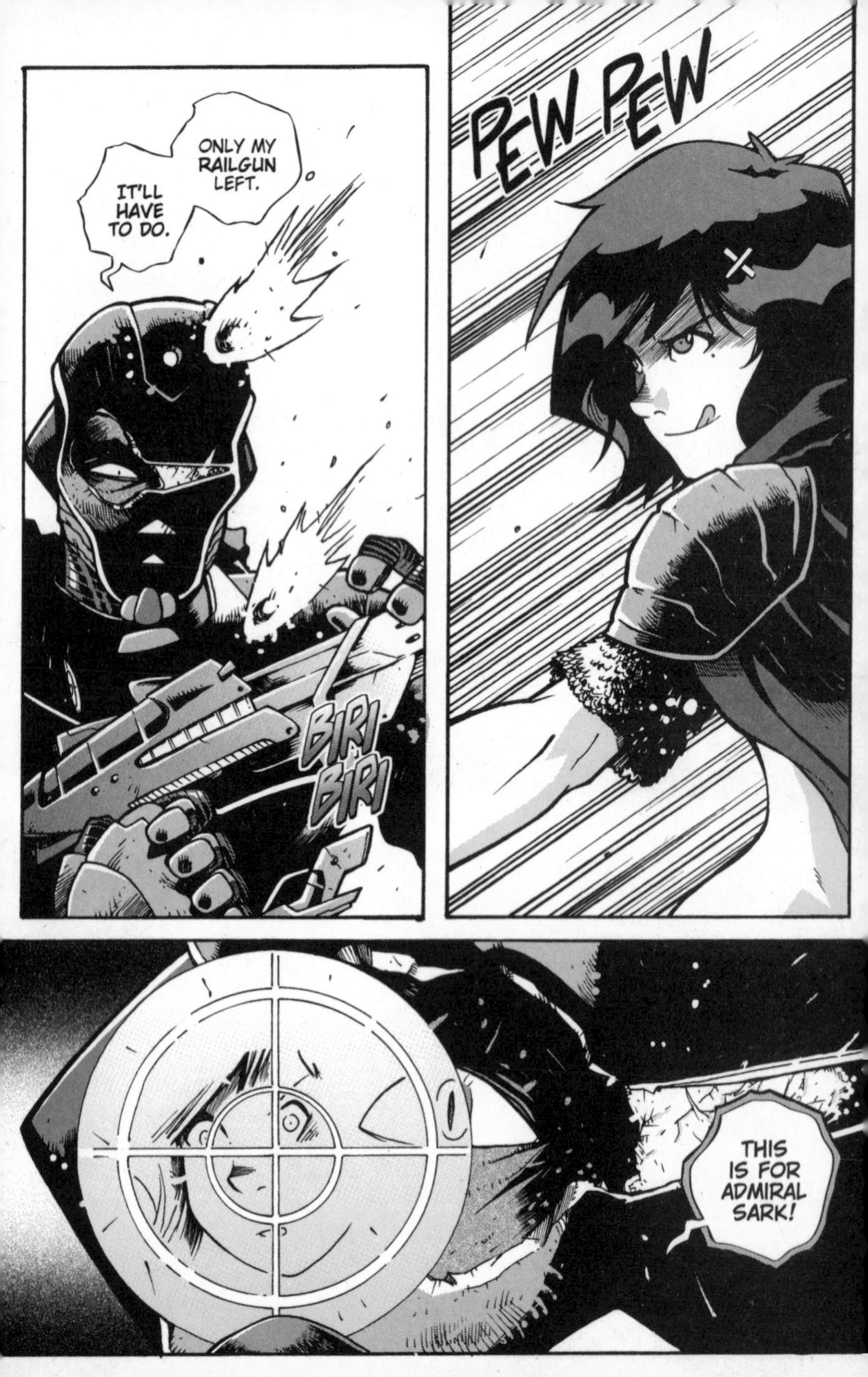
PEW PEW
ONLY MY RAILGUN LEFT.
IT'LL HAVE TO DO.
BIRI BIRI
THIS IS FOR ADMIRAL SARK!

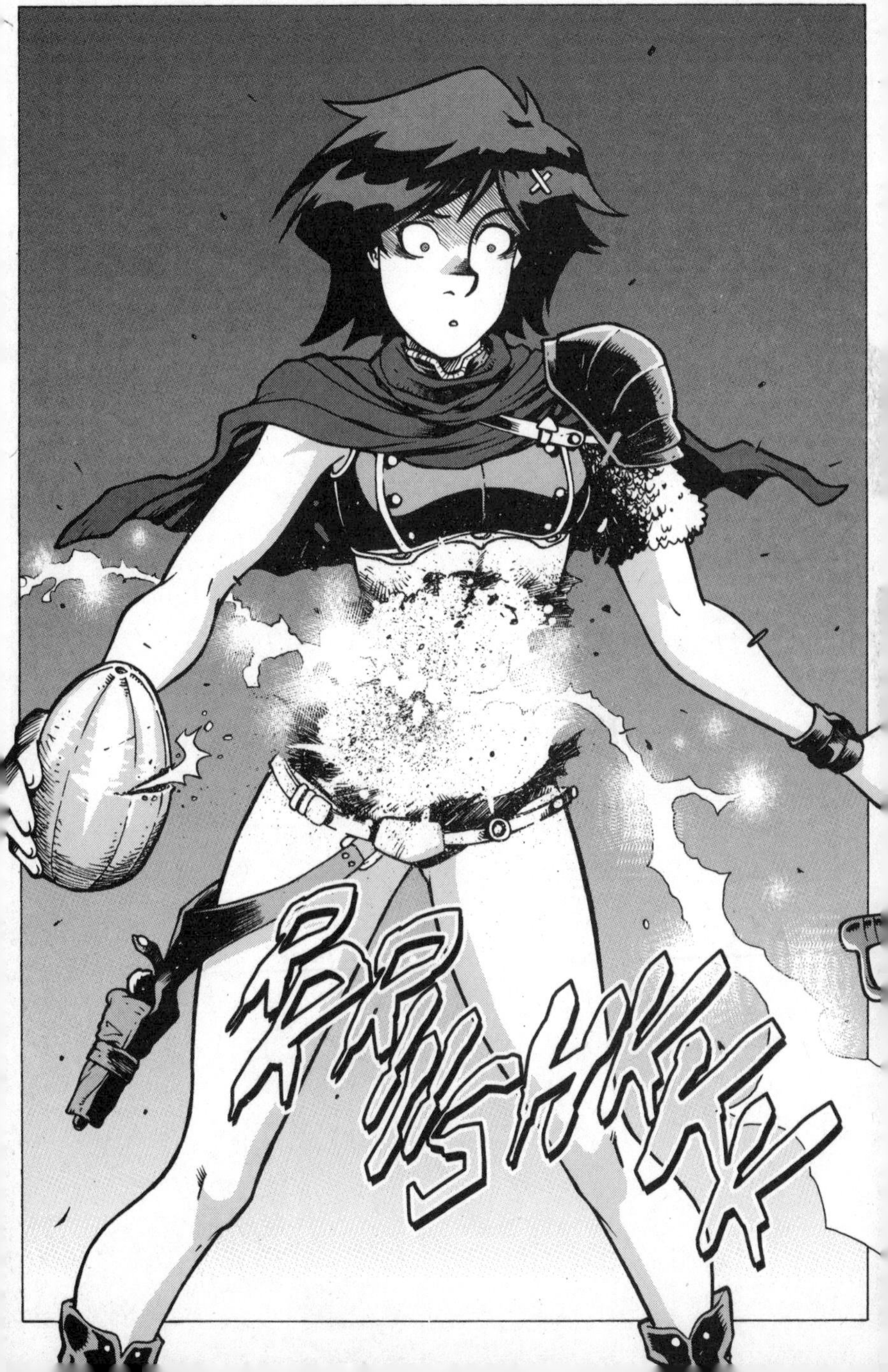
RRIISHHKK

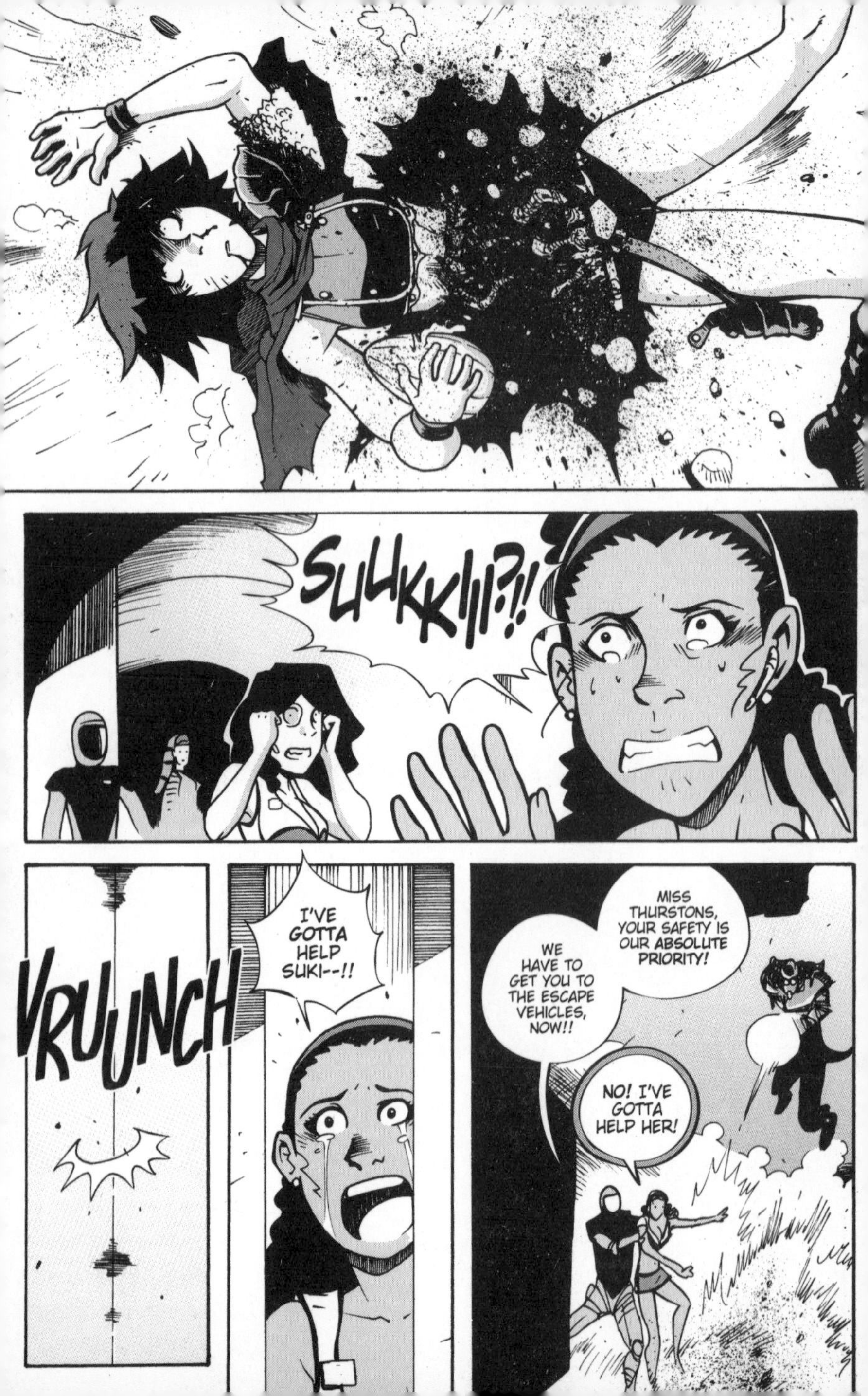
SUUKKIII?!!
MISS THURSTONS, YOUR SAFETY IS OUR ABSOLUTE PRIORITY!
WE HAVE TO GET YOU TO THE ESCAPE VEHICLES, NOW!!
NO! I'VE GOTTA HELP HER!
I'VE GOTTA HELP SUKI--!!
VRUUNCH

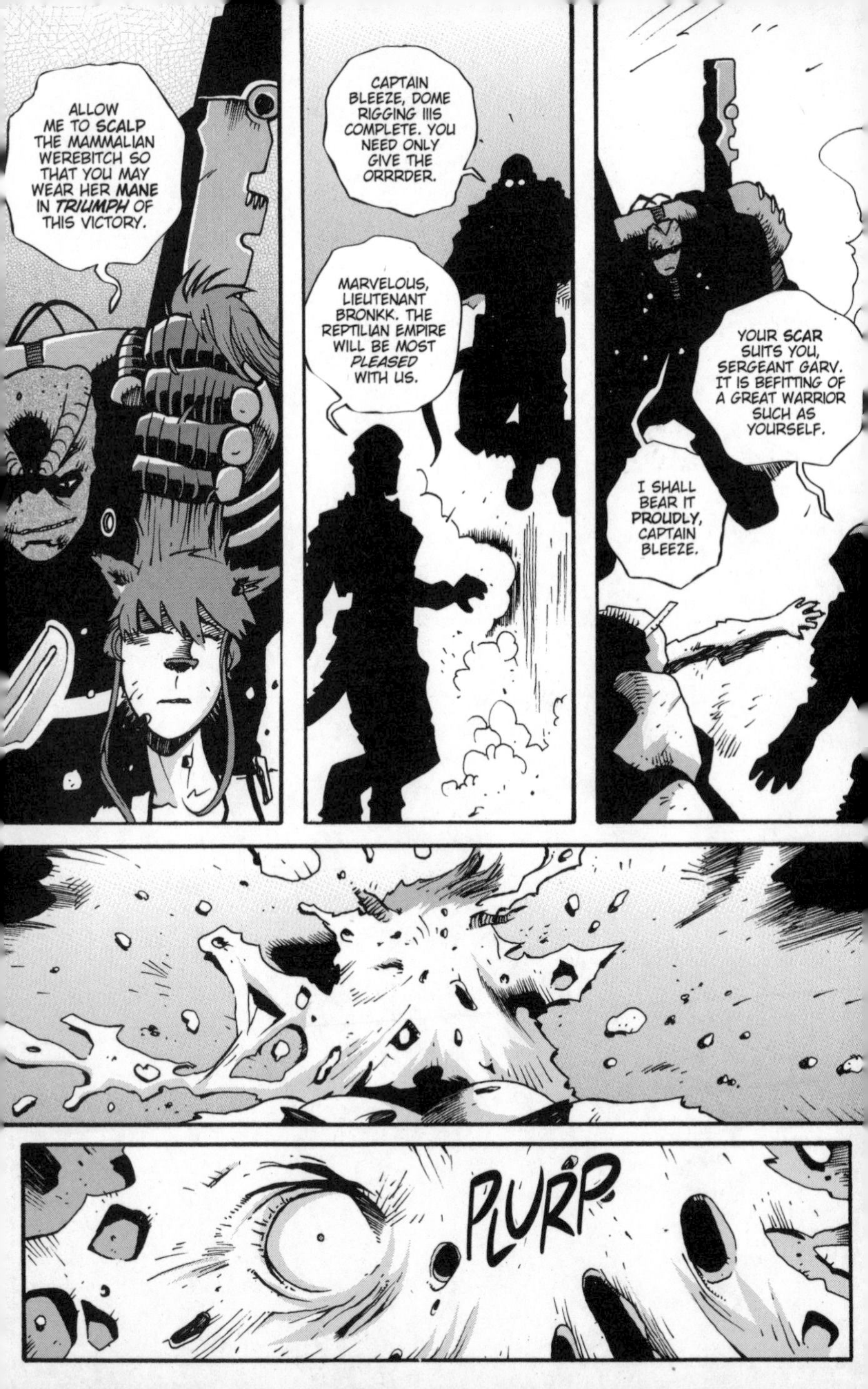
YOUR SCAR SUITS YOU, SERGEANT GARV. IT IS BEFITTING OF A GREAT WARRIOR SUCH AS YOURSELF.
I SHALL BEAR IT PROUDLY, CAPTAIN BLEEZE.
CAPTAIN BLEEZE, DOME RIGGING IIIS COMPLETE. YOU NEED ONLY GIVE THE ORRRDER.
MARVELOUS, LIEUTENANT BRONKK. THE REPTILIAN EMPIRE WILL BE MOST *PLEASED* WITH US.
ALLOW ME TO **SCALP** THE MAMMALIAN WEREBITCH SO THAT YOU MAY WEAR HER **MANE** IN ***TRIUMPH*** OF THIS VICTORY.
PLURP

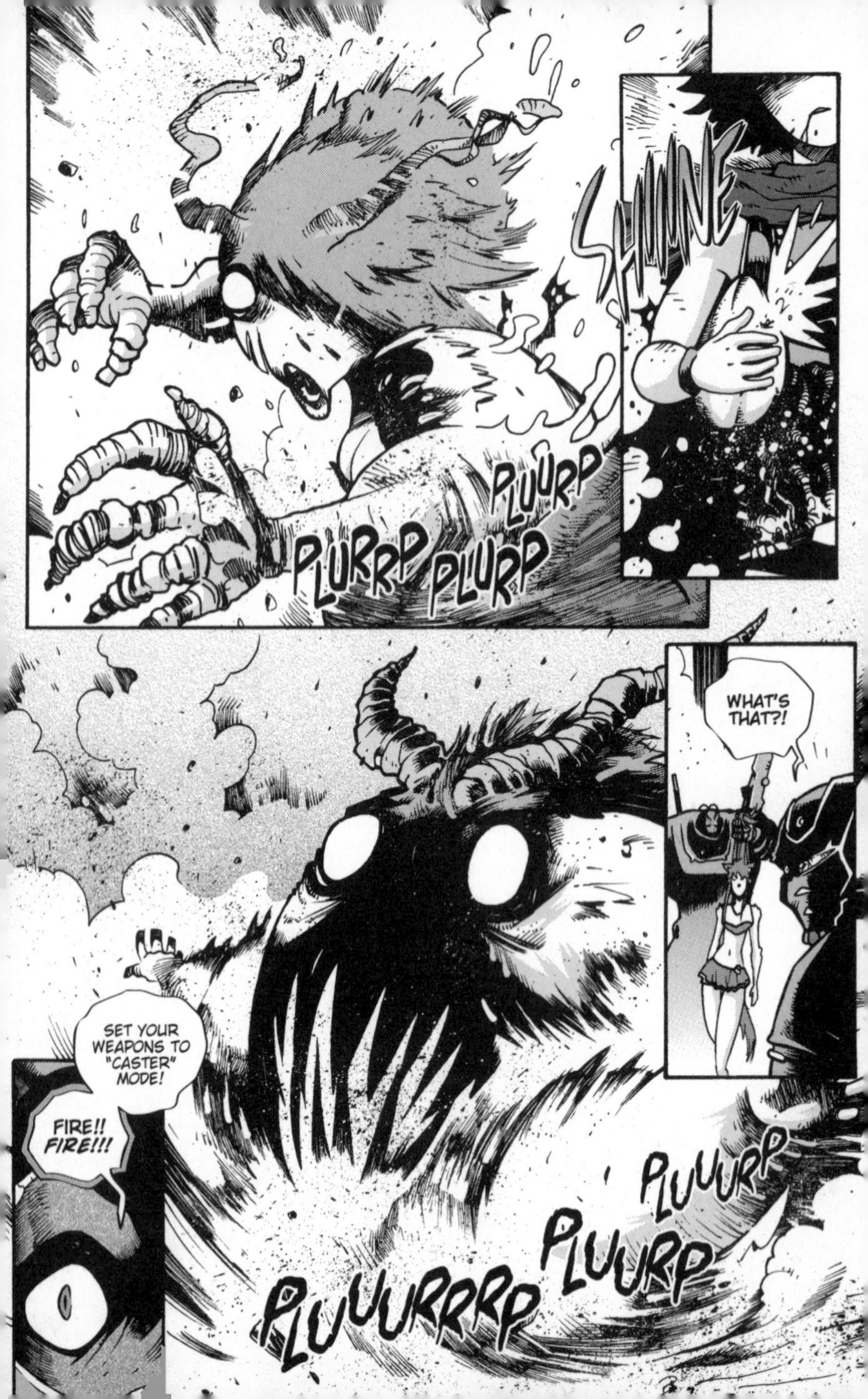
SHIIINE
PLUURP
PLURRP
PLURP
WHAT'S THAT?!
SET YOUR WEAPONS TO "CASTER" MODE!
FIRE!! FIRE!!!
PLUUURP
PLUURP
PLUUURRRP

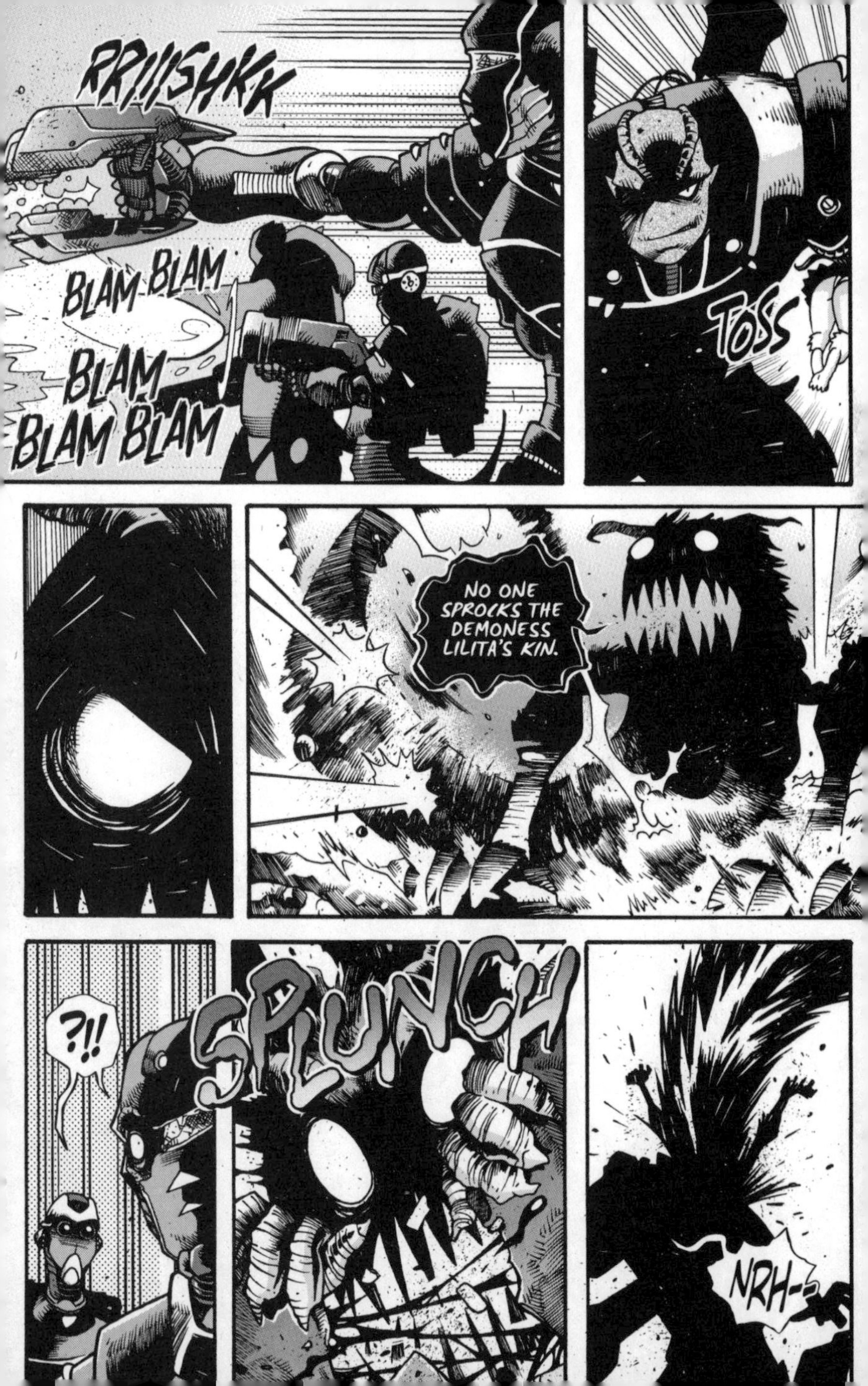
TOSS
RRIISHKK
BLAM BLAM
BLAM
BLAM BLAM
NO ONE SPROCKS THE DEMONESS LILITA'S KIN.
NRH-
SPLUNCH
?!!

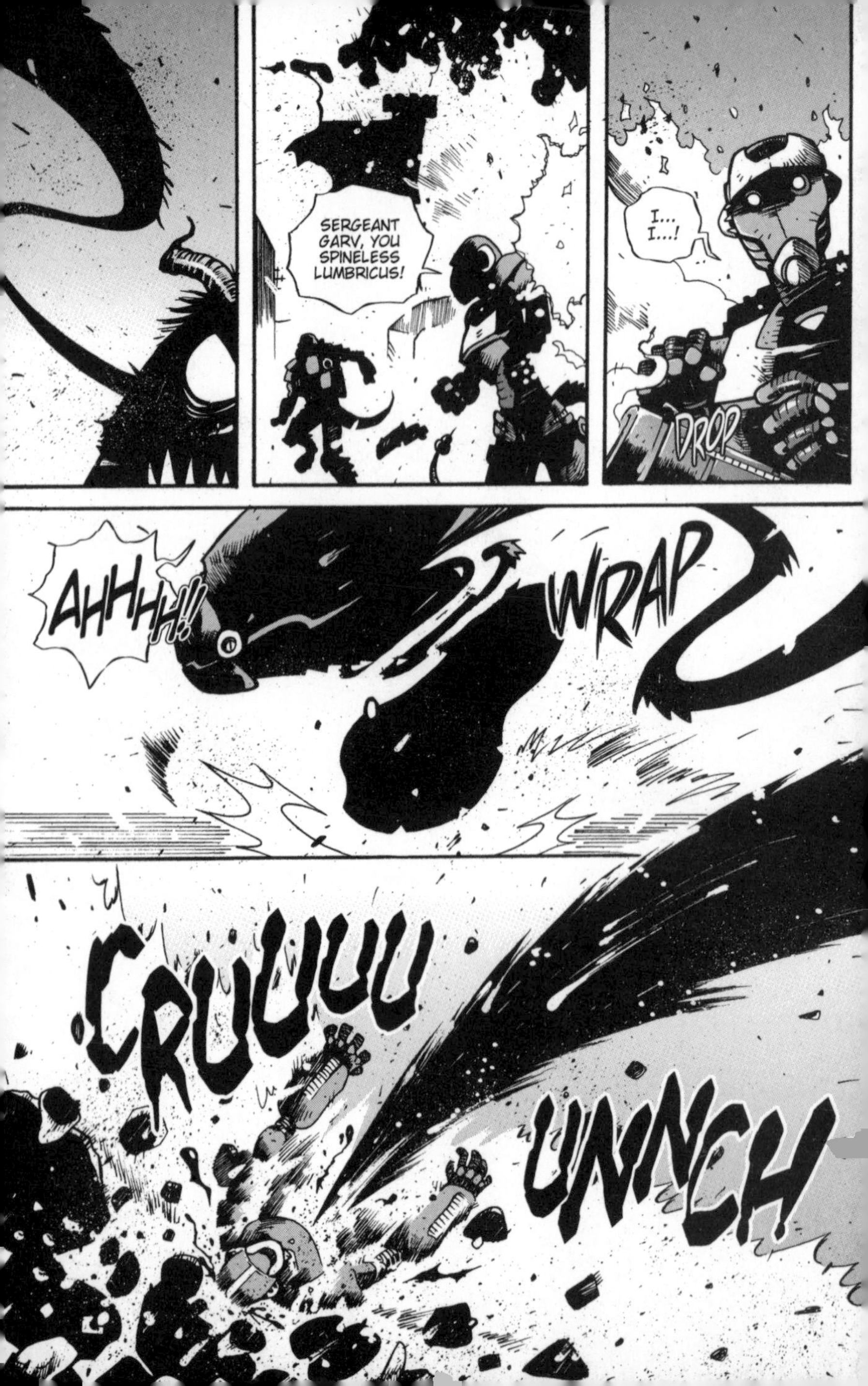
I...,
I...!
DROP
SERGEANT GARV, YOU SPINELESS LUMBRICUS!
WRAP
AHHHH!!
CRUUUU
UNNCH

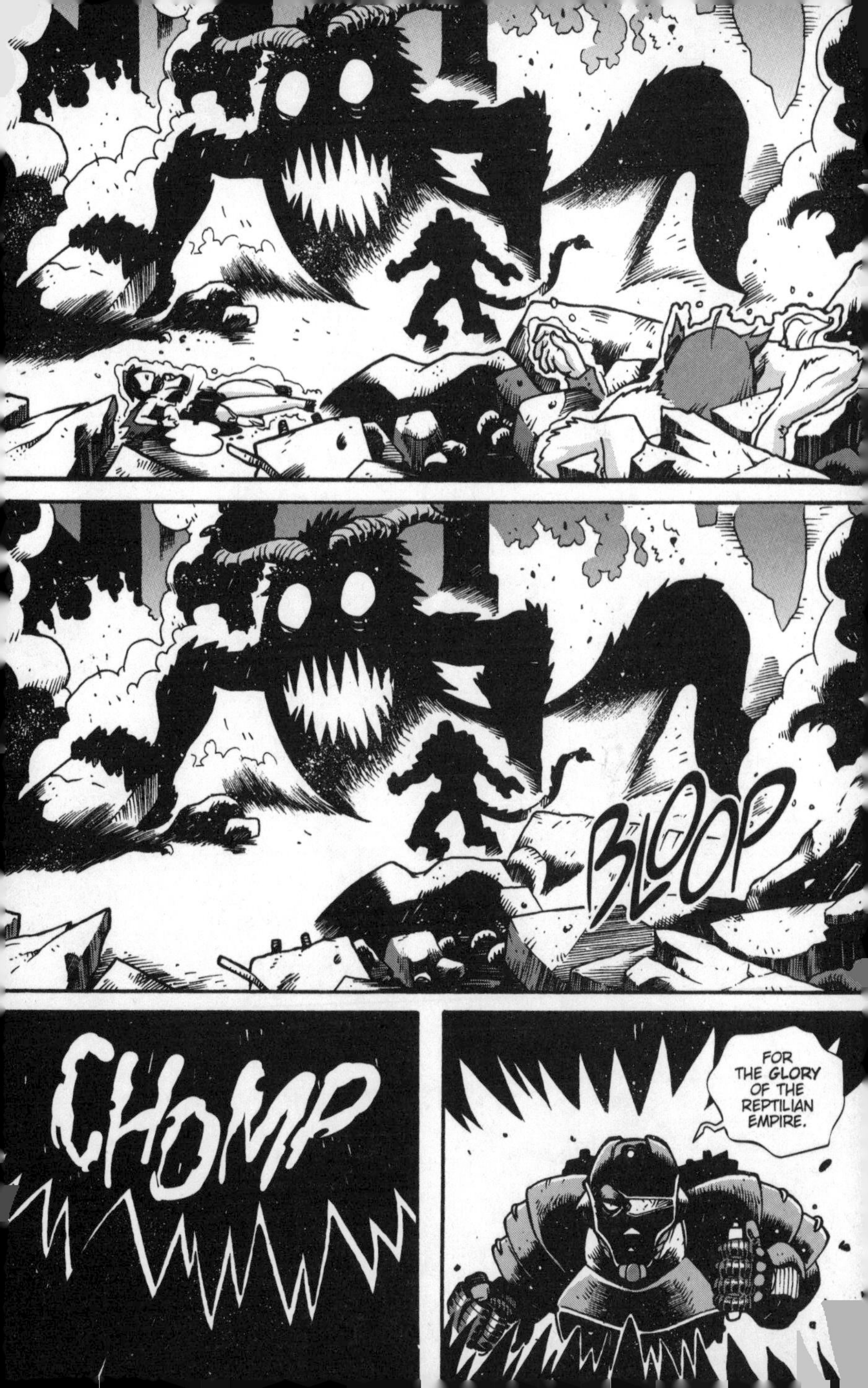
BLOOP
FOR THE GLORY OF THE REPTILIAN EMPIRE.
CHOMP

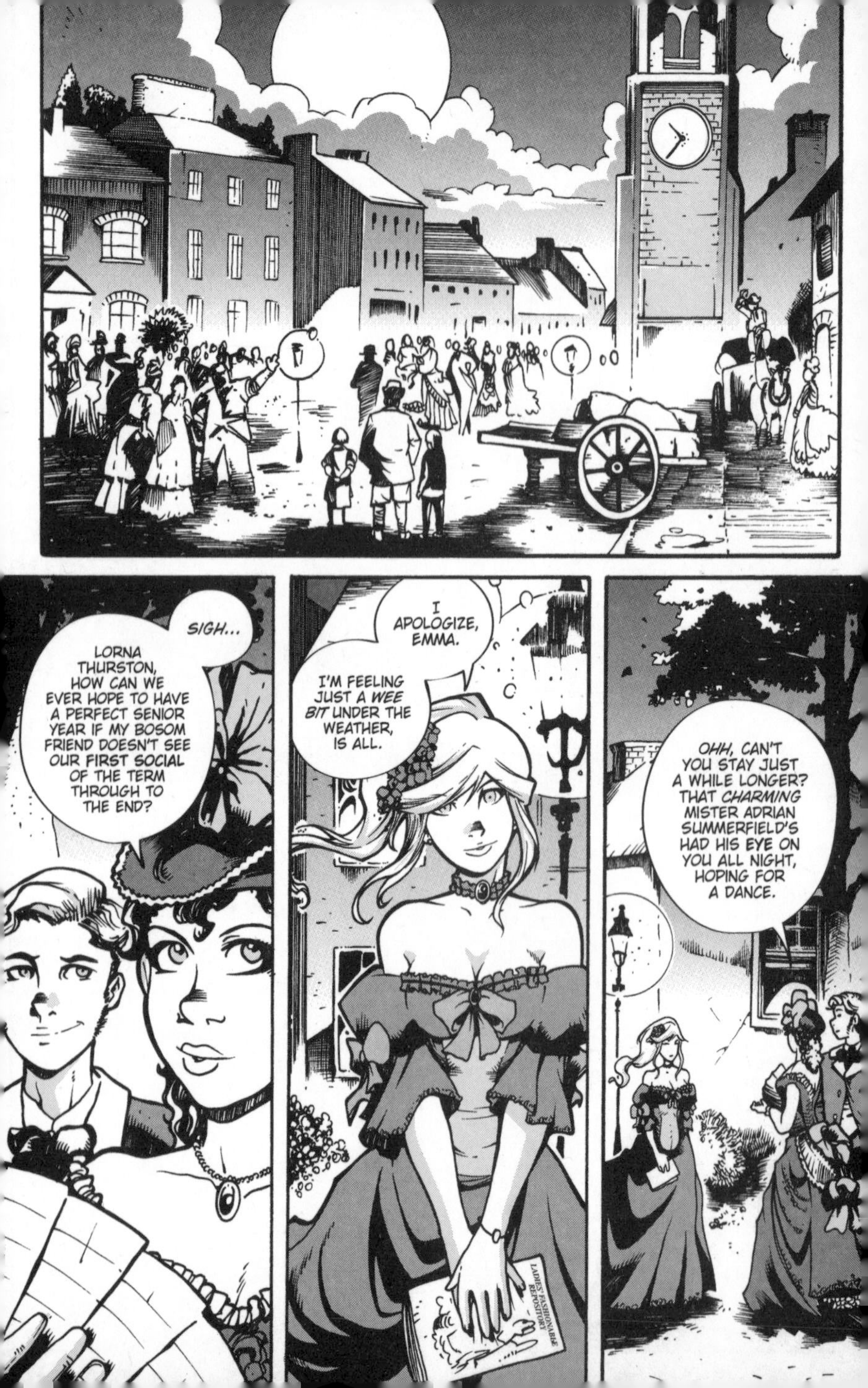
OHH, CAN'T YOU STAY JUST A WHILE LONGER? THAT *CHARMING* MISTER ADRIAN SUMMERFIELD'S HAD HIS EYE ON YOU ALL NIGHT, HOPING FOR A DANCE.
I APOLOGIZE, EMMA.
I'M FEELING JUST A *WEE BIT* UNDER THE WEATHER, IS ALL.
LADIES' FASHIONABLE REPOSITORY
SIGH...
LORNA THURSTON, HOW CAN WE EVER HOPE TO HAVE A PERFECT SENIOR YEAR IF MY BOSOM FRIEND DOESN'T SEE OUR **FIRST SOCIAL** OF THE TERM THROUGH TO THE END?

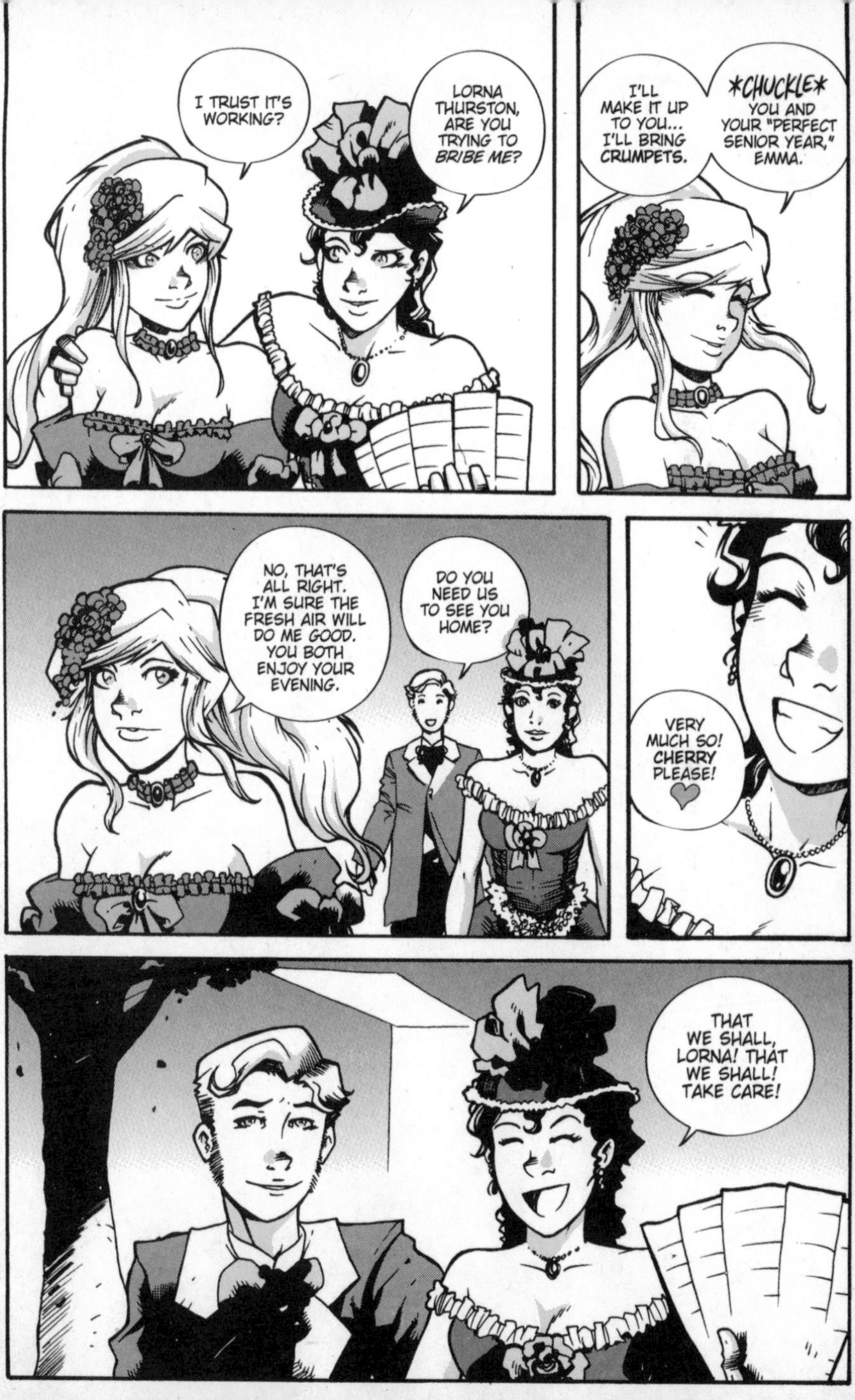
I TRUST IT'S WORKING?
LORNA THURSTON, ARE YOU TRYING TO BRIBE ME?
I'LL MAKE IT UP TO YOU... I'LL BRING CRUMPETS.
CHUCKLE YOU AND YOUR "PERFECT SENIOR YEAR," EMMA.
NO, THAT'S ALL RIGHT. I'M SURE THE FRESH AIR WILL DO ME GOOD. YOU BOTH ENJOY YOUR EVENING.
DO YOU NEED US TO SEE YOU HOME?
VERY MUCH SO! CHERRY PLEASE!
THAT WE SHALL, LORNA! THAT WE SHALL! TAKE CARE!

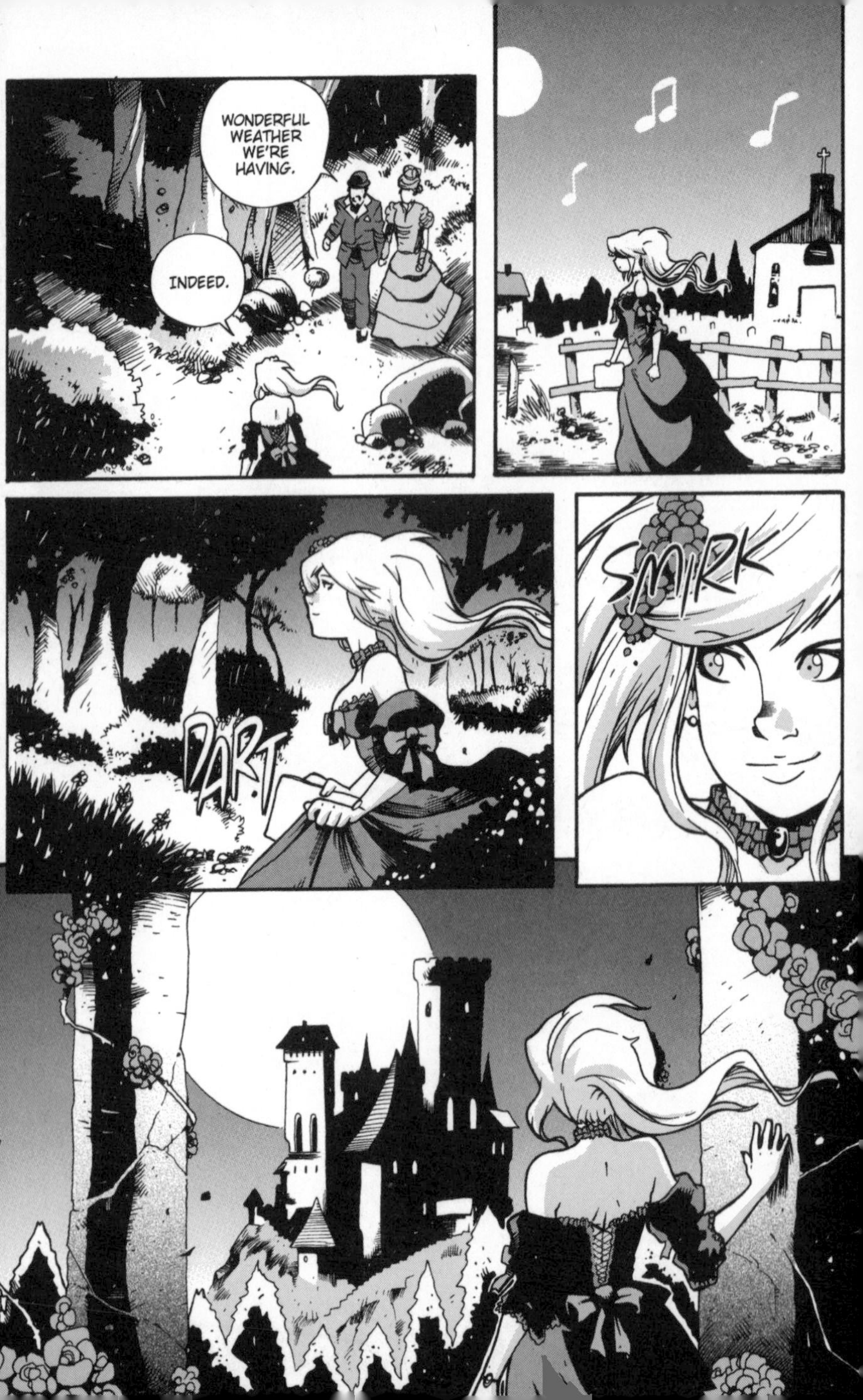
WONDERFUL WEATHER WE'RE HAVING.
INDEED.
SMIRK
DART

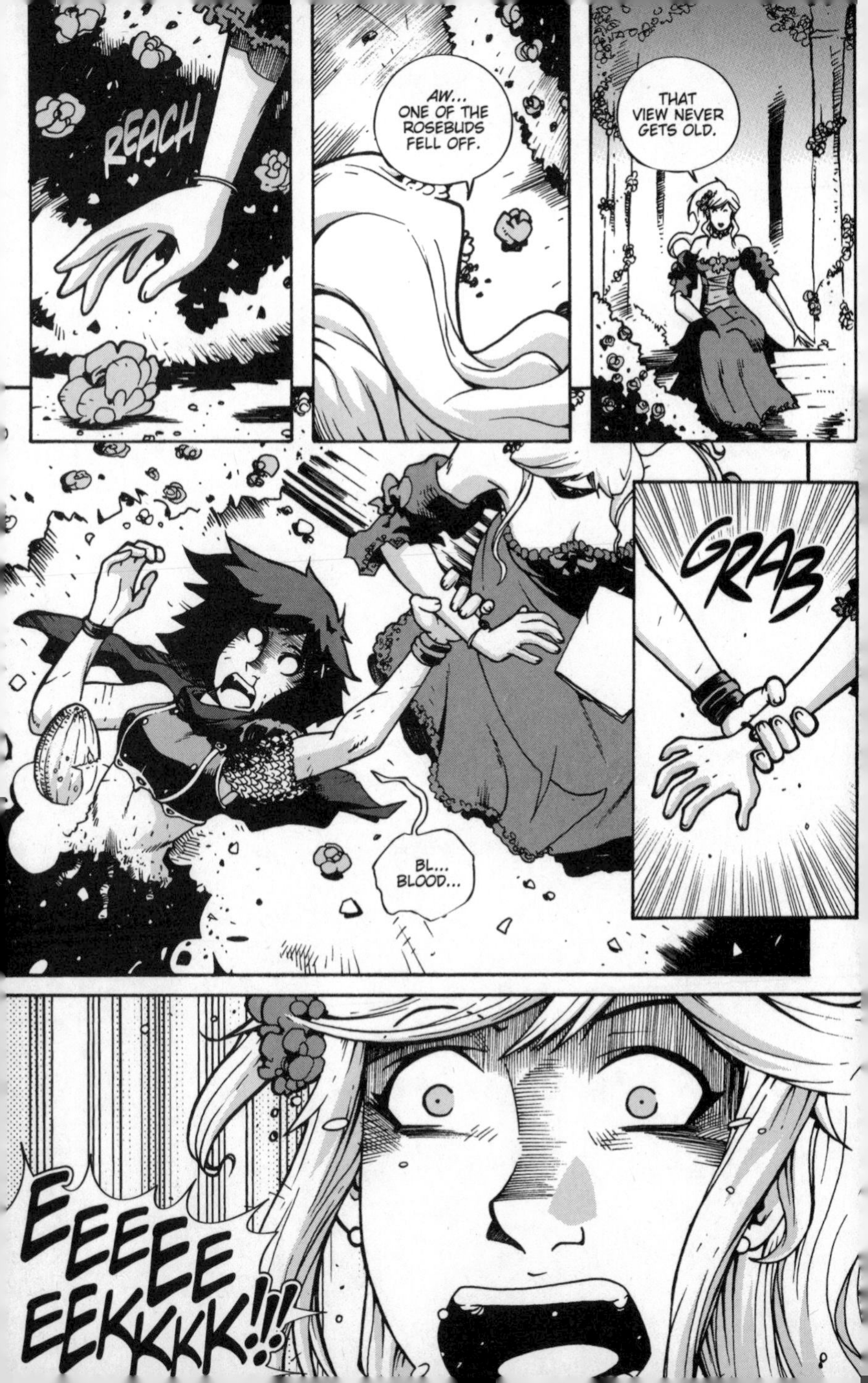
THAT VIEW NEVER GETS OLD.
AW... ONE OF THE ROSEBUDS FELL OFF.
REACH
GRAB
BL... BLOOD...
EEEEEEEEKKKK!!!

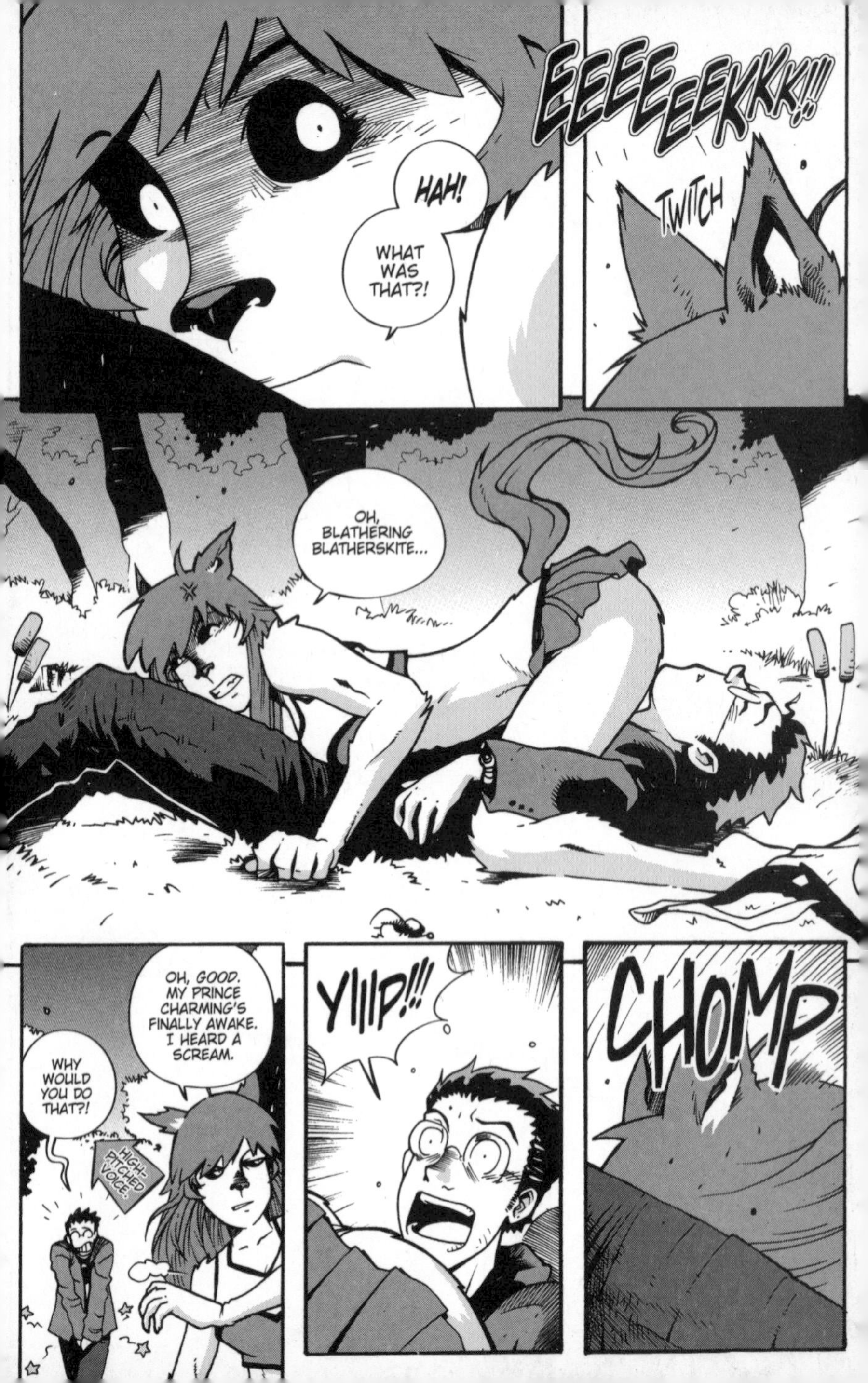
EEEEEEKKK!!
TWITCH
HAH!
WHAT WAS THAT?!
OH, BLATHERING BLATHERSKITE...
CHOMP
YIIIP!!!
OH, GOOD. MY PRINCE CHARMING'S FINALLY AWAKE. I HEARD A SCREAM.
WHY WOULD YOU DO THAT?!
HIGH-PITCHED VOICE.

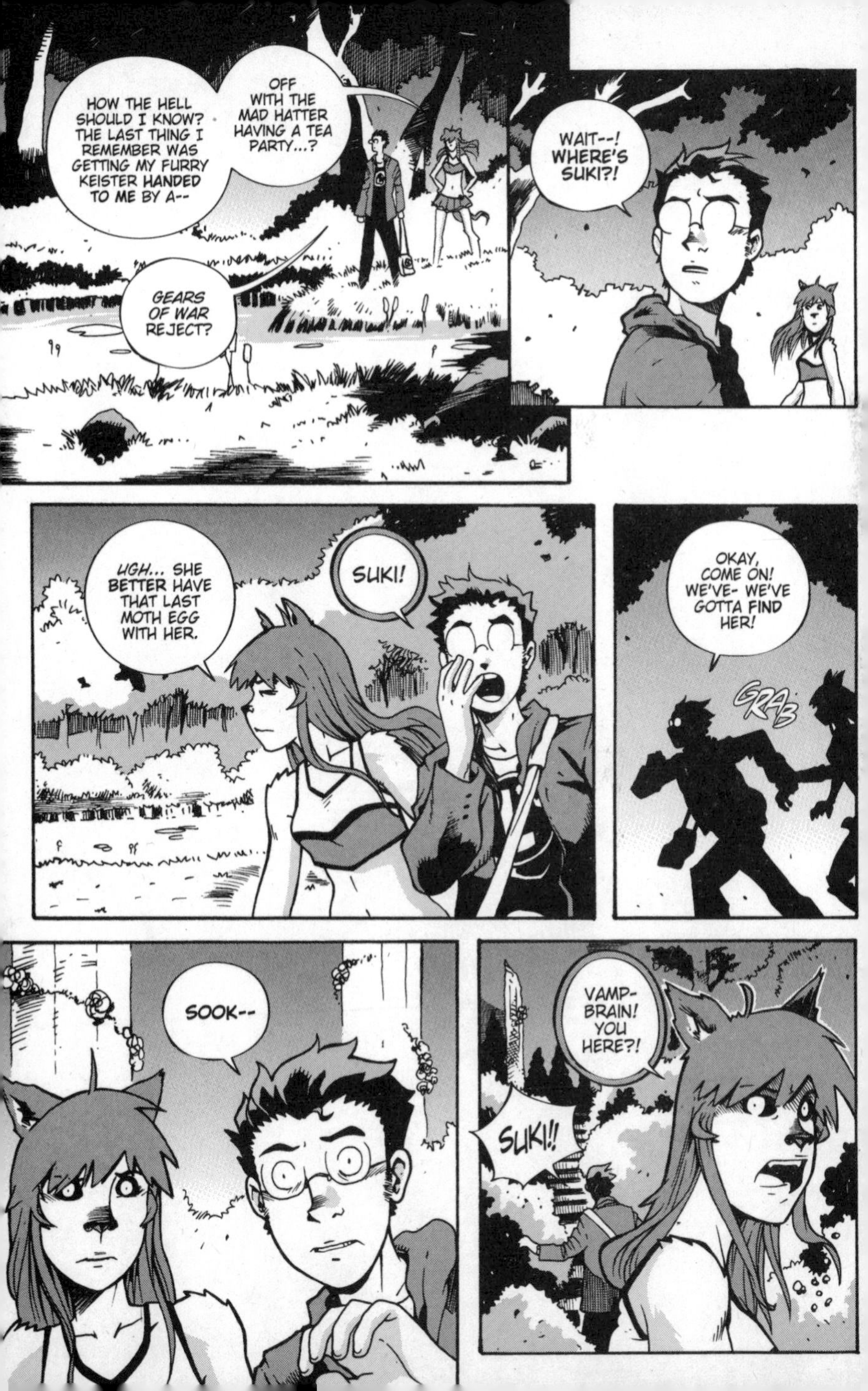
WAIT--! WHERE'S SUKI?!
OFF WITH THE MAD HATTER HAVING A TEA PARTY...?
HOW THE HELL SHOULD I KNOW? THE LAST THING I REMEMBER WAS GETTING MY FURRY KEISTER HANDED TO ME BY A--
GEARS OF WAR REJECT?
OKAY, COME ON! WE'VE- WE'VE GOTTA FIND HER!
GRAB
SUKI!
UGH... SHE BETTER HAVE THAT LAST MOTH EGG WITH HER.
VAMP-BRAIN! YOU HERE?!
SUKI!!
SOOK--

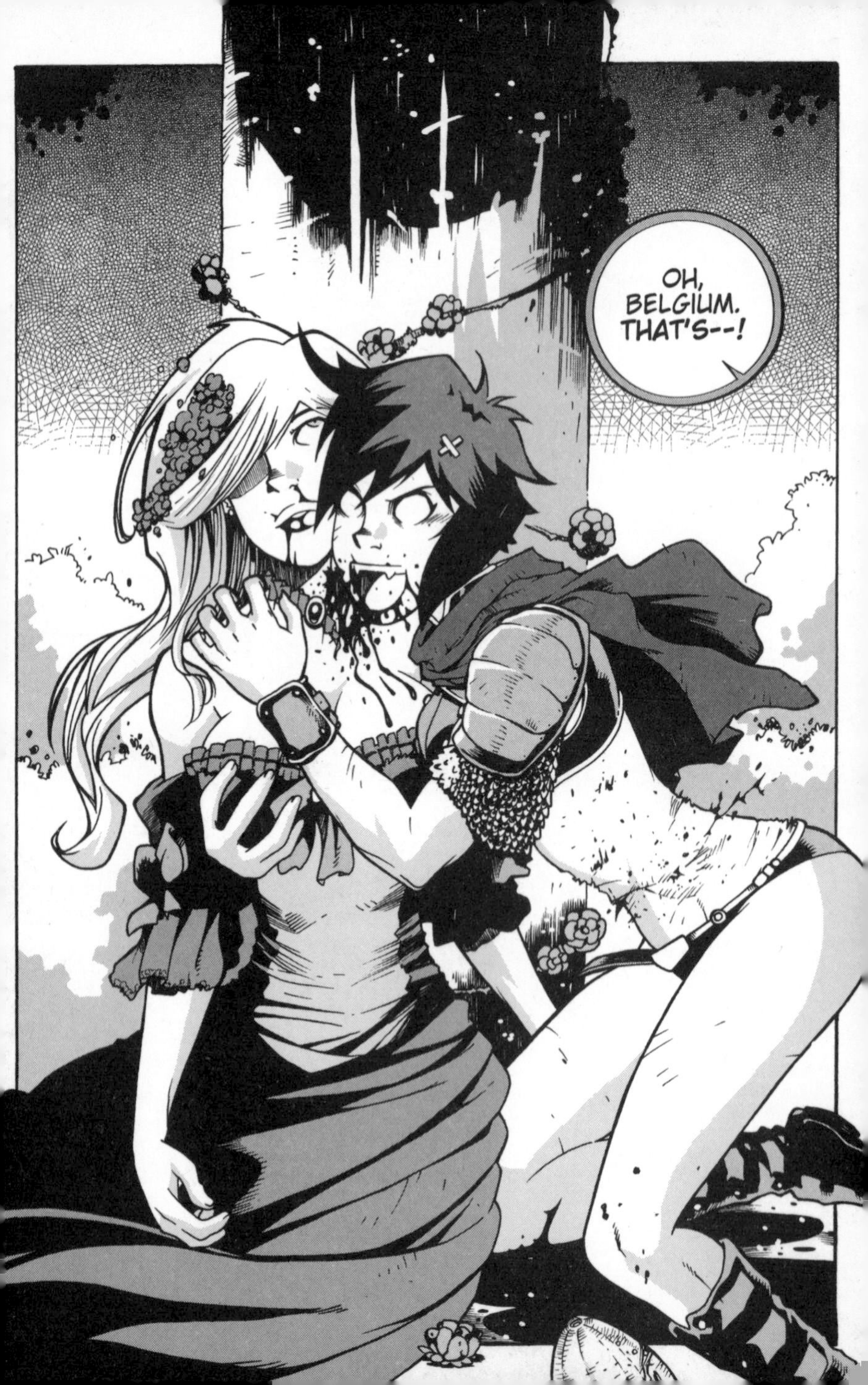
OH, BELGIUM. THAT'S--!

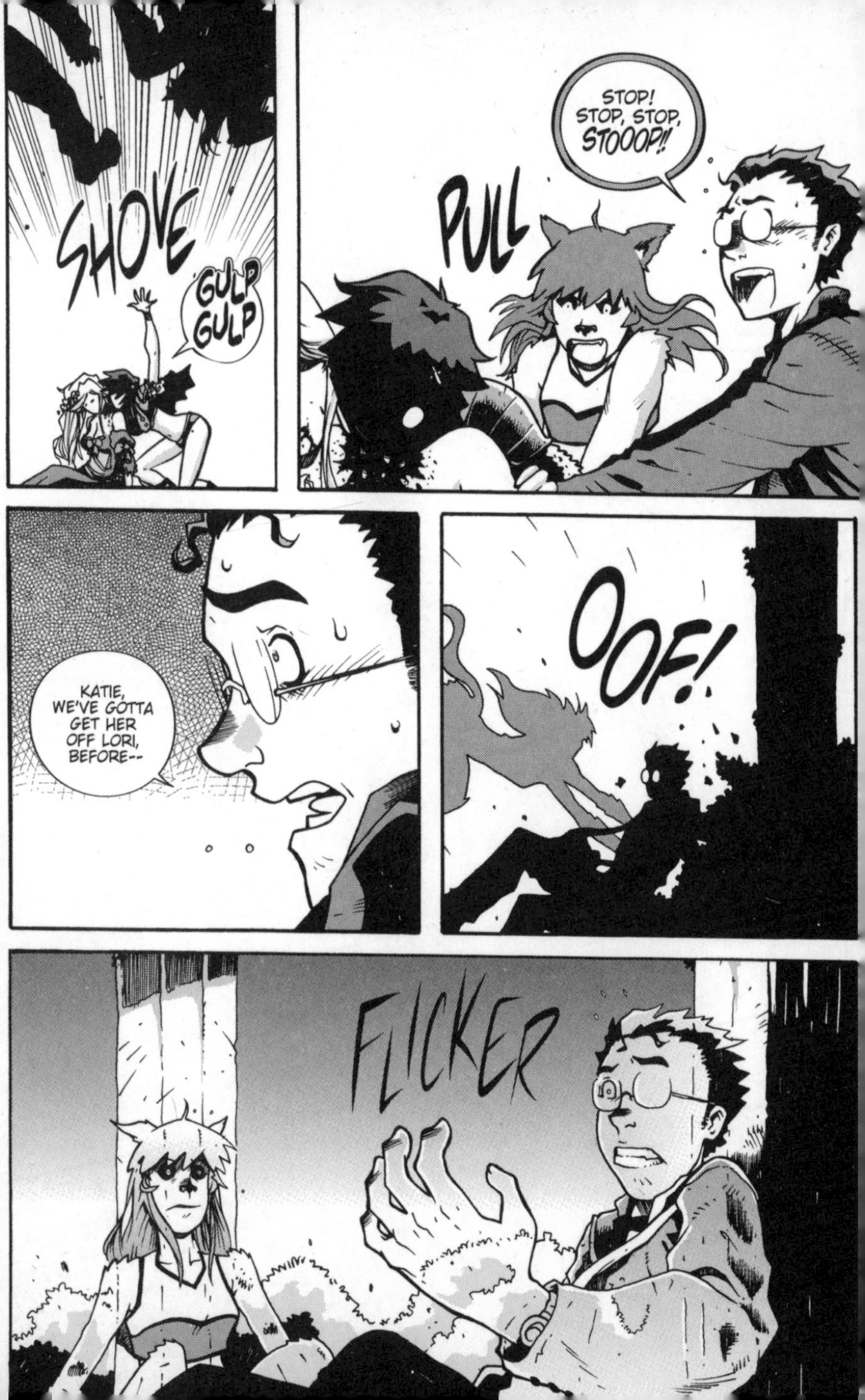
STOP!
STOP, STOP,
STOOOP!!
PULL
SHOVE
GULP
GULP
OOF!
KATIE,
WE'VE GOTTA
GET HER
OFF LORI,
BEFORE--
FLICKER

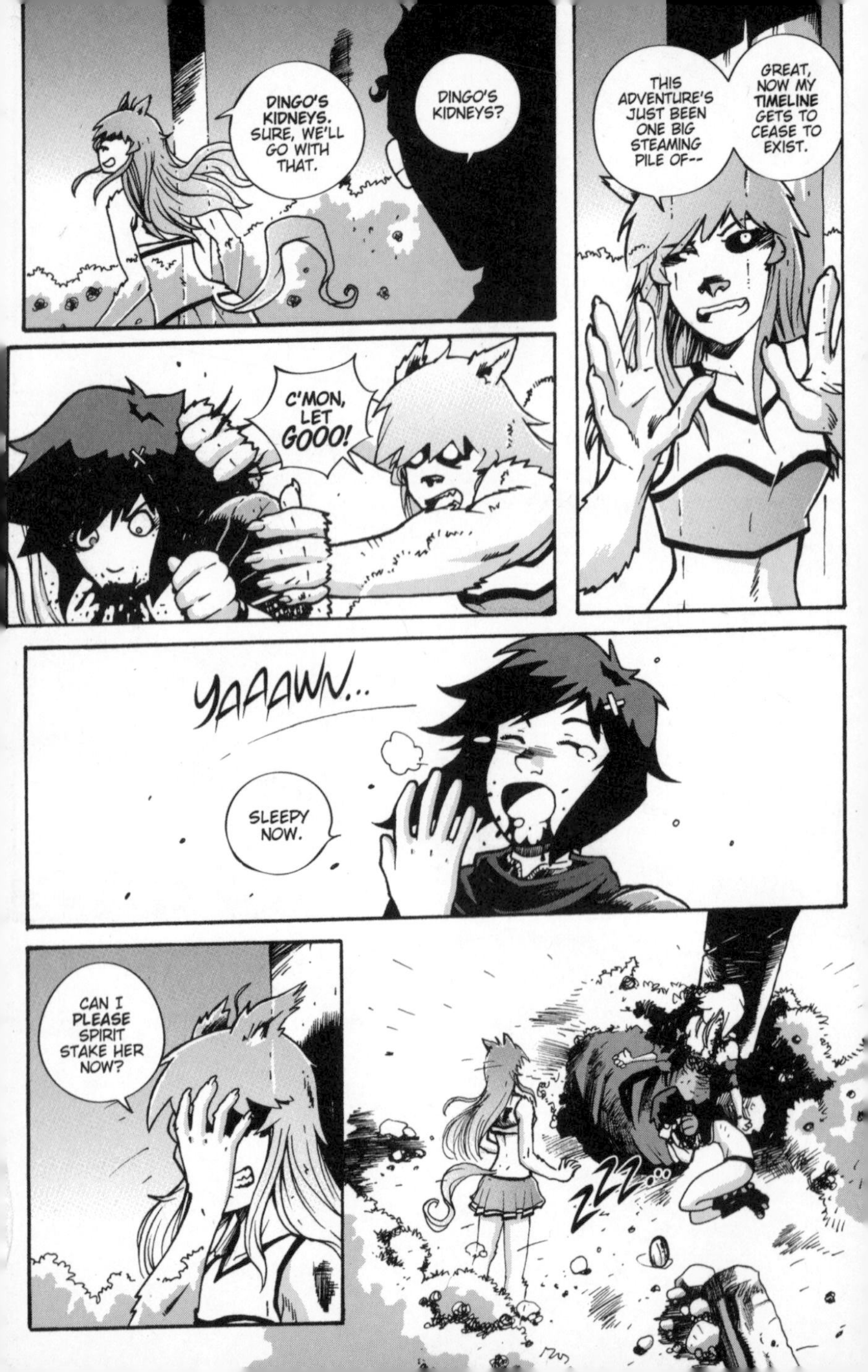
GREAT, NOW MY TIMELINE GETS TO CEASE TO EXIST.
THIS ADVENTURE'S JUST BEEN ONE BIG STEAMING PILE OF--
DINGO'S KIDNEYS?
DINGO'S KIDNEYS. SURE, WE'LL GO WITH THAT.
C'MON, LET GOOO!
YAAAWN...
SLEEPY NOW.
ZZZ...
CAN I PLEASE SPIRIT STAKE HER NOW?

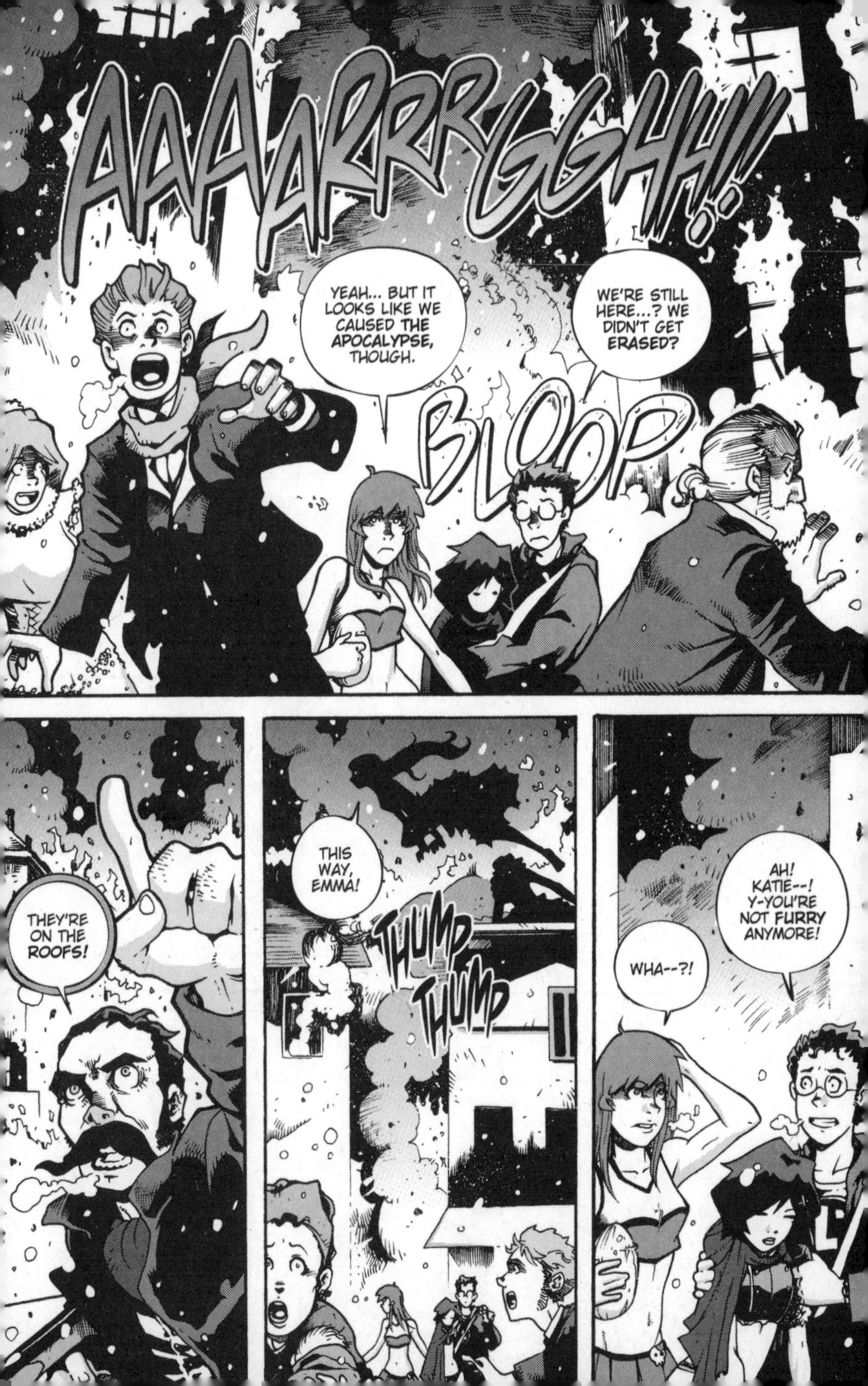
AAAARRRGGHH!!
WE'RE STILL HERE...? WE DIDN'T GET ERASED?
YEAH... BUT IT LOOKS LIKE WE CAUSED THE APOCALYPSE, THOUGH.
BLOOP
AH! KATIE--! Y-YOU'RE NOT FURRY ANYMORE!
WHA--?!
THIS WAY, EMMA!
THUMP THUMP
THEY'RE ON THE ROOFS!

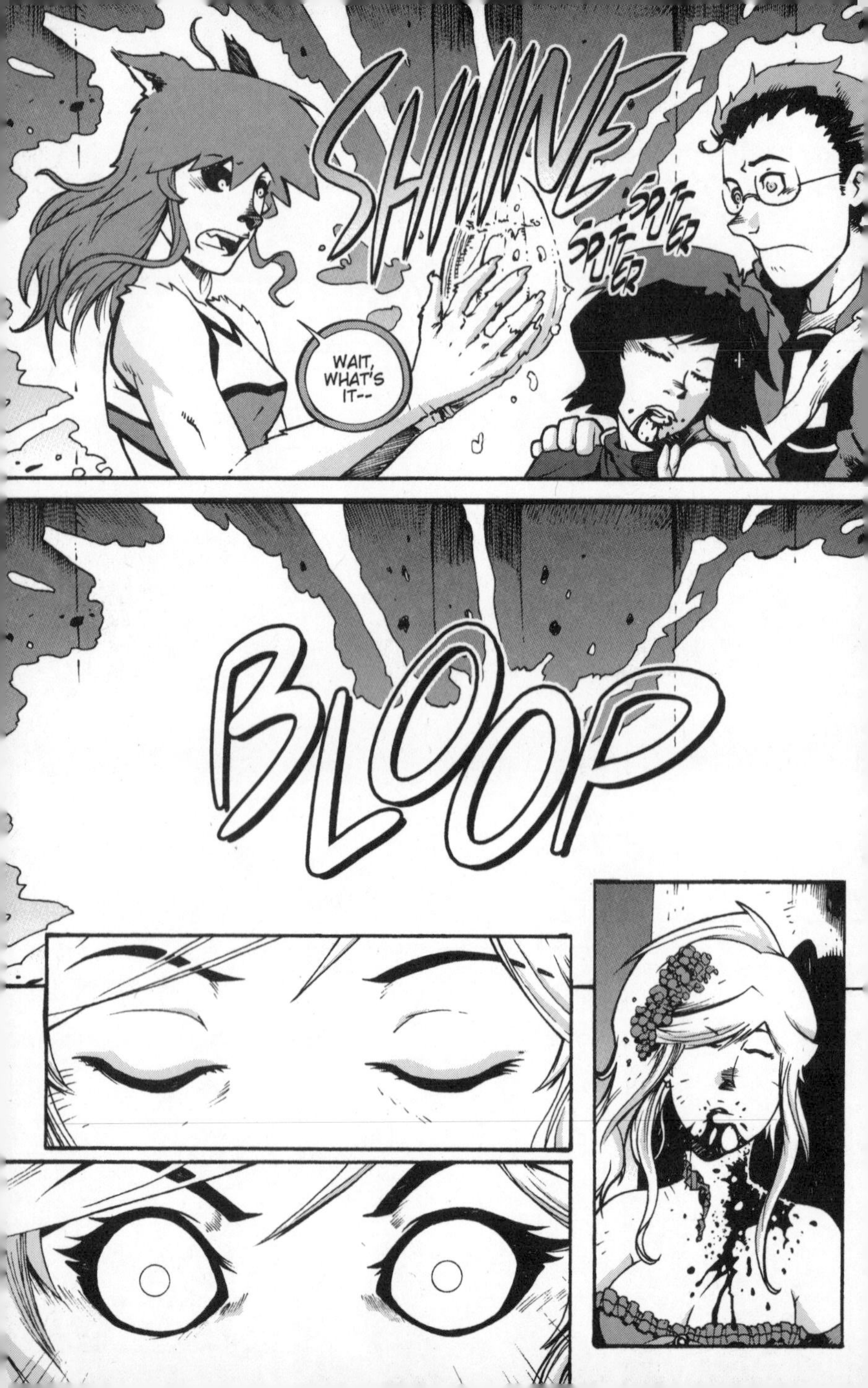
SPUTTER SPUTTER
SHIIINE
WAIT, WHAT'S IT--
BLOOP

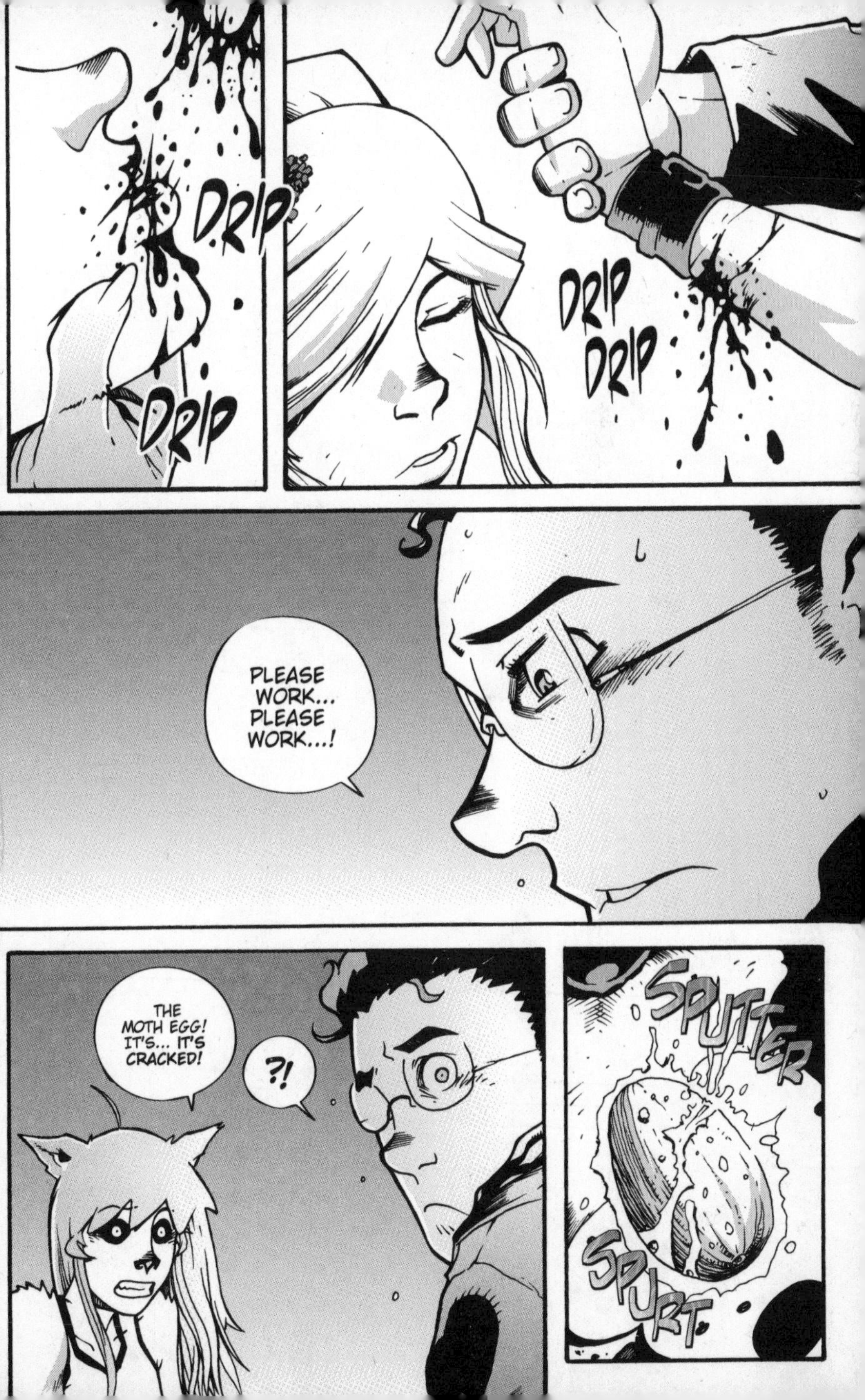
DRIP
DRIP
DRIP
DRIP
PLEASE WORK... PLEASE WORK...!
SPUTTER
SPURT
?!
THE MOTH EGG! IT'S... IT'S CRACKED!

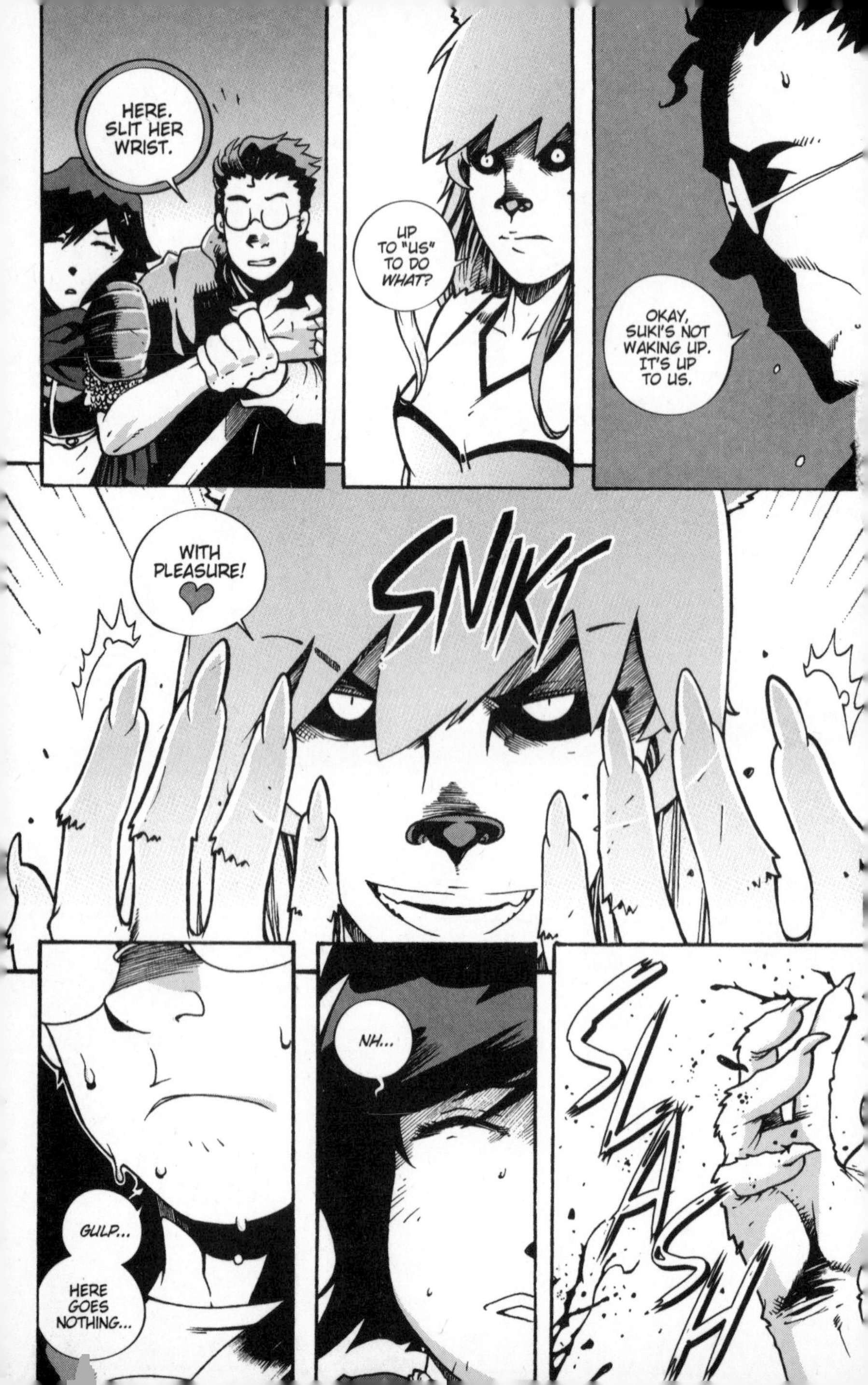
OKAY, SUKI'S NOT WAKING UP. IT'S UP TO US.
UP TO "US" TO DO WHAT?
HERE. SLIT HER WRIST.
SNIKT
WITH PLEASURE! ♥
SLASH
NH...
GULP...
HERE GOES NOTHING...

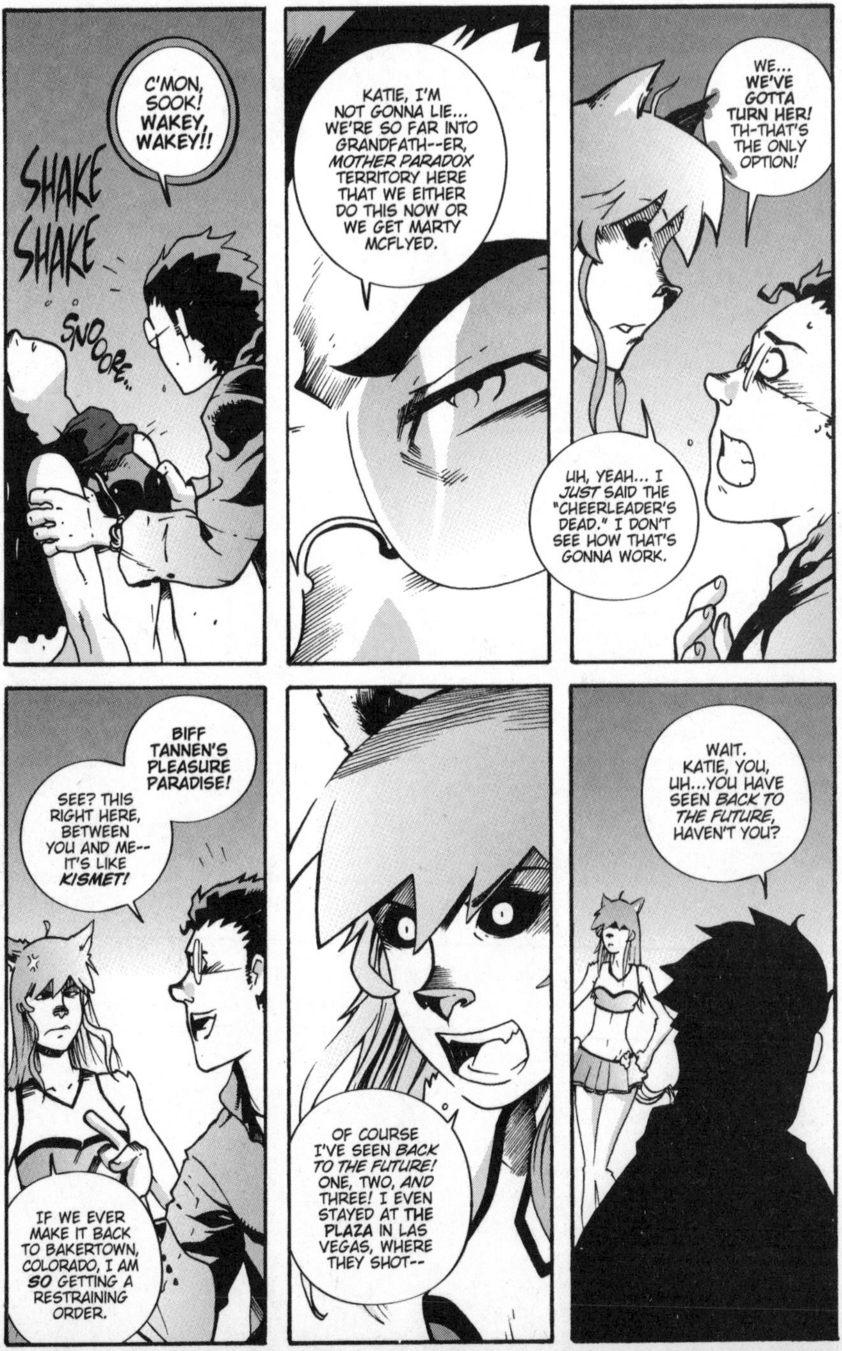
WE... WE'VE GOTTA TURN HER! TH-THAT'S THE ONLY OPTION!
UH, YEAH... I JUST SAID THE "CHEERLEADER'S DEAD." I DON'T SEE HOW THAT'S GONNA WORK.
KATIE, I'M NOT GONNA LIE... WE'RE SO FAR INTO GRANDFATH--ER, MOTHER PARADOX TERRITORY HERE THAT WE EITHER DO THIS NOW OR WE GET MARTY MCFLYED.
C'MON, SOOK! WAKEY, WAKEY!!
SHAKE SHAKE
SNOOORE...
WAIT. KATIE, YOU, UH...YOU HAVE SEEN BACK TO THE FUTURE, HAVEN'T YOU?
OF COURSE I'VE SEEN BACK TO THE FUTURE! ONE, TWO, AND THREE! I EVEN STAYED AT THE PLAZA IN LAS VEGAS, WHERE THEY SHOT--
BIFF TANNEN'S PLEASURE PARADISE!
SEE? THIS RIGHT HERE, BETWEEN YOU AND ME-- IT'S LIKE KISMET!
IF WE EVER MAKE IT BACK TO BAKERTOWN, COLORADO, I AM SO GETTING A RESTRAINING ORDER.

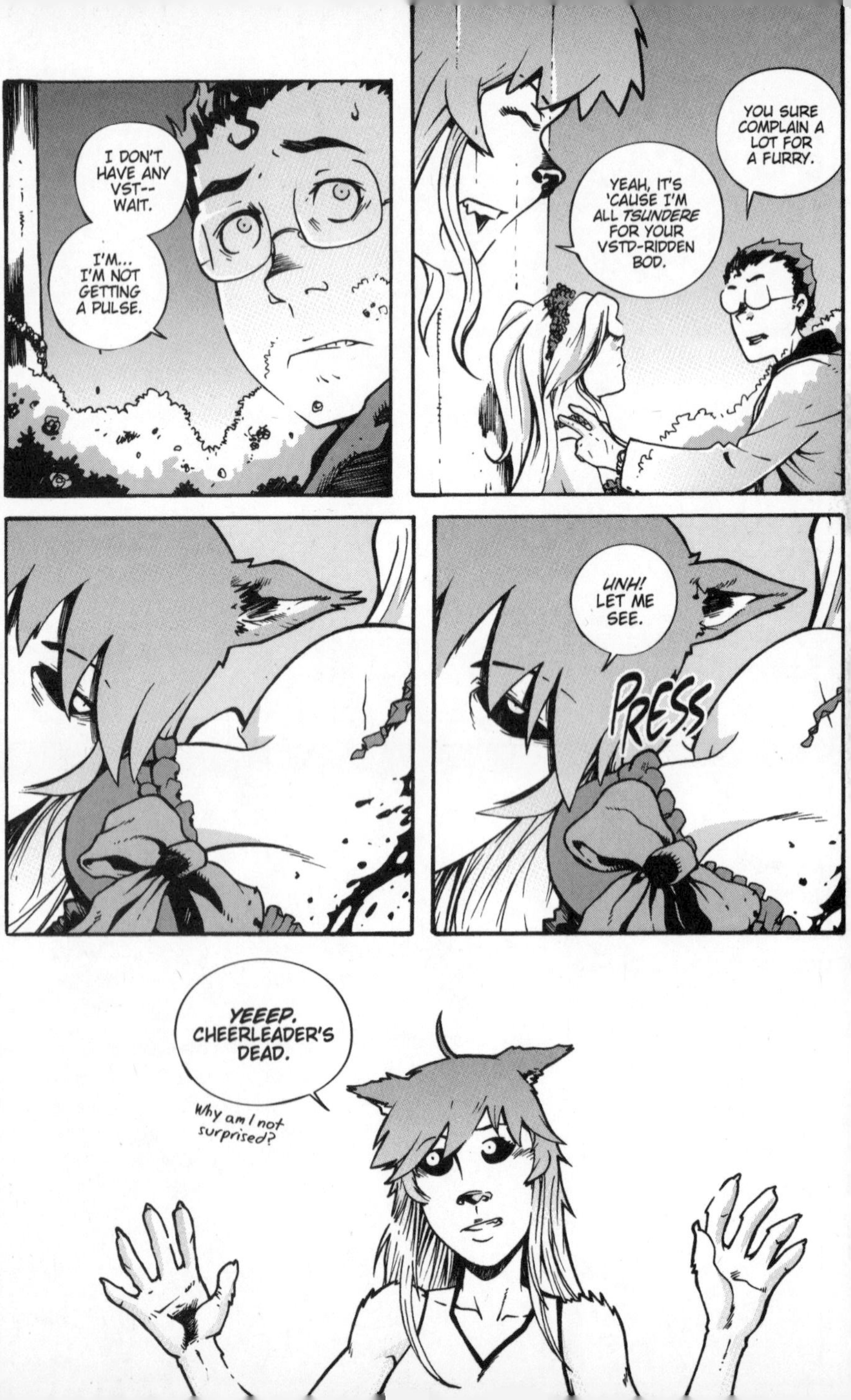

YOU SURE COMPLAIN A LOT FOR A FURRY.
YEAH, IT'S 'CAUSE I'M ALL *TSUNDERE* FOR YOUR VSTD-RIDDEN BOD.
I DON'T HAVE ANY VST-- WAIT.
I'M... I'M NOT GETTING A PULSE.
UNH! LET ME SEE.
PRESS
YEEEP. CHEERLEADER'S DEAD.
Why am I not surprised?

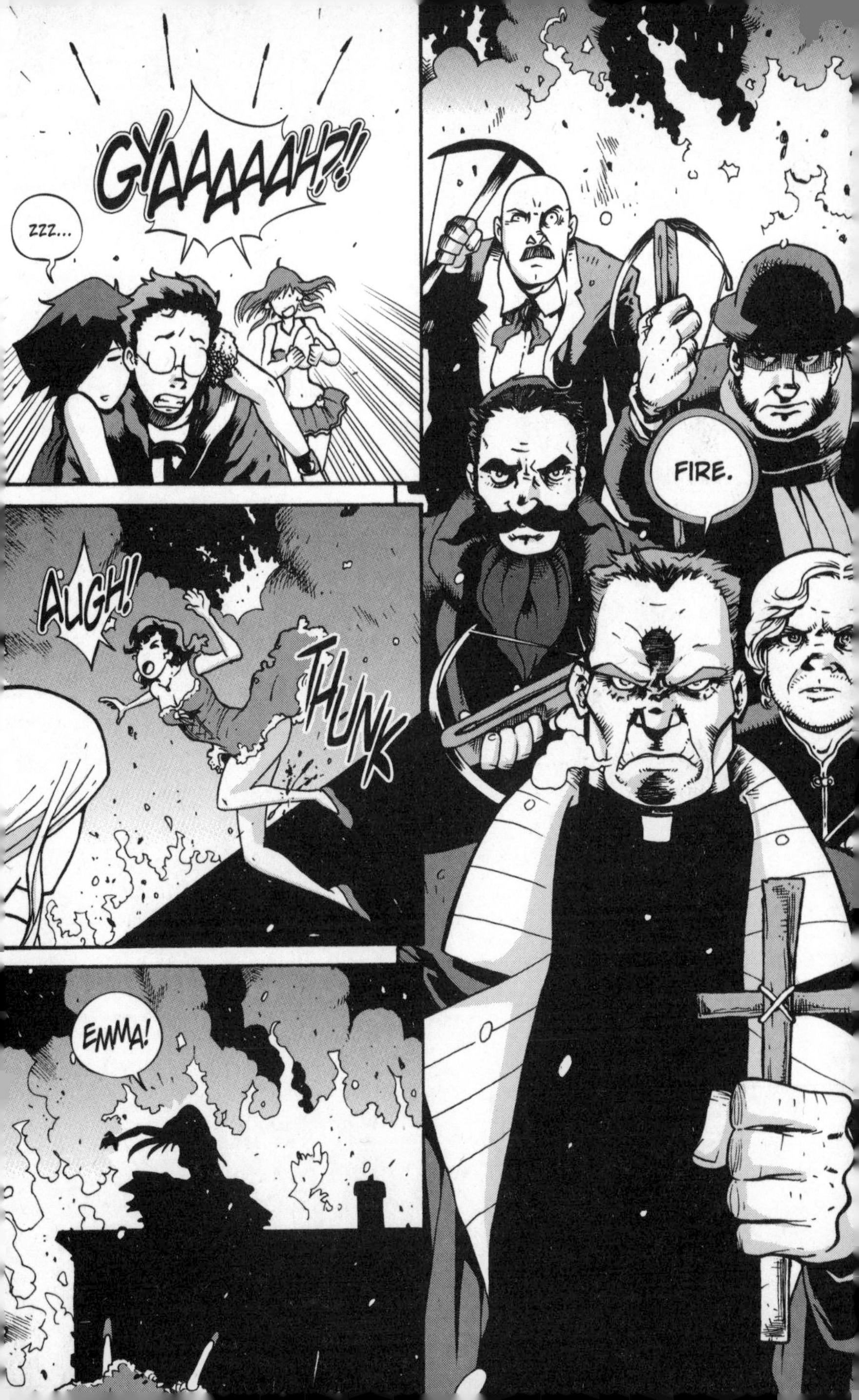
FIRE.
GYAAAAAH?!
zzz...
AUGH!
THUNK
EMMA!

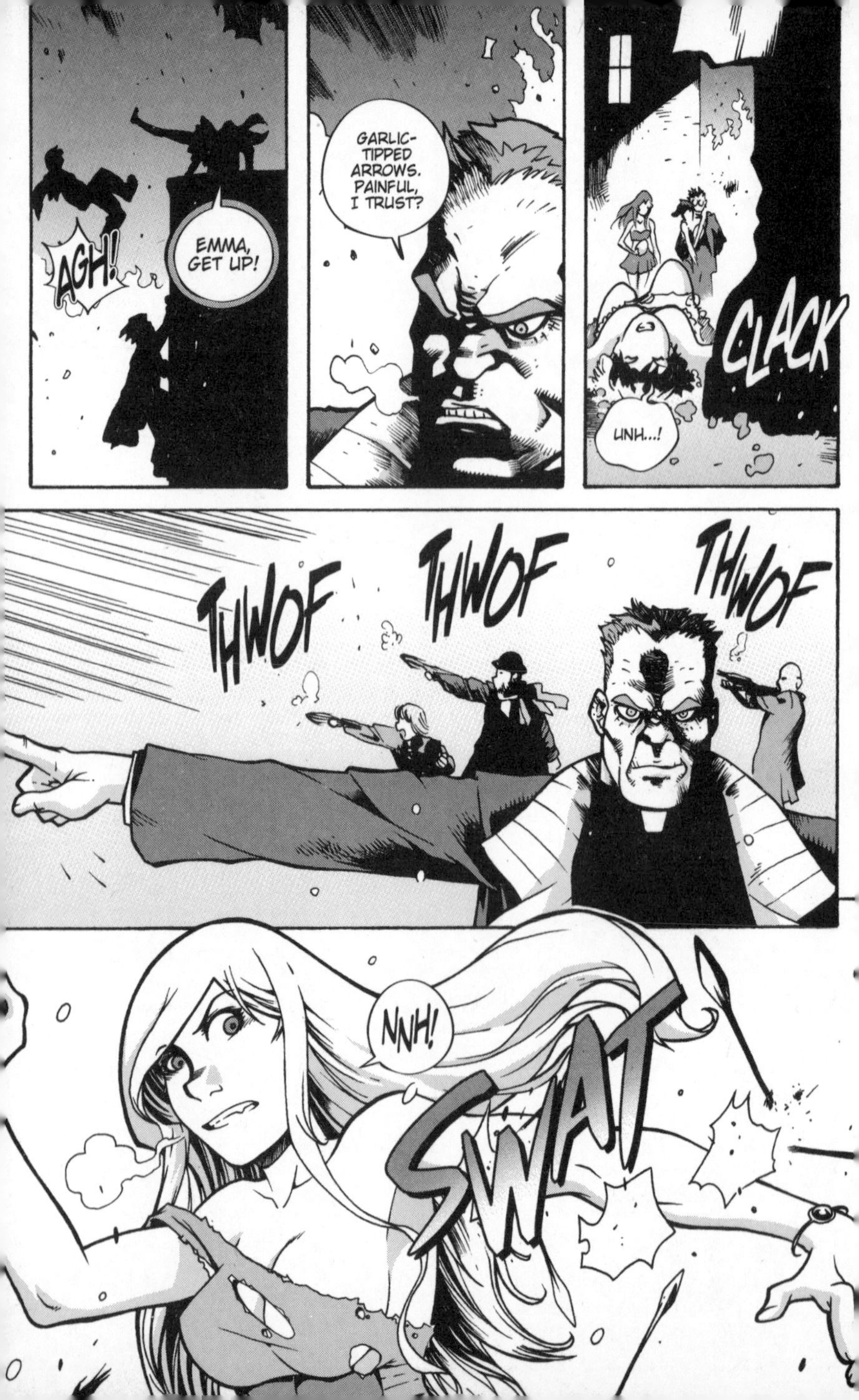
CLACK
UNH...!
GARLIC-TIPPED ARROWS. PAINFUL, I TRUST?
EMMA, GET UP!
AGH!
THWOF
THWOF
THWOF
NNH!
SWAT

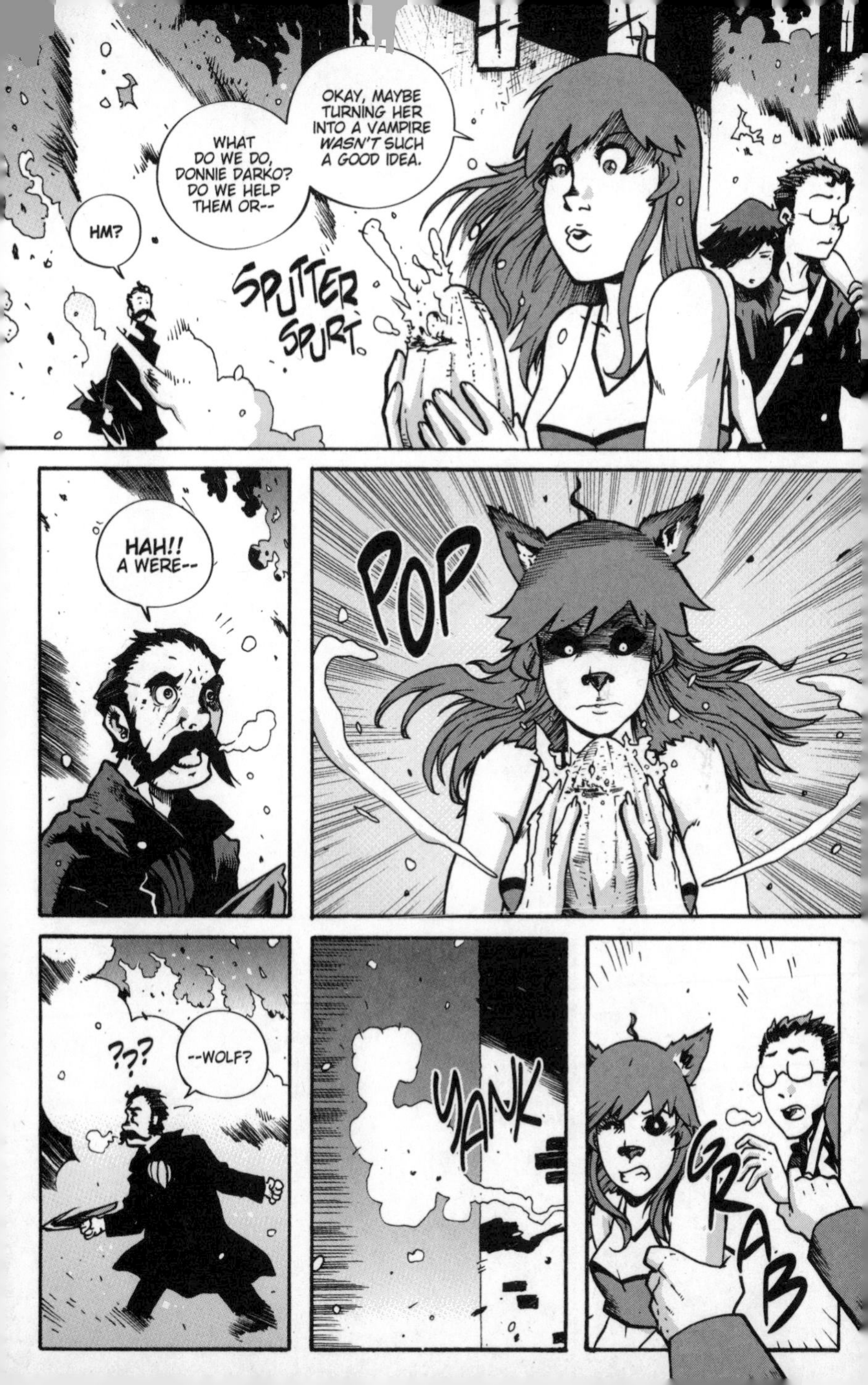
OKAY, MAYBE TURNING HER INTO A VAMPIRE *WASN'T* SUCH A GOOD IDEA.
WHAT DO WE DO, DONNIE DARKO? DO WE HELP THEM OR--
HM?
SPUTTER
SPURT
POP
HAH!! A WERE--
GRAB
YANK
???
--WOLF?

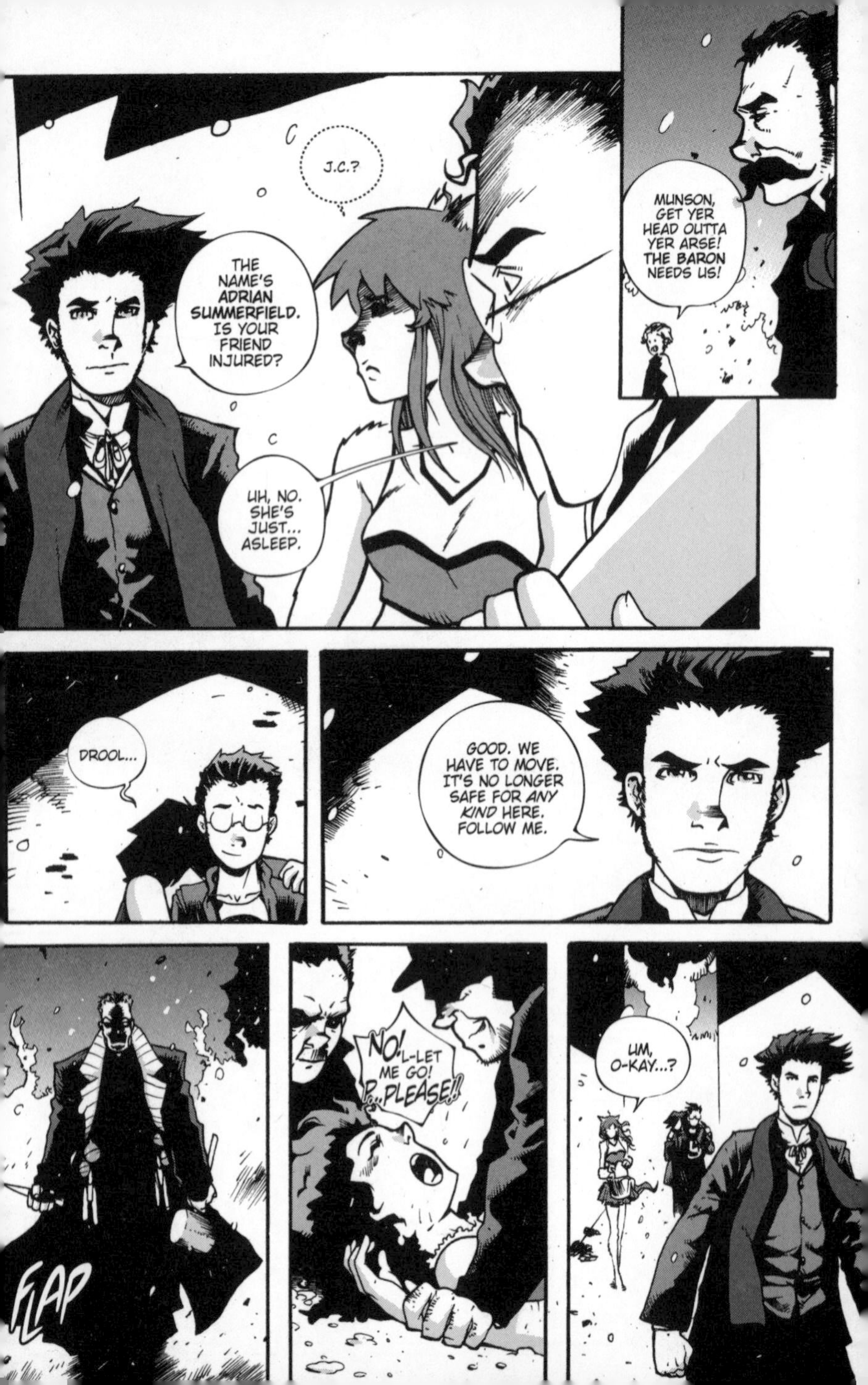
MUNSON, GET YER HEAD OUTTA YER ARSE! THE BARON NEEDS US!
J.C.?
THE NAME'S ADRIAN SUMMERFIELD. IS YOUR FRIEND INJURED?
UH, NO. SHE'S JUST... ASLEEP.
GOOD. WE HAVE TO MOVE. IT'S NO LONGER SAFE FOR *ANY KIND* HERE. FOLLOW ME.
DROOL...
UM, O-KAY...?
NO! L-LET ME GO! P...PLEASE!!
FLAP

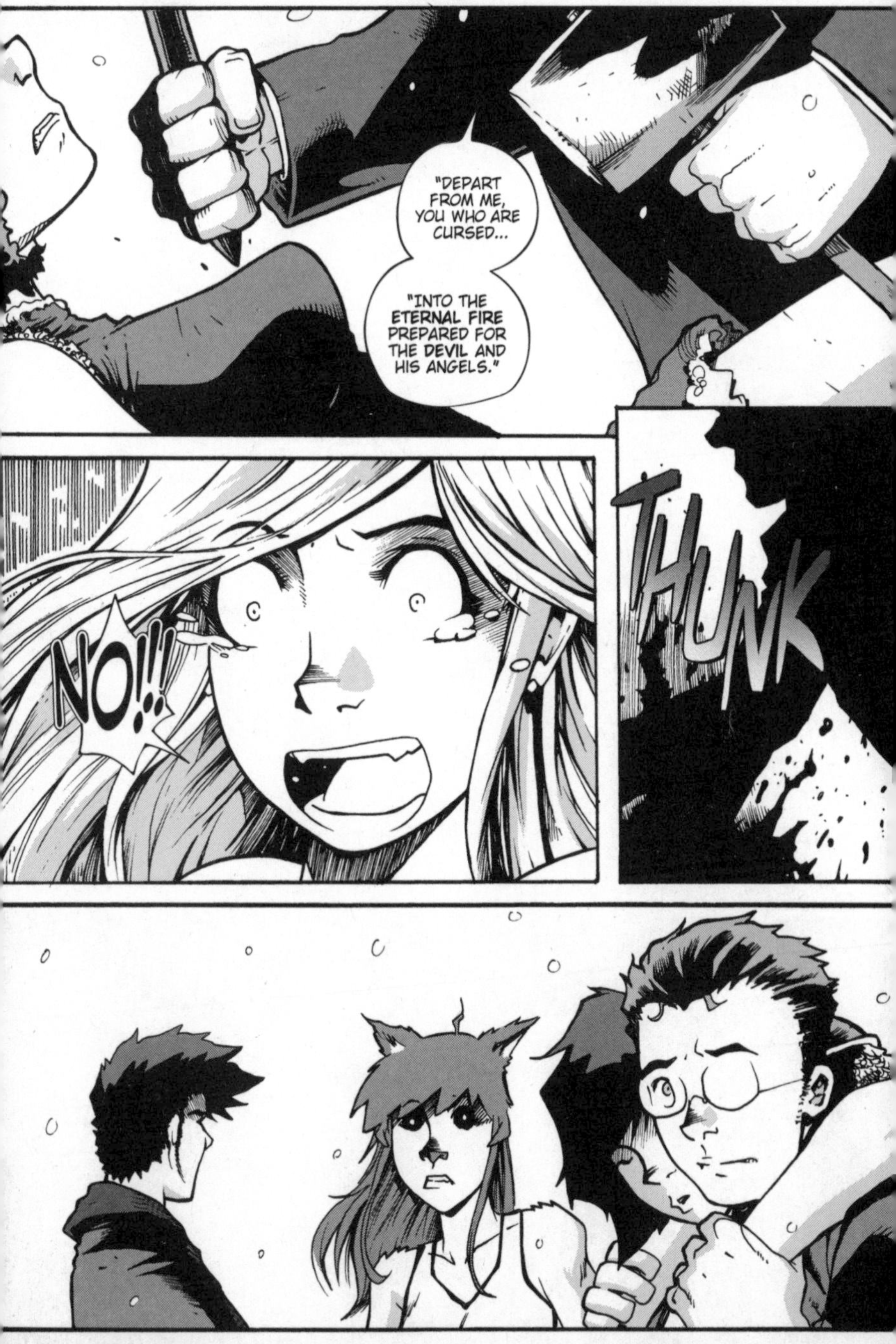
"DEPART FROM ME, YOU WHO ARE CURSED...
"INTO THE ETERNAL FIRE PREPARED FOR THE DEVIL AND HIS ANGELS."
THUNK
NO!!!

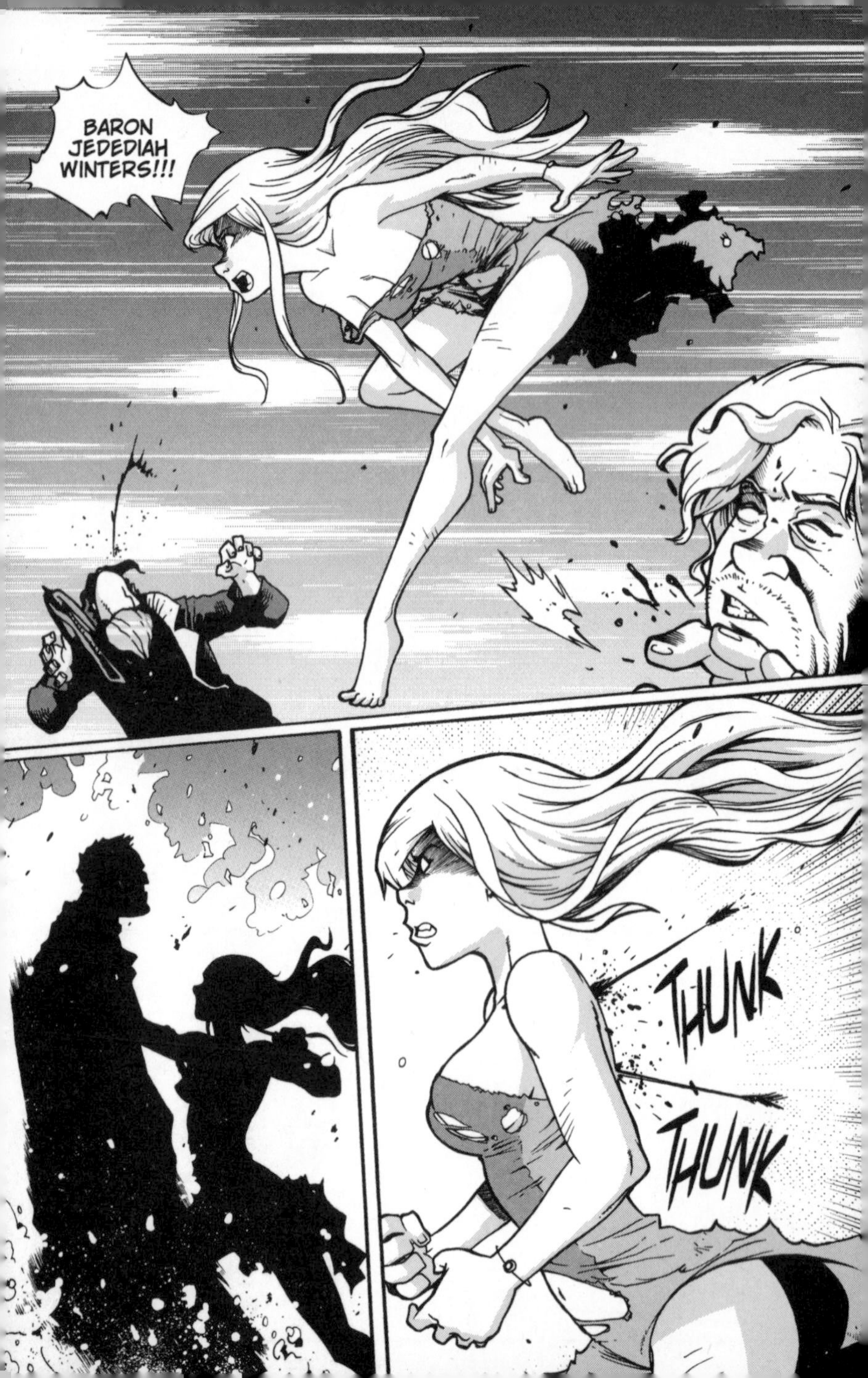
BARON JEDEDIAH WINTERS!!!
THUNK
THUNK

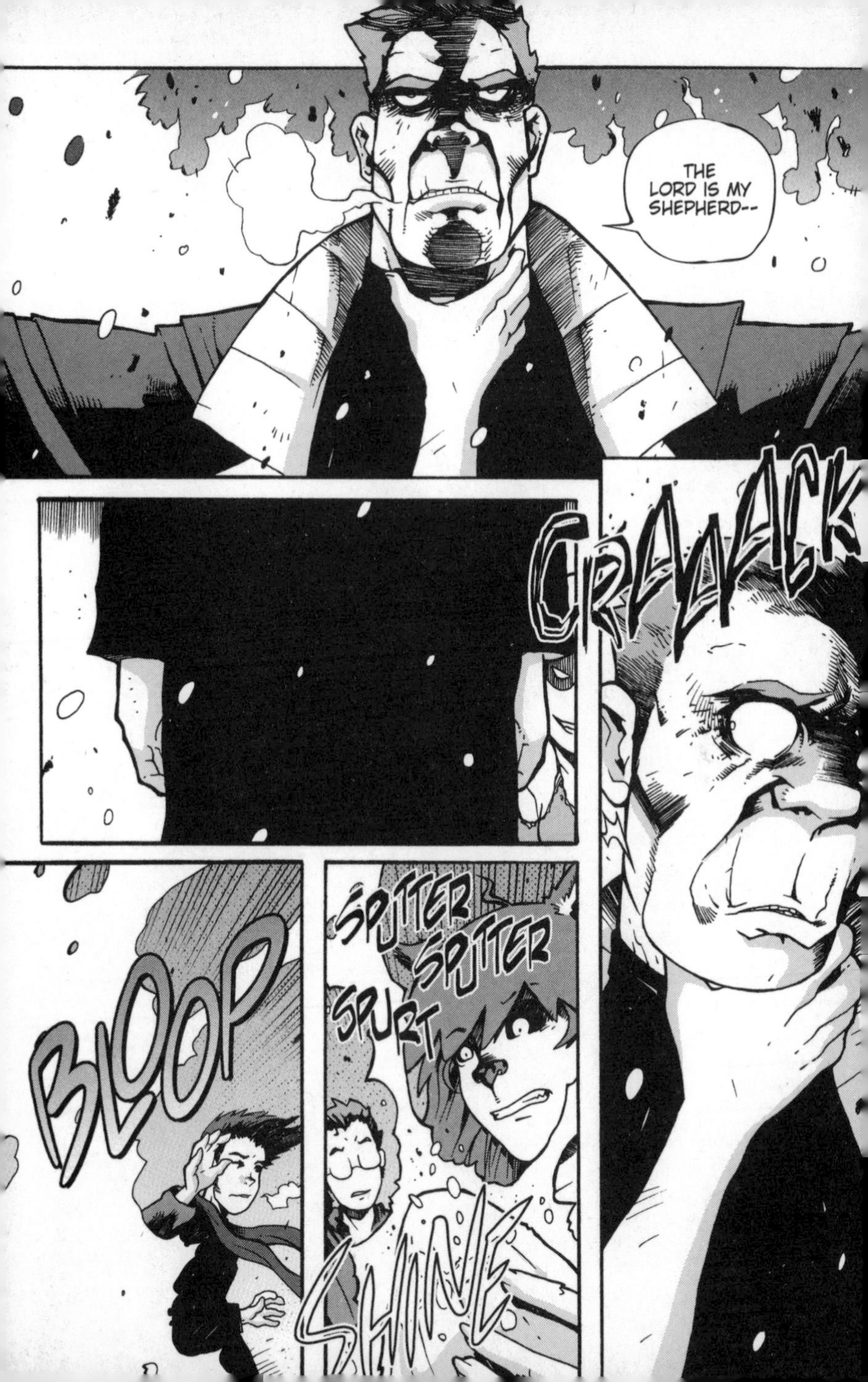
THE LORD IS MY SHEPHERD--
CRAAACK
SPITTER
SPITTER
SPURT
SHINE
BLOOP

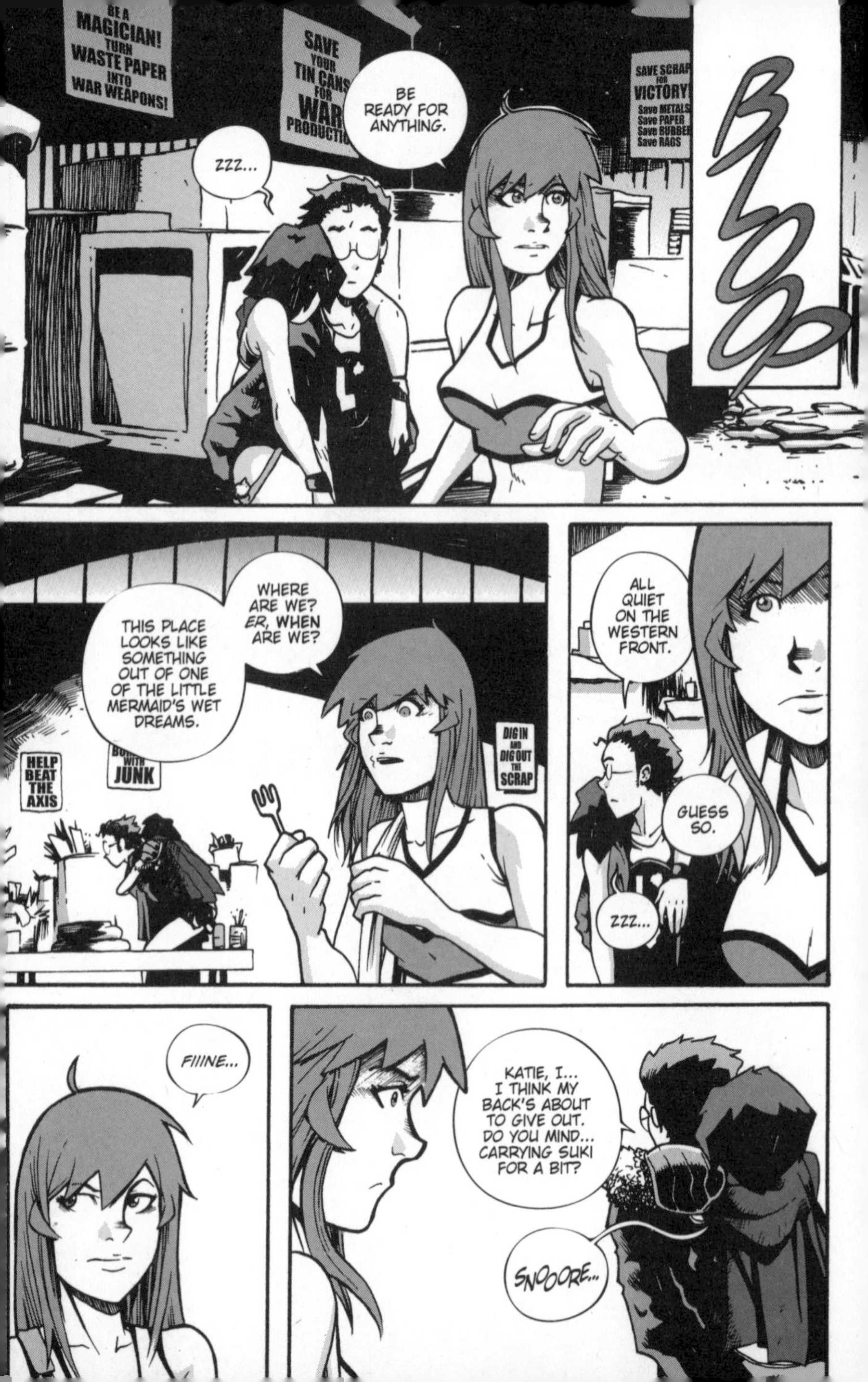
SAVE SCRAP FOR VICTORY! Save METALS Save PAPER Save RUBBER Save RAGS
BE READY FOR ANYTHING.
SAVE YOUR TIN CANS FOR WAR PRODUCTI
BE A MAGICIAN! TURN WASTE PAPER INTO WAR WEAPONS!
ZZZ...
ALL QUIET ON THE WESTERN FRONT.
GUESS SO.
ZZZ...
WHERE ARE WE? ER, WHEN ARE WE?
THIS PLACE LOOKS LIKE SOMETHING OUT OF ONE OF THE LITTLE MERMAID'S WET DREAMS.
DIG IN AND DIG OUT THE SCRAP
HELP BEAT THE AXIS
KATIE, I... I THINK MY BACK'S ABOUT TO GIVE OUT. DO YOU MIND... CARRYING SUKI FOR A BIT?
SNOOORE...
FIIINE...

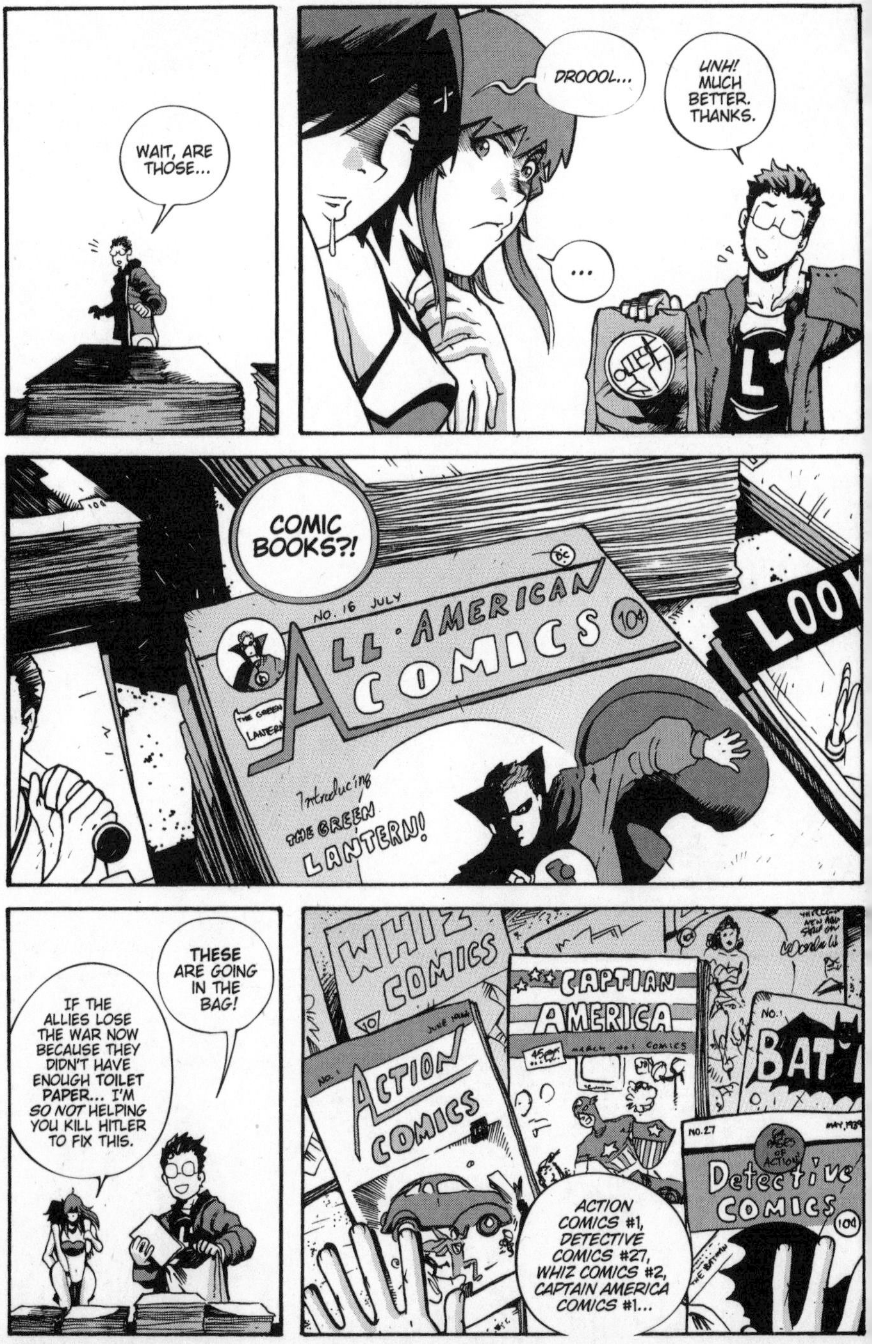
UNH! MUCH BETTER. THANKS.
DROOOL...
...
WAIT, ARE THOSE...
COMIC BOOKS?!
NO. 16 JULY
ALL AMERICAN COMICS
10¢
THE GREEN LANTERN
Introducing THE GREEN LANTERN!
LOO
WHIZ COMICS
CAPTIAN AMERICA
ACTION COMICS
BAT
NO. 27
Detective COMICS
ACTION COMICS #1, DETECTIVE COMICS #27, WHIZ COMICS #2, CAPTAIN AMERICA COMICS #1...
THESE ARE GOING IN THE BAG!
IF THE ALLIES LOSE THE WAR NOW BECAUSE THEY DIDN'T HAVE ENOUGH TOILET PAPER... I'M *SO NOT* HELPING YOU KILL HITLER TO FIX THIS.

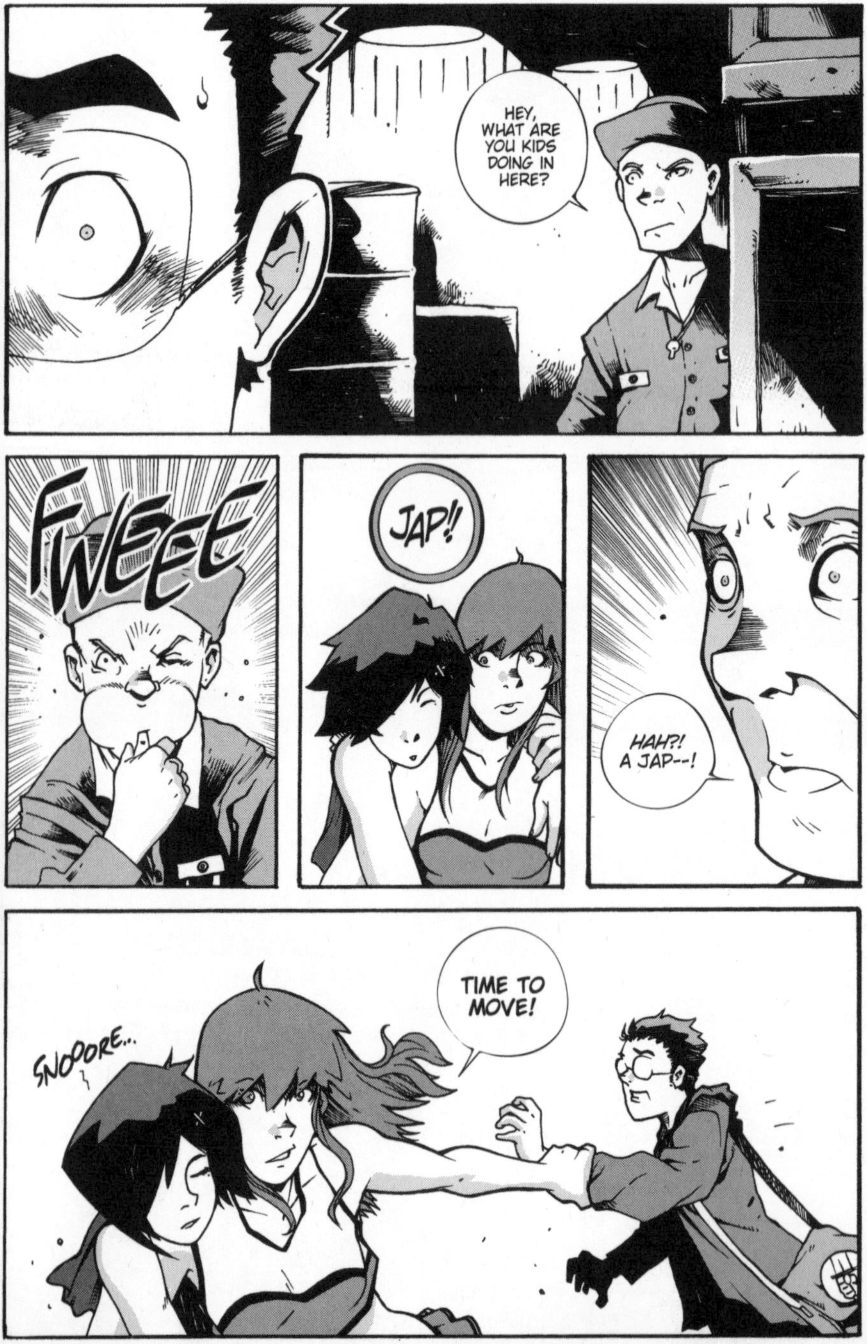
HEY, WHAT ARE YOU KIDS DOING IN HERE?
HAH?! A JAP--!
JAP!!
FWEEE
TIME TO MOVE!
SNOOORE...

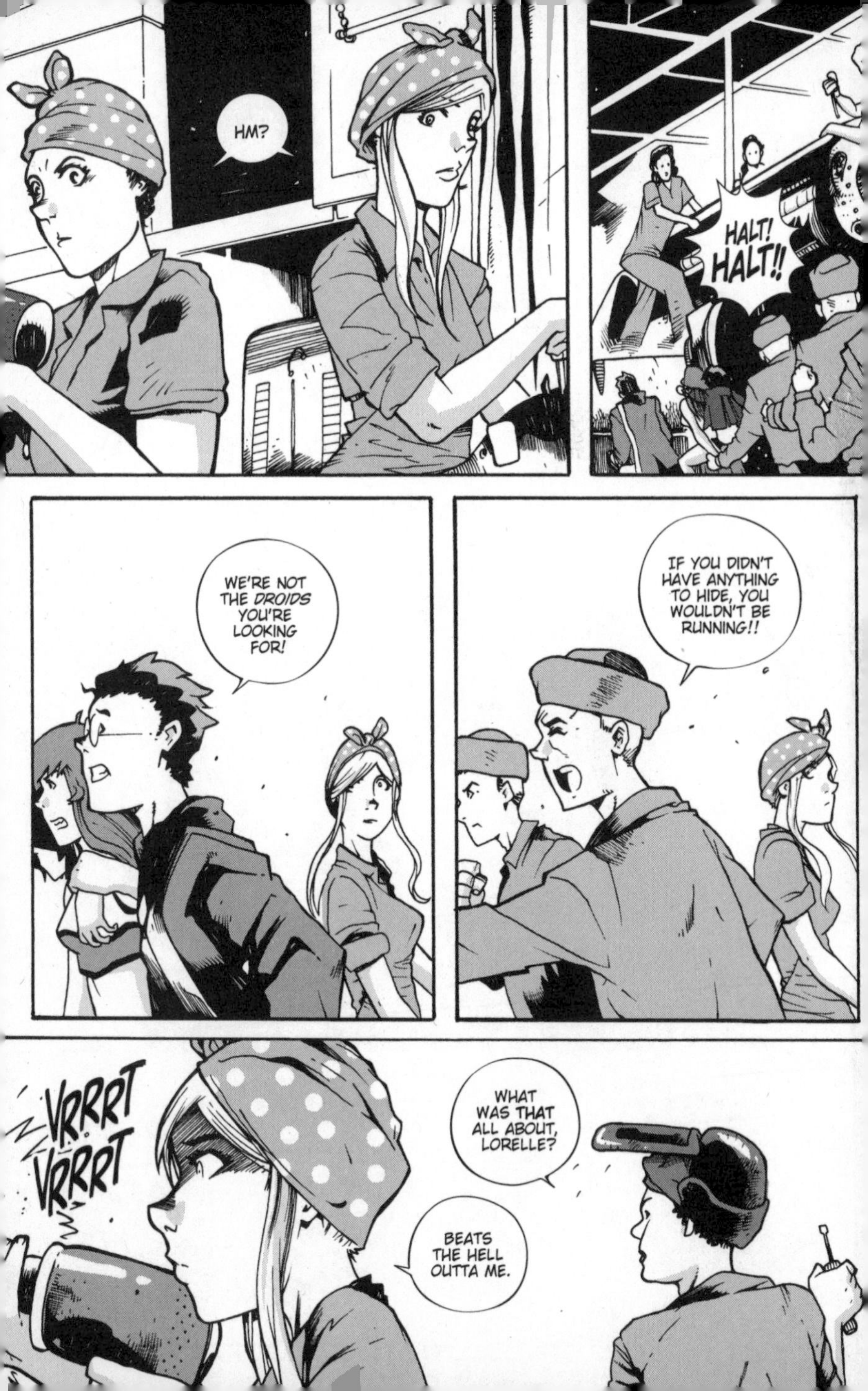
HALT! HALT!!
HM?
IF YOU DIDN'T HAVE ANYTHING TO HIDE, YOU WOULDN'T BE RUNNING!!
WE'RE NOT THE *DROIDS* YOU'RE LOOKING FOR!
WHAT WAS THAT ALL ABOUT, LORELLE?
BEATS THE HELL OUTTA ME.
VRRRT VRRRT

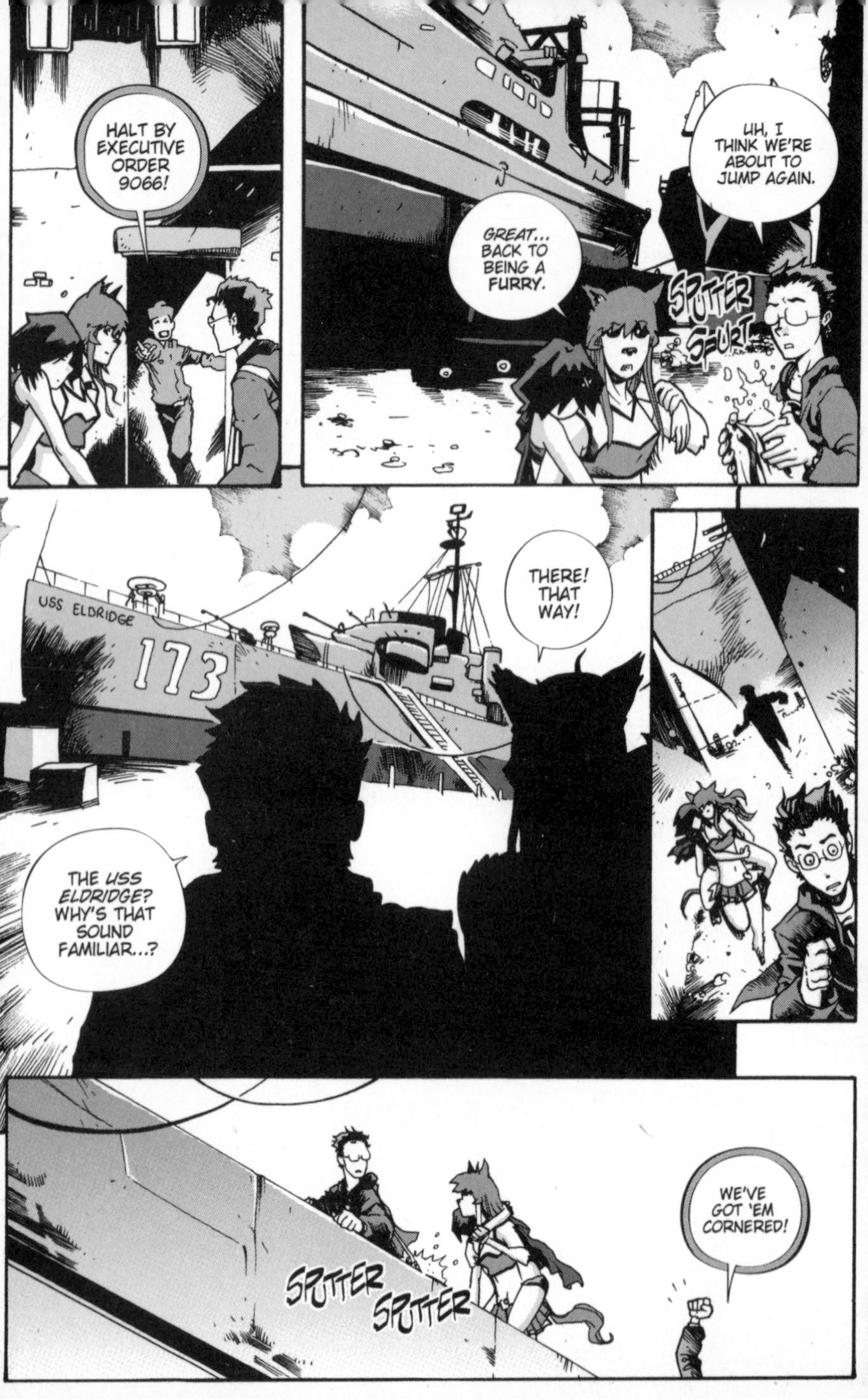
UH, I THINK WE'RE ABOUT TO JUMP AGAIN.
GREAT... BACK TO BEING A FURRY.
SPUTTER
SPURT
HALT BY EXECUTIVE ORDER 9066!
THERE! THAT WAY!
USS ELDRIDGE
173
THE USS ELDRIDGE? WHY'S THAT SOUND FAMILIAR...?
WE'VE GOT 'EM CORNERED!
SPUTTER
SPUTTER

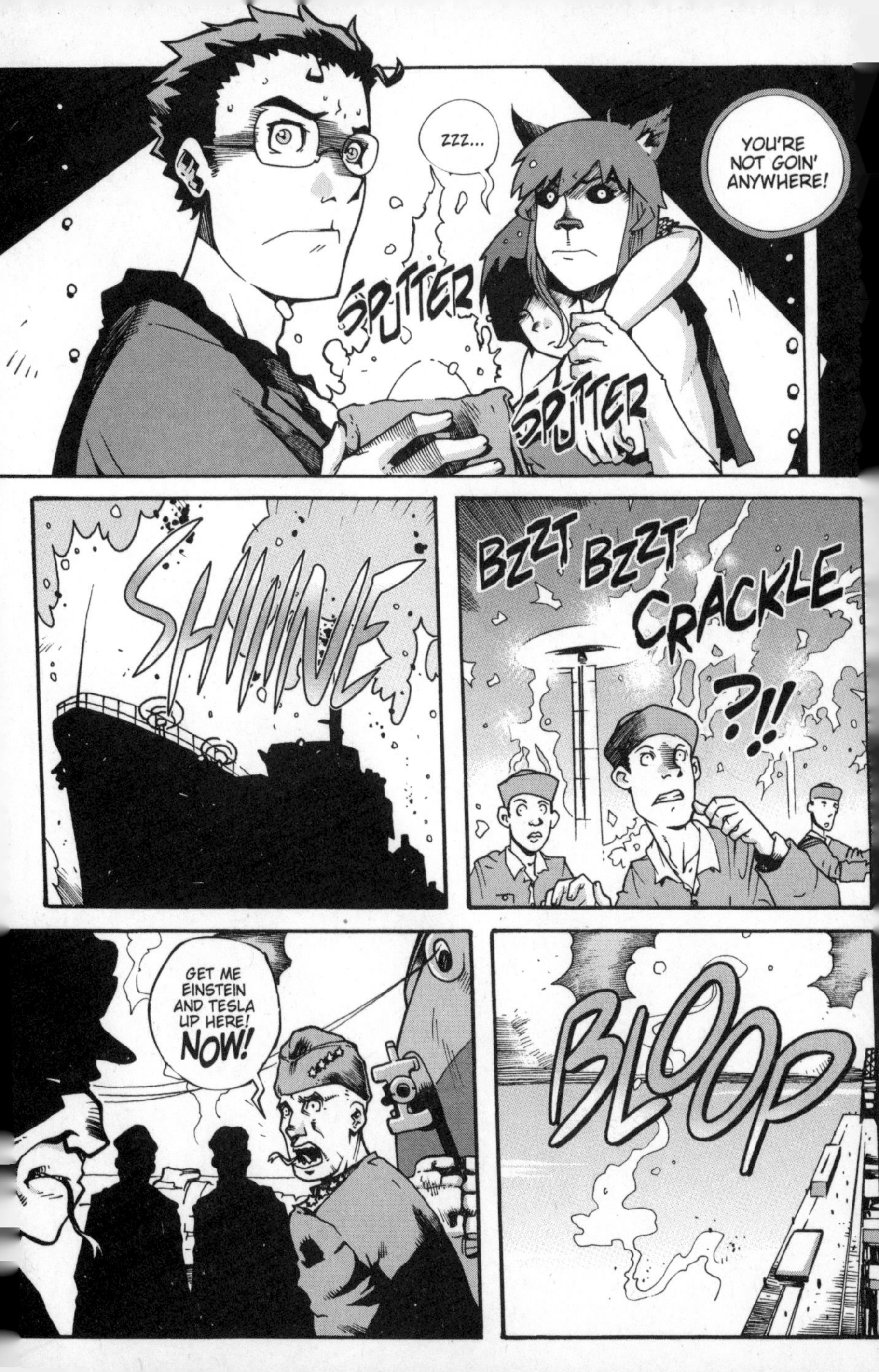
YOU'RE NOT GOIN' ANYWHERE!
ZZZ...
SPUTTER
SPUTTER
BZZT BZZT
CRACKLE
?!!
SHIIINE
BLOOP
GET ME EINSTEIN AND TESLA UP HERE! NOW!

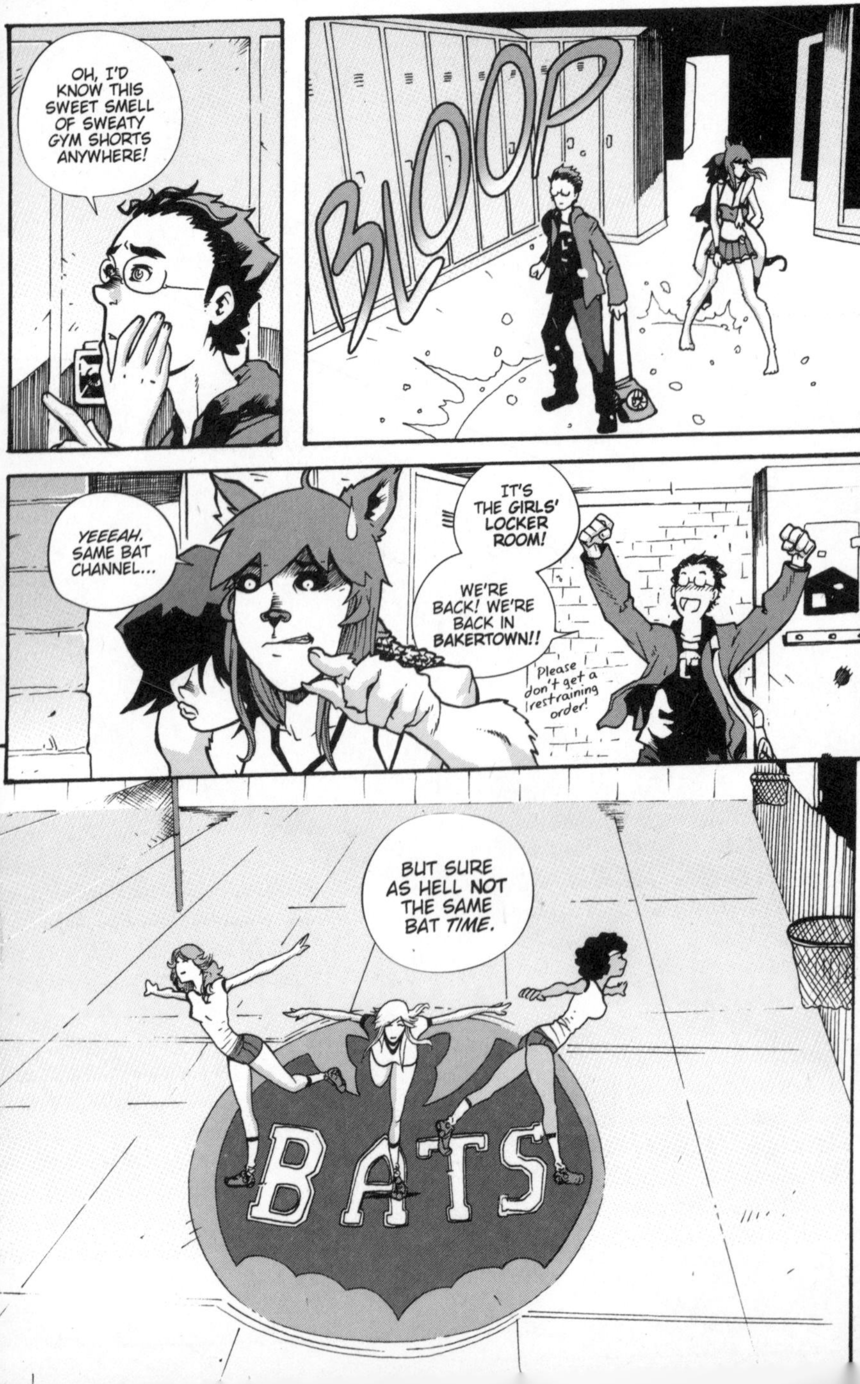
BLOOP
OH, I'D KNOW THIS SWEET SMELL OF SWEATY GYM SHORTS ANYWHERE!
IT'S THE GIRLS' LOCKER ROOM!
WE'RE BACK! WE'RE BACK IN BAKERTOWN!!
Please don't get a restraining order!
YEEEAH. SAME BAT CHANNEL...
BUT SURE AS HELL NOT THE SAME BAT TIME.
BATS

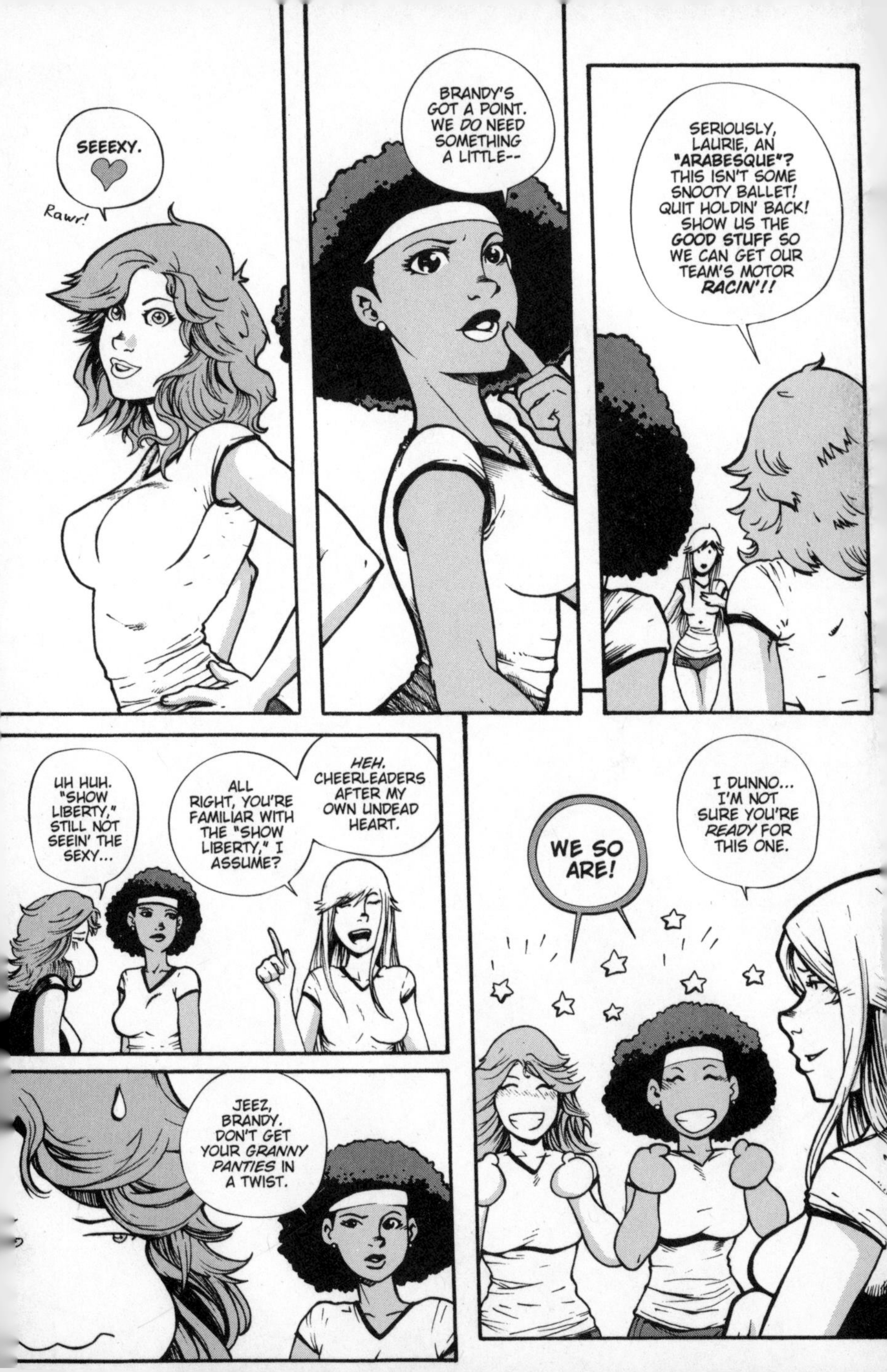
SERIOUSLY, LAURIE, AN **"ARABESQUE"?** THIS ISN'T SOME SNOOTY BALLET! QUIT HOLDIN' BACK! SHOW US THE **GOOD STUFF** SO WE CAN GET OUR TEAM'S MOTOR ***RACIN'!!***
BRANDY'S GOT A POINT. WE *DO* NEED SOMETHING A LITTLE--
SEEEXY. ♥
Rawr!
I DUNNO... I'M NOT SURE YOU'RE *READY* FOR THIS ONE.
WE SO ARE!
HEH. CHEERLEADERS AFTER MY OWN UNDEAD HEART.
ALL RIGHT, YOU'RE FAMILIAR WITH THE "SHOW LIBERTY," I ASSUME?
UH HUH. "SHOW LIBERTY," STILL NOT SEEIN' THE SEXY...
JEEZ, BRANDY. DON'T GET YOUR *GRANNY PANTIES* IN A TWIST.

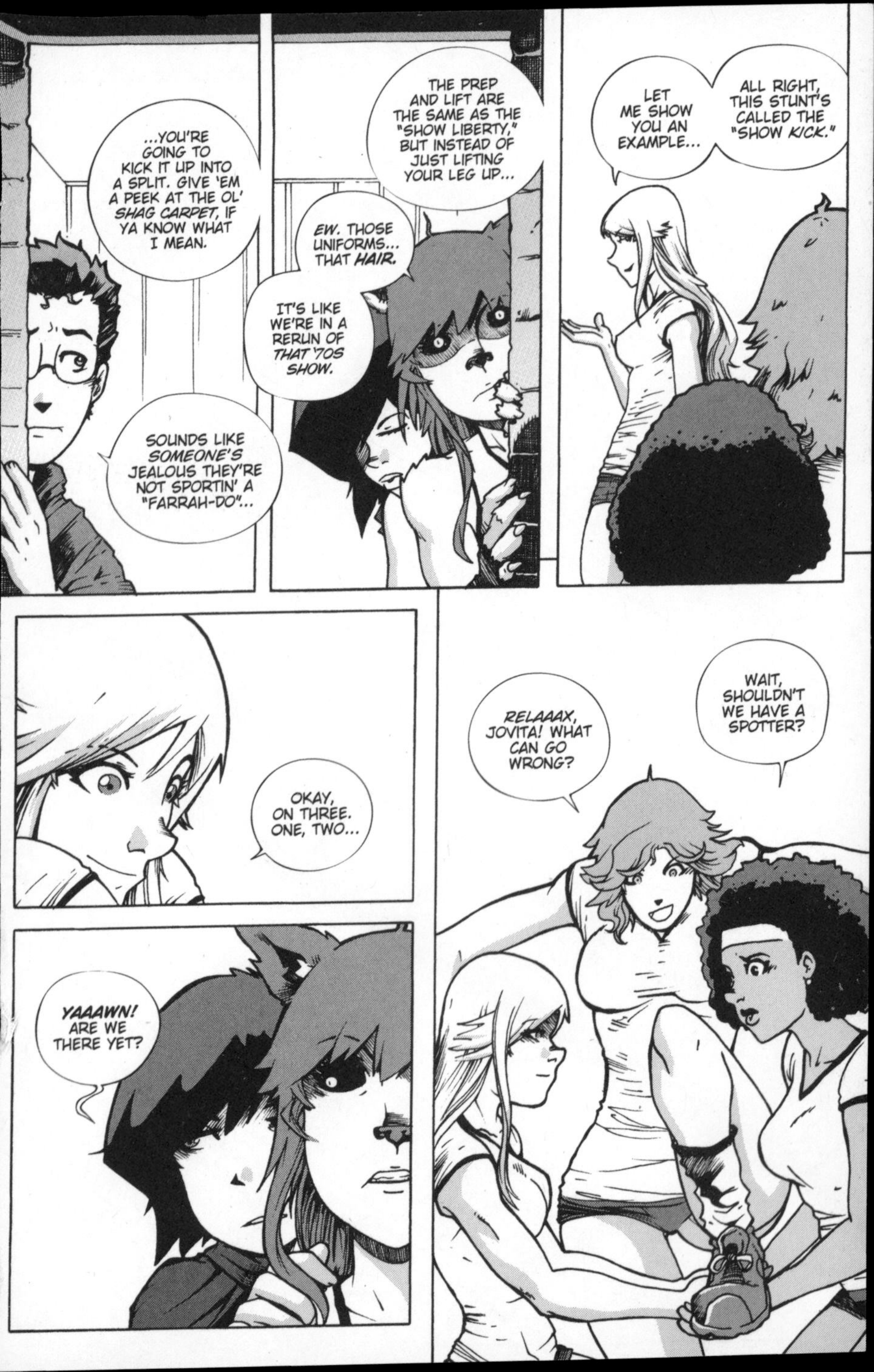
ALL RIGHT, THIS STUNT'S CALLED THE "SHOW *KICK*."
LET ME SHOW YOU AN EXAMPLE...
THE PREP AND LIFT ARE THE SAME AS THE "SHOW LIBERTY," BUT INSTEAD OF JUST LIFTING YOUR LEG UP...
EW. THOSE UNIFORMS... THAT ***HAIR.***
IT'S LIKE WE'RE IN A RERUN OF *THAT '70S SHOW.*
...YOU'RE GOING TO KICK IT UP INTO A SPLIT. GIVE 'EM A PEEK AT THE OL' *SHAG CARPET*, IF YA KNOW WHAT I MEAN.
SOUNDS LIKE *SOMEONE'S* JEALOUS THEY'RE NOT SPORTIN' A "FARRAH-DO"...
WAIT, SHOULDN'T WE HAVE A SPOTTER?
RELAAAX, JOVITA! WHAT CAN GO WRONG?
OKAY, ON THREE. ONE, TWO...
YAAAWN! ARE WE THERE YET?

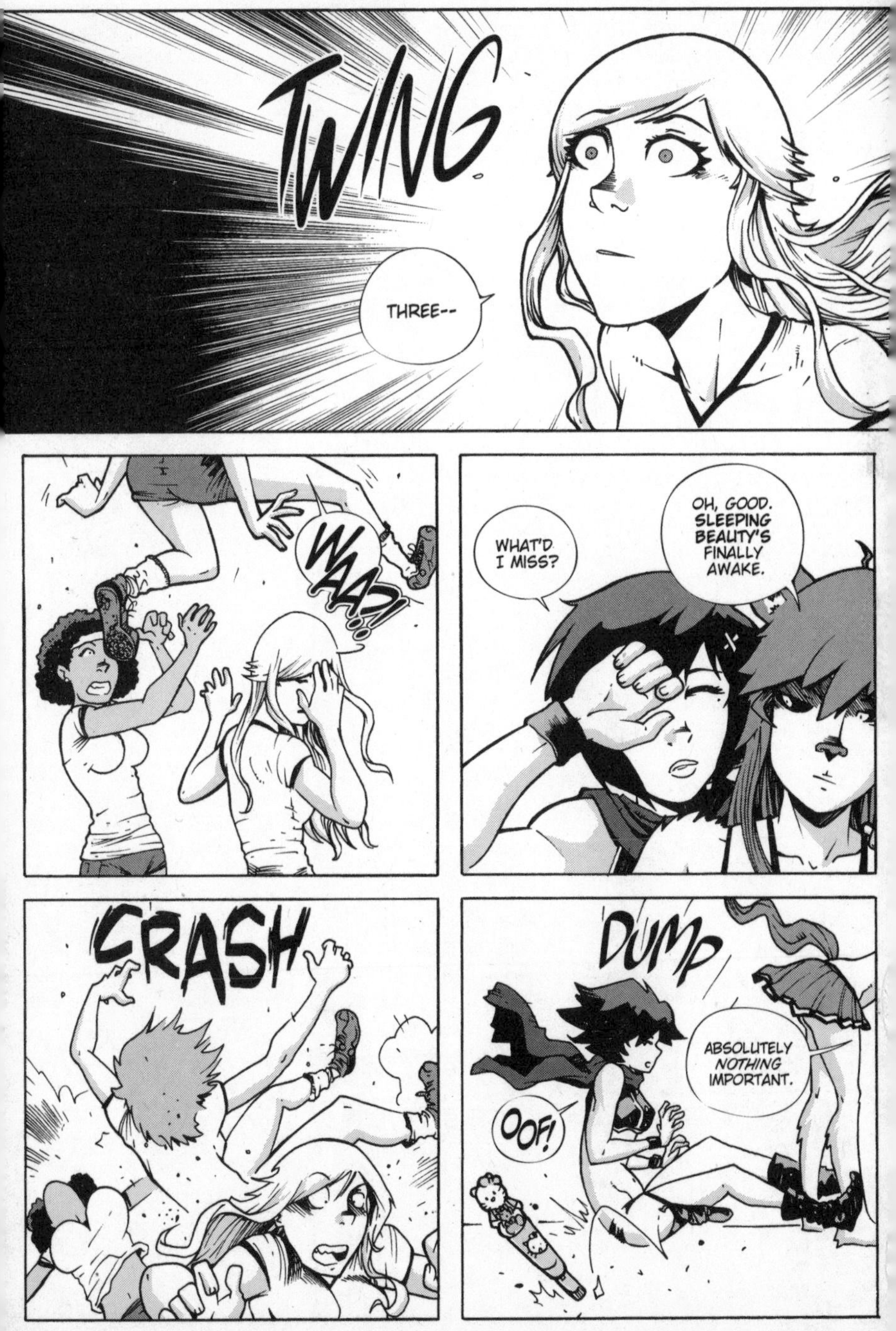
TWING
THREE--
OH, GOOD. SLEEPING BEAUTY'S FINALLY AWAKE.
WHAT'D I MISS?
WAA?!!
DUMP
ABSOLUTELY *NOTHING* IMPORTANT.
OOF!
CRASH

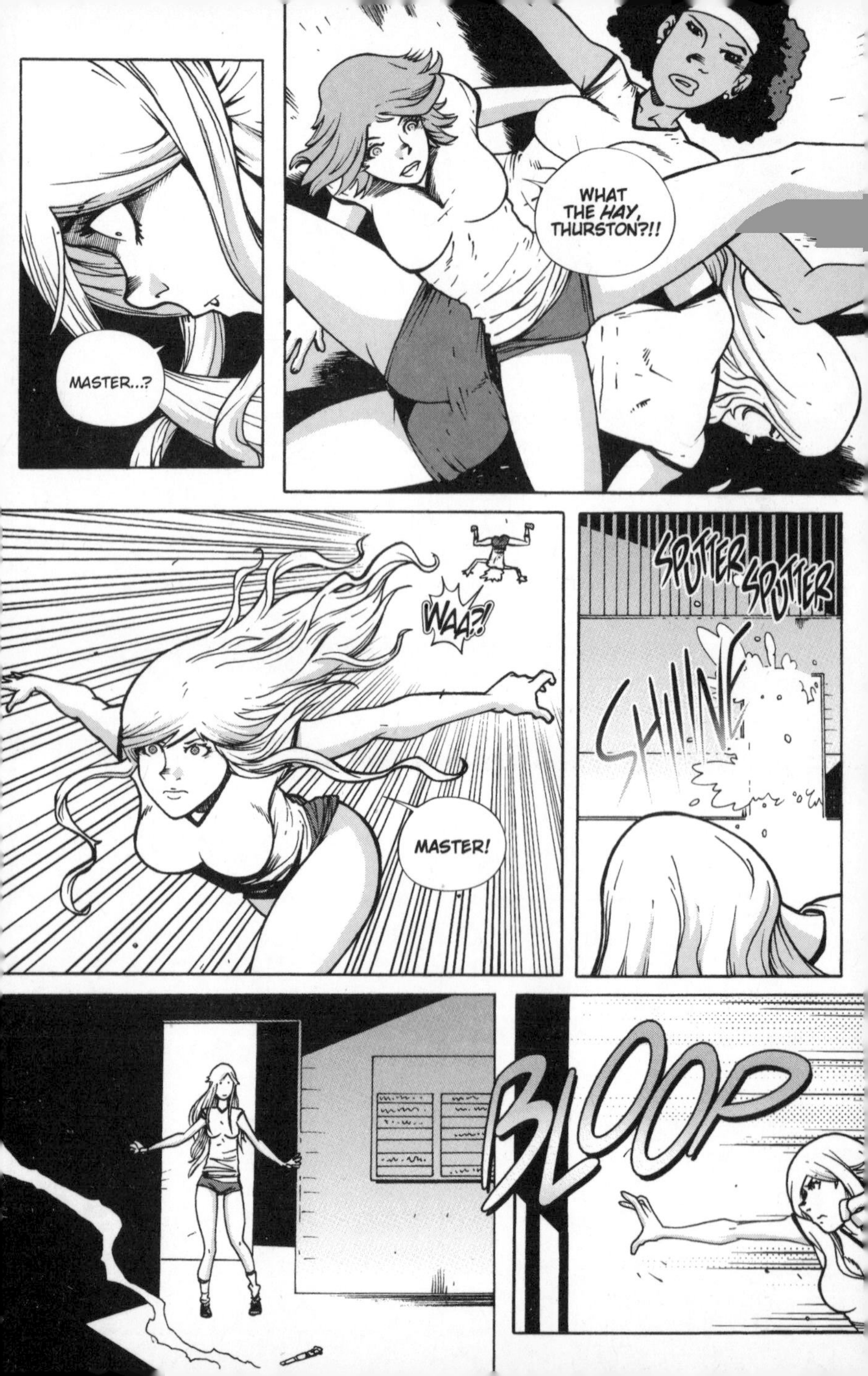
WHAT THE HAY, THURSTON?!!
MASTER...?
SPUTTER SPUTTER
SHIIINE
WAA?!
MASTER!
BLOOP

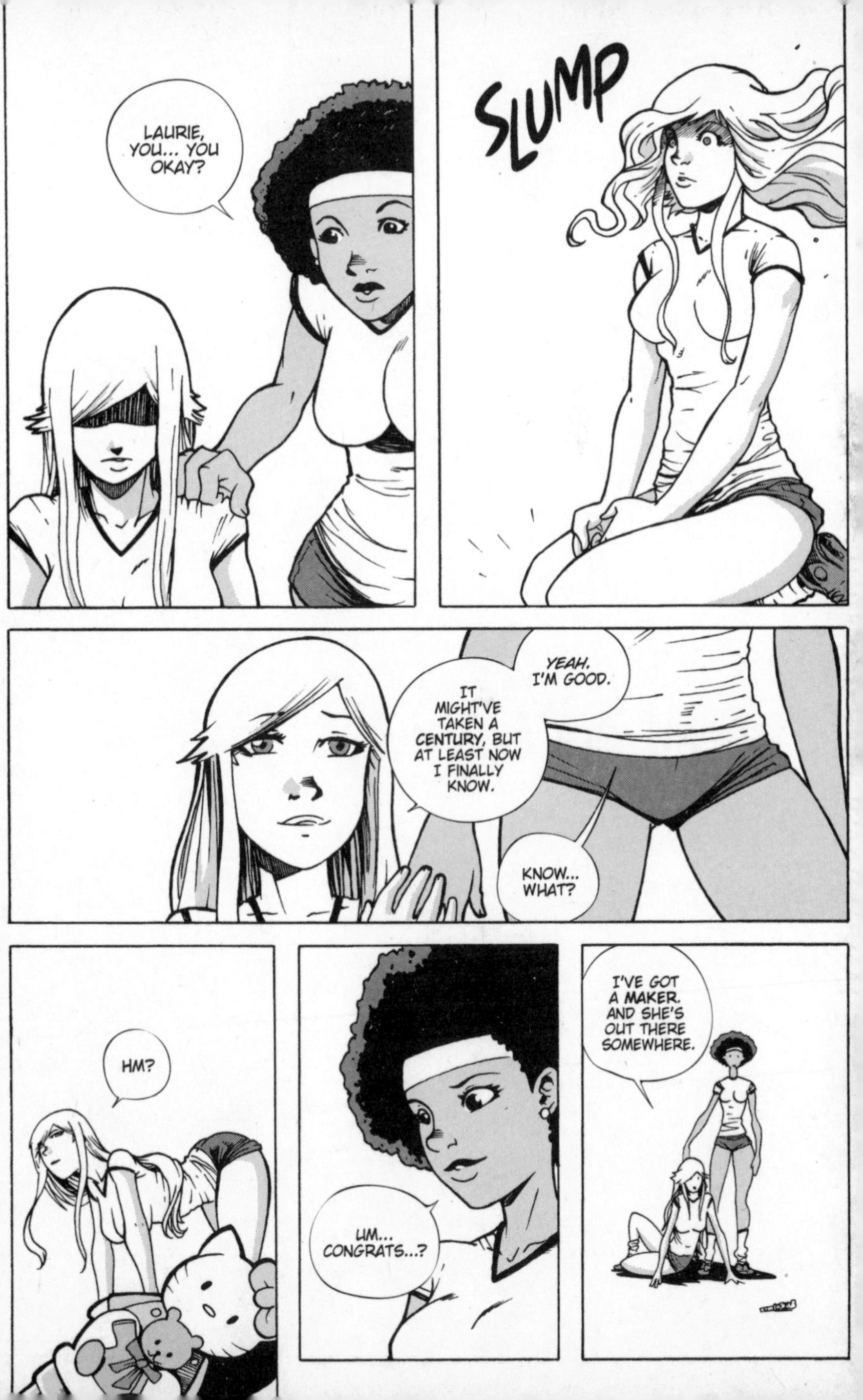
SLUMP
LAURIE, YOU... YOU OKAY?
YEAH. I'M GOOD.
IT MIGHT'VE TAKEN A CENTURY, BUT AT LEAST NOW I FINALLY KNOW.
KNOW... WHAT?
I'VE GOT A MAKER. AND SHE'S OUT THERE SOMEWHERE.
UM... CONGRATS...?
HM?

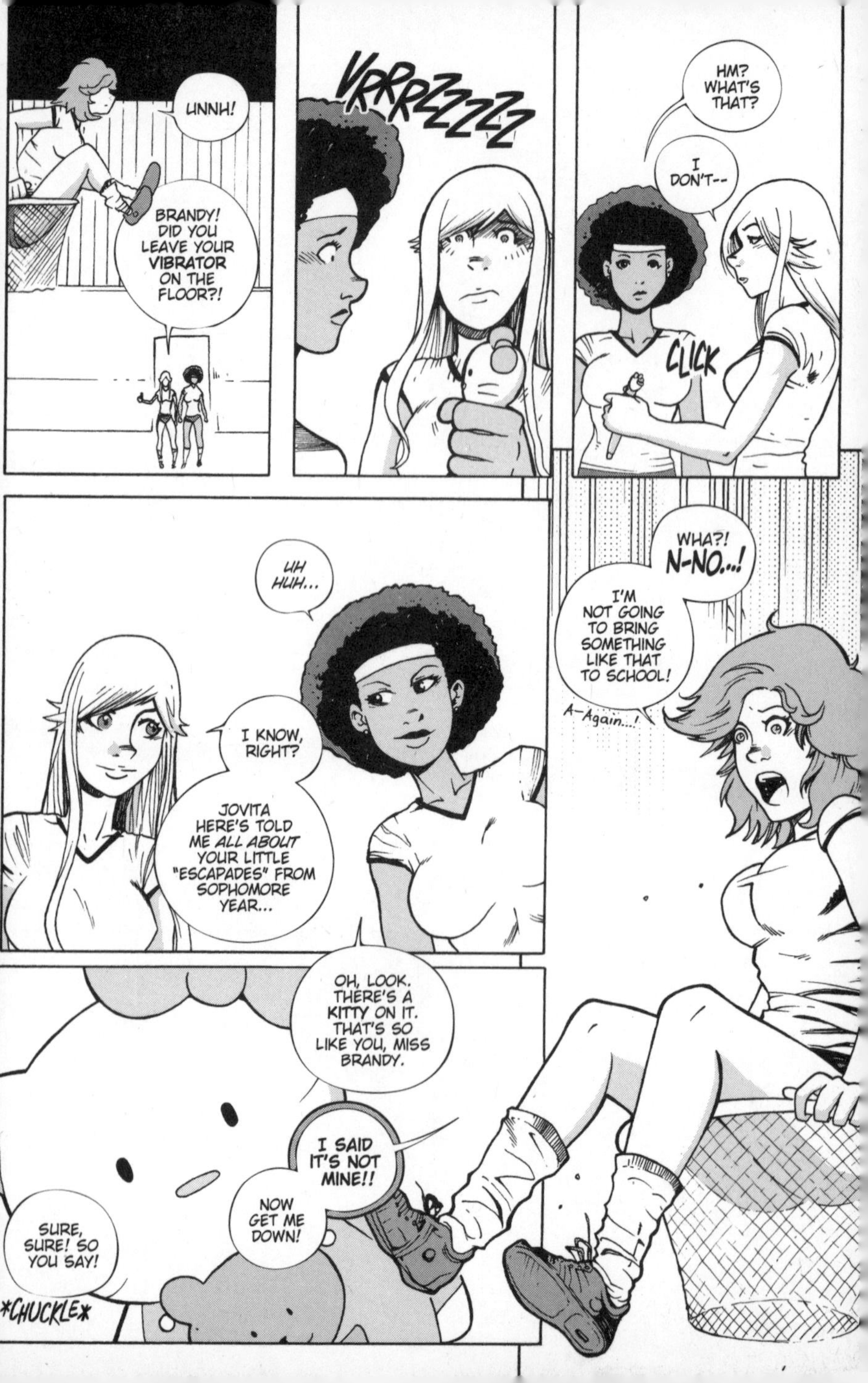
HM? WHAT'S THAT?
I DON'T--
CLICK
VRRRZZZZZ
UNNH!
BRANDY! DID YOU LEAVE YOUR **VIBRATOR** ON THE FLOOR?!
WHA?! **N-NO...!**
I'M NOT GOING TO BRING SOMETHING LIKE THAT TO SCHOOL!
A-Again...!
UH HUH...
I KNOW, RIGHT?
JOVITA HERE'S TOLD ME *ALL ABOUT* YOUR LITTLE "ESCAPADES" FROM SOPHOMORE YEAR...
OH, LOOK. THERE'S A **KITTY** ON IT. THAT'S SO LIKE YOU, MISS BRANDY.
I SAID IT'S NOT MINE!!
NOW GET ME DOWN!
SURE, SURE! SO YOU SAY!
CHUCKLE

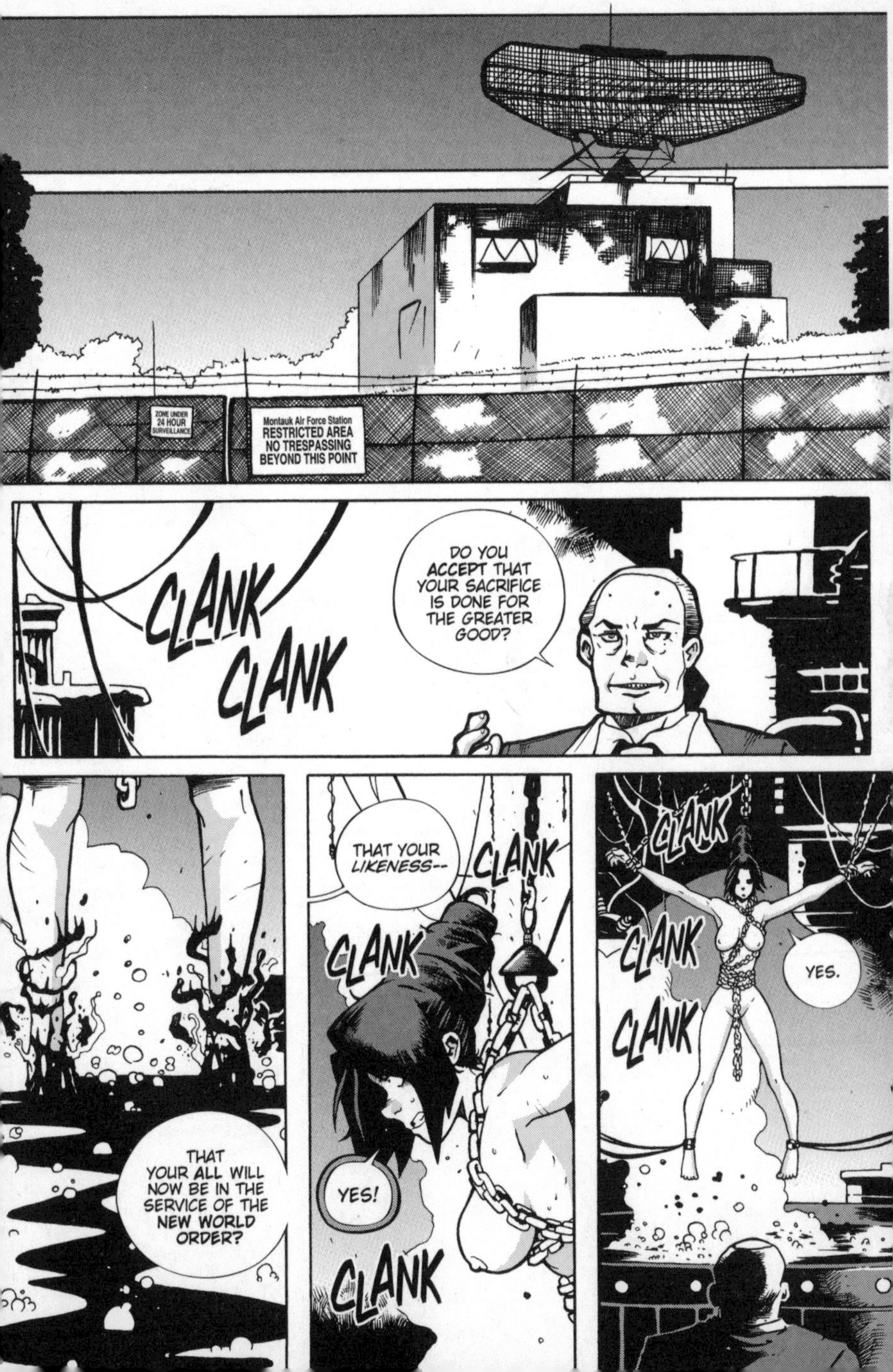
Montauk Air Force Station
RESTRICTED AREA
NO TRESPASSING
BEYOND THIS POINT
ZONE UNDER 24 HOUR SURVEILLANCE
DO YOU ACCEPT THAT YOUR SACRIFICE IS DONE FOR THE GREATER GOOD?
CLANK
CLANK
CLANK
CLANK
CLANK
YES.
THAT YOUR LIKENESS--
CLANK
CLANK
YES!
CLANK
THAT YOUR ALL WILL NOW BE IN THE SERVICE OF THE NEW WORLD ORDER?

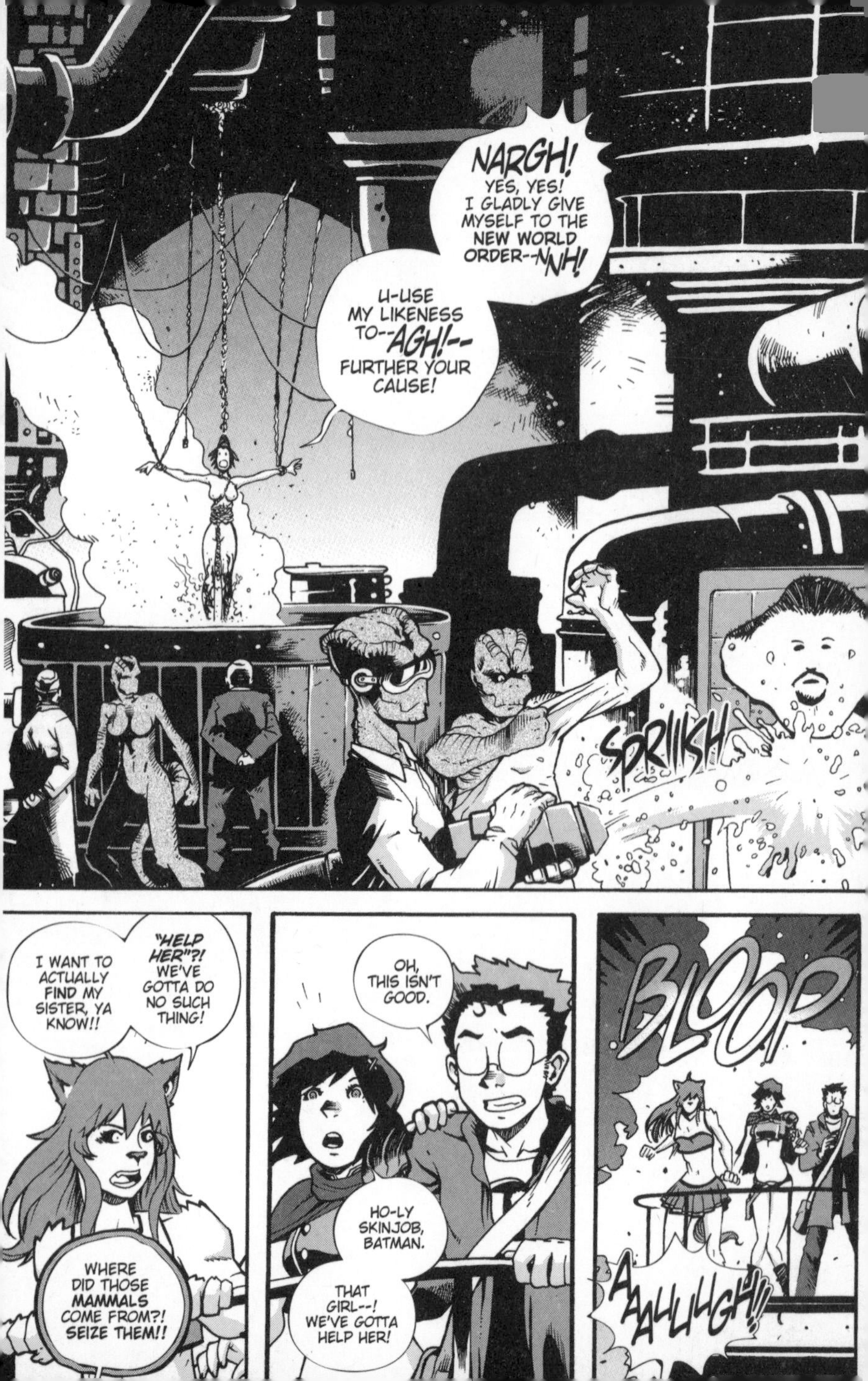
NARGH! YES, YES! I GLADLY GIVE MYSELF TO THE NEW WORLD ORDER--NNH!
U-USE MY LIKENESS TO--AGH!--FURTHER YOUR CAUSE!
SPRIIKSH
BLOOP
AAAUUGH!!
OH, THIS ISN'T GOOD.
HO-LY SKINJOB, BATMAN.
THAT GIRL--! WE'VE GOTTA HELP HER!
"HELP HER"?! WE'VE GOTTA DO NO SUCH THING!
I WANT TO ACTUALLY FIND MY SISTER, YA KNOW!!
WHERE DID THOSE MAMMALS COME FROM?! SEIZE THEM!!

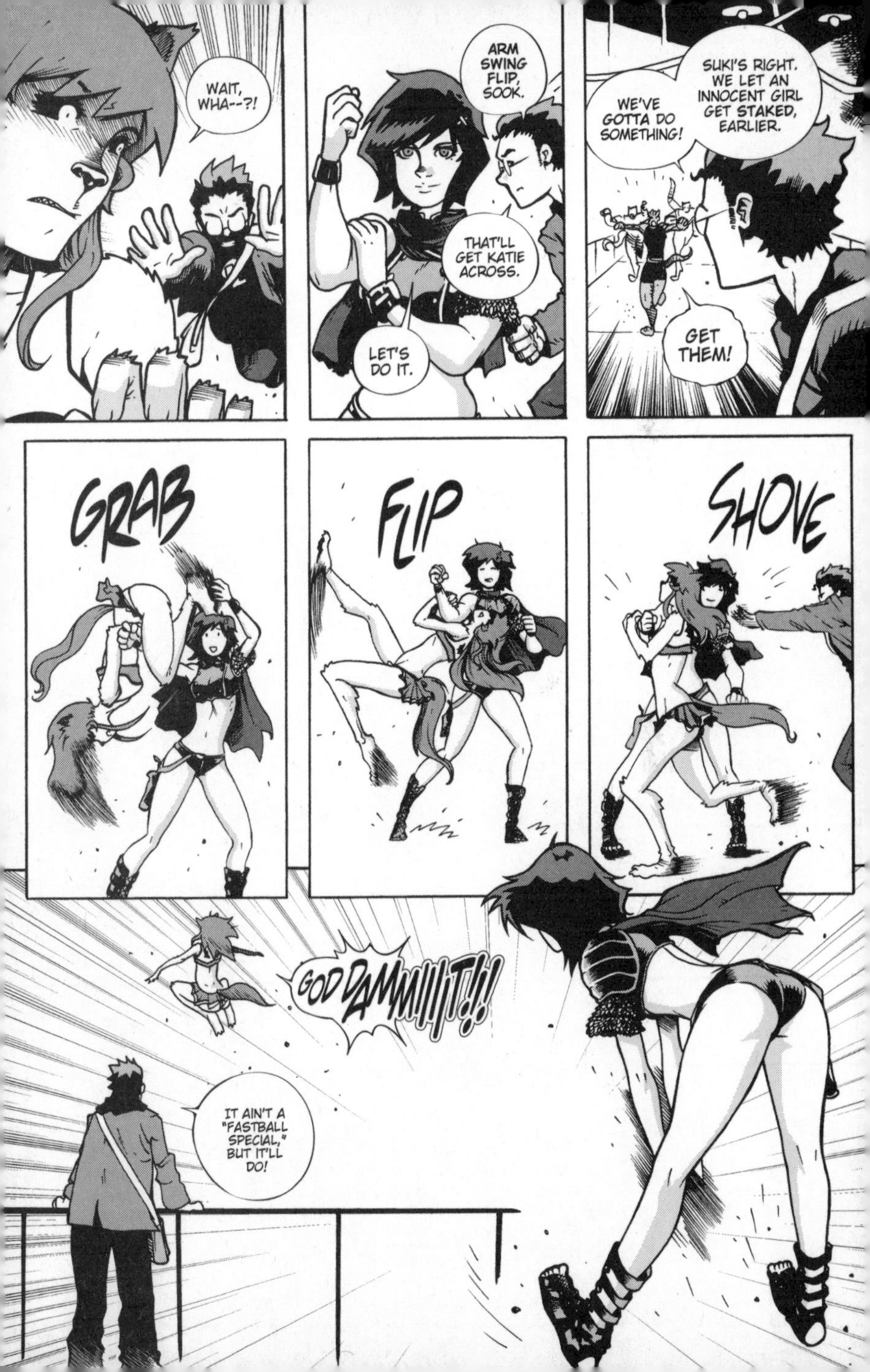
SUKI'S RIGHT. WE LET AN INNOCENT GIRL GET STAKED, EARLIER.
WE'VE GOTTA DO SOMETHING!
GET THEM!
ARM SWING FLIP, SOOK.
THAT'LL GET KATIE ACROSS.
LET'S DO IT.
WAIT, WHA--?!
SHOVE
FLIP
GRAB
GOD DAMMIIIIT!!!
IT AIN'T A "FASTBALL SPECIAL," BUT IT'LL DO!

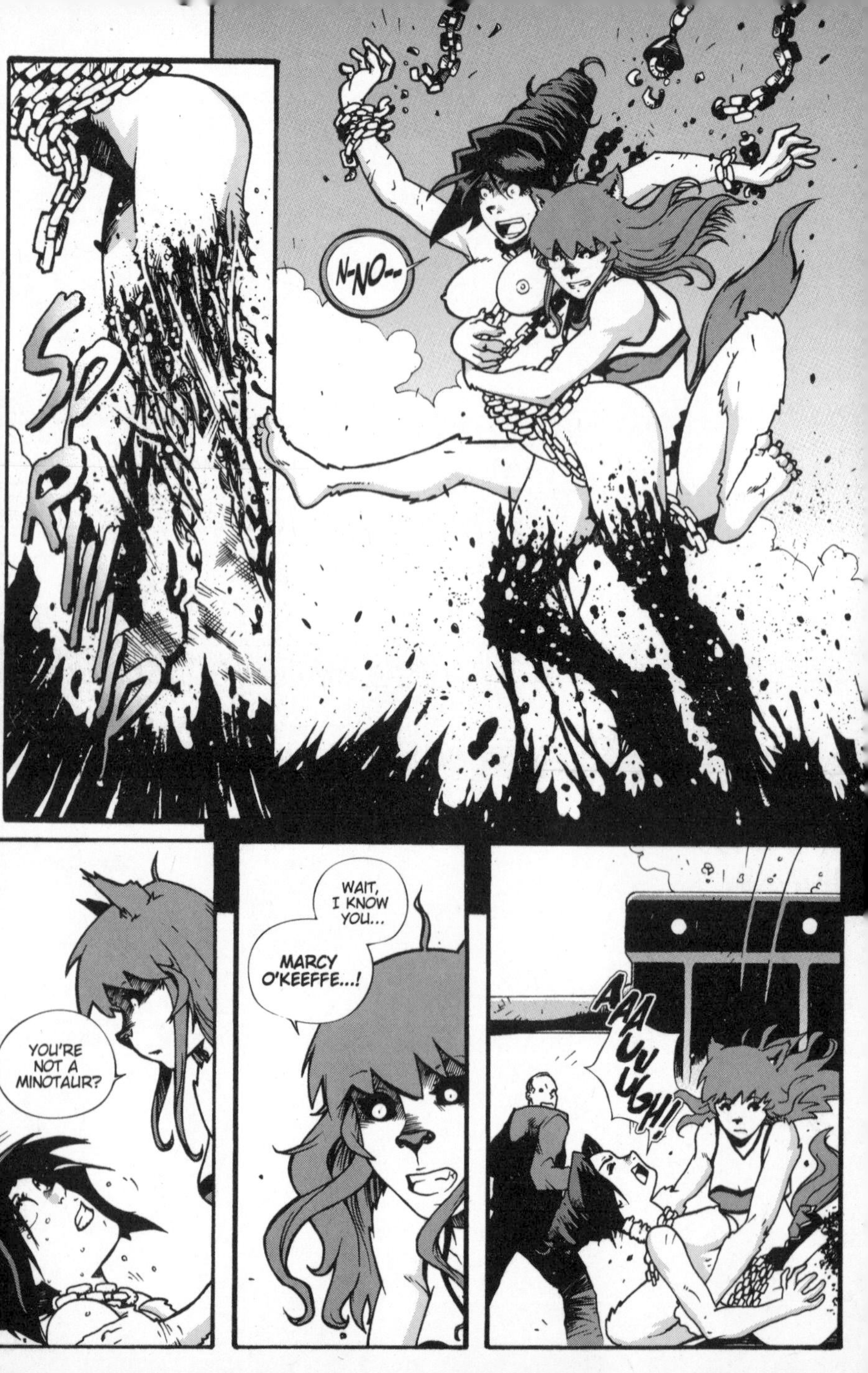
N-NO--
AAAUUUGH!
WAIT, I KNOW YOU...
MARCY O'KEEFFE...!
YOU'RE NOT A MINOTAUR?

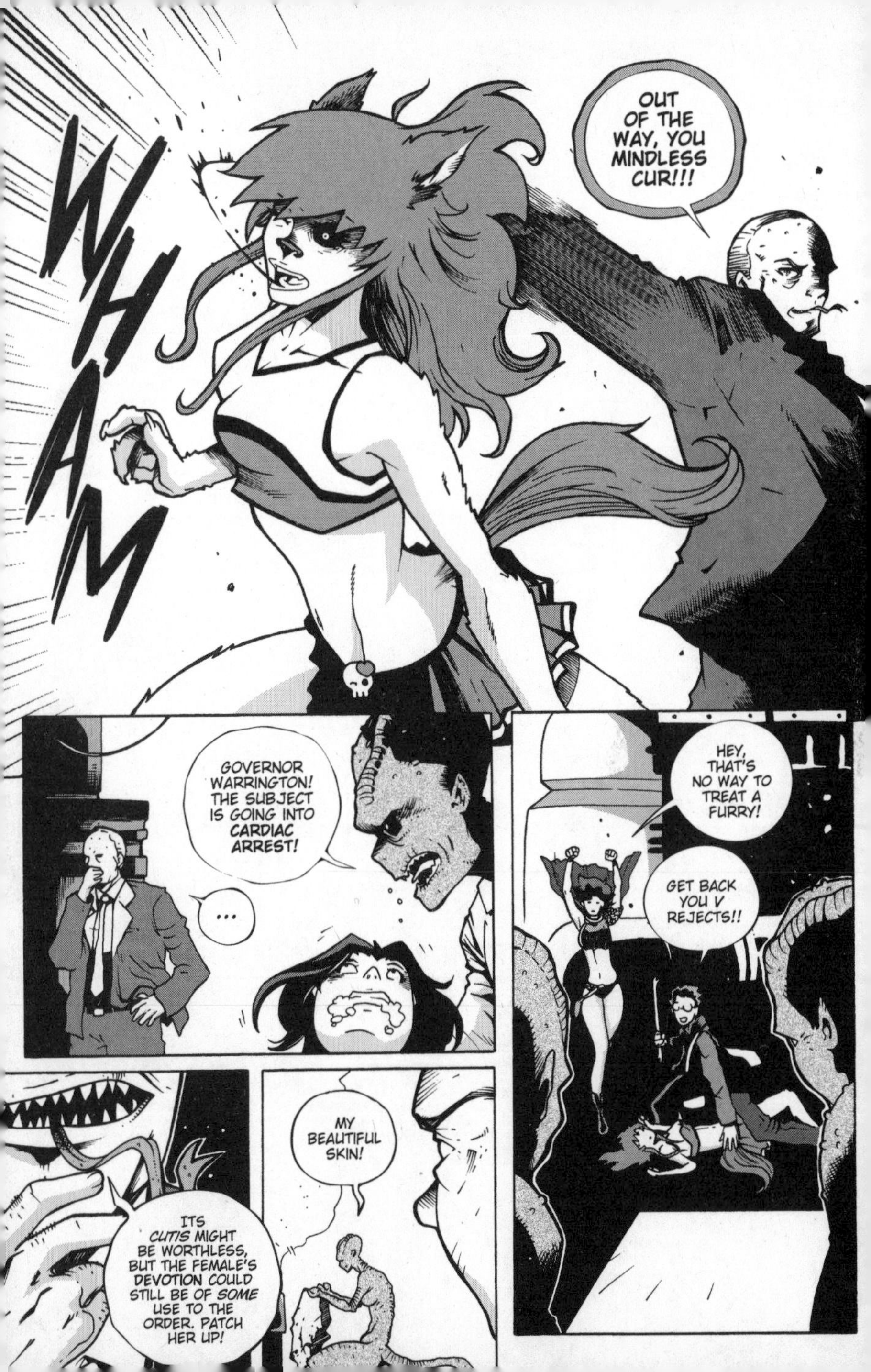

OUT OF THE WAY, YOU MINDLESS CUR!!!
WHAM
HEY, THAT'S NO WAY TO TREAT A FURRY!
GET BACK YOU V REJECTS!!
GOVERNOR WARRINGTON! THE SUBJECT IS GOING INTO **CARDIAC ARREST!**
...
MY BEAUTIFUL SKIN!
ITS *CUTIS* MIGHT BE WORTHLESS, BUT THE FEMALE'S DEVOTION COULD STILL BE OF *SOME* USE TO THE ORDER. PATCH HER UP!

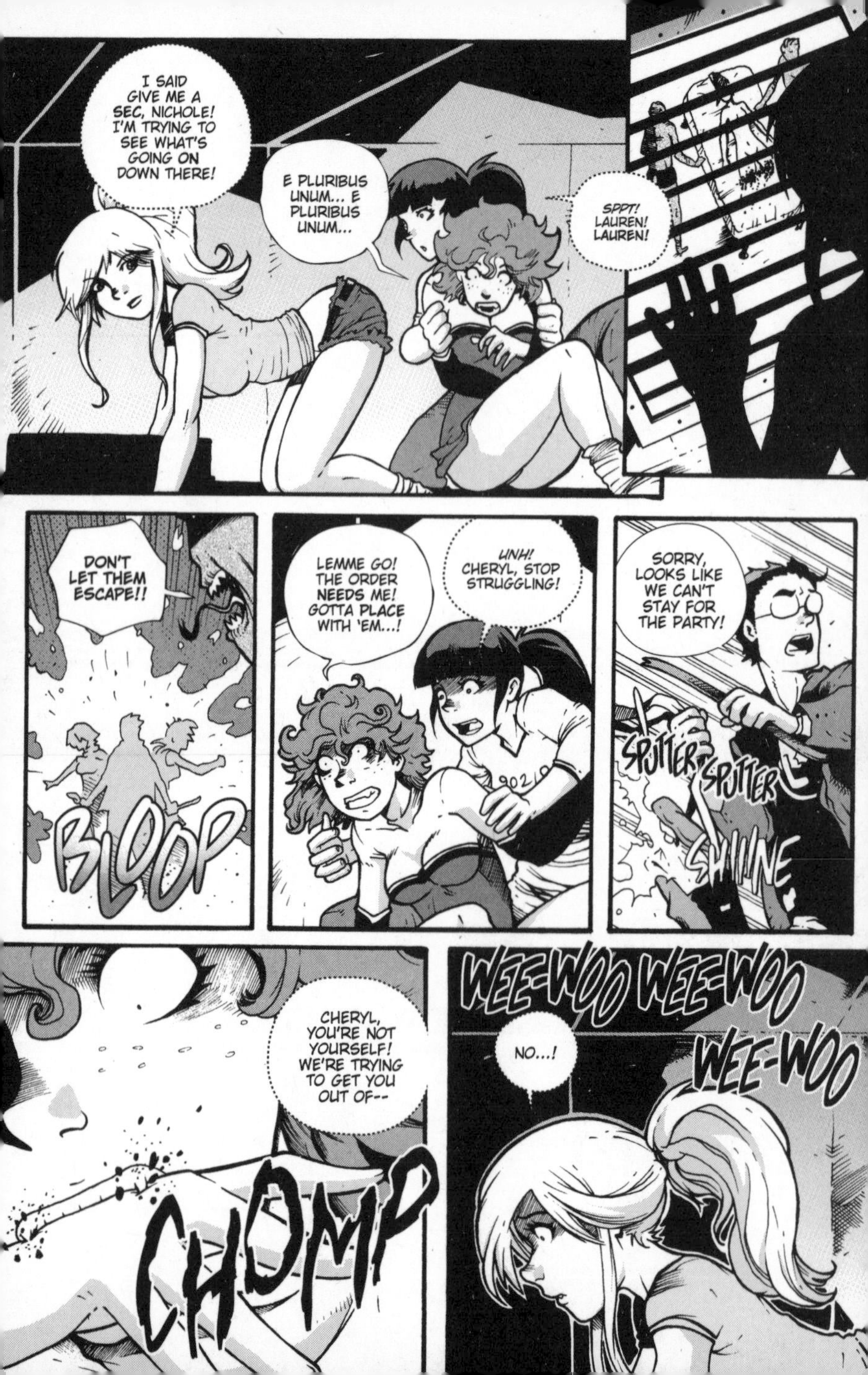
SPPT! LAUREN! LAUREN!
I SAID GIVE ME A SEC, NICHOLE! I'M TRYING TO SEE WHAT'S GOING ON DOWN THERE!
E PLURIBUS UNUM... E PLURIBUS UNUM...
SORRY, LOOKS LIKE WE CAN'T STAY FOR THE PARTY!
SPUTTER SPUTTER
SHIINE
UNH! CHERYL, STOP STRUGGLING!
LEMME GO! THE ORDER NEEDS ME! GOTTA PLACE WITH 'EM...!
DON'T LET THEM ESCAPE!!
BLOOP
WEE-WOO WEE-WOO
WEE-WOO
NO...!
CHERYL, YOU'RE NOT YOURSELF! WE'RE TRYING TO GET YOU OUT OF--
CHOMP

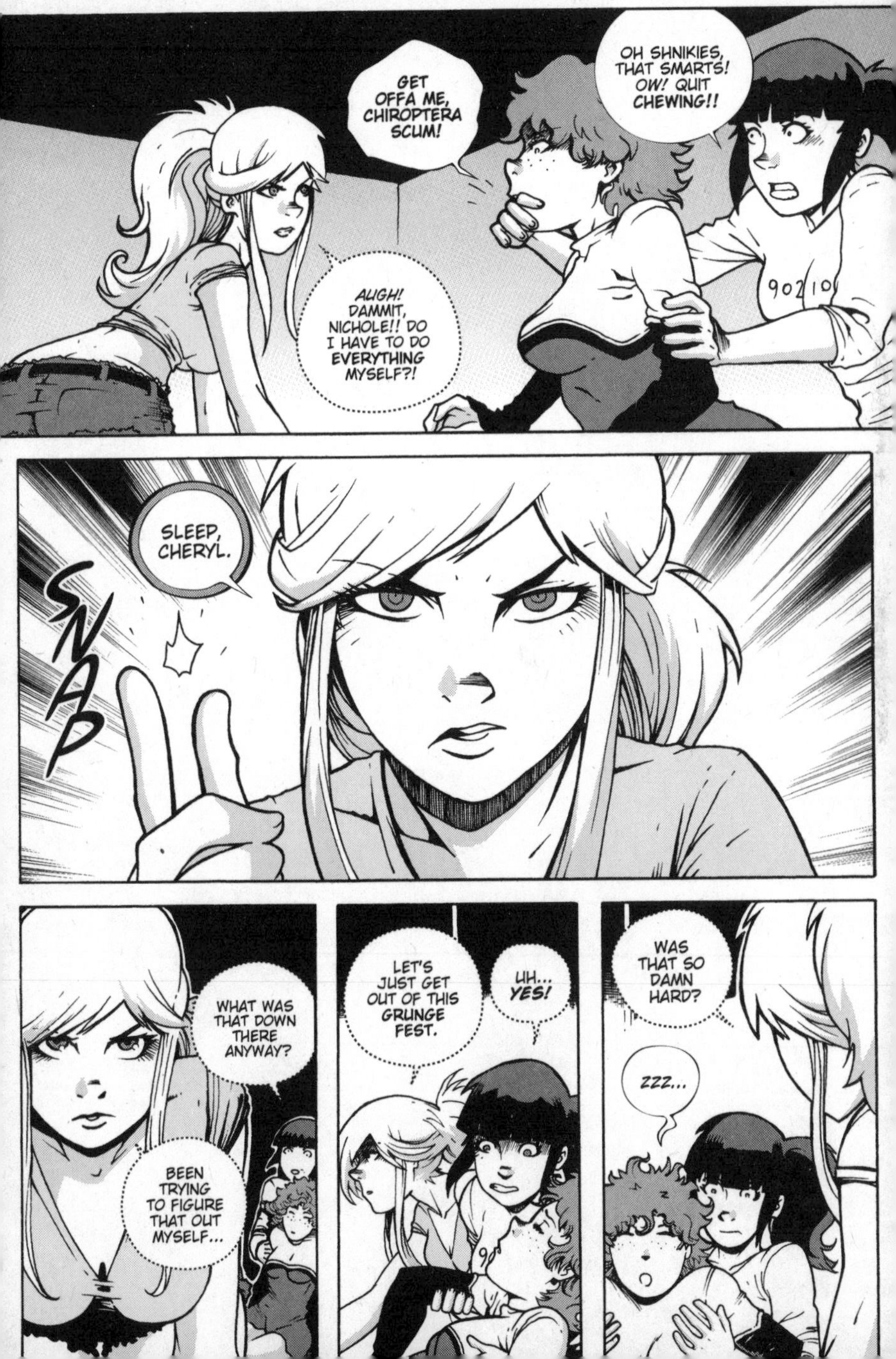
OH SHNIKIES, THAT SMARTS! OW! QUIT CHEWING!!
GET OFFA ME, CHIROPTERA SCUM!
AUGH! DAMMIT, NICHOLE!! DO I HAVE TO DO EVERYTHING MYSELF?!
SLEEP, CHERYL.
SNAP
WAS THAT SO DAMN HARD?
ZZZ...
UH... YES!
LET'S JUST GET OUT OF THIS GRUNGE FEST.
WHAT WAS THAT DOWN THERE ANYWAY?
BEEN TRYING TO FIGURE THAT OUT MYSELF...

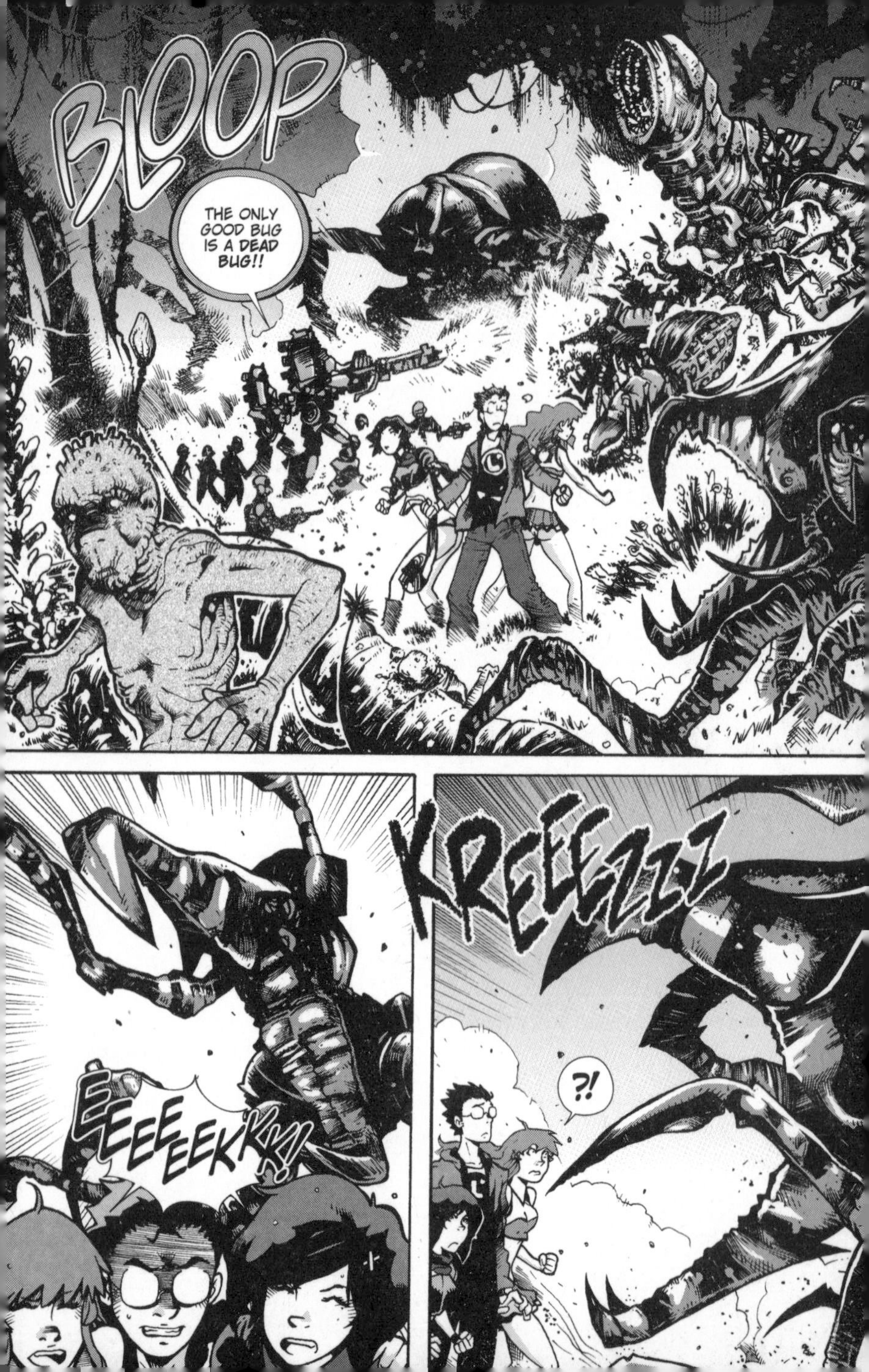
BLOOP
THE ONLY GOOD BUG IS A DEAD BUG!!
KREEEZZZ
?!
EEEEEEKKK!

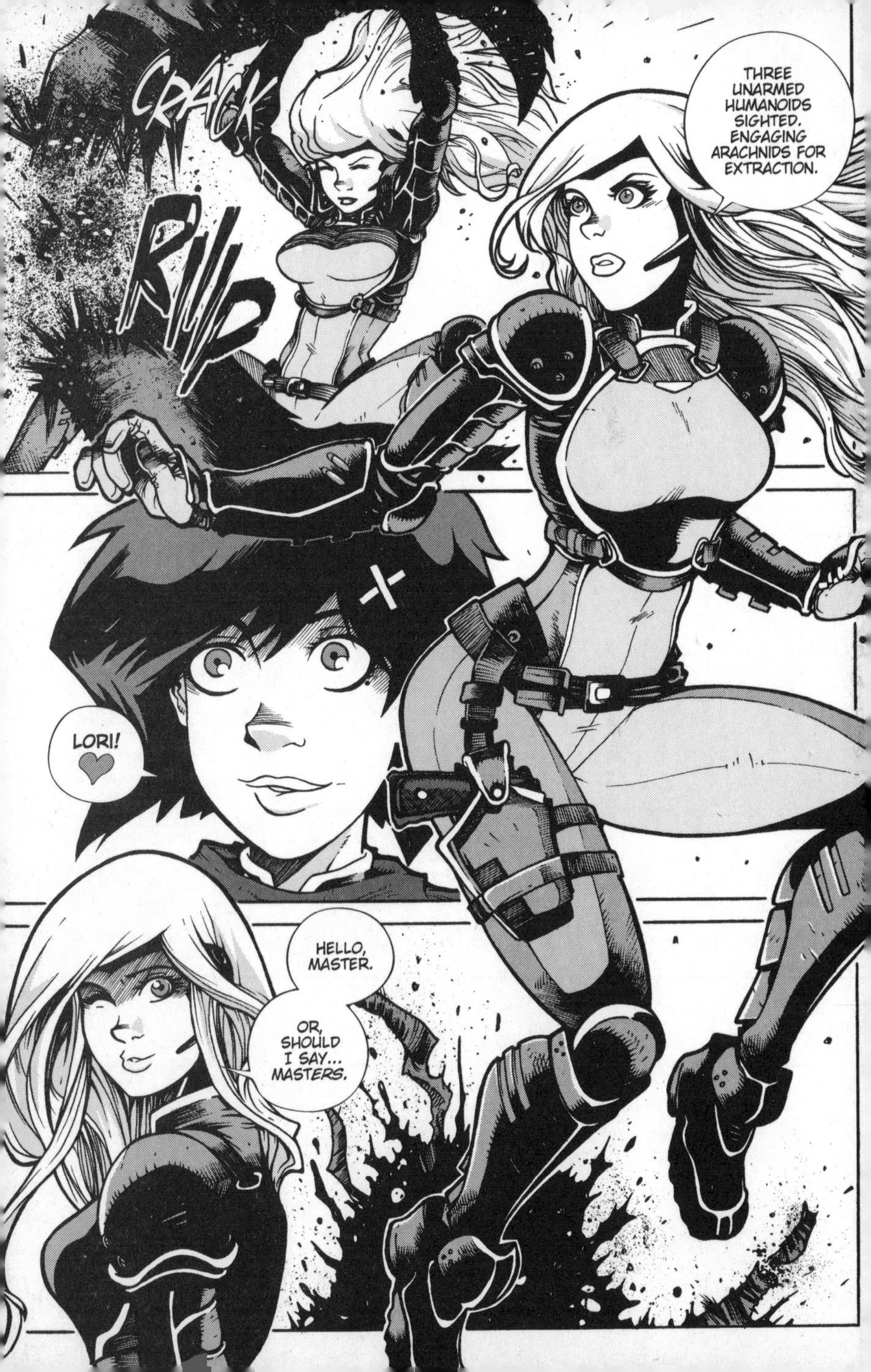
THREE UNARMED HUMANOIDS SIGHTED. ENGAGING ARACHNIDS FOR EXTRACTION.
CRACK
RIP
LORI! ♥
HELLO, MASTER.
OR, SHOULD I SAY... MASTERS.

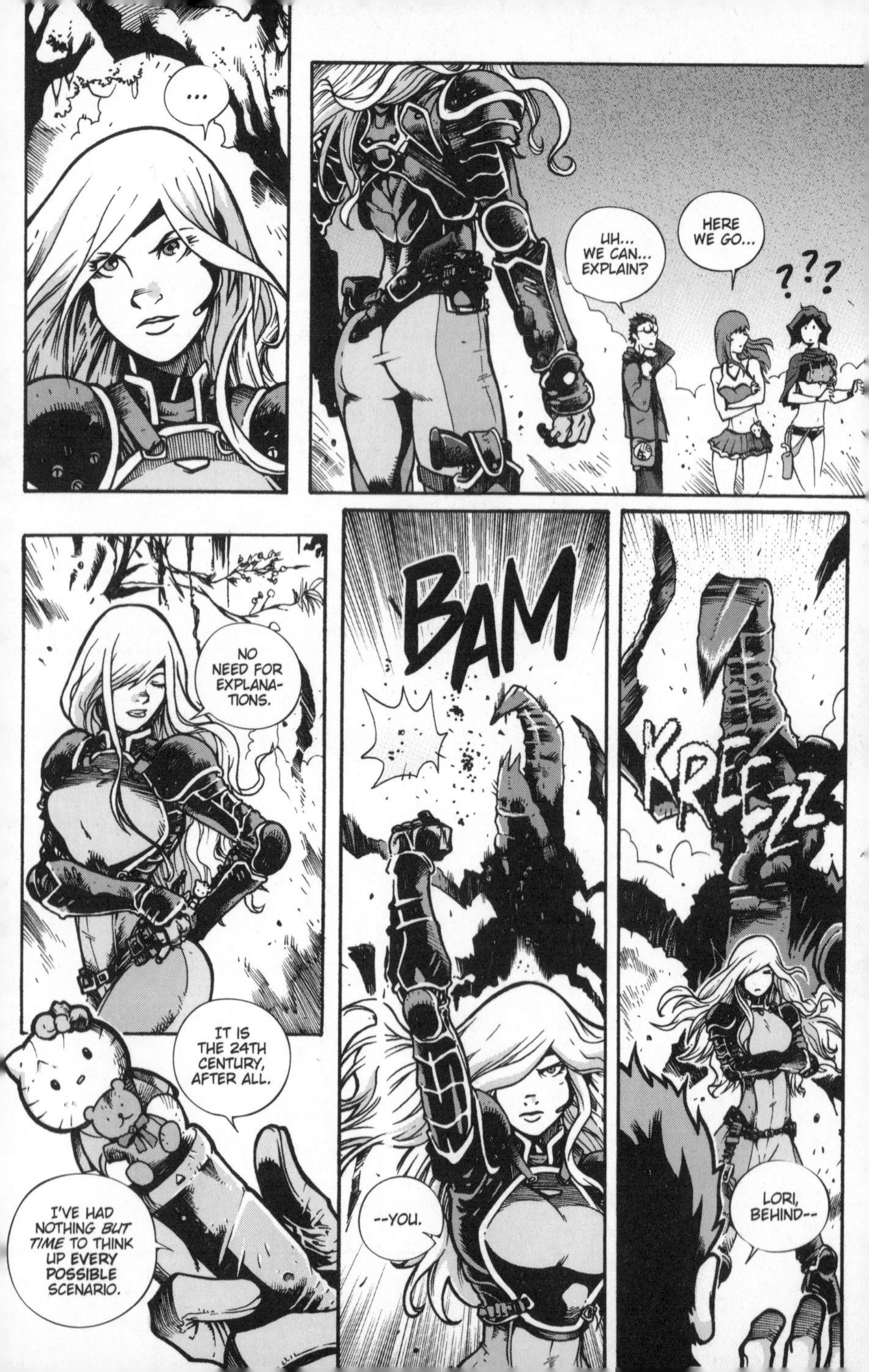
HERE WE GO...
UH... WE CAN... EXPLAIN?
???
...
KREEZZ
LORI, BEHIND--
BAM
--YOU.
NO NEED FOR EXPLANA-TIONS.
IT IS THE 24TH CENTURY, AFTER ALL.
I'VE HAD NOTHING *BUT TIME* TO THINK UP EVERY POSSIBLE SCENARIO.

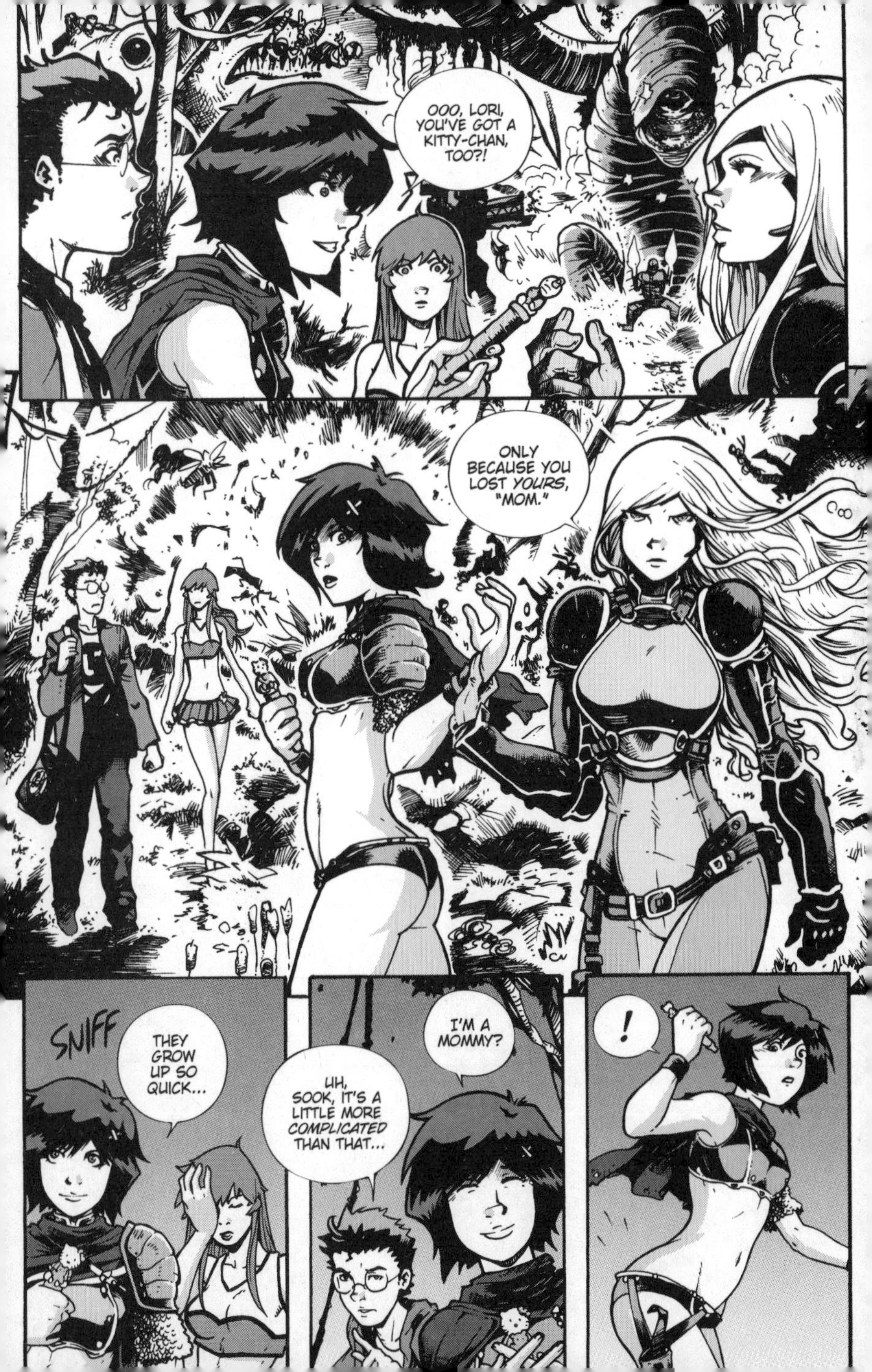
OOO, LORI, YOU'VE GOT A KITTY-CHAN, TOO?!
ONLY BECAUSE YOU LOST *YOURS*, "MOM."
!
I'M A MOMMY?
UH, SOOK, IT'S A LITTLE MORE *COMPLICATED* THAN THAT...
SNIFF
THEY GROW UP SO QUICK...

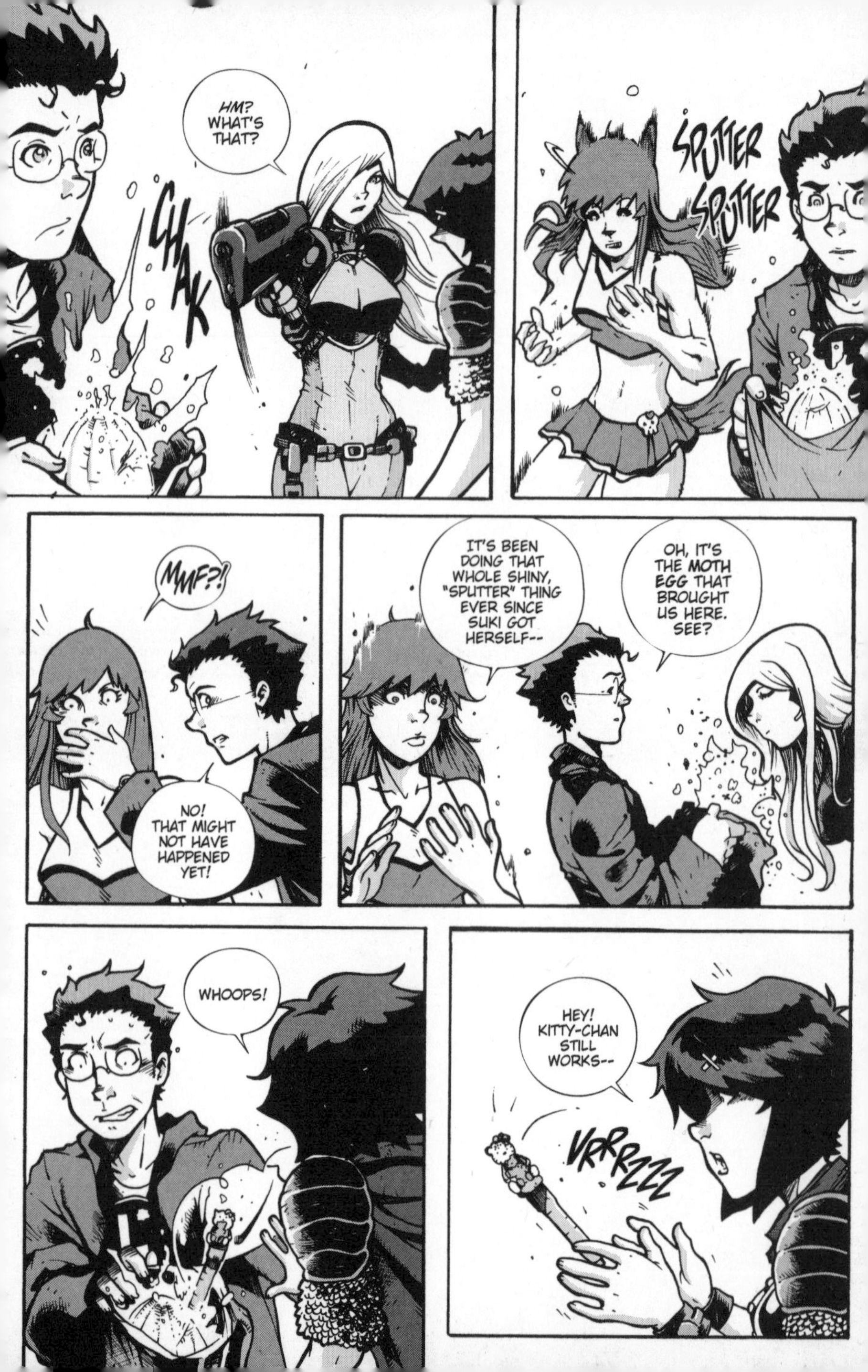
SPUTTER SPUTTER
HM? WHAT'S THAT?
CHAK
OH, IT'S THE MOTH EGG THAT BROUGHT US HERE. SEE?
IT'S BEEN DOING THAT WHOLE SHINY, "SPUTTER" THING EVER SINCE SUKI GOT HERSELF--
MMF?!
NO! THAT MIGHT NOT HAVE HAPPENED YET!
HEY! KITTY-CHAN STILL WORKS--
VRRRZZZ
WHOOPS!

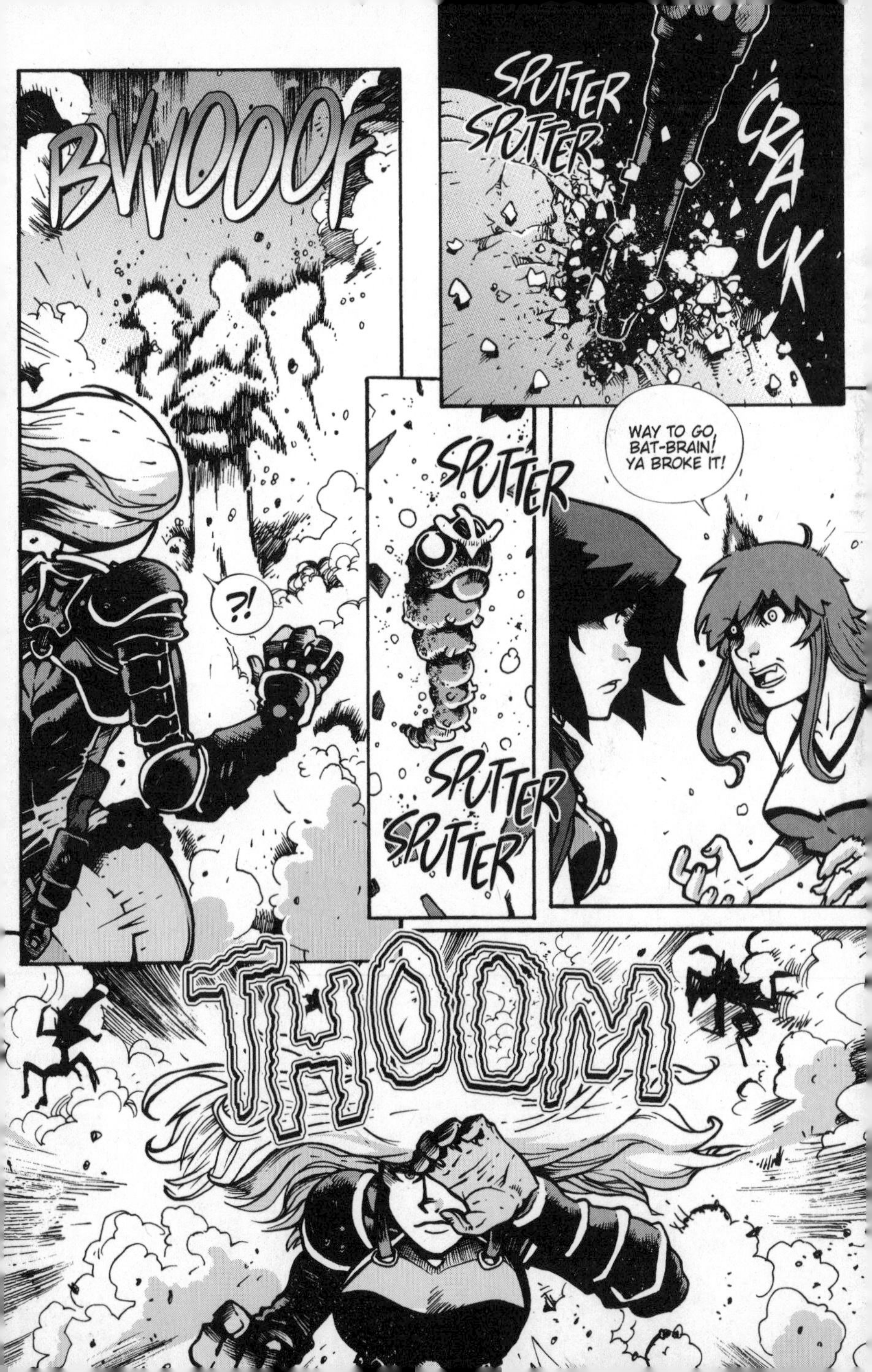
SPUTTER
SPUTTER
CRACK
WAY TO GO, BAT-BRAIN! YA BROKE IT!
SPUTTER
SPUTTER
SPUTTER
BWOOOF
?!
THOOM

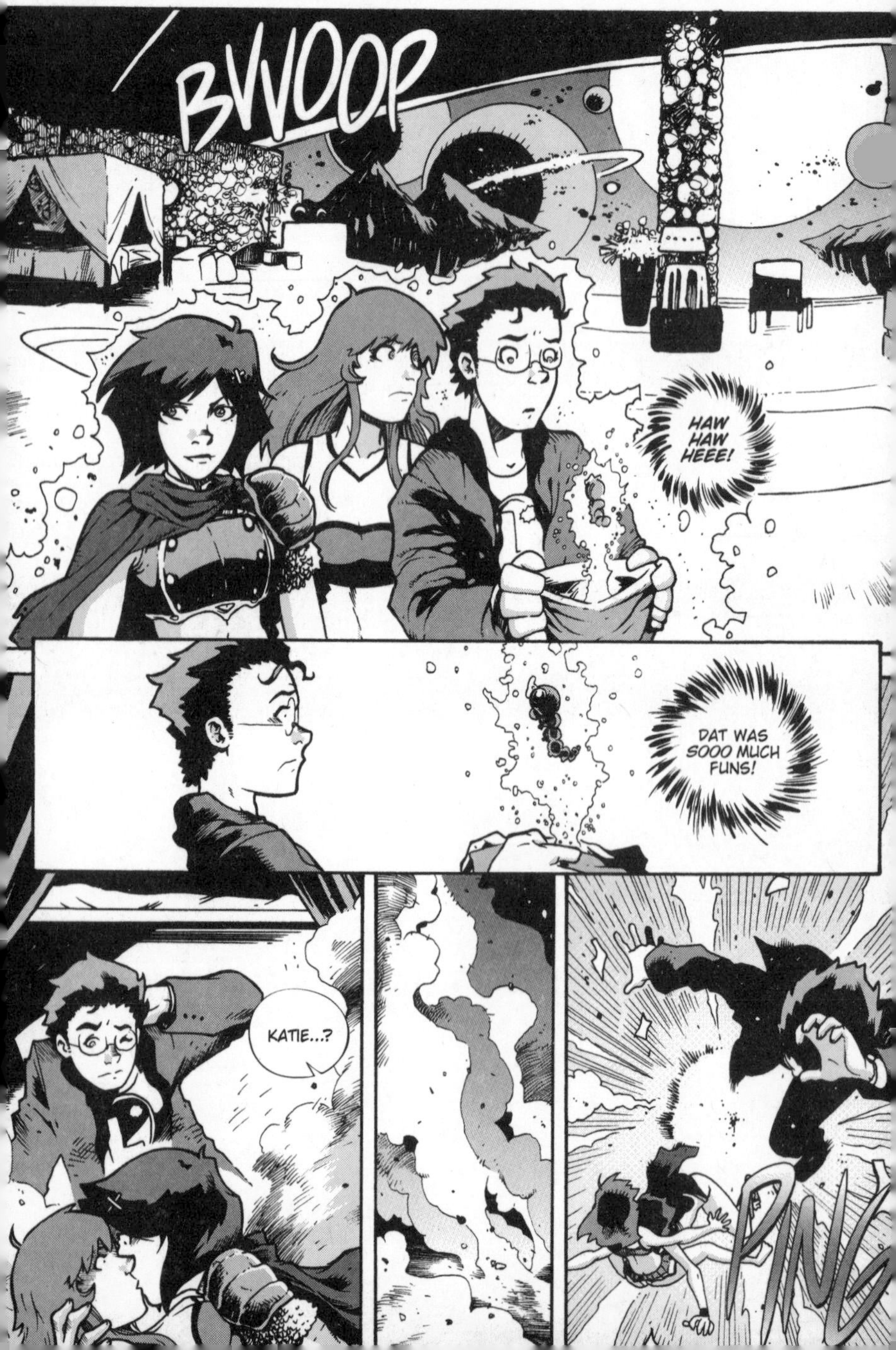
BVVOOP
HAW HAW HEEE!
DAT WAS SOOO MUCH FUNS!
KATIE...?

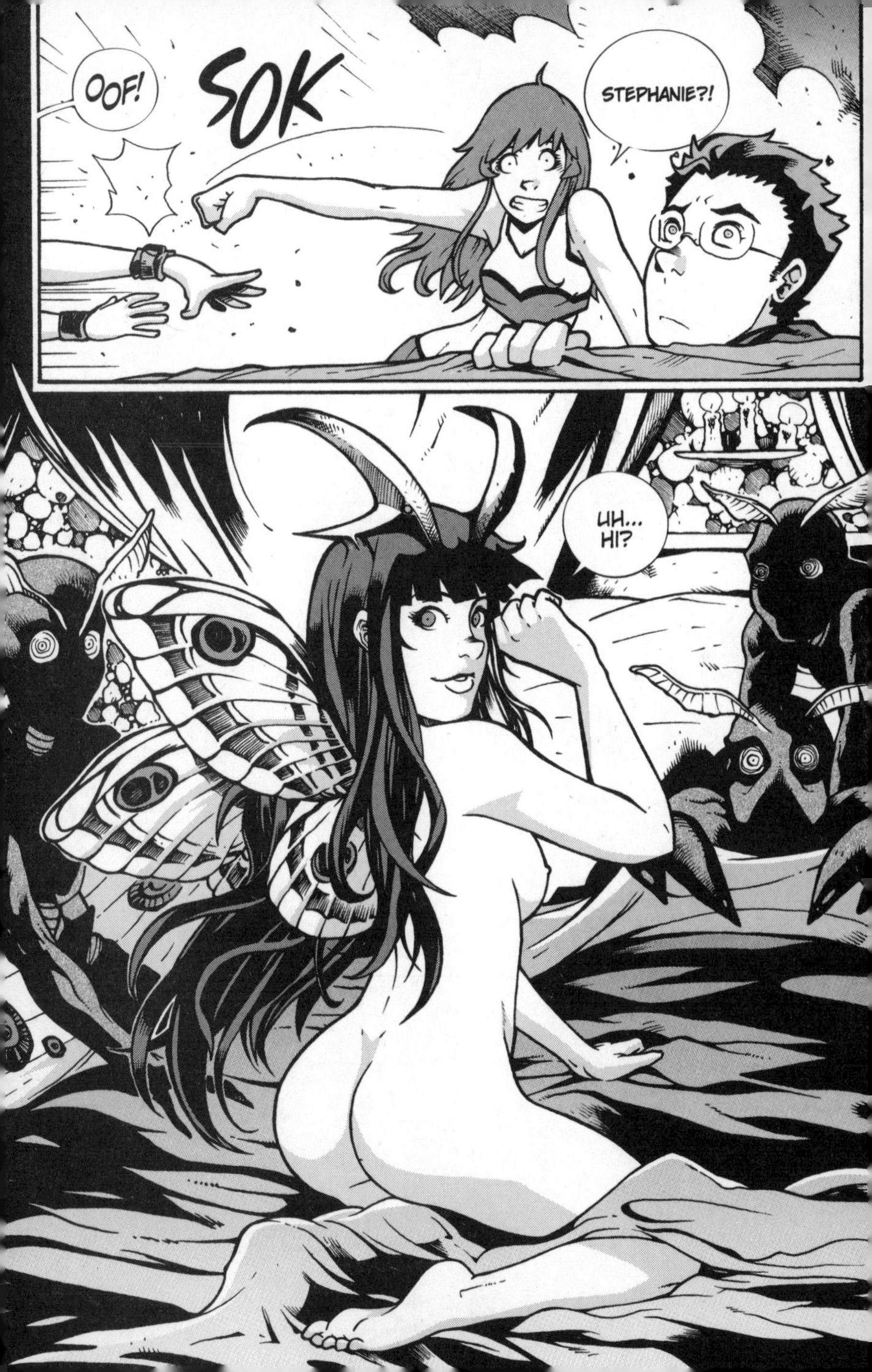
STEPHANIE?!
SOK
OOF!
UH... HI?

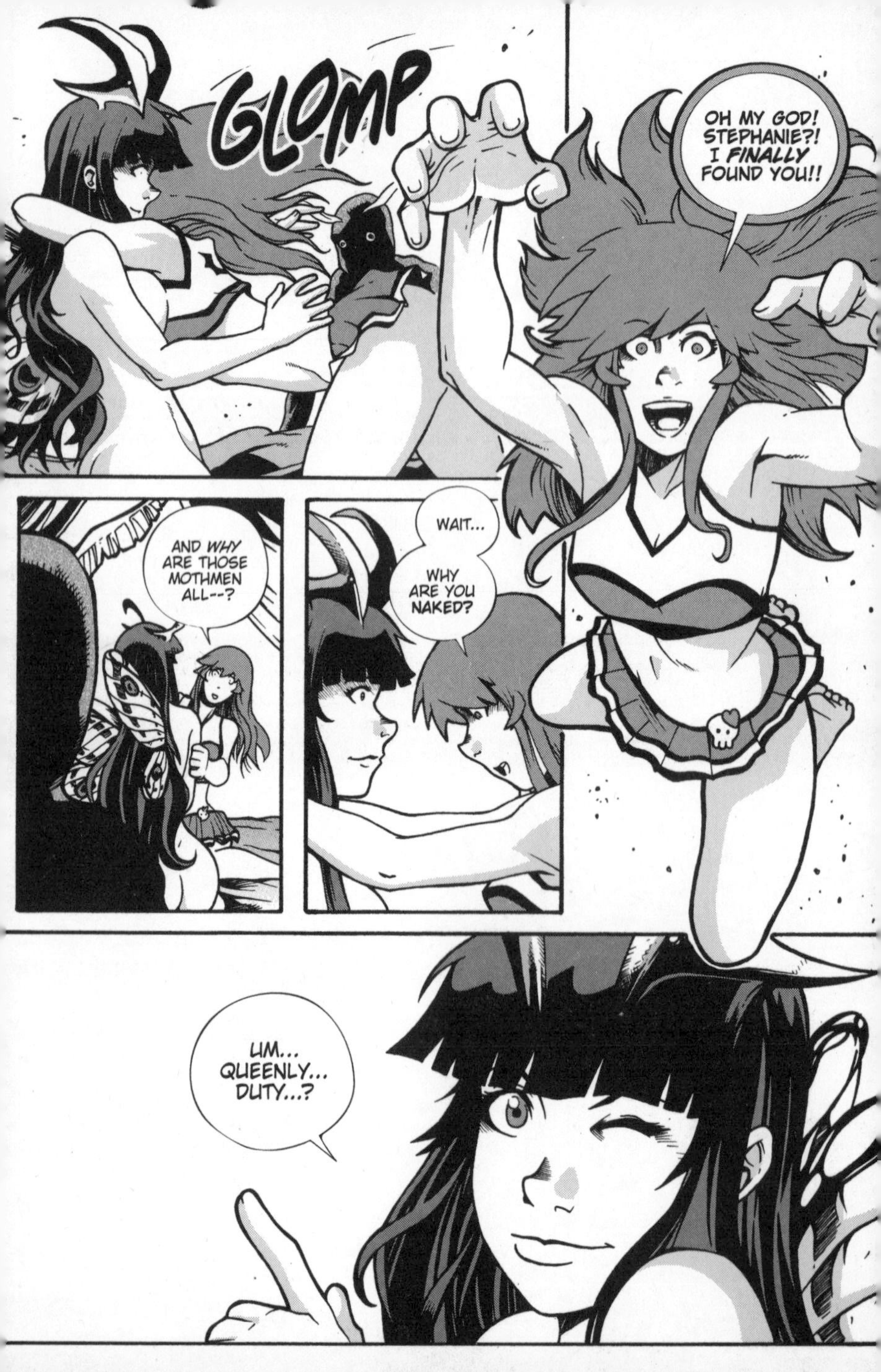
OH MY GOD! STEPHANIE?! I *FINALLY* FOUND YOU!!
GLOMP
WAIT...
WHY ARE YOU NAKED?
AND *WHY* ARE THOSE MOTHMEN ALL--?
UM... QUEENLY... DUTY...?

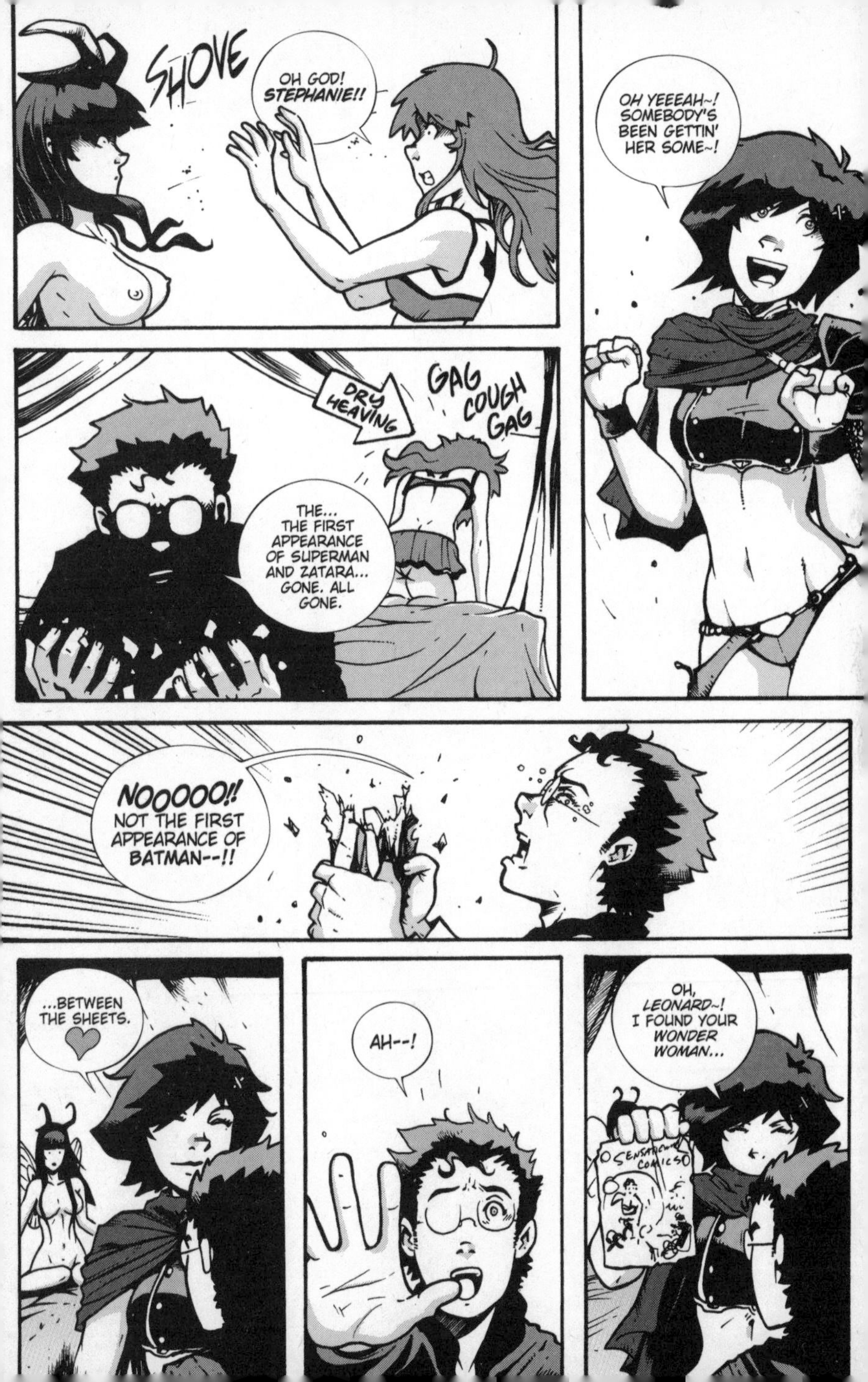
OH YEEEAH~! SOMEBODY'S BEEN GETTIN' HER SOME~!
OH GOD! STEPHANIE!!
SHOVE
GAG COUGH GAG
DRY HEAVING
THE... THE FIRST APPEARANCE OF SUPERMAN AND ZATARA... GONE. ALL GONE.
NOOOOO!! NOT THE FIRST APPEARANCE OF BATMAN--!!
OH, LEONARD~! I FOUND YOUR WONDER WOMAN...
AH--!
...BETWEEN THE SHEETS.

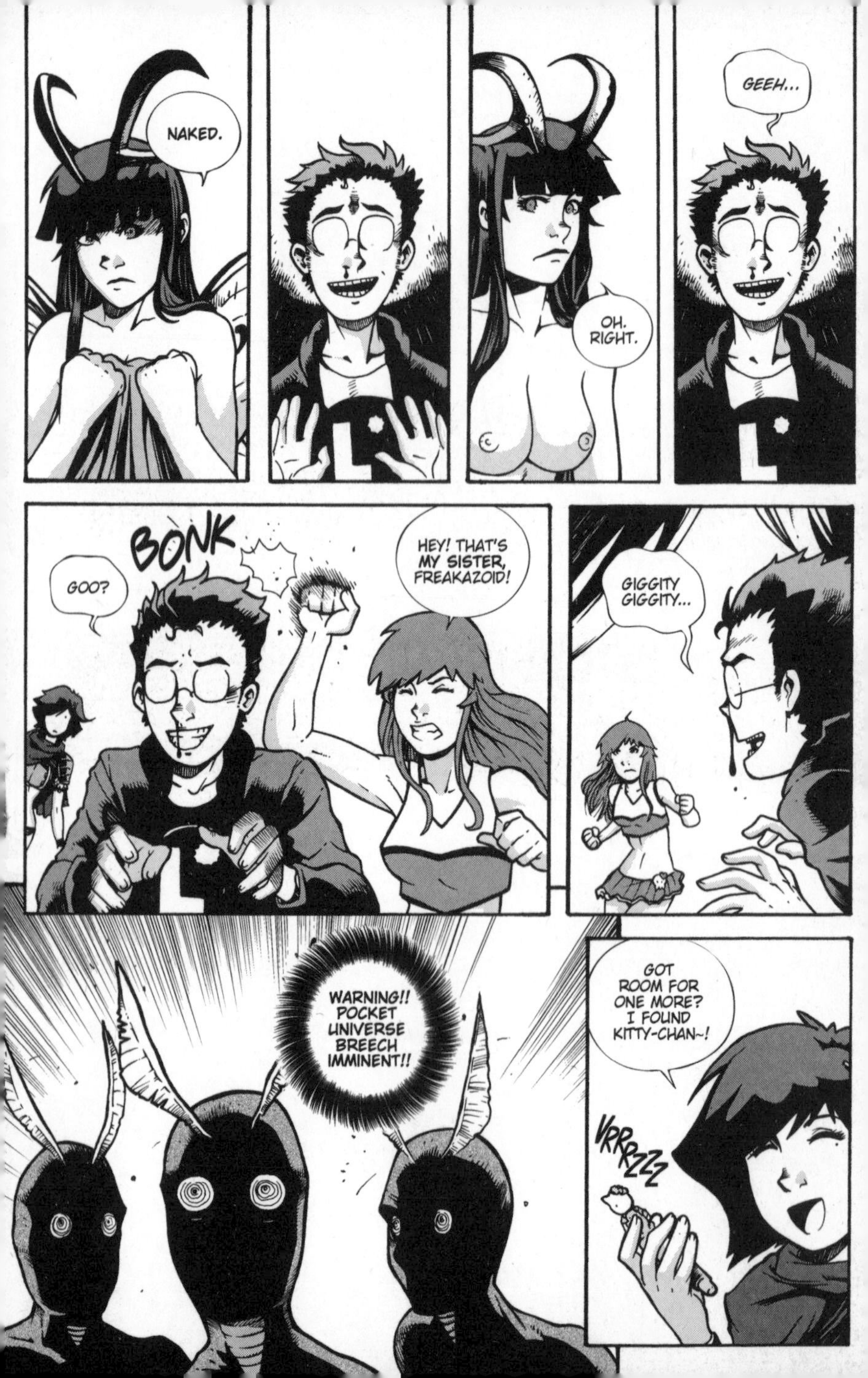
GEEH...
OH. RIGHT.
NAKED.
GIGGITY GIGGITY...
HEY! THAT'S MY SISTER, FREAKAZOID!
BONK
GOO?
GOT ROOM FOR ONE MORE? I FOUND KITTY-CHAN~!
VRRRZZZ
WARNING!! POCKET UNIVERSE BREECH IMMINENT!!

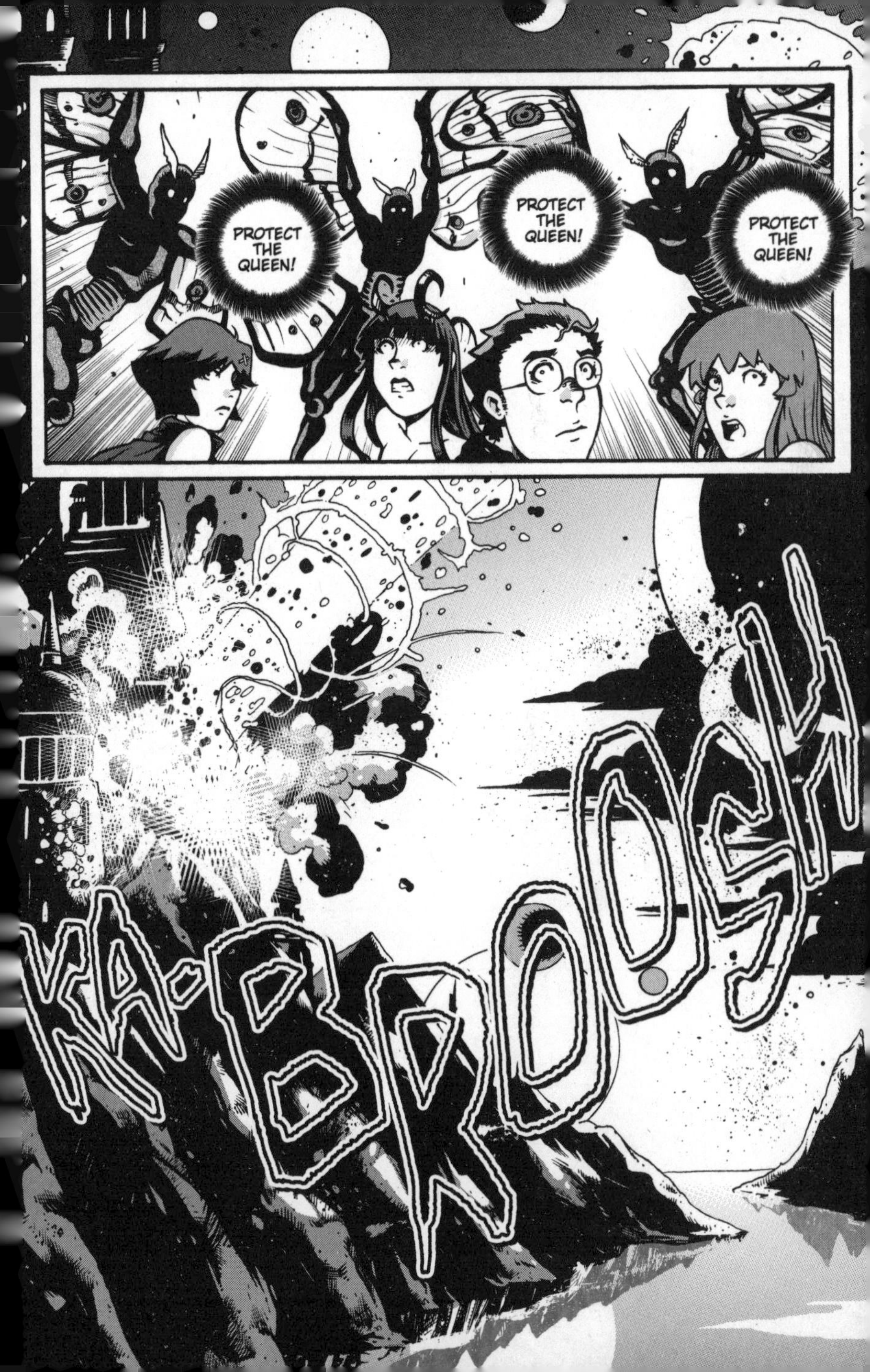
PROTECT THE QUEEN!
PROTECT THE QUEEN!
PROTECT THE QUEEN!
KA-BROOOSH

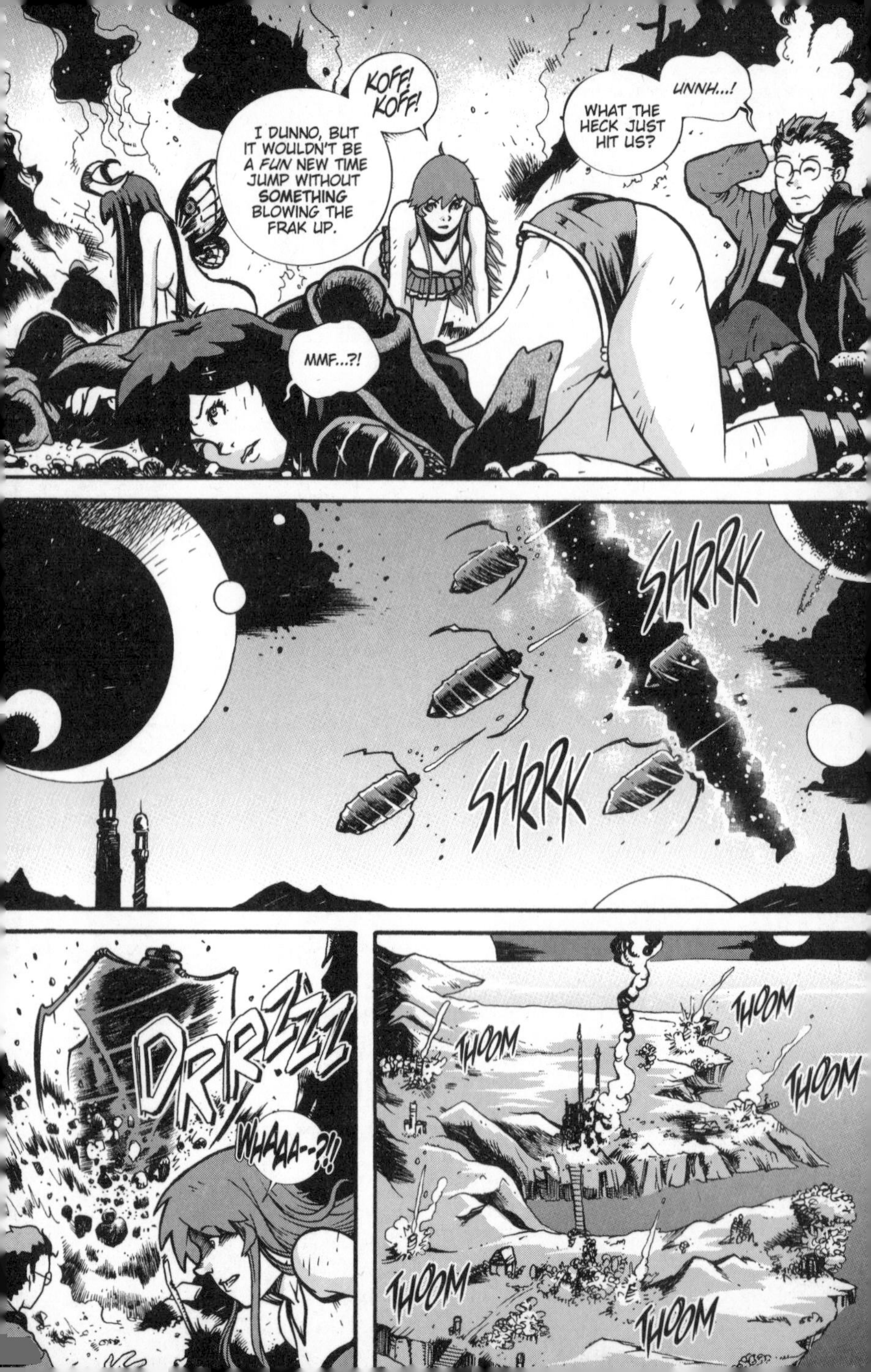
UNNH...!
WHAT THE HECK JUST HIT US?
KOFF! KOFF!
I DUNNO, BUT IT WOULDN'T BE A *FUN* NEW TIME JUMP WITHOUT SOMETHING BLOWING THE FRAK UP.
MMF...?!
SHRRK
SHRRK
THOOM
THOOM
THOOM
THOOM
THOOM
DRRZZZ
WHAAA--?!

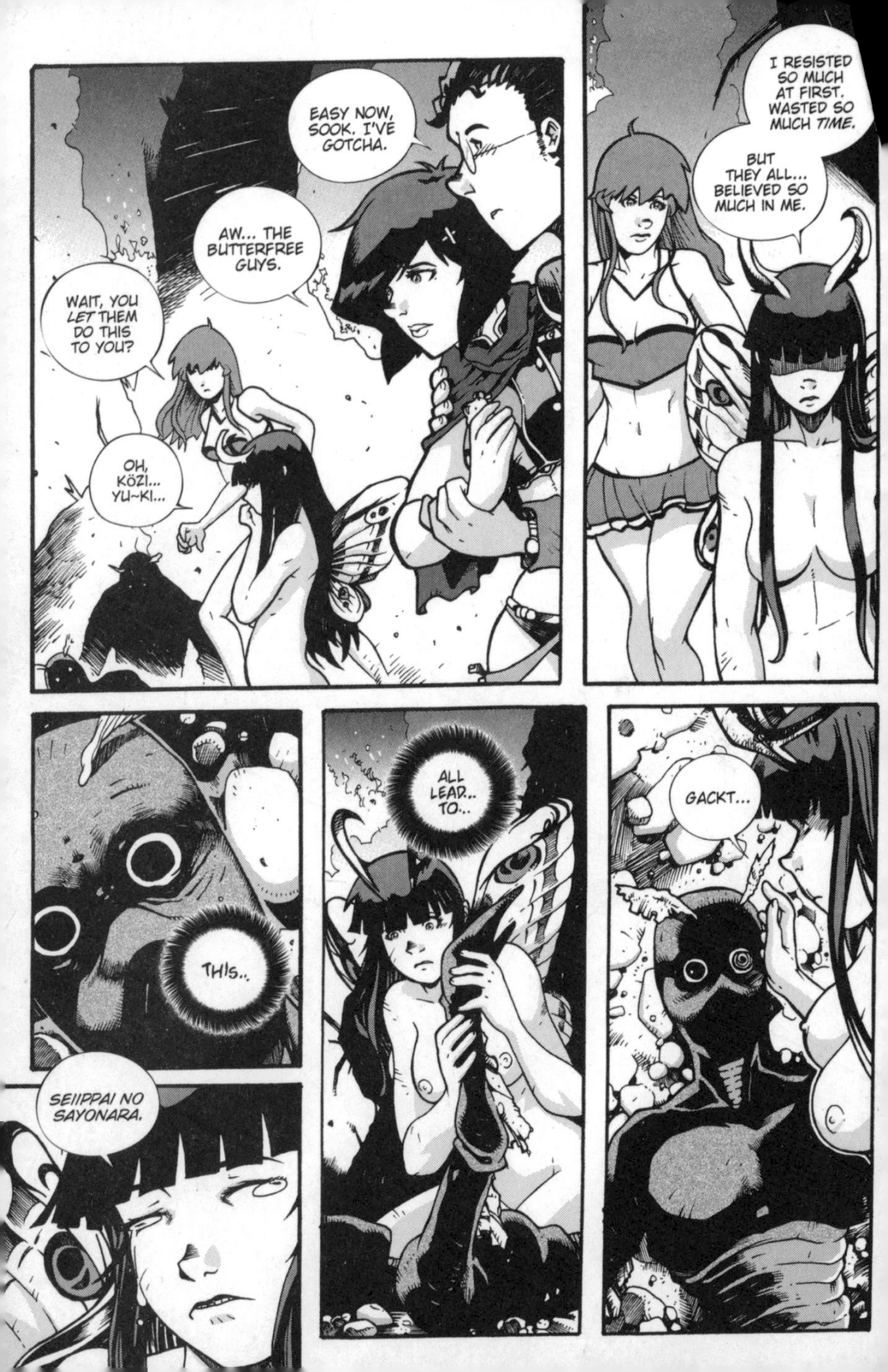
I RESISTED SO MUCH AT FIRST. WASTED SO MUCH *TIME*.
BUT THEY ALL... BELIEVED SO MUCH IN ME.
EASY NOW, SOOK. I'VE GOTCHA.
AW... THE BUTTERFREE GUYS.
WAIT, YOU *LET* THEM DO THIS TO YOU?
OH, KÖZI... YU~KI...
GACKT...
ALL LEAD... TO...
THIS...
SEIIPPAI NO SAYONARA.

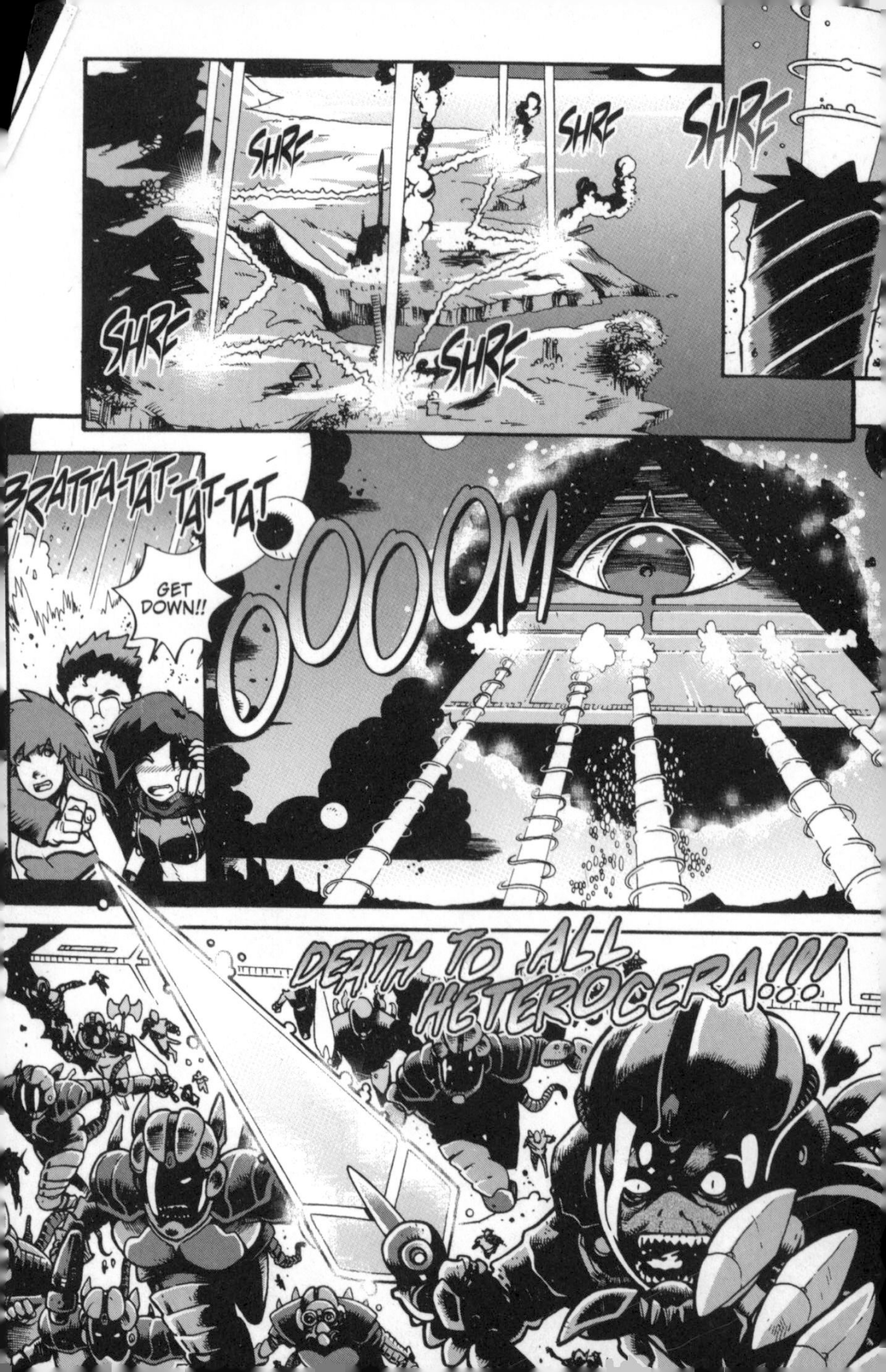
SHRF
SHRF
SHRF
SHRF
SHRF
OOOOM
BRATTA-TAT-TAT-TAT
GET DOWN!!
DEATH TO ALL HETEROCERA!!!

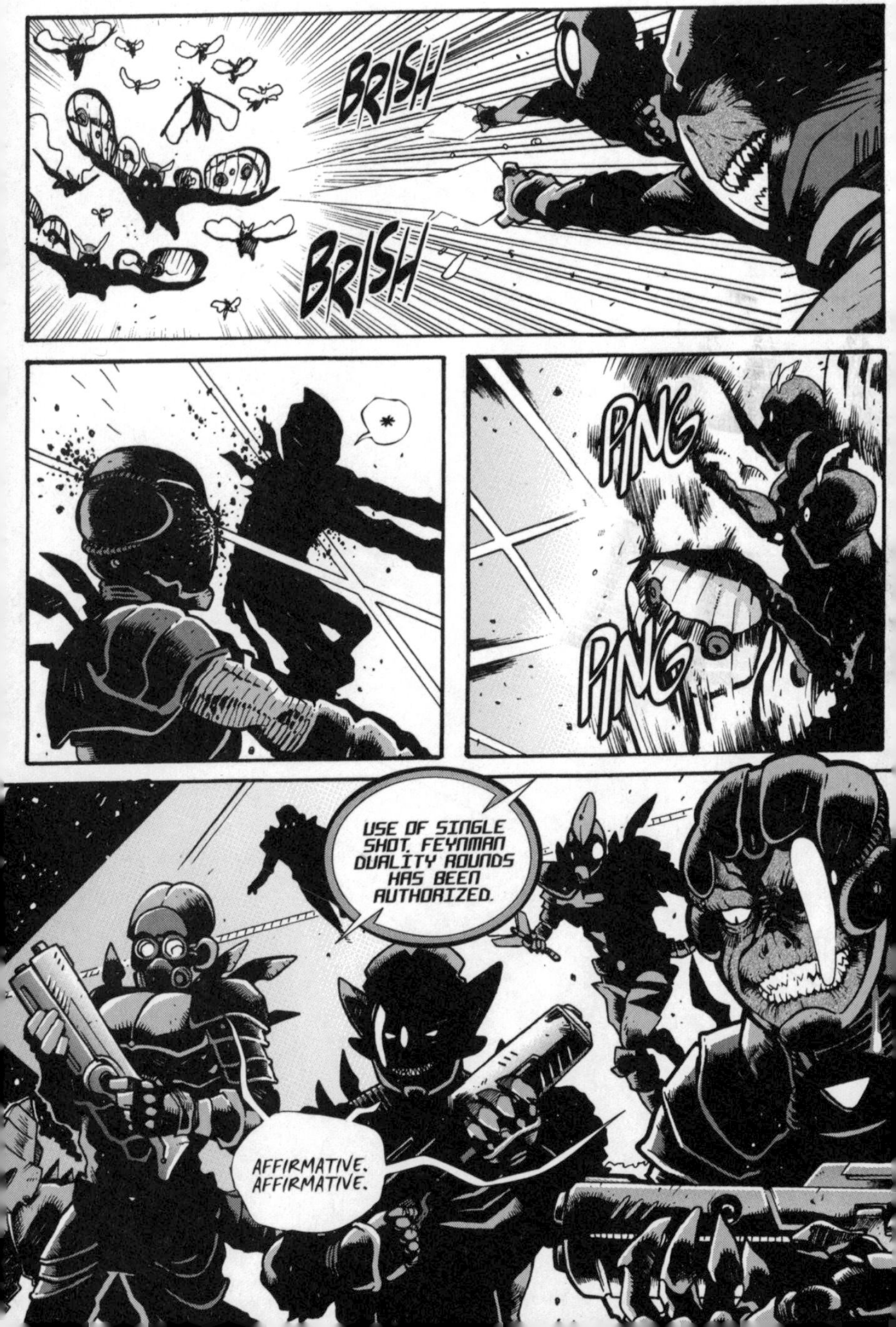
BRISH
BRISH
PING
PING
*
USE OF SINGLE SHOT, FEYNMAN DUALITY ROUNDS HAS BEEN AUTHORIZED.
AFFIRMATIVE. AFFIRMATIVE.

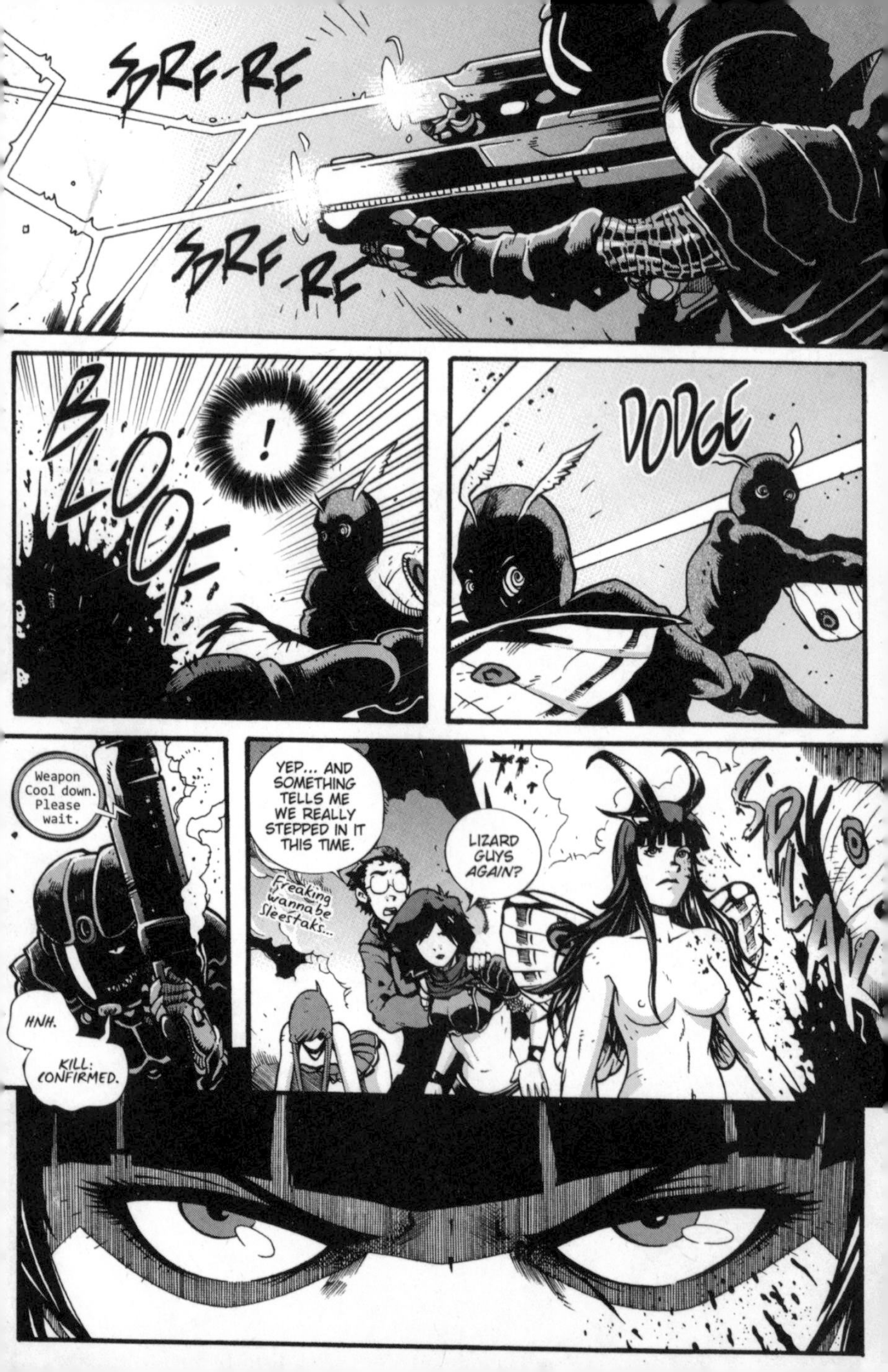

SDRF-RF
SDRF-RF
DODGE
BLOOOF
!
SPLAK
LIZARD GUYS AGAIN?
YEP... AND SOMETHING TELLS ME WE REALLY STEPPED IN IT THIS TIME.
Freaking wannabe Sleestaks...
Weapon Cool down. Please wait.
HNH.
KILL: CONFIRMED.

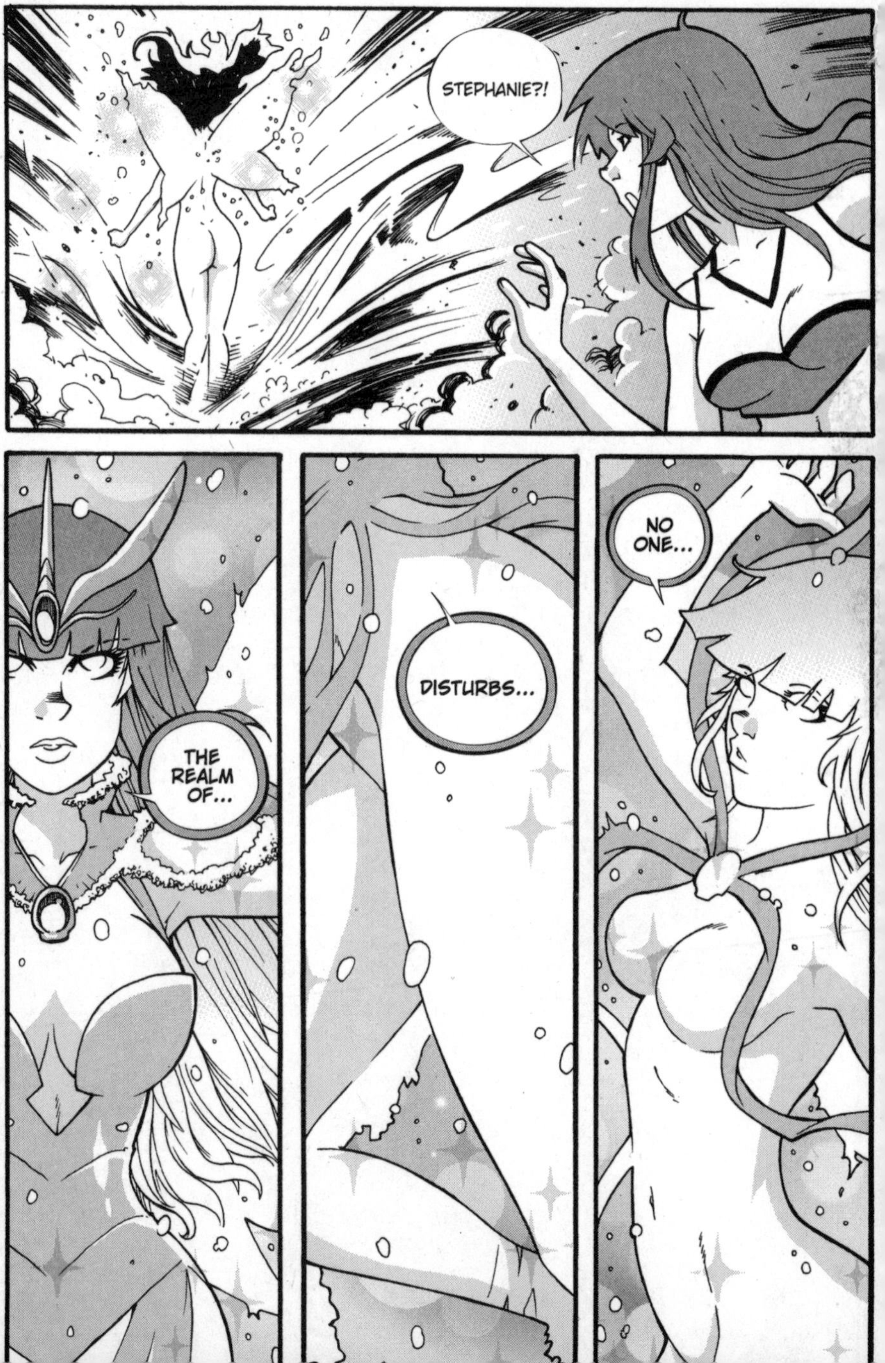
STEPHANIE?!
NO ONE...
DISTURBS...
THE REALM OF...

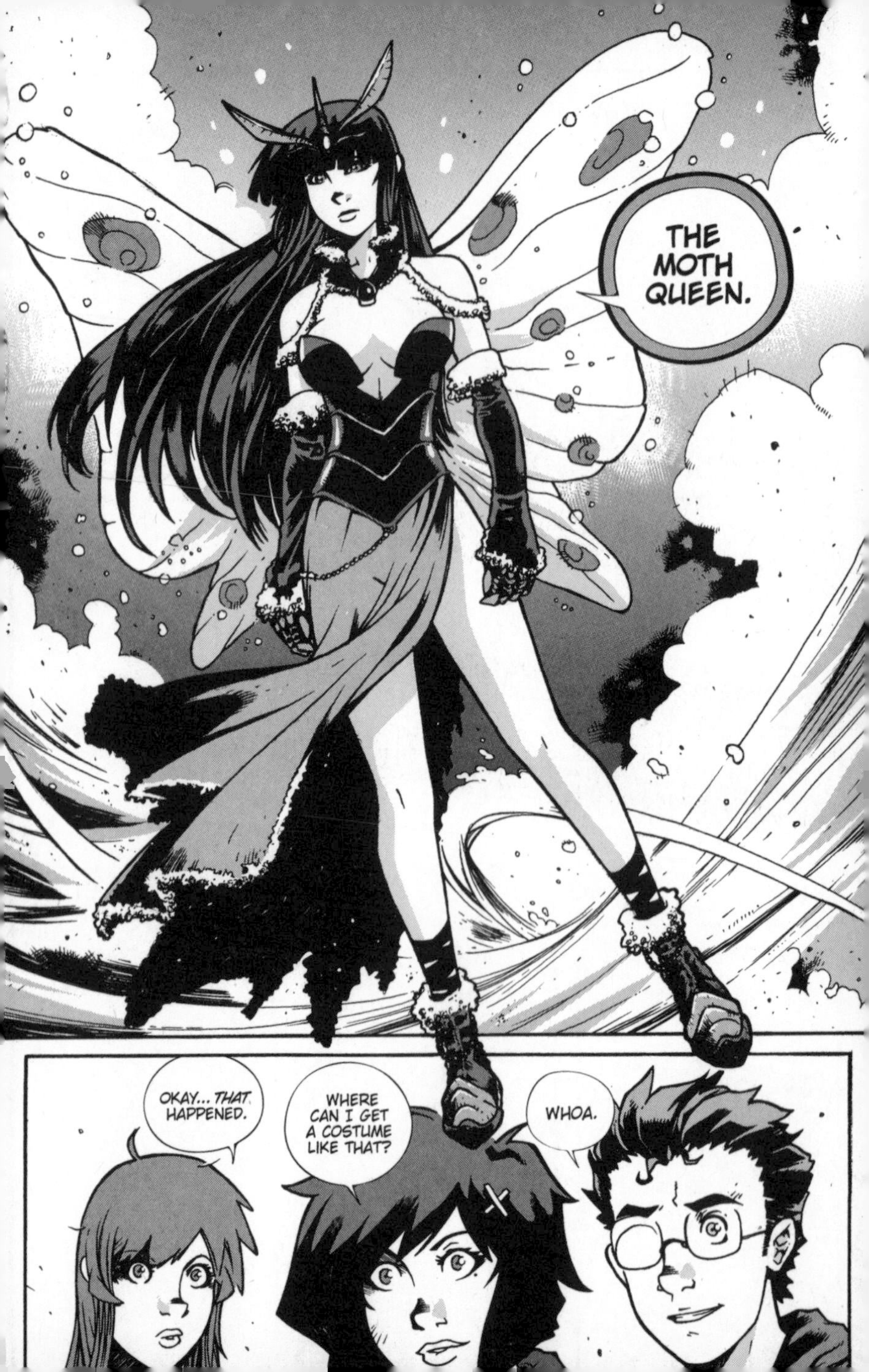
THE MOTH QUEEN.
WHOA.
WHERE CAN I GET A COSTUME LIKE THAT?
OKAY... *THAT* HAPPENED.

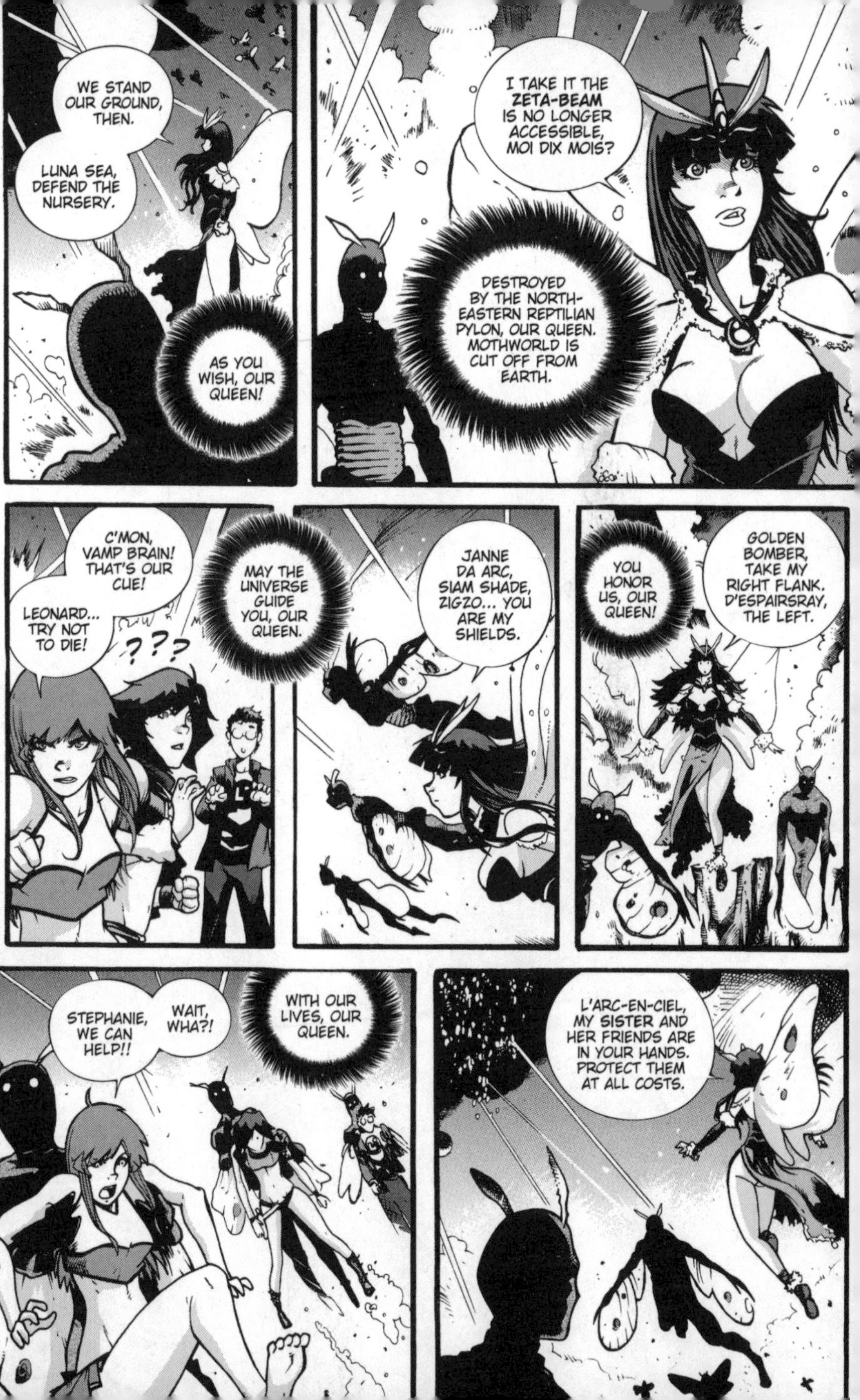
I TAKE IT THE ZETA-BEAM IS NO LONGER ACCESSIBLE, MOI DIX MOIS?
DESTROYED BY THE NORTH-EASTERN REPTILIAN PYLON, OUR QUEEN. MOTHWORLD IS CUT OFF FROM EARTH.
WE STAND OUR GROUND, THEN.
LUNA SEA, DEFEND THE NURSERY.
AS YOU WISH, OUR QUEEN!
GOLDEN BOMBER, TAKE MY RIGHT FLANK. D'ESPAIRSRAY, THE LEFT.
YOU HONOR US, OUR QUEEN!
JANNE DA ARC, SIAM SHADE, ZIGZO... YOU ARE MY SHIELDS.
MAY THE UNIVERSE GUIDE YOU, OUR QUEEN.
C'MON, VAMP BRAIN! THAT'S OUR CUE!
LEONARD... TRY NOT TO DIE!
???
L'ARC-EN-CIEL, MY SISTER AND HER FRIENDS ARE IN YOUR HANDS. PROTECT THEM AT ALL COSTS.
WITH OUR LIVES, OUR QUEEN.
WAIT, WHA?!
STEPHANIE, WE CAN HELP!!

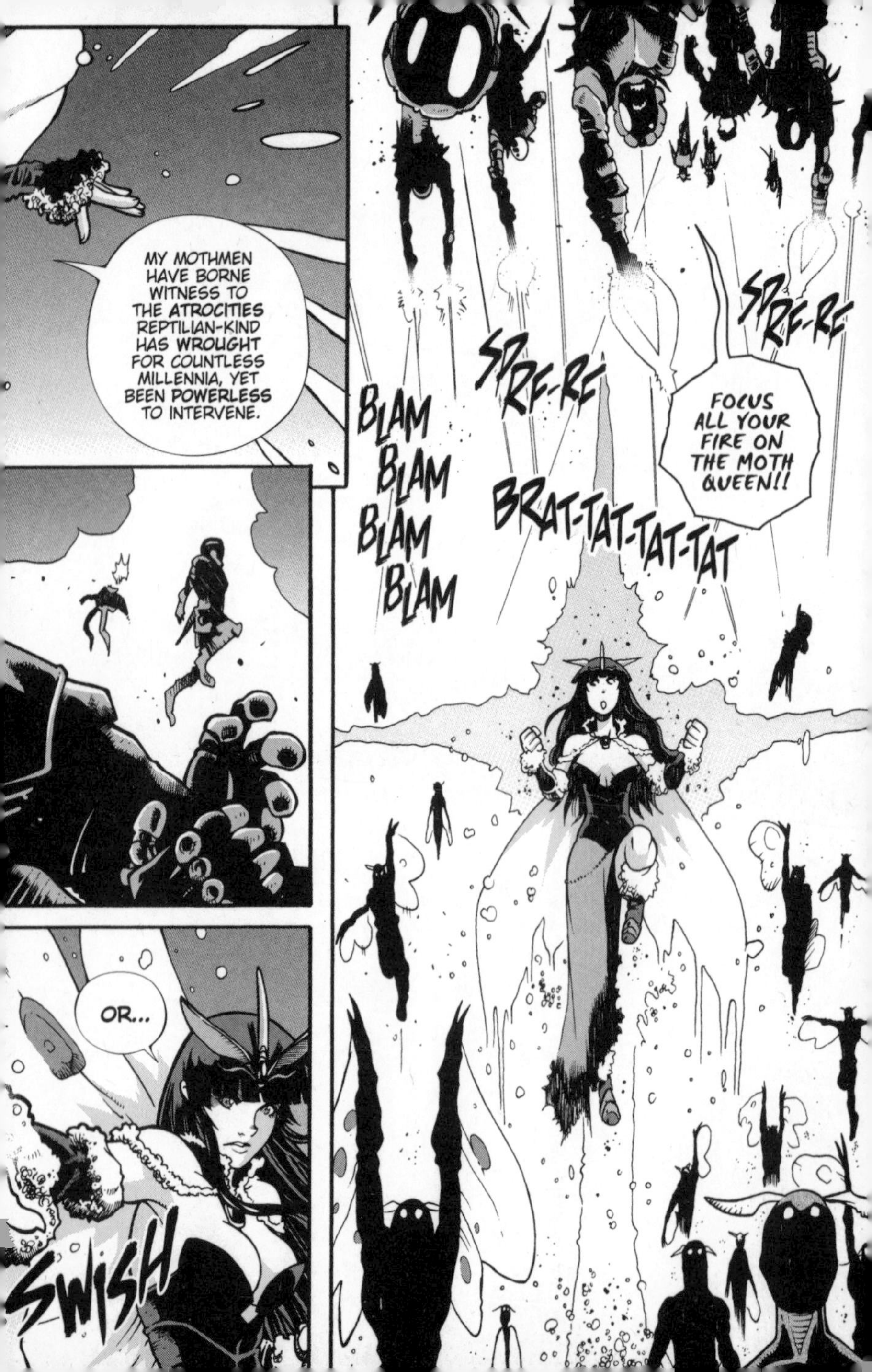

SDRF-RF
FOCUS ALL YOUR FIRE ON THE MOTH QUEEN!!
SDRF-RF
BLAM BLAM BLAM BLAM
BRAT-TAT-TAT-TAT
MY MOTHMEN HAVE BORNE WITNESS TO THE ATROCITIES REPTILIAN-KIND HAS WROUGHT FOR COUNTLESS MILLENNIA, YET BEEN POWERLESS TO INTERVENE.
OR...
SWISH

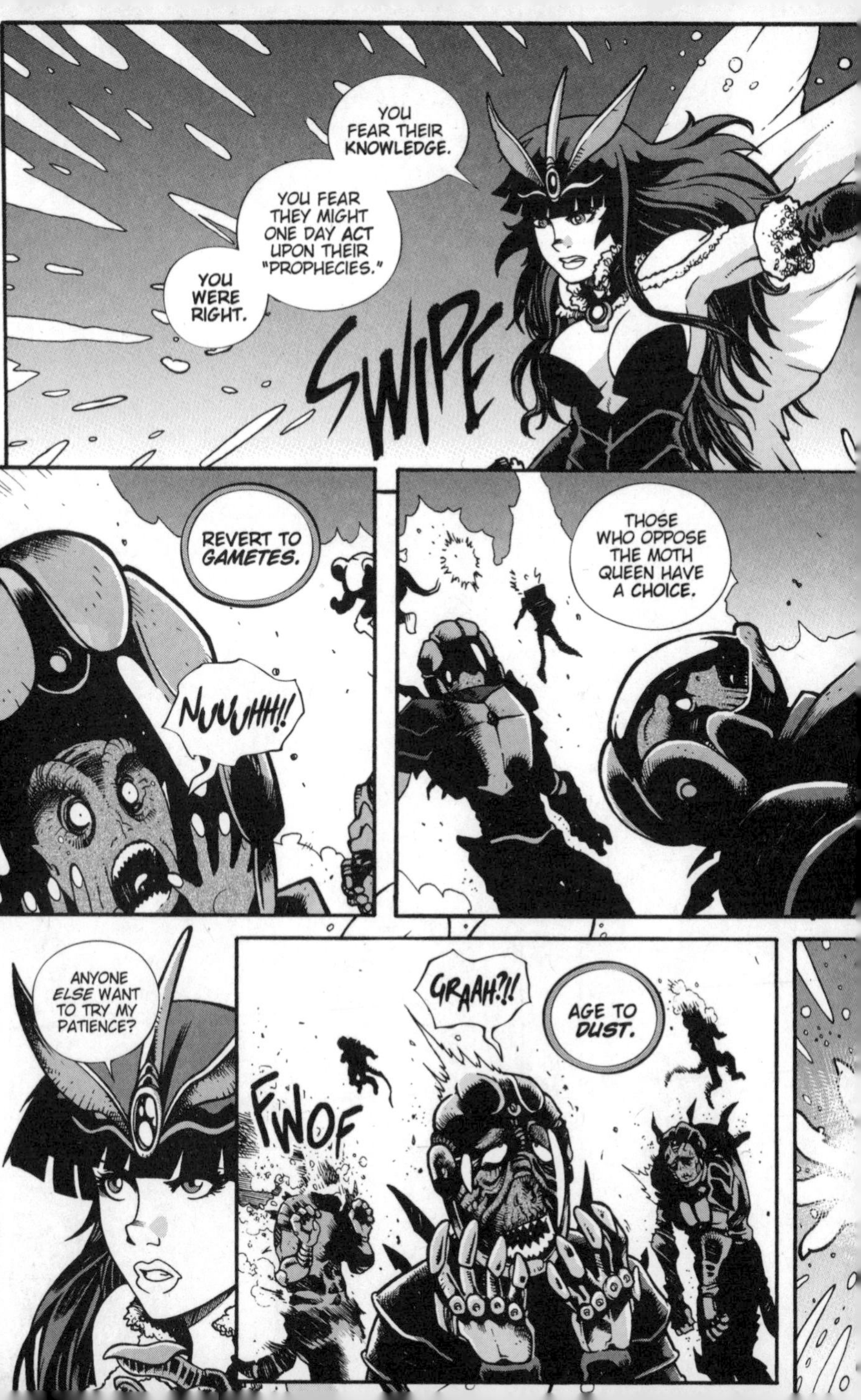
YOU FEAR THEIR KNOWLEDGE.
YOU FEAR THEY MIGHT ONE DAY ACT UPON THEIR "PROPHECIES."
YOU WERE RIGHT.
SWIPE
THOSE WHO OPPOSE THE MOTH QUEEN HAVE A CHOICE.
REVERT TO *GAMETES.*
NUUUHH!!
AGE TO *DUST.*
GRAAH?!!
FWOF
ANYONE *ELSE* WANT TO TRY MY PATIENCE?

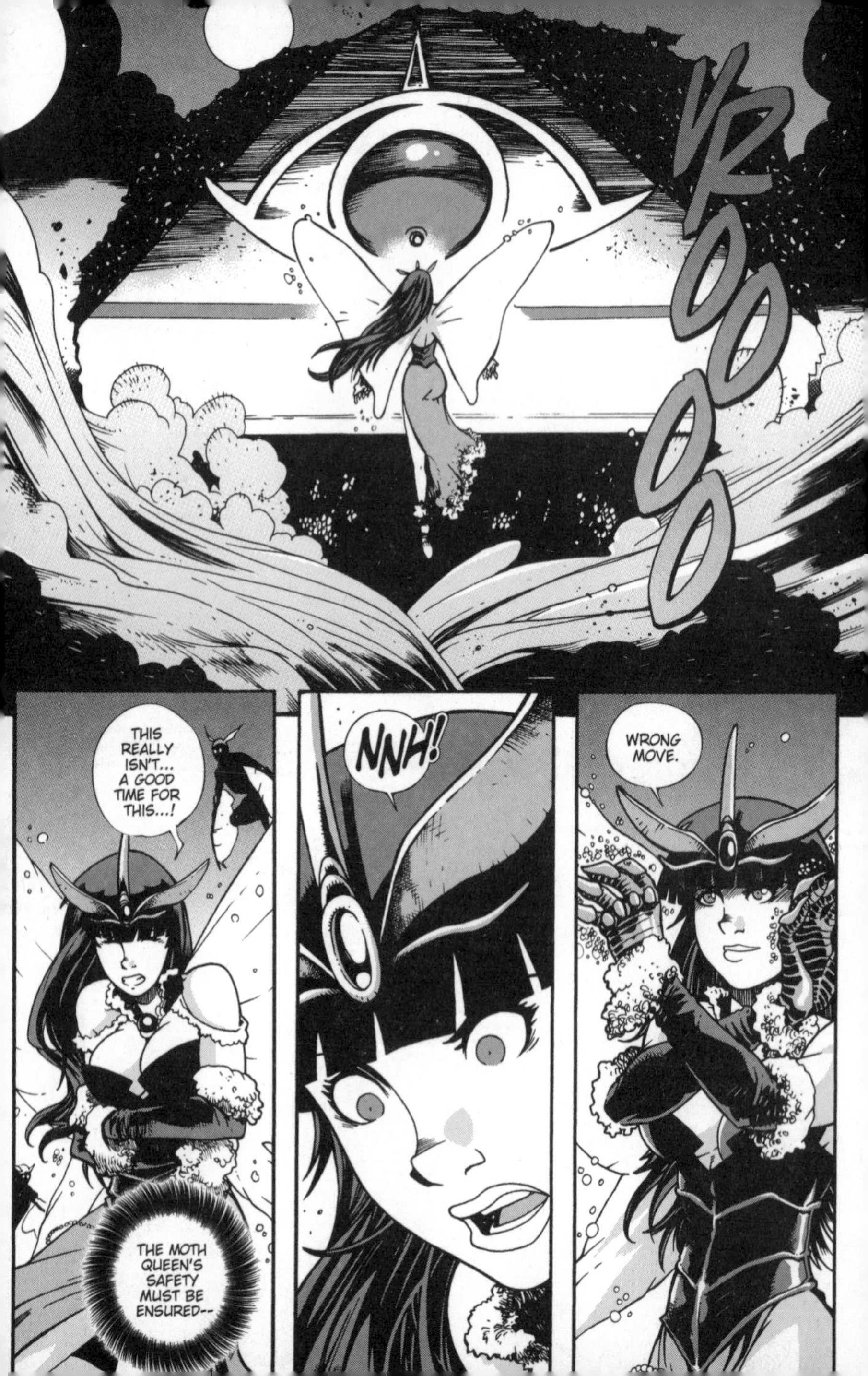
VROOOO
WRONG MOVE.
NNH!
THIS REALLY ISN'T... A GOOD TIME FOR THIS...!
THE MOTH QUEEN'S SAFETY MUST BE ENSURED--

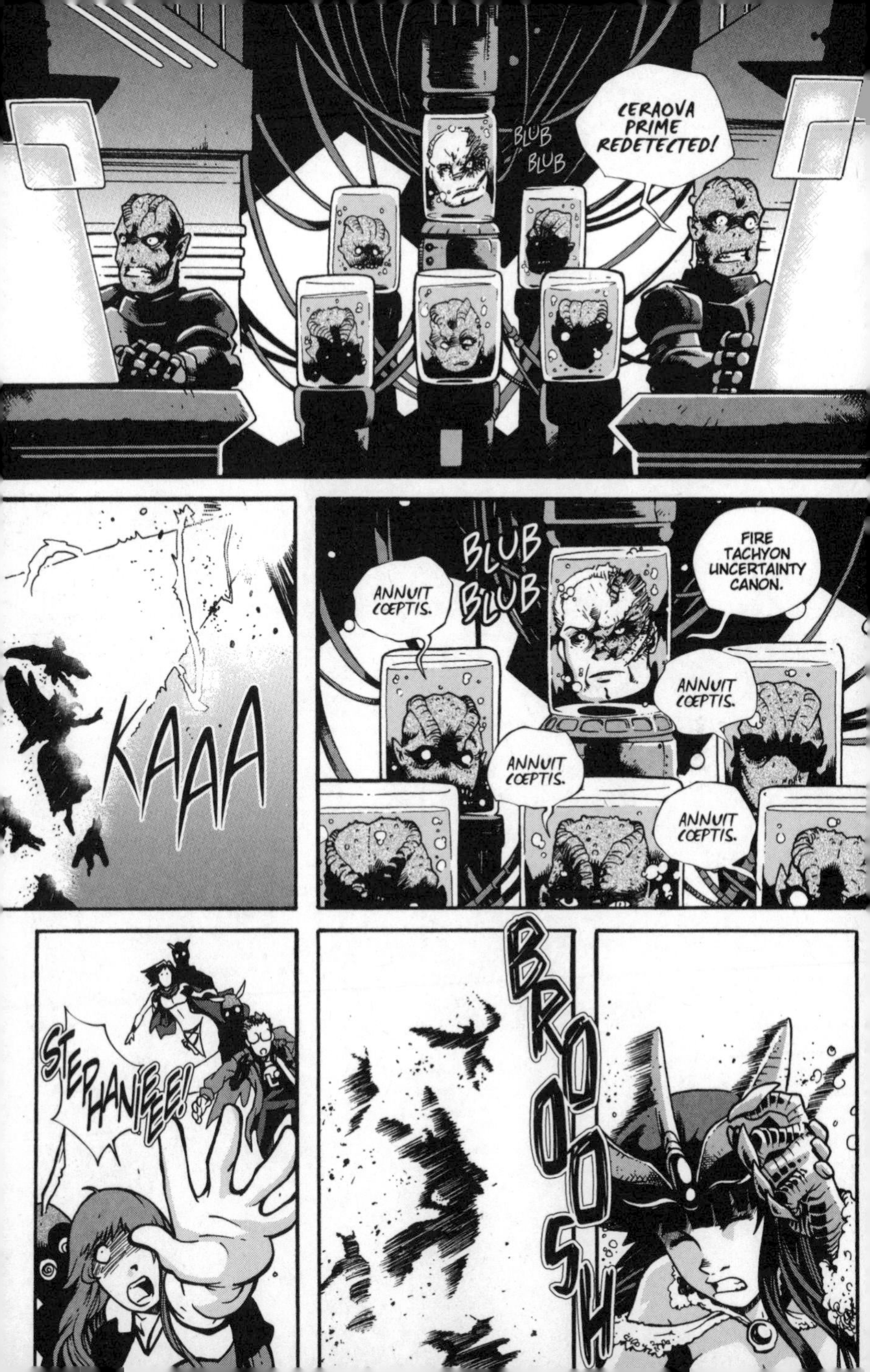
BLUB
BLUB
CERAOVA PRIME REDETECTED!
FIRE TACHYON UNCERTAINTY CANON.
BLUB
BLUB
ANNUIT CŒPTIS.
ANNUIT CŒPTIS.
ANNUIT CŒPTIS.
ANNUIT CŒPTIS.
KAAA
BROOOOSH
STEPHANIEEE!

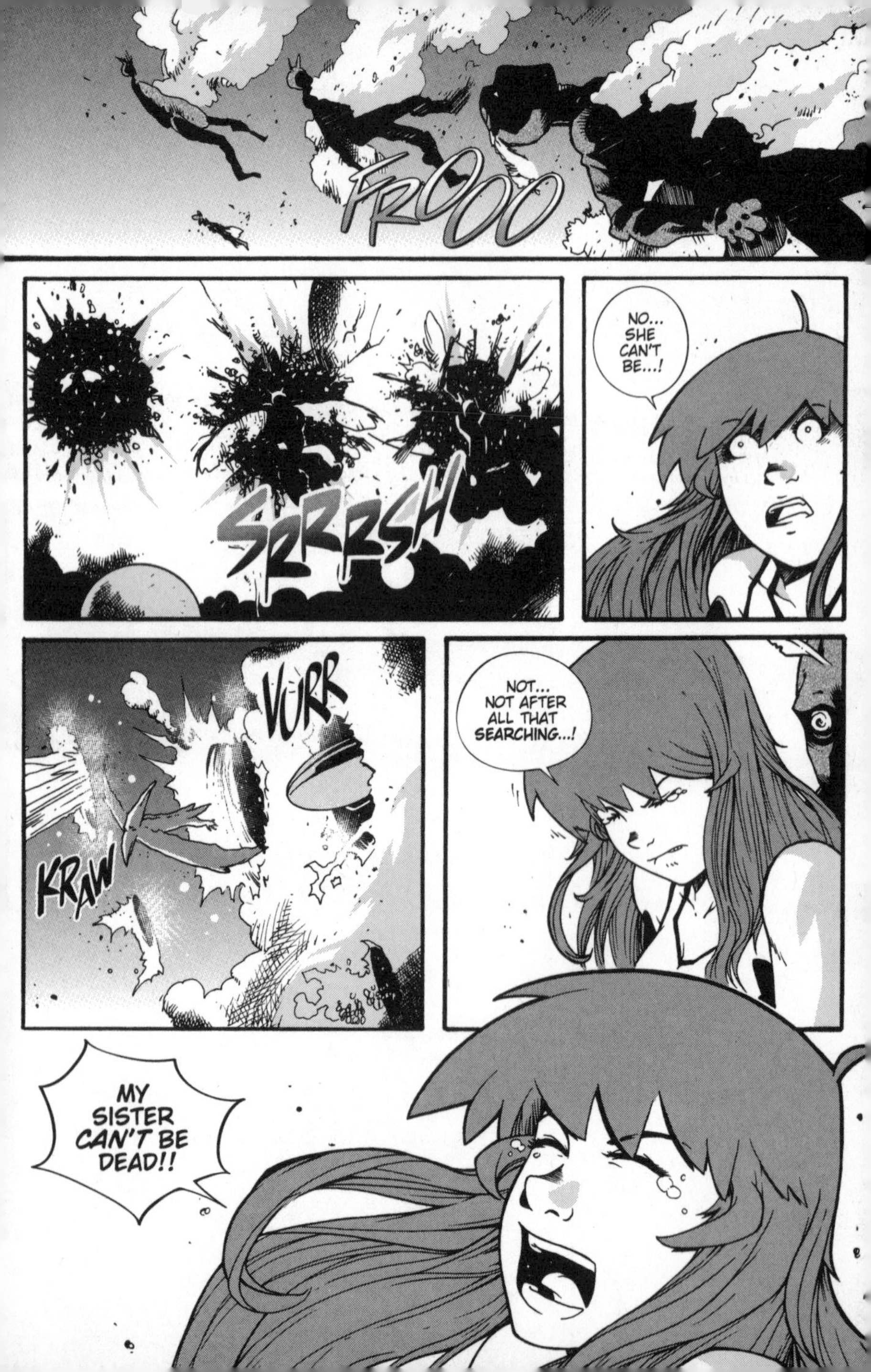
FROOOO
NO... SHE CAN'T BE...!
SPRRSH
NOT... NOT AFTER ALL THAT SEARCHING...!
VURR
KRAW
MY SISTER CAN'T BE DEAD!!

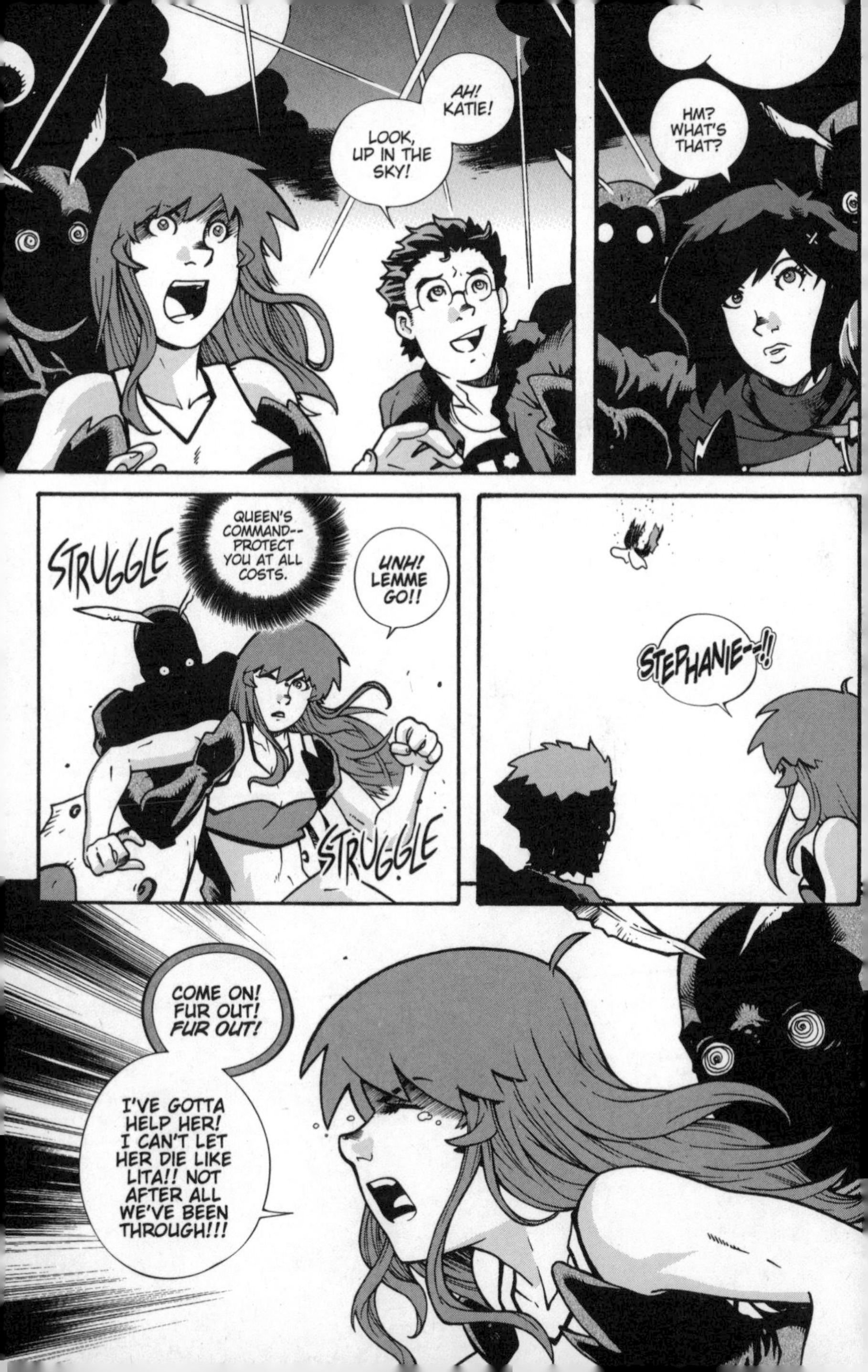
HM? WHAT'S THAT?
AH! KATIE!
LOOK, UP IN THE SKY!
STEPHANIE--!!
UNH! LEMME GO!!
QUEEN'S COMMAND-- PROTECT YOU AT ALL COSTS.
STRUGGLE
STRUGGLE
COME ON! FUR OUT! FUR OUT!
I'VE GOTTA HELP HER! I CAN'T LET HER DIE LIKE LITA!! NOT AFTER ALL WE'VE BEEN THROUGH!!!

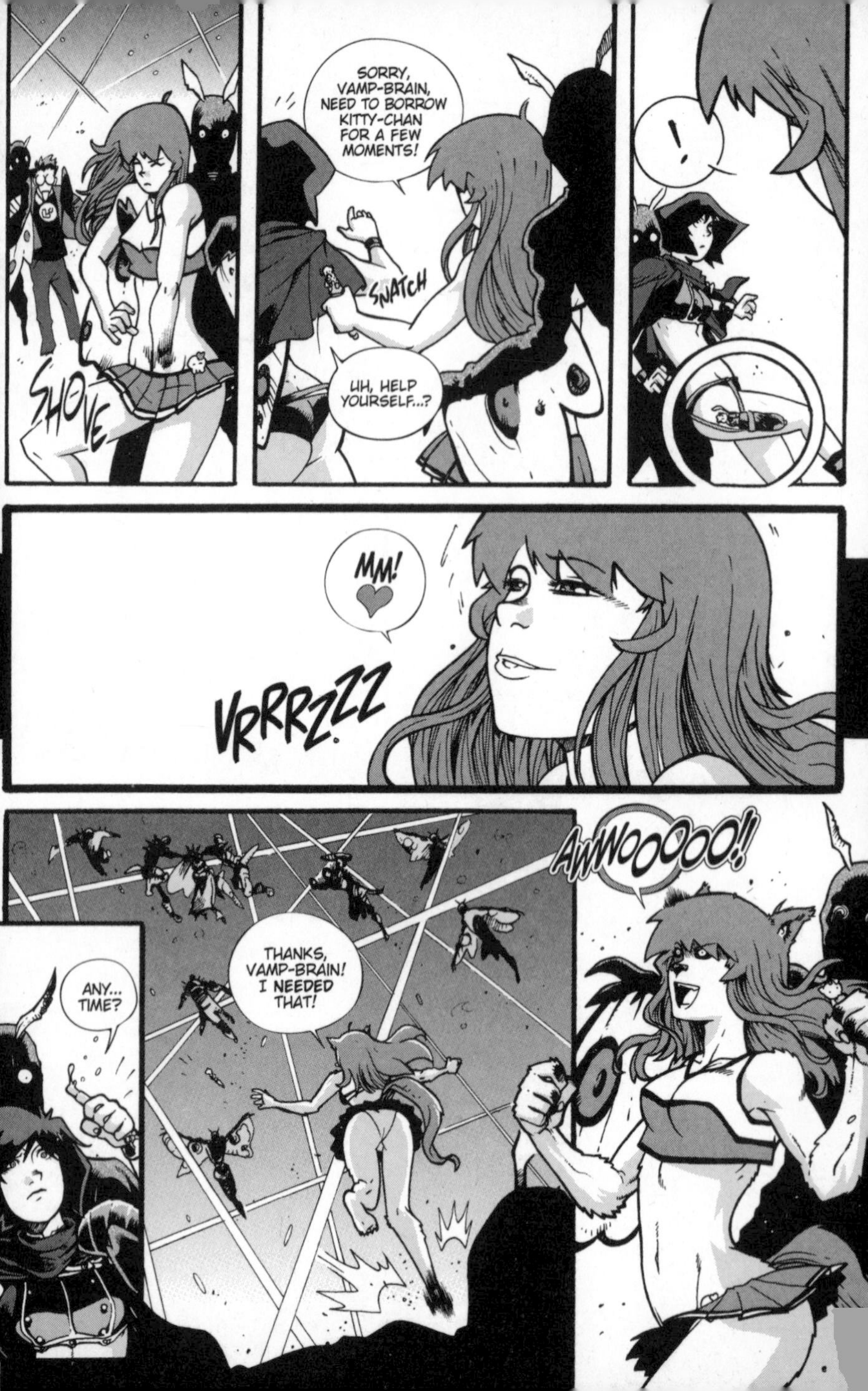
!
SORRY, VAMP-BRAIN, NEED TO BORROW KITTY-CHAN FOR A FEW MOMENTS!
SNATCH
UH, HELP YOURSELF...?
SHOVE
MM! ♥
VRRRZZZ
AWWOOOOO!!
THANKS, VAMP-BRAIN! I NEEDED THAT!
ANY... TIME?

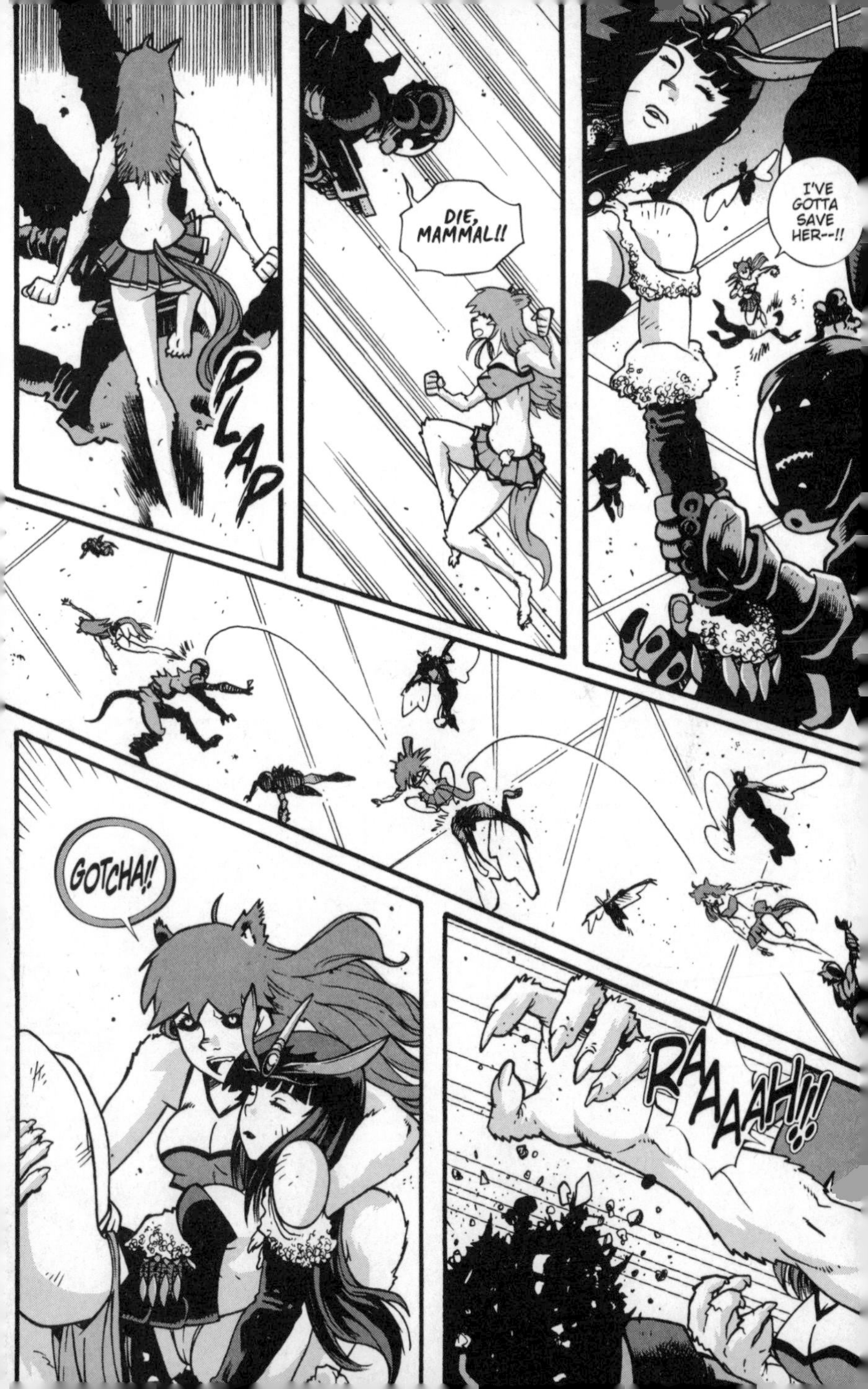
I'VE GOTTA SAVE HER--!!
DIE, MAMMAL!!
PLAP
RAAAAH!!!
GOTCHA!!

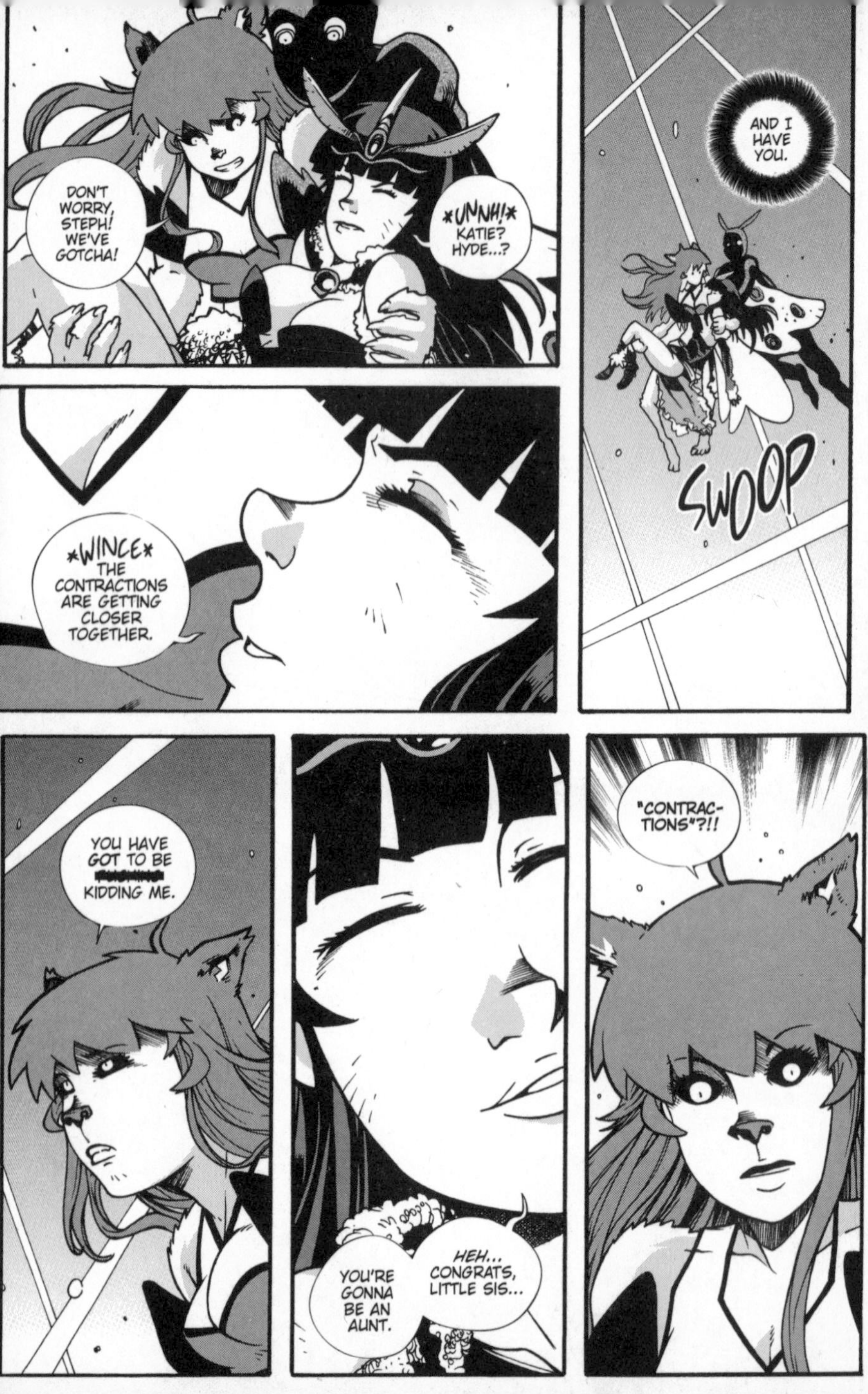
AND I HAVE YOU.
SWOOP
UNNH! KATIE? HYDE...?
DON'T WORRY, STEPH! WE'VE GOTCHA!
WINCE THE CONTRACTIONS ARE GETTING CLOSER TOGETHER.
"CONTRAC- TIONS"?!!
HEH... CONGRATS, LITTLE SIS...
YOU'RE GONNA BE AN AUNT.
YOU HAVE GOT TO BE [redacted] KIDDING ME.

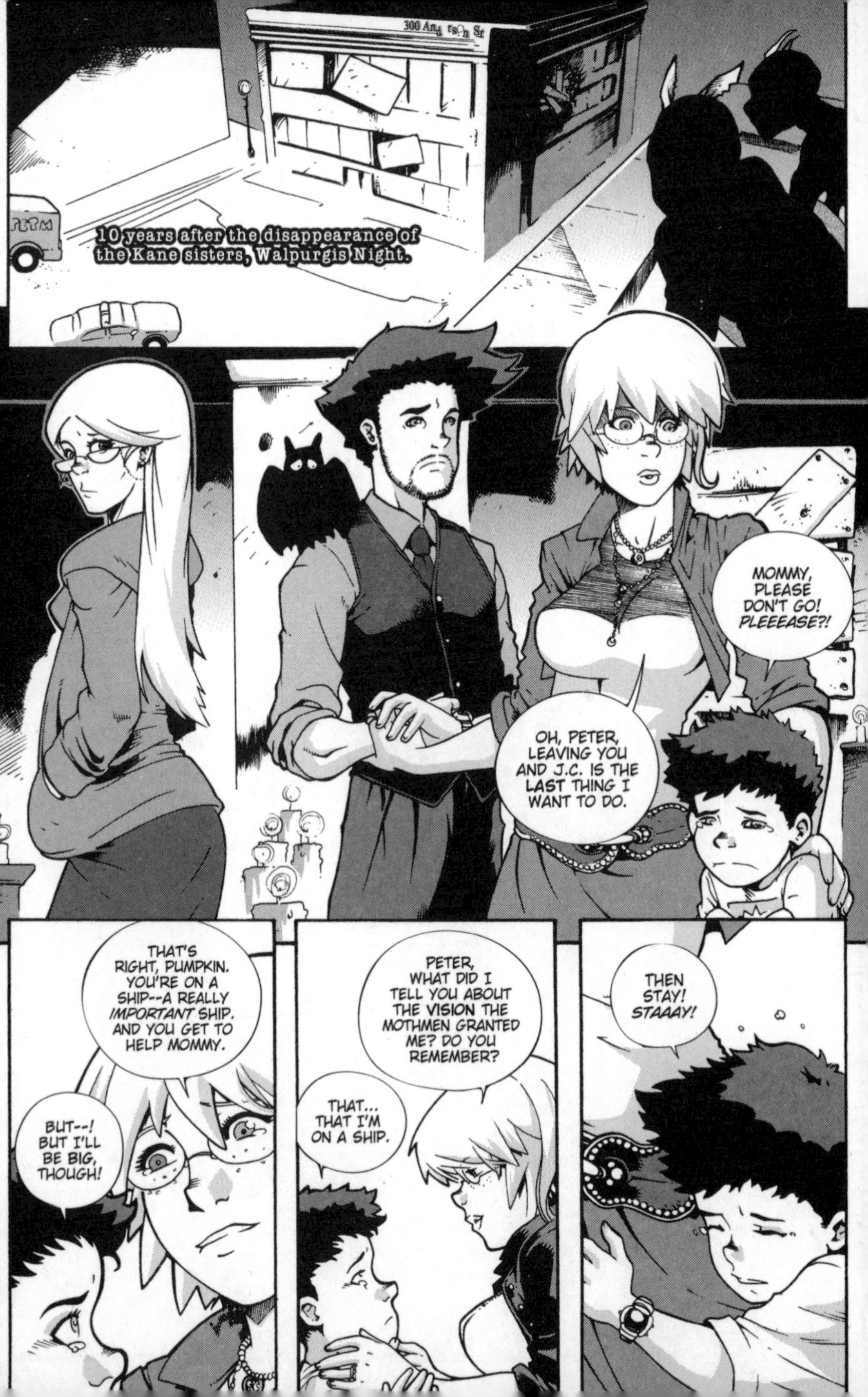
10 years after the disappearance of the Kane sisters, Walpurgis Night.
MOMMY, PLEASE DON'T GO! *PLEEEASE?!*
OH, PETER, LEAVING YOU AND J.C. IS THE **LAST** THING I WANT TO DO.
THEN STAY! *STAAAY!*
PETER, WHAT DID I TELL YOU ABOUT THE **VISION** THE MOTHMEN GRANTED ME? DO YOU REMEMBER?
THAT... THAT I'M ON A SHIP.
THAT'S RIGHT, PUMPKIN. YOU'RE ON A SHIP--A REALLY *IMPORTANT* SHIP. AND YOU GET TO HELP MOMMY.
BUT--! BUT I'LL BE BIG, THOUGH!

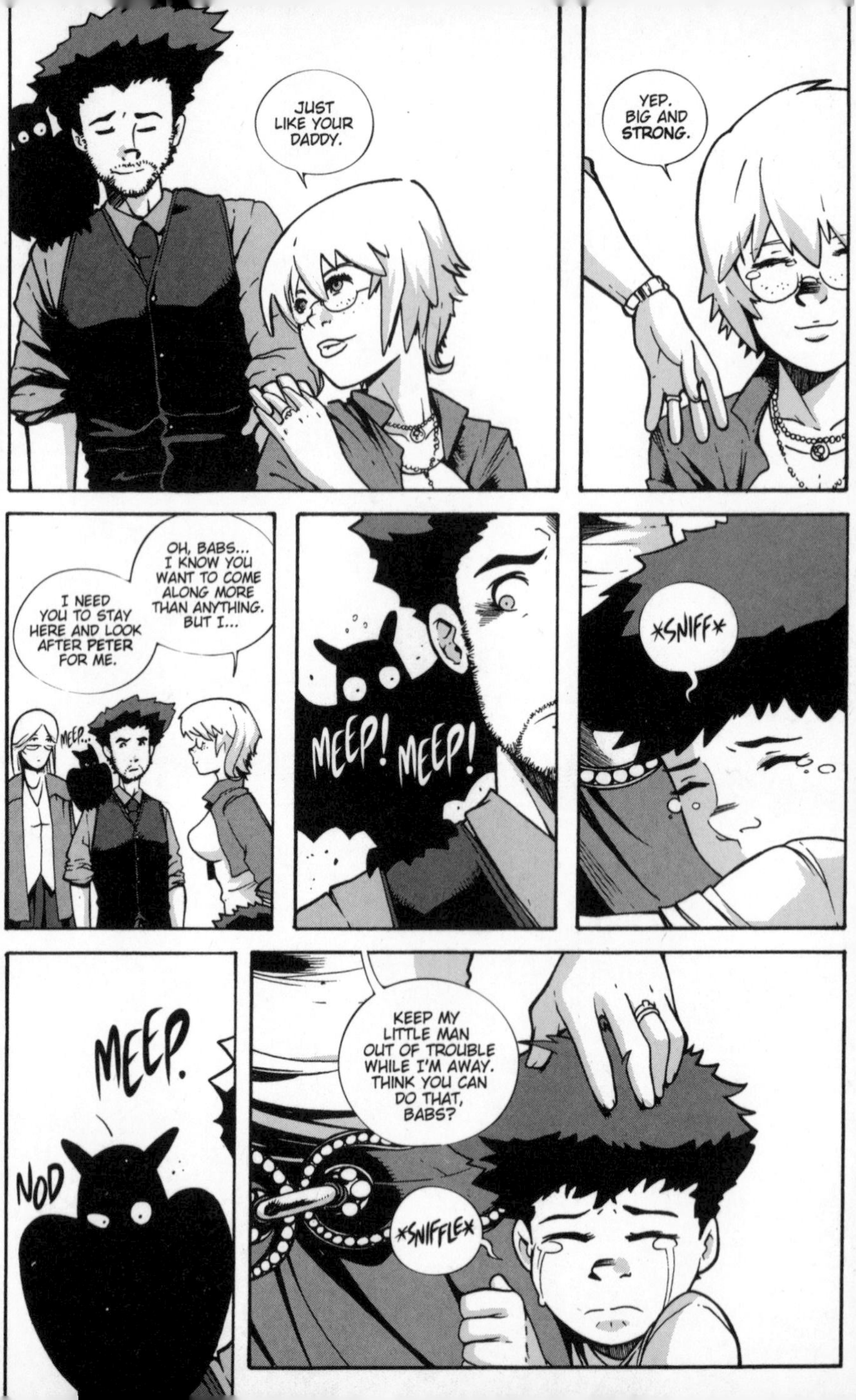
YEP. BIG AND STRONG.
JUST LIKE YOUR DADDY.
SNIFF
MEEP! MEEP!
OH, BABS... I KNOW YOU WANT TO COME ALONG MORE THAN ANYTHING. BUT I...
I NEED YOU TO STAY HERE AND LOOK AFTER PETER FOR ME.
MEEP...
KEEP MY LITTLE MAN OUT OF TROUBLE WHILE I'M AWAY. THINK YOU CAN DO THAT, BABS?
SNIFFLE
MEEP.
NOD

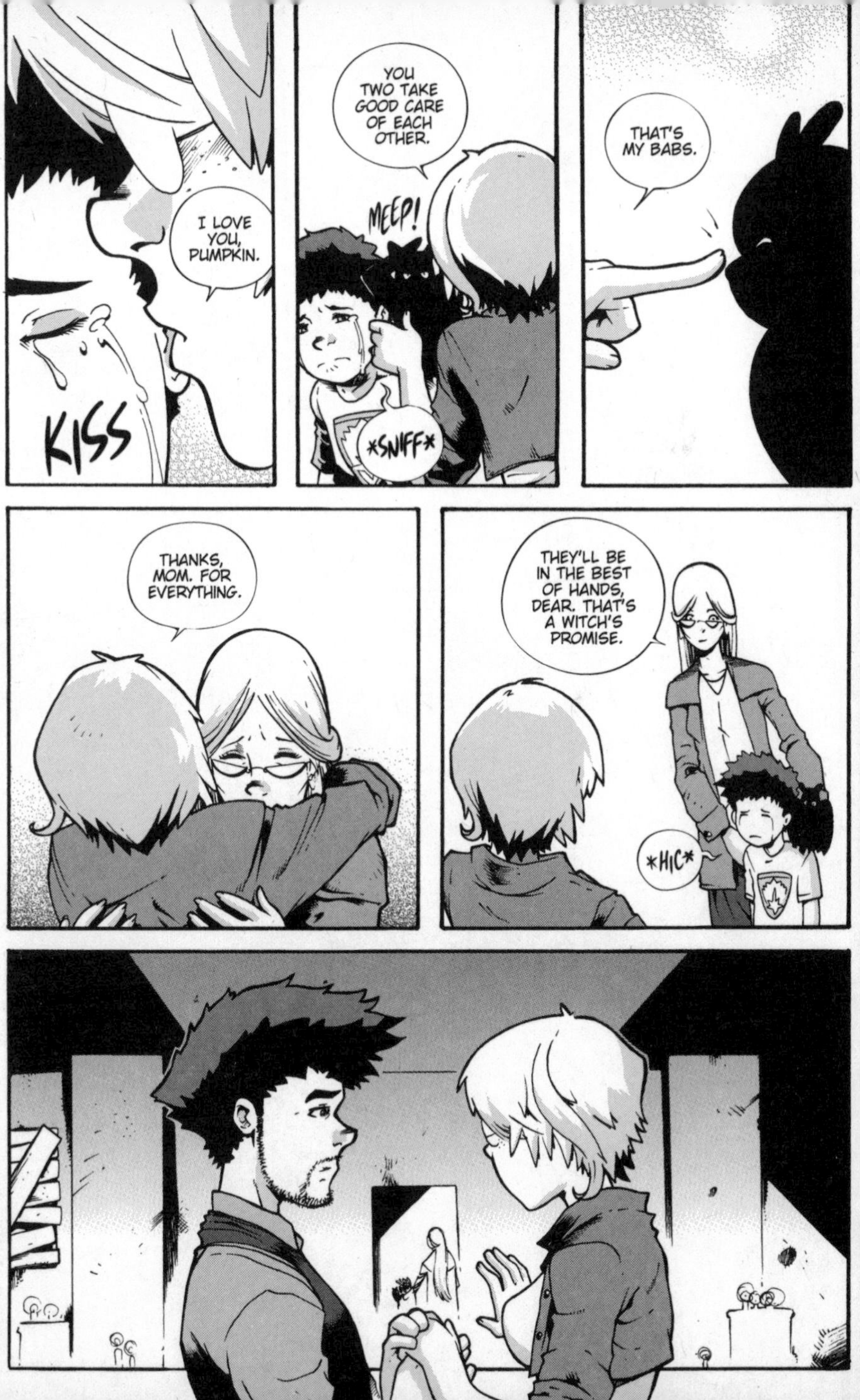
THAT'S MY BABS.
YOU TWO TAKE GOOD CARE OF EACH OTHER.
MEEP!
SNIFF
I LOVE YOU, PUMPKIN.
KISS
THEY'LL BE IN THE BEST OF HANDS, DEAR. THAT'S A WITCH'S PROMISE.
HIC
THANKS, MOM. FOR EVERYTHING.

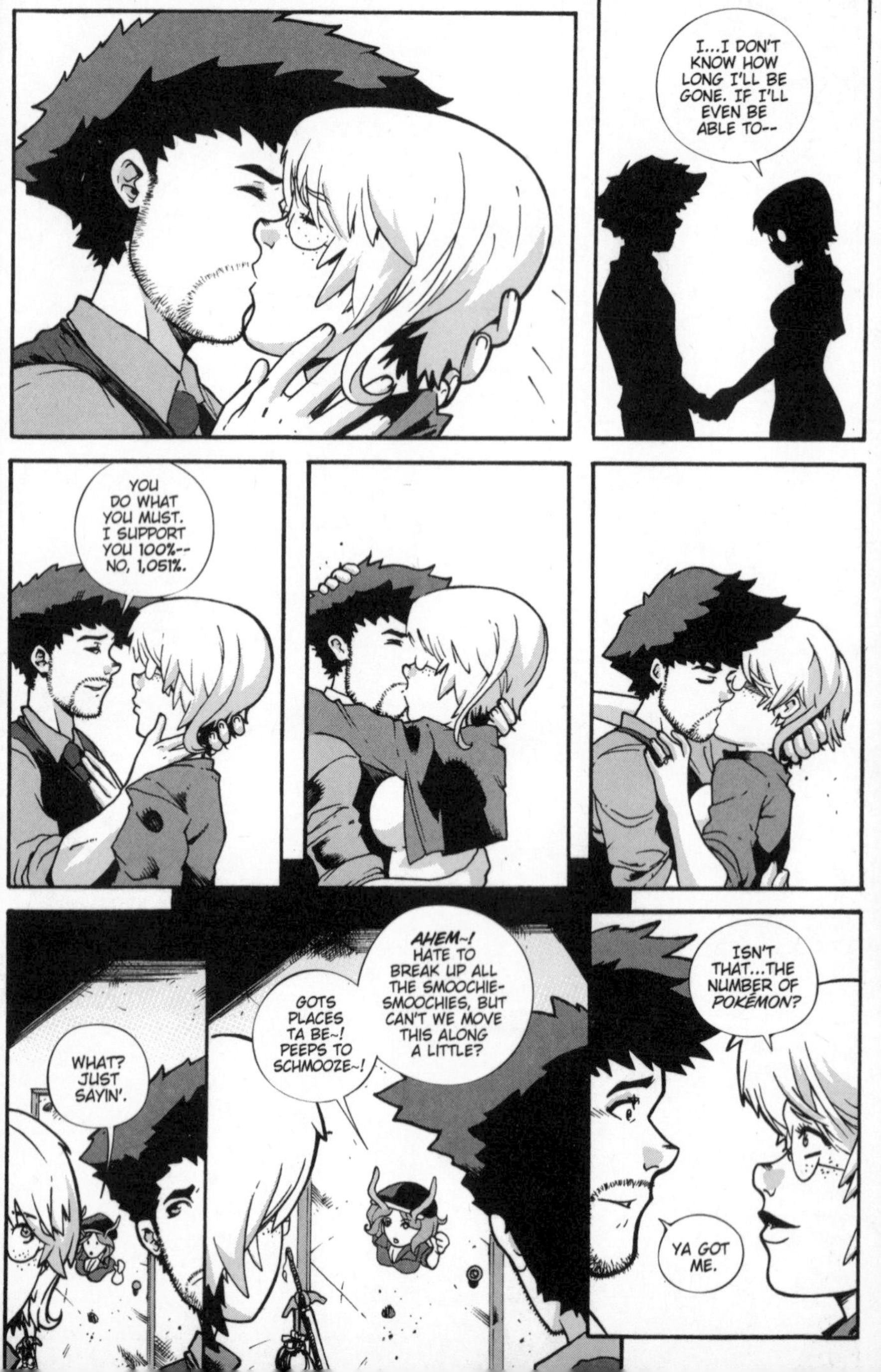
I...I DON'T KNOW HOW LONG I'LL BE GONE. IF I'LL EVEN BE ABLE TO--
YOU DO WHAT YOU MUST. I SUPPORT YOU 100%-- NO, 1,051%.
ISN'T THAT...THE NUMBER OF *POKÉMON*?
YA GOT ME.
AHEM~! HATE TO BREAK UP ALL THE SMOOCHIE-SMOOCHIES, BUT CAN'T WE MOVE THIS ALONG A LITTLE?
GOTS PLACES TA BE~! PEEPS TO SCHMOOZE~!
WHAT? JUST SAYIN'.

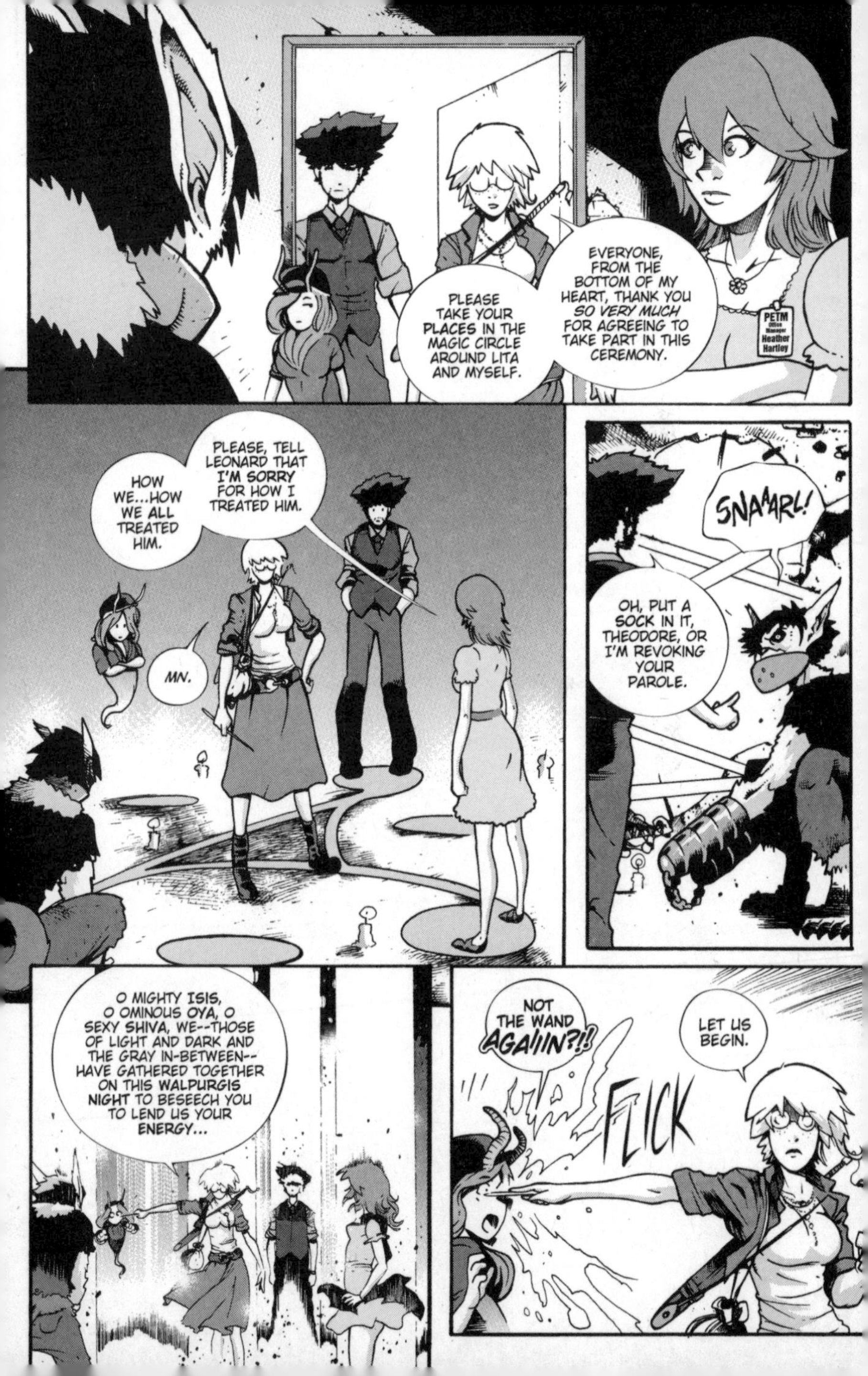
EVERYONE, FROM THE BOTTOM OF MY HEART, THANK YOU *SO VERY MUCH* FOR AGREEING TO TAKE PART IN THIS CEREMONY.
PLEASE TAKE YOUR PLACES IN THE MAGIC CIRCLE AROUND LITA AND MYSELF.
PETM
Heather Hartley
SNAAARL!
OH, PUT A SOCK IN IT, THEODORE, OR I'M REVOKING YOUR PAROLE.
PLEASE, TELL LEONARD THAT **I'M SORRY** FOR HOW I TREATED HIM.
HOW WE...HOW WE **ALL** TREATED HIM.
MN.
LET US BEGIN.
NOT THE WAND AGAIIIN?!!
FLICK
O MIGHTY **ISIS**, O OMINOUS **OYA**, O SEXY **SHIVA**, WE--THOSE OF LIGHT AND DARK AND THE GRAY IN-BETWEEN--HAVE GATHERED TOGETHER ON THIS **WALPURGIS NIGHT** TO BESEECH YOU TO LEND US YOUR **ENERGY**...

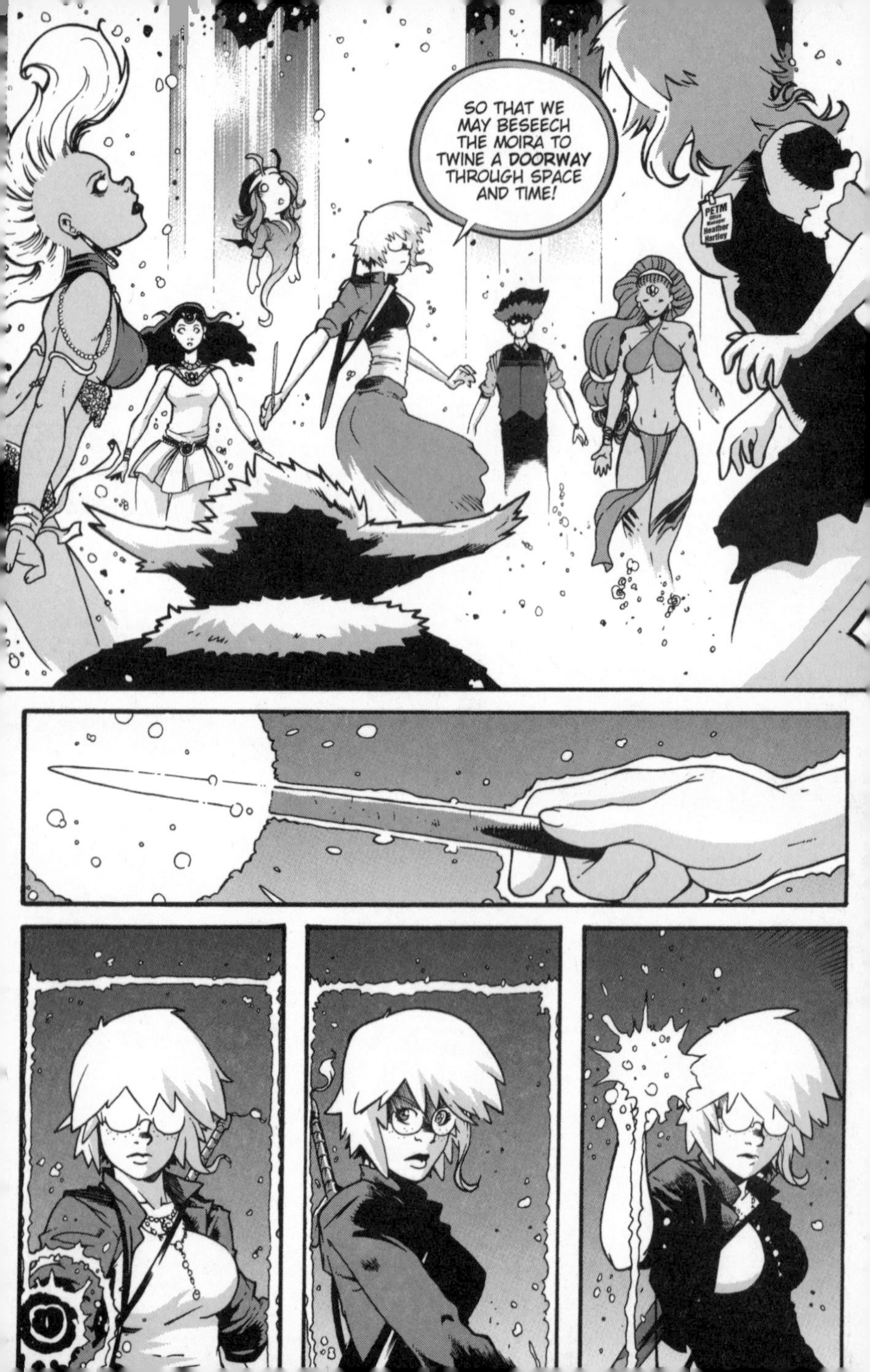
SO THAT WE MAY BESEECH THE MOIRA TO TWINE A DOORWAY THROUGH SPACE AND TIME!
PETM
Heather Hartley

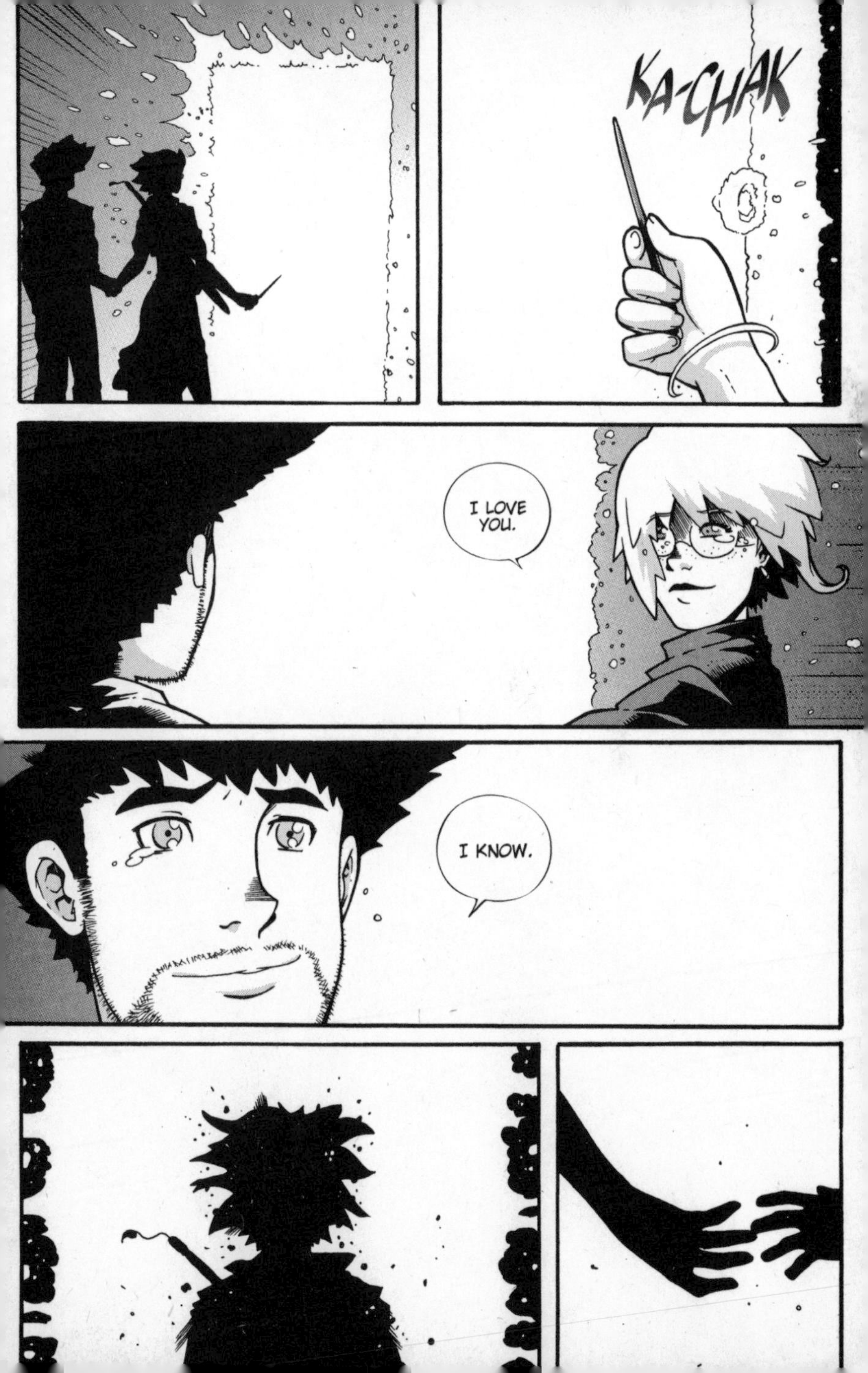
KA-CHAK
I LOVE YOU.
I KNOW.

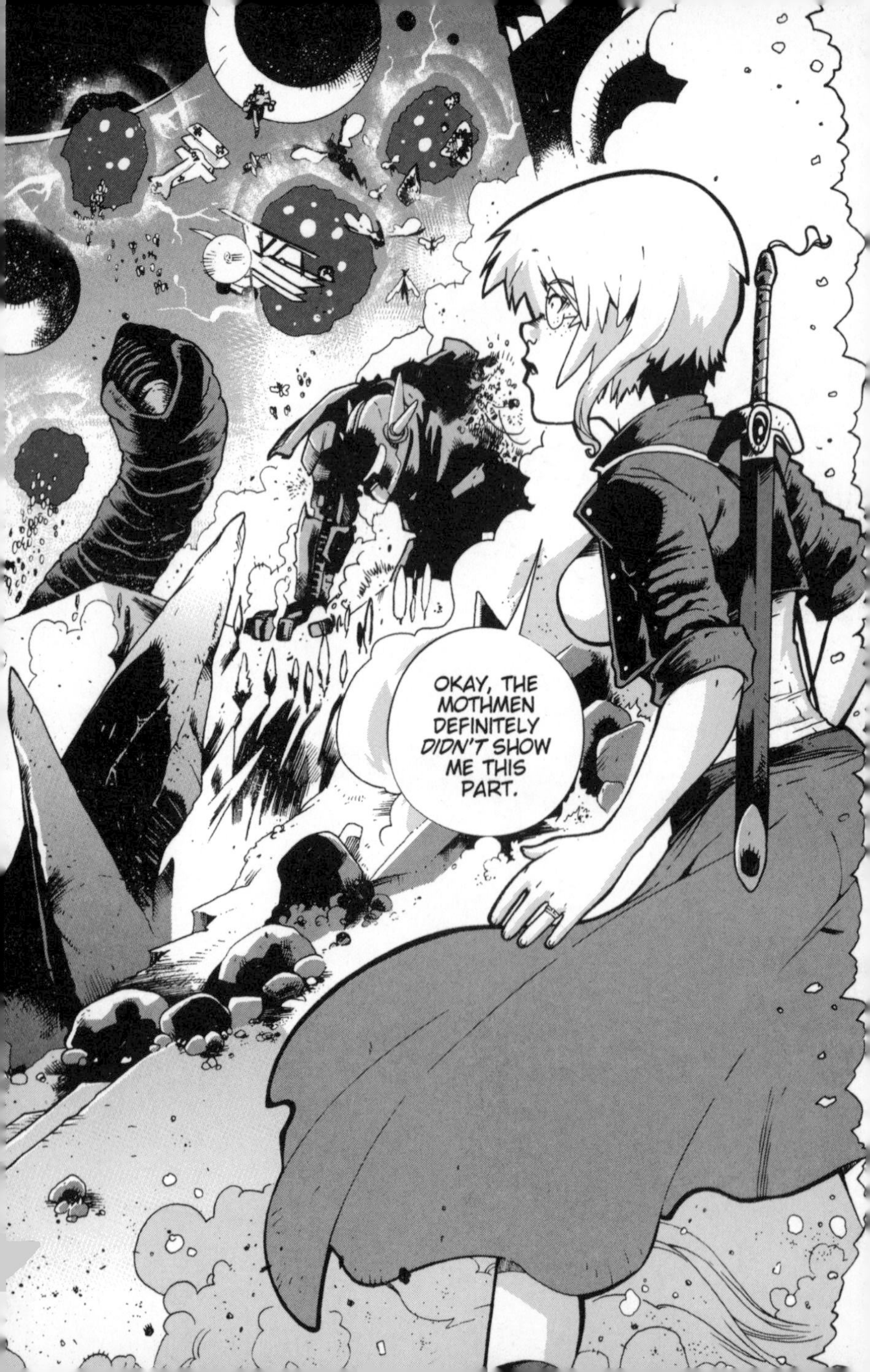
OKAY, THE MOTHMEN DEFINITELY *DIDN'T* SHOW ME THIS PART.

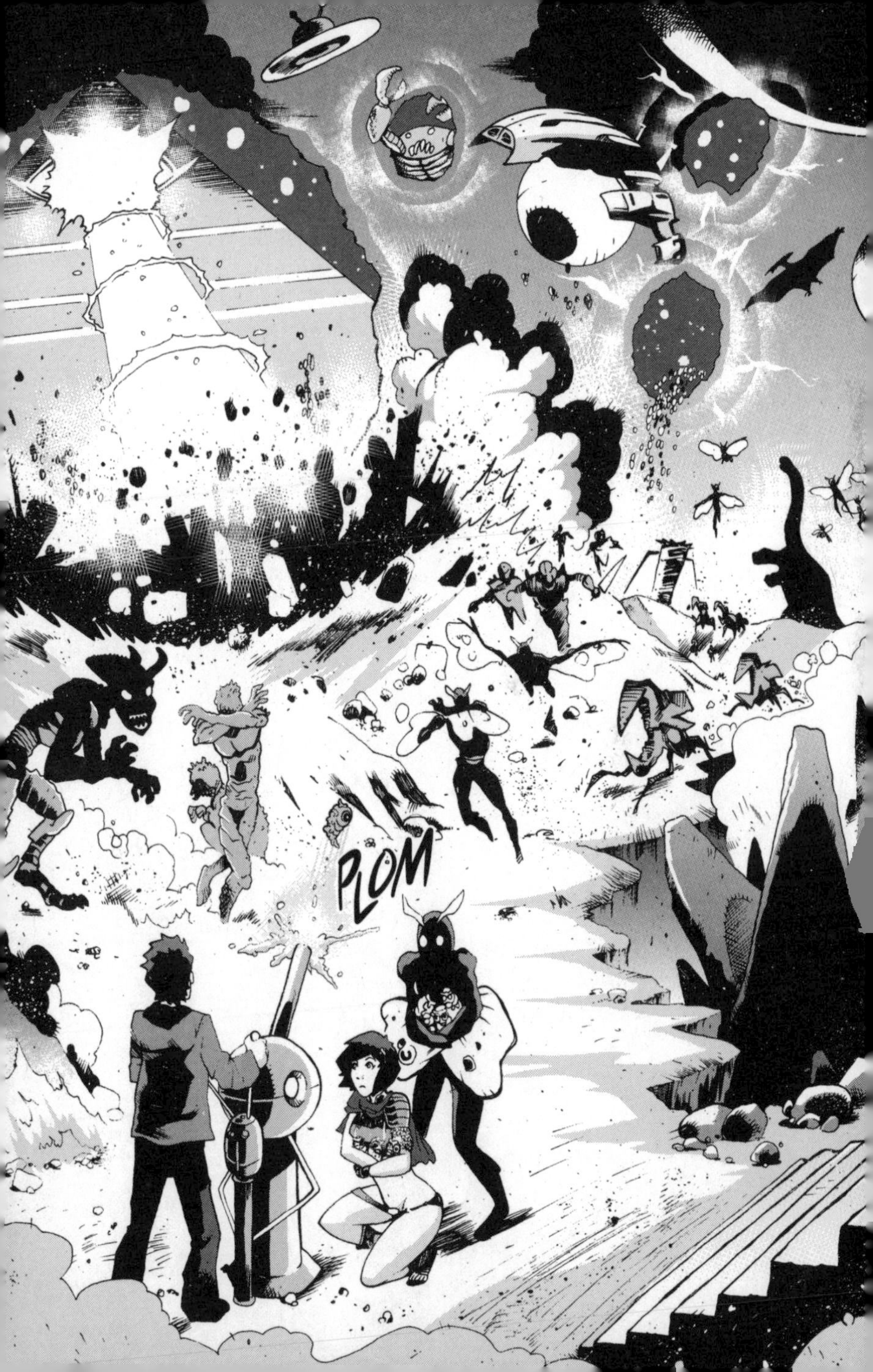
PLOM

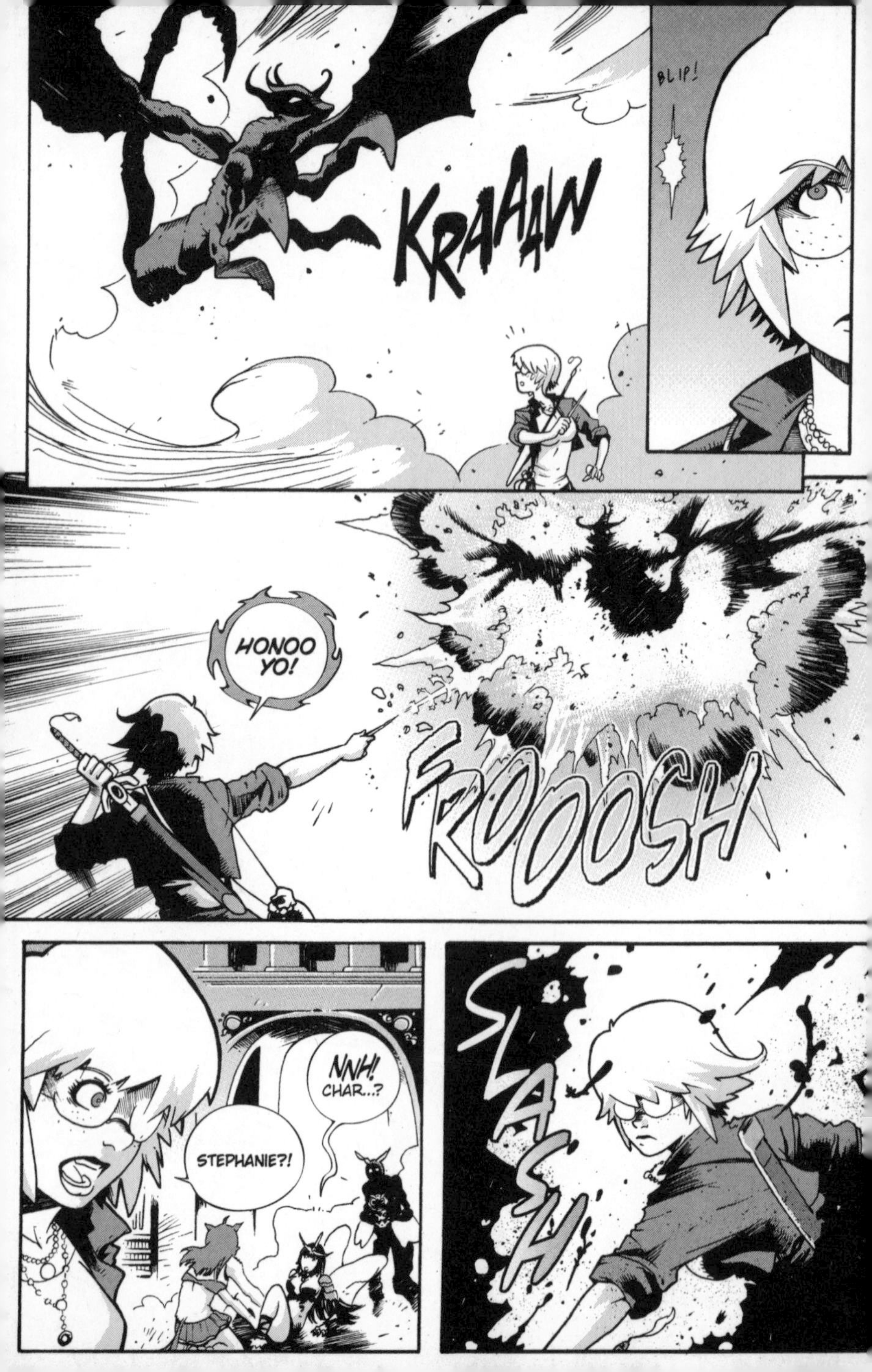
BLIP!
KRAAAW
HONOO YO!
FROOOSH
SLASH
NNH! CHAR...?
STEPHANIE?!

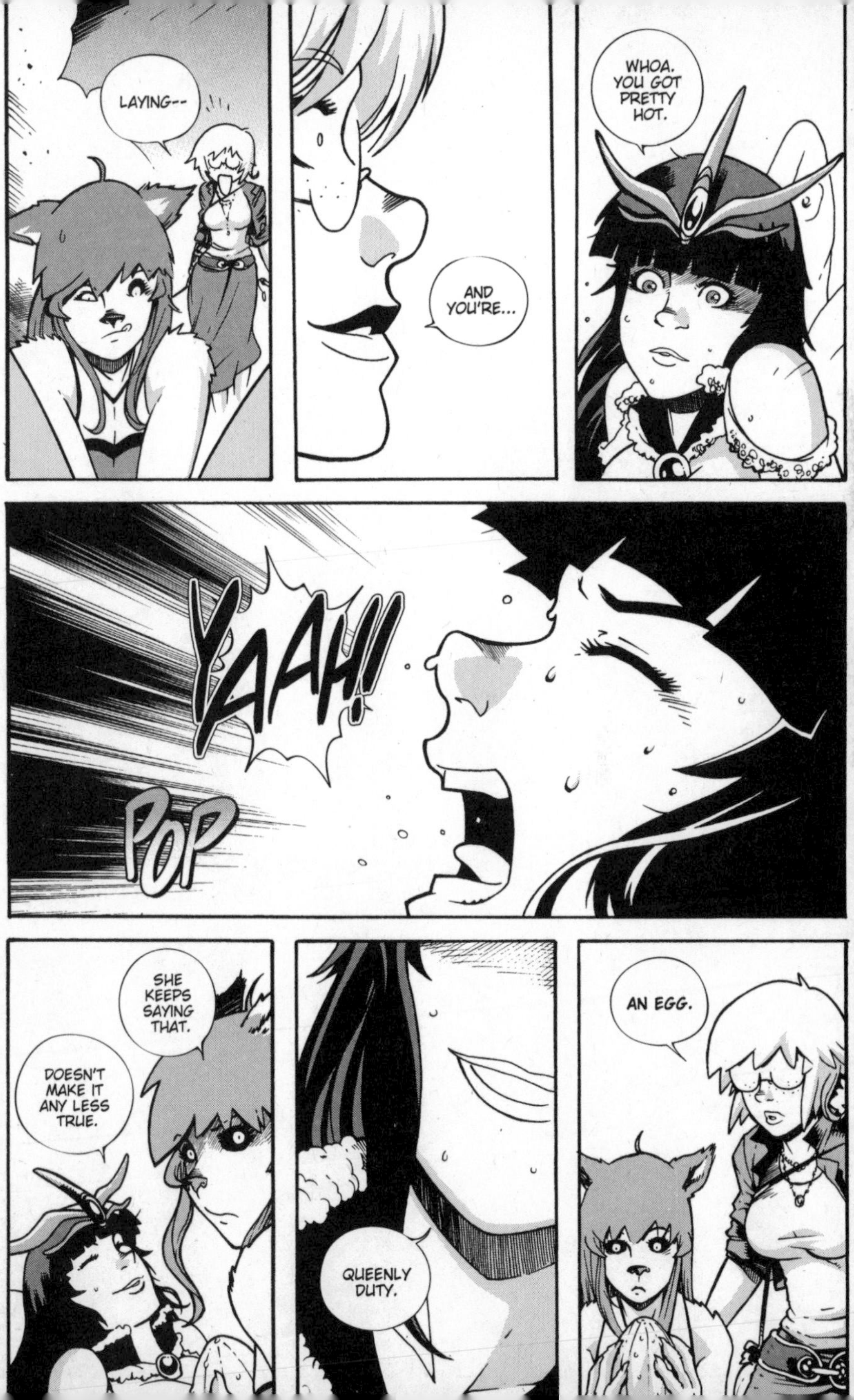
WHOA. YOU GOT PRETTY HOT.
AND YOU'RE...
LAYING--
YAAH!!
POP
AN EGG.
QUEENLY DUTY.
SHE KEEPS SAYING THAT.
DOESN'T MAKE IT ANY LESS TRUE.

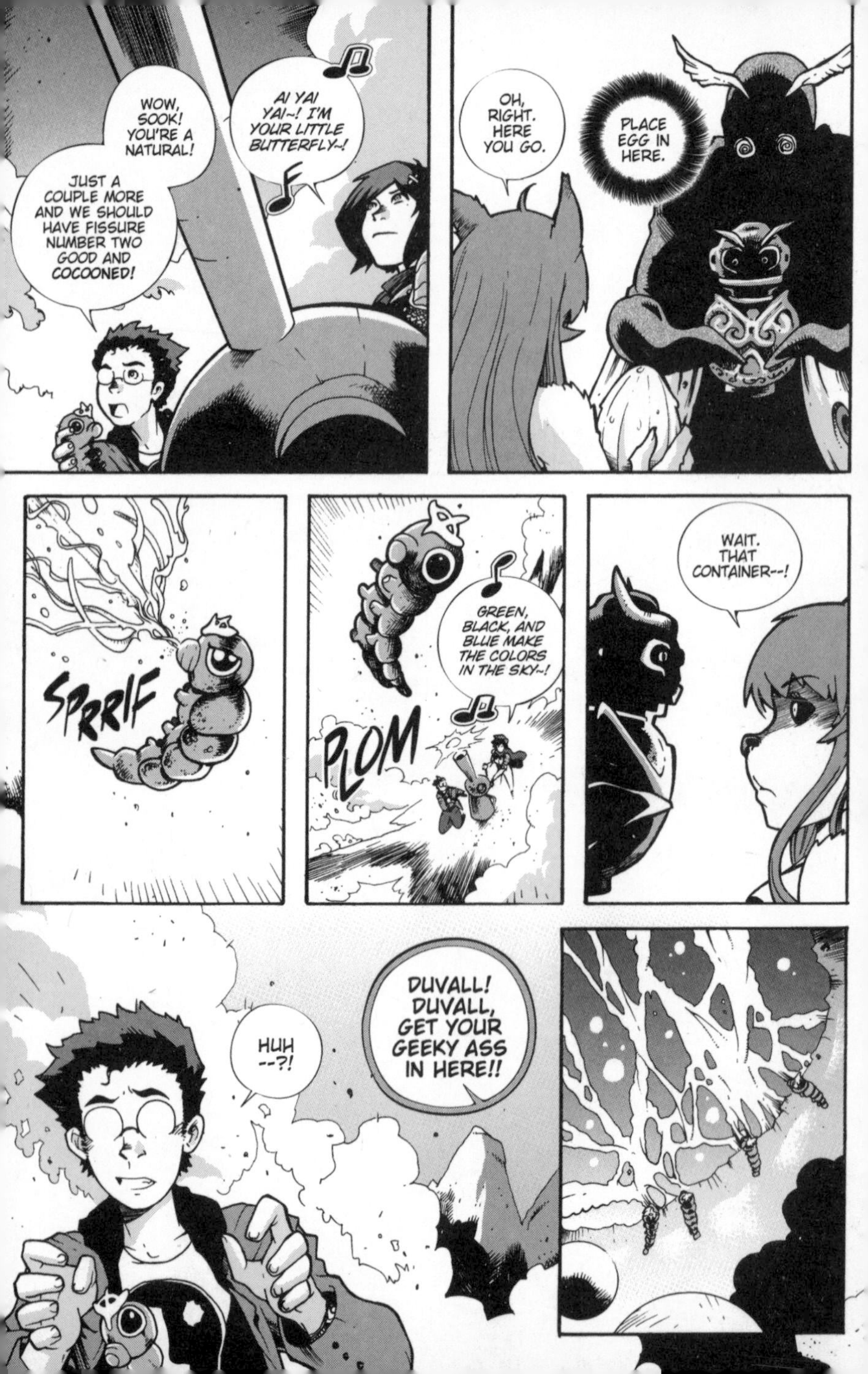
PLACE EGG IN HERE.
OH, RIGHT. HERE YOU GO.
AI YAI YAI~! I'M YOUR LITTLE BUTTERFLY~!
WOW, SOOK! YOU'RE A NATURAL!
JUST A COUPLE MORE AND WE SHOULD HAVE FISSURE NUMBER TWO GOOD AND COCOONED!
WAIT. THAT CONTAINER--!
GREEN, BLACK, AND BLUE MAKE THE COLORS IN THE SKY~!
PLOM
SPRRIF
DUVALL! DUVALL, GET YOUR GEEKY ASS IN HERE!!
HUH --?!

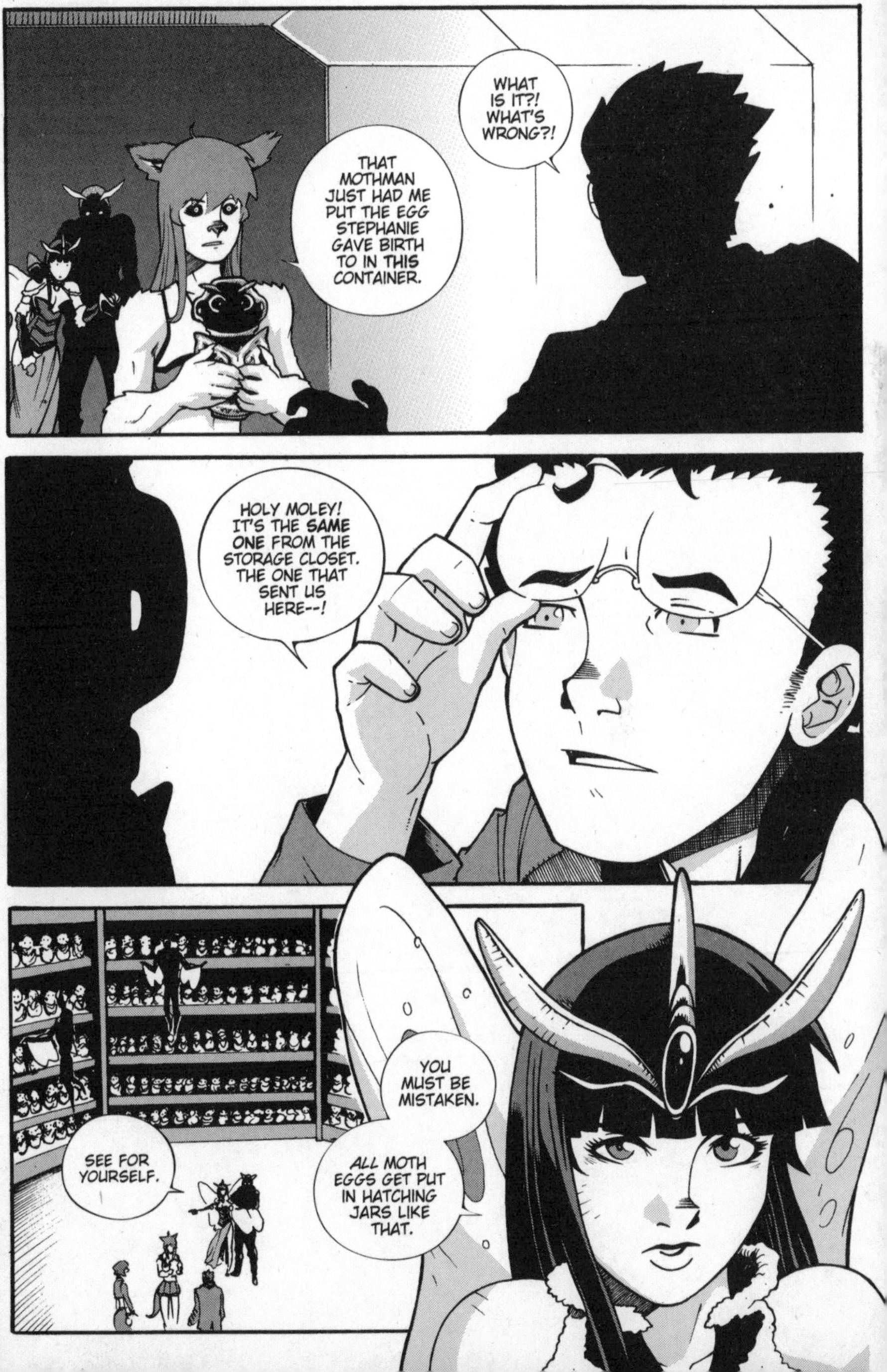
WHAT IS IT?! WHAT'S WRONG?!
THAT MOTHMAN JUST HAD ME PUT THE EGG STEPHANIE GAVE BIRTH TO IN THIS CONTAINER.
HOLY MOLEY! IT'S THE SAME ONE FROM THE STORAGE CLOSET. THE ONE THAT SENT US HERE--!
YOU MUST BE MISTAKEN.
ALL MOTH EGGS GET PUT IN HATCHING JARS LIKE THAT.
SEE FOR YOURSELF.

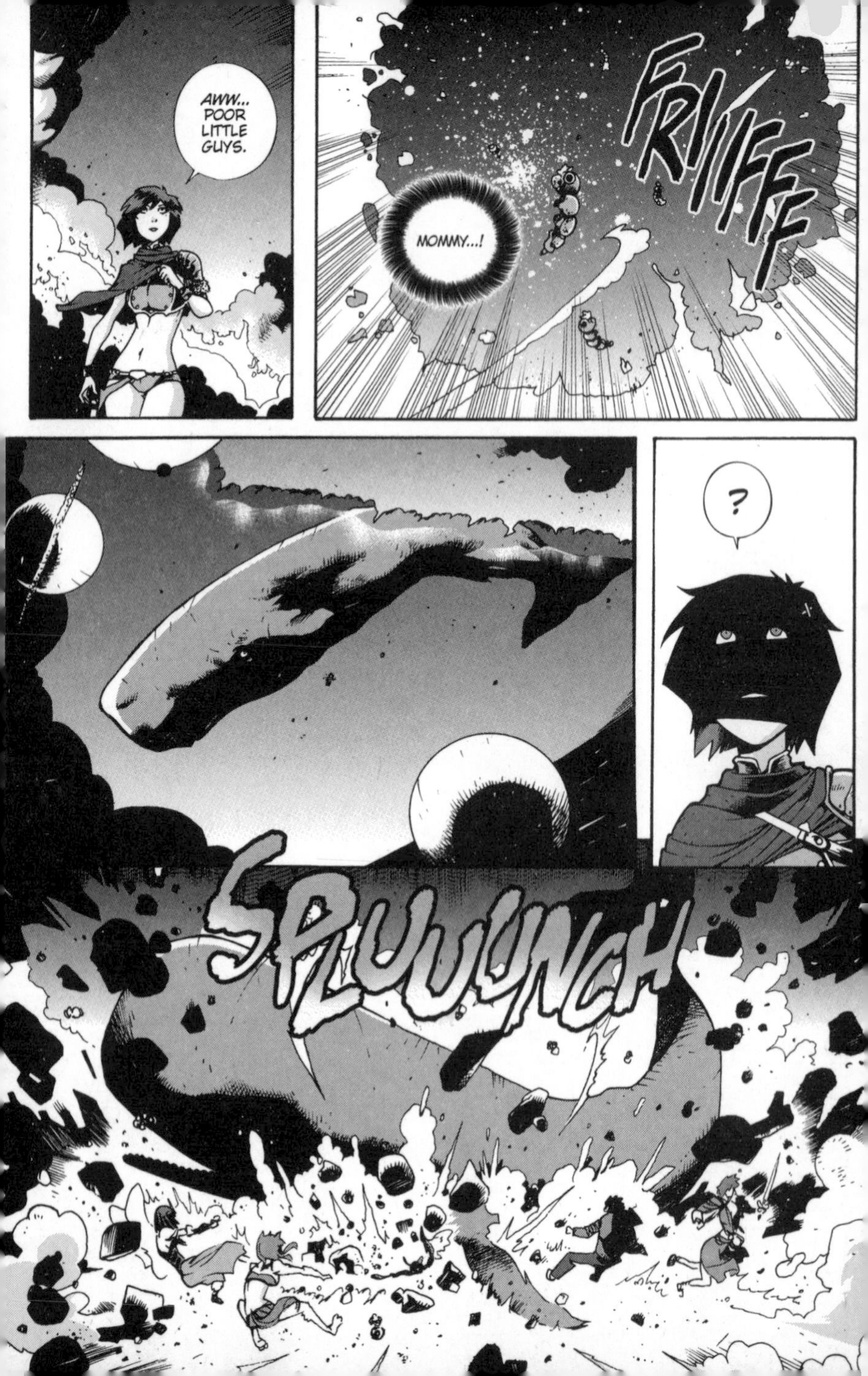
FRIIFFF
MOMMY...!
AWW... POOR LITTLE GUYS.
?
SPLUUUNCH

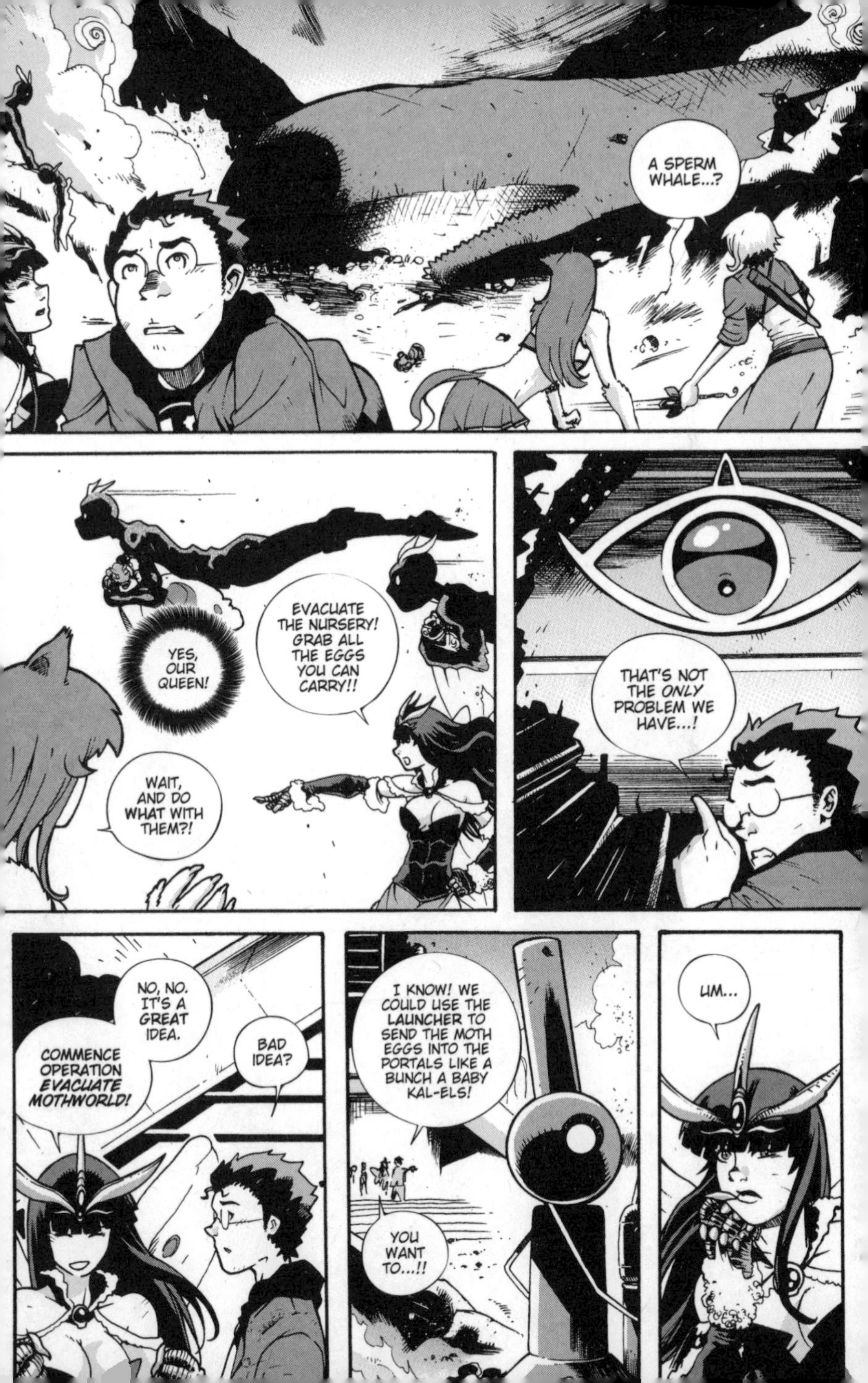
A SPERM WHALE...?
THAT'S NOT THE *ONLY* PROBLEM WE HAVE...!
EVACUATE THE NURSERY! GRAB ALL THE EGGS YOU CAN CARRY!!
YES, OUR QUEEN!
WAIT, AND DO WHAT WITH THEM?!
UM...
I KNOW! WE COULD USE THE LAUNCHER TO SEND THE MOTH EGGS INTO THE PORTALS LIKE A BUNCH A BABY KAL-ELS!
YOU WANT TO...!!
BAD IDEA?
NO, NO. IT'S A GREAT IDEA.
COMMENCE OPERATION *EVACUATE MOTHWORLD!*

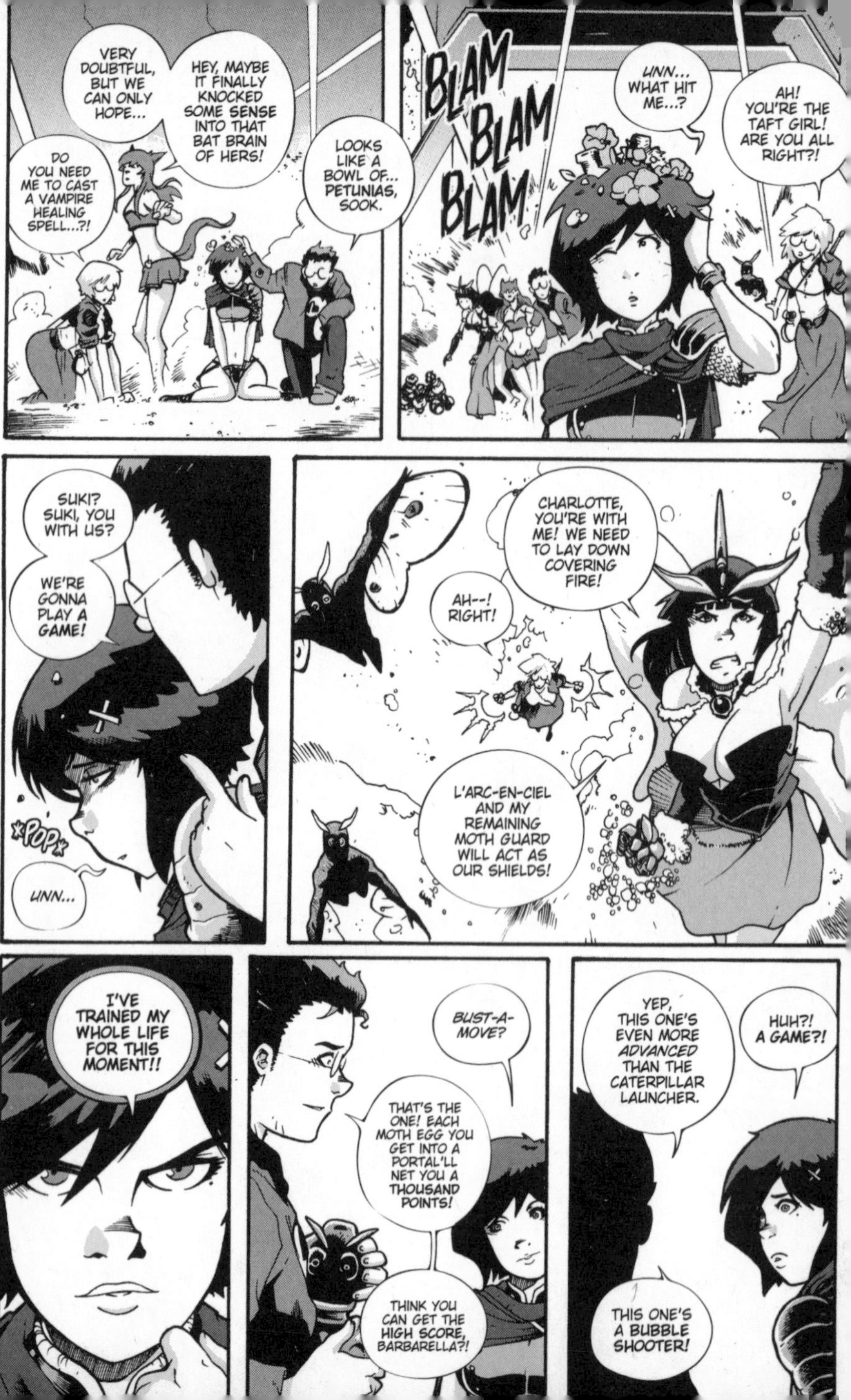
UNN... WHAT HIT ME...?
AH! YOU'RE THE TAFT GIRL! ARE YOU ALL RIGHT?!
BLAM BLAM BLAM
HEY, MAYBE IT FINALLY KNOCKED SOME SENSE INTO THAT BAT BRAIN OF HERS!
VERY DOUBTFUL, BUT WE CAN ONLY HOPE...
LOOKS LIKE A BOWL OF... PETUNIAS, SOOK.
DO YOU NEED ME TO CAST A VAMPIRE HEALING SPELL...?!
CHARLOTTE, YOU'RE WITH ME! WE NEED TO LAY DOWN COVERING FIRE!
AH--! RIGHT!
L'ARC-EN-CIEL AND MY REMAINING MOTH GUARD WILL ACT AS OUR SHIELDS!
SUKI? SUKI, YOU WITH US?
WE'RE GONNA PLAY A GAME!
POP
UNN...
HUH?! A GAME?!
YEP, THIS ONE'S EVEN MORE *ADVANCED* THAN THE CATERPILLAR LAUNCHER.
THIS ONE'S A BUBBLE SHOOTER!
BUST-A-MOVE?
THAT'S THE ONE! EACH MOTH EGG YOU GET INTO A PORTAL'LL NET YOU A THOUSAND POINTS!
THINK YOU CAN GET THE HIGH SCORE, BARBARELLA?!
I'VE TRAINED MY WHOLE LIFE FOR THIS MOMENT!!

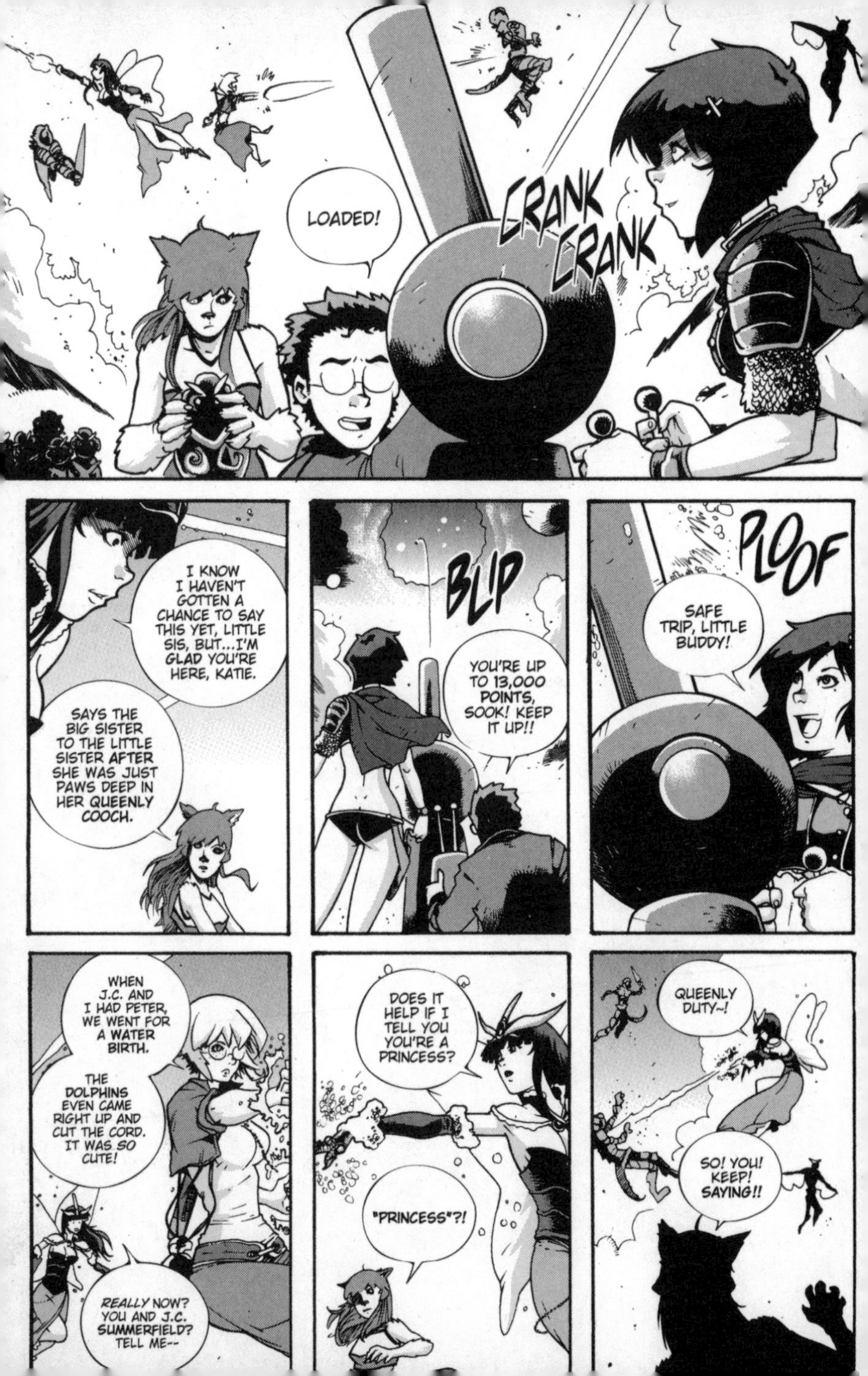
CRANK CRANK
LOADED!
PLOOF
SAFE TRIP, LITTLE BUDDY!
BLIP
YOU'RE UP TO 13,000 POINTS, SOOK! KEEP IT UP!!
I KNOW I HAVEN'T GOTTEN A CHANCE TO SAY THIS YET, LITTLE SIS, BUT...I'M GLAD YOU'RE HERE, KATIE.
SAYS THE BIG SISTER TO THE LITTLE SISTER AFTER SHE WAS JUST PAWS DEEP IN HER QUEENLY COOCH.
QUEENLY DUTY~!
SO! YOU! KEEP! SAYING!!
DOES IT HELP IF I TELL YOU YOU'RE A PRINCESS?
"PRINCESS"?!
WHEN J.C. AND I HAD PETER, WE WENT FOR A WATER BIRTH.
THE DOLPHINS EVEN CAME RIGHT UP AND CUT THE CORD. IT WAS SO CUTE!
REALLY NOW? YOU AND J.C. SUMMERFIELD? TELL ME--

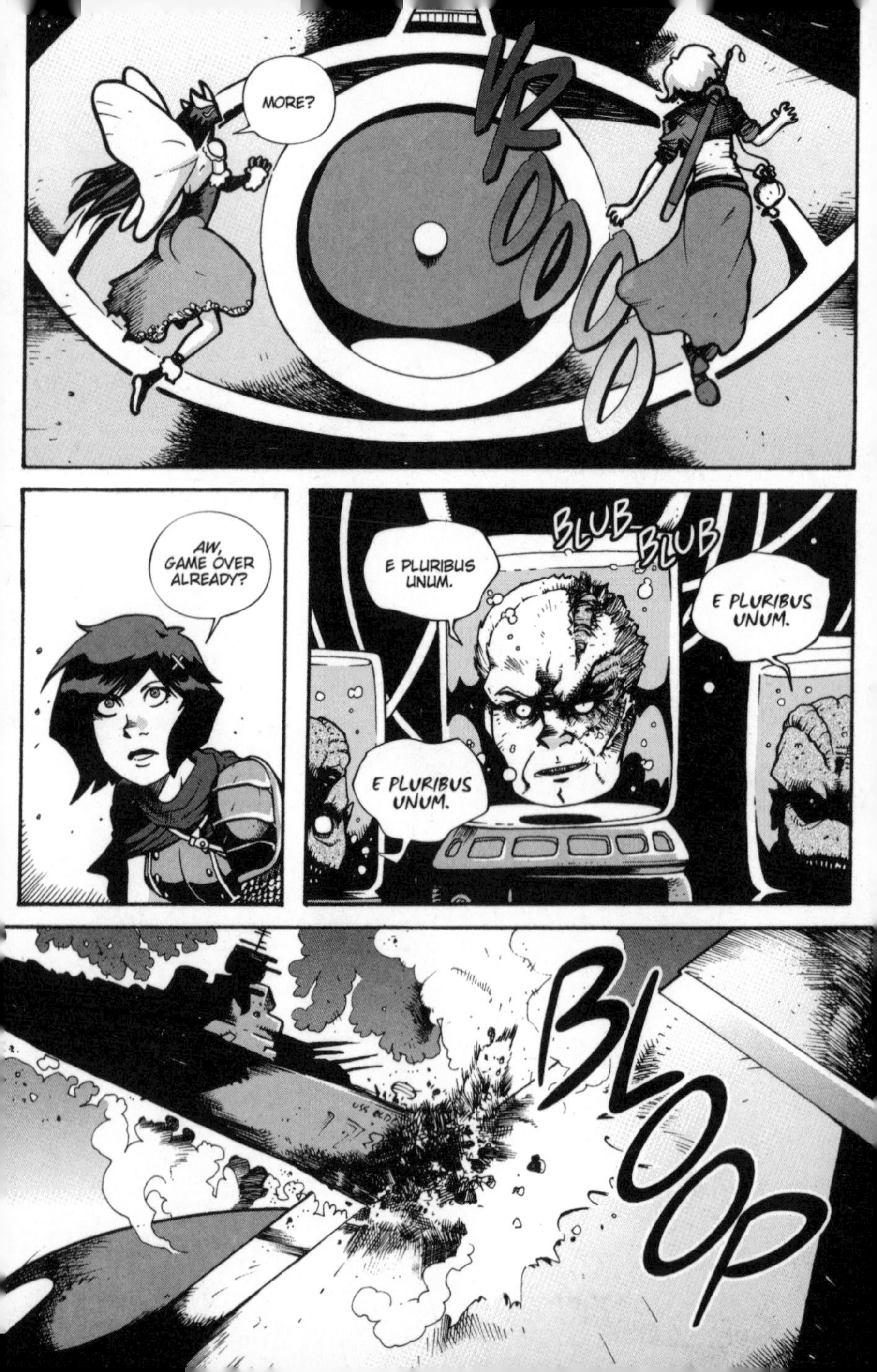
VROOOO
MORE?
BLUB-BLUB
E PLURIBUS UNUM.
E PLURIBUS UNUM.
E PLURIBUS UNUM.
AW, GAME OVER ALREADY?
BLOOP

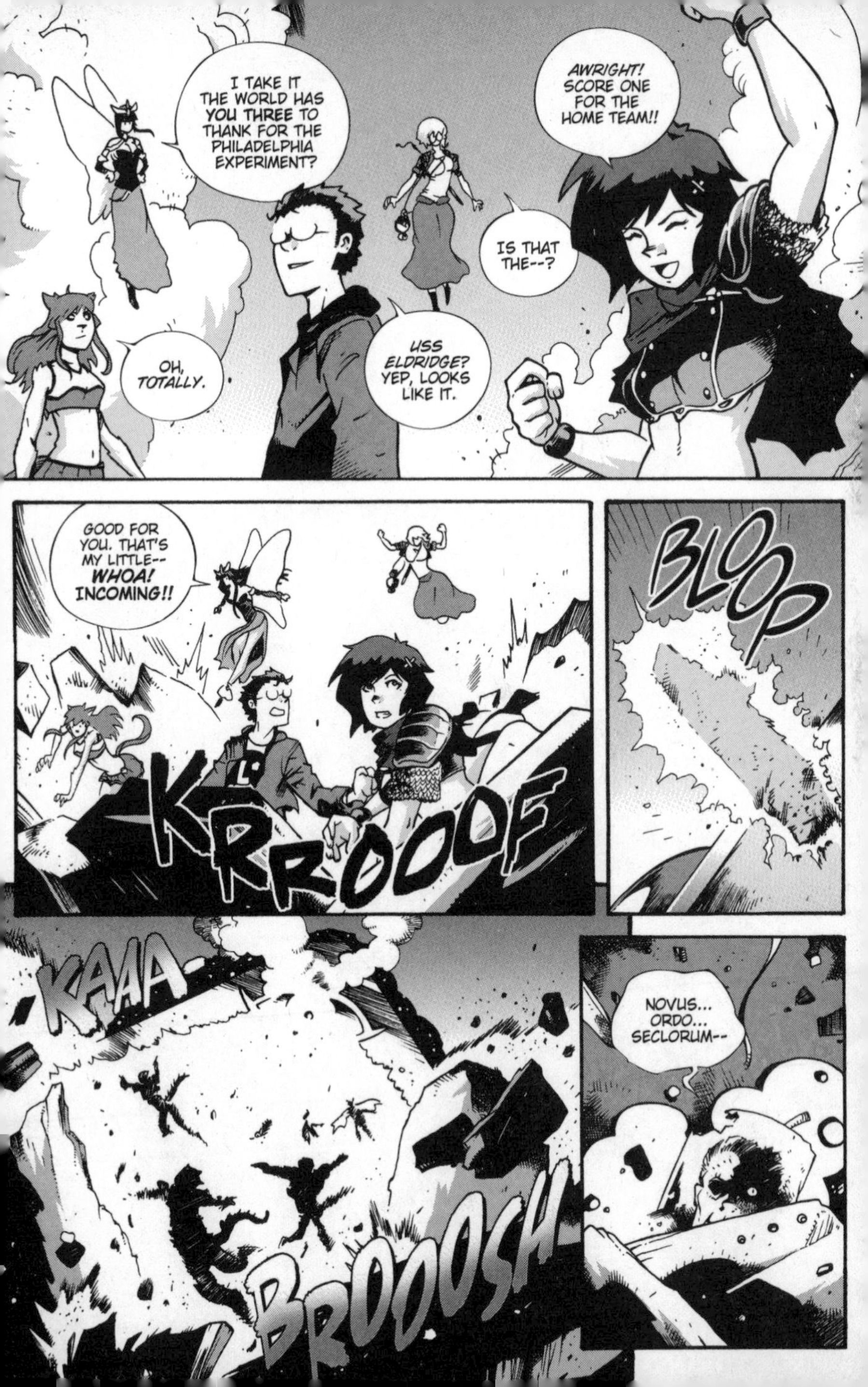
AWRIGHT! SCORE ONE FOR THE HOME TEAM!!
I TAKE IT THE WORLD HAS YOU THREE TO THANK FOR THE PHILADELPHIA EXPERIMENT?
IS THAT THE--?
USS ELDRIDGE? YEP, LOOKS LIKE IT.
OH, TOTALLY.
BLOOP
GOOD FOR YOU. THAT'S MY LITTLE-- WHOA! INCOMING!!
KRROOOF
NOVUS... ORDO... SECLORUM--
KAAA-
BROOOSH

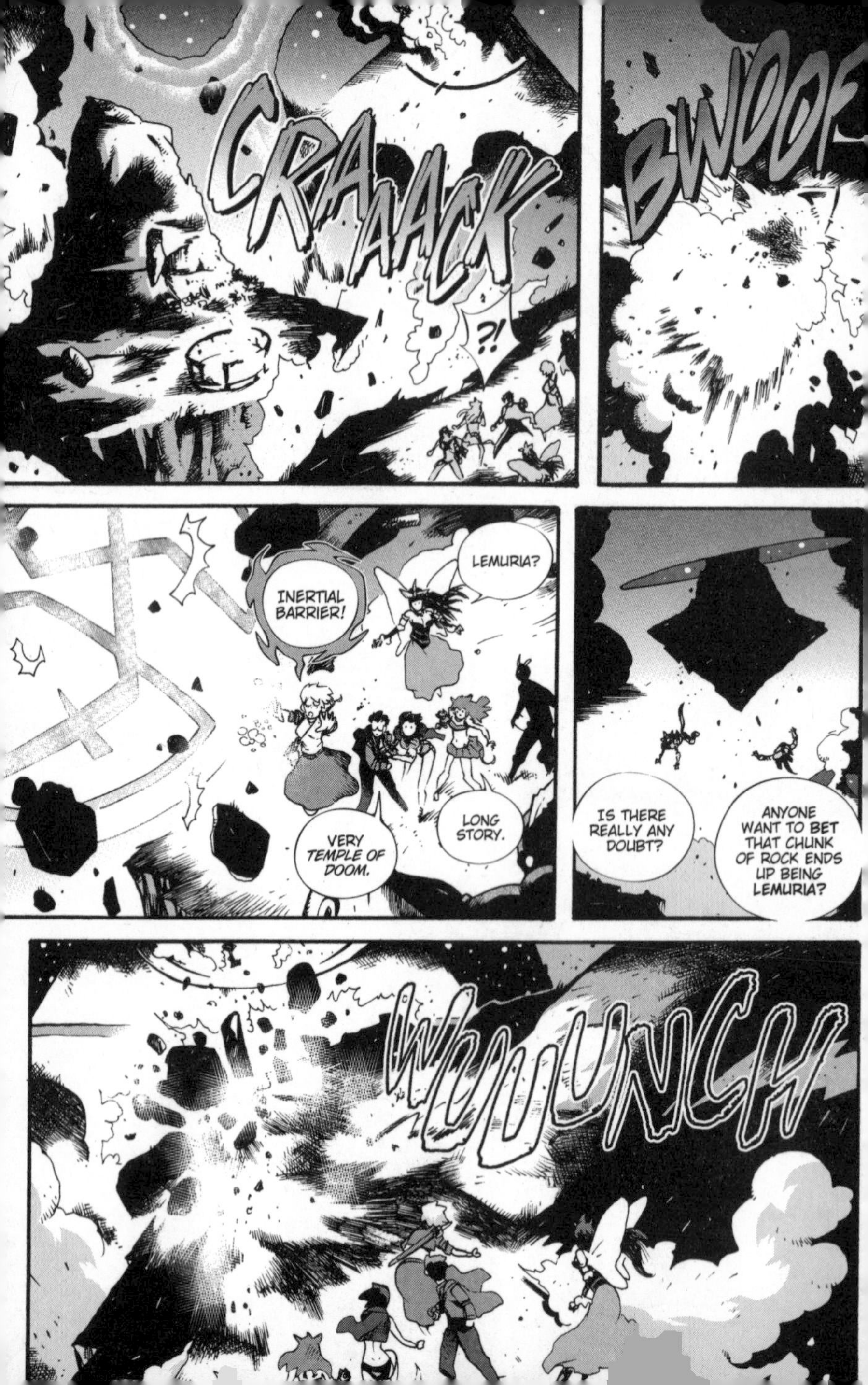
BWOOF
CRAAACK
?!
ANYONE WANT TO BET THAT CHUNK OF ROCK ENDS UP BEING LEMURIA?
IS THERE REALLY ANY DOUBT?
LEMURIA?
INERTIAL BARRIER!
LONG STORY.
VERY TEMPLE OF DOOM.
WHUUUNCH

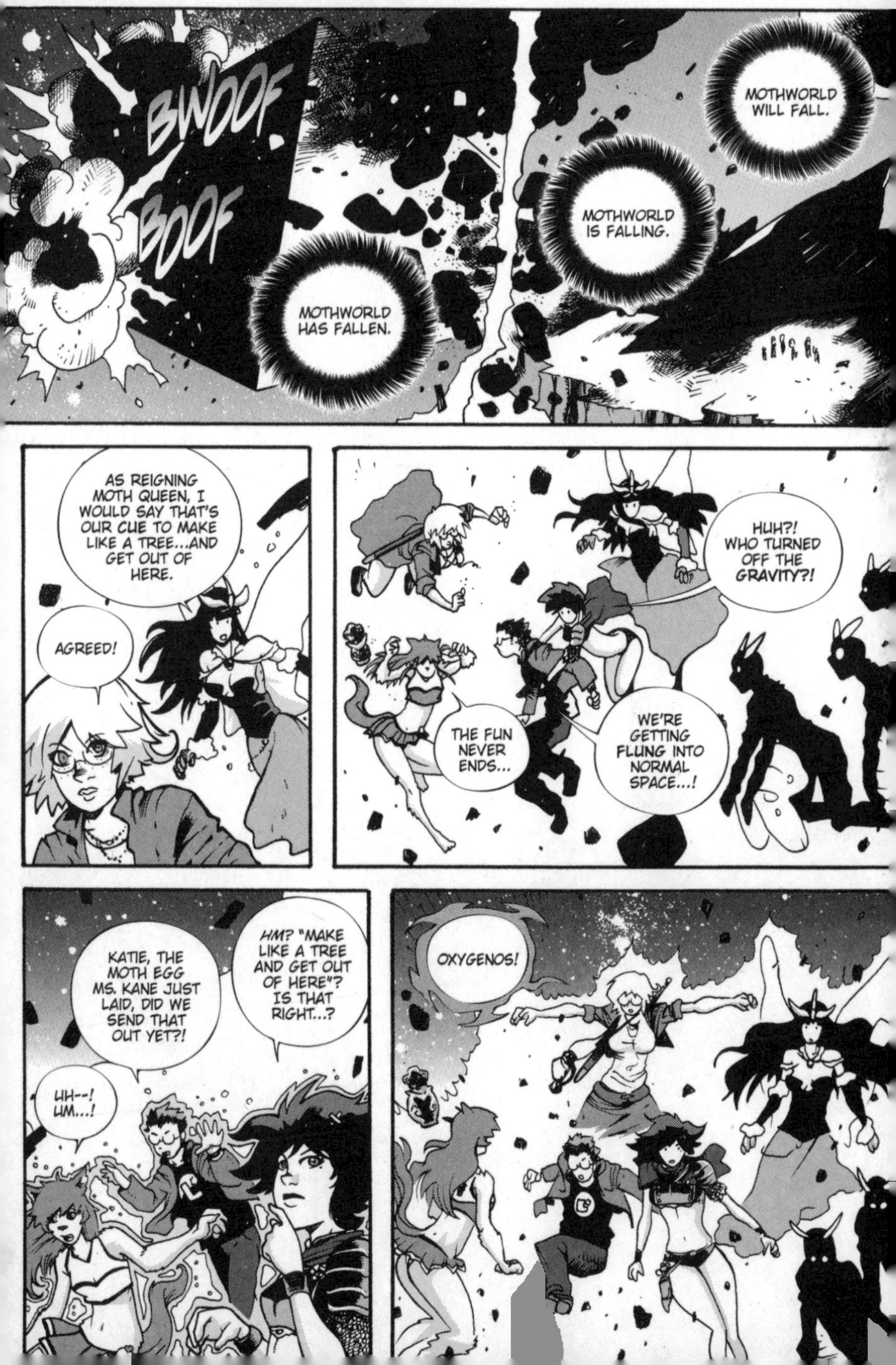
MOTHWORLD WILL FALL.
MOTHWORLD IS FALLING.
MOTHWORLD HAS FALLEN.
BWOOF
BOOF
HUH?! WHO TURNED OFF THE GRAVITY?!
WE'RE GETTING FLUNG INTO NORMAL SPACE...!
THE FUN NEVER ENDS...
AS REIGNING MOTH QUEEN, I WOULD SAY THAT'S OUR CUE TO MAKE LIKE A TREE...AND GET OUT OF HERE.
AGREED!
OXYGENOS!
HM? "MAKE LIKE A TREE AND GET OUT OF HERE"? IS THAT RIGHT...?
KATIE, THE MOTH EGG MS. KANE JUST LAID, DID WE SEND THAT OUT YET?!
UH--! UM...!

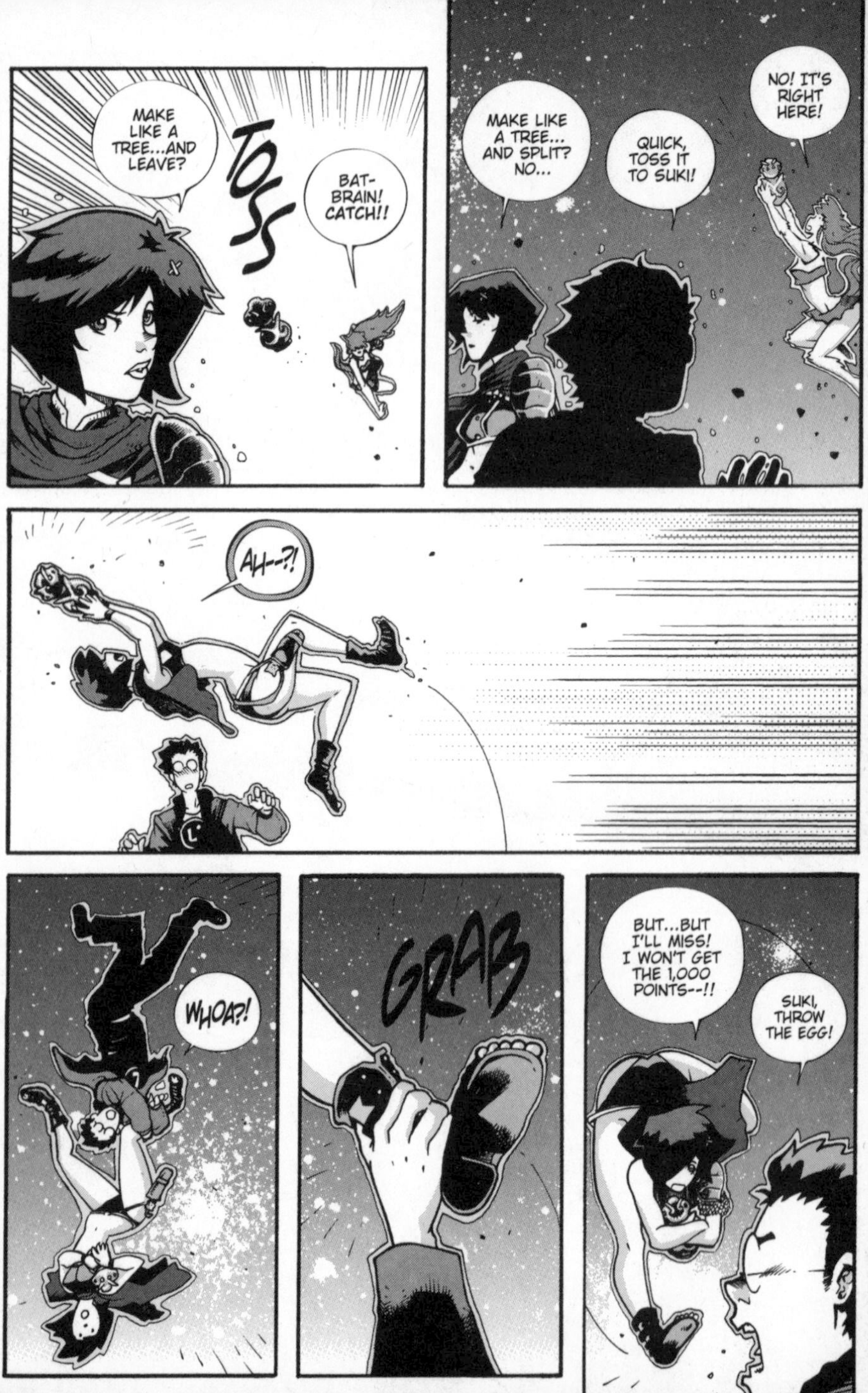
NO! IT'S RIGHT HERE!
QUICK, TOSS IT TO SUKI!
MAKE LIKE A TREE... AND SPLIT? NO...
BAT-BRAIN! CATCH!!
TOSS
MAKE LIKE A TREE...AND LEAVE?
AH--?!
SUKI, THROW THE EGG!
BUT...BUT I'LL MISS! I WON'T GET THE 1,000 POINTS--!!
GRAB
WHOA?!

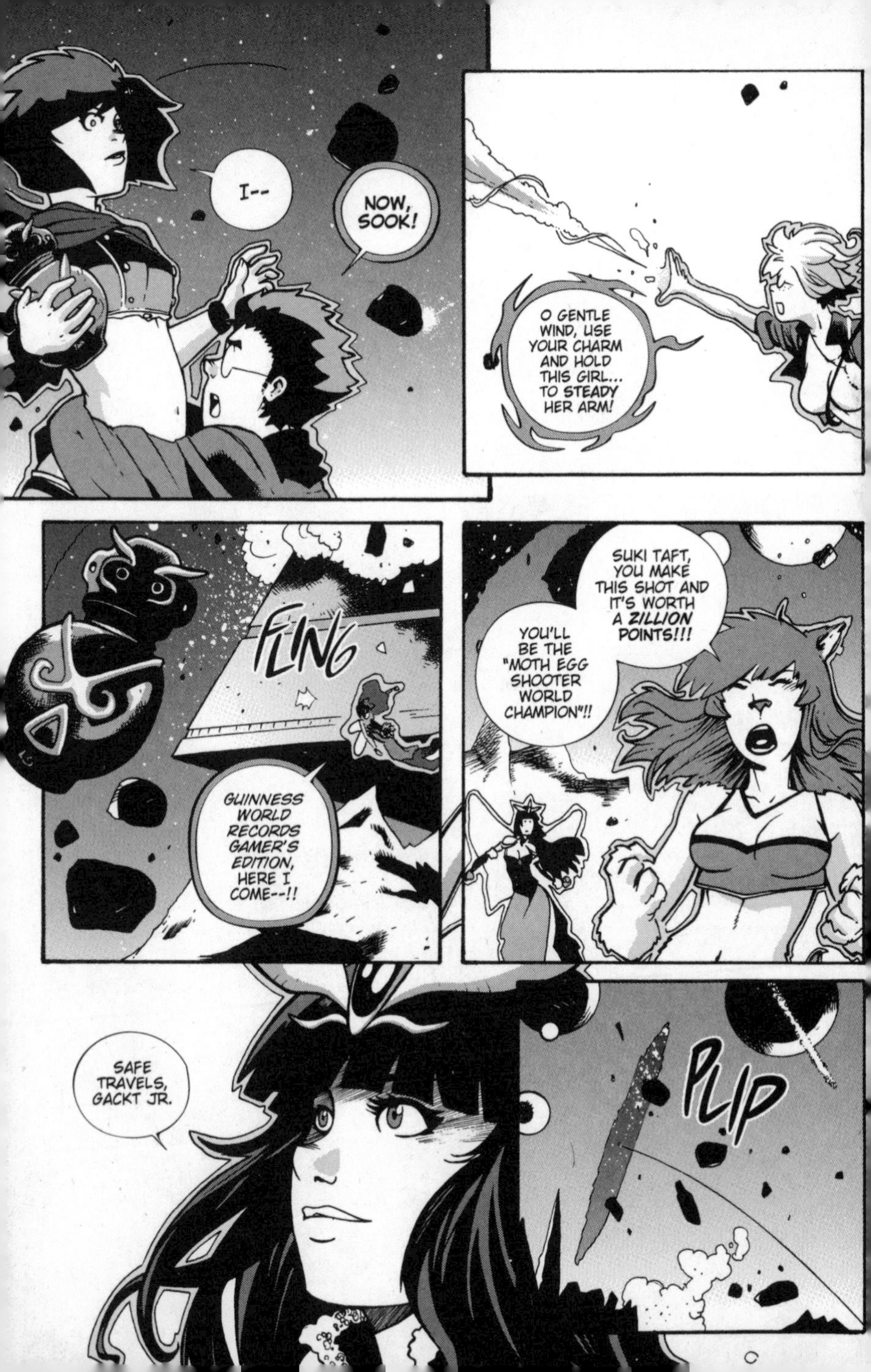
O GENTLE WIND, USE YOUR CHARM AND HOLD THIS GIRL... TO STEADY HER ARM!
NOW, SOOK!
I--
SUKI TAFT, YOU MAKE THIS SHOT AND IT'S WORTH A *ZILLION* POINTS!!!
YOU'LL BE THE "MOTH EGG SHOOTER WORLD CHAMPION"!!
FLING
GUINNESS WORLD RECORDS GAMER'S EDITION, HERE I COME--!!
PLIP
SAFE TRAVELS, GACKT JR.

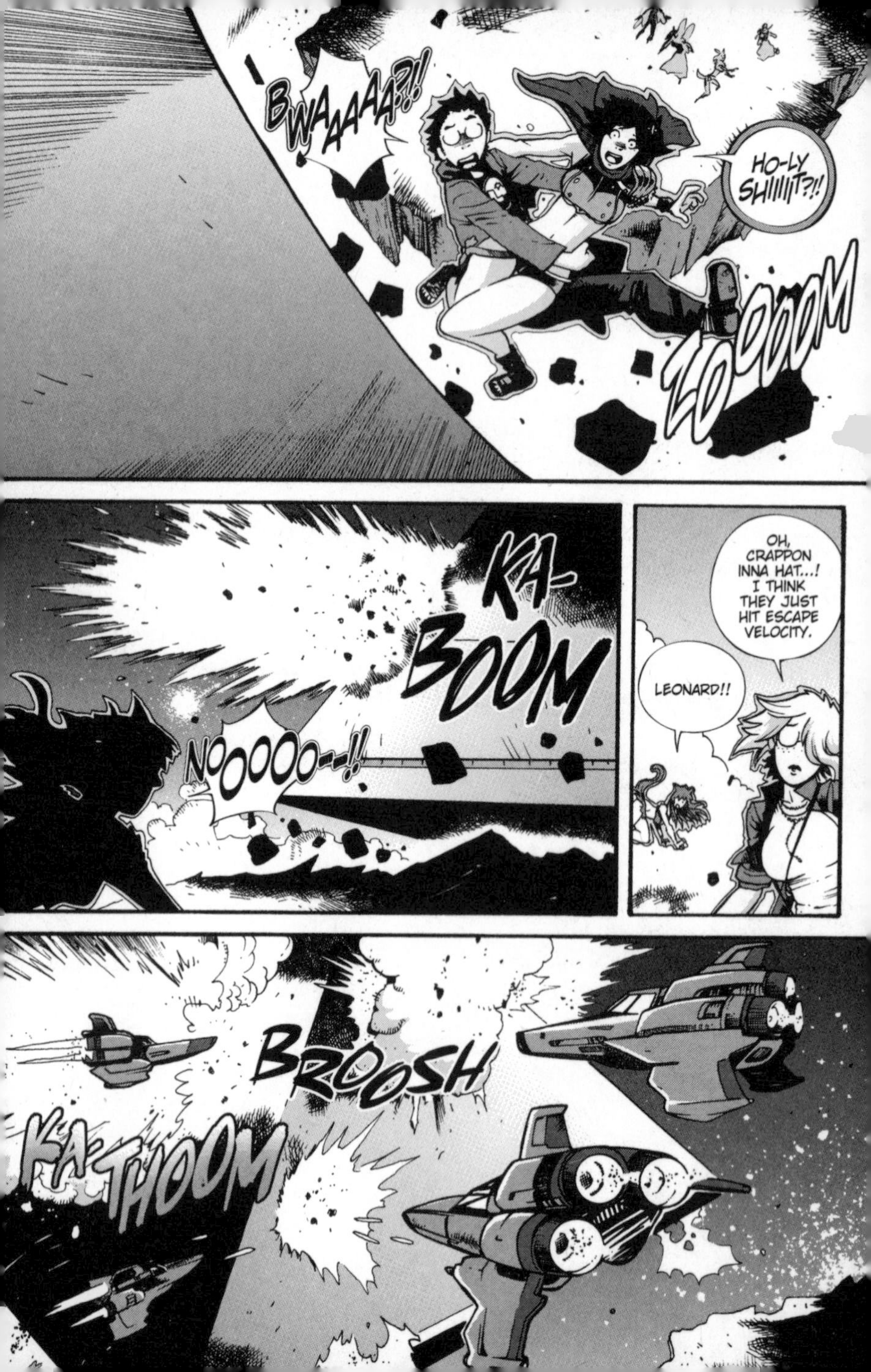
HO-LY SHIIIIT?!!
BWAAAAA?!!
ZOOOOOM
OH, CRAPPON INNA HAT...! I THINK THEY JUST HIT ESCAPE VELOCITY.
LEONARD!!
KA-BOOM
NOOOOO--!!
BROOSH
KA-THOOM

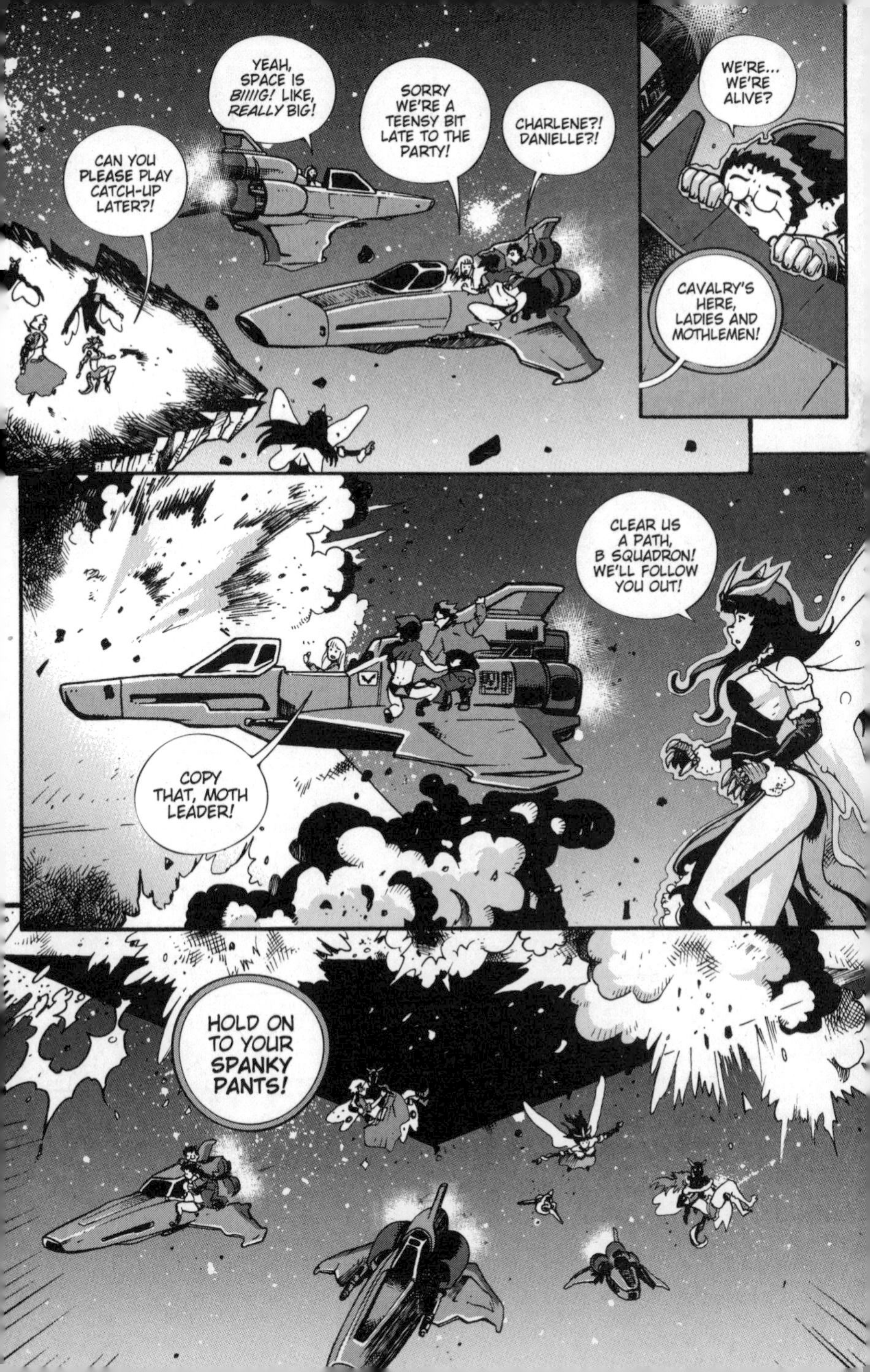
WE'RE... WE'RE ALIVE?
CAVALRY'S HERE, LADIES AND MOTHLEMEN!
CHARLENE?! DANIELLE?!
SORRY WE'RE A TEENSY BIT LATE TO THE PARTY!
YEAH, SPACE IS *BIIIIG!* LIKE, *REALLY* BIG!
CAN YOU PLEASE PLAY CATCH-UP LATER?!
CLEAR US A PATH, B SQUADRON! WE'LL FOLLOW YOU OUT!
COPY THAT, MOTH LEADER!
HOLD ON TO YOUR SPANKY PANTS!

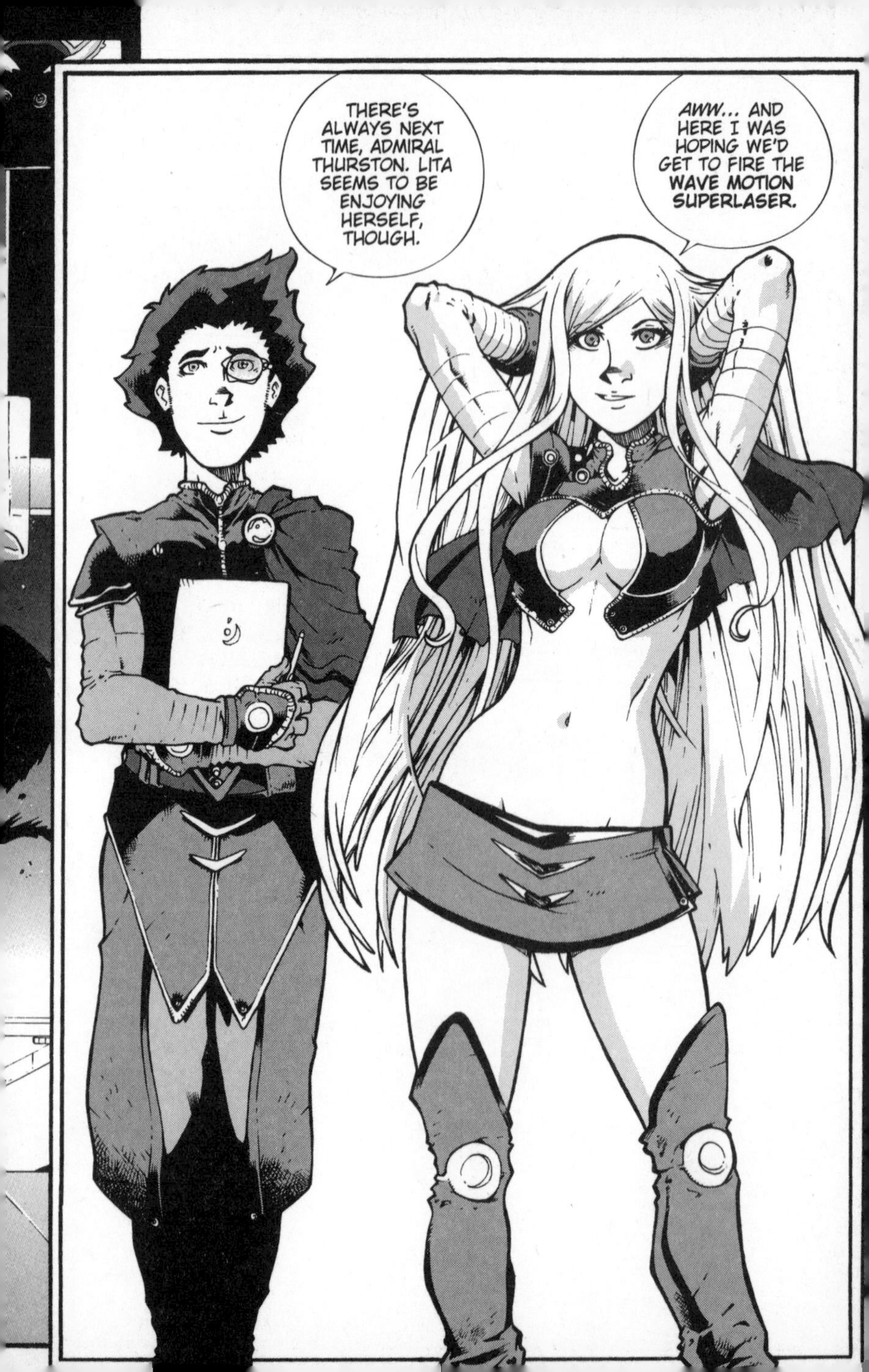
AWW... AND HERE I WAS HOPING WE'D GET TO FIRE THE WAVE MOTION SUPERLASER.
THERE'S ALWAYS NEXT TIME, ADMIRAL THURSTON. LITA SEEMS TO BE ENJOYING HERSELF, THOUGH.

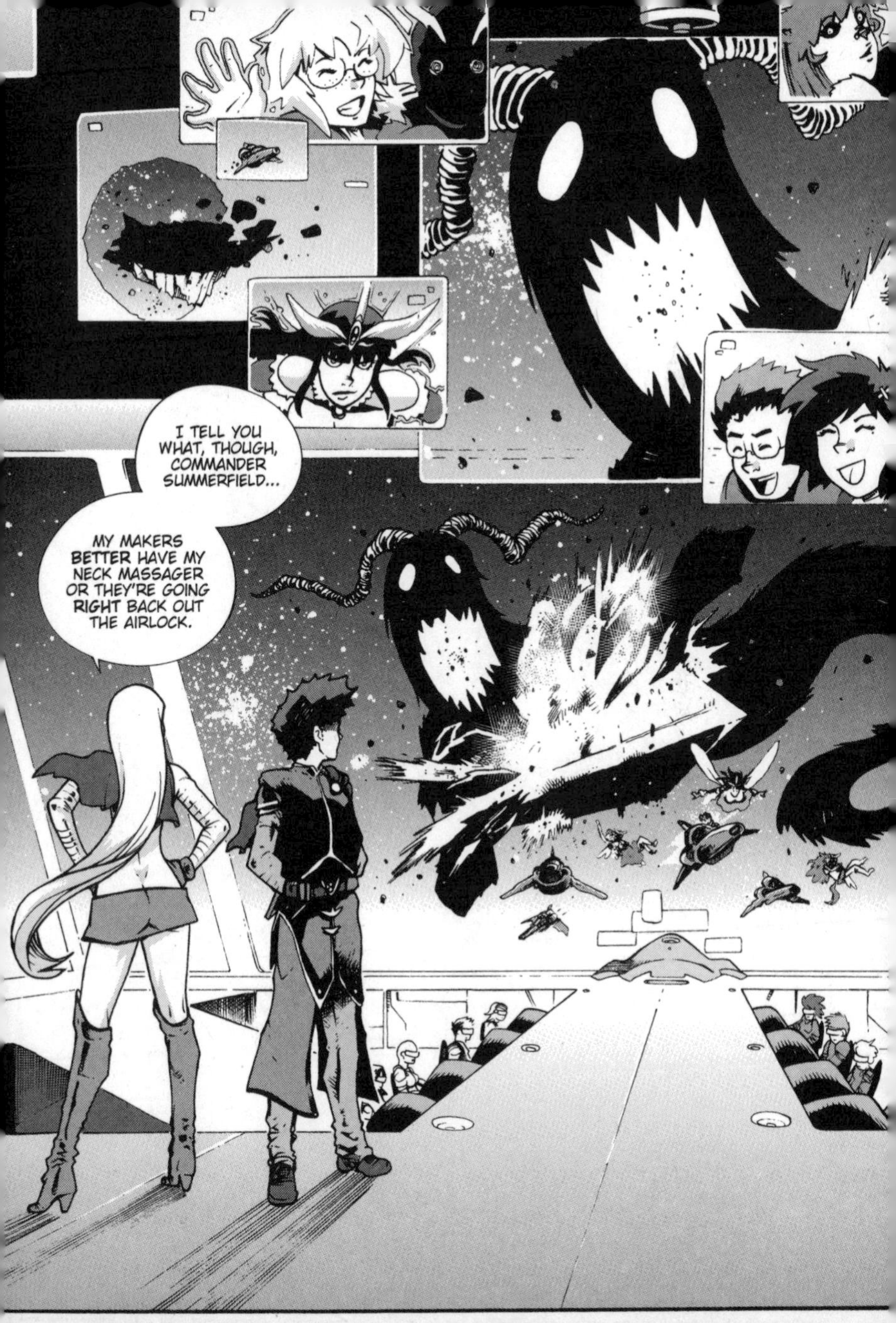
I TELL YOU WHAT, THOUGH, COMMANDER SUMMERFIELD...
MY MAKERS BETTER HAVE MY NECK MASSAGER OR THEY'RE GOING RIGHT BACK OUT THE AIRLOCK.

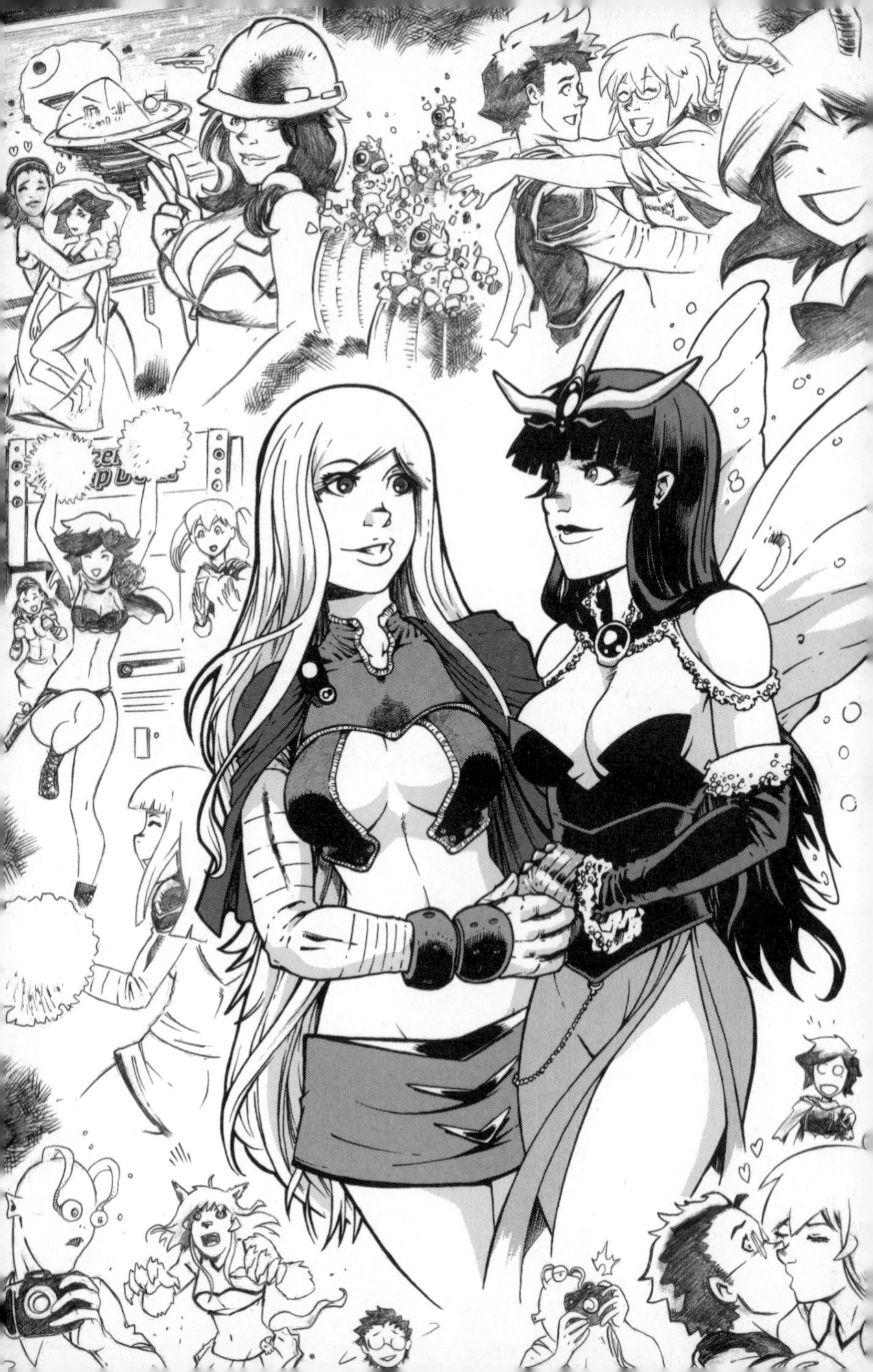

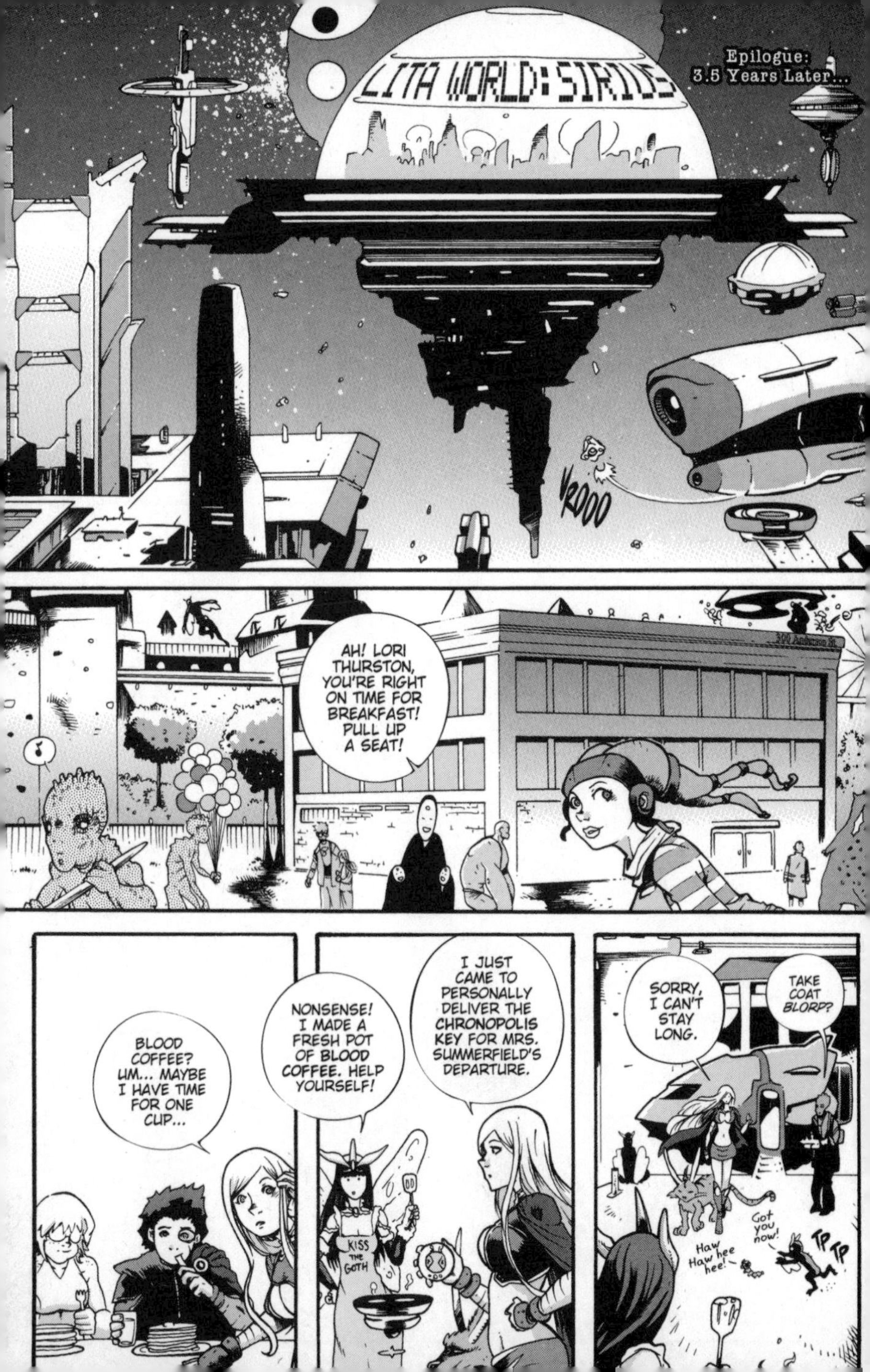
Epilogue:
3.5 Years Later...
LITA WORLD: SIRIUS
VRDOO
AH! LORI THURSTON, YOU'RE RIGHT ON TIME FOR BREAKFAST! PULL UP A SEAT!
SORRY, I CAN'T STAY LONG.
TAKE COAT BLORP?
Got you now!
Haw Haw hee hee!
TP TP
I JUST CAME TO PERSONALLY DELIVER THE CHRONOPOLIS KEY FOR MRS. SUMMERFIELD'S DEPARTURE.
NONSENSE! I MADE A FRESH POT OF BLOOD COFFEE. HELP YOURSELF!
KISS THE GOTH
BLOOD COFFEE? UM... MAYBE I HAVE TIME FOR ONE CUP...

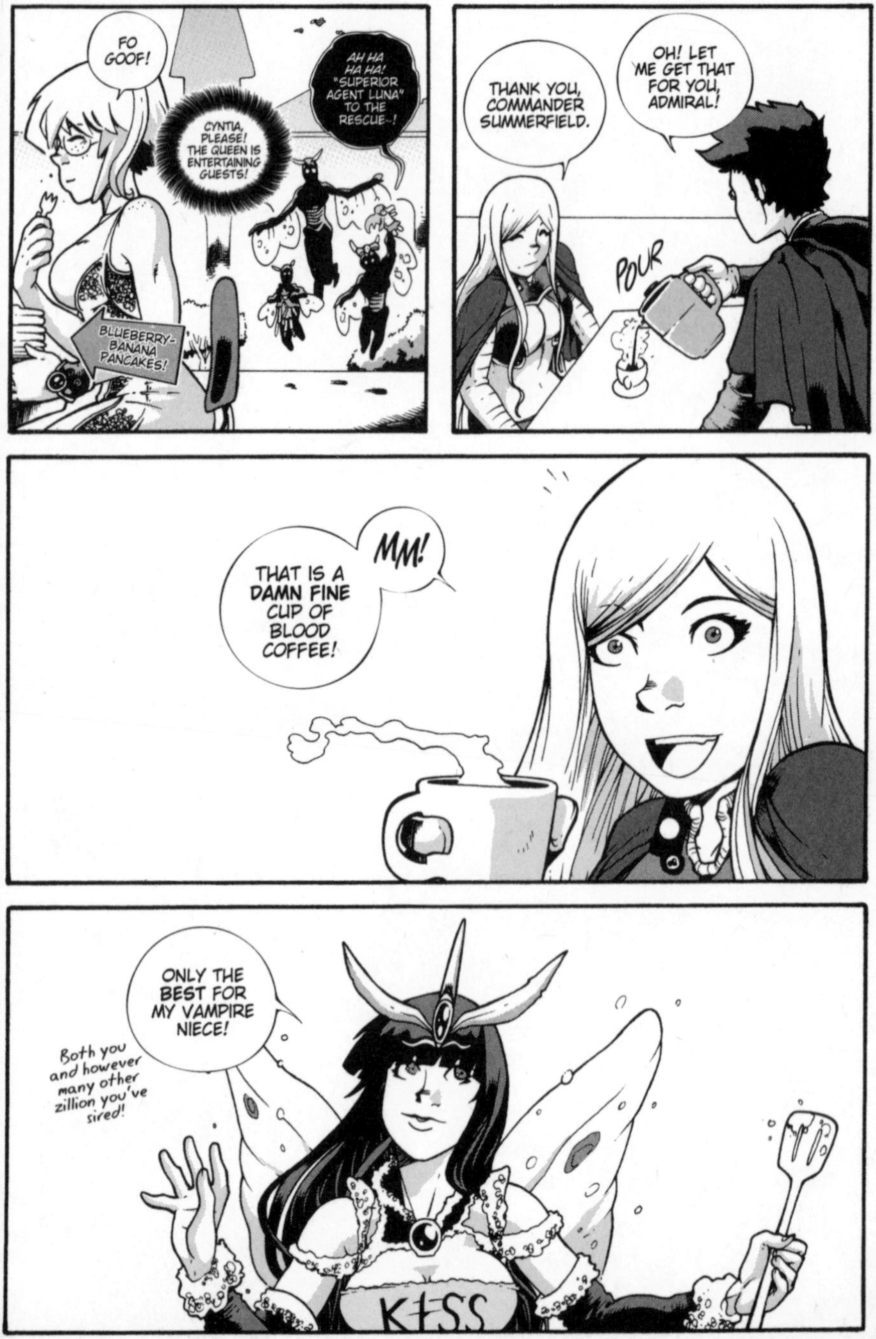
OH! LET ME GET THAT FOR YOU, ADMIRAL!
THANK YOU, COMMANDER SUMMERFIELD.
POUR
AH HA HA HA! "SUPERIOR AGENT LUNA" TO THE RESCUE-!
FO GOOF!
CYNTIA, PLEASE! THE QUEEN IS ENTERTAINING GUESTS!
BLUEBERRY-BANANA PANCAKES!
MM!
THAT IS A DAMN FINE CUP OF BLOOD COFFEE!
ONLY THE BEST FOR MY VAMPIRE NIECE!
Both you and however many other zillion you've sired!
KISS

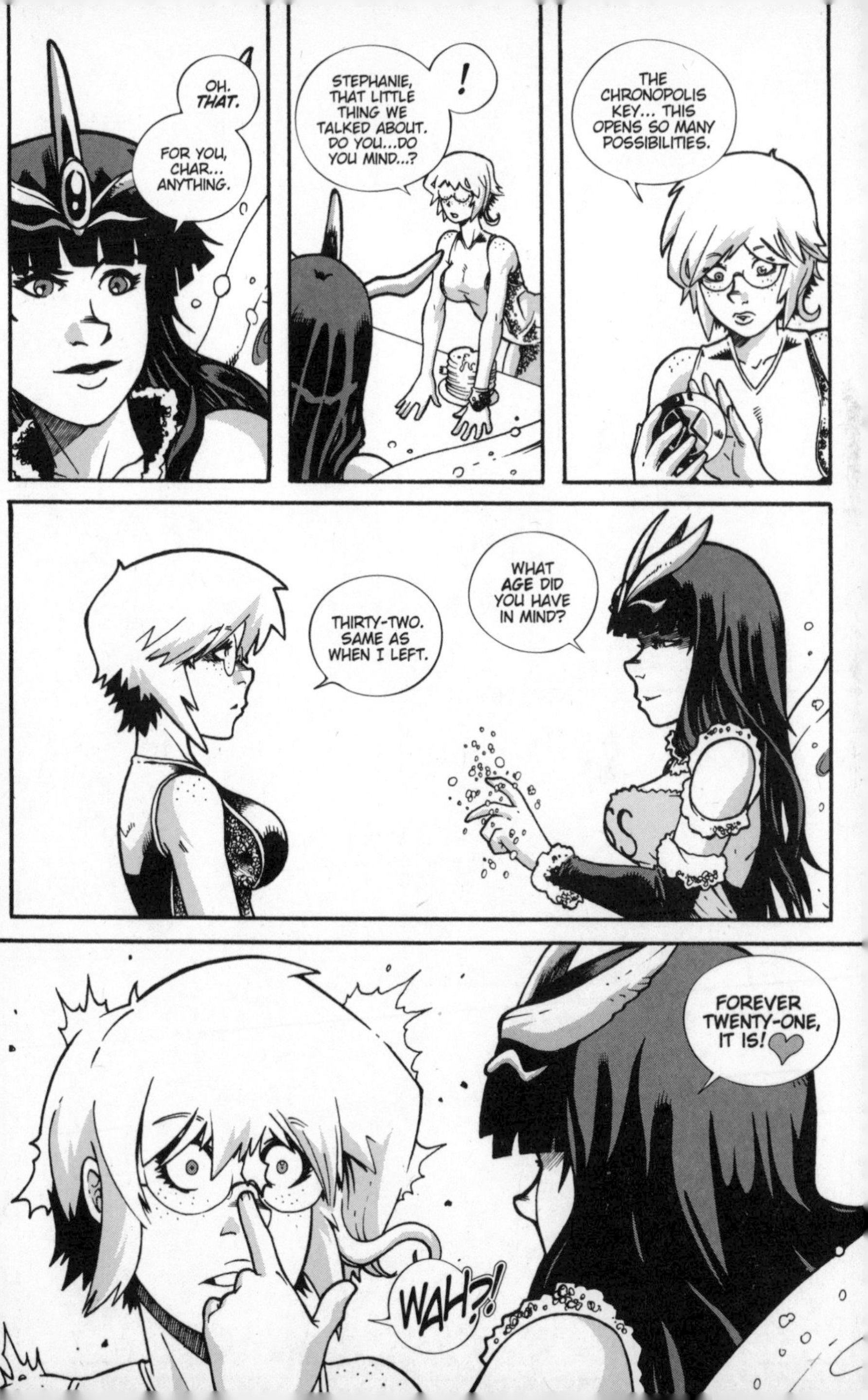
THE CHRONOPOLIS KEY... THIS OPENS SO MANY POSSIBILITIES.
!
STEPHANIE, THAT LITTLE THING WE TALKED ABOUT. DO YOU...DO YOU MIND...?
OH. *THAT.*
FOR YOU, CHAR... ANYTHING.
WHAT AGE DID YOU HAVE IN MIND?
THIRTY-TWO. SAME AS WHEN I LEFT.
FOREVER TWENTY-ONE, IT IS! ♥
WAH?!

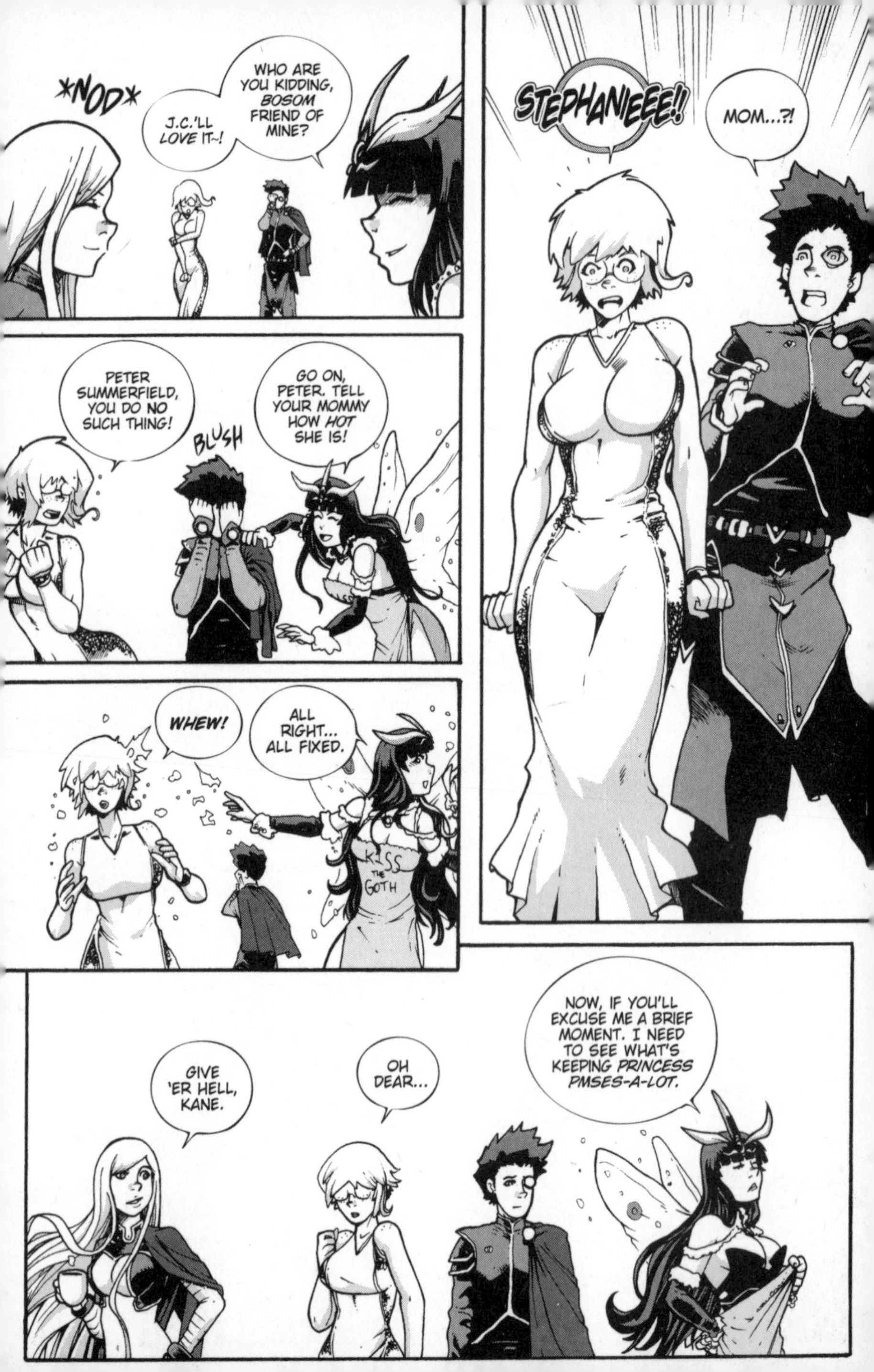
MOM...?!
STEPHANIEEE!!
WHO ARE YOU KIDDING, *BOSOM* FRIEND OF MINE?
J.C.'LL *LOVE* IT~!
NOD
GO ON, PETER. TELL YOUR MOMMY HOW *HOT* SHE IS!
BLUSH
PETER SUMMERFIELD, YOU DO NO SUCH THING!
ALL RIGHT... ALL FIXED.
KISS THE GOTH
WHEW!
NOW, IF YOU'LL EXCUSE ME A BRIEF MOMENT. I NEED TO SEE WHAT'S KEEPING *PRINCESS PMSES-A-LOT*.
OH DEAR...
GIVE 'ER HELL, KANE.

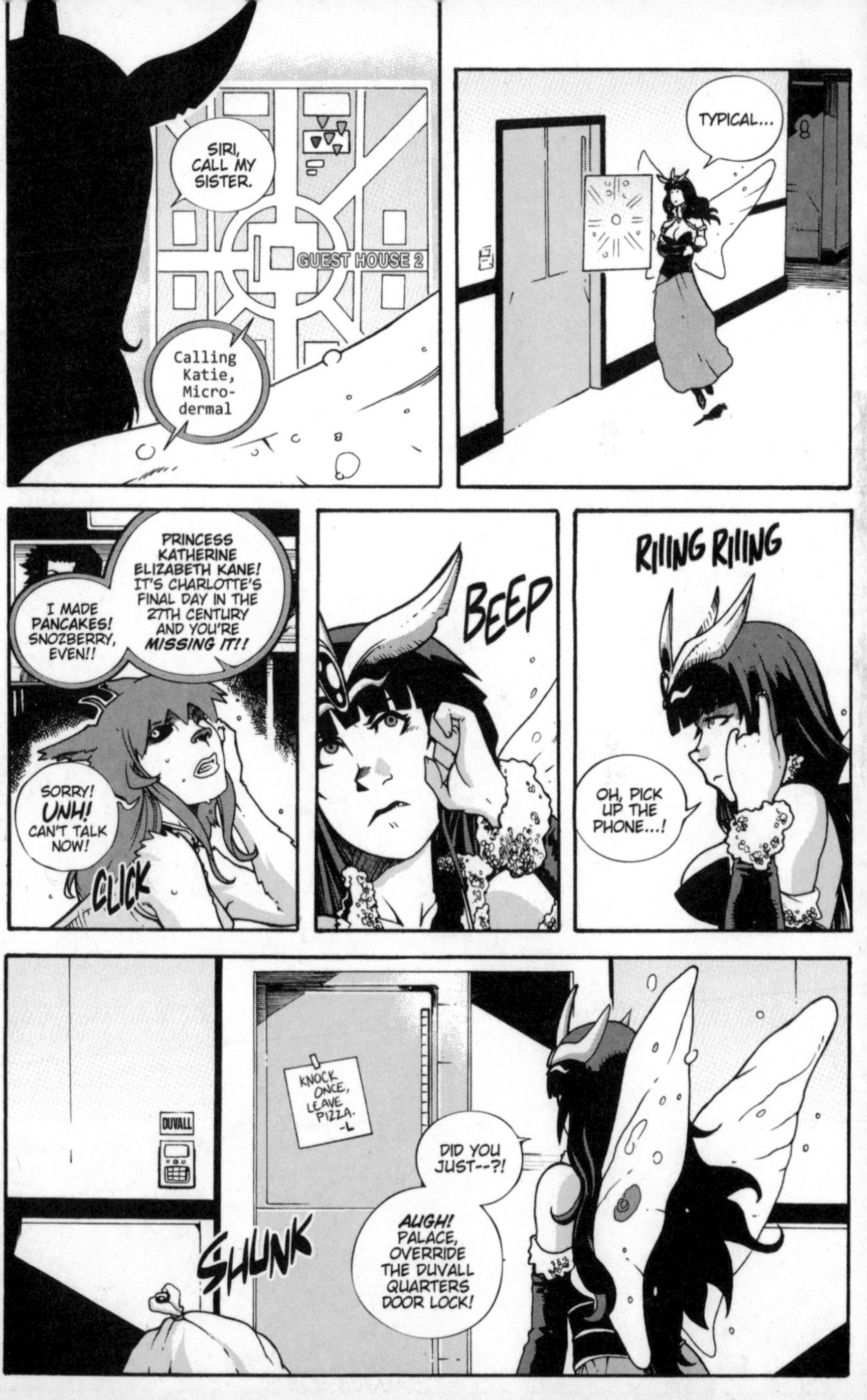
TYPICAL...
SIRI, CALL MY SISTER.
GUEST HOUSE 2
Calling Katie, Microdermal
RIIING RIIING
OH, PICK UP THE PHONE...!
BEEP
PRINCESS KATHERINE ELIZABETH KANE! IT'S CHARLOTTE'S FINAL DAY IN THE 27TH CENTURY AND YOU'RE **MISSING IT!!**
I MADE PANCAKES! SNOZBERRY, EVEN!!
SORRY! **UNH!** CAN'T TALK NOW!
CLICK
KNOCK ONCE, LEAVE PIZZA. -L
DUVALL
DID YOU JUST--?!
AUGH! PALACE, OVERRIDE THE DUVALL QUARTERS DOOR LOCK!
SHUNK

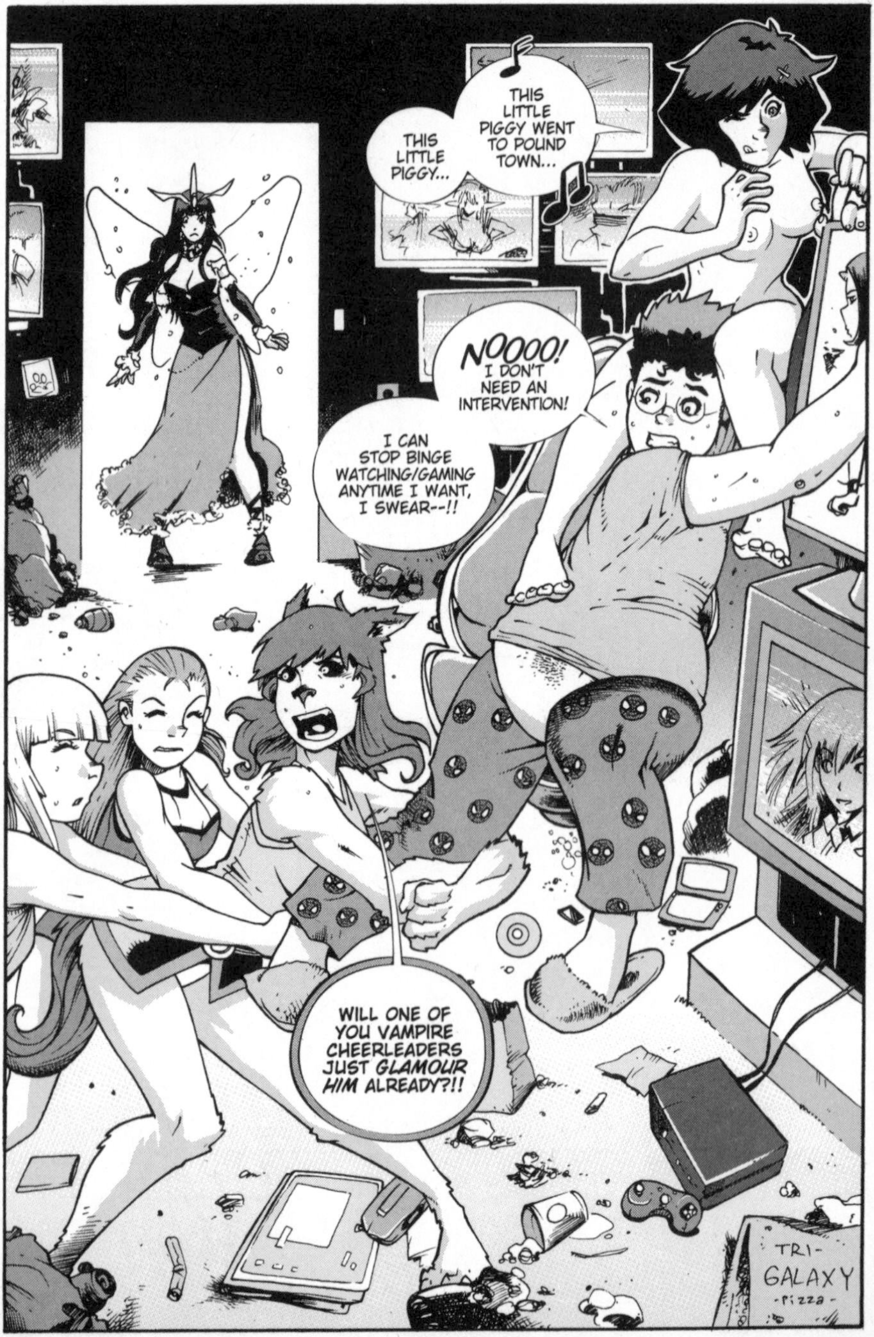
THIS LITTLE PIGGY...
THIS LITTLE PIGGY WENT TO POUND TOWN...
NOOOO! I DON'T NEED AN INTERVENTION!
I CAN STOP BINGE WATCHING/GAMING ANYTIME I WANT, I SWEAR--!!
WILL ONE OF YOU VAMPIRE CHEERLEADERS JUST GLAMOUR HIM ALREADY?!!
TRI-GALAXY -pizza-

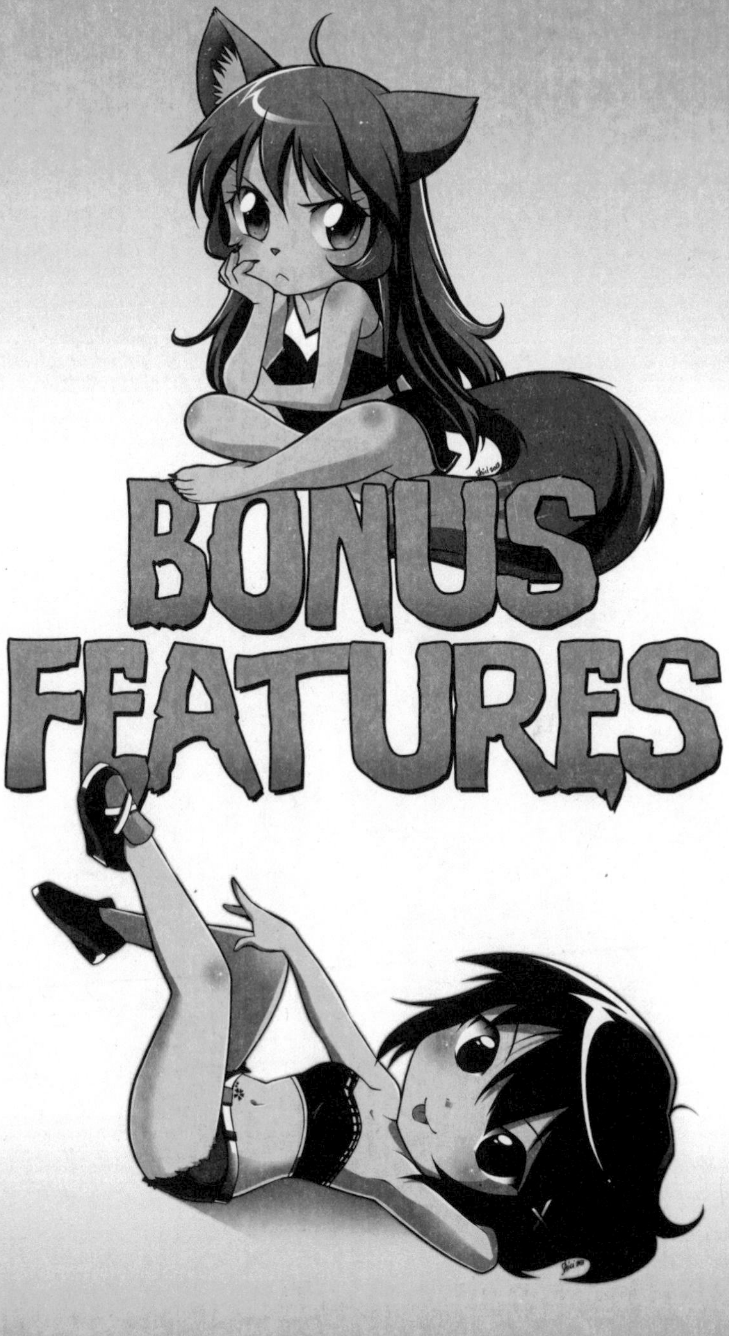
BONUS
FEATURES

VAMPIRE CHEERLEADERS

MICHAEL SHELFER'S CHARACTER DESIGNS

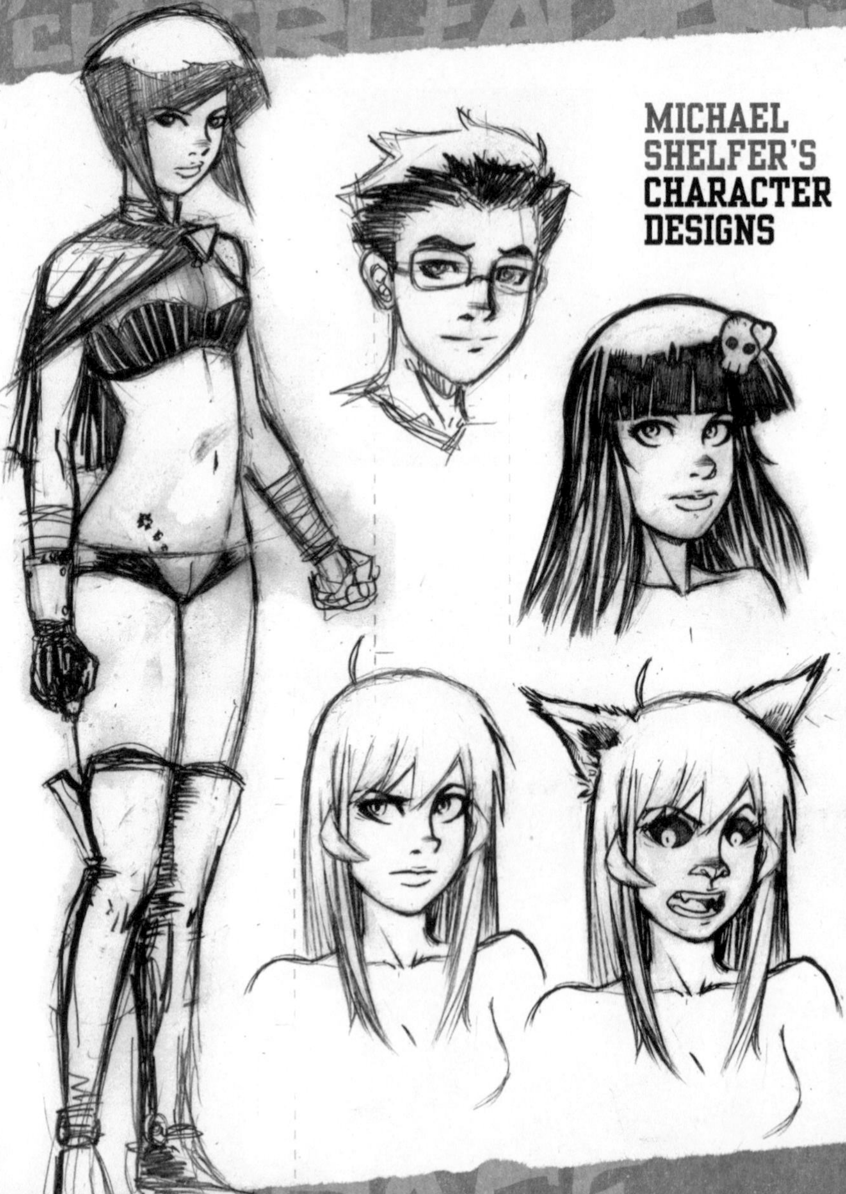

IN SPACE... AND TIME?

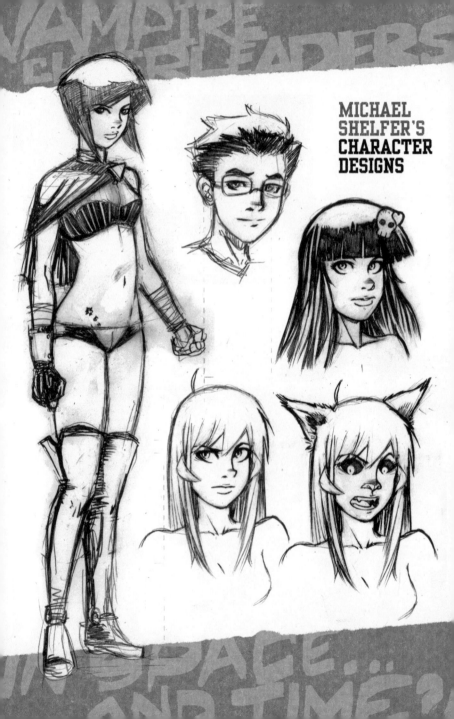

VAMPIRE CHEERLEADERS

MICHAEL SHELFER'S CHARACTER DESIGNS

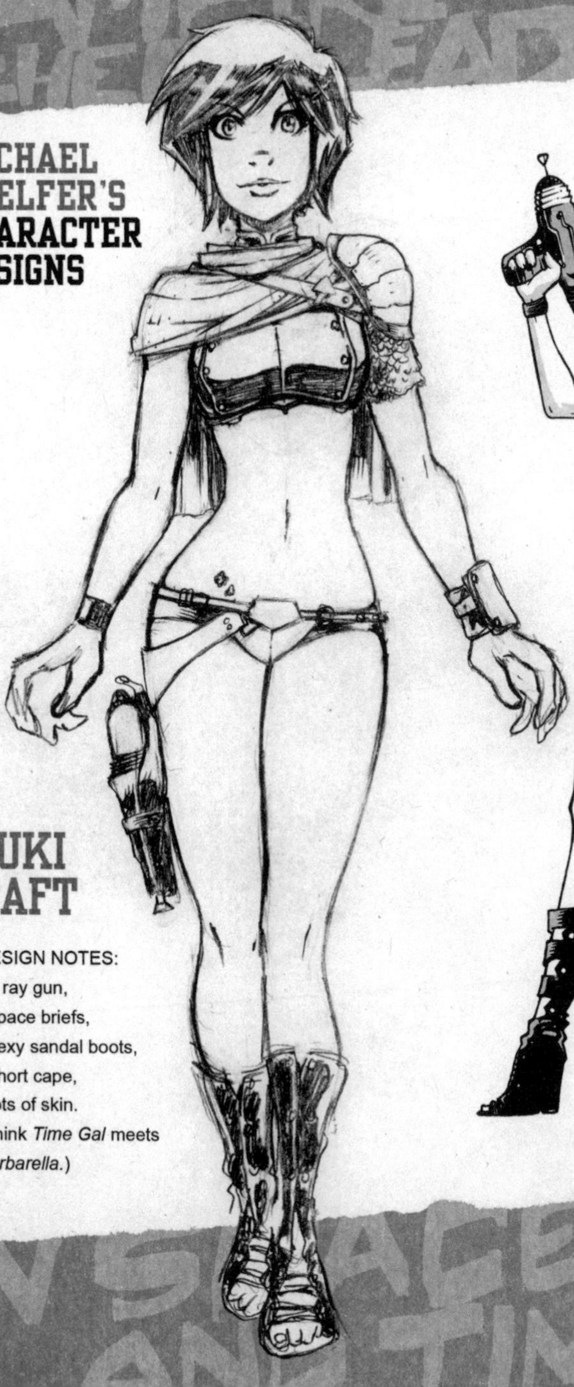

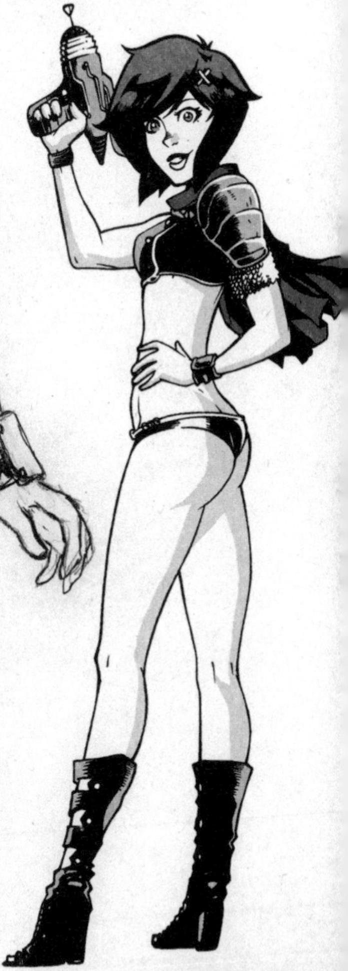

SUKI TAFT

DESIGN NOTES:

- a ray gun,
- space briefs,
- sexy sandal boots,
- short cape,
- lots of skin.

(Think *Time Gal* meets *Barbarella.*)

IN SPACE... AND TIME?

MICHAEL SHELFER'S PENCILS

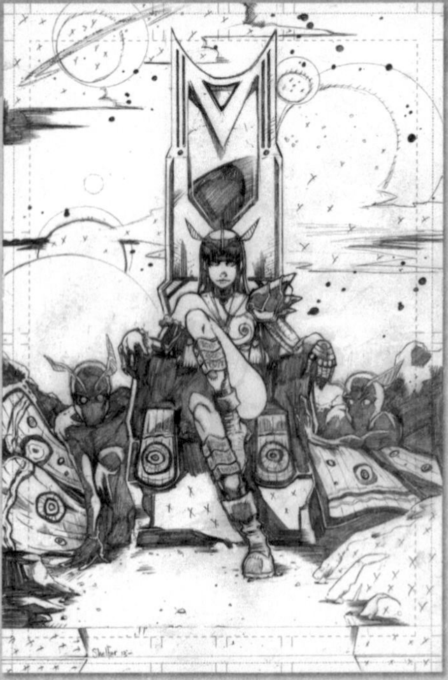

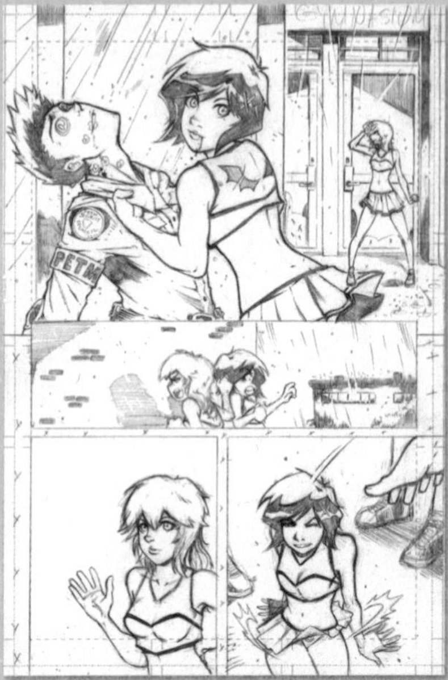

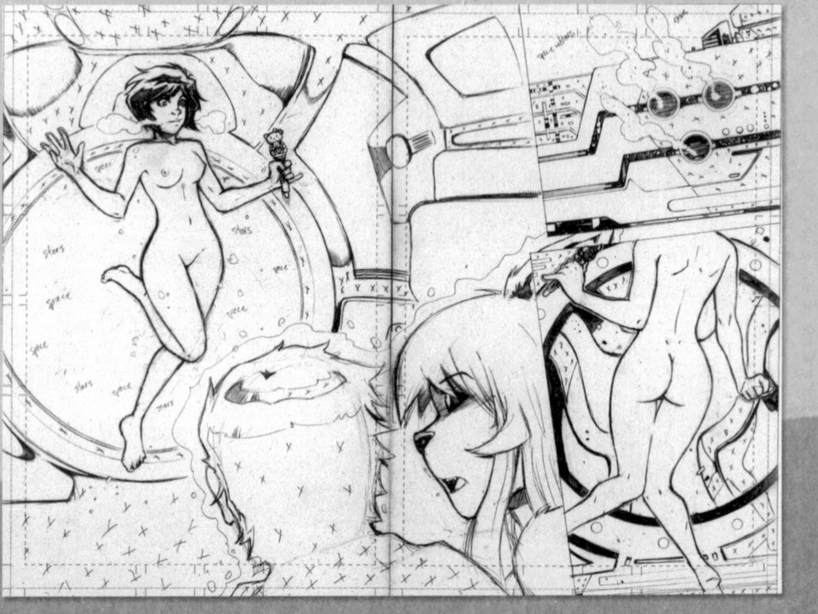

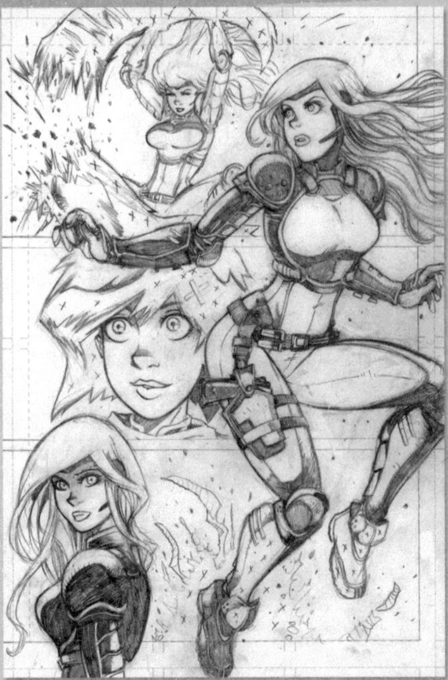

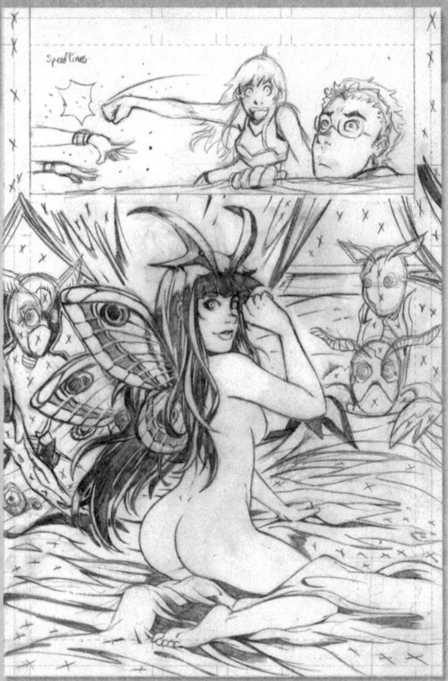
Speedlines

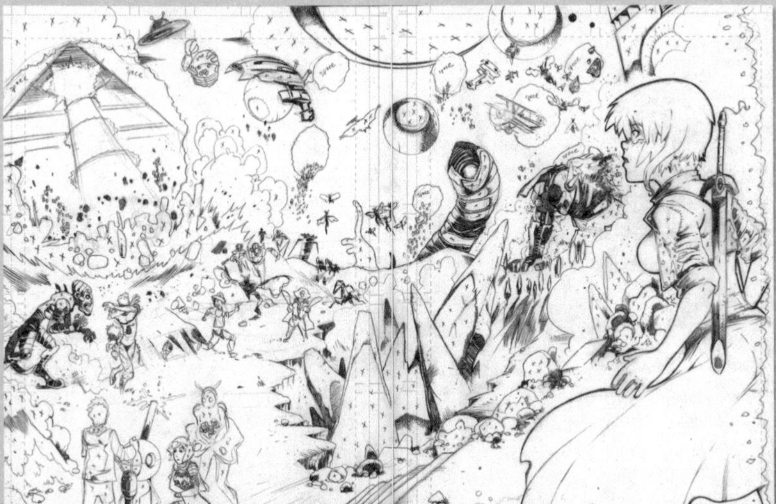

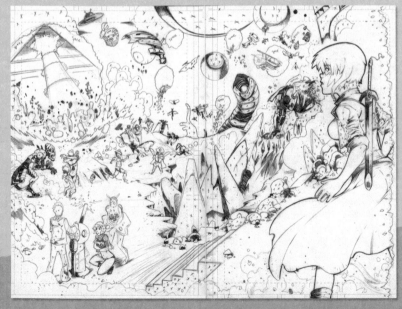

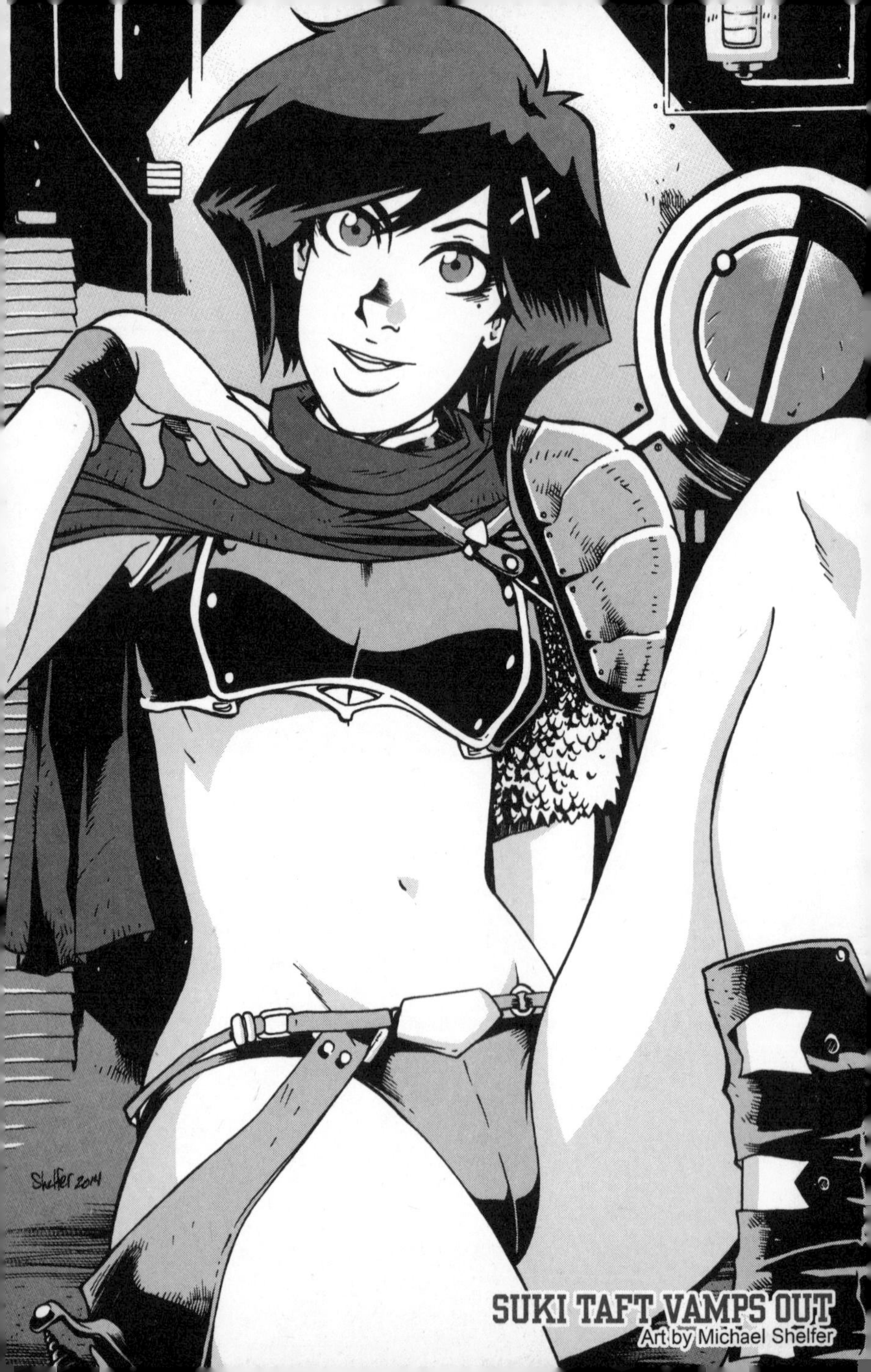
Shelfer 2014
SUKI TAFT VAMPS OUT
Art by Michael Shelfer

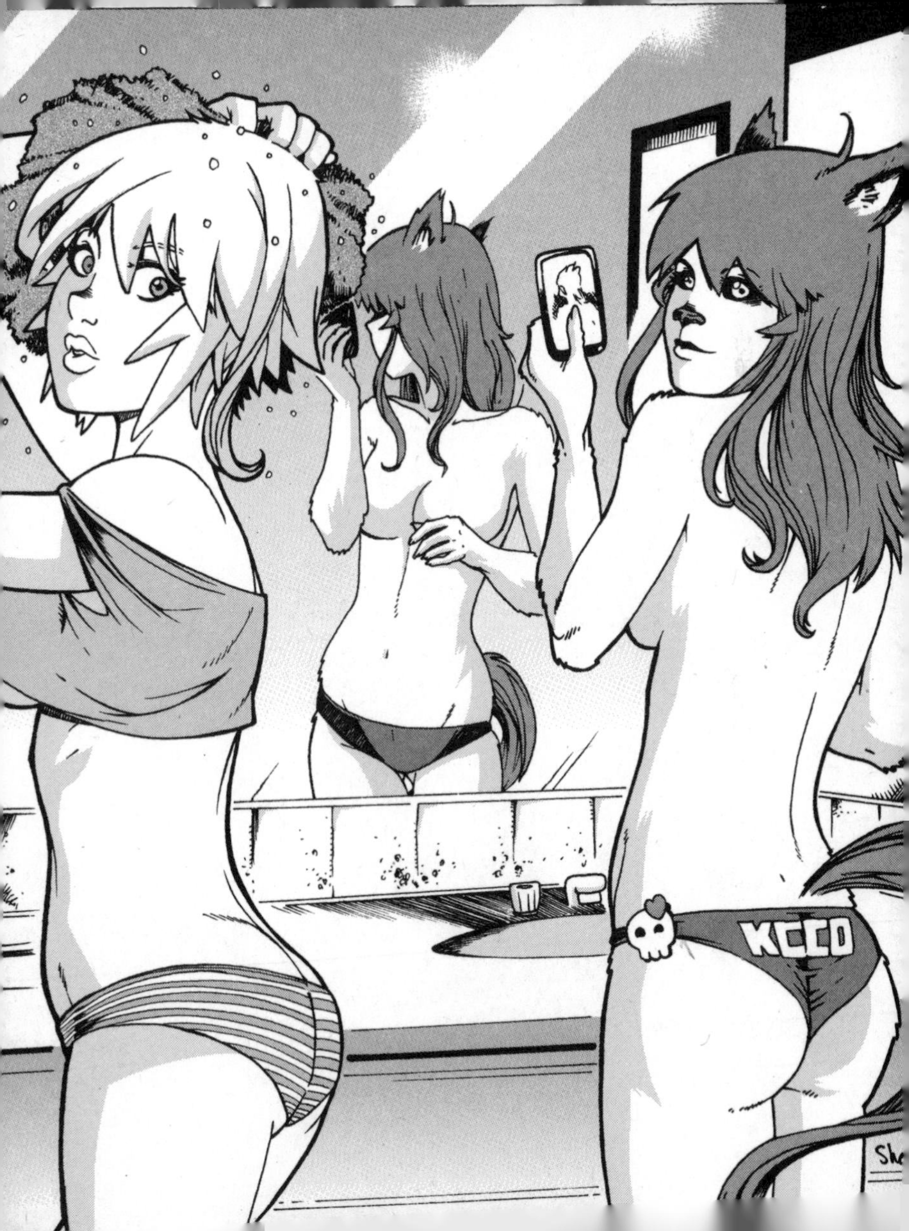
KCCO

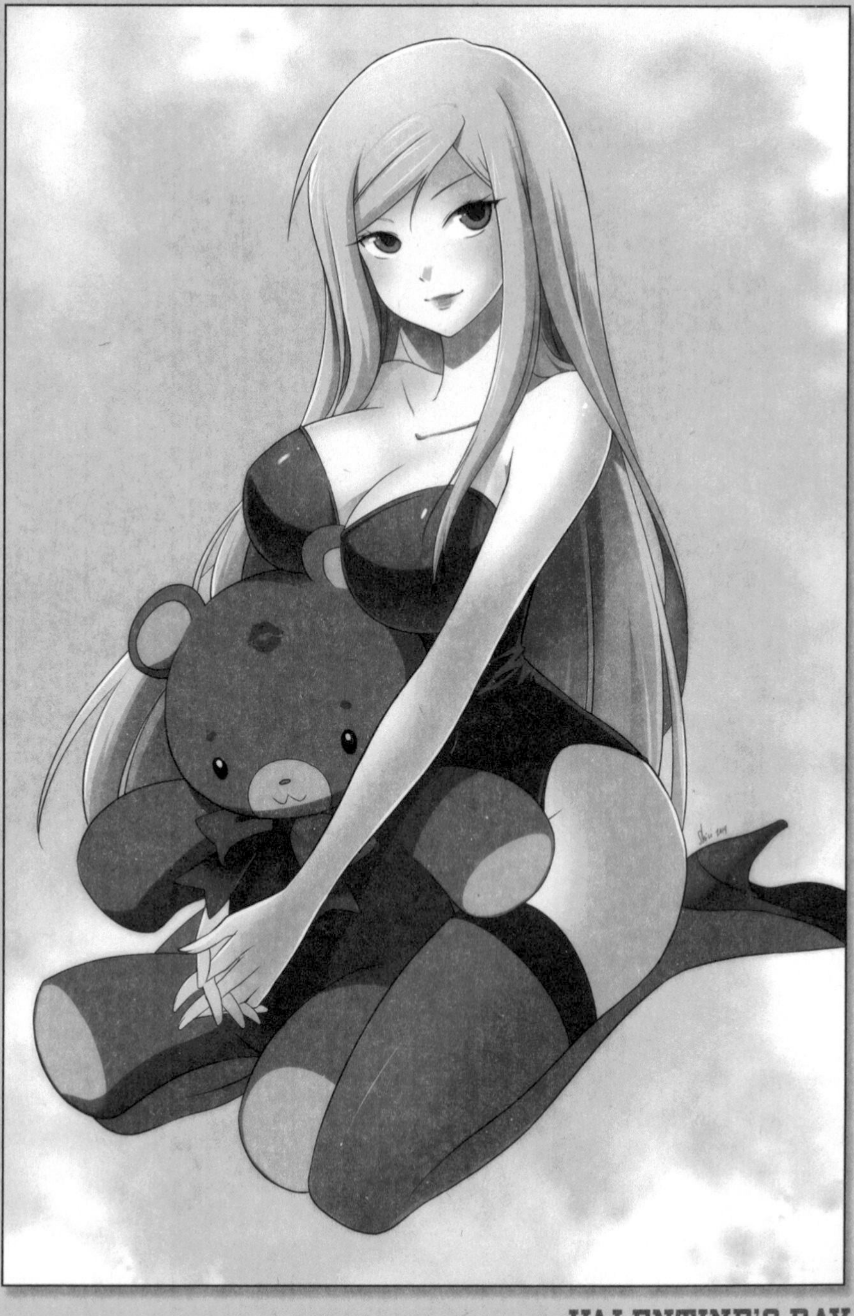

VALENTINE'S DAY

Art by Shiei

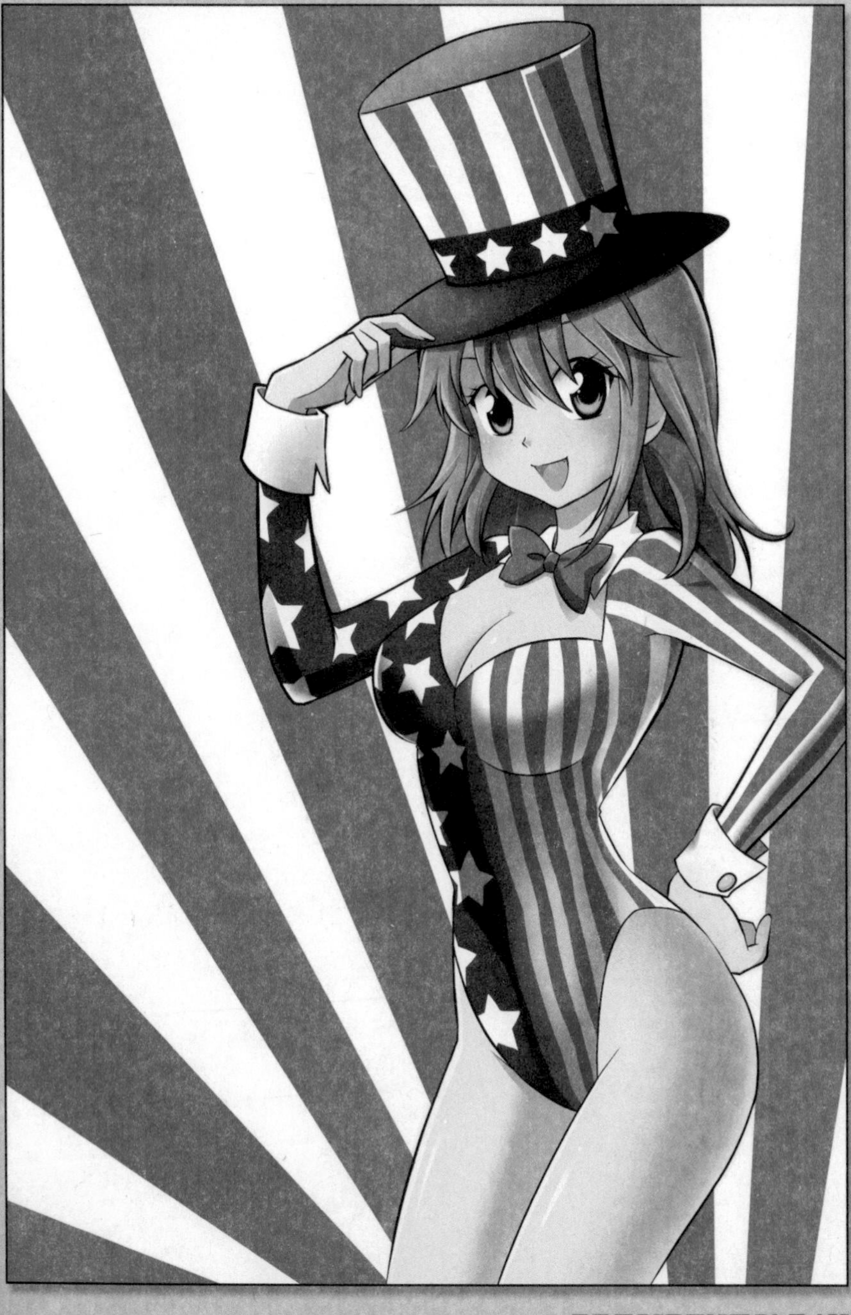

PRESIDENTS' DAY
Art by Shiei

PIN-UP GALLERY

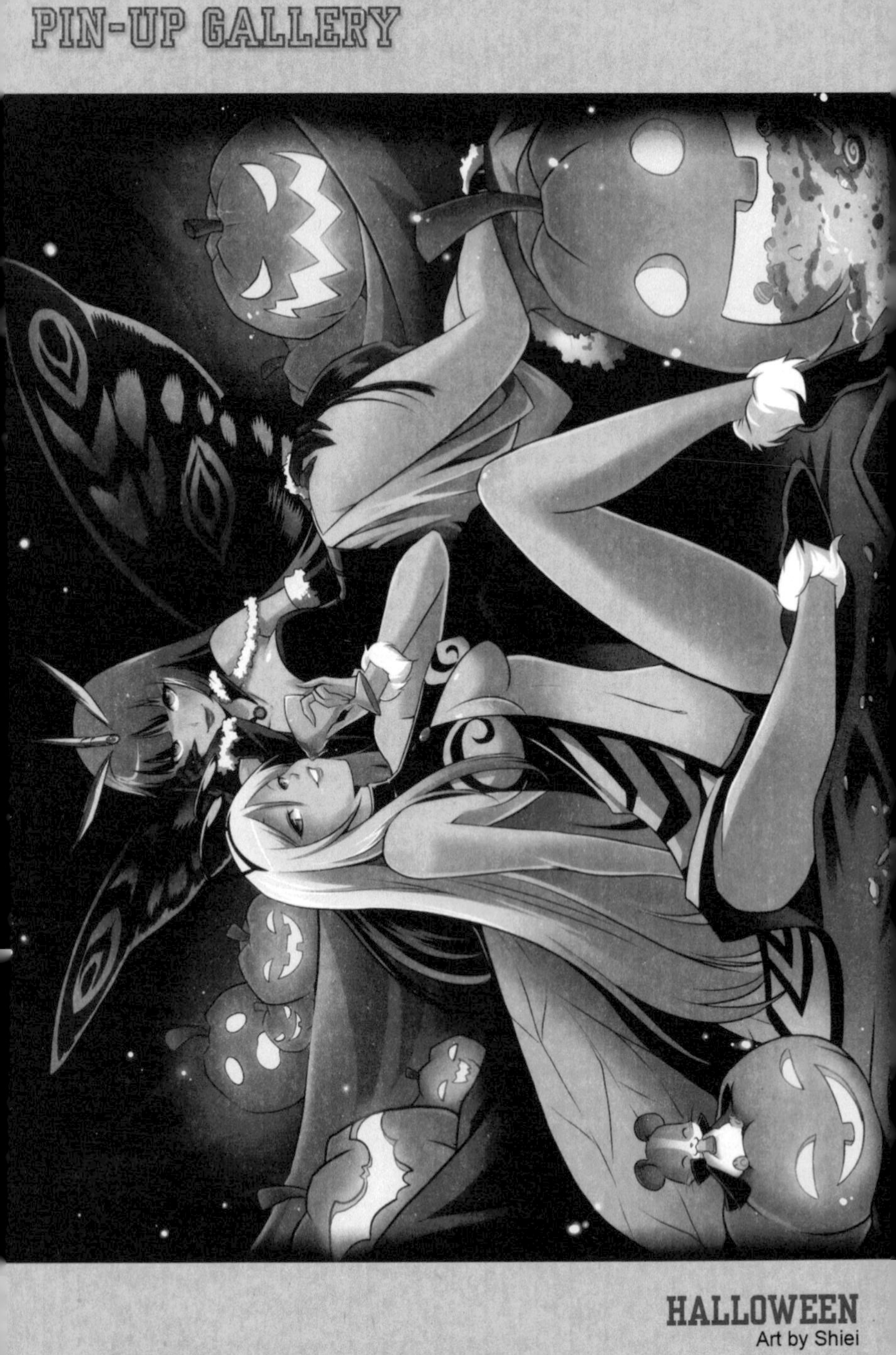

HALLOWEEN
Art by Shiei

PIN-UP GALLERY

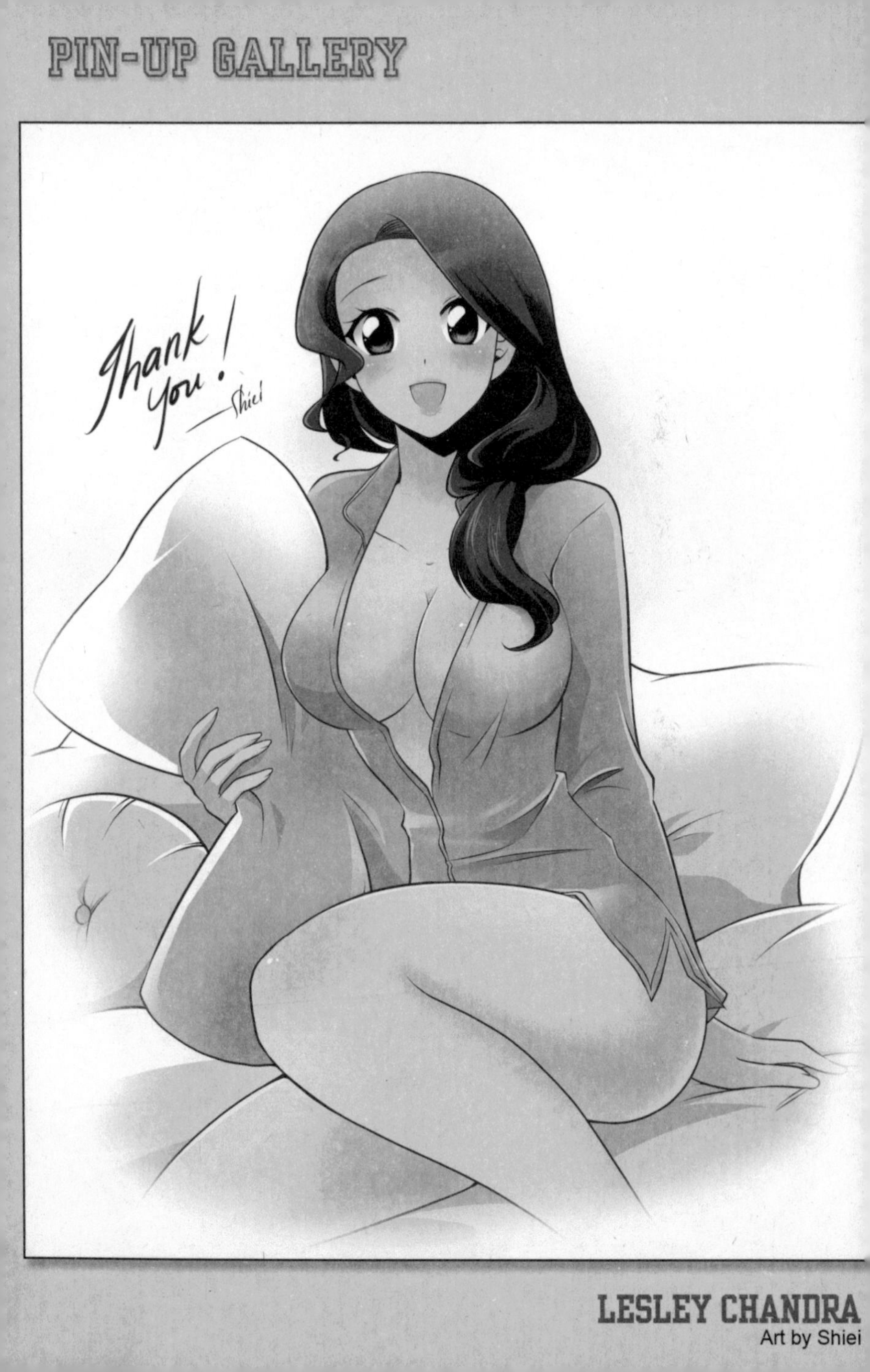
Thank you!
—Shiei

LESLEY CHANDRA
Art by Shiei

PIN-UP GALLERY

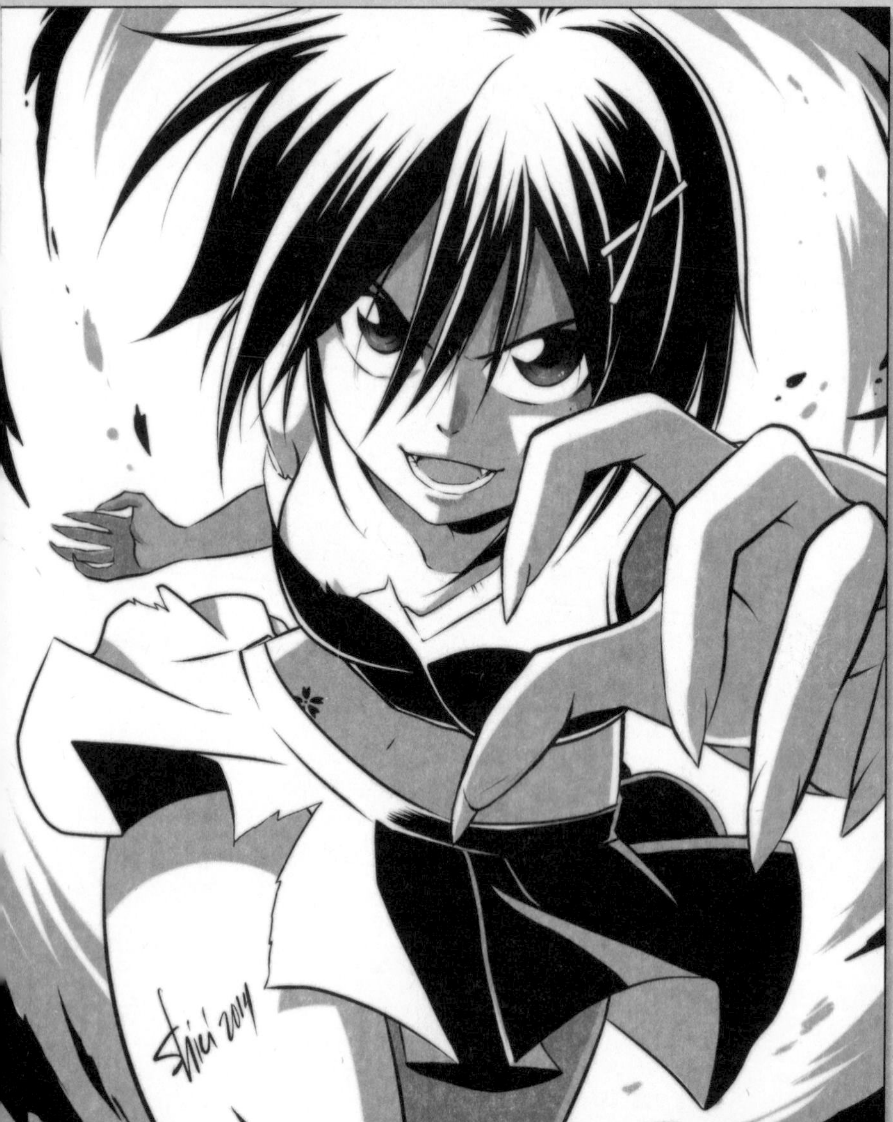
Shiei 2014

SUKI TAFT VAMPS OUT
Art by Shiei

PIN-UP GALLERY

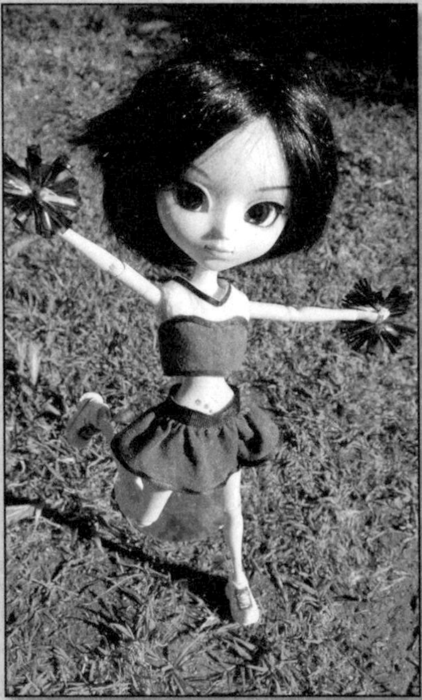

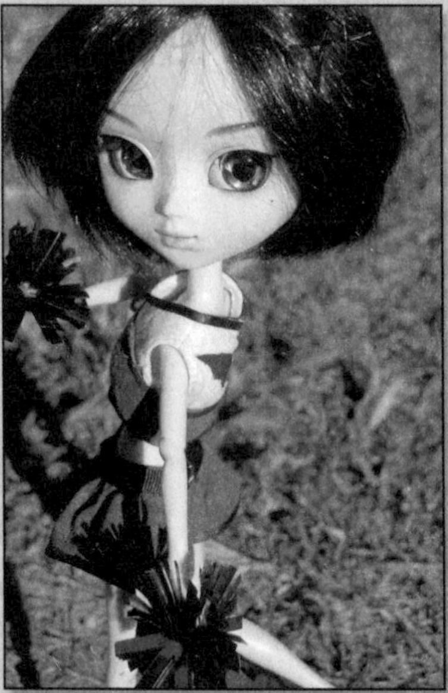

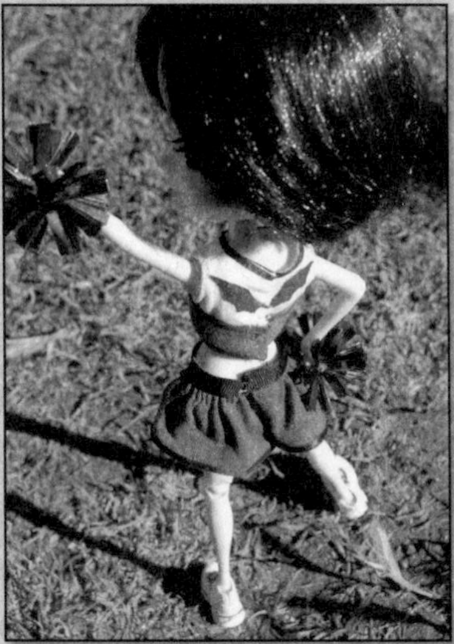

PULLIP SUKI

Doll Customization by Shiei, Costume by Adam Arnold

"Vampire Cheerleaders Get Rescued"

Story by ADAM ARNOLD
Illustrations by MICHAEL SHELFER

INT. CRESSIDA HARROW'S SLAVE WAREHOUSE (MIAMI, FL), NIGHT

The sounds of Cressida Harrow's low-heeled pumps echo loudly as she runs with a bitter scowl on her face down a long, dark corridor lined with horizontal tubes resembling unlit fluorescent light bulbs. (Cressida Harrow should be dressed in a women's business suit with a pair of designer sunglasses on her face.)

> **SFX**
> *Clack! Clack! Clack!*

A ways back, but hot on Cressida's trail is Lori Thurston (barefoot, vamp-faced, and dressed in a tattered smock/toga) followed closely by Stephanie Kane (Jian sword in hand).

> **STEPHANIE**
> *Huff Huff!*
> Sooo... We good about the whole **Prom** thing?
> *Huff!*

> **LORI**
> Want me to **rebreak** that arm?

Cressida reaches the end of the corridor where there is a panel with a button on the wall and a doorway with stairs leading up. Cressida slams her fist down on the button...

Suddenly, there's a bright flash as the entire hallway lights up with intense UV rays and heat.

> **SFX**
> FLAAASH

Lori instantly screams out in pain as her flesh starts to burn and sizzle. Even Stephanie has to stop in her tracks and shield her eyes from the intense brightness of the lights.

Note: This deleted scene occurs immediately following the *Vampire Cheerleaders Must Die!* storyline.

LORI

YYAAAARRGGHH!!!

YOU'RE- YOU'RE *NOT* GETTING AWAY FROM ME!!

SFX

SIIIZZZZZ

Cressida grins devilishly before rushing up the stairs.

SFX

GRIN

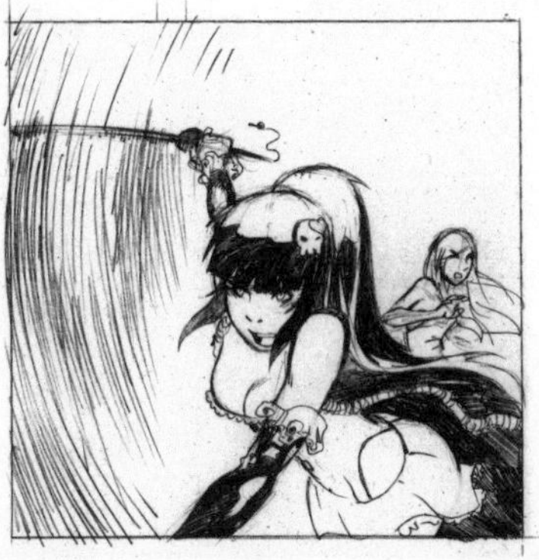

Unable to move forward, and with Lori about to burst into flames, Stephanie does the only thing she can... she slashes her sword in an arching motion, instantly shattering all the lights and sending glass raining down on them.

SFX

SKKIIISH

As she scrambles to her feet, Lori's face is absolutely feral.

LORI

CRESSIDA HARROW!!!

Lori grabs Stephanie's Jian sword by the blade, making it her own.

SFX

GRAB

STEPHANIE

Hey--!

And Lori races up the stairs in hot pursuit of the sole remaining Harrow sister. Stephanie can only try and keep pace.

LORI

RRRRAAAAAAGGGGH!!!

STEPHANIE (TO HERSELF)

Holy vampire cheerleaders, Batman.

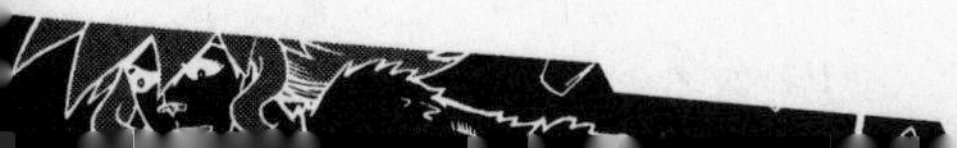

EXT. THE ROOF OF CRESSIDA HARROW'S SLAVE WAREHOUSE, NIGHT

Lori bursts through the stairwell doorway leading out onto the roof of Cressida's bayside warehouse where a helicopter and pilot await on a helipad. Cressida can be seen climbing into the helicopter.

SFX (LORI BURSTING THROUGH DOOR)
BAM

CRESSIDA HARROW
Get us in the air at once!!

PILOT
Yes, Madam Harrow!

We see Stephanie emerge onto the roof. Cressida screams at the pilot...

CRESSIDA HARROW
NOW!!

The helicopter starts to rise into the air.

SFX
Whup Whup Whup Whup Whup

Lori and Stephanie race towards the airborne helicopter.

The helicopter leaves the roof and is over the water... Lori takes a running leap off the roof (Jian sword in hand) and grabs ahold of the landing gear.

Stephanie runs right up to the edge of the building, stopping herself just as she's about to go off the edge.

STEPHANIE
Whoa! Not gonna make *that* jump.

Cressida tosses off her designer shades, and we see her scowling face as she starts stomping her feet down onto Lori, who is trying to climb into the helicopter.

CRESSIDA HARROW
You **worthless** insect!

SFX

STOMP STOMP STOMP

The view shifts back to Stephanie, who is watching the events from the ground. Lori's battle with Cressida unfolds before Stephanie in silhouette...

Lori slashes upward with the Jian, causing a splash of blood to splatter outward.

SFX

SLASH

There's a pained cry from Cressida (grabbing her face, now missing an eye) and a flash sound effect as Cressida uses her gorgon paralyzing powers.

CRESSIDA HARROW
DRRAAAH?!!

SFX
FLASH

And we see a paralyzed Lori fall backwards out of the helicopter towards the water below. The Jian sword tumbles down with her.

Lori and the Jian hit the water with a...

SFX

SPLOOOOSH

With Cressida's helicopter but a tiny speck in the sky now, Stephanie climbs down the fire escape ladder on the side of the building. Reaching the bottom, Stephanie plants her boots on the ground.

SFX

Hup

Stephanie reaches the edge of the warehouse dock and Lori's head emerges from the waters of Miami Bay.

SFX

SPLASH

STEPHANIE (EAGER TO KNOW THE SCOOP)
How'd it go?

                    LORI
              Took her eye.

          STEPHANIE (QUIPPING BACK)
        Good thing she's got **two**. O'Keeffe'd be all
        over me.

                    LORI
            Gonna help me out of the water?

Stephanie looks down at Lori from the dock.

                  STEPHANIE
        You realize you lost my **Jian**, right?

                    LORI
        Get your witch to find it..

          STEPHANIE (QUIPPING BACK)
        Eh... We've already got PETM on our asses.
        I'd hate to have the **EPA** after us also...
        you know, for *boiling all the water out* of
        Biscayne Bay.

Lori glares at Stephanie with a fang-y snarl.

                    SFX
                  GLARE

Lori takes a deep breath and dives under the water.

We see an empty panel where Lori is still submerged.

Then Lori bursts from the water covered in sludge and trash from
the bay of Miami, Stephanie's Jian in hand.

                    SFX
                 SPLOOOSH

Lori lands on the dock in front of Stephanie and thrusts the sword
into the ground inches from Stephanie's feet. The Jian's hilt has
plastic "six pack" rings and sludge on it.

                    LORI
              There! *Happy?*

                  STEPHANIE
              Much obliged.

Suddenly, a voice is heard over the comm device in Stephanie's ear.

SFX (COMM STATIC)
SQUAK

J.C. SUMMERFIELD (VOICE OVER COMM)
The "BATS" are secure.

And the scene quickly shifts to show J.C. Summerfield, Katie Kane, Charlotte Roth, and Leonard Duvall having dispatched Cressida Harrow's burly henchmen and saved the Vampire Cheerleaders (Heather, Lesley, Zoe, and Suki). There are other girls here as well, like the servant girl that Bianca Harrow had in her hotel room during *Vampire Cheerleaders Vol. 2*.

J.C. SUMMERFIELD
Repeat, the **"BATS"** are secure.

In the background, we can see a Heather who's overcome with emotion grabbing onto a very cool-looking Leonard.

HEATHER (TO LEONARD)
Oh- Oh my god...**Leonard?!**
I'm so **happy** to see you!!

LEONARD
Any time, Lady Heather. Any time.

Stephanie replies over the comm.

STEPHANIE
Copy that, A-Team. Meet ya at the **rendezvous**.

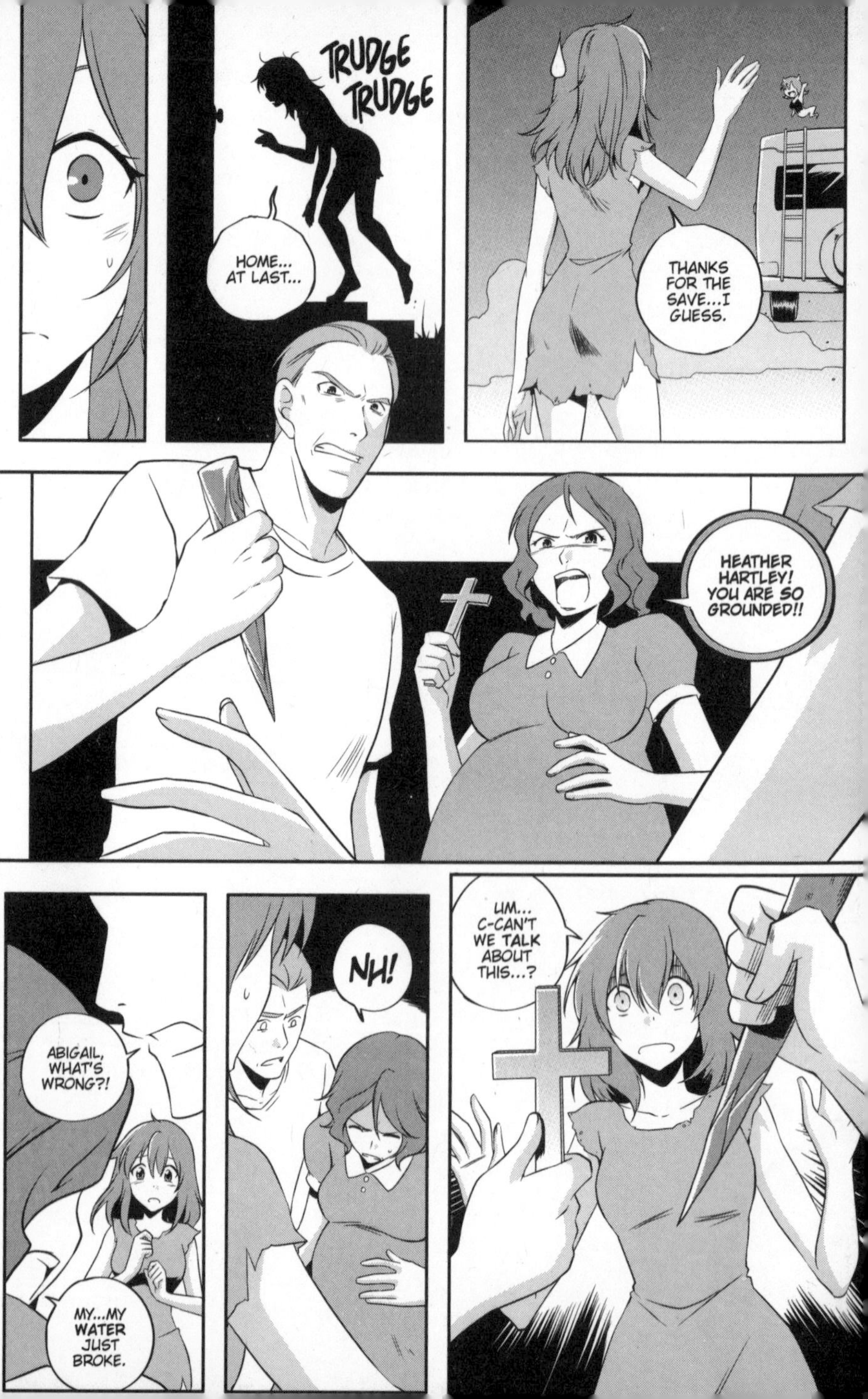
THANKS FOR THE SAVE...I GUESS.
TRUDGE TRUDGE
HOME... AT LAST...
HEATHER HARTLEY! YOU ARE SO GROUNDED!!
UM... C-CAN'T WE TALK ABOUT THIS...?
NH!
ABIGAIL, WHAT'S WRONG?!
MY...MY WATER JUST BROKE.

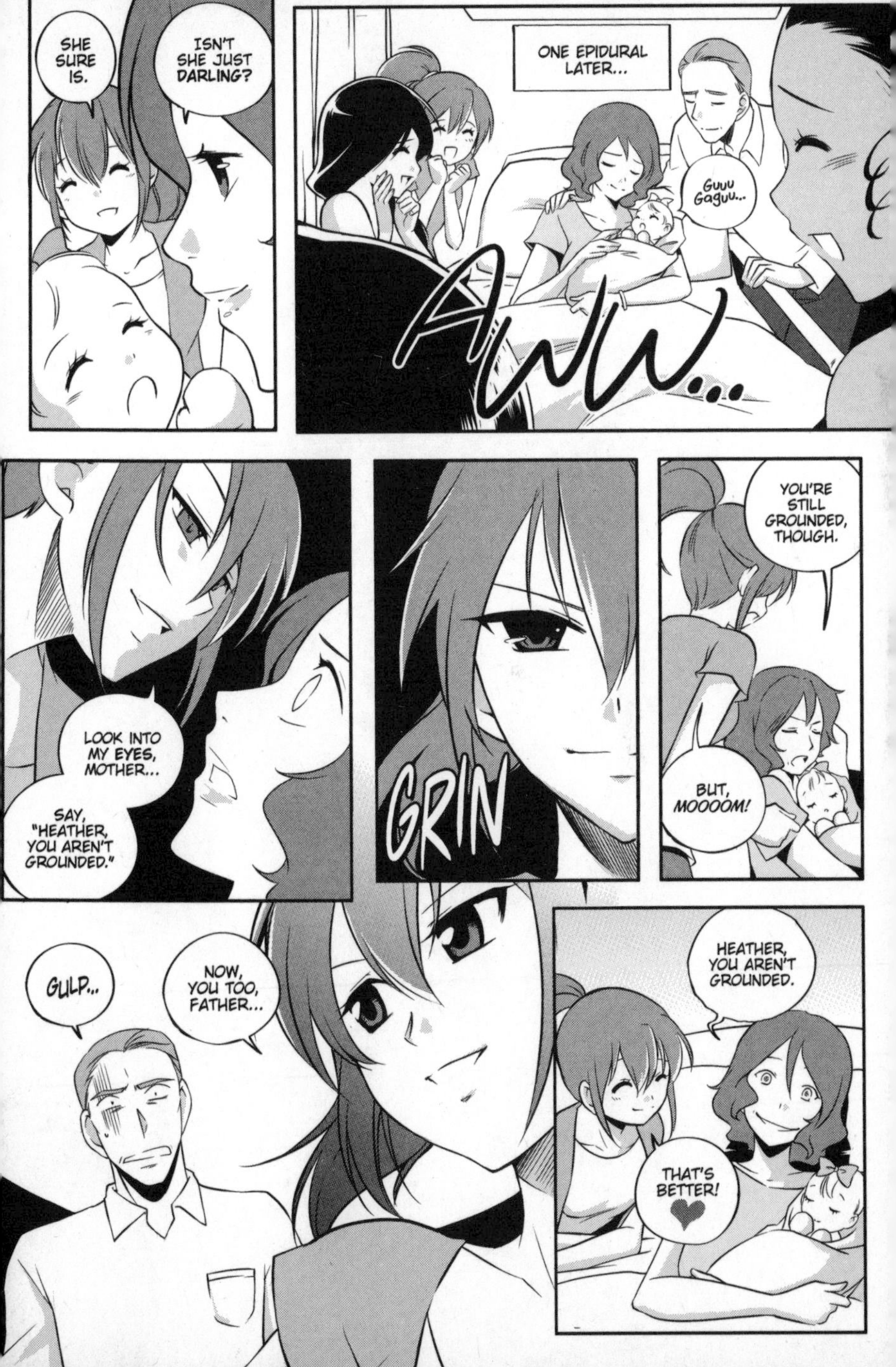
ONE EPIDURAL LATER...
GUUU GAGUU...
AWW...
ISN'T SHE JUST DARLING?
SHE SURE IS.
YOU'RE STILL GROUNDED, THOUGH.
BUT, MOOOOM!
GRIN
LOOK INTO MY EYES, MOTHER...
SAY, "HEATHER, YOU AREN'T GROUNDED."
HEATHER, YOU AREN'T GROUNDED.
THAT'S BETTER!
♥
NOW, YOU TOO, FATHER...
GULP...

VAMPIRE CHEERLEADERS CAMP IT UP!

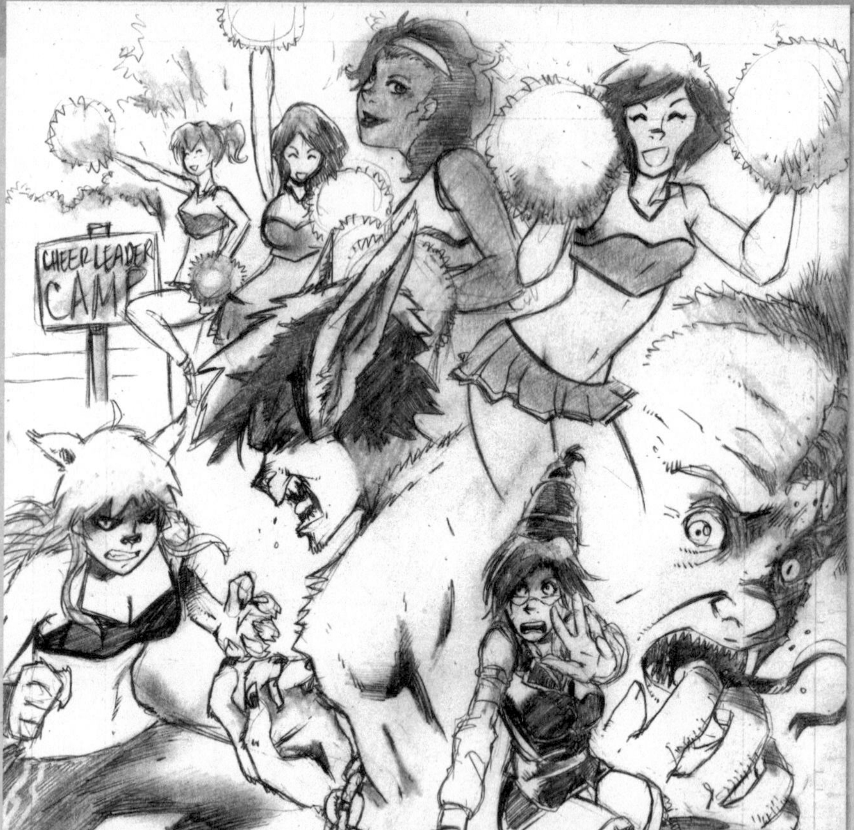
CHEER LEADER
CAMP

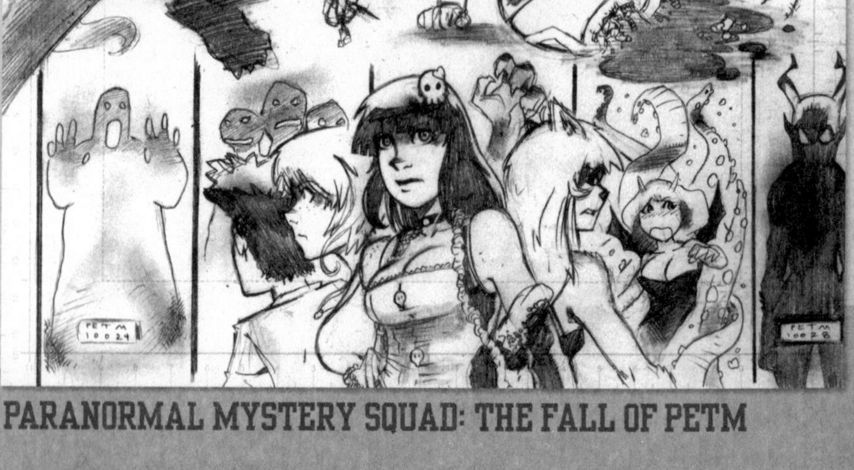
PETM
10028
PETM
10024

PARANORMAL MYSTERY SQUAD: THE FALL OF PETM

VAMPIRE
CHEERLEADERS
PRESENTS

FRANKENBITCHES

SCRIPT BY
ADAM ARNOLD

CHARACTER DESIGNS BY
SHIEI

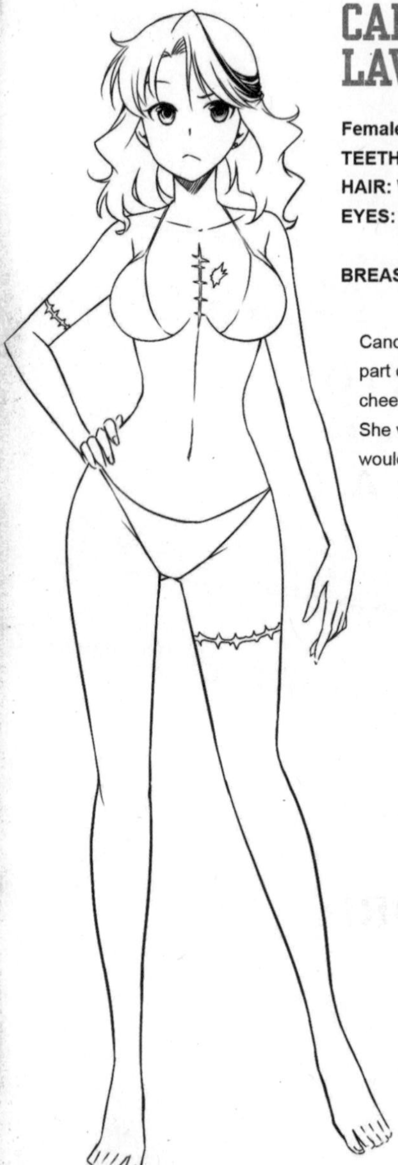

CANDICE LAVENZA

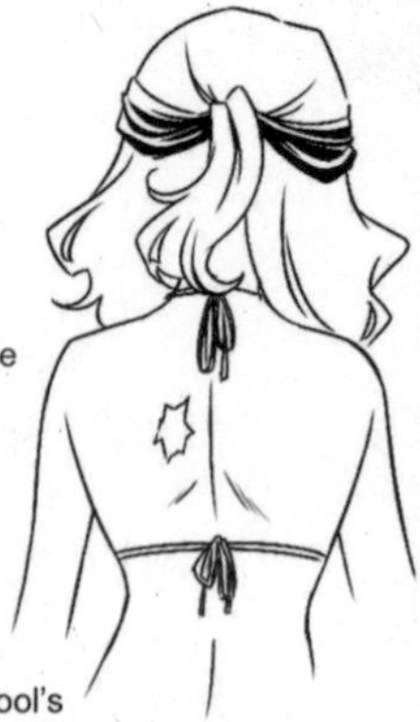

Female, 18, Caucasian
TEETH: Braces
HAIR: Wavy/curly, Dirty Blonde
EYES: Brown/Red (Vampire), Green (Frankenbitch)
BREASTS: C Cup

Candice was originally a part of Bakertown High School's cheerleadering squad, the "Bakertown Bats." She was a ditzy vampire with braces that would "pop" when she bared her fangs.

New "Frankenbitches" Form:
– Candice should retain her braces.
– Candice's blonde hair should also still be wavy/curly, but there are now some Bride of Frankenstein-style black streaks present on both sides.
– Candice's skin color has now turned from suntanned to light green.
– One of Candice's brown/red vampire eyes will have changed to green.
– Running down the middle of Candice's chest (between her breasts) is a vertical line of stitches. Clearly an open-heart surgery scar, still very fresh.
– Candice's chest should also have a visible circular scar from where she was impaled by the gearshift. This scar will be visible on her back as well.
– Her left leg has been totally replaced with another one, so there is a visible scar running around her leg, mid-thigh.
– Candice's right arm has been replaced with someone else's as well. There should be a visible scar running around the middle of her arm to represent this.

FRANKLIN "FRANK" STEINBERG

Male, 21, Caucasian
HAIR: Black
EYES: Brown

Our story's mad scientist. Think Jeffery Combs' Herbert West from *ReAnimator* meets Crispin Glover's *Willard* in appearance. Frank is a medical student at Mooreland State University (MSU). He likes to keep to himself and has trouble meeting girls...so he has turned to making the perfect girl that he can love unconditionally and not at all in a creepy way like a love doll. See, Frank is a hopeless romantic at heart who wants nothing more than true love, but so far...it hasn't happened yet. And now, he's amassed an ever-expanding harem of "Frankenbitches" that are both a help...and a hindrance.

JUSTINE

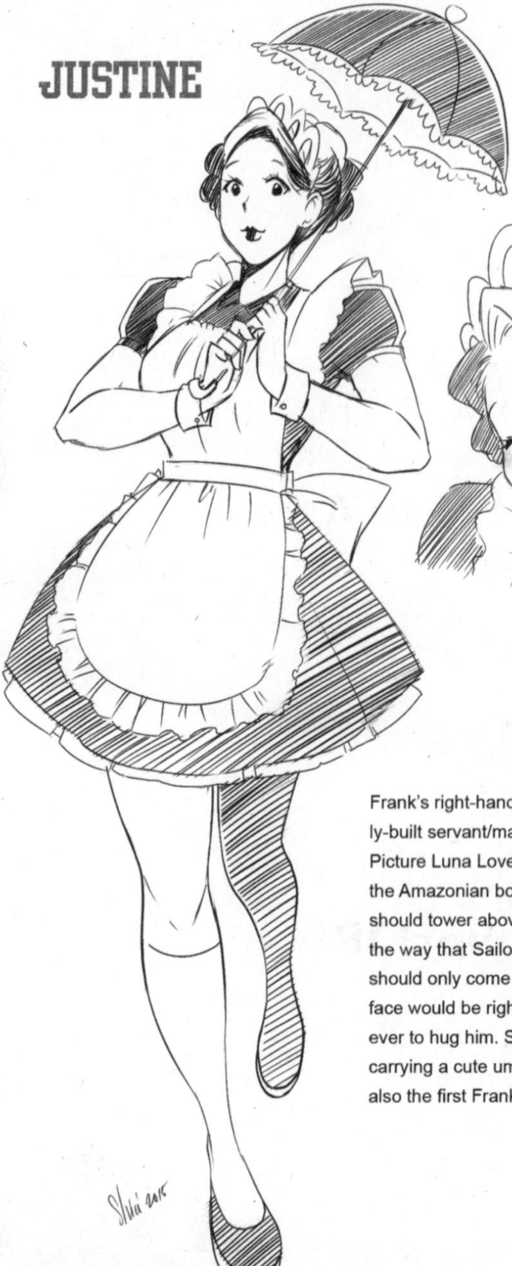

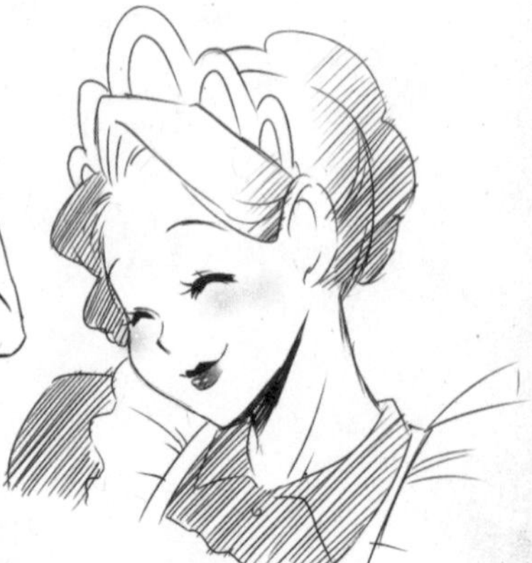

Frank's right-hand woman. Big, powerfully-built servant/maid who wouldn't hurt a fly. Picture Luna Lovegood's airy personality in the Amazonian body of a female wrestler. She should tower above all the other girls much the way that Sailor Jupiter does. Frank's head should only come to her shoulders, so his face would be right at her breasts if she were ever to hug him. She often can be seen carrying a cute umbrella with her. Justine is also the first Frankenbitch that we meet.

INGA & ELSA

A Siamese-twin type Frankenbitch.
2 heads, 2 legs, 2 arms... 3 breasts.
Imagine if "Zaphod Beeblebrox" from
The Hitchhiker's Guide to the Galaxy
were a really cute girl.

She shouldn't have too many
stitches, though, as we don't want
her to seem gross. Inga and Elsa
are constantly at odds with each
other and would like nothing more
than to be in sole in control of their
body...instead of, you know.

MARGIE (MARGARET)

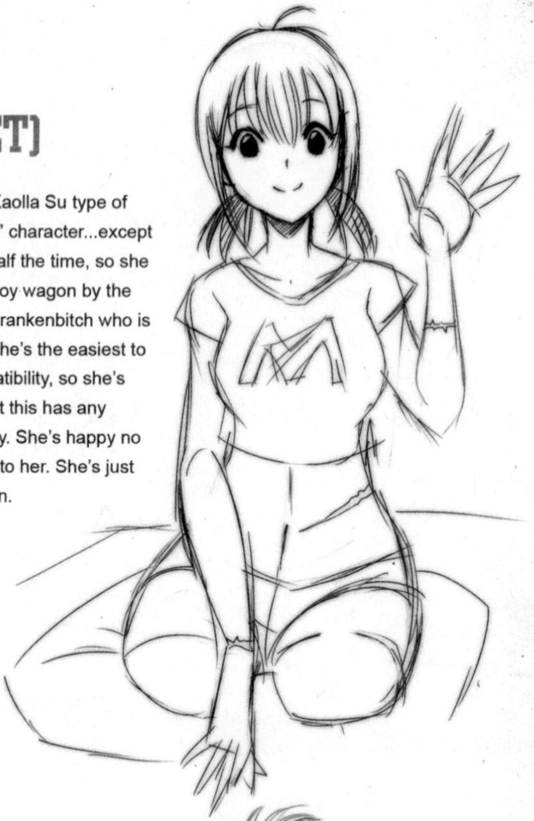

The Morgan McKnight/Kaolla Su type of "always on a sugar high" character...except she doesn't have legs half the time, so she gets pulled around in a toy wagon by the other girls! Margie is a Frankenbitch who is often used for parts as she's the easiest to test for transplant compatibility, so she's never complete...not that this has any impact on her personality. She's happy no matter what Frank does to her. She's just glad to have the attention.

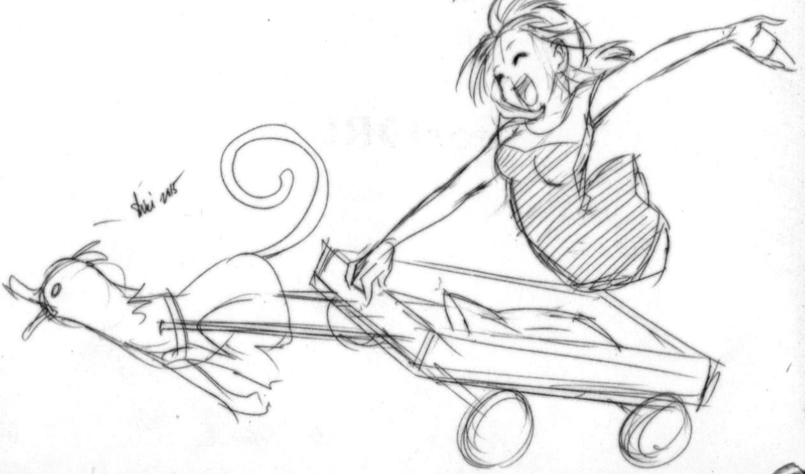

MARY BETH

She looks like the hot blonde daughter (Elly May Clampett) from *The Beverly Hillbillies*...but she's a total ditz who would lose her head if it weren't sewn on. Oh, wait...scratch that. It's NOT sewn on. She literally DOES lose her head all the time. Nothing helps. It just...keeps falling off.

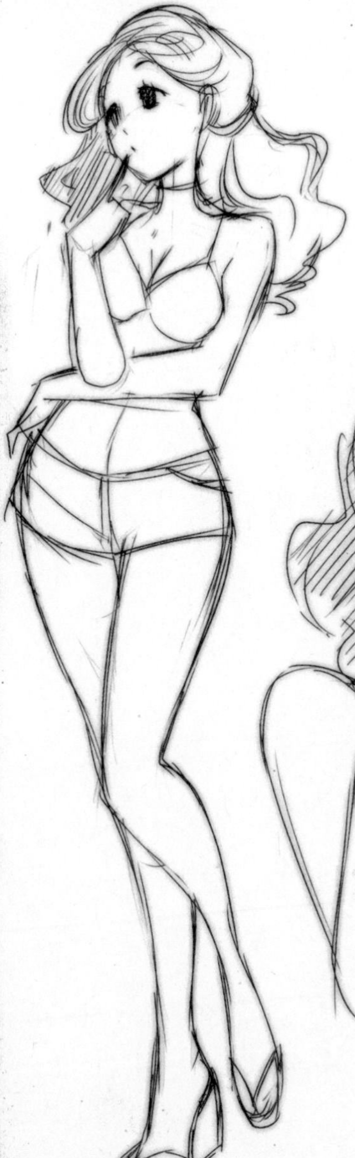

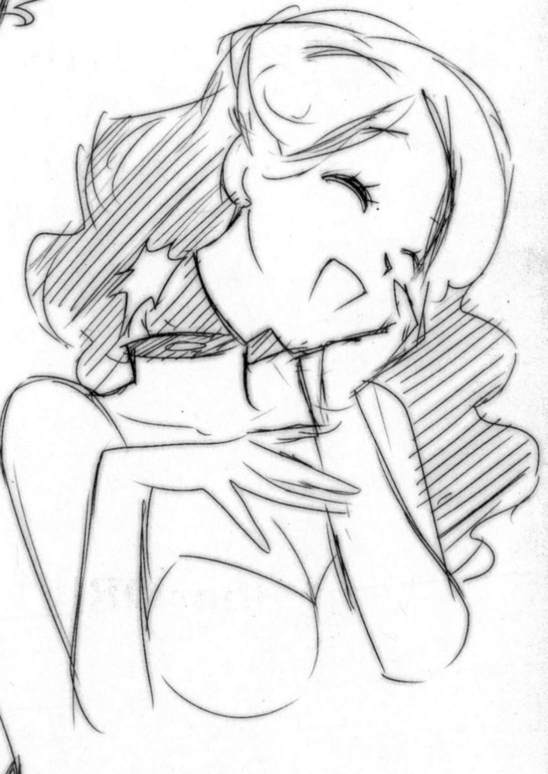

KARLOFF

A cute, cobbled-together pet made from... a monkey's body, dog's legs, and a duck's head. Can't have a harem without a cute pet, right?

EXT. BOTTOM OF INSPIRATION POINT, NIGHT

CAPTION BOX
Inspiration Point

We see a cute bunny on all fours hop out between some pine trees at the base of a cliff. (Readers should think... 'Aww...')

The bunny nibbles on a little leaf, further demonstrating just how cute it is.

Suddenly, a CAR falls from above, hood/engine first, right onto the bunny... and instantly BURSTS INTO FLAMES on contact with the ground!!

SFX
KA-BROOOOSH

We see for the first time **Franklin Steinberg**, his servant/maid creation **Justine**, and **Karloff** the cobbled-together pet. They're standing there dumbfounded at the insane sight they've just witnessed on their evening walk. Justine is holding an open umbrella in one hand.

JUSTINE
See, Frank? The weather lady was right. We
did need our umbrella.

FRANK (SWEAT DROP)
Cloudy with a chance of exploding cars. I don't
think that's *quite* what she meant, Justine...

Karloff starts barking...er...quacking, his leash going tight as he tugs on it towards the car.

KARLOFF
Quack! Quack! Quack!

Karloff breaks free of the leash and runs towards the passenger window of the burning wreckage of the car.

FRANK
Karloff, wait!

We see the passenger-side window of the upside-down car. Flames are lapping from it.

KARLOFF
Quack! Quack! Quack!

Suddenly, the charred left arm/hand of a young woman falls limp to the ground in classic horror movie scare fashion. The fingernails should be nicely manicured and painted purple. While the fingers are touching the ground, the arm itself is hanging from above.

> KARLOFF (SCARED/JUMPING BACK)
> QUACK?!

> CANDICE (GROANING)
> *Unnh...*

We see the poor woman's head for the first time; her wavy hair and trademark braces should make her instantly recognizable. It's **Candice Lavenza**, one of Bakertown High School's cheerleading squad, the "Bakertown Bats," and she should be dressed in her trademark Bakertown High School cheerleading outfit-- now slightly singed and dirty.

Candice should be hanging upside-down in the burning car. While readers will know Candice was impaled through the chest by the car's GEAR SHIFT, our characters won't be able to see this. They'll just assume she's caught on something like a seat belt.
Justine starts to talk to Frank about the situation, head forward.

> JUSTINE
> Oh, Frank, the poor thing. Do you think we
> should...

Justine looks over to where Frank was and we just see an empty dotted outline of where he should be standing.

> JUSTINE
> Frank?

Justine, still clueless, looks around behind her to see where Frank is...

> JUSTINE (CLUELESS LOOK)
> Where'd you...?

...before looking forward to see Frank trying to pull Candice out of the upside-down car's front passenger window (the window should be broken). Frank should have thrown off his suit jacket and rolled up the sleeves of his white dress shirt.

> JUSTINE (DAWNING COMPREHENSION LOOK)
> Oh.

Braving the flames, Frank grabs Candice under her arms...and tries to pull her sizzling body from the wreckage of the burning car.

...before looking forward to see Frank trying to pull Candice out of the upside-down car's front passenger window (the window should be broken). Frank should have thrown off his suit jacket and rolled up the sleeves of his white dress shirt.

>   JUSTINE (DAWNING COMPREHENSION LOOK)
>   Oh.

Braving the flames, Frank grabs Candice under her arms...and tries to pull her sizzling body from the wreckage of the burning car.

>   FRANK
>   Don't worry, I've got you!

>   CANDICE (BARELY CONSCIOUS, AND
>   TOTALLY ON FIRE)
>   *Unnh...*

>   KARLOFF
>   Quack! Quack!

Suddenly, Frank gets singed on his arm. He flinches, grabbing his arm in pain.

>   FRANK
>   **DAGH!**

Justine's eyes light up with alarm at the sight of Frank's pain. Instantly dropping the umbrella, Justine clomps towards the car with heavy footfalls.

>   JUSTINE
>   FRANK!

>   SFX
>   CLOMP CLOMP CLOMP

Justine reaches Frank, who is already back to trying to pull Candice out of the car. Justine is fussing over Franks' arm.

>   JUSTINE
>   Frank, you're hurt.

>   FRANK
>   I'm okay, Justine! **NNH!**
>   Just--just help me! She's caught on something!!

>   JUSTINE
>   Ah--! Yes, of course!

And together Justine and Frank grab Candice by her shoulders and YANK AS HARD AS THEY CAN!

FRANK

YAAAH!

They succeed and they all go tumbling backwards with a THUD.

SFX

THUD

Candice is lying on her back on top of Frank's legs. Frank's eyes instantly widen in sheer horror at the sight of Candice's terrible condition.

- Candice's cheerleading costume is totally burnt, with spots showing her singed skin. There can be a touch of fan service with bits of her bra and panties visible, but no actual nudity.
- Her left leg is totally broken and twisted off to the side. (And burnt, of course.)
- Her right arm is broken as well.
- Her hair is a total mess.
- And worst of all...
SHE HAS A BROKEN-OFF GEAR SHIFT IMPALED THROUGH THE MIDDLE OF HER CHEST!
[Note: the gear shift penetrated Candice's chest just right of her left breast, nearly dead center of her chest. This is around where her 5th/6th ribs would be. Obviously, it missed her vampire heart--hence, she didn't die the true death. This all happened when Candice was kicked onto the gear shift and it punctured her back and came out her chest at the start of *Vampire Cheerleaders Vol. 1*.]

FRANK (IN TOTAL DISBELIEF)
Oh my God. How is she even still **ALIVE?!**

CANDICE (BARELY HANGING ON)
Unn...

JUSTINE (STUNNED EXPRESSION)
Snicker...doodle.

KARLOFF
Quack! Quack!

Frank scrambles to his feet, saying...

FRANK
Justine, quick...!

And we end the scene with a shot of Frank, Justine, and Karloff all racing away from the burning car. Justine is clutching Candice's charred body tightly in her arms. Frank is holding the umbrella up over them as the rain starts to come down.

FRANK

We have to get her back to my **lab!!**

KARLOFF

Quack! Quack! Quack!

EXT. FRANK'S HOME, DARK & RAINING

We open the scene with a shot of Frank's modest two-story dwelling that lies on the fringes of the Mooreland State University campus.

It's early morning, it's still dark out...and the rain's really coming down.

The roof of the house has various lightning rods and Tesla coils, just as you'd expect from a house containing a Frankenstein laboratory.

There's a lightning strike...

SFX

KRA-BRRZZZT

INT. FRANK'S LAB

We shift to inside the house where we have a have a close-up on Candice's sleeping face. She's on a gurney with a bed sheet covering her naked body. She looks a lot better than she did in the first scene. Her hair is tidy and normal (except for the new "*Bride of Frankenstein* streaks") and she doesn't have any soot or burns on her face. In fact, her face looks pretty normal. Peeking out from the sheets, we should see a fresh set of stitches running vertically down the middle of Candice's chest, between her breasts.

Candice begins to stir...

CANDICE

Mn...

Candice's eyes open.

CANDICE

Hm?

Frank is dressed in medical scrubs and is looking down at Candice. He has a doctor's head mirror on.

> FRANK
> Easy now. Don't try to move. Your **stitches**
> need time to heal.

> CANDICE
> My what...?

Candice grabs the sheet with her left hand and pulls it off to reveal her naked body. (Note: Candice shouldn't have a bra here, but she should be wearing panties. Nipple bumps are okay to show.)

For the first time, we see the full extent of Frank's gift...

> CANDICE
> What the **hell** did you *DO* to me?!

> FRANK
> You were hurt--near death.
> I patched you up. Gave you a **new** arm, leg, and heart.
> I fixed you. Made you **better.**

> CANDICE
> **Made me "better"?!**
> **I'M A *VAMPIRE!* I DIDN'T NEED YOU TO FIX ME!!!**

Candice feels a jolt of pain in her chest from the over-exertion.

> CANDICE (WINCING)
> *NNH!*

> FRANK
> I told you not to move!
> Let me see.

Franklin pulls his head mirror down over his eye and takes a close look at Candice's chest.

> FRANK
> *Augh!* You already popped a stitch!

Candice looks really irked that this freaky doctor kid is now staring directly at her bare chest.

Candice has an anger mark/vein clearly visible on her perturbed forehead.

Candice grabs Franklin by the hair and exposes his neck.

CANDICE (ANGER MARK ON FOREHEAD)
That's it, Doctor *Freak*enstein! It's snack time!!

Candice opens her braces-filled mouth and we see her Vampire fangs emerge with a familiar...

SFX
POP

...only to fall right out of her mouth!

SFX
Tink Tink

Candice clasps her hands over her open mouth, her eyes wide with shock.

CANDICE
?!!

Frank picks up the fangs, holding one up, not sure what to make of what he just witnessed.

FRANK
Did your canine just--

Suddenly, the door bursts from its hinges and Inga/Elsa, Margie, Mary Beth, and Justine come spilling into the room. It's one big pile of Frankenbitches!

SFX
CRAAASH!

Mary Beth's head goes rolling across the floor and hits the heater.

SFX
Roll Roll Roll Roll Roll BONK

MARY BETH'S HEAD
OOF!

The girls look positively squished under Justine's Amazonian form.

MARGIE (swirly eyes, squished)
I...I can't feel my leg...

KARLOFF
Quack...

INGA

That's 'cause Franklin gave it to the new girl, dingleberry.

Inga struggles under the weight of Justine.

INGA

GUH!

Justine... you have **got** to lay off the power bars.

JUSTINE

Sorry...

ELSA (squished)

Don't listen to Inga, Justine. You're just--*unh!*--just **big boned**, is all.

From the floor Mary Beth's head speaks up to Candice.

MARY BETH'S HEAD

Hey, newbie!

I'm **Mary Beth!**

What's *your* name~?

Candice can do only one thing...

CANDICE

AAAAAAAAHHHHHHHHHHH!!!

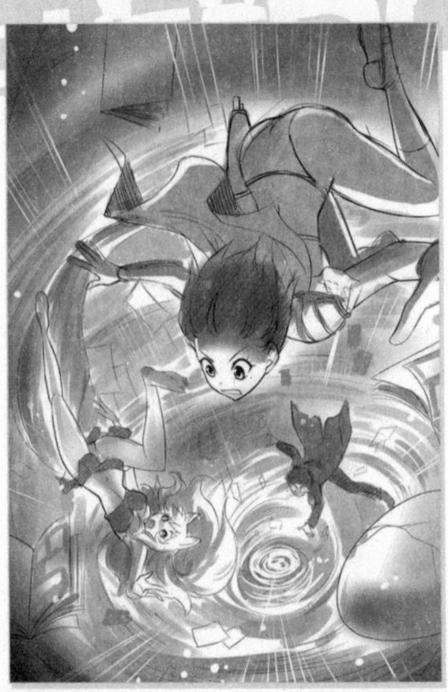

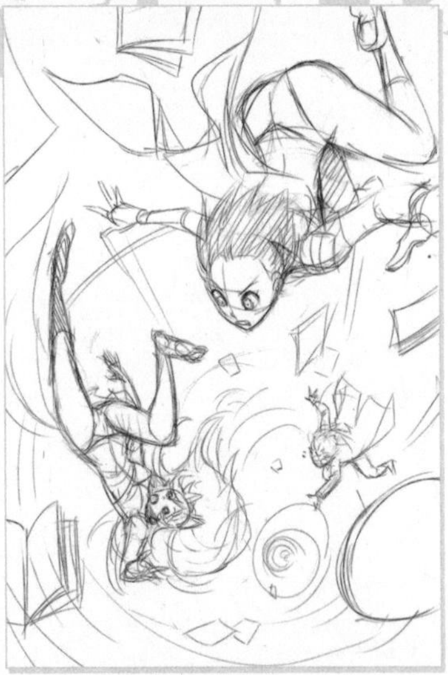

VAMPIRE CHEERLEADERS COVER PROGRESSION

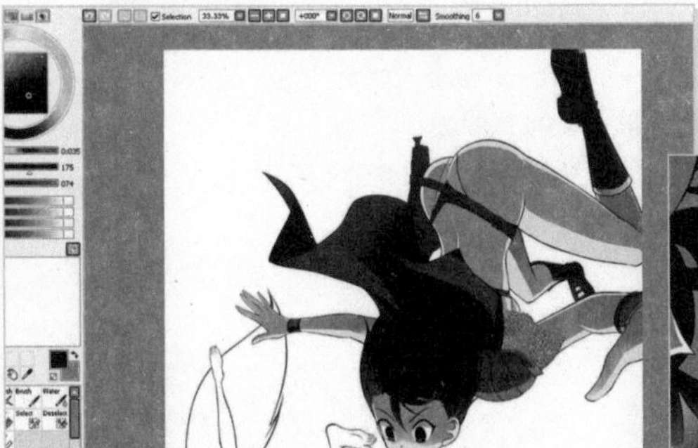
Selection
33.33%
+000°
Normal
Smoothing
6

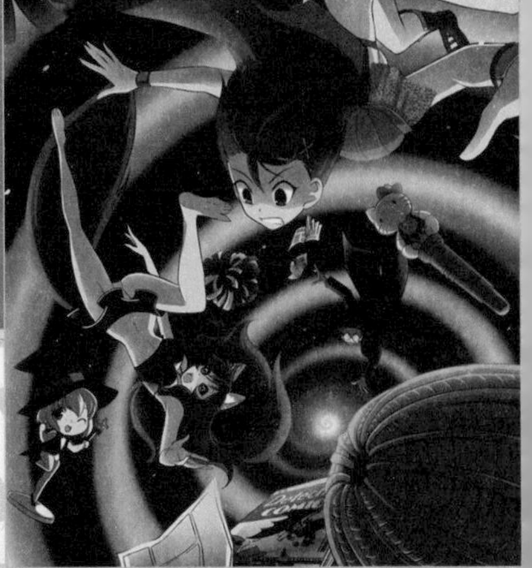

Vampire Cheerleaders Paranormal Mystery Squad & OVA

And so another manga with the *Vampire Cheerleaders* draws to a close. But the story doesn't have to stop here! With ***OVA: The Anime Role-Playing Game***, you and your friends can create new adventures for your favorite characters. What happens next is up to you!

On the following pages, you will see character statistics and new rules designed for *Vampire Cheerleaders*. You'll need a copy of ***OVA*** to play, so visit *www.wiseturtle.com* for information on how to get yours. You can also download free Player Books to introduce you to the game.

So let's go, readers, let's go!

OVA
THE ANIME ROLE-PLAYING GAME
OVA THE ANIME ROLE-PLAYING GAME

Written by Clay Gardner
Original Stories by Adam Arnold
Artwork by Shiei and Ian Cang

STEPHANIE KANE

As the strong-willed, gothy leader of the Paranormal Mystery Squad, Stephanie commands her band of misfits in the quest to quell the cryptid threat...and maybe make some good money while she's at it. The death of her parents fuels her actions with a deep hatred for cryptids that's difficult to keep in check. While the newfound "monstrous" nature of her companions, J.C. Summerfield and her sister, Katie, have softened her somewhat in this regard, Stephanie will still be the first to offer violence as a solution and the last to share sympathy where cryptids are concerned. Her inherent stubbornness and propensity to fly off the handle certainly don't lend to making measured decisions either.

While she has no special powers, Stephanie has honed her skills as a master of the jian, a double-edged Chinese sword. Coupled with her athleticism and capacity to never back down, Stephanie Kane is a force to be reckoned with.

+1	Agile
+3	Attack
+2	Combat Expert
+1	Intuitive
+2	Iron-Willed
+2	Knowledge (Cosplay)
+3	Knowledge (Cryptids)
+2	Quick
+2	Vigorous
−2	Guardian (Char & Katie)
−1	Hatred (Cryptids)
−2	Impulsive
−1	Infamous (Ruthless Cryptid Killer)
−1	Rude
−2	Short-Tempered
−1	Stubborn

Attacks & Combat Stats (HEROIC)

	ROLL	DX	END
Xianghua ARMOR PIERCING; WEAPON Xianghua, Stephanie's beloved jian, proves an adequate solution to many a problem.	5	4	0
Off with Its Head ARMOR PIERCING, EFFECTIVE X2; FINISHER, WEAPON When it comes to putting an end to a fight, Stephanie knows how to do it.	5	6	0

DEFENSE	HEALTH	ENDURANCE	TV
4	40	60	15

KATIE KANE

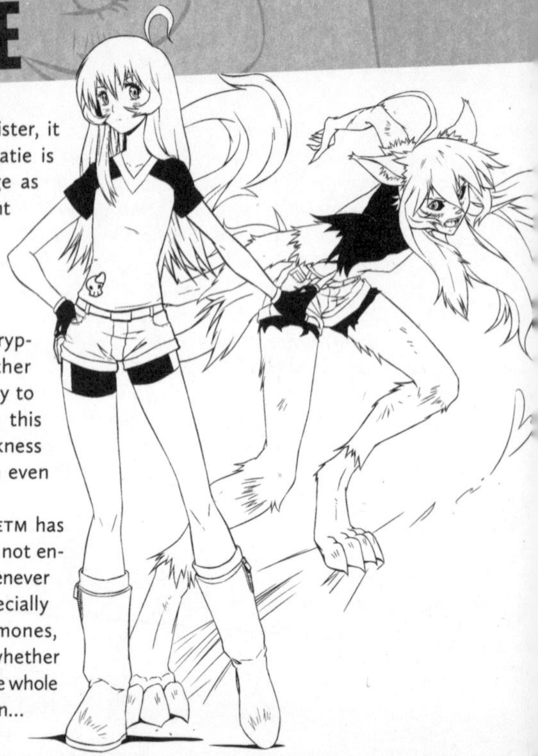

As Stephanie Kane's younger sister, it comes as little surprise that Katie is every bit as difficult to manage as her sibling. Add to that significant helpings of brattiness and teenage angst, and you have a handful no matter how you slice it.

Ever since an unfortunate incident with a lycanthropic cryptid, Katie possesses yet another problematic attribute: the ability to transform into a werewolf! In this form, she possesses great quickness and awing strength but also an even moodier personality!

Although treatment from PETM has helped, Katie's transformation is not entirely reliable or predictable. Whenever she feels intense emotion, especially those related to teenage hormones, she's liable to get her "fur on" whether she wants to or not. Never mind the whole business with phases of the moon…

- +1 *Evasive*
- +2 *Knowledge (Teenybopper Stuff)*
- +5 *Transformation*
  - +1 *Agile*
  - +2 *Attack*
  - +2 *Heightened Sense (Hearing)*
  - +2 *Heightened Sense (Smell)*
  - +2 *Quick*
  - +2 *Strong*
  - +1 *Tough*
  - −2 *Bizarre Appearance*

- −1 *Ageism*
- −1 *Crybaby*
- −1 *Easily Distracted*
- −1 *Short-Tempered*
- −1 *Unique Weakness (Dog Magnet)*
- −1 *Unique Weakness (Unreliable Transformation)*

Attacks & Combat Stats (HEROIC)

Attack	ROLL	DX	END
Tooth & Nail AFFINITY: FURRY **While precision isn't Katie's strong suit, she makes up for it with raw power.**	3	5	0
She's Yiffin' Mad! EFFECTIVE, STUNNING; BREAK; UNWIELDY **You really don't want to make her angry. No, seriously. Just don't.**	3	6	0

DEFENSE	HEALTH	ENDURANCE	TV
3/5	40/50	40	14

CHARLOTTE ROTH

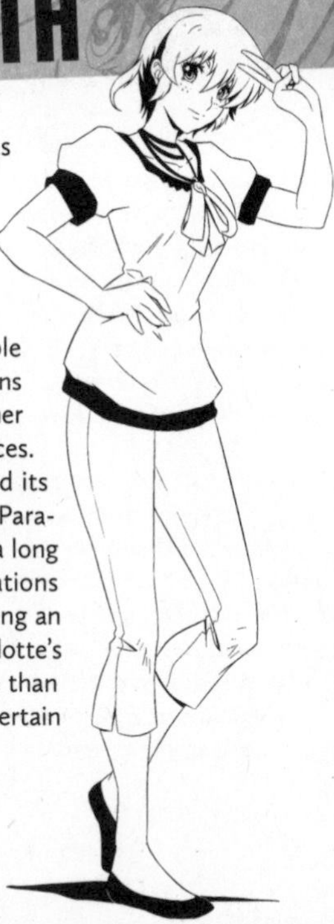

Charlotte and Stephanie have been thick as thieves since childhood due to their parents dragging them around the world on various cryptid-hunting jaunts. Despite the sheer amount of time she has spent in the presence of her hot-headed friend, Charlotte is a kind soul with a warm, likable presence. Unfortunately, all her good intentions fall apart in the heat of the moment, leaving her flustered or, worse, frozen in dire circumstances.

Still, Charlotte's knowledge of Wicca and its spells have proven an invaluable part of the Paranormal Mystery Squad, but each spell takes a long time to cast and involves elaborate incantations and gestures. This always makes precise timing an issue when it comes to her conjurations. Charlotte's powers also have the inclination to do more than she intends, like that time a fire spell razed a certain hotel to the ground...

+2 *Attack*
+1 *Healer*
+2 *Knowledge (Attack Spells)*
+2 *Knowledge (Retro TV)*
+2 *Knowledge (Wicca)*
+2 *Magic, Arcane*
+3 *Sixth Sense*
+1 *Smart*
+2 *Spirit Medium*

−2 *Focus (Magic and Attack Require Wand or Staff)*
−1 *Kind-Hearted*
−1 *Shy*
−1 *Unique Weakness (Combat Paralysis)*
−1 *Unlucky*
−1 *Weak*

Attacks & Combat Stats (HEROIC)

Attack	ROLL	DX	END
Goddess of Wind STUNNING, RANGED, AFFINITY: WIND; DELAYED, ELABORATE GESTURES **A powerful wind knocks foes down.**	4	3	0
Goddess of Ice EFFECTIVE X2, RANGED, AFFINITY: ICE; DELAYED, ELABORATE GESTURES **Char gives an opponent the cold shoulder.**	4	5	0
Goddess of Fire AREA EFFECT X2, EFFECTIVE, RANGED, AFFINITY: FIRE; DELAYED, ELABORATE GESTURES, LOW PENETRATION **She has the power...to light way too many things on fire at one time.**	4	4	10

DEFENSE	HEALTH	ENDURANCE	TV
2	40	40	9

J.C. SUMMERFIELD

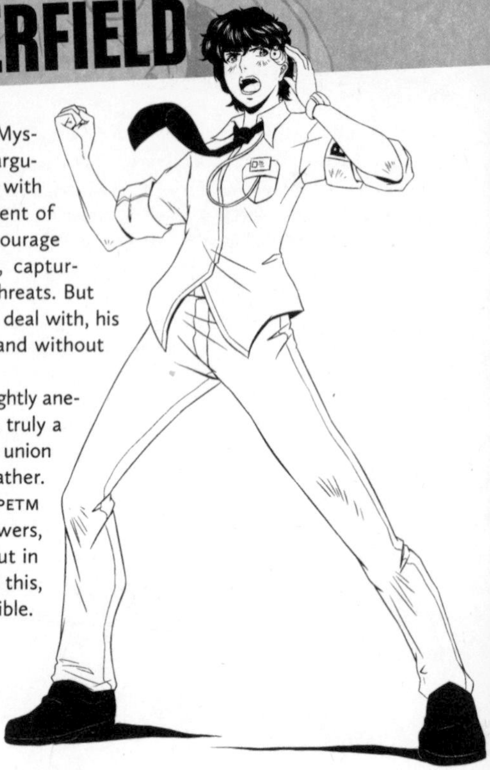

J.C. Summerfield is the Paranormal Mystery Squad's lone male member and, arguably, only voice of reason. As a liaison with PETM (People for the Ethical Treatment of Monsters), J.C. does his best to encourage less drastic measures for handling, capturing, or otherwise subduing cryptid threats. But with three strong-minded women to deal with, his opinion is often overridden quickly and without fanfare.

Even though J.C. appears to be a slightly anemic desk jockey on the surface, he is truly a dhampir, a half-cryptid born from the union of a human mother and a vampire father. While he undergoes treatment from PETM to subdue his symptoms and his powers, the taste of blood will bring them out in full force. J.C. would prefer to avoid this, and outright violence, whenever possible.

+1 *Agile*
+1 *Intuitive*
+3 *Knowledge (Cryptids)*
+1 *Quick*
+2 *Smart*
+3 *Strong*

−1 *Dependency (PETM Treatments)*
−1 *Frail*
−1 *Pacifist*
−1 *Restricted Freedom (PETM)*
−3 *Suppressed Power (Strength Requires Dhampir Form)*

Attacks & Combat Stats (HEROIC)

Attack	ROLL	DX	END
Dhampir Damage AFFINITY: VAMPIRE **While J.C. would rather not make use of force, he's quite capable as a Dhampir.**	3	4	0
Don't Tase Me, Bro PARALYZING X2, RANGED; NO DAMAGE **PETM may be naive, but it's not stupid. Tasers are standard issue.**	3	0	0

DEFENSE	HEALTH	ENDURANCE	TV
3	30	40	9

LORI THURSTON

Lori Thurston is a girl of many talents—and many names if you dig through past yearbooks of Bakertown High. Her position as the head cheerleader of the local Bats football team is hardly surprising. She's beautiful, charismatic, and certainly intimidating enough to command the respect of her fellow squadmates. But Lori is more than a cheerleader, she's a Vampire Cheerleader! Throughout the years, she has relived high school countless times by pretending to be her own daughter. It has become Lori's ceaseless goal to make the Bakertown High cheerleading squad the best it can possibly be. And if that involves turning key members into vampires, well, *c'est la vie!*

Currently, she has a devoted clique of Vampire Cheerleaders at her side, loyal and true despite being prone to infighting. But there's more to life than high school, and in Lori's storied past there's bound to be those that have a bone to pick with this short-tempered vamp!

+3 Agile
+2 Attack
+2 Beautiful
+2 Charismatic
+4 Cheerleader
+3 Glamour
+1 Intuitive
+1 Iron-Willed
+3 Quick
+3 Strong
+2 Tough
+2 Vigorous

-2 Dependency (Blood)
-2 Guardian (The Squad)
-1 Obsession (Cheerleading)
-2 Short-Tempered
-1 Unique Weakness
   (Must Be Invited)
-2 Vulnerability (Back)
-2 Vulnerability (Garlic)
-2 Vulnerability (Sun)

Attacks & Combat Stats (HEROIC)

	ROLL	DX	END
Manicured Maul AFFINITY: VAMPIRE CHEERLEADER Lori has no problem using her devastating strength—even if she might break a nail.	5	6	0
More than a Hickey FATIGUING, IMPAIRING, VAMPIRE; INACCURATE, UNWIELDY Like all vampires, Lori is capable of sucking the very life from her foes.	4	6	0

DEFENSE	HEALTH	ENDURANCE	TV
5	60	40	18

VAMPIRE CHEERLEADERS

Much like cheerleading itself, Lori's squadmates have become a vital part of her life. As vampires, they all have the following Weaknesses in addition to their own: *Dependency −2 (Blood)*, *Unique Weakness −1 (Must Be Invited)*, *Vulnerability −2 (Back)*, *Vulnerability −2 (Garlic)*, and *Vulnerability −2 (Sun)*. You can read more about these and other vampire facts later on in this guide.

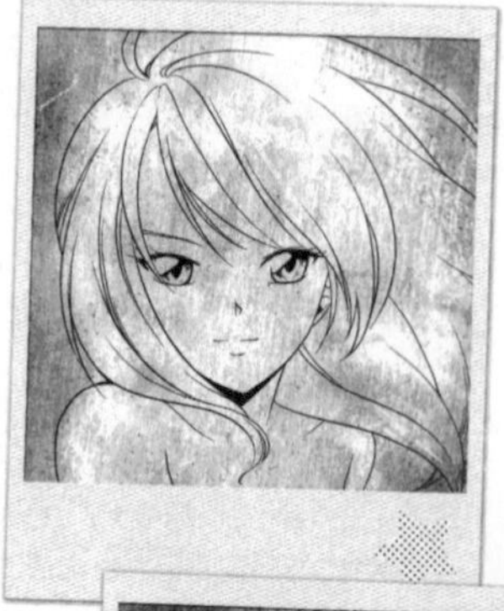

Heather Hartley, despite being the newest member, shows great skill and promise, both as a cheerleader *and* a vampire. However, Heather's previously sheltered life has led her to be drunk with her newfound power. What kindness and propriety she may have once possessed have been shed in favor of being one *seriously* mean girl! The glamour-induced enslavement of her parents is testament to this.

ATTRIBUTES: Agile +2, Attack +1, Cheerleader +3, Cute! +1, Glamour +2, Quick +2, Strong +2, Wealthy +1 (Parent's Bank Account); Impulsive −1, Naive −1

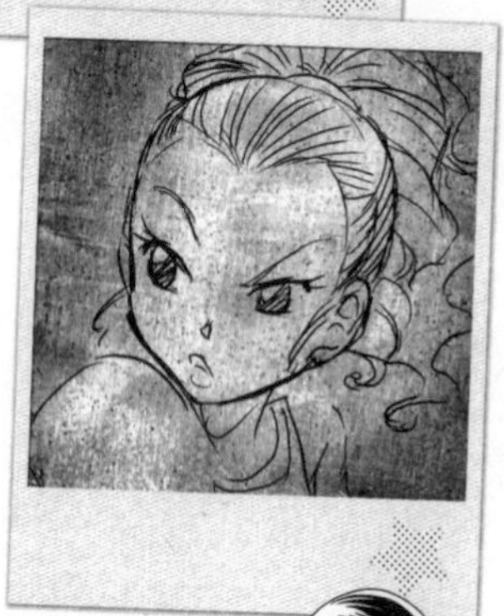

Zoe Weller, co-captain of the Bats and Lori's right-hand vampire, is probably the most level-headed of the bunch. However, her constant rivalry with her fellow co-captain can derail the entire team into a petty fight.

ATTRIBUTES: Agile +1, Attack +1, Beautiful +1, Cheerleader +2, Glamour +2, Intuitive +2, Quick +1, Strong +3; Rival −2 (Suki)

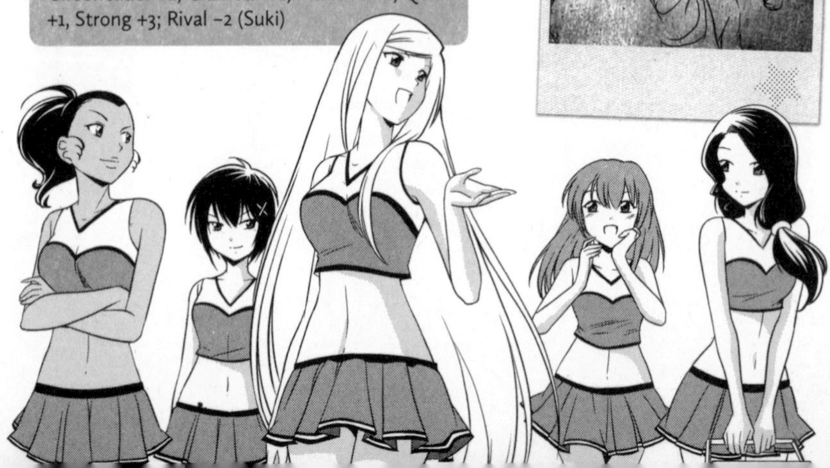

VAMPIRE CHEERLEADERS

Suki Taft, the other co-captain, is the team's bad seed. Equipped with no filter whatsoever, Suki says what's on her mind regardless of the potential consequences, and she has no qualms about using her feminine wiles to get what she wants.

> **ATTRIBUTES:** Agile +2, Beautiful +1, Charismatic +1, Cheerleader +2, Glamour +2, Kitty-chan +0 (Good Vibrations), Quick +2, Strong +3; Compulsion −2 (Speaking Her Mind), Dense −1, Love Magnet −1 (Asian Fever), Rival −2 (Zoe)

Lesley Chandra is by far the smartest of the cheerleaders and puts that aptitude to good use as the team's treasurer. But her academic nature belies a wild side...

> **ATTRIBUTES:** Agile +1, Attack +1, Beautiful +1, Knowledge +3 (Money Matters), Smart +3, Strong +2; Secret −1 (Ms. Kama Sutra)

Leonard Duvall is practically an official squadmate (and even has a few cheerleading moves of his own). However, his fondness for long-time friend Heather and his dateless nerd lifestyle have made Leonard *incredibly* easy to glamour. This resulted in him spending a lot of time as a personal thrall of the Vampire Cheerleaders. But with the glamouring spell now broken, Leonard is exploring what it's like to be his own person (and an amateur adventurer). Even with his newly acquired arsenal of weaponry, Leonard is ultimately just a nice guy.

> **ATTRIBUTES:** Attack +2 (Array of Stakes, Axes, and Other Makeshift Weaponry), Cheerleader +1, Combat Expert +1, Evasive +2, Knowledge +3 (All That is Geek), Knowledge +3 (Drink Mix Master), Smart +2; Kind-Hearted −1, Love Interest −2 (Heather), Vulnerability −2 (Glamouring), Weak −1, Weak-Willed −1

RULES FOR VAMPIRES

Outside of combat or against glamoured extras, one can just assume the target falls unconscious. Upon waking, victims of blood-sucking exhibit feelings of weakness and lightheadedness similar to...well...donating blood. Of course, an especially unscrupulous vampire, or just an especially clueless one, can kill a person by sucking too much blood.

The fangs vampires use for this purpose are retractable, so only the most careless vampires are likely to reveal themselves in this manner.

Vampire Weaknesses

While being able to charm everyone around you—or crush the few who escape your spell—is a very nice capability to have, being a vampire isn't all wine and roses.

Once the stuff of horror films and late-night scary stories, the world has become rife with all matter of *cryptids*. These real-life personifications of spirits, the undead, demons, and the like are prevalent across the globe. Many are peaceful enough, but others are hell-bent on causing mayhem against humankind.

Vampires are just one example of cryptid, but their remarkable charisma and human-like appearance makes it easy for them to integrate into society without notice. (Even as cheerleaders, apparently.) This only makes them all the more dangerous.

Vampire Abilities

Vampires have been feared across the centuries, and for good reason. However, not all of their powers from myth are based in fact. For instance, vampires do *not* turn into bats, mist, or any other dark, floaty things.

Among a vampire's true powers is the ability to **Glamour** others. By gazing into the target's eyes without breaking eye-contact, the vampire may influence his or her actions for the next 24 hours. After that time, or preferably, sometime before that time, the target must be re-glamoured for the vampire to retain control. Those aware of what is going on *can* resist being glamoured and do so against the vampire's *Glamour* dice. Every vampire gains this *Glamour* Ability, though at varying levels.

Vampires also gain **immense strength,** regardless of how weak they may appear. This strength manifests as *Strong +2* at the very least, though older, more powerful vampires can exhibit Levels of +3, +4, or even +5!

Finally, and least surprisingly, vampires gain a new Attack: **Suck Blood** (FATIGUING, IMPAIRING, VAMPIRE; INACCURATE, UNWIELDY).

RULES FOR VAMPIRES

While the story goes that a stake through the heart is the only sure way to kill a vampire, *their back is also very vulnerable.* Damage dealt to this location is twice as effective (again treated as a *Vulnerability −2*).

Finally, vampires have the *Unique Weakness −1 (Must Be Invited)*. They may not enter the dwelling of another person without the express invitation to do so.

Becoming a Vampire

To become a vampire, one must be initiated by another vampire. All of a person's blood is drained from their body and replaced with some of their "maker's" blood. The would-be vampire does not necessarily need to agree to this process, though glamouring would make such reservations of little consequence. Once someone has become a vampire, there is no turning back.

There is one other way to "become" a vampire. Should the relationship between a human and a vampire be consummated, the resulting offspring is born a half-vampire, or dhampir. Though not as strong as a full-blooded vampire, a dhampir can also control some of a vampire's less desirable qualities through treatment.

Cheerleading

To a certain breed of vampire, cheerleading is serious business. Abilities like *Agile* and *Performer* are perfect fits for this high school vocation, but *Charismatic*, *Quick*, and *Strong* can also factor into some rolls.

But if you like, you can bring cheerleading even more into focus for your games. Create a new *Cheerleader* Ability, or perhaps split it up into various aptitudes, like *Pep*, *Tumbling*, *Aerials*, and so on. Just don't forget the words!

Purple & Black! Bats, let's fly! Press the attack! To Victo-rye! Goooooooo, Bats!

Vampires have a *Dependency −2* for blood. If forced to skip a regular "meal," vampires will receive a −2 to all actions until they are able to bloodfeast again. Given enough time, a vampire that does not drink blood will die.

Vampires have several unusual vulnerabilities. First off, *garlic* is an incredibly toxic substance. If vampires ingest it (or drink the blood of someone who has spiked their bloodstream with massive amounts of it), they will receive DX 2 Damage versus a Defense of zero. Consider this *Vulnerability −2* for all other purposes.

Sunlight, too, can prove a serious hazard to a vampire. However, loads of sunscreen is ample protection from the sun's rays...at least for a while. But should a vampire have to face daylight without the protection of sunscreen or heavy clothing, they will receive DX 2 Damage versus a Defense of zero. Consider this *Vulnerability −2* for all other purposes.

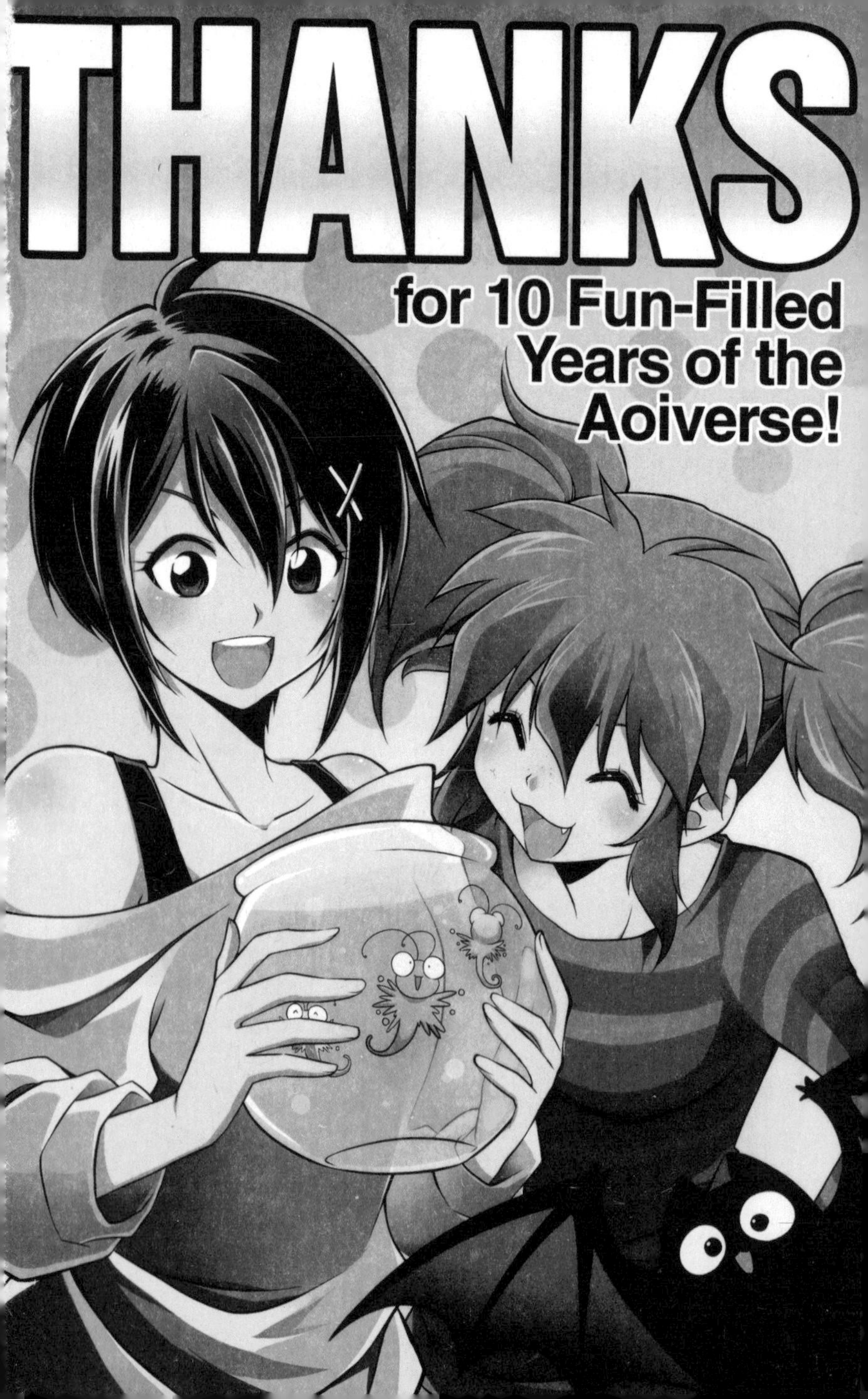
THANKS
for 10 Fun-Filled Years of the Aoiverse!